European Stories

Intellectual Debates on Europe in National Contexts

Edited by
Justine Lacroix and Kalypso Nicolaïdis

OXFORD

UNIVERSITY PRESS

OXFORD
UNIVERSITY PRESS

Great Clarendon Street, Oxford OX2 6DP

Oxford University Press is a department of the University of Oxford.
It furthers the University's objective of excellence in research, scholarship,
and education by publishing worldwide in

Oxford New York

Auckland Cape Town Dar es Salaam Hong Kong Karachi
Kuala Lumpur Madrid Melbourne Mexico City Nairobi
New Delhi Shanghai Taipei Toronto

With offices in

Argentina Austria Brazil Chile Czech Republic France Greece
Guatemala Hungary Italy Japan Poland Portugal Singapore
South Korea Switzerland Thailand Turkey Ukraine Vietnam

Oxford is a registered trade mark of Oxford University Press
in the UK and in certain other countries

Published in the United States
by Oxford University Press Inc., New York

British Library Cataloguing in Publication Data
Data available

Library of Congress Cataloging in Publication Data
Data available

Typeset by SPI Publisher Services, Pondicherry, India
Printed in Great Britain
on acid-free paper by
MPG Books Group, Bodmin and King's Lynn

ISBN 978–0–19–959462–7

3 5 7 9 10 8 6 4

To our children

Acknowledgements

Most of the research that led to this volume was sponsored by RECON (Reconstituting Democracy in Europe), a five-year (2007–11) European Integrated Project supported by the Sixth Framework Programme for Research of the European Union. Coordinated by ARENA – Centre for European Studies at the University of Oslo – RECON includes twenty-one partner institutions across Europe and New Zealand.

Part of the research was also sponsored by the Action de Recherche Concertée 'Resisting Europe. Social and Political Responses to the Process of European Integration' (2006–10) supervised at the Université libre de Bruxelles by Professors Jean-Michel De Waele, Justine Lacroix, Pieter Lagrou, and Paul Magnette.

The chapters were discussed in two conferences held in April 2008 at the Institute for European Studies, Université libre de Bruxelles and in April 2009 at the European Studies Centre, St Antony's College, Oxford University. We would like to thank the Institute for European Studies at Université libre de Bruxelles; St Antony's College, the Department of Politics, and the Maison française at Oxford University for their generous administrative or financial support. Justine Lacroix would like to thank St Antony's College for the Deakin fellowship which allowed her to spend the academic year 2008–9 in Oxford in order to complete the volume with Kalypso Nicolaïdis.

This project benefited from the invaluable comments of Timothy Garton Ash, Ian Krastev, Diane Pinto and Jan Zielonka. Our thanks also go to Gabi Maas for the scrupulous and insightful editorial help she provided throughout the whole process.

The project would not have been possible without Dominic Byatt's belief in its merits from the beginning and Sarah Parker's supportive management style. Our thanks to both of them and their support team at Oxford University Press.

Table 16.1 was previously published in Chapter 8 ('Framing the European Union in national public spheres') of *The Making of a European Public Sphere: Media Discourse and Political Contention*, edited by Ruud Koopmans and Paul Statham (Cambridge: Cambridge University Press, 2010).

Acknowledgements

Table 16.2 was previously published in Chapter 4 ('The public sphere and the European Union's political identity') of *European Identity*, edited by Jeffrey T. Checkel and Peter J. Katzenstein (Cambridge: Cambridge University Press, 2009).

Table 16.4 was previously published in *Framing Europe*, by Juan Díez Medrano (Princeton: Princeton University Press, 2003).

Contents

Contents

Part VI. One Story or Many?

List of Figures

List of Tables

List of Contributors

Daniel Barbu is Professor of Political Science and Director of the Graduate School of Political Science at the University of Bucharest. He has been a visiting professor at the University of Pittsburgh, at the Central European University (Budapest), and at the Institut d'Etudes Politiques of Bordeaux. He is the author of *Die abwesende Republik* (Berlin: Frank & Timme, 2009) and editor of *Studia Politica: Romanian Political Science Review*.

Antonio Barroso is a graduate student at the School of International and Public Affairs, Columbia University. He holds an MA in European Political and Administrative Studies from the College of Europe (Bruges) and a BA in Political Science and Sociology from the University of Granada. He has worked for the Centre for Sociological Research and the Centre for Political and Constitutional Studies (Ministry of the Presidency, Spain). His main research interests are EU treaty reform and EU foreign policy.

Muriel Blaive is a historian and project leader at the Ludwig Boltzmann Institute for European History and Public Spheres in Vienna, Austria. She is working in a socio-political perspective on the communist and post-communist period in Central Europe, especially on Czechoslovakia/the Czech Republic. She is the author of *Grenzfälle: Österreichische und tschechische Erfahrungen am Eisernen Vorhang* (with Berthold Molden, Weitra: Bibliothek der Provinz, 2009), as well as of the volume *Une déstalinisation manquée. Tchécoslovaquie 1956* (Brussels: Complexe, 2005).

Francis Cheneval is currently Visiting Professor of Political Theory at the Université libre de Bruxelles and Lecturer at the University of Geneva. His contribution to this volume was written during his 2008–9 term as Senior Associate Member at St Anthony's College, Oxford.

Carlos Closa is a professor at CSIC-Madrid. He has been Deputy Director at the Centre for Political and Constitutional Studies, Madrid (CEPC) and member of the Venice Commission for Democracy through Law of the Council of Europe. He was formerly Senior Lecturer in Political Science at the University of Zaragoza (Spain) and lecturer at the Universidad Complutense de Madrid and Jean Monnet Fellow at the European University Institute (EUI), Florence, Visiting Fellow at the Centre for European Studies (Harvard University), and Visiting

Professor at the College of Europe (Bruges). He is Associated Researcher at the Real Instituto Elcano de Estudios Internacionales y Estratégicos (RIE).

Ahmet Evin, currently senior fellow at the Transatlantic Academy, Washington, DC, and visiting scholar at the Johns Hopkins University, teaches at Sabanci University, where he was the founding dean of Faculty of Arts and Social Sciences, and a founding member of Istanbul Policy Center. Professor Evin has previously taught at New York University, Harvard, Hacettepe (Ankara), University of Pennsylvania (where he also served as Director of the Middle East Center), Hamburg, Bilkent, and Northwestern University. He has also served as Director of Education of the Aga Khan Trust for Culture, Geneva. His publications include: *The Origins and Development of the Turkish Novel* (Minneapolis: Bibliotheca Islamica, 1983), *Modern Turkey: Continuity and Change* (Opladen: Leske and Budrich, 1984), *State, Democracy and the Military: Turkey in the 1980s* (with Metin Heper, New York: de Gruyter, 1988), *Turkey and the European Community* (with Geoffrey Denton, Opladen: Leske and Budrich, 1990), *Politics in the Third Turkish Republic: A Case Study in Transition to Democracy* (with Metin Heper, Boulder: Westview, 1994) and *Towards Accession Negotiations: Turkey's Domestic and Foreign Policy Challenges Ahead* (with Natalie Tocci, Florence: Robert Schuman Centre, 2004).

Nora Fisher Onar obtained her DPhil in International Relations from the University of Oxford, and is currently a faculty member of the Department of Political Science and International Relations of Bahçeşehir University in Istanbul, Turkey. She has published extensively on Turkish domestic and foreign policy issues, with articles in journals such as *Middle Eastern Studies*, the *International Journal on Minority and Groups Rights*, and *Turkish Studies*.

John Erik Fossum is Professor of Political Science at ARENA, Centre for European Studies, University of Oslo, Norway. He is substitute coordinator of the European Commission-funded five-year Integrated Sixth Framework Project RECON (Reconstituting Democracy in Europe). He has written extensively on democracy, identity, and constitutional issues in Europe and Canada. Recent books include *The European Union and the Public Sphere* (co-edited with P. Schlesinger, London: Routledge, 2007) and *The Ties that Bind* (co-edited with J. Poirier and P. Magnette, Brussels: Peter Lang, 2009).

Michael Freeden is Professor of Politics, Director of the Centre for Political Ideologies at the University of Oxford, and Professorial Fellow of Mansfield College, Oxford. His books include *The New Liberalism: An Ideology of Social Reform* (Oxford: Clarendon, 1978), *Liberalism Divided: A Study in British Political Thought 1914–1939* (Oxford University Press, 1986), *Ideologies and Political Theory: A Conceptual Approach* (Oxford University Press, 1996), *Liberal Languages: Ideological Imaginations and 20th Century Progressive Thought* (Princeton: Princeton University Press, 2005). He is the founder-editor of the *Journal of Political Ideologies*.

Magdalena Góra received her MA and PhD in Political Science from the Jagiellonian University, Krakow. Her PhD (2007) tackled the issues of relations between Poland and Israel after the Second World War. Her academic interests include processes of EU enlargement, contemporary Polish foreign policy, and Polish–Jewish and Polish–Israeli relations. She works at the Institute for European Studies of the Jagiellonian University.

Katy Hayward is Lecturer in Sociology in the School of Sociology, Social Policy and Social Work at Queen's University Belfast. Among her publications are *Irish Nationalism and European Integration* (Manchester: Manchester University Press, 2009), *The Europeanization of Party Politics in Ireland* (ed., London: Routledge, 2010), and *Political Discourse and Conflict Resolution* (ed., London: Routledge, 2011).

Cathrine Holst is Senior Researcher at ARENA – Centre for European Studies and Postdoctor at the Department of Sociology and Human Geography, University of Oslo. She has published in political theory, feminist theory, philosophy of science, and Norwegian intellectual history. Among her recent publications are 'What is philosophy of social science?' (*International Studies in the Philosophy of Science*, 3/2009) and 'Nussbaum versus Rawls' in *Nature and Rational Agency*, ed. Trygve Wyller and Kjartan Koch (Frankfurt am Main: Peter Lang Verlag, 2009).

Justine Lacroix is Professor of Political Science at the Université libre de Bruxelles. She is the author of *Michaë Walzer: Le pluralisme et l'universel* (Paris: Michalon, 2001), *Communautarisme versus libèralisme* (Brussels: Editions de l'ULB, 2003), *L'Europe en procès: Quel patriotisme au-delà des nationalismes?* (Paris: Editions du Cerf, 2004), and *La pensée française à l'épreuve de l'Europe* (Paris: Grasset, 2008). In 2008–9, she was Deakin Visiting Fellow at St Antony's College, Oxford University.

Ulrike Liebert is Professor of Political Science, Jean Monnet Chair and Director of the Centre for European Studies, University of Bremen. Her major interests include research projects and teaching activities at the European University Institute/Florence, the University of Heidelberg, the Universidad Autonomà/Barcelona, and Cornell University, in the fields of democratic theory, comparative democratization, and European integration. She is a co-coordinator of Reconstituting Democracy in Europe (RECON, Sixth FP, ARENA/Oslo, 2007–11).

Zdzisław Mach is Professor of Sociology at the Jagiellonian University, Krakow, specializing in social anthropology and European studies. He obtained his MA in sociology in 1978 and his PhD in 1984. Between 1993 and 1999 he was the Dean of the Faculty of Philosophy, and since 1993 he has been Director of the Institute of European Studies. He is also Professor at the School of

Administration, Bielsko-Biała (Poland) and Permanent Visiting Professor at the Centre for Social Studies, Warsaw. He has held visiting professorships and fellowships at many academic institutions in the important European and American universities. He supervises several international research projects dealing with European integration, democracy and collective identity, transnationalization of the social movements in Europe in the twentieth and twenty-first centuries, and the social meaning of the Holocaust.

Nicolas Maslowski is Lecturer in Sociology at Charles University and Head of the Collegium Minor in Prague.

Juan Díez Medrano is a Professor at the University of Barcelona and a Senior Researcher at the Institut Barcelona d'Estudis Internacionals. He is the author of articles and books on the topics of nationalism, ethnic conflict, and European integration. Among these are, 'The effects of ethnic competition and ethnic segregation on political conflict in the Basque country, 1988' (*American Sociological Review*, 1994), *Divided Nations* (Ithaca: Cornell University Press, 1995), 'Nested identities: National and European identity in Spain' (with Paula Gutiérrez: *Ethnic and Racial Studies*, 2001), *Framing Europe* (Princeton: Princeton University Press, 2003), and 'Distance matters: Place, political legitimacy, and popular support for European integration' (with Mabel Berezin: *Comparative European Politics*, 2008). He is a recipient of the Alexander von Humboldt Foundation scholarship (1995) and of the Einaudi Chair in International and European Studies at Cornell University (2006).

Jan-Werner Müller teaches in the Politics Department, Princeton University, and directs the Project in the History of Political Thought, University Center for Human Values, also at Princeton. He is the author of *Constitutional Patriotism* (Princeton: Princeton University Press, 2007), *A Dangerous Mind: Carl Schmitt in Post-War European Thought* (New Haven: Yale University Press, 2003), and *Another Country: German Intellectuals, Unification and National Identity* (New Haven: Yale University Press, 2000).

Kalypso Nicolaïdis is Professor of International Relations at Oxford and a member of the EU reflection group on the Future of Europe (2020–30). She was Associate Professor at the Kennedy School of Government, Harvard University and has also held visiting professorships around Europe. Her publications appear in numerous journals including *Foreign Affairs, Foreign Policy*, the *Journal of Common Market Studies, Politique Etrangère*, and *Raison Publique*. Her books include *The Federal Vision: Legitimacy and Levels of Governance in the United States and the European Union* (Oxford: Oxford University Press, 2001), *Under the Long Shadow of Europe: Greeks and Turks in the Era of Postnationalism* (Leiden: Brill, 2009), *Mediterranean Frontiers: Borders, Memory and Conflict in a Transnational Era* (London: IB Tauris, 2009), and *Whose Europe?* (Oxford: Oxford University Press,

2003). More information can be found on her website: <http://www.sant.ox.ac.uk/esc/knicolaidis/>.

George Pagoulatos is Associate Professor of Politics at the Department of International and European Economic Studies of the Athens University of Economics, and a Visiting Professor at the College of Europe in Bruges. He received his doctorate in Politics from the University of Oxford. His research focuses on European integration and the EU and Southern European political economy. He is a board member of various academic and civic organizations and a regular contributor to the Sunday edition of the main Greek centrist newspaper *Kathimerini*. He has edited, authored, and co-authored five books, and published extensively in leading journals.

Janie Pélabay is a researcher at Sciences-Po Paris (Cevipof). Prior to this, she was a researcher within the European Governance Program at the University of Luxembourg, Deakin Visiting Fellow at the University of Oxford, as well as a post-doctoral researcher as a Marie Curie Fellow and within the RECON framework at the Université libre de Bruxelles. She holds a PhD in political philosophy from the University of Paris-Sorbonne.

Mario Telò is Vice-President of the Institute of European Studies, Université libre de Bruxelles, and Professor of Political Science, International Relations as an Honorary 'J. Monnet Chair' at the ULB; Member of the Royal Academy of Belgium; President of the International Garnet PhD school and Central Coordinator of the Erasmus Mundus Doctoral Program GEM (Globalization, Europe, Multilateralism) 2009–15; and Visiting Professor in European, American, Asian Universities. He served as a consultant to the EU Commission and the Presidency of the EU and the European Parliament. Among his books are *European Union and New Regionalism* (ed., Aldershot: Ashgate, 2007); *Europe: A Civilian Power?* (Basingstoke: Palgrave, 2005), *International Relations: A European Perspective* (Brussels, 2008 and Ashgate: Aldershot, 2009).

Georgios Varouxakis is Reader in History at Queen Mary, University of London. He is the author of *Mill on Nationality* (London: Routledge, 2002) and *Victorian Political Thought on France and the French* (Basingstoke: Palgrave Macmillan, 2002) and the co-author of *Contemporary France: An Introduction to French Politics and Society* (London: Arnold, 2003). He is also the co-editor of *Utilitarianism and Empire* (Lanham, MD: Lexington Books, 2005) and *John Stuart Mill – Thought and Influence: The Saint of Rationalism* (London: Routledge, 2010).

Xenophon A. Yataganas received PhD degrees from the Universities of Athens and Paris in European Law and Philosophy of Law respectively. He was Fellow of the Haag Academy of International Law and Harvard University. He served as Legal Advisor at the Legal Service, Senior Member of President

Santer's Cabinet and Head of the Financial Legislation Unit of the European Commission, Advisor to the Greek Minister of Foreign Affairs and to the President of the Republic of Cyprus. He has published books and articles on European topics in Europe and the USA. He teaches Public Law at the Athens Law School, serves as Scientific Director of the Hellenic Centre of European Studies and Research (EKEME), and collaborates with the European Public Law Centre (EPLC).

Note on the Jacket Illustration

Europa's Dance is meant to be enigmatic, the charts to its meaning lay in the very mystery of the Cosmos itself, from which so much of modern philosophy and science find their compass. It celebrates the primal human joy to be alive, timelessly where Europe, free, allows this natural hope in us all to be undiminished.

Hidden in the painting are images of Europe spinning through the Milky Way, stars lightly adorning the bodies of the dancers, an abstracted central DNA Double Helix, and different perspectives of European geography which will always be a reality of different cultures seeing diversity, solidarity and unity simultaneously in a Post Einstein world. What is above is reflected in more earthly terms below. The imagery pays homage to the softer aspects of Mediterranean values from which so much of Europe's culture is infused and engendered. The European logo becomes a soft halo of beneficence. The map of Europe becomes a canvas ready for many dreams to go a-dancing.

The painting says "Can't you hear the timeless music of existence that binds us all in the deepest core of our dreams and DNA? Dance. Dance. Dance. All your thinking will be better for it. And so will all our shared European dreams."

Debra McEachern

European Stories: An Introduction*

Justine Lacroix and Kalypso Nicolaïdis

Romanians see Europe as an ethical hazard, the Germans as (still) their best chance for national atonement; the Spaniards as the key to their democracy and the Italians as the guarantee of their unity; and so on. These may be but simplistic clichés, as each national debate *in* Europe *about* Europe pits schools of thought against schools of thought, ideology against ideology, national trope against national trope. Nevertheless, they belong to distinctly different national debates about the twenty-first-century project that is the European Union, its relationship to the history of its respective peoples, and the promises or threats that it may hold for their various national projects today.

This book is about the constellation of different 'European stories' woven by these national debates, and ultimately what their overlaps and divergence might tell us about Europe itself. It is not yet another study of the European or national public spheres, but rather an exploration of intellectual debates on the European Union in distinct national contexts. More precisely, it focuses on the visions and interpretations of European integration proposed since the early 1990s by so-called 'public intellectuals', i.e. political philosophers, scholars, editors, or writers whose opinions contribute to framing public attitudes.

The term 'public intellectuals' – though commonly used in the US – might sound like a pleonasm to many in Europe who consider that an 'intellectual' is by definition a public figure. Yet we believe that it remains useful, since in reality not all those who engage in 'intellectual' occupations seek to address a wider public. Put differently, we use 'intellectual' in the cultural sense, to identify those figures 'regarded as possessing some kind of "cultural authority", that is who deploy an acknowledged intellectual position or achievement in addressing a broader, non-specialist public' (Collini 2006: 46). Consequently,

* We are grateful to all the participants in the European Stories workshop and especially to Timothy Garton Ash, Michael Freeden, and Ivan Krastev for their insightful comments on earlier drafts of this introduction. We would also like to thank Diana Pinto and two anonymous referees from Oxford University Press.

the 'intellectual' considered in this volume is a scholar who addresses a lay public either in a national or a transnational context, but is not necessarily politically active in the sense of the French *intellectuel engagé*. As Michael Freeden points out in his chapter, this leaves the question open as to whether his object is to *interpret* or *change* the world.

Naturally, therefore, the book is also concerned with the reception of intellectuals' debates and thus the source of their authority, to be found in the ways in which citizens listen to, are influenced by, or even in some cases defer to their 'European stories'. Of course, the public may also ignore or reject these debates. While the very definition of intellectuals and their place in society varies greatly between European countries, national debates among these intellectuals all shape – and reflect, in more or less distorted ways – the dominant opinions of their fellow citizens. Moreover, intellectuals influence the way in which their country is perceived by other Europeans, and thus the evolving relationship between European peoples.

Ironically, perhaps, this also means that for the most part the intellectuals considered in this volume are not specialists of the European Union; and nor is this book a comparative study of the state of the art of 'European studies' across Europe. Paraphrasing Collini, we could say that the intellectual considered in this book is a person who deploys an acknowledged position in a certain field of research in order to address a different topic – in this case European integration. Thus, Jürgen Habermas was recognized as one of the most prominent thinkers of our time well before he turned to the subject of Europe in the early 1990s; Marcel Gauchet and Pierre Manent were well established as, respectively, a theorist of democracy and a historian of liberal political thought before they published their first articles on Europe in the mid-2000s. Inevitably, these intellectuals originate from a plurality of disciplines – from political theory to public law, philosophy, contemporary history, political sociology, and even literature. As a result, the chapters present different disciplinary emphases reflecting both national intellectual traditions and their authors' own bias – political theory in the case of the chapter on France, law for Spain, or history for Britain.

However, it should be clear that this book is not a 'who's who' of European intellectuals – a topic which has already given rise to an important literature, whether one considers the voluminous body of academic writings on the role of intellectuals at the European[1] or the national level.[2] Our objective is to compare and contrast intellectual debates *on* Europe rather than the role of intellectuals

---

[1] See for instance Bauman 2007; Eyerman 1994; Jennings and Kemp-Welch 1997; Lemayrie and Sirinelli 2003; Lepenies 2007; Lilla 2001; MacLean, Montefiore, and Winch 1990.

[2] See for instance Bellamy 2001; Bozóki 1999; Collini 2006; Jennings 1993; Moses 2007; Müller 2003; Ory and Sirinelli 1992; Stapleton 2001; Winock 1997.

in Europe.[3] We focus on the *content* of the discourses rather than their actors. Indeed, there is an almost complete lack of literature on the way in which European integration has been addressed by intellectuals since the birth of the European Union in 1992. In articulating the distinct European narratives that emerge from these debates, we hope to deepen understanding of the multi-faceted nature of the European process as a whole.

Moreover, this book does not aim to provide a comprehensive history of the intellectual debates on 'Europe' in the *longue durée*. Although this story remains to be written,[4] we have chosen to focus on the 'history of the present' (Timothy Garton Ash) and the recent turning points at which intellectual debates on the EU have come to life. Of course, each country has its own initial 'European moments' – the 1992 ratification of the Maastricht Treaty in France, the 1993 Constitutional Court decision in Germany; and further back in time, the 1975 accession referendum in Britain or even the heydays of dissidence in the ex-Czechoslovakia or Poland. Consequently, even if each chapter embeds its story in the national intellectual tradition and its predominant 'obsessions', which usually indeed goes back several centuries, most of the debates analysed are predicated on the existence of the European Union.

'European stories' is a collective attempt at contrasting distinct visions of European integration across Europe, exploring differences not only in ultimate diagnosis, but also between the very terms of the debate in various national contexts. How is the European Union framed in different intellectual debates? How is the evolving European polity conceived? What do these differences in turn tell us about the European Union? Are the concerns raised and the assumptions made in these various historically bounded settings part and parcel of a shared *problématique*? Or are they irrelevant to one another? To what extent can we observe a cross-pollination between these national debates, or at least echoes from one arena to the other?

We are aware of no comparative study as yet addressing these issues and based on in-depth analysis of the national normative debates underpinning them. This volume stems from our conviction that the time is ripe to explore such a fascinating avenue of research and to take stock of recent convergences between political or legal theorists increasingly interested in the EU on one hand, and mainstream EU scholarship increasingly interested in normative matters on the other.

In this introductory chapter, we first provide a brief overview of debates over Europe in the *longue durée*, and then try to explain the (near) absence of

---

[3] On the latter question, see for instance Charles 1990; Lemayrie and Sirinelli 2003; Trebitsch and Granjon 1998.

[4] There are very few recent books on the history of the idea of Europe before 1957. See Curcio 1958; Duchenne 2008; Duroselle 1965; or Renouvin 1949. For a philosophical point of view, see Cheneval 2005.

intellectual debates on European integration during the Cold War. In the third section, we suggest that the myriad of visions and positions on the EU in the last two decades can be clustered around three distinct normative models, so that variants of these models can be found across national contexts. Finally, we provide an outline of the volume as a whole through an overview of its various chapters.

Europe invented: Post-war eras across centuries

It might seem anachronistic to use the term 'intellectual' to encapsulate the various visions of Europe found in the literature before the nineteenth century, since the word itself was not used in avant-garde literary circles before the end of the 1890s (Jennings 1993). Some actually identify the decisive moment as the Dreyfus Affair, more precisely 1 February 1898 when Maurice Barrès mocked as a 'protestation des intellectuels' the text signed by some 1,200 scholars endorsing Emile Zola's charges against the Dreyfus trial. So while the term entered common parlance with a pejorative connotation, 'as often in such cases, those to whom it was applied came in time to claim it proudly as a self-description' (Collini 2006: 21). However, even if the concept itself was not coined before the nineteenth century, one can – along with Francis Cheneval, who in the following chapter draws on both the sociological definition provided by Jacques Le Goff and the metaphysical theory of Alain de Libera – retrospectively consider as 'intellectuals' the various scholars who, since the end of the thirteenth century, have led a life of research independent from direct secular or ecclesiastic control.[5]

Accordingly, early thinking on 'Europe' can be traced back to the emergence of what Le Goff termed a *communauté de clercs*, whose profession lay in philosophy and the teaching of their thought. As recounted in the next chapter, historians have found no fewer than 182 European unification projects authored between 1306 and 1945 (Foerster 1967). We will not give a potted history of these 'European visions', but simply highlight three crucial moments in the story, namely the Enlightenment, the interwar years, and the immediate post-1945 era.

---

[5] European unification seems to have entered the history of ideas with Pierre Dubois (1255–1312). A student of Thomas Aquinas and Siger de Brabant at the University of Paris, Dubois outlines in his treatise *De Recuperatione Terrae Sanctae* what appears to be the oldest proposal for a confederation of kingdoms founded on the authority of international arbitrage, to be entrusted neither to papal nor imperial authority but to a secular council representing each member of the federation. Though this plan had no immediate impact, it seems to have influenced several later projects for European unification, as late as the mid-nineteenth century in the writings of Ernest Renan for instance (Voyenne 1954).

It is nothing new to say that Europe has been born and reborn from the ashes of wars. But we must be wary of reading pre-Enlightenment visions of Europe with hindsight and assuming that greater unity was always necessarily associated with progress. Indeed, before the Enlightenment, the idea of 'Europe' tended to be advocated as a way to *resist* change, in the context of a growing desire for strict state independence from imperial or papal power – 'ideas that were infinitely more novel at the time than those of Dante or Dubois' (Duroselle 1965: 73). It was the state which became the object of intellectuals' attention in the century that culminated in the peace of Westphalia (1648), notably through the work of state sovereignty theorists such as Jean Bodin (1530–1596) or Hugo Grotius (1583–1645). Even the idea of federalism, which was to greatly influence Europeanism itself, was first developed (albeit inspired by Biblical covenant principles) by Johannes Althusius (1563–1638) to apply to emerging states and their constituent parts. In the ensuing struggle over the direction of European state-building, Althusius lost to Bodin and the statists who extolled the virtues of unified states, whether under a king or a ruling elite (Nicolaïdis and Howse 2001). In this spirit, Westphalia entrenched the emerging European system in a state-centric notion of peace between European rulers, predicated on the mutual (albeit conditional) respect for state sovereignty.[6]

It was perhaps not an accident, therefore, that the 'European crisis of conscience', to quote a seminal work (Hazard 1953), came precisely in the wake of this consolidation of the nation-state system in Europe at the end of the seventeenth century. Let us call this phenomenon an intellectual *contrapunctual*, a balancing act in the realm of ideas. As political thinkers in this divided community of nations began to explore the promise of secularism and denounce the perils of absolute power, it became an embarrassment to be reminded that their common Christian identity was uniquely what united them. Instead, 'Europe' 'filled the need for a designation with more neutral connotations' (Davies 1996: 7). From this time onwards, we are no longer dealing with a few disparate mentions, a few dozen scattered references to Europe per century. Instead, 'there will be hundreds, thousands, millions' (Duroselle 1965: 105). At the same time as the Neapolitan thinker Giambattista Vico dedicated his magnum opus 'To the Academy of Europe', a proliferation of

---

[6] It is noteworthy that the idea of perpetual peace through deeper continental cooperation reappeared at the very beginning of the Thirty Years War which led to Westphalia in *Le nouveau Cynée ou Discours des Occasions et Moyens d'établir une Paix générale et la liberté de commerce pour tout le monde*, a treatise published in 1623 by the cleric and mathematics master Emeric Crucé. This was not, however, a 'European idea', since Crucé had appealed to Louis XIII to promote the idea of a truly international organization that would extend not only to the Christian kingdoms but also to Turkey, China, Japan, or Persia. The Duc de Sully's project (1620/1635), better known as the *Grand dessein d'Henri IV*, was more clearly centred on Europe and its equal partition between a certain number of powers, of which none would be permitted to take precedence over the others. Under this plan, a Christian Council would represent fifteen states and would be assisted by a permanent senate of sixty members (four for each state).

pamphlets referred to Europe in their title, whether in *L'Europe savante, L'Europa letteraria*, or *Histoire littéraire de l'Europe*.

Encapsulating the spirit of the times, the Pennsylvania legislator and English quaker William Penn, dubbed by Montesquieu as the 'modern Lycurgus', published his 1693 *Essays towards the present and future peace of Europe*. Like previous projects, this plan called for the creation of a body uniting the sovereign princes of Europe into a single and permanent contract, with a number of representatives per state according to the relative size of their populations and economies, a rotating presidency, and decisions taken by a three-quarters majority. More radically, Penn's Diet – which, like that of Crucé, included Turkey and Russia – would have access to an army to enforce its decisions.[7] Little wonder that such proposals were not considered seriously by the powers that be.

One that was taken seriously, in contrast, was the *Projet pour rendre la paix perpétuelle en Europe* (1713–17), formulated by Abbé Charles Irénée de Saint-Pierre and proposing a five-point plan founded on a permanent alliance between European sovereigns; the submission of all sovereigns to the decisions of a European senate; a contribution from all states to the shared costs of the alliance; collective action against any party violating the terms of the pact; and revision of the terms by simple majority, except on fundamental matters such as modification of borders. Criticized for its utopian tone – notably by Voltaire, who rebaptized its author the 'Abbé Saint-Pierre d'Utopie' – the project nonetheless introduced the notion of a collective security conditional on the sovereignty of law, as well as the idea that 'an organised society of States must guarantee the rights of States'. Such innovations were praised by Leibniz, Rousseau, and Kant, to name only three of the authors who (without necessarily endorsing all elements of the Abbé's analysis) praised and – in the case of Jean-Jacques Rousseau – commented prolifically on the project.

With hindsight, however, the Abbé de Saint-Pierre's project (to be analysed in more depth in the next chapter) was eventually eclipsed by the final unification plan of the century, 'the last milestone of 18th-century cosmopolitan utopias' (Duroselle 1965), namely Immanuel Kant's *Zum Ewigen Frieden* of 1795. As is well known, the Könisberg philosopher advocated a Federation of Free States, specifying that no state would be permitted to intervene by force in the constitution or government of another (Article 5). In other words, Kant positioned himself against any form of cosmopolitanism liable to lead to conflation of national characters through absorption of one state by another, and similarly against any merging of nation-states into a new polity (Raulet 1997: 123). Within the Federation of Free States envisioned by Kant, states could not be required to renounce sovereignty in order to merge into a 'superstate', a

---

[7] In 1710, another quaker, John Bellens, would propose highly similar ideas to the British Parliament in a project entitled *Some Reasons for a European State*.

structure which in Kant's view could not be republican and would inevitably take the form of an absolute monarchy.

To be sure, there is considerable controversy in the literature on the nature of Kant's cosmopolitanism and the difference between what can be referred to as the first versus second Kant, or the statist versus cosmopolitan emphasis in his writings (Hurrell 1990). Yet, we can at least say safely here that the Kant of *Perpetual Peace* was searching for a third way between absolute state sovereignty and the absolute transcendence of such sovereignty. Kant thus identified a three-tier legislative structure applicable to political organization within and between states. State law would regulate relations between citizen and state, as well as amongst the citizenry. International law would regulate relations between sovereign and fully autonomous states. Cosmopolitan or transnational law would meanwhile set the parameters of a third dimension allowing for the establishment of juridical relations between foreigners and host states, as well as among foreigners themselves. In Kant's thinking, this cosmopolitan law was confined to the single condition of universal hospitality: it allowed for the free circulation of people (and ideas) while excluding the right to take up permanent residence outside one's own country (Cheneval 2005; Raulet 1997: 127). As we shall see below, the interpretation of Kant's theory continues to animate a large swathe of the theoretical debate on Europe. What is clear is that 150 years after Westphalia, while the idea of Europe has come to prevail as a moral alternative to Christianity, it remains a complement to the idea of European nations.

It would take more than a century and the most bloody war in human history, however, to generate a second wind of intellectual passion for Europe. Indeed, bracketing the Enlightenment as pre-history, the interwar period has been described by some historians as the 'first golden age' of the European ideal among intellectuals (Lemayrie 2008), who across Europe quickly came to equate a united Europe with the cause of peace (Frank 2002: 315). Some estimate at over six hundred the number of articles (excluding those in the daily press) and academic works published on the question of European unity between 1919 and 1939, and principally between 1925 and the start of the 1930s (Chabot 2005).[8] At the same time, numerous new 'European movements' were created from London to Denmark and Vienna, devoted to furthering the unification of the Continent.[9]

---

[8] Journals dedicated at least in part to Europe included: André Gide's *La Nouvelle Revue Française*, focusing on Franco-German exchanges; Louise Weiss' *L'Europe nouvelle*, which published a series of articles *inter alia* around the theme of international cultural cooperation; José Ortega y Gasset's *La Revista de l'Occidente*; *Revue Européenne*; and *Europe*.

[9] These include the European Unity League, founded in London in 1913; the *Les Etats-Unis des Nations européennes* or *Scandinavian Initiative*, instigated around 1924 in Roskilde (Denmark) by Dr Heerfordt; and the *Comité Franco-Allemand d'Information et de Documentation* established by the Luxembourgeois industrialist Emil Mayrisch in 1926. Another project, instigated by Prince Karl-Anton of Rohan, led to the creation in 1923 of the Vienna-based *Kulturband* as well as the *Fédération des Unions intellectuelles* in Paris.

Yet such newfound European fervour often needed more than the simple idea of peace to substantiate itself. Take, for instance, perhaps the most famous movement at the time: *Paneuropa*, founded in 1923 by the Czech Richard Coudenhove-Kalergi. The world order envisaged by the movement was organized around vast global empires – Panamerica, the British Empire, the Soviet Union, Panasia, and finally Paneurope – the latter noticeably excluding Russia and Great Britain. However, Coudenhove-Kalergi remained vague on how to implement his plan for European integration, merely calling for a political confederation modelled on the United States and based on an arbitration treaty and a customs union. More to the point, he shared with numerous other prophets of European unification in the interwar years the conviction that European political decline was due above all to a 'crisis of conscience' which could only be alleviated by a moral revolution. Indeed, this culturally pessimist vision of a united Europe fell little short of a brand of mystique in which European political integration was intimately bound up with the advent of a new spiritual direction (Chabot 2005).

The moral dimension of Europeanism is at the core of Julien Benda's *Discours à la nation européenne* (a paraphrase of Fichte's *Speeches to the German Nation*) of 1933. In this essay, largely forgotten today, the French thinker made a vibrant plea for a Europe of reason and universalism to stand up against the dangers of particularism embodied in the national 'nettle'. For Benda, the unity of Europe would not grow out of economic or material interests, but rather out of education and ethics. Contrary to what the title of his book may suggest, the ethics in question dictated that Europe remain free of any nationalism on a larger scale, as European unity could only have moral value if 'far from being an end in itself, it is but a moment in our quest for God, when all instincts, all marks of pride and selfishness have disappeared' (Benda 1992: 126). Benda called on his fellow European intellectuals to drive home the point that nationalism as such was morally compromised (Müller 2006: 129), and that European unification would herald the victory of reason and abstraction over pragmatism and particularism.

The impact of this intellectual effervescence on Europe's political life was not trivial. It contributed to and was stimulated by Aristide Briand's project of a 'European federation' in his 5 September 1929 speech on the necessity of a 'sort of federal link', and the memorandum of May 1930 on the organization of a 'European Federal Union' further elaborated by Alexis Léger (the poet Saint-John Perse). The intellectual melting pot culminated in the interviews held in Paris between leading literary figures on 16–18 October 1933. Directed by Paul Valéry, the group brought together Georges Duhamel, Aldous Huxley, Hermann von Keyserling, Salvador de Madiaraga, Jules Romains, and others. The atmosphere, however, had changed over the preceding years: the failure of Briand's project against the backdrop of Hitler's accession to power cast an ominous shadow over events, and indeed as of 1933 European unification projects declined rapidly. Moreover, when Europe was invoked, it was increasingly not just as a reaction to nationalism in the abstract but against a particular incarnation thereof, for instance the social democracy of the Weimar Republic or of the popular front. To some extent, the very fact that so many intellectuals had seen in Europe the incarnation of 'pure' values, as opposed to the materialist values of mass production and consumption prevailing in the US and the USSR, muted their reaction to Hitler's rise to power – even leading some to acquiesce. It is perhaps in part due to this tainted heritage that the first golden age of the European movement now represents a moment when 'intellectuals appear to have played a role that they would never recover' (Lemayrie 2008: 239).

Nevertheless, the initial effect of the Second World War appeared similar to the First, albeit unsurprisingly without the moral certitudes.[10] The second 'brief golden age of intellectuals' commitment to European affairs', in Lemayrie's words, speaks of a desire to return to the pre-war brand of European humanism, but this time around with a much greater focus on political organization and polity-building. Indeed, the key idea of the immediate post-war era speaks to a collective desire to transcend nationalism along a path well trodden across the Atlantic, namely federalism. Altiero Spinelli symbolizes this trope, penning the first federalist manifesto for Europe in 1941 (along with his colleagues Ernesto Rossi, E. Colorni and Colorni's wife Ursula Hirschman) and creating the *Movimento Federalista Europeo* in 1943. This would eventually become a pan-European federalist movement with the creation of the Union of European Federalists in 1946 (in collaboration with Alexandre Marc – previously founder of *La Fédération*, a pioneer interwar group).

But while the movement was able to draw on the aura of the Resistance to elicit significant 'idealist' following in the immediate post-war years, it failed to connect effectively with political realities of the time. As they grew in numbers, federalists 'simply wrote ... as if the mere recommendation by well meaning advocates unburdened by a reactionary political past, of a rational formula for the "sensible" reorganization of the continent's political arrangements was all that was required given the postwar catharsis, to bring it about' (O'Neill 1996: 27). Soon the movement would split between those embracing the pragmatism of Monnet's methods and those who preferred to remain with the pure vision (although it would reunite in the post-Cold War years). But perhaps more notable than their disagreements was simply intellectuals' rapid loss of interest in the European question. Hence the European intellectuals' paradox: as the

---

[10] There were still representatives of this sensibility, such as Denis de Rougemont who organized a series of meetings in Geneva under the umbrella theme of 'The European Spirit'; contributions were made by Karl Jaspers, Salvador de Madariaga, Albert Camus, Julien Benda, and others. Rougemont also directed the *Centre Européen de la culture* (1950) and presided over the *Congrès pour la liberté de la culture* (1951), the latter counting among its participants Hannah Arendt and Raymond Aron.

European project finally turned into reality, intellectuals turned away from it (Bachoud, Cuesta, and Trebitsch 2000: 11).

Europe ignored: Perversity, diversion, and disillusion

How can we explain this European intellectuals' paradox? Why were intellectual and political activism so far apart during these Cold War decades? We see three categories of arguments.

Perversity. Firstly and obviously, for many of these intellectuals, especially former members of the Resistance, the very idea of European unity had been tainted beyond redemption by the most lethal plan yet for European unification, namely Hitler's New European Order. 'Many intellectuals and bureaucrats across the continent enthusiastically supported the project and a whole ideology – which was not simply identical with Nazism – built around ideas of peace and specific European values' (Müller 2007; see also Case 2008). In short, the idea of a united Europe had only recently helped justify war, not peace, with the assent of many of the intellectuals who had taken up its cause in the interwar period. Even the term 'Community' had been tainted by its use under the Pétain regime.

Diversion. Secondly, at least from the late 1950s onwards Europe had become a diversion from the two great causes of the era: the Cold War and decolonization. In these two defining conflicts Europe was simply on the wrong side for significant parts of the left-leaning intelligentsia. How could one be *against* American domination and colonial oppression and *for* Europe? More specifically, the new geopolitical context marked the end of the natural equation between Europeanism and universalism (Bachoud, Cuesta, and Trebitsch, 2000: 12). In the interwar period, it was still possible to believe that Europe signified universalism because it prefigured the eventual construction of a lasting world peace. In spite of rising anti-colonialism, one could believe in the bright side of nineteenth-century universalism, the idea that other parts of humanity should have access to progress and modernity exemplified by Europe. After 1950, in contrast, as European states struggled with the aftermath of their civil war turned World War and their often bloody decolonization, it had become clear that Europe's 'Other' could only be its own past. By all means let Europe look for ways to overcome such a past through economic cooperation, but this should be seen as a particularist cause, neither generous nor universal (Frank 2000).

This new cluster of associations with Europe (Hitler, Auschwitz, conquest, colonialism) might help to explain why so many intellectuals after 1945 were often indifferent or even opposed to the European Community (Müller 2007). André Rezler, director of the *Centre européen de la culture* created immediately after the Hague Congress of 1948, thus suggested that the 'de-Europeanization' of intellectuals in the 1950s and 1960s was first and foremost a result of their 'bad conscience' stemming from the violence perpetrated by or in the name of Europe (Rezler 1976, quoted by Frank 2000).

Disillusion. Thirdly and finally, many leading intellectual figures rejected the European cause out of disillusion with the actual project of European integration as it came to be. Even those who were 'true Europeans' did not like what they saw. The EEC was identified with a Europe of 'tradesmen' and technocracy, narrowly economic in nature, and devoid of the kind of commitment to values and spiritual uplifting with which they had identified Europe in the interwar period. Witness for instance the evolution of review *Esprit* in France. Led by figures such as Emmanuel Mounier, Joseph Rovan, or Alfred Grosser, it remained staunchly committed to Europe between 1945 and 1948, when the promotion of peace, federal Europe, and Franco-German reconciliation were the order of the day. But it progressively 'de-Europeanized' over the following years, calling the ECSC a 'false Europe' existing only on economic foundations (Frank 2000). And when the debate on the European Defence Community (1954) raged in the French parliament and other political forums, most intellectuals remained silent or came out against the project.

These stances and their motivations stand in stark contrast with the kinds of debates which emanated from the 'other Europe' during this period. Interestingly, during the first three decades of European integration, it was on the other side of the iron curtain that anti-totalitarian engagement contributed to reflections on European civilization – notably through the idea, found under various guises in the works of the Pole Czesław Miłosz, the Czech Jan Patočka, or the Hungarian István Bibó – that 'European identity is consubstantial with the idea of liberty, and must be founded on an effort at critical reflection rather than simple subservience to a tradition' (Laignel-Lavastine 2000: 30). The idea of a Europe grounded in the ethics of responsibility is at the heart of dissident thought. Against nationalism and ultraliberalism, intellectuals like Bibó or Patočka revisited the question of European universalism in light of their own dispossession of what they saw as European values. Bibó defined European civilization as emancipation of the weakest and legal restraint of the powerful, while Patočka, chief spokesman of Charter 77 alongside Václav Havel, associated European culture with the chance of providing a space for resistance both to totalitarianism and to an exclusively market-based economic rationality. Dissident reviews – *Kultura* in Poland, *Svedectivi* in Czechoslovakia, *La Nouvelle alternative, Lettre internationale* – all engaged in trans-European intellectual exchange. It could be argued that to this day the intellectual attitude on Europe in these countries remains 'politicized' by the fact that pro-European ideas were often carried by exiles and dissident circles.

To be sure, Europe started to make a timid comeback in Western intellectual circles in the mid-1970s as they belatedly picked up on the critique of totalitarianism long expounded by their Eastern counterparts. The shockwaves created by the publication of Alexander Solzhenitsyn's *Gulag Archipelago* in 1974, combined with the Helsinki process and the Cambodia tragedy which opened many eyes to the impasse of communism, led in 1978 to the creation of the *Comité des intellectuels pour l'Europe des libertés*. This marked the revival of a liberal intellectual thrust and its convergence with non-Marxist currents on the left, including on the part of converted ex-Marxists (Lemayrie 2008: 242). In this regard, the example of the French sociologist Edgar Morin is significant. A communist until 1951, fighting for decolonization and the 'third world' in the 1950s and 1960s, he remained opposed to European integration until the early 1970s when he understood that 'Europe was a poor little dear thing. I became neo-European because I saw that Europe was ill' (Morin 1987). Like him, with the decline of Marxism, many European intellectuals progressively came back to a more realistic (and democratic) cause in the form of European integration (Frank 2002: 324). To simplify greatly, in the three decades following the signing of the Treaty of Rome, the *perversity school* waned with the fading echoes of the war, except in some ultranationalist British circles; and the *diversion school* lost its relevance or at least its intensity as both decolonization and communism lost their mobilizing potential. The *disillusion school* certainly did not disappear to the same degree, and the anti-materialist, anti-capitalist, anti-globalization critique of the EC/EU has since remained alive and well. But, as in Edgar Morin's case, a growing number of intellectuals came to see that it was precisely its anti-utopian quality that could be the grounds for embracing it, with eyes open and without illusions.

Nevertheless, from the signing of the Treaty of Rome to that of the Maastricht Treaty (1992), European integration attracted precious few 'public intellectuals', especially popular political philosophers. There were plenty of intellectuals *in* Europe but few intellectuals *on* Europe. The political scientists and other social scientists who remained engaged with the European project spoke and published in restricted circles disconnected from the public sphere. Only with the end of the Cold War, the project of reunifying the continent through the EU, and the dual launch of political and monetary union at Maastricht did the intellectual class as a whole finally wake up to a Europe which had undergone a profound metamorphosis since its inception.

What European polity? Three normative visions of the European Union

European intellectuals have had a lot of catching up to do over the past two decades. The European Union has continued to expand its remit to politically sensitive areas of action from money to migrants and defence, giving rise to public debates over its very nature as a polity. As pointed out by Kaelble, this politicization process was certainly heightened by intellectuals' rediscovery of Europe as a topic of analysis. 'This ended a long period of disinterest and disdain with which intellectuals, for the most parts, had treated the area of the EU since the 1950s – as a small, purely economic, technocratic, culturally unattractive, and conservative project' (Kaelble 2009: 194).

To be sure, before Maastricht and the end of the Cold War, academics focused on the different dimensions of integration (legal, institutional, economic, social, political) either descriptively, historically, or analytically – asking what were the drivers of integration or the causes of resistance to it. However, they very rarely delved into the normative questions attached to the process. But since the early 1990s, the 'question of Europe' has emerged as a bone of contention among major figures of contemporary political thought across the continent. Intellectuals with no prior interest in the European Union have come to recognize its relevance to larger philosophical problems, from the relative merits of liberal, communitarian, or republican paradigms for democracy within and beyond the state to the moral significance of political boundaries and geographical borders in cosmopolitan thinking. While some intellectuals continue to embrace the EU as the promise of a polity *beyond nationalism*, others have come to question a 'Community model' based on technocracy, market power, and depoliticization, not least the former dissident intellectuals in Central and Eastern Europe.

Whether or not difficult referenda reflect an erosion of the so-called 'permissive consensus', it appears that the public debates associated with the ratification of the Maastricht Treaty have at last opened the valves for theorizing on the legitimacy of the European Union. As the story goes, the sheer volume and impact of decision-making at the European level erodes the legitimacy of the democracies that provide its foundations, without acquiring a generally recognized democratic legitimacy in its own right. We may or may not agree with this diagnosis, but what matters to us here is that this very perception has served as a trigger. Now convinced that 'the EU matters', intellectuals across Europe have increasingly come to debate the actual, potential, or desirable existence of a European public sphere, a European identity, or a European people, and the relationship between these and their national counterparts. Still, the debate remains largely compartmentalized across member states, disciplines, and issue areas. Debates over the advent of a transnational civil society or a European public space, the question of the democratic deficit in the European Union, or of constitutional patriotism and the like have almost become specific and separated theoretical research subjects.

This volume attempts, however, to discern broad cross-national patterns across member states. We argue that one can discern two main debates. The first is the perennial debate between those who call for continent-wide unity and those who defend European nations as the only legitimate political units. Underlying this first debate have usually been historically contingent ideas on the best way to secure progress or the public good, be it peace, prosperity, morality, or the good life. In other words: does progress, whatever it may mean, lie with more or less Europe? What is the promise or fear behind the cause of uniting the Continent?

The second debate builds on the first at a higher level of complexity, and could be termed the 'search for a third way', whereby certain thinkers seek to demarcate themselves from either side of the first debate, coming up instead with political designs which neither reify nor deny state-level sovereignty, seeking instead to tease out the conditions for upholding 'unity in diversity' (to borrow a contemporary phrase). This second debate leaves questions of substantive progress in the background in order to privilege the question of diversity and pluralism per se: can we have both Europe and its states, cooperation and sovereignty together? How can we preserve diversity while seeking to pursue common goals?

So, since Maastricht, a philosophical triangle which stems from two debates can be identified across member states, albeit under different variants. Even if not all the authors that have contributed to the framing of this conceptual map would qualify as 'public intellectuals', we believe that this triangle can help to locate the intellectual debates on Europe across various countries. This is summarized in Figure 1.1.

At one end of the first opposition, we find what we may call the 'national civic' or 'statist' school, who essentially criticize the EU in the name of the nation-state. At its most general, this school of thought is based on the idea that the cradle of both modern democracy and the welfare state is the nation-state, which arguably cannot be reproduced as such at the European level. As democracy presupposes a community with a common language and common representations which originates in a shared history and exists thanks to its very differences from other communities, and as Europe does not – or cannot – meet such prerequisites, the idea of a European democracy is an aporia. Similarly, the

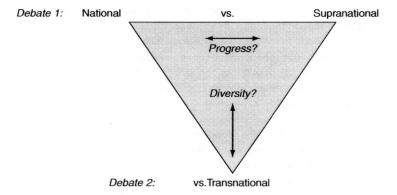

Figure 1.1 European Stories: The debates

mutual sacrifices required by social justice suppose the kind of mutual trust and identification found within bound political communities.

Here, the European Union is not apprehended as a theoretical, political object per se, but rather as a label used to describe a process of de-compartmentalization of national markets and standardization of rules and regulations promoted by technocratic regulatory bodies. Consequently, European integration is not considered as progressive but rather as a threat to both collective self-determination and/or social justice – the two major achievements of the contemporary nation-state. This school of thought could itself be divided into two strands – a conservative strand which sees Europe as a threat to national identity and cultural values, and a progressive strand which insists on seeing the nation-state as the best way to guarantee self-government and social justice. As shown in this volume, many prominent thinkers from Norway to the United Kingdom, France, or the Czech Republic offer variations on this theme.

In contrast and at the other end of the spectrum are all those who equate more Europe with progress, what we may call the 'supranational' school. Europe is seen as the promise of economic, social, moral, and eventually political progress by virtue of its anti-nationalist and anti-hegemonic features, premised on the assumption that it constitutes a new territorial scale where democratic principles may spread. A federal Europe would also be the only way to 'rescue' the achievements of the national welfare state – achievements that are threatened by the pace of globalization. The advocates of this conception of Europe acknowledge the fact that a common language and shared values are necessary to consolidate a democratic political community, but they argue that these have been the result of a long historical process when unfolding at the nation-state level and that a similar process may take place at the European level. Clearly there are disagreements within this school itself, including on the necessary conditions for the emergence of a true continental democracy (whatever this may mean), or the development of a European public space underpinning and ultimately embodying European political identity. But all seem to agree that these developments are desirable to the furthering of the European cause. Conceived as a supranational project, the ideal-type Europe of this school of thought would potentially be a multinational federal state.

There are of course many intellectuals in Europe today who have taken up the flame of the European cause – as shown in this volume. Foremost among them, Jürgen Habermas has come to embrace this last vision in his later work (Habermas 2001b, 2006b; Habermas and Derrida 2005), inspiring *inter alia* an upsurge in intellectual support for an EU Constitution. For him, however, the concept of a permanent alliance between peoples envisioned by Kant in the *Perpetual Peace* was incompatible with Kant's own presuppositions. Indeed, in the 'Doctrine of Right', the first part of the *The Metaphysics of Morals*, Kant grounded the general principles of law on human rights and should not logically have considered that individual liberty depended on state sovereignty (Habermas 1996). It was according to this logic that Habermas declared himself in favour of a European federal state: 'I support the idea of a European Constitution, and consequently of the adoption by Europe of a new principle of legitimacy and of Europe acquiring the status of a State' (Habermas 2001c: 102).

This first-order debate between the statist or national school and the supra-national school which we find in different form across member states does not, however, exhaust Europe's intellectual landscape. Indeed, there are also those who oppose both sides in this first debate by advocating a third way between the two, or rather a way to transcend this age-old opposition. Here, the debate revolves more around the challenge of accommodating radical diversity within a polity in the making than around that of progress as such. If both sides of the first debate share a fundamentally state-centric outlook, the third way sees Europe as a new kind of polity.

This third school of thought may be called 'transnational', although one of its earlier variants was misleadingly referred to as 'post-national'. It upholds the view that Europe is a body of regulations, procedures, rights, and norms destined to 'tame' national democracies, and shares with the champions of the 'national civic' approach the idea that democracy can only really exist – at least at this stage of history – within the framework of the nation. But this school also diverges from statist views in so far as it considers that the European 'constraint' is not the source of some form of dissolution of national democracies, but rather a potential means of perfecting them (Bellamy and Castiglione 1998 and 2003; Weiler 2001). Accordingly, the EU's main asset is the constitutional discipline that it imposes on the member states, for example the ban on any form of discrimination based on nationality. For many of those identifying with the transnational vein, Europe is more a constitutional polity than an evolving democracy, and the mechanisms that allow citizens to take part in European decision-making processes are a means for the promotion of individual rights rather than the necessary condition for the emergence of a shared civic culture.

Though they belong to the same third 'family', some of these scholars do not content themselves with a vision of Europe in which democracy would be confined to the strict limits of national space. The EU is more than a confederation of states since its peoples are also connected through multi-faceted and deep forms of political and historical mutual recognition, what Nicolaïdis refers to as a 'demoï-cracy' in the making (Nicolaïdis 2004a: 101). This interpretation of the cosmopolitan paradigm is now supported notably by authors such as Jean-Marc Ferry (2000 and 2005), and is grounded on an alternative reading of Kant to that proposed by Habermas. For these authors, Habermas failed to see that the permanence of states and of their rights according to the principles of equal liberty was essential in the making of a cosmopolitan state 'which cannot simply be buttressed on the universal constitutionalization of fundamental rights, but should stem from the constitutional recognition of the fundamental rights of the peoples' (Ferry 1998: 11). The EU represents a 'federalism of free states' or a federal union rather than a federal state as defined in the second article of Kant's *Perpetual Peace*. A federation of states differs from a federal state in as much as it precisely allows for the persistence of the sovereignty principle for its constituent parts (Beaud 2007). In its original sense, a federation is defined as a durable union based on a free convention (*foedus*). Understood as a third way between a federal state system and a confederation, the federal union thus transcends the sacrosanct distinction between domestic public law and international law. According to these authors, cosmopolitanism would be some form of voluntary legal integration of free states based on regular and organized deliberation, and not on their subordination to a higher authority. The mutual recognition of European nations may pave the way for the emergence of a shared civic culture without necessarily heralding the advent of a federal Europe. The European polity should thus give birth to a federation of states *and* peoples.

In short, in the words of Francis Cheneval in the next chapter, we move from an incremental to a transformative logic, whereby a change of geographical level (from nation to Europe, or for that matter to the world) should not consist in simply reproducing the same pattern on a different scale. In this sense, the idea of Europe as a 'third way' between the national and supranational logics (as we present it here) chimes with Cheneval's depiction of a Europe struggling to exist between the patriotic trope (which may be found in either) and the universal cosmopolitan one. In many aspects, the three models identified sit very well with the three Democratic Orders identified by Eriksen and Fossum in framing the RECON project,[11] namely the 'Audit Democracy' – in which the union is derived from the member states; the 'Federal Multinational Democracy' – in which the union is recognized as a sovereign state, in accordance with international law; and the 'Regional European Democracy' – in which polity sovereignty is multi-dimensional and shared among levels (Eriksen and Fossum 2007).

These core debates over the nature of the European polity are not, of course, the only controversy that animates the national intellectual debates pertaining to the EU. Morever, the aims and forms of national normative debates vary greatly since they reflect the core characteristics embedded in each national political culture. Intellectuals approach the topic of European integration equipped with a cultural repertoire that tends to vary along social, political, and national lines and includes values, knowledge, *habitus*, stories, memories, and worldviews upon which they draw more or less consciously. Put differently, concepts such as democracy, citizenship, or the republic as well as values, ethics, or norms are now at the core of debates that inextricably link the

---

[11] RECON is an Integrated Project supported by the European Commission's Sixth Framework Programme for Research (2007–2011).

'national' and the 'European'. This book explores some of the ways in which these different meanings come together to weave a mosaic of European stories.

A roadmap of the volume

The book proceeds in six parts. The introductory part lays out some general analytical building blocks on European intellectuals and European debates. The next three parts group countries according to the classic chronology: the 'old' founding member states (Part II); states who joined either in the first enlargement in 1973 or in the 1980s before the end of the Cold War (Part III); and three new members from Central and South-East Europe (Part IV). We group these two latter states under the label the 'Returners'. This title might be misleading since the countries of the former Soviet bloc had never left Europe, although their leaders used the rhetoric of exclusion/return as a means of strengthening their case for early EU membership.[12] To the extent that they were returning to Europe, so were Greece, Portugal, and Spain: all were returning from dictatorship to democracy. And yet, the title is still justified by the fact that the Mediterranean countries had not been isolated and cut off from Western Europe in the way that the countries of Central and Eastern Europe had been. Part V adds two non-members – Norway and Turkey. Finally, Part VI offers two concluding sets of remarks, one on the relation across Europe between the intellectual public sphere and public opinion across member states; the other a defence of narrative diversity in the EU through an elucidation of the various debates covered in the book.

Since we argue that these intellectual debates on Europe are country-specific, this book should ideally have included a chapter on each 'European' country. Even short of this ideal, one might regret the absence of a chapter on Belgium, Luxembourg, and the Netherlands among the 'Founders', on Denmark among the 'Joiners', or on Portugal among those Mediterranean states who joined between 1980 and 1986. It is also a great pity to do without the states who joined in 1995 – Austria, Finland, and Sweden – or Hungary among our 'Returners'. We firmly believe that all the national intellectual debates around Europe deserve all our attention in a comparative perspective. They all contribute to the framing of our 'European stories', even though it would be naïve – albeit politically correct – to deny that some national debates are more influential than others.

This book does not aim to provide a comprehensive overview of all the national intellectual debates on Europe. More modestly, our ambition is to open the way for new research on this topic which will eventually cover the

---

[12] We owe this remark to an anonymous referee.

many countries not considered here. Ours is an ongoing project – to be continued individually and collectively. The sample of countries chosen here is not necessarily representative. We did however try to cover as many as possible of the attributes we deemed important in discussing national stories about Europe. We therefore sought to discuss old and new EU members, members and non-members, Southern, Nordic, Western, and Eastern countries, large, medium, and small states, mainstream Catholic and non-Catholic cultures, periphery versus core, etc. Such a range we believe provides enough comparative leverage to convey the variety of European stories which can be found across Europe without overwhelming the reader.

Clearly, no simple grouping of European countries can be satisfactory when we consider the many strands, meanderings, and conflicts that characterize each national debate over time, as well as the many echoes and contrasts between these debates. Europe takes on many faces and elicits countless narratives in all these contexts. It can be *invented* and reinvented from the ashes of the past; it has been *othered* by those who still 'go to Europe' when they cross their borders, or conversely *possessed* by those who believe that they are at its core; it has long been *imagined* as a community to which one did not yet or quite belong, *appropriated* as a project of one's own, *enlisted* at the service of various national projects, or seen as rightfully *returned*; it has been alternatively *reified, revered, resented,* or *defied* . . . Often, it is simply *ignored*. Sometimes, all of the above can be found in the same country. And so we try to convey this effervescence as best we can.

I *Themes*

In Chapter 1, Francis Cheneval analyses the ambiguous status of the European intellectual in a European integration process understood as the attempt to overcome self-centred patriotism in the name of universal principles. He shows that European intellectuals adhering to universal principles find themselves caught between two rationales – the rationale of political particularity and closure on the one hand, and that of cosmopolitan integration on the other. The challenging question is thus how European intellectuals can defend European institution-building and political consolidation when the process is in strong tension with cosmopolitan ideals. Such a conceptual incertitude between Euro-patriotism and cosmopolitan tendencies is evident in the recent evolution of Jürgen Habermas, whose discrepancy between an initial plea for critical and rational identities and a more recent glorification of the European model might well illustrate a structural problem of European integration theory faced by many European intellectuals over time. Yet Cheneval admits that it is easier to criticize Habermas' statist view of the EU than to conceive an alternative path of successful European integration. Ultimately, the productive tension between particularity and universalism seems to remain the hallmark of (European) intellectualism.

However, as pointed out below, over the past two decades European integration has indeed undergone profound transformations, from an elite process conducive to progressive supranational sovereignty pooling to deeper processes of constructing a European polity and European society. The struggles between different ideological projects over national boundaries in elections and referenda have been conducive to politicization, and have replaced mass public 'permissive consensus' by 'constraining dissensus' (Hooghe and Marks 2009). Consequently, in Chapter 2, Ulrike Liebert analyses the dialectics of national intellectual discourses on Europe from the perspective of the controversial issue of democratic legitimacy in Europe. She scrutinizes the contents of national intellectual contributions to this debate during the most recent critical and contentious debate over European political development, from 2001 to 2009. She argues that European democracy debates oscillate between a communitarian vision that cherishes democracy in collectivist terms and a liberal vision that celebrates diversity, individual rights, and legal constitutionalism. Echoing the normative triangle presented in this introduction (although with a different focus), she then considers 'European demoï-cracy' and 'constestatory democracy' as innovative proposals that aim to square the circle of unity and diversity. Here, the third way is not, as we suggest, between sovereigntists and supranationalists; rather, it is (similarly) between both of these seen as communitarians on one hand, and the liberal tradition on the other (which we would include in the third way, but which admittedly has not attempted to integrate the arguments of communitarians).

In Chapter 3, Michael Freeden begins by asking the question 'What is an intellectual?' He draws for this on Mannheim's definition, according to which in every society there are social groups whose special task is to provide an interpretation of the world for that society. He argues that all social views might be contestable interpretations of a moving and fluctuating reality, rather than historically anchored truths. Moreover, he points that the recent 'flashiness' associated with being an intellectual, combined with lower barriers to entry, has somewhat undermined intellectuals' authority in our liberal societies. From this analytical background, Freeden raises some doubts about considering 'intellectuals' as 'story-tellers', as we try to do in this book. He reminds us that telling stories is an act of imagination and interpretation, less of rational critique, whose authors are for the most part not intellectuals. He also sheds a new light on the overused concept of 'democratic deficit', pointing out that we would be hard pressed to imagine a democratic arrangement that would not produce such a deficit of one kind or another. Consequently, intellectuals need to ask which necessarily inadequate combination of political features has the most chances of durable implementation, given the main cultural features of European countries. In addition, intellectuals should remain modest by recognizing that a common legal and political framework is never devoid of ideological content.

II *Founders*

In Chapter 4, Jan-Werner Müller discusses the peculiarities of the *German* debate on the EU. It is not surprising that most politicians and intellectuals in West Germany have long been favourably disposed towards the idea of European unification – to the extent that Euroscepticism remains almost a political taboo. The country was effectively a semi-sovereign polity until 1990; its national traditions had been thoroughly thrown into question by Nazism, to the extent that many intellectuals on the left actually equated National Socialism, nationalism, and nation-statehood. Yet it would be wrong to say, even given the absence of anything resembling a systematic Eurosceptical tradition, that German politicians and intellectuals have always been uniformly pro-European for the same reasons. It is often forgotten that the plans of the federalist movement were conclusively sidelined after 1945, or that proponents of a unified democratic-socialist Europe were thoroughly frustrated. Meanwhile politicians, while using idealistic pro-European rhetoric, often advanced German interests 'in Europe's name' (to use Timothy Garton Ash's formulation). In a less obvious way, German ideals of European unification have often been projections of the country's own supposedly post-national trajectory after 1945. However, beginning in the mid-1990s, there has been a harsher tone among politicians regarding Europe, independent of party affiliation, while constitutional lawyers have also increasingly asserted the need to rein in the ECJ and affirm the nation-states as ultimate *Herren der Verträge* (masters of the treaties). Intellectual opinion, meanwhile – on the EU constitutional debate in particular – has increasingly split: on the one hand, there are those hoping for continuous supranational constitutionalization (which appears almost as a last utopia), on the other there has been a marked celebration of legal pluralism and fragmentation of international law. Müller argues that these correspond broadly to the theoretical legacies of Jürgen Habermas and Niklas Luhmann respectively.

In *France*, since the hard-won ratification of the Maastricht Treaty in 1992, the European issue has emerged as a bone of contention among French intellectuals. In Chapter 5, Justine Lacroix argues that the current French controversy over Europe is embedded in an even more salient debate on the very nature of democracy. More specifically, the French debate over the EU's democratic legitimacy has revolved around the connection between rights and boundaries, and around the appropriate locus for democracy. As to the meaning attached to 'rights' in democratic politics, Europe is either conceived as the symptom of a 'religion of law', which supposedly undermines democracy; or conversely blamed for its incapacity to implement the human rights it endlessly claims to represent. To be sure, the different perceptions of Europe, seen either as an 'undefined' and 'open' space or an 'exclusive' entity centred on its own particularities, are in total contradiction. The chapter's title, 'Borderline Europe', refers to an object that lends itself to such starkly contrasting representations. In spite of these differences, Lacroix shows that there is no equivalent in the French intellectual circles to the model of federal supranationalism advocated in Germany by Jürgen Habermas. French intellectuals writing on Europe almost all insist on the nation as the main locus for political socialization, but they disagree on whether the EU constitutes an unwelcome motor for the dissolution of national communities or a promise to move beyond the sole nation-state framework.

Chapter 6 on *Italy* by Mario Telò focuses on the intellectual impetus for and roots of the rise of the large domestic consensus in favour of a federal European Union achieved in Italy during the First Republic (1947–92), and addresses the role of intellectuals in explaining the continuities and discontinuities found in ideas about Europe between the First and the Second Republic (1992–2008). The main argument made is that the current normalization of a pro-European intellectual presence in Italy maintains national particularities and distinctive features which cannot be explained without what the French historian Fernand Braudel called a *longue durée* approach. The intellectual debate combined with sixty years of the process of Italian integration into Western Europe is understood as part of long term trends within national and cultural history. This historical construction is powerful enough to counterbalance both past and recent tendencies of discontinuity. More precisely, bipartisan centripetal convergences about EU Treaty ratification, the process of Europeanization of policies and institutions, and a certain decline of the classical Euro-federalist approach, are making the hypothesis of a normalization of the Italian debate about the idea of Europe quite realistic.

III Joiners

In Chapter 7, Georgios Varouxakis offers a critical account of debates on 'the question of Europe' in *British* intellectual life since the issue of membership of the EEC arose in earnest with Britain's first application in 1961. Varouxakis starts with some reflections on the role that perceptions and representations of British and English history have played in shaping the peculiarities of British attitudes towards 'Europe' and Britain's relation to it in the twentieth century. He then goes on to analyse the nature and major characteristics of British intellectuals' debates on the EEC and the issue of British membership from the time of the first British application for entry, in 1961, to the time of the referendum that confirmed Britain's continued membership in 1975. The rest of the chapter then focuses on contemporary intellectual debates on 'Europe' and the EC/EU and analyses both the specific contributions of individual thinkers/'intellectuals' and the major characteristics that can be identified as peculiar to UK debates on the issue. Although British politicians and journalists have traditionally been categorized as being either 'pro-European' or 'Eurosceptic', the picture that emerges as far as 'intellectuals' are concerned is more complex than a simple binary distinction of 'pro-' and 'anti-'. The peculiarities of Britain's position due to its history, its post-imperial hangover, and its so-called 'special relationship' with the United States are discussed as major factors affecting British debates on Europe.

In Chapter 8, Katy Hayward argues that the Irish nation is the principal character in the 'European stories' recounted in *Ireland* and that their dominant theme is always nationalism – official, moderate, and progressive, but nationalism nevertheless. The 'No' results of the first referenda on the Treaty of Nice in 2001 and the Treaty of Lisbon in 2008 may be seen, therefore, as not merely consequences of the changing economic status of Ireland but also as signifiers of the need for a new conceptualization of the relationship between 'nation' and 'Europe' in the twenty-first century. The problem is not so much that of growing Euroscepticism – as indicated by the high opinion among the Irish public of EU membership and its benefits – but an absence of public reflection on the purpose and path of further European integration. Consequently, Hayward argues that there is an urgent need for a fresh vision of Ireland's place in the future European Union, one which requires a depth and a boldness that can only be realized by a new wave of intellectual engagement in this national debate.

In Chapter 9, George Pagoulatos and Xenophon Yataganas argue that the prevalent European story among Greek public intellectuals has equated Europe with progress, identifying the country's modernization challenge with catching up with Europe. Consequently, pro-European supranationalism has been the most vocal opposition pole of the debate, struggling against a long tradition of cultural gravitation towards Eastern Orthodoxy, ethnocentrism, a nostalgic communitarian vision of an unadulterated past, a 'culture of the underdog', or – to follow a more systematic typology – the statist/national school of thought. The independence versus integration, nationalism versus supranationalism divide has been the most salient one in the Greek public intellectual debate. Such ideological polarization, however, has been mitigated by the emergence of a 'third pole', a middle of the road 'transnational' school of thought, which was given impetus by the increasing complexity and mishaps of the European integration project, and especially the disenchantment following the rejection of the European Constitutional Treaty. This transnational school of thought is gathering pace among Greek intellectuals who are principally European scholars.

In Chapter 10, Carlos Closa and Antonio Barroso show that *Spanish* intellectuals have long shown a 'benign neglect' towards the EU and European integration. As a result of the link established between democratization and Europe, the latter occupied an almost totally uncontroversial position. This provoked a vacuum which specialized intellectuals tried to fill. More precisely, public lawyers have assumed a central role in discussion on the EU and this has had the effect of turning it into a kind of arcane domain for specialists. Through a number of case studies, Closa and Barroso argue that it is the notion of constitutional tolerance as articulated by Joseph Weiler (2001) that best fit with Spanish intellectual debates on Europe. The insertion of Spain into the European constitutional architecture is broadly conceived as a way of perfecting national democracy.

IV *Returners*

In Chapter 11, Magdalena Góra and Zdzisław Mach aim to describe and understand the contemporary *Polish* debate about Europe against the background of the development of views on Europe in the twentieth century. The starting point for their analysis is the regaining of the state's independence in 1918 and the accompanying debate about the place of the newly established country in interwar Europe. The continuity and change in Polish debate on Europe over the years are crucial to understanding how the perception of Europe in Poland is constructed nowadays. In the second part of the chapter, the problem of re-orientation of the place of Poland in a changing Europe is discussed. Moreover, the authors present the phenomenon of being 'east of the West and west of the East', as the country's location is often described. The chapter concentrates on reconstruction of the major voices regarding the costs and benefits of integration processes, as well as the self-perception of Poles as Europeans.

In Chapter 12, Daniel Barbu deconstructs the transformations undergone by the language and the enactment of political and intellectual consent to the process of European integration by *Romanian* academia and public intellectuals. Drawing on a mainstream literature rooted in the works of two iconic figures of Romanian culture, Mircea Eliade and Constantin Noica, he argues that Europe was, and still is, almost canonically considered in Romania by those who speak out in the public space as both a convenience in terms of free trade and freedom of movement and as an ethical hazard. Barbu shows that Europe is chiefly conceived more as a source of regulations (*acquis communautaire*) than a new type of polity Romanians have to join, make theirs, and eventually help to build. Accession to the European Union was mainly described as a historical technique marshalled from above, as a political device of extracting consent – under the promise of promoting such social goods as welfare and political pluralism – from a national society characterized by an ahistorical identity unstained by either communism or liberalism. According to this line of thinking, shared also by the spokesmen of the culturally dominant and (semi-)established Church (Greek Orthodox), through the language of constitutionalism, democracy, and human rights Europe tends to sponsor the emergence of a standardized 'recent man', exactly as the ideology of state socialism used to enforce the model of the 'new man'.

In Chapter 13 on the *Czech Republic*, Muriel Blaive and Nicolas Maslowski start off by recalling that the past is like a toolbox, a heritage which can be used in political thinking according to its potential for thought and action. The Czech heritage has been mobilized in two opposite directions in relation to 'Europe': in an ethnic and isolationist, nationalist direction which rejects Europe as a danger (Václav Klaus) and in a humanist direction emphasizing individual responsibility, the heritage of the Enlightenment, and dissidence (Václav Havel). In particular, Blaive and Maslowski underline that 'Central Europe' can be considered as an 'intellectual gate' which predetermines attitudes on Europe as a whole. According to them, a pro-European stance is not only a political issue but is also closely linked to certain attitudes on the domestic front relating to decentralization and civil society. Central Europe, Europe, humanism, human rights, civil society, ecology were historically shaped as one and the same weapon against the communist regime and they still go hand in hand today. Conversely, the Klaus trend, despite its professed anti-communism, appears largely as the heir to pan-Slavism and former anti-Western propaganda. In many aspects, Klaus' denunciation of 'Europeism' as a substitute ideology to socialism echoes some part of the Romanian debate.

V *Outliers*

In Chapter 14 on *Norway*, John Erik Fossum and Cathrine Holst examine how a select number of Norwegian academic intellectuals have conceived of Europe, the European integration process, and Norway's relationship to the rest of Europe. More precisely, they discuss their approach in relation to three conceptions of the European Union: as a problem-solving entity; as a value community; and as a rights-based union. Echoing most of the other chapters in this book, Fossum and Holst's findings suggest that the most important single dominant obsession could be said to boil down to 'the national issue'. The great majority of Norwegian public intellectuals frown at the notion of Europe as a democratic anchor, and instead insist that the EU is a democratic curse, which Norway should stay away from. The European project and European governance are seen to have profoundly negative effects on the role of politics, autonomy, agency, sovereignty, and republican ideals. The same can be said of how Norwegian public intellectuals consider the relationship between Europe-as-values and Europe-as-prosperity. There is a strongly held conviction that Europe is a 'rich man's club', a conviction that has remained unscathed throughout the last two bouts of EU enlargement because of a subtle shift to Europe-as-a-businessman's club, and fountain of an all-permeating neoliberal economics.

Observers, both inside and outside *Turkey*, often assert that there is something exceptional about the country's place in Europe. Assessing whether this is the case, Nora Fisher Onar and Ahmet Evin trace, in Chapter 15, continuity and changes in several schools of thought on Europe from the inception of Ottoman Westernization to the present. They then turn to key moments in the 1999–2009 period during which debates on Turkey's place in Europe were particularly intense in light of acquisition of EU candidate status in 1999. Fisher Onar and Evin argue that certain features of Turkish discourse are constant both over time and across the political spectrum at any given time. These include a tendency to see 'Europe' as a ubiquitous and monolithic actor, and the perception that the 'European experience' offers a menu for change from which some items may be ingested and others ignored. Other aspects of intellectuals' engagement of Europe, however, appear contingent upon the proclivities of the individuals in question and the intellectual traditions to which they adhere, as well as on evolving domestic and international contexts. The interplay between the more constant and more contingent features of discourses on Europe means that views span from those who advocate a selective engagement to those who call for unequivocal convergence with that which they understand Europe to represent.

VI *One story or many?*

Finally, Part VI provides two contrasting chapters in conclusion. In Chapter 16, Juan Díez Medrano focuses on citizen representations and, more generally, on views on Europe expressed by actors in the public sphere. While occasionally these actors are intellectuals, they are more often than not politicians or representatives from interest groups. Their views on Europe are sometimes inspired by those of public and scholarly intellectuals, but only partially overlap with them. Either because European stories lose their national-specific narrative structure as they travel from intellectuals to public actors and citizens, or because public actors and citizens autonomously develop their representations of Europe, the fact is that national public spheres portray the European Union and the European integration process and imagine the future of the European Union in very similar ways. Therefore, Medrano argues that viewed from the public sphere and the citizens' perspective, the most relevant story to be told about the European Union is one of similarity. However one uses the term 'identity' in connection with European integration and the European Union, what one sees is that public actors and citizens share very nearly the same 'European story', with similar cross-national representations of the European Union and a common political identity project.

Conversely, Janie Pélabay, Kalypso Nicolaïdis, and Justine Lacroix argue in the Conclusion that it is neither desirable nor possible to promote a unique, homogenized, and official vision of what it means to be European. As evidenced by the essays in this book, the EU polity is significantly marked, supported, or challenged by a great variety of diverging and competing – though reasonable – stories about Europe. Hence the question of how to accommodate this mosaic of European stories: how could and should they participate in a public process of agreement on the European project? What is the epistemological status given to these competing candidates for European 'story-telling'? Which normative constraints have to regulate their participation in such a process? How to engage in the narrative enterprise without eventually erasing the diversity on which it is entirely based? Based on an overview of European intellectual stories, their conclusion examines what is both theoretically and practically at stake in the very idea of 'narrative diversity' once applied to the EU.

Part I

Themes

1

Lost in Universalization?

On the Difficulty of Localizing the European Intellectual

Francis Cheneval

'Mind the gap': Europe between country and cosmos

> Let us grasp the idea that there are two commonwealths – the one, a vast and truly common state, which embraces alike gods and men, in which we look neither to this corner of the earth nor to that, but measure the bounds of our citizenship by the path of the sun; the other, the one to which we have been assigned by the accident of birth....Some yield service to both common-wealths at the same time – to the greater and to the lesser – some only to the lesser, some only to the greater.
>
> (Seneca 1958: 187–9, *On Leisure* IV.1, trans. Basore)

Seneca reminds us of a fundamental normative problem of political action, the problem of allegiance to the particular and bounded political community versus obedience to universal moral laws. The analysis of the endeavours of European intellectuals in this chapter will show that the underlying dichotomy between country and cosmos continues to pose a fundamental problem for intellectuals who aspire to give political meaning to Europe. In their effort to achieve an integrated or federated political Europe, be it supranational or transnational, intellectuals seem to get lost in between the two normative realms of country and cosmos. Their political conception of Europe, be it supranational or transnational, has to be defended against the allegation that it represents a 'half way house' (Nicolaïdis 2004a: 101). Intellectuals in Europe have indeed often shifted between the defence of allegiance to a bounded national polity on the one hand and a cosmopolitan creed pleading for a community of mankind on the other. Few have defended a distinct political realm of justice for Europe. And from both the nationalist and the cosmopolitan point of view, Europe has appeared to some as a political *non lieu*, an imagined community, undone in the name of cosmopolitanism as soon as conceived by the idea of overcoming national sovereigntism.

We may qualify this statement. Cosmopolitanism, although embracing the world at large, was conceived in Eurocentric terms and amounted to European imperialism rationalized by universal validity claims (Cheneval 2002; Pagden 2000). Patriotism was more transparent as it rejected the grand designs of European integration on the same grounds that it rejected cosmopolitanism, as a morally void synonym for imperialism, authoritarianism, and absolutism. In the debates opposing patriotism to cosmopolitanism, intellectuals either found strong grounds for legitimating their particular political community or for transcending it in the name of universal reason. For the latter, Europe was a transitional category, hard to pin down from any possible point of view, be it in hermeneutically oriented narratives or in normative conceptions.

In this chapter, I try to come to a deeper understanding of the idea of European political integration as it is defended by certain European intellectuals. I shall show that the political conception of Europe, presented in the introduction to this volume as an object of two debates opposing nationalism, supranationalism and transnationalism, not only has difficulties in being determined within these paradigms. European supranationalism and transnationalism both face difficulties also because some of their main arguments have strong cosmopolitan implications. The political conception of Europe is thus confronted with the hiatus between polity and cosmos and, seemingly, a loss in universalization. Some cosmopolitan intellectuals react to this difficulty by shifting back to the concept of sovereignty they tried to overcome. They plead for a European federal state and a closed supranational political community. With the Abbé de Saint-Pierre and Jürgen Habermas, I present examples of this ambiguity from the Enlightenment period as well as from contemporary discussion.

Another group of European intellectuals, however, also minds the gap between the national and the global but offers a different, genuinely Kantian reading of the cosmopolitan position. Furthermore, some intellectuals of this strand conceive a theory of democracy detached from a fixation on a singular demos. For reasons that I shall explain in the next two sections, both groups can be considered *European* intellectuals. I shall also argue that the latter position has more coherence and moral truth. However, the condition of philosophical validity of a conception needs to be distinguished from a theory of historical realization. If the geopolitical scenario of 'multi-polarity without multilateralism' (National Intelligence Council 2008: 81) imposes itself in the next couple of decades, European intellectuals will find it increasingly difficult to defend the third way of Europe as a decentred, open-ended multilateral political process rather than a classic federal state in the making (or unmaking).

The concept of the 'intellectual' will be analysed in further detail later. At this point, I will very briefly justify why Eurosceptic and anti-European intellectuals, such as those for instance mentioned in the chapter on the French discussion by Justine Lacroix or the chapter on the debate in the Czech Republic, will not be treated in this chapter. While they are of course European intellectuals according to a geographical and contextual conception, their rejection of a political meaning of Europe and of European integration has the consequence that they avoid the problem under discussion here: for them it is clear that their (and anybody's) country is the nation-state of origin or adoption, and they argue that it is better for things to remain that way.

'De nobis ipsis silemus'

Before the European intellectual's problem with the hiatus between patriotism and cosmopolitanism is further addressed, the difficulty of defining the (European) intellectual and the role of the European intellectual in European integration needs further explanation. First, studies on intellectuals written by people considering themselves as intellectuals are always in danger of representing an exercise in irrelevant narcissism. Intellectuals like to present themselves as protagonists of revolutionary change, as reasonable legislators of humanity, as solitary prophets crying in the desert, as impartial judges of past and future generations, and so forth. No task, no idea seems lofty enough for their brilliant minds, moral integrity, and limitless imagination. In order to avoid vain self-referential discourse in the treatment of this topic we could follow Mark Lilla (2001) and limit this chapter to a critique of the disastrous political role of many twentieth-century European intellectuals – without forgetting their implants in the United States. In numbers far too great, directly or indirectly, by conviction or defeatism, by calculus or naïveté, intellectuals have contributed to the defence of totalitarian systems, mostly in the name of higher social standards and superior forms of civilization.[1] Furthermore, and maybe happily so if we consider Lilla's point, one cannot but admit to the fact that a large majority of twentieth-century intellectuals have neglected the project of European integration – unlike many of their medieval, Renaissance, and Enlightenment counterparts, or even unlike many thinkers of the nineteenth century up until the First World War (Cheneval 2002).

But such negative and critical discourse on intellectuals, albeit necessary and cathartic, holds the danger of playing the role of the superior judge of intellectuals, made easy by the *ex post* point of view of any critique. Faced with this difficulty, it might be advisable to remember the very first phrase of Kant's

---

[1] Cf. The critique of Jaspers against Heidegger quoted in Lilla 2001: 34–5.

Critique of Pure Reason. It is a quote from Francis Bacon's preface to his *Instauratio Magna*: 'About ourselves we shall remain silent when undertaking the task of science.' According to one possible interpretation of this phrase, and leaving aside the hermeneutic history of reception of Kant's transcendentalism, intellectuals (at least philosophers and scientists) should thus avoid mixing science with a discourse about themselves, be it as individuals or as a group.

However, Mark Lilla does not exclusively cast judgement on intellectuals of the past. In his opinion, contemporary intellectuals also fail to recognize the profound danger of the 'politique du désespoir théologique' or of the passion for political perfectionism.[2] Lilla thinks that illiberal and deconstructivist intellectuals risk repeating the errors of the past. They give indirect or direct support to political theories with potentially totalitarian consequences. The reason for the potential 'dérive totalitaire' is a lack of clarity about the coercive nature of political authority and the inaccessibility of the political for any kind of religious or morally idealistic engineering that follows from this. Any theory about authoritative collective action will thus have to put a check on authority as much as it would like to define the political as realization of the best possible form of common good life, and therefore make it as powerful as possible. Even if one does not agree with the content of Lilla's accusations – I think that he makes a very valuable point – the defence or accusation of passionate intellectuals engaging in critical discourse shows that making intellectuals a subject of critical reflection is an important part of political theory – at least of a political theory that tries to relate analytical political theory to historico-hermeneutical reflection.

What is an intellectual?

As has been made clear in the introduction to this volume, a further difficulty of this subject matter stems from the somewhat elusive concept of the intellectual. The following paragraphs do not present a comprehensive conception of the intellectual. They simply add a few reflections to the thoughts offered in the introduction to this book. Following in the footsteps of Antonio Gramsci and Jacques Le Goff, we could adopt a sociological definition of intellectuals. Le Goff (1985) identifies intellectuals as a group of people emerging at the end of thirteenth-century Europe who, protected by their status at the faculty of arts at the university, led a life of research, discussion, and writing in relative independence from direct secular or ecclesiastic political domination. Intellectuals are thus the product of institutional differentiation and secularization of society in general, and of the foundation of the university in particular. Antonio

---

[2] Lilla 2001: 193–216.

Gramsci's distinction between organic and critical intellectuals is in relation to this conception and finds an institutional grounding. The critical intellectual was thus born in the medieval faculty of arts, an institution that was increasingly emancipating itself from the primacy of theology at the end of the thirteenth century. Intellectuals thus ceased to be theologians with direct links to ecclesiastical hierarchy.

In contrast to the sociological position discussed above, Alain de Libéra has developed a metaphysical theory of the intellectual. He links the term 'intellectual' more directly to a theory of the intellect, and considers intellectuals as people defending an independent status of the intellect, not only with regard to political authority but also to the world of material causation in general. In his *Penser au moyen âge* (2001), Alain de Libéra considers intellectuals as philosophers who affirm the immaterial or independent nature of the intellect and who try to live according to theoretical or moral principles that are derived from reason alone. An intellectual is thus a person who affirms theoretical and moral truths that are independent from and superior to positive or causal proof.

The difference between the sociological conception of Le Goff and the metaphysical conception of de Libéra merits further analysis which cannot be provided in this chapter. The debate shows, however, that conceptualizing the intellectual implies far-reaching philosophical choices. We can consider different degrees of radicalism and of self-conceptions of intellectuals. The politically sensitive version of the intellectual is a person who makes a claim for the independence of intellectual analysis vis-à-vis political and historical realities. As shown by Lilla, political reality is structured in a such a way as to transform any idealistic religious or moral design of political power into authoritarianism or totalitarianism. Many intellectuals tend to fail to take into account the coercive nature of real political authority, a characteristic which often increases and becomes unchecked when directly linked to absolute truth and transcendent morality.

However, this inherent danger of political 'theology' and its various religious and secular manifestations is no reason to abandon intellectual aspirations in all things political. There is room and need for an intellectual attitude seeking reflexive equilibrium between mental experiments, rational calculus, empirically accessible hypotheses, and interpretative historical reflection of short and long *durée*. Workers of the mind who constantly enact such mental and discursive practices in public and in more protected spaces of academia can be called intellectuals. It is of little importance whether such figures are physicists, journalists, writers, philosophers, etc. Ideally, intellectuals are tireless seekers of better arguments and better proofs in open debates. They are responsible for historical memory and future generations. Their field of action was never limited to the university, although the existence of universities has considerably facilitated their existence and social reproduction. As figures like Dante Alighieri show, in the thirteenth and fourteenth centuries there were already intellectuals with absolutely no links to the university. Not only was the cosmopolitan Dante a total autodidact, something he has in common with his patriotic Enlightenment counterpart Rousseau, he was also the first public intellectual defending European unity with philosophical arguments. For many centuries, the intellectual's field of action was the exchange of arguments, interpretations, and normative social models in public spaces.

What is a European intellectual?

Another difficulty we are facing lies in the adjective 'European' that qualifies the intellectuals we are focusing on in this book and chapter. If we accept that intellectuals operate in public spheres, it seems difficult to claim the existence of 'European' intellectuals, at least in our times. Plenty of studies demonstrate the absence or fragmentation of a European public sphere. Second, Jeffrey Goldfarb's *Civility and Subversion: The Intellectual in Democratic Society* shows that the *habitus* of public intellectuals is situated in the national public sphere (Goldfarb 1998). In an article under the title 'The Role of Intellectuals in Twentieth-Century Europe' written as introduction to an edited volume on intellectuals, Jeremy Jennings affirms a similar idea: 'Each of our countries . . . offers markedly different paradigms of the relationship of the state to nation and of the place of the intellectual within the process of state building and the creation of a broader public culture' (Jennings 2000: 785).

As an exception confirming the rule, one could refer to Jürgen Habermas. He has recommended that the European Union adopt a constitution and that Europeans consider 'constitutional patriotism' as the centrepiece of European political identity. Constitutional patriotism would consist in a common acceptance of a number of principles that found the normative framework of the European Union's institutions. European constitutional patriotism would replace national patriotism, at least a certain form of national patriotism characterized by identity struggles and ugly gestures of exclusion. Constitutional patriotism claims the normative advantage of being based on universally recognizable principles and of being free of discriminatory connotations on ethno-national, cultural, and religious grounds.[3]

For the purpose of this chapter it is important to remember that the concept of constitutional patriotism was coined by Dolf Sternberger in the national context of Germany's confrontation of its national-socialist past (and, at the time, its socialist present of the GDR) and efforts towards intellectual rebuilding of a liberal nation.[4] Habermas himself first used the concept in this context

---

[3] For an early presentation and defence in English see Lacroix 2002.
[4] For a Hegelian conception of European constitutional patriotism and and account of the genealogical critique see Müller 2007.

in order to determine the only form of patriotism possible after national-socialism. The concept was developed to break with nationalistic passions and their manifestations in totalitarian regimes of left and right. Its adaptation to a European discourse thus seems more than adequate. But the problem is that constitutional patriotism has not enjoyed the same positive reception by a wider European public as it has in Germany. Other European nations, and the EU as a unit, form contexts of reception of this concept that differ from the German debate of the 1960s and 1970s in fundamental ways. Smaller countries of Eastern Europe who see themselves primarily as serial victims of imperialism, of German National Socialism, and of Soviet communism in the twentieth century will find their own value-based patriotism quite legitimate. This might help in explaining why Habermas' constitutional patriotism with cosmopolitan overtones has not found the same resonance in Europe at large as in post-Second World War Germany (Lacroix 2004b: 145–89).

Does this mean that it would be wrong to consider Jürgen Habermas a European intellectual? After all, he tries to give public discourse a universal normative ground and European character, and reaches out to intellectuals in other European countries to further what he thinks is good for Europe (and the world). Habermas and similar intellectuals (any list of them would be incomplete and is therefore not given) should be considered *European* intellectuals, but the counterarguments help us determine the concept more precisely. It is important not to use the concept of a European public sphere as sociological *sine qua non* for the definition and identification of the European intellectual. Although a European public sphere comparable to national public spheres does not exist, debates on Europe are part of many national public debates and national media arenas in Europe.

A culturally divided country such as Switzerland does not have a unified public sphere in the strict sense of the term, and yet is considered a solid liberal democracy (Tresch and Jochum 2005). This is plausible because what exist in Switzerland are common political institutions and separated public spheres in which national political questions are discussed. Participation of political and intellectual elites across the linguistically separated public spheres exists, but is very limited. The necessary condition for democratic deliberation in culturally and linguistically diversified countries is not a unified public sphere but the existence of common political institutions which install local political deliberation and mutual opening of public spheres. As Habermas says, Europe does not need a unified public sphere, but rather the mutual opening up of public spheres towards each other. Without common institutions and procedures such as meaningful elections and well coordinated referenda, this opening up is likely to be difficult and overridden by respective national issues.

The European intellectual could thus be conceived as a person who actively participates in public discussions on European issues in a national or transnational context. Beyond this mere description I would also take a more normative stance and define the European intellectual as a person who engages in discussions criticizing, affirming, and projecting common European institutions and actions. The critical European intellectual distances himself from nationalism without abandoning national heritage. He or she therefore measures the consequences of national democratic politics for citizens of other European states, and for the other European states themselves. In order to do this, the European intellectual monitors the results of the common institutional framework in bringing national interests and the interests of citizens of other European states into a better balance. This guiding principle of seeking the common interest was also one of the leading ideas of Jean Monnet, as described in his memoirs.[5] It is thus a concept that unites practitioners and intellectuals of European integration. This volume offers ample evidence of the richness and broad scope of intellectual action deployed in the debate about the normative value and historical meaning of European institutions, policy processes, and cultural life.

The dilemma of the European intellectual

In this section, the considerations presented in the introductory part of this chapter on the ambiguous stance of European intellectuals towards a political conception of Europe are illustrated with some concrete historical examples. The process of globalization notwithstanding, terms like 'fatherland' or 'homeland' whose meaning can be traced back to the Latin term 'patria', and its vernacular versions in many languages, are still part of intensive political and intellectual discussions. They seem to point to a deeply human need to feel attached to a community of security and communication and to the fact that the great majority of human beings make their formative experiences in the context of such communities. The essentially political dimension of these communities stems from their role as lender of the last resort and ultimate asylum of economic and social security.

Before expanding on this reflection, it can be recalled that the German researcher Rolf Hellmut Foerster (1967) has counted 182 projects of European unification between 1306 and 1945. There may be more, there may be less; it is not the exact number which is of importance. These projects have been put forward by persons who could be called 'European intellectuals'. Their projects differ from each other, but they all contradict Hegel's point that the owl of Minerva only starts her flight when night has fallen, that is to say in the mode of historical hermeneutical reflection on what has already occurred. Intellectuals have projected and counterfactually anticipated European integration

[5] Monnet 1997: 97: 'La clé de l'action se situait pour moi dans cette règle: Considérer l'exposé du problème dans son ensemble et à la lumière de l'intérêt général'.

according to criteria and with imaginative designs that cannot be directly traced back to the Roman Empire or other historical experiences. But in doing so, they risked neglecting their real homeland in favour of an imagined European political union, at least in the eyes of their patriotic critics. At the same time, they also risked betraying their own cosmopolitan values in favour of Euro-centrism.

The Abbé de Saint-Pierre serves as example to illustrate this point. He was an active participant in the intellectual life of the Parisian *salons* of his time, especially the *salon* of Madame Dupin. In his *Projet pour rendre la paix perpétuelle en Europe* the Abbé proposes the foundation of a 'European Union' (Saint-Pierre 1986b). Jean-Jacques Rousseau contributed to its promotion by writing the *Extrait du Projet de paix perpétuelle*. But in fact he was deeply critical of the *Projet*. This brought him into a difficult position, being the private secretary for Mme Dupin – a great admirer of the Abbé. Rousseau thus wrote a second piece on Saint-Pierre, the *Jugement sur le Projet de paix perpétuelle*, which remained unpublished during his lifetime.

Being a man of the church, the Abbé projected the European Union as a union of the eighteen principal 'Christian Sovereigns' of his time, including Russia. But in the course of his work, he justifies this union by principles and reasoning which claim universal validity and recognition beyond Christian faith. Public reason and religion sustaining the particular power interests of Western monarchs were thus only partially dissociated from each other. The Abbé himself recognized this inherent tension in his work:

In my second Draught I took in all the Kingdoms of the World; but my Friends observ'd to me, that even though in following Ages most of the Sovereigns of Asia and Africa might desire to be receiv'd into the Union, yet this Prospect would seem so remote and so full of Difficulties, that it would cast an Air of Impossibility upon the whole Project; which would disgust all the Readers. (Saint-Pierre 1714: viii)

The Abbé conceived a project of universal political integration on the grounds of reasonable principles, comprehensible and valid to humankind. Confronted with a first critical reception, he seems to have reduced it to the closed horizon of the Christian Sovereigns. But even within the more limited framework of his explicitly 'Christian' project, Saint-Pierre defended the idea of political integration beyond what he perceived as Europe at his time. In a paragraph dedicated to the question of membership of Turkey in the European Union he again quotes his Eurocentric contemporaries:

One of my friends who would like the Turk to be chased from Europe instead of making a treaty of commerce with him or receiving him in the Union as member, proposes that the Union go to war with Turkey in order to give to the Poles what the Tartars . . . own on the Black Sea and to give to the Emperor the coasts of the Black Sea all the way to Constantinople.[6]

---

[6] This later added section with objections had not been included in the 1714 English translation. Here translated by the author from Saint-Pierre 1986b: 306–7.

To this indecent proposal the Abbé responds: 'I doubt that the majority of Princes of Europe would like to assume such heavy costs instead of simply receiving the Turk into the European Union' (Saint-Pierre 1986b: 307). The Abbé thus seems to vacillate between an argument in favour of a distinctly Christian Union whereby the Christian religion is territorially bounded to Europe, and reasonable pragmatism with cosmopolitan tendencies. The latter, universal aspect of the argument is very strong because it serves as a normative basis for the overcoming of state sovereignty and for the unification of Europe. To overcome the state of nature among sovereigns, to consolidate peace and foster prosperity by trade, and to pursue these goals by a federal union is not something that makes sense only for Christians, nor should it be reduced to the Christian world. On the contrary, the limitation to Europe and the hostility to Turkey and the rest of the world invalidates the claims to peace and prosperity and represents a reversion to the traditional logic of exclusion and confrontation.

In trade matters, the Abbé formulated a universal principle of non-discrimination that comes very close to the most-favoured-nation principle of today's WTO: ''Tis the chief Point in Commerce, that no one Nation be preferred to another, and that all be equally free to come to sell and buy Merchandizes' (Saint-Pierre 1714: 120). But his reasonable universalism was not limited to international commerce. In security matters, the Abbé also proposed an argument of universal validity:

For either the two Pretenders make a part, and are Members of some permanent Society, or they do not make a part of it: If they do not make a part of it, their Differences cannot be terminated by Laws, nor, consequently, by the Judges or Interpreters of Laws; as they have the Misfortune to be destitute of the Advantages of perpetual Commerce and of permanent Society, so also have they the Misfortune to be destitute of the Advantage of Laws, which distribute to every one what lawfully belongs to him. Thus, to obtain what each of 'em looks upon as his Right, they are unhappily oblig'd to surprize on another by Deceit, or to destroy each other by Force, that is, by War. (Saint-Pierre 1714: 3)

Saint-Pierre stands for a European intellectual who tries to argue in favour of a unification of Europe on the ground of reasonable principles. He thereby faces the problem that the arguments which make integration beyond the particular sovereigns of Europe look reasonable also stand in the way of a closure of Europe at its borders, wherever these might be supposed to run. The most-favoured-nation principle is reasonably acceptable if applied universally. Overcoming the state of nature will bring peace only if all are on board a common security structure, and if Europe does not form a new closed unity confronting the rest of the world. Consequently, Saint-Pierre's principles and arguments are in contradiction with a closed political union of Europe as much as he would like to argue in favour of it. Saint-Pierre conceives a process of economic and federal integration which has its historical origins in Europe but ought to remain open to the world at large. He represents the type of European intellectual who conceives universal principles and reasonable argumentation in favour of European integration in such a way that a European political particularity is at the same time questioned in the name of an incremental cosmopolitanism.

European intellectuals like Saint-Pierre are thus not necessarily at ease with a principle of closure of Europe, not just because they question this principle for the national or domestic level but also because they propose a change of principle, a constant process of political, economic, and security integration which should not stop at Europe's borders (however they might be conceived). There is an inherent conceptual incertitude in this kind of literature on European integration, because a Euro-patriotic and a cosmopolitan tendency are advocated at the same time.

Many contemporary European intellectuals take a position not far removed from this, or if anything even more complex. This can be illustrated by taking up an example previously mentioned. The principle of non-discrimination in trade matters has become the basis of multilateral trade law (GATT 1947). It has thus gone well beyond Europe and is in principle recognized by the 153 member states of the WTO. The European Union, on the other hand, has seen the light of day and maintains its internal market because it could profit from special exceptions from the principle. Europe has thus exported a universally recognized principle of non-discrimination but has had to make a step back towards 'discriminatory' practices in order to integrate. European intellectuals adhering to universal principles find themselves caught between two rationales, the rationale of political particularity and closure in the name of Europe on one hand and the rationale of cosmopolitan integration on the other. As the example shows, there is no easy way out of this dilemma simply by stating that the European state is a step towards the world state. As will be discussed in more depth in the next paragraph, cosmopolitanism implies a change of principle away from the consolidation of closed and exclusive political units in confrontation with each other towards the unbundling of borders and differentiated integration among multilateralized states.

A manifestation of this incremental cosmopolitanism can be detected in the differentiated and overlapping integration formed by NATO, the WTO, the EU, the Council of Europe, the Eurozone, the Schengen Treaty, etc. The clash of the two rationales can be illustrated by the fact that the collective security systems of the UN and NATO, the guarantees of human rights, and the multilateral trade system go well beyond Saint-Pierre's closed, armed, and Christian European Union. Cosmopolitan institution-building is well on its way and any European intellectual faithful to universal principles has to be its first advocate. The challenging question is thus how European intellectuals can defend European institution-building and political consolidation when this process violates or is in strong tension with cosmopolitan progress in trade law and security. As a nation-building process, European integration would not arrive until very late in European intellectual history. In other words, the pivotal question is: can the European intellectual defend a political particularity of Europe when faced with the reality that the world at large, or at least some multilateral institutions, have started to internalize the very same universal principles that once served as normative foundation for overcoming the nation-state in a context limited to Europe? The Euro-nationalist intellectual might exist, but he or she has a hard time because patriotism favours levels of political integration lower than that of Europe, yet at the same time the principles and political strategies which go beyond patriotism also seem to go beyond Europe.[7] Freedom, non-discrimination, and mutual recognition are all principles of universal validity, yet they do not delineate a specifically European territory. The same is true for all security strategies which attempt to avoid repeating the security dilemma on a continental level.

Towards a European motherland

In this section, I would like to come back to the question of European constitutional patriotism as defended by Jürgen Habermas and others following in his footsteps (or not too far off). Taking the stance of a *législateur* as defined by Rousseau, the German philosopher has proposed that Europe give itself a constitution and that it construct the core of its identity around the universal constitutional principles which can be accepted by everybody on the grounds of reasonable deliberation (Lacroix 2004b). According to the idea of constitutional patriotism, the feeling of belonging to a community can continue to exist on the national and sub-national levels as long as these political structures do not violate universal principles established by a European constitution. These principles ought to be tolerance, freedom, equality, a certain degree of solidarity, and respect for the integrity of the person. The ultimate motive for adherence to the European Union and the added value of identity would not be another specific cultural or tradition-based identity, but rather adherence to universalizable principles and their realization in a new political structure. Original accounts of the 'Europeanness' of such constitutional patriotism show that the latter does not consist in specific norms, values, or principles

---

[7] 'In short, the "federal" emerged prior to or in contrast with the "state" before the two converged; only by questioning the attributes of the nation-state that federalism inherited in the course of history can we recover the federal vision. This does not mean seeking to retrieve the federal ideal type from the vagaries of history. It simply means, in Europe, that our vision is of a federation of nation-states, not a federal state; and, in the United States, that the federal state is only one contemporary element of a more lasting federal vision. This also means that such a federal vision is relevant to governance at the world level, albeit in muted form. This is, in other words, a federal vision beyond the state' (Nicolaïdis 2001: 441).

that only count for Europe, but in a historical practice of integration which has created a normative moral surplus for Europe that can be described in the above-mentioned principles. European constitutional patriotism can thus be understood as constitutional patriotism situated in Europe (Müller 2007: 119–39; Nanz 2006).

But in spite of the intellectual soundness of his own cosmopolitanism, Jürgen Habermas concedes that the political construction of Europe needs closure, boundaries, and defined competencies for every level of governance. He sees the finality of European integration in the foundation of a federal state. This European state would be a sort of new 'fatherland', but the patriotism of its citizens would be limited to constitutional patriotism. The question to ask is not if constitutional patriotism is an intellectually appealing concept but whether it has sufficient force of mobilization to unite Europe's citizens. Habermas himself seems to have given a negative answer to this question in the famous and widely discussed article co-signed with Jacques Derrida which appeared in several major European papers on 30 May 2003. Habermas sees in the mobilization of the masses against the United States' war in Iraq the emergence of a European identity. The adhesion to abstract constitutional principles seems to be an insufficient unifier, in need of an element of passionate mass mobilization against an 'other'. Moreover, Habermas seems to follow the political theology of despair and to engage in the politics of fear when he writes: 'there is only one alternative to the forging of a European identity: the old continent will vanish from the world's political scene'.[8] From a realist point of view one has to admit that the confrontation with the 'other' is useful, maybe necessary in the formation of collective political identity. The problem with Habermas' argumentation is not the lack of rationale, but the coherence of his position when compared with the moral and cosmopolitan foundation of his normative political theory. As I argue in this chapter, this lack of coherence, this example of cosmopolitanism losing its nerve, is not a problem specific to Habermas, but a structural problem of European integration philosophy which many European intellectuals have faced over time and continue to face. In the quoted paper, Habermas is seeking to rescue a political conception of Europe and attempts to fill the political void between patriotism and cosmopolitanism. Faced with the fear that a Europe of constitutional patriotism might get lost in universalization, he tries to engage with the seemingly unavoidable politics of friend and foe.

This posture of a world-power EU triggers the question of whether a strong and unified Europe, capable of confronting the other powerful states of the world, could possibly correspond to the principles of European integration as it has been successfully realized so far. Would Europe not fall back into the logic of

---

[8] Habermas 2004: 'Zur Herausbildung einer europäischen Identität gibt es daher nur eine Alternative: Der alte Kontinent verschwindet von der weltpolitischen Bühne.'

nationalism and exclusion that it has successfully overcome in the five decades of its political existence by a functionally differentiated and politically de-centred integration? For a long time this question was not at the forefront of European intellectual debates because the economic dimension of European integration was sufficiently technical to keep the political implications beneath the radar of philosophical critique. Today, the question of the political aims of European integration is urgent, and divides intellectuals. Some seek to found a supranational European federal state, taking some existing federal state as their paradigm; others plead in favour of a decentred and functionally differentiated Europe which prefigures a cosmopolitan evolution towards a unification of mankind and avoids the regression to nationalism and the security dilemma. We can diagnose a division of European intellectuals into European statists on the one hand and multilateralists or cosmopolitans on the other. The statist might defend a supranational or transnational Europe, but it is clear that many intellectuals defending the transnational conception of Europe also have strong cosmopolitan tendencies. Among the European statists there are intellectuals like Habermas who propose that Europe should counterbalance the United States of America and other powerful nation-states, and play a major role in world politics. In a multi-polar world of powerful nation-states, the decentred EU of functionally differentiated integration has difficulties in positioning its institutional conception. The EU is under pressure to become a unified and efficient actor, or even to adapt to the principle of national sovereignty upheld by the superpowers and many other nation-states.

Other intellectuals do not seek a major world-political role for an integrated Europe, arguing that it should rather be a sort of 'Big Switzerland' as proposed by Denis de Rougemont,[9] concentrating on economic development and a humanitarian foreign policy with a strong tendency towards neutrality when the great powers clash in war or armed conflict. De Rougemont, one of the advocates of the European federal state, has written about Switzerland what could be true for Europe: a people need not be powerful to be happy – assuming the Swiss are happy (de Rougemont 1965b). But even in this merely civilian rationale (difficult for the EU because an essential aspect of Switzerland is its small size and relatively simple multicultural structure) we seem to arrive at the same problem: Europeans do not form a happy people, because they do not form a people. And in order to form a people, an opposition of friend and foe and passionate mobilization against the 'other' seem unavoidable, even in the thought of cosmopolitan European intellectuals like Jürgen Habermas.

---

[9] De Rougemont 1965a: 65: 'My belief is that the only unity which is compatible with the genius of Europe itself, with its past, with its realities and its present vocation, is unity in diversity, a strong and flexible union of which Switzerland has perfected the prototype: and that means federalism.'

It is easier to criticize Habermas than to conceive a different path of successful European political union. While it seems plausible to apply a cosmopolitan theory to existing political communities and nation-states in order to liberalize them and open them up to each other, the process of constitution of a political community seems to be more resistant to the evacuation of an exclusionary concept of the political. But it is clear that a political concept of friend and foe, of exclusion, and of a strong sovereign Europe[10] is at odds with an incremental European political integration based on universal principles of transnational freedom rights, mutual recognition, and non-discrimination, and on the rationale of overcoming the security dilemma by decentred and territorially differentiated functional integration. According to this paradigm, European integration is about overcoming an absolutist reading of national sovereignty, about constructing interdependencies and shared multilayered identities. A regression to identity politics, an advocacy of passionate Euro-patriotism or Euro-nationalism are in flat contradiction with the idea and method of European integration as it has been applied so far. This is true for the liberal-cosmopolitan position as well as for more liberal-conservative positions. After all, it was Denis de Rougemont who wrote: 'The will to unite will be healthy if it tends to eliminate the virus of nationalism, not to offer it greater scope by creating a continent transformed into a super-nation and saddled with a super-nationalism' (de Rougemont 1965a: 64). Very much in line with today's conceptions of diversity without division and in line with a Habermasean mistrust of economic integration without political integration, de Rougemont defends a conception of unity which avoids two opposite extremes: a Europe made up of separate 'fatherlands' ('fatherland' is according to de Rougemont a 'fundamentally incorrect expression') and complete unification without federalism.

To avoid the pitfalls of closure and exclusion inherent in such a design, certain intellectuals argue in favour of a political Europe without a statist finality. According to Ferry (2005), the juridical foundations of the EU were anticipated two centuries before its actual creation in Immanuel Kant's *Towards Perpetual Peace* (1795). Ferry thus defends a cosmopolitan Europe which is compatible only with the transnational conception of Europe as mentioned in the introduction to this volume. Furthermore, this transnational conception would need to remain open to further and ultimately cosmopolitan multilateral integration.[11] In accordance with Kant, Ferry does not identify the 'cosmopolitan idea' with the idea of a world state or of the state according to the modern concept (Ferry 2005: 121–41). Rather, it represents a threefold structure of public law: (1) the internal structure of the law of the state (*ius civitatis*); (2) the public law instituted among the states' peoples (*ius gentium*); (3) the cosmopolitan law of transnational civil rights of individuals (*ius cosmopoliticum*).

[10] For such a position also see also Morgan 2005.
[11] See also "Pour un cosmopolitisme processuel", in Cheneval 2005.

45

Kant's cosmopolitan idea envisages an interconnected institutional progress on all three levels (Cheneval 2005: 165–246). According to Ferry, the European Union's constitutional legal structure incorporates all three levels of the Kantian cosmopolitan design. It contains states with a democratic *ius civitatis*, a structure of international law (*ius gentium*), and a system of transnational civil rights which further develop Kant's idea of *ius cosmopoliticum* by the freedom of movement and residence alongside economic and political rights and protections. Any attempt or proposition to reduce the EU to one of those dimensions of public law is flawed and does not take into account the other necessary elements of its structural design. For instance, the proposal to portray the EU in the image of a supra-nation-state would mean reducing it to the *ius civitatis*, Kant's first article of *Perpetual Peace*, and disregarding the international and transnational dimensions.

On the other hand, an analysis of the EU in terms of classic internationalism or intergovernmentalism is blind to the institutional connection to national legislative and constitutional structures, as well as to the transnational rights guaranteed by supranational jurisdiction. Neither is the EU only a system of transnational rights detached from inter-state law and national political community. According to Ferry, the EU's rationale ('raison') consists in this threefold and irreducible institutional differentiation of its public law. To this static structural design is added a dynamic imperative to keep pushing the realm of institutionalized cooperation beyond its borders as far as possible. Ferry is keen to point out that even a common security policy can be integrated into this cosmopolitan and decentred conception of the EU. It may give itself an instrument of common defence and yet still respect national sovereignty by virtue of the possibilities of abstention and formal consent that are in place. Ferry quotes a report by the *Institut des hautes études de la Défense nationale* (2003) that outlines the goals of the Common Foreign and Security Policy as limited to turning the EU into a respected actor whose voice is heard.

Following a formulation by Mario Telò and Paul Magnette from 1996 that has lost nothing of its relevance, the proposal of a threefold structure of the EU can be based on an empirical diagnosis:

The inexistence of a European super-state or of a European nation constrains us to imagine the process of a long construction of a transnational European society and, at the same time, original institutional forms. EU enlargement increases internal heterogeneity and multiplies cultural, social, religious, and political diversities. This prohibits any illusion of the formation of a European people. Common sovereignty has to reside on several 'demoi' and not one single 'demos'. (Telò and Magnette 1996: 14–15)

The cosmopolitan idea of Europe thus evokes a structure of supranational, intergovernmental, and national institutions. Thinkers like Jean-Marc Ferry, Jan-Werner Müller, and Patrizia Nanz have no difficulty in attaching a sort of constitutional patriotism to such a cosmopolitan Europe. The weakness of emotional intensity which Europeans manifest towards these decentred structures is not seen as a deficit, but rather as sign that the political can be conceived and realized beyond pathological and confrontational divides of friend and foe. Paul Magnette has pointed to the negative consequences of a reductionism which projects the EU in the image of the traditional nation-state and disregards the cosmopolitan, i.e. international and transnational dimensions. There is a solid correlation between a strong identification with Europe and xenophobia. The more a singular political identity of Europe is promoted, the greater the potential for exclusion and opposition towards a real or imaginary internal and external 'other' becomes (Magnette 2007). The paradoxical effect of political consolidation of the EU is thus a reduction of tolerance within its own borders. The very idea of unity in diversity would be undermined. Other studies of social psychology show that internal tensions of a group grow in proportion to the development of a collective identity. Magnette explains this phenomenon in relation to the EU with the fact that collective identity politics are led by a large internal group which projects its own vision on Europe.

Magnette points to Jürgen Habermas' concept of a federal state of Europe as distinctly 'German'. Such generalizations of particular visions reduce internal reciprocal tolerance: The mistrust which the Germans and French demonstrate towards the Poles can be explained by the fact that these two founding countries of the EU project their socio-economic and political model onto the EU and that they perceive Poland as Atlanticist and liberal, and therefore as diverging from the European norm. Such strategies of declared identity by nations seeing themselves as senior to others necessarily backfire. The peoples judged as deviant from the European norm perceive these judgements as hostile and as a denial of recognition. Unless a stronger Union is based on a consensual process of mutual recognition, the resulting 'common identity' can considerably weaken reciprocal tolerance and undermine the project of integration. Forced homogenization that is out of touch with mutual respect among the different peoples of Europe or activates xenophobia towards third parties is in contradiction with the cosmopolitan finality which European integration claims to serve (Licata and Klein 2002; Magnette 2007; Mummendey and Waldzus 2004: 59). Aspirations towards an 'Europe-puissance' via a unified European state revive the socio-pathological elements of politics which the European integration process intended to overcome in the first place. Such a dynamic is not compatible with the rationale of differentiated, decentred, and consensual integration. European 'statism', especially the impatient variety, is thus bound to mobilize resentment and passionate xenophobia in order to achieve a political union that does not seem to produce itself swiftly by functional integration.

Also from other, non-Kantian theoretical points of view that are oriented towards pluralist conceptions of democracy, certain European intellectuals defend a political conception of Europe but reject a European federal state or at least a process of integration by forced identity politics (Nicolaïdis 2001). Forms of non-state federalism or the threefold structure of the EU as based on national, international, and transnational institutions are portrayed as the political model consistent with the European core ideal of overcoming the security dilemma and the confrontational politics of friend and foe in the international and national realms of politics. The statist model, on the other hand, revives socio-pathological processes and thereby undermines the polit-ical originality of the European project. According to these 'truly European because truly cosmopolitan' intellectuals, the political originality of the EU lies in the strong reduction of essentialist confrontation between closed political entities through interlinked institutions and increased functional integration, creating a web of cross-cutting cleavages and interests. These cosmopolitan European intellectuals are 'Euro-patriots' in the sense that they value the basic rationale of European integration and the 'acquis' of European institution-building. They seek to construe Europe on the basis of the universally accept-able principles of reciprocity, non-discrimination, and mutual recognition. Any particular political community based on these principles contains within itself an opening towards similar political entities.

This brings us back to the initial question of whether European intellectuals defending the cosmopolitan structure of the EU are citizens without a country. The answer is in the negative. First, because the cosmopolitan structure as conceived in the terms of Kant's three definitive articles of *Towards Perpetual Peace* contains the statespeoples in its first and second pillar. Also, the concept of multilateral democracy or demoi-cracy values individual peoples and sees them as normative reference. An affiliation to the – albeit transformed and multilateralized – nation-state as the fundamental community is not only possible but necessary in order to uphold a politically solid cosmopolitan structure. Second, the threefold cosmopolitan structure has enough political elements to become in itself a country of transnational citizenship. The term 'country' ('Land', 'pays', 'pais', 'paese', etc.) is more open than Seneca's com-munity of birth or the term 'fatherland'. 'Country', 'Land', 'pays', etc. contains a meaning of transmigration beyond narrowly conceived borders. This cosmo-politan country is not the same as the 'fatherland' of emotional allegiance and primary formative experiences, nor is it identical to the abstract moral universe. It is rather a sort of 'motherland' of public reason, transnational modes of existence and citizenship, and of a situated constitutional patriotism that is not a fruit of abstraction but of the practice of European integration.

But this emerging transnational and incrementally cosmopolitan dimension of the political has an extremely fragile status. There is a discrepancy between the EU's internal demand for a decentred and differentiated structure of gover-nance and outside demands for unified, reliable, and swift agency of the EU. The multi-polar structure of world politics upheld by existing and emerging powers, all of which are consolidated nation-states with a strong tendency towards 'multi-polarity without multilateralism' (National Intelligence Council 2008), poses a challenge to a cosmopolitan, multilateral Europe. It might push the EU towards a statist paradigm despite itself, with all the pathological consequences that this implies. The second reason for this structural fragility is related to this status of the EU as an original and non-replicated political body. The quote from Seneca illustrates this, as it leaves no room for a commonwealth between country and cosmos. In this light, European intellectuals seem to have no other choice than to argue either in favour of a European country or to put Europe in the otherworldly heaven of a moral kingdom. This chapter has shown, however, that there are European intellectuals who have chosen the arduous task of making plausible the notion that the promising originality of Europe's existing and functioning political construction lies in between a statist vision and cosmopolitan morality.

2

Contentious European Democracy

National Intellectuals in Transnational Debates*

Ulrike Liebert

Introduction

In the wake of the fall of the Berlin Wall, the cultural historian Wolf Lepenies depicted 'the greatness and misery of European intellectual life' as an oscillation between 'melancholy and utopia' (Lepenies 1992: 20). If the accomplishment of the European Union's Eastern enlargement in 2004 drove such dreams home, the failure of the project of establishing a 'Constitution for Europe' changed the tide shortly after. Since then, has melancholy among intellectuals prevailed, driven by the 'inadequacies of the world they live in and which they are not able to change'? Or have utopian energies been fuelled again by the intellectual 'inhibition of action and transference of unsatisfied dreams from this world to a better one' (Kwiek and Lepenies 2003: 331)? This chapter revisits these questions about the 'homo Europaeus intellectualis' in the light of contemporary contentions over 'Europe's democracy' and their transnational dynamics.

Ultimately, democracy beyond the state has become an issue of discursive public contestations at the global scale (Dryzek 2006). In twenty-first-century 'Europe in contention', the so-called democratic deficit has conspicuously fuelled mass public politicization (Magnette and Papadopoulos 2008), replaced people's permissive consensus by 'constraining dissensus' (Hooghe and Marks 2009), and further aggravated these trends by the seminal experiment of uniting the deepening and enlarging union of states by a common constitution.[1] Thus, the questions of whether the EU requires popular or democratic or other forms of legitimacy, and if so, how the European would-be polity could be

---

* I am grateful for valuable suggestions and comments to both editors of this book, to Michael Freeden, and to the participants of the workshop at Oxford University, 30 April and 1 May 2009.

[1] For an analysis of mass media debates about the EU's constitutional treaty ratification in six old and new member states, see Liebert 2007.

transformed into a democratic and effective system of governance, have been dubbed 'one of the thorniest of all contemporary problems of democratic theory and constitutional politics' (Offe 2003: 22).[2] Even scholars and intellectuals who used to deny the question of democracy for an allegedly intergovernmental and regulatory regime have belatedly admitted that coming to terms with the 'democratic deficit' is 'the deepest question Europeans face today' (Majone 2010; Moravcsik 2006: 590). Hence, exploring how intellectuals think and engage across contending discourses and borders in a still divided Europe is critical. It will shed light on one of the most contested political ideas, and also on how these contestations have shaped Europe's 'communicative space in the making' (Fossum and Schlesinger 2007).[3]

For exploring the discursive construction of a legitimate European political order, the insights into the national narratives that this book provides are crucial. Yet a transnational approach is also needed if we want to understand intellectual exchanges that transcend national discourses. Arguably, a transnational dynamic has become a defining feature of the most recent European constitutional debate, from Laeken to Lisbon.[4] More than any previous episode of European contemporary history, this tormented chapter has brought intellectual ideas about democratic life in Europe into public light, from academia into the general public, and from national into transnational debate.[5]

Mapping ideas about democracy in Europe entails taking into account different theoretical, practical, and comparative questions, namely: (1) What does

---

[2] See also Föllesdal and Hix 2006; Mény 2002; Moury and de Sousa 2009; Offe and Preuss 2006.

[3] Here, I conceive of 'intellectuals' as interpreters of our world who enable us better to understand ourselves and to gain an understanding of who we are and what we should be – and, beyond interpretation, of how ideas can motivate social or political agency for changing the world. See Michael Freeden, Chapter 3 of this volume.

[4] At the Laeken Summit in December 2001, Heads of States and Governments of the EU-15 established the Convention on the Future of Europe, a representative deliberative body mandated to draft an EU Treaty. The resulting 'Treaty establishing a Constitution for Europe' was signed in Rome in October 2004, but rejected by popular referenda in France and the Netherlands in May and June 2005. After a two year 'reflection period', an Intergovernmental Conference negotiated the Reform Treaty of Lisbon, signed in December 2007. The ToL failed ratification by referendum in Ireland in June 2008, but passed parliamentary ratification procedures and a number of National Constitutional Court proceedings in the remaining EU-26. After a second successful referendum in Ireland, and after having been signed by the reluctant Czech and Polish Presidents, Klaus and Kaczynski, the Treaty of Lisbon entered into force on 1 December 2009.

[5] I have adapted Richard Posner's 'media mentions' strategy (cf. Posner 2003) to the European multilingual context for selecting national intellectual contributions to the debate on democracy. I divided this into two steps: a first list contained a comprehensive range of academics and intellectuals originating in EU member states who over the last ten years have published on questions of democracy in Europe. Drawing on this list, I then produced a table showing the sixty 'public intellectuals' with the highest number of 'media mentions', calculated on the basis of the Google News Archive for the period 2000–2009 and covering five languages from 'old' and 'new Europe': English, French, German, Polish, and Czech. See Table 2.1.

democracy in contemporary Europe mean normatively, that is which values are attached to it? (2) To which institutional forms are these normative ideas wedded in the European context? (3) What misfits exist between facts and norms? and (4) What kinds of agency will it take to put such normative ideas into practice? After all, these democratic ideas will vary, depending on how public intellectuals position themselves regarding the *longue durée* semantic traditions of their national cultural contexts (Münch 2008).

Anticipating my findings in a nutshell, I will make a threefold argument. Firstly, I contend that intellectual disagreements about the European political order do not reflect incompatibilities between idiosyncratic national discourses, that is how 'the' Germans and 'the' French (or 'the' Continental Europeans) think and talk differently from, say 'the' British, Irish, Polish, or Czechs. As epitomized by leading European public intellectuals, for example the Dahrendorf–Habermas debate – first on positivism in German sociology, later on Europe and democracy – contentious issues have sometimes first fuelled domestic debates before spilling over into transnational intellectual controversy.

Secondly, intellectual positions in Europe can no longer be divided into two categories only, such as those proposed by Isaiah Berlin during the Cold War. In dealing with Europe's ideological history, Berlin was preoccupied with the question of the origins of totalitarian thinking, and came up with a division among 'monists', whom he nicknamed 'hedgehogs', and 'pluralists', whom he dubbed 'foxes'[6] – the former being the bad guys and the latter the good. Here, I will argue that at both ends of this divide we can now find discourses that are no longer merely nation-statist, but also European and supranational. More importantly, instead of pitting supranational 'monist' discourses on the one hand against national 'pluralist' discourses on the other, I discern a third discursive strand that has emerged more recently. Mapping onto the conceptual triangle that Justine Lacroix and Kalypso Nicolaïdis propose for characterizing national debates about Europe,[7] this third pole emerges from the 'search for a third way', typically escapes binary thinking, and is aimed at reconciling 'unity' and 'diversity'. Examples for this third category can be found, as I will demonstrate, in the republican camp, where the meanings and requirements of democracy beyond the state have been renegotiated.

Thirdly, I suggest that contentious issues of democracy in Europe have fuelled intellectual debates and exacerbated traditional ideological differences. At the same time, these differences have inspired creativity and innovation, in

---

[6] Referring to Archilochus' saying 'The fox knows many things, but the hedgehog knows one big thing', Berlin marks 'one of the deepest differences which divide writers and thinkers, and, it may be, human beings in general'; see Berlin 2009 [1953]: 3.

[7] Lacroix and Nicolaïdis depict the 'search for a third way' as one that seeks to come up 'with political designs which neither reify nor deny state-level sovereignty, seeking instead to tease out the conditions for upholding "unity in diversity"'; see the introduction to this volume, especially Figure 1.1 'European Stories: The debates'.

content as well as in practice. As a result, European intellectual debates have engendered a multilingual conceptual network, connecting competing narratives about democracy in the European context and coming up with illuminating conceptual innovations.

Accordingly, I will reconstruct the European democracy debate in three steps. To start with, I review unifying ideas of political community that cherish democracy in the terms of single, universal, organizing principles that have been wedded to the national as well as to a supranational state. Next, I map ideas of pluralism and liberal democracy that celebrate diversity, and display sympathy for a confederation of states rather than for a supranational federal state. In the third part I survey ideas for reconciling these binaries. The concluding section draws a few lessons from the European democracy debate.

Cherishing unity: Monistic ideas of Europe as democracy

Monistic ideas of democracy are attached to notions of a homogeneous demos or people that is conceived as collective, either in pre-political communitarian or in republican forms. In the first case, the demos is defined by unifying ideas such as ethnicity, nation, and religion. In the second case it relies on social cohesion, social solidarity, or shared ethical values. In any case, a democracy that is understood in collective terms requires the institutional form of the sovereign state. If the collectivist-statist frame is then attached to the European level, it either mutates into utopia or into a nightmare: on the one hand, a European democratic state understood as a collective presents the ultimate 'finality' or target of European integration that is embraced by European federal democrats; on the other hand, it appears as a spectre that haunts 'methodological nationalists' or nation-state democrats.

Nation-statist meaning of democracy in Europe

Democracy coded in a national or statist language in the singular has traditionally resonated strongly with Continental European thinking, originating in Rousseau as well as in Herder and Fichte, and taking on traditionalist, conservative, leftist, and post-Marxist – but also communitarian and Christian – persuasions. This family of discourses has travelled widely across Europe and most national intellectual debates. For instance in France, Pierre Manent has come up with the idea that only a national – different from a civic – republic founded on 'Christian community' will be capable of constituting a 'political body'.[8] Within the Polish debate, Zdzisław Krasnodębski, one of the foremost

---

[8] Manent 2007; see Justine Lacroix, Chapter 5 of this volume.

intellectual architects of Polish conservative reforms, drew on the Solidarność movement and communitarian ideas to counter post-1989 liberal deconstructions of Polish national history and commemoration. He proposed 'Polish civil religion' as a symbolic structure, based on an 'ethics of solidarity' and Christianity for understanding 'the Polish experience in light of ultimate and universal realities', and thus the 'unified Polish political nation' in non-ethnic terms (Krasnodębski 2008: 207).[9] And in Great Britain, the cradle of liberal democracy, preoccupations with national sovereignty have flourished as well. In recent British debates on Europe, conservative and right-wing as well as left-leaning intellectuals converge in defence of the nation, for instance Noel Malcolm on the one hand or David Miller on the other.[10] In sum, in contemporary discourse, unifying ideas of the demos or democratic community vary, but attach value above all to national sovereignty, and sometimes to Christianity. They continue to refer to the national level but have also been scaled up to the European level, mutating into the vision of a European demos and the search for a 'European soul' or identity.

Admittedly, none of these conceptions of a European identity followed the image of an ethnically homogeneous people. Instead, 'shared values' and 'myths' – or, alternatively, 'constitutional patriotism' – have been put forward in the search for the idea expected to provide the bonds and, eventually, help constitute a European identity. While some looked back to antiquity and European history to determine the normative foundation of a European identity, others affirmed a self-reflexive concept of reason. An intersubjective transformation of modernity, and an open-ended formation of European identity in the framework of Europe-wide constitutional principles, would arguably promote a shared sense of 'European constitutional patriotism'.

For the culturalist project, the European identity of the early twenty-first century could not be built from a European constitution, but only from a pre-existing community defined by common values.[11] A culturally founded European community needed values, historical narratives, and symbols as the foundation for political belonging. The 'Christian Occident', 'the Enlightenment', or 'fifty years of European integration' were screened as promising

---

[9] See also Góra and Mach's discussion of Krasnodębski's critique of 'liberal deconstruction', in Chapter 11 of this volume.

[10] See for example Miller 2007. For Noel Malcolm, democratic politics only works well in a political community founded on the same customs, political traditions, and language, and thus, a kind of politics that could hardly be 'writ large in Europe', as Varouxakis points out in Chapter 7 of this volume.

[11] Tasked to 'take stock of the spiritual and cultural dimension of an enlarged Europe' and to determine 'the intellectual foundations of the Union', a European expert panel convened under the auspices of the European Commission under Commission President Romano Prodi in spring 2002, and was coordinated by Krzysztof Michalski. Participants included Kurt Biedenkopf, Jutta Limbach, Ernst Böckenförde, Rainer Bauböck, Ute Frevert, Anton Pelinka, and Ulrike Lunacek (Michalski 2006).

cultural resources for a collective European identity that would augment the EU's capacity to act. For maintaining the 'specifically European' democratic and social way of life, universal values were required as reference points for identity-building.[12]

The project of a 'European civil identity' in the 'postnational constellation' took an alternative approach. First of all, a European identity was deemed necessary for maintaining the 'specific European way of life' and for coping with the challenges of globalization, denationalization, and enlargement.[13] Then, as to the resources for this endeavour, the 'civic European identity' was neither constructed from old Europe's past splendours, nor did it merely stereotype 'Europe as non-America', as Timothy Garton Ash and Ralf Dahrendorf suspected.[14] Instead, Habermas clarified that the mental 'habitus' of Europeans was based on individualism, rationalism, and activism, and thus applied to the whole West (Habermas 2006b). At the same time, he and Derrida claimed that these values found specific expression in the European context, different from the USA: for instance, Europeans displayed more negative attitudes than Americans to the death penalty and to the 'liberal' play of market forces; they were more sceptical regarding the promises of progress, thought more in social terms, felt more empathy with the weak. Moreover, common European historical experiences, traditions, and accomplishments, Habermas argued, were what constituted European citizens' consciousness of a shared political fate that had endured in the past and would jointly shape the future.

Against this backdrop, Habermas and Derrida trusted that Europeans would be capable of developing a particular type of civic identity. In particular, Habermas conceived 'European constitutional patriotism' as a novel form of a non-national political identity, based on principles of democratic constitutionalism and political order that are negotiated among the diverse parts and shared by common consensus.[15] Against such recent 'Europatriotic temptations', Justine Lacroix has insisted on Habermas' initial plea for critical and rational identities and their reflexive distance towards existing political practices (Lacroix 2009). Moreover, in the context of Eastern Europe, these ideas have not been embraced, but rather met with disappointment and contention. From the 2003 horizon of the new would-be members knocking at the EU's door, Imre Kertesz interpreted these ideas as 'arrogant theory', aimed at excluding the upcoming Eastern members from 'core Europe', and evoking the 'paradox conveniences' that Western Europe had enjoyed during the Cold War and that it was reluctant to give up. Summing up Kertesz's words: 'in the first

---

[12] Michalski 2006; Nida-Rümelin and Weidenfeld 2007.
[13] Habermas and Derrida 2003.
[14] Ibid.; see also the response by Dahrendorf and Garton Ash (2003).
[15] See Jan-Werner Müller, Chapter 4 of this volume.

moments of the Iraq war, everything that had been established at Luxembourg and Strasbourg fell apart'.[16]

Institutional form of European democracy in unitary perspective

Precisely because of such dramatic failures, European public intellectual debate was expressly concerned with what the unifying idea of Europe as a democracy, if raised to the EU level, would require in institutional terms. The question about what was needed to reconstitute the European Union had long moved centre stage. In terms of institutional configuration, a federal multinational democracy is often portrayed as one where the Union's borders would be set in accordance with European identity and where democratic legitimacy would rest on popularly elected bodies based on representative democracy at all levels; here, representative government, based on political equality and majority rule, would not remain the reserve of the nation-state but would be implemented also at the supranational level (Eriksen and Fossum 2009: 37). Accordingly, in the context of the Laeken process at the beginning of the twenty-first century, a series of visions about the ultimate 'finality' or target of European integration were proposed by German Foreign Minister Joschka Fischer. In his legendary Humboldt University address in Berlin in May 2000, Fischer argued for a transition from an association of states to a European federation.[17] Jürgen Habermas followed suit. Making the case for 'Why Europe needs a Constitution' (Habermas 2001b), he laid out how to reconceptualize post-national constitution-building as a virtuous circle. In this model, different anticipations stimulated and reinforced each other mutually in a circular process, enhancing the development of European political parties, of a European civil society, and a European political public sphere. These were not pictured as prerequisites of European constitution-making, but rather as outcomes of synergistic interactions that would accompany it. Following this approach, European constitution-building would function as a focal point of European identity and transnational solidarity which, in turn, would help construct the EU's constituency (Habermas 1998: 154ff.). In the aftermath of the Laeken process, Habermas succeeded, if not in making the contentious idea of a European constitution popular throughout all camps, at least in placing an intensely discussed issue on the European public agenda:

The challenge before us is not to invent anything but to conserve the great democratic achievements of the European nation-state, beyond its own limits. These achievements include not only formal guarantees of civil rights, but levels of social welfare, education

---

[16] Imre Kertesz, 'Rede zum Jahrestag der Deutschen Einheit', 3 October 2003, in Magdeburg (reproduced in *Frankfurter Allgemeine Zeitung*, 8 October 2003; author's translation).
[17] Joschka Fischer, 'Vom Staatenverbund zur Foderation – Gedanken uber die Finalität der europäischen Integration', in *Bulletin der Bundesregierung* (Nr. 29, 24 May 2000), 1–12.

and leisure that are the precondition of both an effective private autonomy and of democratic citizenship...A European constitution would...constitute a necessary, not a sufficient condition for the kind of policies some of us are inclined to advocate. To the extent that European nations seek a certain re-regulation of the global economy, to counterbalance its undesired economic, social and cultural consequences, they have a reason for building a stronger Union with greater international influence...From this perspective, the European project can be seen as a common attempt by the national governments to recover in Brussels something of the capacity for intervention that they have lost at home. (Habermas 2001b)

As is well known, the debate provoked by Fischer and Habermas by no means remained an exclusively intra-German affair. Their ideas converged, for instance, with Larry Siedentop's *Democracy in Europe* (2001), or with *The Idea of a European Superstate* by Glyn Morgan (2005), a work that delved deeply into British Eurosceptic discourses in order to develop a compelling justification for why Europe's security interests required a European supranational state.[18] Although he could more accurately be called a politician writer than a public intellectual, Guy Verhofstadt's advocacy for *The United States of Europe* (2006) also gained currency in nearly every national public debate and was translated into most European languages. Stefan Collignon (2009), meanwhile, further developed Habermas' justification of a European constitution as a means for preserving Europe's social model by offering compelling political economic reasons to support a social European constitution that would enhance Europe's capabilities for producing public goods – namely, EU governance of financial and economic crises, fighting unemployment and inflation, and redressing other social deficits.

Misfits between democratic norms and European practices

The seminal venture of intellectually conceiving a constitutional project for the European Union not only became vital to opening a new chapter in European constitutional politics; it was also influential in provoking Eurosceptic opposition and rejection from many different camps. Oppositional 'EU deficit-discourses' took two directions, a centre-right and a leftist conservative one. In the German context, they came from conservative thinkers, notably German political scientist Peter Graf von Kielmansegg[19] and Dieter Grimm, a legal scholar and judge of the German Constitutional Court.[20] In the vein of cultural pessimism, and based on the 1993 Maastricht judgment by the German Federal

---

[18] See also Varouxakis, this volume.

[19] In 2006, Graf Kielmansegg received the 'Cross of Merit, First Class' (*Bundesverdienstkreuz 1. Klasse*) from the Federal Republic of Germany in honour of his achievements for promoting dialogue between the social sciences and political practice.

[20] In 1999, Dieter Grimm was awarded the 'Great Cross of Merit with Star and Shoulder Ribbon' (*Großer Verdienstorden mit Stern und Schulterband*) by the Federal Republic of Germany.

Constitutional Court, Kielmansegg (1996) constructed the 'democracy dilemma' of European integration. As a consequence of European integration, he argued, democracy was caught in an irresolvable dilemma: assuming that democratic legitimacy rested with the people, which he defined by a collective identity, a community of remembrance, and a common public sphere, and given that these prerequisites did not exist at the European level, crises of the EU were inevitable. Therefore, Kielmansegg did not discount an ultimate failure of the European integration process in a general sense. And as long as these presumed preconditions for a European demos were not in place, Grimm also rejected the particular project of a European constitution.[21] In his contributions to the German and transnational Eurosceptic discourse, Grimm questioned the European constitution on normative grounds too. Accordingly, from the viewpoint of a Europe of sovereign nation-states, a European identity was deemed unnecessary for the legitimacy of the EU's authority, since it was derived from the democratic member states. As Hauke Brunkhorst showed, this argument was flawed. It was premised on assumptions that can no longer be seen as steadfast in the post-national constellation: the notion of a sovereign people, or demos, is locked into that of the nation-state (Brunkhorst 2007: 40ff.).

Fatalistic warnings against a constitutional democratic European order were not the privilege of centre-right conservative thinkers. They have converged with those on the left, including post-Marxists and critical theorists, as well. For instance, Claus Offe shared the view that European integration had increasingly affected member societies and diminished the opportunities for citizen participation in decision-making. He firmly believed that European democratic self-governance based on input legitimacy was always less sustainable, since European identity was weak and cross-border solidarities among constituents scarce (Offe 2003: 269). As a matter of fact, this was more than an expression of the traditional German belief that a European demos in the singular was needed as a requisite for enhancing a European democracy. Paradoxically, this belief complemented negative views on the impact of European integration on national democratic politics, autonomy, sovereignty, and republican ideals.[22] Such cultural pessimist ideas of a democratic 'race to the bottom' attained popularity in Nordic Eurosceptic discourse too. Norwegian intellectuals, for instance, were reported to 'insist that the EU is a democratic curse, which Norway should stay away from'.[23] By contrast, Nordic fatalism about the fate

---

[21] Grimm 1995. See also Müller, this volume.

[22] Eurosceptic slogans have turned into book titles on the German market, such as *Europa – Der Staat, den keiner will* ('Europe – the state that nobody wants'), *Die sieben Todsünden der EU* ('The seven lethal sins of the EU'), *Das Europa-Komplott – Wie EU-Funktionäre unsere Demokratie verscherbeln* ('The European conspiracy – how EU bureaucrats sell out our democracy'), to give a few examples.

[23] See John Erik Fossum and Cathrine Holst, Chapter 14 of this volume.

of democracy in the European Union ran squarely counter to Southern enthusiasm. For instance, Italian or Spanish public discourses did not blame the EU for domestic democratic deficits, but rather acclaimed it for its democratic benefits, that is for enhancing the consolidation and stabilization of domestic democracy.[24]

The French variety of the nation-statist Euro-critical discourse in the context of a multi-religious and multicultural, liberal Europe took inspiration from Pierre Manent's work. In the view of this French philosopher, the fate of self-government in Europe could not but be seen critically as it depended on the national form of the liberal state that, 'hand-in-hand' with the 'Christian nation', made self-government possible. Taking issue with the European form of democratic governance, Manent claimed that this 'neither truly represents nor governs the individuals whose rights it aims to maximize', and underscored that 'the consent of the individual must be balanced by a broader cultivation of that civil and religious "communion"', by one that allegedly 'informed every authentically human community' (Manent 2007: 71).

In sum, nationalist or statist democratic frames of reference for painting Europe negatively can be found in conservative as well as leftist Eurosceptic discourses, in the British as well as in the German and French debates. On the left, national allegiance and the statist form of democracy were seen as almost as indispensable as on the right, although on different grounds.[25] Whether the 'dilemma of democracy due to European integration', the non-existing 'European demos', the missing European public sphere, or the lack of European identity, all these ideas erected cognitive impediments to rethinking democracy in more innovative and constructive terms. Under these conditions, for as long as the national statist frame of reference for thinking about Europe shaped mass perceptions, public opinion, and political behaviour on European politics, the institutional model of 'derivative democracy' at Union level coupled with representative democracy confined to the formally sovereign nation-states (Eriksen and Fossum 2009: 35–6) was most likely to prevail.

Celebrating diversity: Liberal thinking about democracy in Europe and its tensions

Had we adopted a pluralistic lens, most of these unifying presuppositions for either a Europe of multiple national communities or as one democratic

---

[24] See Mario Telò, Chapter 6 of this volume; and Carlos Closa and Antonio Barroso, Chapter 10.

[25] Leftist statism was more instrumental, due 'to progressive, left-wing politics of welfare and redistribution, because people will not accept the burdens of taxation and welfare if they do not feel a strong identification with those who might be the beneficiaries of such schemes'. See Varouxakis, this volume.

community would have fallen apart. From a pluralistic view, and fore-grounding the disparity of interests among the enlarged European citizenry, Armin von Bogdandy objected that even a concept of European identity that was defined by democratic constitutional patriotism might be 'crypto-normative' and 'thus dangerous', since it submitted citizens to enormous expectations. Should a 'liberal polity', von Bogdandy asks, not be better guided by the long-term self-interest of the citizens than by a common identity (von Bogdandy 2005)? Similarly, French writer Claude Lefort and historian Pierre Rosanvallon have made the case that strictly speaking 'the people' is an empty space. Against the grain of the 'artificial and perverse vision of social unity', Rosanvallon has argued: 'The people in a democracy is always a fragile people, ever incomplete and never a fused bloc. Instead of magnifying an unlocalizable unity, it is a matter, on the contrary, of ever making clear the tensions of life together, to allow the attempt to overcome them' (Rosanvallon 2006: 213).

Liberal-democratic ideas

Sometimes liberal (-democratic) ideas about how to conceive Europe have been portrayed as if they were first and foremost a British province.[26] This claim merits three qualifications: to start with, liberal (-democratic) ideas had long gained purchase on the other side of the Channel, too. They resonated in Continental, Southern and Eastern European intellectual and political life, for instance in the writings of Raymond Aron[27] or Norberto Bobbio[28] or Václav Havel,[29] to name but a few quite different thinkers. The liberal paradigm made inroads into mainstream political and social philosophy as well as legal thinking in Germany and spilled over into public debate.[30] Furthermore, it should not be forgotten that Britain's towering figures in post-Second World War liberal philosophy and history were refugees and expatriates from the Continent. There were namely Karl Popper, the philosopher of Austrian origin, Isaiah Berlin, the historian of ideas of Russian origin, and Ralf Dahrendorf, the German-British sociologist. In the dialectics of British–Continental European exchanges, this 'sceptical generation' between the wars had been defined by the experience of two devastating totalitarianisms in Europe, and prepared

---

[26] See Varouxakis, this volume.

[27] See Lacroix, this volume.

[28] See Telò, this volume.

[29] Václav Havel was awarded the Prize For Freedom of the Liberal International in 1990. See <http://www.liberal-international.org/editorial.asp?ia_id=707> (accessed 15 February 2010).

[30] A liberal paradigm shift in Continental European intellectual thought derived from the German School of Critical Theory, and specifically the political social philosophy of Jürgen Habermas, who established the democratic public sphere as one of its key anchors. Public and European legal scholars of German origin made the case for reconciling social and liberal constitutionalism: most notably Werner Maihofer, legal scholar, German Minister of Home Affairs, and President of the European University Institute.

the intellectual ground on which subsequent generations of liberal public thinkers in and on Europe could build. However, liberal thought did not escape tensions and contentions: not only on the part of outspoken enemies to the open society, but sometimes also that of illiberal thinking in the disguise of liberal rhetoric.

Liberal perspectives on Europe clearly diverged from Continental European intellectual efforts at conceiving the European demos in the singular. For liberal philosophers, the image of an open society had to be grounded on epistemological falsification and political pragmatism, as Karl Popper authoritatively established. Isaiah Berlin, preoccupied with understanding the intellectual origins of the two totalitarianisms in Europe, developed an influential critique of 'monism', that is of utopian and totalizing streams in modern political thinking, foremost from Continental Europe.[31] For a liberal historian of ideas in the footsteps of Isaiah Berlin, it appeared unpromising if not perilous to apply the unifying template of a political collective to the complexities of any political order, including a European one. Rather, liberal interpreters of the Enlightenment message attached the highest value to pluralism, believing that this was furthered by 'negative liberty', that is individual rights for freedom from state or private intervention.[32] As Ralf Dahrendorf argued, democracy is 'domesticated conflict'.[33] But modern social conflict is not 'domesticated' by a form of democracy as the rule of all, or of the majority; rather, it relies on 'anti-utopian' devices, such as moderate market liberalism, the rule of law, and parliamentarism. Moreover, democratic conflict domestication required the socialization of a type of liberal personality that is immune to totalitarian temptations.[34] Referring to Dahrendorf's depiction of the 'liberal icons', the Arons, Poppers, and Berlins who – unlike many of their cohort – had kept their distance from the totalitarian movements of the Left and the Right, Habermas noted:

The representation does not leave any doubt about the model character of this attitude. It is the love for freedom which immunizes these intellectuals against the temptations of the totalitarian century.[35]

---

[31] Isaiah Berlin introduced his liberal doctrine in 'Two Concepts of Liberty', his 1958 inaugural lecture as Chichele Professor of Social and Political Theory at Oxford; and further developed it in his book *Liberty* (Berlin 2002).

[32] Berlin's *Four Essays on Liberty* were first published in 1969 and have become a continuously discussed standard text of liberalism.

[33] Ralf Dahrendorf believed that the distribution of *power* is the crucial determinant of social structure, where the essence of power is the control of sanctions, enabling those who possess power to give orders and obtain what they want from the powerless; see Dahrendorf 1959.

[34] This *leitmotif* defined Dahrendorf's four earliest books: *Class and Class Conflict in Industrial Society* (1959); *Homo Sociologicus* (1958); *Gesellschaft und Freiheit* (1961); and *Gesellschaft und Demokratie in Deutschland* (1965).

[35] Jürgen Habermas, keynote speech at panel discussion 'On liberty: The Dahrendorf questions', marking the eightieth birthday of Lord Dahrendorf, 1 May 2009, St Antony's College,

Overall, the impact of liberalism on modern European political thought has not been without contention. For liberals it may not only be difficult to fight anti-liberalism in practice. While attaching value to personal dignity and private property, to universal human rights and free expression, to religious tolerance and equality of opportunity, they also may have problems in upholding common values such as social equality, cohesion, and solidarity. As Richard Münch ambivalently argued, the semantic construction of a European social order that is modelled on liberal constitutionalism, and thus based on the rule of law, ethical individualism, and individual and human rights (Münch 2008: 58ff., 341ff.), does not come without costs; the 'dialectics of transnational integration' correlates with 'national disintegration'. Likewise, the institutional correlates of liberal values include limited and transparent government, popular sovereignty and national self-determination, respect for privacy, the rule of law and science; while those of social democrats and social liberals were more concerned about the fate of the welfare state under the liberal banners of an unfettered 'free market economy' and 'free international trade'.[36]

Institutional forms of a liberal-democratic Europe

Liberal questions and ideas also inspired thinking about power and democracy in the 'turbulent fields' of European regional integration. As early as 1976, Ernst B. Haas took up Dahrendorf's question as to whether the desirable expansion of scope in the activities of the European Community ought to be accompanied by the growth in centralized power demanded by the Commission.[37] In fact, Dahrendorf had always rejected the functional logics ('Sachlogik') by which Jean Monnet, Robert Schuman, or Sicco Mansholt had constructed the European Communities. In his theory as well as his practice of EU politics, he actively and successfully championed an integrated European market, and even more so international trade liberalization. On this position, Dahrendorf joined hands with one of the most prolific British political writers and public intellectuals debating Europe in a pronouncedly liberal vein, Timothy Garton Ash, to warn against European separatism.[38] Contrary to Habermas and Derrida, both advocated a 'European pillar in the free world', that is an economic and security 'association of democracies', constituted as an 'open society' of about forty

---

Oxford University, with Fritz Stern and Timothy Garton Ash; published as Habermas 2009 (author's translation).

[36] See 'Freiburger Thesen', adopted by Federal Party Congress by the German Liberal Party (FDP), Freiburg im Breisgau (27 October 1971).

[37] Dahrendorf 1973, quoted by Haas 976.

[38] In *Free World: Why a Crisis of the West Reveals the Opportunity of our Time* (2004), Garton Ash made his case against attempts at profiling European world power by constructing a regional identity in opposition to that of the US.

states. Garton Ash, in particular, called Europe to resist the dangerous myth of a European nationalism and to embrace instead the permanent peaceful and regulated competition between different models of economic, social and political orders, and promote democracy not as a value in itself but as a means for the pursuit of political objectives such as of liberty, good government and just laws (Garton Ash 2004: 268; 295–7, 299).

In these liberal terms of diversity and competition among EU democracies, supranational representative or participatory democratic institutions appeared neither a necessary nor a desirable asset. Nevertheless, comparing the uneventful elections to the European Parliament to the drama of US presidential elections, Garton Ash praised the 'discreet charm of Eurodemocracy', as a 'postmodern Euro-drama taken from the Franco-German arts channel Arte, with subtitles', a movie by Buñuel and not a blockbuster by Spielberg:

> The cast consists of hundreds of characters, most of them totally unknown to most viewers. (Pöttering? Who, where, why or what is Pöttering?)...If you look at the biographies of the more than 700 members of this new parliament, you find former dissidents, writers, scholars, unionists, economists and youth activists, as well as the usual dreary party functionaries, from 25 different countries. A collection of people infinitely more diverse and interesting than the US Congress; a kind of anthology of European history over the past half-century. Out of that history, and this complex political system, comes a politics of peaceful negotiation, consensus and compromise, not of high noon and winner-takes-all. Less dramatic, less fun, to be sure; but not necessarily worse. Given the choice between a Cheney and a Pöttering, I'd choose Pöttering any day. I say: let Europe keep Pöttering on.[39]

If passionate engagement for Europe, especially among young people, was lacking, Europe was to be blamed for having lost its 'plot', namely its 'true history of freedom' epitomized by the peaceful 'evolutions'[40] in East Central and Eastern Europe.

European democratic deficits from liberal perspective

Measured by liberal-democratic ideas, European Union legitimacy deficits loomed large. Yet, confronted with Europe, liberal ideals have sometimes degenerated into liberal rhetoric, sometimes used as justifications for British obsessions with European war memories and idiosyncratic nationalist fears of a European superstate. Such antagonizing insinuations have depicted the

---

[39] Timothy Garton Ash, 'Take two for democracy. The US election is a Hollywood blockbuster, but Europe's arthouse version is a better movie to be in', The Guardian, 28 October 2004 <http://www.guardian.co.uk/politics/2004/oct/28/eu.uselections2004>.

[40] See Timothy Garton Ash and Timothy Snyder, 'The Orange Resolution', New York Review, 28 April 2005.

European Union as just another name for the bad guys, for a 'totalitarian' and ultimately a German project for hegemony in Europe, aimed at belatedly winning the Second World War and fighting the British, this time with centralized European bureaucratic rather than military means.[41]

Contrasting with this dark side, the 'European democratic deficit' thesis had initially a constructive spin, placing the issue on the European agenda.[42] Ralf Dahrendorf should be credited as an early analyst of the 'two great problems of all modern public orders' that characterized the 'huge institutional experiment' of the European Community already in the early 1970s, namely the inefficiency of its 'huge machinery' and its 'unbearable deficit of democracy' (Dahrendorf 1973: 221). While numerous critics have blamed the EU for failing to engage ordinary citizens, others have also come up with remedies for fixing this gap. Notably, Simon Hix has suggested that the EU should and could reproduce the patterns of pluralist party democracy established in the nation-states. Making the case for a true, albeit limited, democratic politics in the EU, Hix advocated competitive European parliamentary elections and the formation of EU party government.[43]

On the other hand, to put the home-grown democratic deficits in focus, Colin Crouch (2004) has coined 'post-democracy' as a term that has successfully travelled from Italy to the UK and from there across Continental Europe. It has served the purpose of putting the European democratic deficit talk in critical perspective. In democratic practice, Crouch suggested, political decision-makers had become more inclined towards business and economic elites; workers' organizations had lost out against free markets and international corporate regimes; and social movements remained little more than 'fig leaves' that had lost sight of socially important issues such as quality of life and appropriate forms of political community. Moreover, in the age of 'post-parliamentarism', representative democracy no longer responded to the requirements of social constituencies and courts no longer offered a last resort for individual or class action either. In sum, post-democracy analysts warned that democratic promises of equality as well as liberty were lost.

Faced with these three discourses – European democratic scepticism, European democratic reform optimism, and post-democratic fatalism – liberal thinkers had not yet convincingly answered the crucial 'Dahrendorf question', namely

---

[41] Such nightmares have been haunting the British audience of the tabloid press, among them notably the *Sun*. For an analysis of the British print media coverage of the European Constitution debate during the ratification period, see Packham 2007.

[42] It seems incorrect to attribute the 'European democratic deficit' thesis to David Marquand, a British journalist and author of the book *Parliament for Europe* (1979). As Ralf Dahrendorf, then European Commissioner, argued in 1973, European federalist Altiero Spinelli and the 'pragmatist' Andrew Schofield should be credited for an earlier diagnosis of the EC's deficit of democratic legitimacy (Dahrendorf 1973: 218–21).

[43] In this partly polemical book/long treatise, Hix (2008) outlined a 'Commission Presidency contest' as an innovative scenario for the 2009 European Elections.

'Can European democracy survive globalization?' (Dahrendorf 2001). In view of low voter turnouts around the world, people had apparently lost faith in elections and mistrusted parties, at the national as well as at the European level. Yet, after discussing the shortfalls of a number of democratic reform alternatives, Dahrendorf left his conclusion in the air: 'so rethinking democracy and its institutions must be a top priority for all to whom the constitution of liberty is dear'.[44] The debate about the perils of liberal democracy entailed the issue of democratic practice, that is how public intellectuals imagine – and eventually engage with – the social, political, or institutional agency they deem fit for addressing them.

European democratic agency

On the practical side, liberal ideas have deeply impregnated post-fascist Italian and German intellectual cultures and political reconstruction after the Second World War. Forty years further on, they have also fuelled peaceful regime transformations beyond the eastern borders of the European Community. Dahrendorf's passionate 'love for freedom' coupled with political realism notably resonated strongly after the fall of the Wall with East and Central European reformers, to whom he predicted: 'You can make a constitution in six weeks, for economic recovery you need perhaps six years, for freedom to take social roots however sixty years.'[45] Given their attraction to values of freedom, it could hardly be a surprise that Continental European intellectuals, sixty years after the Second World War, had progressively turned to thinking about the demos, whether national or European, as a plurality.

Still, it came as a shock that post-communist democratic consolidation might not have been successful, but that East Central Europe was backsliding.[46] Some twenty years after the demise of the Soviet regime, some of the new democracies were still haunted by deeply illiberal pockets of totalitarian legacy. As the Jewish-Hungarian Nobel prize laureate writer Imre Kertesz pointed out, from East and East Central European perspectives, the 'liberty of self-determination' and 'Free Europe' were relatively short-lived, compared to the 'long and dark shadows' from the 'fortuneless century'; here, despite the 'immortality of the

---

[44] *Taipei Times*, 16 May 2003, p. 9. One might add that six years later, Dahrendorf, in response to the same question that Habermas put to him, praised non-electoral and non-majoritarian institutions of democracy, namely courts and the British Upper House (notes by author, from panel, Oxford, 1 May 2009, see note above).

[45] I owe this point to Timothy Garton Ash's address in honour of Sir Ralf Dahrendorf on his eightieth birthday, St Anthony's College, Oxford University, 1 May 2009. Garton Ash pointed out that these revolutionary transformations in 1989 fell into the time when Dahrendorf directed St Antony's College and, together with Garton Ash, sponsored renowned programmes for supporting the reform processes in East Central European states.

[46] For instance, see "Is East-Central Europe backsliding?", special issue of *Journal of Democracy* (October 2007), 18 (4).

camps' the 'survival of survivors' had not yet become a right taken for granted, and the question 'will Europe rise again?' was still unresolved.[47] While Western European democratic cultures had grown as the result either of military defeat and subsequent re-education – or, as Kertesz claimed, of successful revolutions – in Eastern Europe they were the outcome of the totally unexpected demise of the Soviet Union:

> It . . . happened much as the unexpected fall of an oak, . . . It was an event without destiny . . . To be sure, there had been the Berlin workers' upheaval of 1953, the Hungarian revolution of 1956, the Prague Spring of 1968, the Polish Solidarnosc movement of 1980: all schools of bitterness. . . . At the end, the peoples here had lost the belief that they could change their destiny. All wished for the break-down, but nobody . . . has willed it. . . . there was no deed' (Kertesz 2003: 172, author's translation)

The twentieth century's traumatic crises of human civilization have imprinted East Central European political cultures with lasting traces such as right-wing extremism, anti-Semitism, and xenophobia. For the sake of national sovereignty and the principle of diversity, such developments have been largely ignored as making up part of the member states' idiosyncrasies. However, European liberal constitutionalists might be misled in assuming that European liberal norms do not require local roots in the member states, while 'democratic sovereigntists' might undervalue the necessity of implementing international human and European fundamental norms for consolidating national democratic cultures (Benhabib 2009).

Reconciling diversity with unity: Contestatory European demoi-cracy

Above, I started by reviewing Continental European political philosophy as one, though not the only, source for conceiving democracy in unifying terms. I then portrayed British liberal pluralism as a hub for diversifying ideas of democracy, also making it clear why such geographical/intellectual ideal types are misleading. I thus illustrated that the European public intellectual debates on democracy in Europe provide discursive constructions of unity as well as deconstructive discourses of diversity. In a critique of the unitary thinking of Dieter Grimm, Hauke Brunkhorst has shown that in the context of denationalization and globalization, the binaries on which this is premised are exposed to continuous deconstruction.[48] In what follows, I will review ideas about democracy in

---

[47] These quotes are titles from essays and speeches by Imre Kertesz, included in his book *Die exilierte Sprache: Essays und Reden* (2003).

[48] As Hauke Brunkhorst argues, Grimm's premise is informed by a conception of legal constitutionalism based on three binary dualisms: (1) an unbridgeable gap between state/politics and society; (2) a state organization law which is detached from the individual rights

Europe that deliberately aim at a third way, overcome binary thinking, and reconcile unity with diversity.[49]

There are a number of original propositions. For resolving the conundrum of moulding the 'contradictory sovereignties of the parts...into a whole', Yves Mény called upon the 'Convention on the future of Europe' to invent a new kind of democratic system, 'a system which as yet has no name', that is – drawing on Habermas' term – a European 'post-national democracy'.[50] Giuliano Amato came up with the term 'hermaphrodite' for depicting the hybrid nature of the European Union: 'Such a hermaphrodite responds to the needs and the demands of the globalized world, by definition a world where not just states but also individual persons are active supranational actors', thus 'blurring the border between international agencies and constitutional ones'.[51] From a neo-corporatist perspective, Colin Crouch and Wolfgang Streeck have conceived the 'diversity of democracy' in terms of corporatism, social order, and political conflict (Crouch and Streeck 2006).

In more analytic terms, the conceptions of 'European demoi-cracy', and 'contestatory democracy' respond to the call for squaring the circle of unity and diversity. In the present context, and without any ambition to do justice to these innovative conceptions, I will limit myself to highlighting their underlying ideas regarding (1) norms, (2) misfits between norms and practices, (3) institutional forms, and (4) agency.

Republican norms of European democracy

Philip Pettit's conception of 'contestatory democracy' offers a device for reconstructing democracy not only in the national but also in the international realm. Republican ideas of democracy cover a discursive space between two

---

of the citizens, thus leading to an apolitical understanding of rights; (3) a duality of international law, as a result of which state sovereignty together with the foreign policy prerogative of the executive are separated from the sovereignty of the people, which is limited to domestic policy; this leads to 'the subordination of international law to state sovereignty and to democracy being encapsulated within the borders of the nation state' (Brunkhorst 2007: 40ff.).

[49] Assuming a dialectics underlying the dynamics of European transnational intellectual debate, the intellectual attitude behind 'unity' thinking could be depicted as 'constructive', that behind 'diversity' thinking as 'deconstructive', and, accordingly, that of the non-binary third approach as 'reconstructive'. The third type of discourse comprises a variety of liberal, radical as well as cosmopolitan ideas and authors such as, on the one hand, Rémi Brague, Umberto Eco, or Hans Magnus Enzensberger, and, on the other, Jean Baudrillard, Pierre Bourdieu, Etienne Balibar, Susan George, Manuel Castells, Ulrich Beck, or Gerard Delanty.

[50] Mény 2002. In this headline article on the eve of the Convention, Mény adopted Habermas' notion of the 'post-national constellation' for diagnosing the transformation of the nation-state in the context of globalization and European integration (Habermas 1998). See also Mény's elaboration of this argument (Mény 2009).

[51] Amato 2006: 33.

antipodes, democratic politics in the singular – that is the political body in the tradition of Rousseau – and the dispersal of power in contestatory configurations of democracy, notably in Pettit's political philosophy. In the first case, the concept of republic borders on that of a pure democracy understood as the unrestricted rule of the majority, that is of the people (singular) which collectively exercises power, directly or indirectly through elections. In the second case, the republic is conceived to secure freedom as non-domination by combining majority rule with the rule by many, that is, by the people as a plurality of citizens who transform the unity (of the nation, or state). The distinction of 'electoral democracy' and 'contestatory democracy' emphasizes the two traditions of majoritarian and republican democracy that Pettit brings together.[52] In other words, he squares the circle by sequencing a first component that looks at unity, and a second one that is concerned with diversity.

Kalypso Nicolaïdis has coined the term of a European 'demoi-cracy' for capturing a multitude of intertwined democracies, arguing that 'the EU is neither a union of democracies nor a union as democracy; it is a union of states and of peoples – a "*demoi-cracy*" – in the making' (Nicolaïdis 2004a, 2004b). Here, the focus is on the territorial dimension of the democratic process or federal ideas that prompt a 'third way' for reconciling diversity with unity. 'European demoi-cracy', in these terms, depicts a new kind of political community that is defined by 'the persistent plurality of its peoples—its demoi'.[53] This model departs from a Europe of segmented, coexisting national democracies as much as from a European supranational federal state, erected on a collective identity. The republican principle of 'constitutional tolerance' is adopted for legitimating a kind of diversity that is premised on the acceptance of a shared destiny with 'others' (Nicolaïdis 2004a; Weiler, Mayer, and Haltern 1995. 'Mutual recognition', cosmopolitan principles, and norms of European multiculturalism are established as devices for securing unity in a radically pluralist community of others, where the stable existence of peoples (bounded imagined communities) rather than groups is firmly acknowledged (Nicolaïdis 2007).

Ulrich Beck and Edgar Grande have foregrounded international human rights and cosmopolitan law for Europe, too, arguing that the cosmopolitan moment should correct or forestall vicious dynamics among its different parts. While 'European demoi-cracy' is concerned with the political other, Beck and Grande's 'cosmopolitan Europe' aims at refining the perception of 'the cultural

---

[52] Pettit defines contestation 'as a means to solve problems of representation or of the direct influence on legislative bodies'; it 'supplements the mechanisms of inclusion into legislation and does not replace them. The need to include all those affected in the procedures and institutions of legislation problematizes the limitation of democracy to contestation.' See Pettit 2006a and 2006b.

[53] In 'We, The Peoples of Europe', Nicolaïdis (2004a) proposes 'demoi-cracy' as a solution to the EU's perennial lack of a clear cut model of democratic legitimacy. Similarly, James Bohman (2007) has suggested a move 'from demos to demoi' for conceiving transnational demoi-cracy.

other', framing a transnational discourse of reconciliation in a Europe of clashing communities of memories. Arguably, through 'the total devastation and cruelty experienced' and 'the immeasurable suffering and guilt that the nationalistic warmongering Europe brought to the world', Europe had become 'more sensitive to the internalised measures of self-criticism, more open and at the same time more resistant in the struggle for a peaceful, post-religious humanity' (Beck and Grande 2004: 159).

Misfits between republican norms and European practices

Third-way authors are concerned about misfits between democratic norms and practices in the European Union in different ways from supranationalists or intergovernmentalists. They do not take issue with judicial activism by the ECJ[54] in as far as this may help secure the freedom rights of minorities. They do not question the political weakness of the Council, joint decision-making deadlock, or structural policy gridlock to the extent that these result from domestic contestatory constituencies. Adopting third-way perspectives, we will question the legitimacy of current EU governance practices from another respect. For instance, we should ask whether the aggregation of citizens' preferences and majority rule – both supposed to secure effective co-decision-making by the Council and the European Parliament – are also equipped with mechanisms for transparency, for accountability, or for individual or collective access to national and European courts. Such mechanisms are required for affected minorities to ensure protection of rights or redress injustices of majority rule through contestation, civil society participation, or representation in the public sphere.

Institutional forms of a European republic

As intellectuals have conceived a great many innovative ideas of 'contentious European democracy', many of these will have to wait to be formalized, eventually constitutionalized, and possibly institutionalized. In any event, these ideas will help assess institutional practices, with an eye to the future of democracy in Europe. Regarding existing or emerging institutional forms that put 'third-way democracy' ideas into practice, there are a number of propositions. They can be grouped in four clusters: federal, parliamentary, deliberative, and legal.[55]

---

[54] See, for instance, the call by Roman Herzog, former Federal Constitutional Court President and Chairman of the EU Convention drafting the Charter, 'Stoppt den Europäischen Gerichtshof!' ('Stop the ECJ!'), *Frankfurter Allgemeine Zeitung*, 8 September 2008.

[55] For comprehensive assessments of EU democratic reform proposals, see in particular Schmitter 2000; Warleigh 2003.

Firstly, British scholars and public intellectuals have prepared the ground for bridging the federalist divide. Key institutional features include federal constitutionalism – that is, a territorial configuration that comprises constitutional, governance, public, and civil-sphere components that leave room for a plurality of power centres and peoples. In this context, John Pinder has pioneered two ideas. On the one hand, he established that after the demise of de Gaulle it was time for the UK to join in the project aimed at the 'United States of Europe'. On the other hand, he sought to justify federalism as not being alien but rather an inherent part of the British (Scottish) political tradition (Mayne and Pinder 1990; Pinder 1969).

Secondly, as to the electoral components of a democratic Europe, Pinder had claimed that national parliamentary democratic traditions together with the European Parliament would provide the appropriate 'foundations of democracy' for the EU (Pinder 1999). Moreover, Erik Oddvar Eriksen and John Erik Fossum have made the case for measuring 'democracy beyond the nation state' by the quality of deliberation that leads to Community law and the deliberative quality of the public institutions that encourage such debates – the public spheres (Eriksen and Fossum 2009; Fossum and Schlesinger 2007).

Also, for 'contestatory' procedures as a supplement to electoral institutions, Bohman has proposed that 'democracy across borders' might require not only transnational governance arrangements and deliberative transnational democratic publics but also transnational civil society networks (Bohman 2007). In this context, deliberation procedures would be linked to decision-making, that is to the 'aggregative' mechanisms of majority rule, on the one hand, and also to contestation, that is mechanisms for minority protection, on the other hand.

Ideas of a 'third way' and a 'contestatory European demoi-cracy' also resonate with the German Constitutional Court's Lisbon ruling. By this judgment, the GCC established the constitutional principle of 'integration responsibility' and, applying it to Germany, required the Bundestag to strengthen its muscles for a more effective oversight of EU political decision-making by the executive. Also, the 2009 Lisbon ruling took a decidedly civic stance for replacing the ethnic conception of the German demos than its 1993 Maastricht judgment suggested. Yet, while devaluing the contribution of the European Parliament as the EU's most prominent majoritarian institution to its democratic legitimacy, the GCC confirmed litigation procedures and mechanisms for minority protection against unjustified majority. To sum up, the German judges provide 'mixed messages' – a reasoning not without tensions.[56]

[56] The German Federal Court issued its Lisbon ruling on 30 June 2009, confirming the constitutionality of the Lisbon Treaty, but also mandating the German legislator to implement institutional reforms for strengthening the role of the national legislature in EU policy-making; see Liebert 2010.

Contestatory constituencies of a European republic

Finally, tackling the issue of agency – that is the question of the EU's constituency – is a matter of theoretical, formal, and substantive ideas. Theoretically, the European demoi-cracy would replace the absent European demos by the plurality of peoples. In formal-legal terms, Anne Peters has made the case for a mixed constituent subject. Accepting that there is no homogeneous European people, she identifies three types of constituent subjects in the EU: the European peoples as the associated – including, but not exclusively, aggregated – citizenries of the member states; member state governments – in intergovernmental as well as transgovernmental terms; and a 'pouvoir constituant mixte' composed by peoples as citizens as well as member states (Peters 2000). In substantive terms, 'mobile citizens', social movements, and 'organized civil society' have surfaced as agents that do matter in the politics of contestatory European demoi-cracy. Moreover, non-national citizenship has become another key to the most pressing problem of the European polity, that is its search for legitimacy:

It is this embryonic form of non-nation-based citizenship which suggests an entirely new construction of the 'we' in the field of political action. Might Union citizenship define a new political identity, a new 'we' which is able to shape the fates of people in a new manner? . . . To conclude, the problem of European democracy is not that there is no European demos . . . The EU's political vision derives its legitimacy from being appropriate to a world where people have become neighbours and still remain strangers to each other. This genuine political and institutional innovation is the contribution of Europe . . . (Offe and Preuss 2006: 200)

For the third way to 'European demoi-cracy' that has been mapped out here, courts, individual, and collective rights are necessary preconditions for legal contestation. In this perspective, 'political constitutionalism' would be lopsided if it were to privilege constitutional forms of representative democracy, while rejecting legal constitutional foundations for contestatory practices (Bellamy 2007).

Conclusion: Beyond utopia and melancholy

Starting in pre-Constitution Europe, the intellectual debate that was kicked off by the futile search for the 'finality of European integration' has come a long way since. One of the most ambitious ideas had to be abandoned, namely that of establishing a 'Constitution for Europe'.[57] Moreover, in post-Constitution Europe, the idea of 'European constitutional patriotism' had to be shelved, as

---

[57] Joschka Fischer, 'From Confederacy to Federation: Thoughts on the Finality of European Integration', Humboldt University Berlin, 12 May 2000.

well. Yet, the challenges, crises, and changes of Europe's political and institutional order have not necessarily spread melancholy among European intellectuals. Rather, the debate on the future of Europe has fuelled vital debates about European democracy and greatly encouraged transnational exchanges among them. Populist rhetoric continues to cast these debates in the terms of national sovereigntist versus supranational antagonism, thus reflecting the traditional clash between monist and pluralist thinking. Many public intellectuals, in turn, have searched for ways out of these binary traps. A variety of third ways have emerged from the dynamics of cross-border exchanges and mutual learning. In the light of innovative as well as realist ideas, sterile stereotypes start losing out, including that of the 'European democratic deficit' or the famous 'No European demos' thesis. Instead, less unitary lenses have been constructed, from the early 'post-national democracy' to that of 'contestatory democracy', 'European demoi-cracy', 'cosmopolitan values', or 'European civil society'. These ideas provide new frames of reference for a more reconciliatory thinking in a still divided Europe. They do not require a formal constitution, nor are they necessarily constrained by popular dissensus.[58] Some of these ideas have already entered European institutional arenas and reshaped their practices, for instance the European Parliament.

A recent episode will illustrate this point. In his plenary speech to the European Parliament, Czech President Václav Klaus challenged the very institution which had called him to present the Czech programme on behalf of the EU's rotating presidency for the first half of 2009. 'Since there is no European demos – and no European nation', Klaus declared, 'this defect cannot be solved by strengthening the role of the European Parliament.'[59] While a number of protesting MEPs walked out, the European Parliamentary President acknowledged Klaus' view as 'an expression of the diversity in Europe' and affirmed that in the 'European democracy... everyone can express his or her own opinion'.[60] Echoing as well as transcending the earlier controversy of Dieter Grimm and Jürgen Habermas,[61] this dispute in the European Parliament can be read as an instructive manifestation of how the binary terms of negotiating a democratically legitimate European order have started changing.

In sum, twenty years after the end of the Cold War, the lessons to be drawn from the public debate about the future of democracy in Europe neither suggest

[58] 'EU politicization' or the 'mobilization of mass public opinion with regard to EU policies and institutions' is the mechanism that has shifted European integration away from a context of 'permissive consensus' to one of 'constraining dissensus'; see Hooghe and Marks 2009: 211.

[59] Václav Klaus, plenary speech to the European Parliament, 30 January 2009; for Klaus' role in the Czech intellectual debate, see Muriel Blaive and Nicolas Maslowski, Chapter 13 of this volume.

[60] Ibid.

[61] Debating the feasibility of a European Constitution in the absence of a 'European demos': see Grimm 1995; Habermas 2001b.

a melancholy-driven 'homo Europaeus intellectualis' nor one whose utopian energies were fuelled primarily by an inhibition to act. Instead, European public intellectuals have started engaging with transnational discourses that contribute to the making of a European communicative space, and, arguably, to constructing third ways for escaping past and present dilemmas.

Table 2.1 60 Public intellectuals debating Europe 2000–2009

AUTHOR	Other NATION. ORIGIN	ENGLISH	FRENCH	GERMAN	POLISH*	CZECH*	ANY LANGUAGE*
Amato, Giuliano	I 1520	1,720	284	225	24	0	(11,500)
Balibar, Etienne	F	36	70	11	0	0	365
Baudrillard, Jean	F	198	70	57	13	0	2,870
Bauman, Zygmunt	PL	119	11	14	51	(24)	1,910
Beck, Ulrich	D	81	40	134	13	13	1,710
Benhabib, Seyla	TÜR 17	31	1	12	0	0	189
Berlin, Isaiah	UK	699	8	29	7	0	3,350
Bobbio, Norberto	I 159	8	4	3	2	1	2,510
Bogdandy, Armin Von	D	4	1	10	0	0	27
Bourdieu, Pierre	F	287	197	56	3(25)	(2)	3,720
Brague, Rémi	F	22	33	10	1	0	238
Brunkhorst, Hauke	D	2	0	7	0	0	32
Castells, Manuel	SPA 186	87	18	7	5	0	1,720
Cichocki, Marek	PL	72	5	86	61	6	324
Collignon, Stefan	D	12	9	11	0	0	45
Crouch, Colin	UK	12	3	3	0	0	168
Dahrendorf, Ralf	D, UK	140	44	137	21	1	2,460
Dehousse, Renaud	BEL	13	42	2	0	0	54
Derrida, Jacques	F	639	197	157	22(138)	(26)	5,000
Eco, Umberto	ITA	799	133	120	56	(103)	11,600
Enzensberger, Hans M.	D	84	19	415	10	5	2,920
Garton Ash, Timothy	UK	1,020	50	122	129	55	2,700
Gauchet, Marcel	F	47	170	1	1	0	638
Giddens, Anthony	UK	339	60	39	9(48)	12	2,860

Ginsborg, Paul	UK, ITA	77	2	9	0	0	536
Grimm, Dieter	D	11	1	37	1	0	235
Habermas, Jürgen	D	548	176	557	61	28	5,170
Havel, Václav	CZ	7,710	915	645	131	(5,430)	(28,900)
Hix, Simon	UK	49	4	4	1	0	182
Kershaw, Ian	UK	209	20	32	19	4	1,570
Kertesz, Imre	HUN	348	52	119	14	0	3,340
Kielmansegg, Peter Graf	D	0	0	19	0	0	73
Konrad, György	HUN	28	9	59	7	2	267
Krasnodebski, Zdzisław	PL	0	0	4	35	0	327
Leggewie, Claus	D	21	4	99	5	0	564
Lepenies, Wolf	D	21	6	98	9	2	402
MacCormick, Neil	UK	121	18	12	1	0	308
Magnette, Paul	BEL	34	152	6	2	3	(1,480)
Maione, Giandomenico	ITA	8	0	0	3	0	32
Manent, Pierre	F	41	53	2	5	(1)	239
Mény, Yves	F	47	40	6	0	2	216
Michnik, Adam	PL	442	75	83	284	87	(4,520)
Morin, Edgar	F	40	211	14	8	0	2780
Mouffe, Chantal	BEL	34	0	11	4(30)	2	330
Negri, Antonio	ITA	29	39	12	1	1	1,030
Nicolaïdis, Kalypso	GRE	30	4	6	12	1	74
Nida-Rümelin, Julian	D	14	5	130	0	0	932
Offe, Claus	D	11	1	13	0	2	156
Pettit, Philip	IRE	9	3	0	0	0	258
Pinder, John	UK	17	0	1	1	0	?

(continued)

Table 2.1 Continued

AUTHOR	Other NATION. ORIGIN	ENGLISH	FRENCH	GERMAN	POLISH*	CZECH*	ANY LANGUAGE*
Rancière, Jacques	F	25	30	2	4	0	515
Rodrigues, Maria João	POR 115	31	13	15	1	0	188
Rosanvallon, Pierre	F	15	115	2	10	0	467
Savater, Fernando	SPA 830	38	33	15	12(54)	1	6,820
Scharpf, Fritz	D	14	5	14	1	0	58
Schwan, Gesine	D	99	7	549	393	2	(5,897)
Siedentop, Larry	UK	48	1	4	1	1	102
Sloterdijk, Peter	D	31	44	180	14	5	2,150
Van Parijs, Philippe	F	21	8	2	1	1	177
Zizek, Slavoj	SLOVE	222	35	43	10	9	2,560

* Figures are calculated by Advanced Google News Research; the figures indicate numbers of news articles mentioning 'Europe' published by the author in English, French, German, Polish, or Czech during the period 2000–2009; figures in parentheses refer to authors holding at least temporarily a public office. The second column refers to author's nationality and number of news articles published in native language only if different from the five languages covered by the table. The final column presents the total number of news articles published in any of the languages covered by Advanced Google News Research.

3

On European and Other Intellectuals

Michael Freeden

In a collection of essays as valuable and wide-ranging as this, focusing as it does on Europe as well as on national and European intellectuals, many of whom are supposed to be engaged in a conversation on European integration, there may be some merit in pausing to raise the questions: What is an intellectual? What is a national or European intellectual? And what do we mean by 'European integration'? I will devote most of this chapter to the first, and then offer very brief remarks on the second and third.

'In every society there are *social groups* whose special task it is to provide an interpretation of the world for that society.' Thus Karl Mannheim, writing some eighty years ago about the 'intelligentsia' (Mannheim 1936: 10). For him a crucial feature of the intelligentsia (and I refer to that term as a collective noun for intellectuals, rather than as a designation for a cultural class) is their detachment from socially determined or inspired viewpoints. (Indeed, that perspective later metamorphosed into conceptions of a rootless intelligentsia, as in Russian usage: see Jennings and Kemp-Welch 1997: 7.) While Mannheim's general approach is to be lauded, it regrettably led him to two related errors of analysis. The one was the expectation that intellectuals would converge on a single perspective of understanding; the other was to assume the possibility of unadulterated detachment. The first error – appealing to an evidential basis of epistemology – still linked Mannheim to the Marxist tradition: the removal of false or partial perspectives would enable scientific social knowledge to claim its rightful, objective status, if not absolutely then with reference to a specific historical situation (Mannheim 1936: 78–9, 86). The possibility that even free-floating intellectuals might create a multitude of perspectives did not occur to him. Free-floating would, after all, only be possible in a reasonably free society, and that would *ipso facto* be one in which many viewpoints cohabited.

The second error – appealing to a neutral-rational basis of epistemology – put an exaggerated premium on the possibility, even desirability, of 'objective' detachment, or at least a 'total orientation' or a synthesis produced by a 'relatively classless stratum' (Mannheim 1936: 153–4, 161). It made a sharp distinction between 'truth' and 'ideology' – a distinction that was often then directed to differentiate between 'good' and 'bad' intellectuals: those who were committed to the virtuous and the reasonable, and those who treacherously put their skills at the disposal of manipulative and mendacious states and governments. In an extreme version of that approach, Louis Feuer (1975: 110, 190) called the latter 'marginal' or 'semi' intellectuals. Though that was not Mannheim's view, he did not consider the possibility that all social views might be contestable interpretations of a moving and fluctuating reality rather than historically anchored truths, and that ideologies are competitions over the control of the languages of interpretation – many of which are plausible and meet the requirements of reflective distance that intellectuals are supposed to fulfil (Freeden 1996).

It is important that we realize which of the many senses of 'intellectual' are deployed in a project that is dedicated to exploring what European intellectuals are and what they may be contributing to a state of 'being European'. One crucial dividing line is whether intellectuals are there to provide understanding or to stimulate action. In a sense that distinction is partly spurious since non-random action must emanate from some understanding or other. But it is frequently the case that intellectuals are believed to be charged with the responsibility to *change* the world, not 'merely' to *interpret* it, in Marx's disdainful phrase. Their vital hermeneutic role – that of enabling a society to understand itself – has frequently been overtaken by those intellectuals who assume a pontificating or missionary role. The question 'what should we be?' has left the question 'what are we?' far behind. It also diminishes the process of transformation from the one question to the other which has been seen as a feature of intellectual work (Shils 1968). Maybe that was always so, but it is also at risk of re-attaching itself to a peculiar arrogance and elitism. Being an intellectual is an elite activity, and an ideological activity, and ideologies are often tempted to mask their inevitable partiality (which is not the same as falsehood, because falsehood assumes the availability of truth) by employing myths of non-evaluative neutrality or special insight that serve, among others, to protect the status of intellectuals. Some intellectuals are not only ideologists in the broad sense – that is perfectly normal – but ideologues: they possess a doctrinaire and often totalizing prescriptive view of the world, and from there it is but one step to regard intellectuals as dangerous manipulators at the service of ruthless rulers and their belief systems. Conviction then becomes not a vessel through which to channel social responsibility but a poisoned chalice. However, you can possess an ideology without being an ideologue, and it is mistaken to suggest that 'old-type' intellectuals engaged through ideologies which have now lost their appeal (Fleck, Hess, and Lyon 2009: 5).

The intellectuals discussed in this volume are understood in the specific sense of having specialized in thinking about, and in prescribing plans for, society. Yet intellectuals should be interpreters – that signified their essence for Mannheim – at least as much as they are prescriptionists. Their role as proper intellectuals is also to be engaged in the Weberian objective of *Verstehen*. Edward Shils saw this as perceiving, experiencing, and expressing 'a general significance in particular, concrete events' (Shils 1968: 399). That view was also captured by Julien Benda, whose famous definition of the intellectual or, more accurately, the 'clerk', referred to all those non-realists and non-materialists 'whose activity essentially is *not* the pursuit of practical aims, all those who seek their joy in the practice of an art or a science or metaphysical speculation' (Benda 1955: 30). As Shils noted, 'the belief in the intrinsic and practical value of scientific knowledge has also contributed to the increase in the size of the intellectual stratum' (Shils 1990: 287). This kind of intellectual is now mostly to be found amongst the ranks of academics, though it must also be emphasized that some academics are closer to being technicians than intellectuals. That said, a distinction needs to be maintained between specialist academics, with their contribution to European integration policies, and non-expert 'prophetic' visionaries with messages to large audiences.

At any rate, when some chapters in this book relate to political theorizing about Europe as primarily normative, they seem to mean the attempt to implement a value agenda, usually a political one. Perhaps there are two senses of 'normative' lurking here. According to Alan Montefiore (1990: 201), 'an intellectual is anyone who takes a committed interest in the validity and truth of ideas for their own sake'. For Montefiore, this is a normative commitment with political responsibilities, as truthfulness is 'a political virtue' and 'a major determinant of the nature of the public or political space in which the community conducts or contests its affairs' (Montefiore 1990: 228). Responsibility itself becomes a normative desideratum, or at least a prescriptive good. But the notion of normativity enmeshed in intellectual activity seems to blur two separate facets: that of advocating specific substantive values that societies should implement (in fact, a typical function of ideologies), and that of committing to a particular social practice. That practice itself may be viewed in two very different lights: the one relates to the pursuit of truth and the other to the pursuit of critical reflexivity without insisting on truth's singularity, or even attainability. So there are two different kinds of responsibility here. We can attach value to various ways of thinking about the world which, given a suitable audience, become ways of intervening in the world; and we can attach value to the ways in which we meet the high professional standards our vocation as critical thinkers requires.

The project of this volume also claims that intellectuals are story-tellers, but story-telling is more about identity than prescription. Telling and understanding stories is *not* the normative part of political theory, and there may be a tension between the two. True, there are (unreliable) pseudo-narratives about a better future (some utopian thinking displays that characteristic) but most narratives link past to present. We therefore should look far more closely at the actual maps of political thinking and discourse currently available across Europe. The prescriptive plans for Europe's *future* can only be significantly analysed as the *current* voices and stories of Europe's cultural make-up, however diverse and competing, yet we spend much of our efforts on examining the merits or demerits of the content of the proposals – many of which aren't stories at all, but relate to the specifics of governance or to issues of democratic transparency – rather than what such debates tell us about the thought-patterns of Europe now (some chapters pull in different directions here).

What seems to have changed in recent treatments of intellectuals? First, our understanding of intellectuals has become more individuated, more the outcome of the performative and communicable celebrity status that many of them seek for themselves, aided by the power of the mass media, rather than connected to the diffusion of what used to be known as high culture.[1] Those intellectuals also possess the short shelf-life associated with the mass media (Fleck, Hess, and Lyon 2009: 8–10). Second – and here Mannheim shared an important insight with Gramsci (even as he also shared with the latter the unsupported conviction that societies would witness converging blocs of ideas) – being an intellectual is not invariably a matter of specialization, training, or skills, but a position that any intelligent and perceptive individual can cultivate. Mannheim's free-floating intellectuals could emerge from anywhere. He wrote of the intelligentsia that they are 'increasingly recruited from constantly varying social strata and life-situations' (Mannheim 1936: 12). Gramsci asserted that 'all men are intellectuals ... but not all men have in society the function of intellectuals' (Gramsci 1971: 9).

In sum, the recent 'flashiness' of being an intellectual has combined with a potentially greater access to that position. This has had an immediate effect on the authority that intellectuals have either claimed or have had assigned to them by popular belief through their expertise, particularly those who have worked in areas of knowledge that have traditionally had high esteem. Traditional sources of authority were partly ascriptive – relating to the standing of one's occupation – and partly what Weber termed 'charismatic': relating to perceptions of uniqueness or greatness that consumers of intellectual discourses projected onto salient individuals. The mounting contestation of values and of knowledge itself – a product of a liberal society – has undermined the solidity and assurance of that authority. This reflects the tendency of intellectual debates increasingly to adopt the form of clashes and competitions over insight and understanding, not of pronouncements about truth or wisdom,

---

[1] On the function of intellectuals in disseminating high culture see Shils 1968: 410.

inasmuch as those latter qualities have been played down under sceptical criticisms from relativists, pluralists, and post-structuralists. Intellectuals can only flourish in an ideological framework that is liberal, and that encourages diversity of outlook, though they can nonetheless survive in non-liberal cultures at some cost and risk to themselves. But being an intellectual in a liberal culture should involve relinquishing strong claims to one's authority.

There is a further issue at stake. In liberal societies, and that is the assumption of the European enterprise, the expectation is that intellectuals contribute to democratic life. However, they are not necessarily linked to the normative upholding of democracy, nor is reflective critique a typical feature or outcome of democratic politics, particularly when the mass media are concerned. This is another way of looking at the flow of impact between intellectuals and liberal democratic societies. Are intellectuals charged with the responsibility for maintaining and improving liberal democracies, or are their specific practices the product of ideologies sustained by liberal democracies? For my part the defender and propagator of democracy is one kind of European intellectual, but excluding others seems to be arbitrary. I fear that will not tell us enough about how European intellectuals think.

Implicit in many of the above approaches is the rather unfortunate phrase 'public intellectual', a phrase that implies that there are private intellectuals. Not so in Mannheim's conception; the very notion of an intellectual emerged from traditional societies where certain groups monopolized 'the right to preach, teach, and interpret the world' (Mannheim 1936: 10). I suspect that there is some confusion between a 'public intellectual' and a 'politically minded intellectual'. Politically minded intellectuals are those with clear ideational agendas by which to change the social world or to conserve it, though these agendas change from person to person; they are some of the creators and purveyors of ideologies, though non-intellectuals will also engage in ideological dissemination, if not production. Intellectuals in that mode attempt – successfully or not – to exercise discursive power over their societies, and in the specific case of Europe also over neighbouring societies. Put differently, they engage (though not alone) in one of the central features of the political: the distribution of significance to values, ideas, ends, and policies – the production of views and statements on what is more important than what; or which is more urgent than which (Freeden 2005). That is what intellectuals do, but they are hardly alone in so doing. Politicians, bureaucrats, journalists, lawyers are no less, maybe more, important in producing and disseminating ideas about Europe.

And if we insist on retaining the term 'public intellectual', the relevant questions then should be: *What* is public about intellectuals? What is the public domain they inhabit? And, most importantly: *Which* publics do they address? Many commentators on this question assume that all this entails a new relationship with a general public (Davis 1997: 262). The introduction to this volume refers to the view that intellectuals address a 'broader, non-specialist public'. Yet most people designated as intellectuals who discuss European integration do no such thing. They talk to highly specialized publics, or audiences, of bureaucrats, governing elites, journalists, or, most probably, other intellectuals (and academics). We need to home in on micro-analysis.

In his chapter, Francis Cheneval does four helpful things with the idea of the intellectual. He alerts us, without using the term, to the ideological rifts among European intellectuals, many of whom turned out to be ideologues with totalitarian tendencies. He is firmly wedded to the view that regards true intellectuals as seeking reflexive equilibrium. He is also quite right in identifying intellectuals as purveyors of passionate as well as rational discourse. Indeed, emotion and forms of bonding and commitment need to stretch beyond the partially rational, partially emotional support that has been voiced in the name of Habermasian constitutional patriotism. That proposal is designed to appeal to intellectuals but, regrettably, will not animate a people or a continent – those are the mechanics, not the organics, of a social vision. And he problematizes the notion of a European intellectual as distinct from a local intellectual, but ends by imposing two restrictive conditions. The first is set by the editors: defining European intellectuals in terms of the content of their discourses – directed towards European issues – and not the actors. But there is a third way, to which I shall return – investigating European intellectuals in terms of the particular cultural identifying features they exhibit. The second constraint introduces the normative dimension of assessing the consequences of a 'common Europe' for national democratic practices, to which I referred above. Ultimately, for Cheneval democrats are intellectuals; non-democrats are ideologues. Ideally, perhaps; effectively, no.

I want to identify three issues regarding Ulrike Liebert's chapter and her very able examination of different kinds of democratic theory in a European context (libertarian, communitarian, and republican). First, she refers importantly to the European demos, but this raises a problem. Intellectuals *talk* about the demos incessantly – but do they engage it? Do *they* give way to listening to current demotic narratives? Is the vernacular voiced or heard in the debates of intellectuals, or is it side-stepped, silenced, and replaced by intellectual discourse? Could it be that even if intellectuals are recruited from broad sections of society, they adopt similarities in style, if not in content, which re-establish distance between them and the 'demos'? Mannheim made the point that, 'we are not concerned here with examining the possibilities of a politics exclusively suited to intellectuals' (Mannheim 1936: 160). It seems to me that some of the discussions in this volume gravitate towards that possibility. If this project is among other things about story-telling, politically minded intellectuals are not the main story-tellers in their societies: telling stories is an act of imagination and interpretation, less of rational critique. They are told by politicians, writers, religious office-holders, ordinary dissidents, elementary school-teachers, artists. Some may be political intellectuals, most are definitely not, and many are not intellectuals at all except in an impossibly loose sense of the term. So do the stories of intellectuals matter that much? And, as there are many European stories, to which should we be listening, given that we cannot take all equally seriously?

Second, in assessing the normative value of different democratic approaches, the overused phrase 'democratic deficit' reappears. My question here is: What democratic arrangement would produce *no* deficit? The problem is obvious: democracy is not a monolithic concept, but contains elements many of which are in zero-sum relationship to each other; or, at least, we possess no algorithm for establishing their relative weight. There is no possible construct that will simultaneously optimize the equality, liberty/self-determination, participation, communal decision-making, and accountability components of the concept of democracy. The question is rather: Which of the many possible deficits are we – or are Europeans more generally – most prepared to tolerate? That seems to me to be the vital issue that intellectuals need to address. Not necessarily, which inadequate combination is the best (there is no conceivable uncontroversial answer to that) but which inadequate combination has the most chances of durable implementation in the context of the main cultural features of European countries?

Third, Liebert identifies some very influential European intellectuals – Habermas is of course the prototypical example – in terms of the conceptual frameworks in Europe that they have launched. She refers to 'public intellectuals' and 'national intellectuals' but avoids the term 'European intellectuals'. However, much of her chapter is not about public-political or national intellectuals but shifts to academic intellectuals who do not necessarily perform on a public political stage. These are the professional semi-private debates of the kind this group of scholars is having at the moment (tellingly, the chapters of this volume were at an earlier stage only accessible by typing in a code, and some of them admonished against citation!).

Finally, some thoughts about European integration. I was struck by Kalypso Nicolaïdis' phrase about Europe as a place where Europeans 'feel at home abroad' but I think that goes far beyond institutional integration or common criteria of citizenship, beyond federal-type organizations, committing to de-mocratization, defining borders, and regulating markets. Being a European is also a question of cultural affiliation and orientations, not identical ones but possessing broad family resemblances: kinds of music, leisure pursuits, modes of socializing, experiencing an affinity to certain physical and natural environ-ments, patterns of rhetoric, expectations of dietary variety, social welfare and health practices, an acceptable range of views on religion, standards of courtesy and how we talk to strangers, forms of moral outrage. Most of those have strong political dimensions as well. Moreover, what is distinctly *politically* European requires exploring strong mutual relationships among separate but roughly contiguous states, and a vague sense of a shared past (much of it unsavoury) that should on the whole not be repeated in a shared future. But otherwise, is the 'process of Europeanization' about forming a political entity called Europe or about becoming European?

Let me put this slightly differently. There is a problem in referring to individual intellectuals, as some authors in this volume do, while still using the collective term 'European intellectuals'. That lumps different categories together. There are academics who are not, strictly speaking, European intellectuals but professional intellectuals who comment on Europe. And there are also intellectuals who may think *about* Europe, but it is also conceivable that they may think in a European fashion, or – more likely – in three or four such modes of thinking '*Europeanly*', with a certain set of shared, or at least overlapping, values. Clearly, we are not referring to European values simply as those produced in geographical Europe – in which case they will be extremely broad, as Europe was one of the major loci of culture and 'civilization', though of course it also produced 'non-civilized' thinking such as fascism. The alternative is to see those ideals as a certain *family of values* in the here and now. And if so, we are methodologically torn between endowing them retrospectively with three competing adjectival classifications: Are we looking for 'good' values, 'typical' values, or 'common' values? If they are good, are we looking for the best arguments that Europe can produce, even if they have little chance of being common? If they are typical, is it in the sense of being concentrated in culturally heavyweight parts of Europe, and are they typical of some groupings in those geographical or cultural areas more than others? And if they are common, does that imply consensus or merely a looser overlap that also contains variations *within* each value?

Those who regard diversity and pluralism as a *sine qua non* of European integration – and I think they are right – must, however, take note that all forms of integration, whether unitary or federalist, imply a common legal and political framework. The catch, of course, is that such frameworks are far from procedurally neutral. They are ideologically rich and entail an artificial consensus that may fly against the very values of diversity and pluralism themselves. That is of course inevitable and as long as intellectuals recognize that this is what they are doing, as long as they are modest and circumspect about their own intellectual ambitions, possibilities, and failings, as long as they do not attempt to seize cultural leadership unilaterally, we can continue to take them seriously.

Part II

Founders

4

In the Shadows of Statism

Peculiarities of the German Debates on European Integration*

Jan-Werner Müller

—In Memory of Ralf Dahrendorf—

The people must be given a new ideology. It can only be a European one.

(Konrad Adenauer, 1952)

What forms the common core of a European identity is the character of the painful learning process it has gone through, as much as its results. It is the lasting memory of nationalist excess and moral abyss that lends to our present commitments the quality of a peculiar achievement.

(Jürgen Habermas, 2001)

How do German intellectuals debate European integration? A short answer might be: they don't. Of course, especially after the Maastricht Treaty and the famous (some would say infamous) Maastricht decision of the German Constitutional Court, there have been wide-ranging discussions about the nature of the EU as a polity, as well as its practical and normative perils and promises – and the 2009 Lisbon decision of the Court has given such debates a new impetus. Moreover, some of the protagonists of these discussions – Jürgen Habermas and the late Ralf Dahrendorf for instance – are among the very few thinkers on the continent who have a claim actually to be both 'national' and genuinely European intellectuals. Nevertheless, what has to be stressed is that compared with other major controversies in the German public sphere 'Europe'

* This essay draws on ideas and arguments I first developed in Müller 2000, 2003, and 2007. The section on anti-statism is adapted from my chapter 'Three constitutionalist responses to globalization' in Macedo and Tullis, forthcoming. For comments and suggestions I am grateful to Mattias Kumm as well as the editors and the participants in the workshop in Oxford on 30 April and 1 May 2009.

has elicited few real passions. Different debates – about the Nazi past and national identity in particular – truly came to shape parts of German political culture. While they arguably rendered Germany a more liberal country in the long run, the details were not always pretty: many of these debates created clearly separated 'intellectual camps', fostered a climate of mutual suspicion and personal recriminations, and often enough centred on false normative or practical choices.

None of this can easily be said about the German debates on European integration. The main reason is that most politicians and intellectuals have long been favourably disposed towards the idea of European unity – to the extent that Euroscepticism as a principled suspicion of integration (and as a set of nationalist feelings) remains almost a political taboo. If anything, Germany has sometimes witnessed what Ralf Dahrendorf (2004: 195) once called Euro-fundamentalism (*Europa-Fundamentalismus*), where further European integration is presented as an unquestioned, or even unquestionable, good. Perhaps only Italy among the larger states (another de facto semi-sovereign polity until the early 1990s) is comparable in having such a broad intellectual consensus on European integration.

At the same time, I would argue, the relatively un-polemical nature of German debates on Europe – in comparison both with other German debates and with debates in France and Britain – have also led to a rather sophisticated level of discussion, both in terms of how the EU is described and in terms of what is politically prescribed. One reason is simply that, given the large political consensus, debates about the basics of European integration have, so to speak, 'migrated' into legal discourse (which has drawbacks, of course, but also almost by itself ensures that these debates – unlike polemical debates elsewhere – have at least some connection with what the EU actually is as a legal entity, in contrast to imaginary Brussels superstates).[1] To be sure, German ideals of European unification have often been projections of the country's own supposedly post-national trajectory after 1945: this is especially true of conceptions of constitutional patriotism and a welfare state at the European level. But there is nothing wrong per se with drawing lessons from one's national history for Europe, as long as it is done in a suitably modest and transparent way. Hence the emphasis in this essay will not be on trying to 'unmask' just how German some of the main arguments in the debates really are; or how intellectuals might be pursuing their very particular agendas 'in Europe's name'. Rather, the question is whether some of the conceptual languages shared by different factions (or sometimes, everyone) in the German Europe debates might be more of a help or a hindrance to comprehending the nature of the EU as a polity, and to what extent they might usefully go beyond some of the categories and

---

[1] Thanks to Christoph Möllers on this point.

positions outlined in the introduction to this volume. I will also ask whether the normative and practical prescriptions formulated in these languages can ultimately transcend a German environment and meaningfully spill over into other contexts (or even that ever elusive thing: a genuinely pan-European intellectual debate).

Statist legacies

Germany emerged late as a nation-state, compared to France, Britain, or Spain – and even then it actually called itself a *Reich*. Ideals of continental (as opposed to colonial) empire – often based on the memory of the glory days of the Holy Roman Empire – loomed large in the political imagination, even after German unification in 1871 (not least because so many German-speakers appeared to have been left outside the state).[2] In fact, Bismarck's Reich strangely oscillated between a self-conception as nation-state and empire; arguably one of the ways its leaders sought to achieve a proper national identity was to pursue policies often associated with imperialism (this happened primarily within the state, as opposed to traditional colonialism). The theorists of the Third Reich would eventually draw on this legacy; and arguably the Nazis themselves attempted to create a European (and eventually global) empire in the form of a nation-state.[3] In short, Germany's identity as either state or empire has remained uncertain for a very long time – in fact right up to 1990. 'Europe' has thus also played an ambiguous role in the political imagination – especially as potentially always a necessary part of a German empire or, after the German division, as an indispensable element for overcoming Germany's deeply problematic statehood.

After 1945, as a semi-sovereign polity, West Germany had an eminent interest in constructing a united Europe: it could hope to gain some measure of moral rehabilitation and practically try to enlarge its room for manoeuvre by advancing its interests 'in Europe's name' (Garton Ash 1993). West German intellectuals also explicitly propounded ideals of a European federation as a response to the Second World War and the atrocities of Nazism. For instance, the founders of the *Gruppe 47*, the most influential grouping of politically engaged writers in the first two decades after 1945, very much subscribed to the federalist idealism which had emerged from the various European Resistance movements. National traditions had been thoroughly put in question by Nazism, to the extent that many intellectuals on the left actually equated National Socialism, nationalism, and nation-statehood. Thus transcending the nation-state became a prime moral imperative. It was largely forgotten that Hitler had also invoked an

---

[2] This aspect has been strongly brought out in Winkler 2007.
[3] This observation was given its most coherent form by Alexandre Kojève in his 1945 'Outline of a Doctrine of French Policy' (Kojève 2004).

emphatic, normatively loaded notion of 'Europe' (in contrast to Bolshevism and 'Americanism') in order to justify his empire-building.[4]

As is well known, most of the conceptions of European unity that had emerged during the war were already defeated by the end of the 1940s (Niess 2001). Subsequently, left-wing intellectuals concentrated their energies on criticizing what they perceived as the 'restoration' of the German state (even if in a divided form) as well as deeply compromised political and intellectual traditions. They were not hostile to European integration as it actually unfolded in the 1950s (though some saw the Common Market as the exact opposite of the democratic socialist Europe they had hoped for) – but they also did not perceive it as a real counterweight to what they felt was going morally and politically wrong in the Federal Republic. Often European unity was criticized as a specifically Christian Democratic project and hence included in the charge of a post-war conservative 'restoration' which had crushed progressive aspirations.

Literary intellectuals and philosophers were not the only ones to debate and contest the meaning of the post-war political constellation. In Germany public jurists (*Staatsrechtslehrer*) have long played an important and prestigious role in proposing concepts for comprehending (and normatively justifying) essentially political arrangements. As individuals, a significant number of them have had ready access to high-quality newspapers and magazines.[5] In a sense, they were the most likely group of intellectuals to argue about European integration in the 1950s and 1960s.

Yet by and large they did not. They were deeply split about the nature of semi-sovereign West German democracy itself, essentially dividing into a 'Schmitt school' – that is, followers of Carl Schmitt – and a 'Smend School': students of Rudolf Smend, who unlike Schmitt was still teaching after 1945. The basic line of separation ran between an ideal of a unitary state with a unified, hierarchical administration, on the one hand, and, on the other, the vision of 'social integration' through a mutual penetration of state and society, and a daily effort by all citizens to make constitutional democracy a lived reality – similar to Renan's famous idea of a *plébiscite de tous les jours* (Günther 2004; Müller 2003, part II). Schmitt's followers were highly sceptical vis-à-vis the newly established Constitutional Court (to which none of them would be elected until the early 1980s); they insisted on formalism and textualism, as opposed to the Court's 'approach of "balancing values"'; and they often effectively deployed the language of democracy to contest its legitimacy. They also diagnosed

---

[4] See Mazower 2008. In 1945 Hitler was still to claim: 'I am the last chance for Europe.'

[5] To give just one example: the *Frankfurter Allgemeine Zeitung* has a special page on 'Staat und Recht', where both journalists and public law professors write – often in a professorial manner that would be unimaginable in other countries' broadsheets.

a general weakening, or even death of the state – properly understood – as a result of ever more interest-group pluralism. In short, in their eyes, sovereign statehood was threatened more from the inside, from society, than by international or supranational law from the outside.

Yet the very deep disagreements about statehood and democracy which characterized the conflicts between members of the Schmitt and Smend schools did not really translate into a major split about the nature and meaning of European integration. Rather, public jurists were relatively open to the possibility of transferring elements of democracy and constitutionalism to a supranational level and to a European *Rechtsgemeinschaft* in particular. The leading interpreter of European integration was undoubtedly Hans Peter Ipsen, who coined the concept of *Zweckverband funktionaler Integration* (purposive association of functional integration – no more elegant translation seems available or possible) to describe European integration (see in particular Ipsen 1972 and 1973). The term suggested a thoroughly technocratic understanding of the process: European nation-states had come together to create public authorities for highly specific economic and technological purposes which could be accomplished more efficiently at the supranational level.[6] Most public jurists – including those of the Schmitt school – agreed with this characterization and had no normative problem with the phenomenon as such – except Schmitt himself, who wrote in 1978 that 'whoever immerses himself in the more than thousand pages of the standard work of H. P. Ipsen ... will be overcome by deep sadness. The global political forces and powers, which are struggling for world unity, are stronger than a European interest in the political unification of Europe' (Schmitt 2005 [1978]: 932).

Still, while what appeared to be a kind of technocratic consensus seemed to reign at least until the 1980s, one should not underestimate the lasting legacy of a number of axioms and conceptual commitments which had characterized *Staatsrechtslehre* since the late nineteenth century – what Christoph Möllers (2008: 16) has called the 'deep grammar' of the discipline. These surfaced in the debates on West German statehood in the 1950s, but, arguably, they were also to structure some of the debates about European integration in the 1990s and in the early twenty-first century. I shall briefly outline these, before moving on to an analysis of contemporary debates.

First, much of German political thought has long been characterized by the central place it holds for an emphatic, normatively heavily loaded concept of the *state* (Hennis 1959; Möllers 2000). This concept was essentially imprinted with an image of the nineteenth-century monarchical executive as the essence

---

[6] Ipsen had been active as a commissioner in occupied Belgium during the Nazi era; there is still considerable controversy to what extent some of his later thoughts continued parts of his legal thinking from the 1930s and 1940s. See Joerges 2003.

of statehood (Möllers 2008: 16).[7] Often a strict dividing line was drawn between state and society, with the state as an institution pursuing the general interest being located above and beyond society. In the nineteenth century parliament was viewed as an agent of society, representing the particular interests of individual citizens and of groups vis-à-vis the state – understood, again, as essentially a monarchical executive. In many cases – though not always – the conceptual state–society division thus had deep anti-democratic implications (Schönberger 1997).

A second long-lasting conceptual legacy was the opposition of *Staatenbund* (a federation of states) and *Bundesstaat* (a federal state) – which originated with the founding of the Second Reich (Möllers 2008: 19).[8] Many conceptual innovations (such as *Staatenverbund*) have been designed to overcome this dichotomy – and yet it has haunted German legal and political thought now for more than a century.

Finally, there is the conceptual division between state and constitution, and, more particularly, the recurrent argument that statehood is a precondition of constitutionalism of any sort (as well as democracy).[9] Related was the assumption that while statehood persists (in the form of a functioning administration), constitutions tend to come and go. The classical formulation of this thought was provided in 1924 by Otto Mayer, the founder of administrative law during the empire: *Verfassungsrecht vergeht, Verwaltungsrecht besteht* ('constitutional law fades, administrative law stays').[10] To be sure, legal languages that took constitutionalism – and not statehood – as their conceptual linchpin became more influential in the 1970s and 1980s (thus creating a clear conceptual opposition between *Staatsrechtslehre* and *Verfassungsrechtslehre*). There was also a sense, however, that debates in 'state theory' – long privileged in German political thought – were de facto being sidelined by the authoritative interpretations of the Basic Law which were emanating from Karlsruhe, the seat of the Constitutional Court, along with the Bundesbank the most respected institution of the old West Germany (Schlink 1989).[11]

---

[7] Broadly speaking, the multiplicity of meanings of the state in the German tradition is not least due to the influence of Jellinek's state theory, which sought to combine legal/normative and social/descriptive elements, and the fact that many state theorists precisely do not disentangle these elements. Beyond that, Germany's problematic statehood has led to an aspirational conception of the state as reflecting or creating 'unity' (*Einheit*) where none might have existed. See also Lepsius 2004.

[8] Also in this context, statehood and sovereignty were dissociated – so as to enable the states within the newly unified German empire to remain states, while Germany as a whole was supposed to be sovereign.

[9] For a classic formulation see Böckenförde 1999.

[10] Mayer claimed in the introduction to the third edition of his classic textbook that not much new material had to be included – this after a world war, the fall of the monarchy, a revolution, etc.

[11] Möllers has gone so far as to argue that constituent power (and 'constitutional populism'), which during Weimar had still been located with the president, actually migrated to the Constitutional Court in the Federal Republic: see Möllers 2007.

Still, the monumental handbook of German *Staatsrecht*, which began to be published in the mid-1980s and whose register (and tenth volume) was completed in 2000, appeared as a clear sign that statist thinkers were not going down without a fight. The eve of the Constitutional Court's Maastricht decision thus saw a kind of stalemate between what one might call the statist and constitutionalist schools of thought (which, at this point, could no longer really be identified as following in the respective traditions of Schmitt and Smend).

Maastricht and after: Contours of a debate

There are two long-term trends in contemporary German intellectual life which arguably began with unification and which have at least indirectly touched on European integration.[12] First, the left had long rejected not just nationalism, but even a German nation-state as such as inherently dangerous for its neighbours and the world at large. Günter Grass famously opposed German unification in 1990 with precisely this argument, warning of a 'monster' that might be created by bringing West and East Germany together. For similar reasons the left had long been favourably disposed to European integration – even if this position remained, for the most part, theoretically very underdeveloped and often had little to do with the actually existing European Community (and other actually existing European countries, for that matter).

These deep-seated fears of Germany – and the moral–political imperative of self-containment which followed from them – slowly disappeared during the 1990s.[13] When a Red-Green government came to power in 1998, Chancellor Gerhard Schröder could afford to take a much more assertive stance vis-à-vis Brussels – without worrying that this would exact large political costs among pacifists and anti-nationalists (groups whose numbers dwindled further with the interventions in Kosovo and Afghanistan and who today are for the most part integrated into the *Linkspartei*).

At the other end of the political spectrum, a newly assertive right – who in fact called themselves the 'New Right' – briefly flourished in the mid-1990s. Its intellectual protagonists called for a 'more self-confident nation', willing to question old ties to Western Europe (and the West more broadly) and prepared

---

[12] Another aspect which is worth mentioning but which I cannot elaborate here is the relative retreat of writers from debates about Europe. The post-Maastricht debates have been dominated by philosophers, historians, and public jurists (who arguably oscillate between roles as experts and intellectuals). Very crudely put: the absence of major writers like Grass and Martin Walser from the debates on Europe has something to do with the fact that they simply do not have the same moral (and emotional) dimension as the debates on national identity in the wake of Nazism.

[13] Instead there emerged a consensus that constitutional patriotism and cultural particularity could coexist in what Ralf Dahrendorf called a 'heterogeneous nation-state': see Dahrendorf 1994.

to pursue its national interest much more vigorously. This movement faded almost as quickly as it had arisen, not least because its members seemed unable actually to formulate 'national interests' – and the means of pursuing them – that were significantly different from what was happening in the waning years of Helmut Kohl's Chancellorship anyway.

Thus simultaneously a strong current of anti-nationalism was coming to an end and a new form of assertive nationalism had been successfully resisted by most intellectuals at the time when Maastricht and the subsequent European Treaties were negotiated. At the same time, a less idealist view of Europe – one also less informed by memories of war and atrocity – was gaining ground, culminating in Schröder's more assertive stance described above (see also Lübbe 1994). When in 2000 the influential literature professor Karl Heinz Bohrer – one of contemporary Germany's most brilliant thinkers and an acerbic critic of the *bien-pensant* left – attacked left-liberal German politicians' enthusiasm for a post-national Europe as rooted in an attempt to escape a nation-state which no longer had an idea of itself, he seemed already to be tilting at windmills.[14] The flight forward from a non-existent national identity into 'Europe' might still have been the fancy of some disintegrating intellectual milieux; but it was hardly government policy.

This is not the place to review the well-known arguments of the German Constitutional Court's Maastricht decision in any great detail (see Alter 2003: 104–8 on the decision). Its chief architect, Paul Kirchhof (who also coined the term *Staatenverbund* which the Court used to describe the EU), brought in some of the main statist assumptions long prevalent in German legal thought: that only statehood 'guarantees' democracy, human rights, and constitutionalism; that only states enable people to appreciate freedom, develop a sense of law and justice, etc.; that states and nations are indissolubly linked; and that statehood can only ever be imagined and function as the recognition of 'pre-political' givens such as a common language, the family, etc.[15] Paradoxically, the Court also saw itself as the main defender of democracy, despite the fact that its own position and the extraordinary importance of constitutional review in the German context were at least somewhat problematic from the point of view of democratic theory. And in fact, the strong defence of a substantial notion of democracy by Karlsruhe seemed to have some echoes of the stance Schmittians had taken in the name of democracy *against* the Court in the 1950s and 1960s.

[14] Bohrer 2000 also charged that Germans' enthusiasm for Europe was rooted in a preference for organicist *Ganzheitsdenken* (thinking in wholes).

[15] Just to be sure that I am not caricaturing: see for instance Kirchhof 1993: 63, which begins with the resounding statement: 'The legal strength of Europe lies in its states.' My point is not that all these ideas are completely wrong or normatively dubious – statism means that there are numerous un-argued (and empirically un-verified) assumptions about *the* state (and not its particular functions or agencies) as cause, explanatory category, or moral agent.

Opinion on the decision was split among intellectuals and public jurists.[16] The judges' criticism of the European Court of Justice, the red lines drawn to prevent *ausbrechendes Recht* (essentially: *ultra vires*), and the self-positioning of the Court as the real guardian over the country's remaining sovereignty and Germans' basic rights: all these were seen by critics as a highly defensive reaction to European integration and as a reaffirmation of the statist strands of German legal and political thought. In their eyes, an ideal of *Staatlichkeit*, or statehood, which had to be defended against the Union, appeared to be largely an invention of the judges – unlike basic rights and democracy it finds no substantive mention in Basic Law, and neither does sovereignty (Möllers 2008: 73).[17] Particular scorn was also heaped on the notion that further transfers of sovereignty were inadmissible as long as there existed no democratic structures at the European level – which in turn depended on a homogeneous European people. Especially the term 'homogeneity' – apparently taken straight from Carl Schmitt's writings on democracy – raised red flags on the left-liberal side of the political spectrum.[18] These highly controversial claims about democracy, however, could in principle be separated from the Court assuming the role as gatekeeper vis-à-vis European law.

At least two options seemed now available for opponents of the Court's ruling on Maastricht: think through what it would actually take to establish democracy on the European level – and, at least to some extent, accept the Court's claims that democracy required the possibilities of forming a supranational public opinion; or secondly, as much as possible to try to separate the concepts that the Court had firmly linked: democracy, constitutionalism, state, and 'homogeneous people'. In other words, they could attempt to disaggregate traditional understandings of constitutionalism and democracy and see whether the European Union – as apparently a new kind of polity – might not generate functional equivalents of democracy and constitutionalism as traditionally understood and thereby alleviate the anxiety that European integration would create ever more supranational normative powers without proper accountability.[19] These basic challenges remained the same with the Amsterdam and Nice Treaties, which, however, never generated the same level of controversy as Maastricht (and which were never connected by statists to emphatic notions of sovereignty and peoplehood in the way that it had happened with the Maastricht decision).

---

[16] I am not discussing here popular opposition to the Maastricht Treaty itself, which was of course centred on the currency union and the loss of the Deutschmark.

[17] Unless one reads the essence of article 20, paragraph 1 to be: 'The Federal Republic of Germany is a state', as was done by Paul Kirchhof (when the actual wording happens to be: 'The Federal Republic of Germany is a democratic and social federal state').

[18] To be fair, the Court actually cited Schmitt's Social Democratic opponent Hermann Heller – who had also used the term 'homogeneity'. There was some speculation as to whether the Court had consciously tried to evoke an authority of the Weimar era who had been theoretically opposed to Schmitt in order to pre-empt criticism. See for instance Ipsen 1994: 17.

[19] On this challenge in general see the exceptionally rich article of Walker 2008.

Joschka Fischer's famous Humboldt Speech in 2000 – when the then German foreign minister called for a debate about the EU's *finalité* and possibly the further constitutionalization and democratization of the Union – gave a spur to proponents of both visions. But it also intensified the resistance of those speaking the traditional languages of German state theory.

In the following I will outline the main fault lines and intellectual cleavages that have emerged after Maastricht and which to some degree have been reinforced by the 2009 Lisbon decision. While not in any way a representative of debates in the German world of legal philosophy and EU law, pride of place nevertheless belongs to Jürgen Habermas, consistently the most outspoken German intellectual on the EU.

Habermas: A state of nation-states, resisting neoliberalism

The first of the two paths outlined above was essentially taken by Jürgen Habermas, whose position has undoubtedly been the most important reference point in the German debates on the European Union. Habermas, very much building on his philosophical work on democracy and the public sphere, argued for the creation of a European space of public opinion-formation as one of the crucial elements for a proper European democracy – and a proper feeling of European political solidarity. The latter mattered, because the EU also afforded a unique opportunity to salvage the achievements of the European national welfare states from a 'neoliberal' onslaught, which might result in post-egalitarian 'market societies'. In other words, for Habermas the European project had a significant defensive or protective purpose. He sometimes went so far as to claim that a European *Gemeinschaft* served primarily to save a European culture and *Lebensform* (way of life): see for instance Habermas 2001a, 2001b.

To be sure, there were other arguments for European integration, too: the creation of an independent military capacity as a way of implementing an understanding of humanitarian interventions as foreshadowing a future cosmopolitan law (*Weltbürgerrecht*) which Habermas advocated – rather than justifying such missions on the basis of the enlarged national interests of liberal states such as the United States and Britain. And, furthermore, there was still the concern to contain a newly unified Germany within larger European structures – a worry that has however somewhat faded in Habermas' recent political interventions on Europe.

Still, the socio-economic and, broadly speaking, cultural reasons were decisive: Europeans, based on their non-neoliberal 'normative self-understanding', should use the Union to make their influence among the 'global players' felt and work towards a re-regulation of the world economy. Habermas stressed that Europeans were not called upon to invent something radically new; rather, they were to create a new entity mainly to serve the conservation of their previous achievements. At the same time, Habermas recognized that a Europe based on intergovernmental negotiations was incapable of generating any form of emotional support and loyalty for Europe as a 'state of nation-states' – while a symbolic act of founding a new political form might well do so.[20]

Habermas rejected the no-demos thesis of the German judges and claimed that a 'people' should not be understood as a pre-political community of fate (*Schicksalsgemeinschaft*) characterized by a common history and language. Rather, historically, nation and republic had mutually strengthened each other in a 'circular process', with the end result of a civic sense of solidarity which no longer depended on pre-political factors such as language and ethnic ties. This – Habermas admitted – 'painful process of abstraction' might in some manner be repeated at the European level: it would take the creation of a European civil society, a European public opinion, and a shared European political culture.

The question was then, of course, how these three 'functional requirements' might be met. Habermas was cautiously optimistic that a constitution – or, more precisely, discourses about a constitution – could serve as a kind of 'catalyst'. This was especially the case if Europeans could vote on a constitution in a continent-wide referendum; such a momentous popular decision was bound to be preceded by cross-border communications about the political future of the Union. But he also offered more mundane suggestions: the EU should be able to raise its own taxes; and as the shift of power to Brussels became more visible, interest groups of all kinds might cooperate more closely across borders and develop a distinctly European character. Not least, the existing national public spheres might be transformed: not in the sense of fusing to create one supranational public sphere, but in the sense of a 'mutual opening' for each other's debates. Ideally, national media should start commenting on other countries' controversies, thereby enlarging the sensitivity for the main cleavages of public opinion elsewhere.

Habermas' calls for such a united Europe in many ways culminated in the appeal he penned in May 2003 (co-signed by Jacques Derrida) on the occasion of the second Iraq War and the large anti-war demonstrations in many European cities.[21] According to Habermas, a 'rebirth of Europe' had

---

[20] Witness his saying: 'For that one needs common value orientations. No doubt the legitimacy of a regime also depends on its efficiency. But political innovations such as the creation of a state of nation-states require the political mobilization for aims which appeal not just to interests but also to people's feelings.'

[21] Derrida and Habermas 2003. The manifesto was published simultaneously in France's *Libération*. Umberto Eco and Gianni Vattimo joined the initiative by writing in Italian newspapers, while Adolf Muschg and Fernando Savater debated 'European Identity' in Switzerland and Spain respectively. Apparently, not a single intellectual ready to defend Europe could be found in Britain. But there was at least an honorary European among the Anglo-Saxons: Richard Rorty, who called on the more 'civilized' Europeans to play the role of world policeman in a piece in *Süddeutsche Zeitung*. Translations of the piece itself and of the debate it sparked can be found in Lévy, Pensky, and Torpey 2005.

occurred on 15 February 2003. On that particular day, millions had marched on the streets in Rome, Madrid, Paris, Berlin, and London against the impending war. This, according to Habermas, had been the moment when a common European consciousness came into focus. This consciousness was supposedly based on shared, and for the most part painful, historical memories of violence and atrocity sparked by national rivalries. Precisely the history of intra-European conflicts (and their eventual resolution) had given Europeans a peculiar capacity for recognizing – and accepting – differences and living with permanent conflicts in the present, as well as a thoroughly reflexive and self-critical attitude towards their own traditions. Finally, according to Habermas, Europeans had become much more sensitive to violence: against the background of the experience of totalitarianism and the Holocaust, they were said to have developed a stronger sense of threats to personal and bodily integrity (and, as a consequence, oppose the death penalty and work for its abolition elsewhere in the world).

Habermas has defended this vision of a strong Europe struggling to save a particular way of life very consistently. Every apparent setback – the French and Dutch referenda in 2005, the Irish referendum in 2008 – has made him appeal all the more urgently for bolder measures to provoke cross-border European debates and enable the formation of a genuinely European political will (Habermas 2008). He has also tried to intervene practically in other countries' debate in a way that is clearly to exemplify the kind of cross-border engagement for which he has been calling time and again – an example being the appeal to French voters published in *Le Monde* before the referendum on the Constitutional Treaty in May 2005.

What is one to make of this position, against both the background of Habermas' own work and the context of German debates on Europe? Very much in line with some of his larger theories of modernity, Habermas has recast the European experience as a 'learning process' – a notion not without overtones of traditional conceptions of progress. While modernity itself is always ambivalent – it has a Janus-face, to allude to one of Habermas' favourite metaphors – Europeans have come to accept this ambivalence and remain sensitive to modernity's dark side as well as its inner tensions. Contrary to caricatures of Habermas as a naïve philosopher of consensus, he has praised the particular European capacity for institutionalizing and living with conflict, as well as generating an always fragile 'solidarity with strangers'.

One can debate whether this is an accurate picture of various European mentalities – but one can hardly reject this story simply because it is *also* a story of progress and 'achievement'. Rather, the moral danger appears to be that 'European identity' becomes a reified and highly restrictive notion, while politically it is far from clear that any 'core Europe' would actually function (or, if it functions, not lead to a quasi-nationalist Euro-Gaullism, as Ralf

Dahrendorf and Timothy Garton Ash charged in an attack on Habermas' and Derrida's appeal).[22]

While the post-war West German experience has profoundly influenced Habermas' view of Europe, it would be wrong to reduce his vision to a mere projection of West Germany's supposed post-national trajectory. To be sure, Habermas has been highly suspicious of nationalism, the nation-state, and any normative justifications of the principle of national self-determination. But contrary to a view of Habermas as intent on cleansing all national cultures of their particularity – effectively eradicating them – Habermas has precisely always insisted on the need to defend the integrity of cultures and 'lifeworlds', while combating the aggressive political tendencies that can be generated with national passions. His appeal has not been for a European superstate, but for an entity that ultimately respects and preserves difference. In that sense, his position might better be described as post-national*ist* rather than as post-national (see also Cronin 2003).

The truly problematic aspect of Habermas' position – one rarely debated in the German context – is the assumption that, for all its diversity and difference, there really exists in Europe a clearly discernible social democratic consensus whose salvation would justify the creation of a 'state of nation-states'. It is arguably here that the de facto social democratic consensus from which Germany has not deviated even under right-wing governments is made into a pan-European story – when the actually existing Europe admits of much more institutional and normative variation – not least after 2004. Obviously, this is not a sufficient argument to discredit Habermas' call for the EU as an instrument to combat neoliberalism – but it calls for a clearer normative and practical, as opposed to historical, defence of the supposed common European *Lebensform*, especially if the latter is not actually in the end just another word for *Schicksalsgemeinschaft*.

Somewhat sceptical (not Eurosceptical) responses: Moderate statism and the search for a coherent anti-statism

Habermas' position has been consistently attacked from two diametrically opposed perspectives: on the one hand, critics have reaffirmed the point that the preconditions for democracy at the European level do not exist

---

[22] Dahrendorf and Garton Ash 2003. Many philosophers and historians have criticized Habermas for now proposing a substantive European identity, instead of the fluid, reflexive processes of identity formation that he used to advocate in his writings on Germany and in his social theory more broadly. I am sympathetic to some of these criticisms, although Habermas' conception of 'European identity' still contains a heavy emphasis on learning processes – the fact that some of the outcomes of these processes might also instil pride is not enough to discredit Habermas' position as somehow having turned communitarian or Euro-nationalist.

(conceptually and/or empirically). On the other hand, he has been charged with still being too statist, for failing to recognize sufficiently that the EU – as a political entity *sui generis* – should not be made to conform to any pre-existing models, including that of a 'state of nation-states' (a criticism which it seems Habermas eventually accepted: he came explicitly to argue that national federations could not serve as models for the EU).[23]

The most distinguished critic along the former lines has undoubtedly been Dieter Grimm, a former judge on the Constitutional Court (see Grimm 1995, 2005a, 2005b). Grimm shares Habermas' belief in broadly speaking social democratic values – and he even shares many of Habermas' assumptions about the nature of democracy and its dependence on the public sphere. He has contended, however, that the empirical conditions in the EU are simply not there to enable the formation of a European public sphere. And he disagrees that the project of constitution-making could serve as a catalyst for creating a genuinely European public discourse. In fact, Grimm – sharing some of the traditional assumptions of *Staatsrechtslehre* – suspects that 'non-state constitutionalism' could simply be an oxymoron. The inflationary use of the language of constitutionalism might be a sure sign of the success of de facto constitutionalism in the post-war world – but it essentially loses its meaning without a proper object, which still happens to be in the first place a state.

However, as far as the connection between constitution and state is concerned, Habermas and Grimm did not necessarily disagree. Habermas did not shy away from using the s-word when portraying his ideal of the EU as a force among the 'global players' – although in recent writings he has moved closer to a form of non-state or post-state constitutionalism, especially in his calls for a constitutionalization of international law.

Grimm, however, did explicitly disagree with the many public jurists who argued – not just in Germany – that the EU was developing a new form of constitutionalism and that, in principle, traditional understandings of statehood and constitutionalism could be disentangled. If the latter is correct, other kinds of public authority, and even institutions not seen as political at all, could potentially be constitutionalized. Accordingly, advocates of 'multilevel constitutionalism', basing their thought very much on the experience of the EU, have recently been extending their models to the global scale (in the process also trying to overcome the dichotomy of *Bundesstaat* and *Staatenbund*). Public jurists like Ingolf Pernice see their conception of the EU as a form of pluralism, denying that the legal architecture of the Union ultimately needs a kind of

---

[23] Prominent in this regard has been the work of Ulrich Beck, who uses the term 'cosmopolitan' to denote his theory of the EU as a means of preserving and fostering diversity and difference – even if 'multicultural' might actually be more appropriate. Some of Beck's ideas clearly resonate with Marcel Gauchet's vision of Europe, even if Gauchet is much more critical of Europe's 'silent cosmopolitan revolution' and has significantly more statist inclinations. See Beck and Grande 2004.

Kelsenian *Grundnorm* (basic norm) and that only legal monism can provide a secure and coherent foundation for constitutions coexisting at different levels. Other proponents of *Verfassungsrechtslehre* have shied away from this kind of pluralism; some have tried to capture the ultimate unity of the political and legal experience of Europe in increasingly complex compound concepts such as *Verfassungsverbund* (constitutional association) and *Verfassungskonglomerat* (constitutional conglomerate). Few – in fact none – of these have caught on in more general discussions of Europe, however.

Other theorists have pushed even further in trying to dissociate state and constitutionalism completely and to formulate a much more radical vision of legal and regulatory pluralism. Very much working in the tradition of Niklas Luhmann's systems theory, they have argued that the decisive issue has long ceased to be how to tame and constrain absolutist state power, and, by implication, that concerns about the constitutionalization of partial extensions of the modern administrative state into the supranational realm are far less important than even the discussion around the EU would suggest. Rather, the challenge now is to develop a 'societal constitutionalism' which effectively constrains the exercise of power by non-state actors. Put differently: the hope is not for the emergence of a European or even global constitutionalism that limits the power of states – a vision that according to defenders of 'societal constitutionalism' (such as Gunther Teubner, drawing on David Sciulli's work) remains caught in a state-centric logic; rather, advocates of such constitutionalism already observe the formation of 'civil constitutions' negotiated by private or semi-public actors – corporations, associations, unions, NGOs, etc. These 'constitutions' will not necessarily cohere or ever establish a global hierarchy of norms; in fact, a unified global law – and thus a global constitutionalism, let alone a global state – will not materialize. Instead, global law is inevitably diffuse and fragmented, in fact sometimes so blatantly contradictory that collisions between different legal regimes constantly have to be negotiated in a pragmatic fashion (see Fischer-Lescano and Teubner 2006; Teubner 2007). The global village (and not just the European village) turns out to be, as Gunther Teubner has put it, 'global Bukowina'.

To be sure, the proponents of multilevel and societal constitutionalism only occasionally reach a wider audience – hardly any of them are public intellectuals in the way that Habermas is: they do not really touch on the moral self-understanding of the polity. But an account of the major intellectual 'cleavages', as far as European integration is concerned, would be incomplete without them.

The overall picture, then, looks something like this: a linchpin of public debate has been Habermas' position – even if within academia his advocacy of a European 'state of nation-states' in the name of a European way of life has had relatively few followers. Within academia (and sometimes spilling over into the high-quality press, radio, and, less so, television), there has been increasing polarization. On the one side, one finds statists, who have regarded the EU and the ECJ in particular with increasing suspicion; on the other side, there are what one might call post-state constitutionalists, who are in principle willing to detach the notions of statehood, constitutionalism, and democracy, and who take a favourable, sometimes outright enthusiastic view of the EU as a political, legal, and administrative laboratory.

It is very schematic, but perhaps not unduly reductionist, to argue that at least some of the statists are really nationalists who employ the language of democracy and sovereignty to protect the cultural integrity of Germany; while some of the constitutionalists are not just post-national*ist*, but seek to be entirely post-national in according nationality no ethical significance whatsoever.

Having said this, I must emphasize one absence: it is striking that the lines in public debate are rarely drawn with reference to ideas of the nation or even to particular German historical experiences. Put succinctly: European integration is regarded with suspicion in the name of statehood and promoted in the name of the welfare state. For neither side, it seems, does democracy play a major role. For the advocates of multilevel constitutionalism, democracy is a topic – but the democratic deficit either disappears or is seen with a great deal of equanimity once the particular and novel nature of the EU is properly understood.

This might somewhat change in the aftermath of the Court's decision on the Lisbon Treaty in June 2009. The Court asked the German parliament to rework the law accompanying the incorporation of the Lisbon Treaty (*Zustimmungsgesetz*), mainly in order to strengthen the role of the Bundestag – specifically mandating that the Bundestag had to consent effectively to abandon the German veto in Council of Ministers decisions. While it is too early to tell what the long-term effect of the decision on German debates might be, it seems clear already that unlike the Maastricht decision, the ruling was seen less as an expression of traditional German statism and more as informed by legitimate concerns about democracy and national parliamentarism in particular. To be sure, some critics of the decision saw a clear continuity with Maastricht: the Court essentially reaffirmed its role as ultimate guardian of the German constitution in the process of European integration; more subtly, it continued the trend to reconstruct and defend sovereignty and statehood in the name of democracy. In their eyes, it also radically devalued the contribution of the European Parliament to democratic accountability, essentially arguing that only an increased role of the German parliament in intergovernmental negotiations could alleviate anxieties about the fate of democracy in the process of integration (Halberstam and Möllers 2009; Möllers 2009). In that sense, the decision could also be read as a repudiation of any attempt to find pluralist and transnationalist alternatives between supranationalism and nationalism.

Some conclusions, some comparisons

The German debates on Europe have deployed inherited vocabularies of political and especially legal thought – how could it be otherwise? Thus the peculiarities of the German view of the state survive to some extent to this day in the controversies surrounding the Union and, in particular, the supposed threats to *Staatlichkeit* which it poses. Yet, inherited languages have not just been an obstacle to comprehending the potentially novel institutional features of European integration. The exceptionally rich past debates on empire and nation-state, federalism and international law, have also served as a resource for creatively rethinking and potentially transcending state-centric perspectives.[24]

The German debates have also – sometimes explicitly, sometimes implicitly – drawn on the apparent 'success story' of post-war West Germany, in which constitutionalism is supposed to have played a significant role. In particular, the increasing legitimacy of the German Basic Law – despite the absence of a popular founding moment as well as any discernible constituent subject over time – has often informed a relatively relaxed view of the potential democratic shortcomings of supranational constitutionalism.[25] Just as the German constitution became legitimate through a *plébiscite de tous les jours* – rather than a foundational *plébiscite d'un jour* – a European constitution, or so it has been argued, might gain legitimacy over time.

At the same time, the constitutionalization of European and international law has been presented as a highly desirable *normative* project – prompting a critic to charge that international law finally appeared to find its home 'in a (Germanic) language of universal reason' (Koskenniemi 2007: 3). Arguably, this heavy normative weight placed on constitutionalism – and even just the languages of constitutionalism with all its conceptual innovations – is a direct legacy of the constitutionalist success story of West Germany.

In general, ideals of democracy and parliamentary sovereignty have not haunted the German debates as they have in France and Britain: no deep opposition is perceived between individual rights and democracy as a collective project (even if historically the distinction between liberalism and democracy played a large role in German anti-liberal thought); and while sovereignty is

---

[24] Two recent examples: the idea of *Verfassungsvertrag* and the concept of *Indigenat*, proposed (or recovered) by Günter Frankenberg and Christoph Schönberger respectively. Or witness even Habermas saying very broadly in his reply to Dieter Grimm that 'European identity can . . . mean nothing other than unity in national diversity; and perhaps German federalism, as it developed after Prussia was shattered and the confessional division overcome, might not be the worst model'. As said above, Habermas eventually retreated from advocating models drawn from the experience of nation-states.

[25] Historical misinterpretations have also played some role – for instance the idea that the Federal Republic was founded by the *Länder*, when in fact it was the political parties in the *Parlamentarische Rat* that brought the Federal Republic into being.

strongly defended by statists, it is not identified exclusively with the Bundestag. Also, religion and 'civilizational identity' have been largely absent from debates on Europe's borders. It is true that recently a number of social democratic historians have spoken out against admission of Turkey to the EU – mostly, one suspects, because an ever larger Union would destroy the very possibility of a core Europe resisting neoliberalism and preserving the supposed social democratic consensus that is Europe's particular achievement.[26] In any event, Christianity has *not* been a main argument in this context.

Instead of civilizational and cultural arguments, then, concerns about *Staatlichkeit* have loomed large – both among defenders of a highly normative conception of statehood and among those who arguably have gone to the other extreme of anti-statism (thereby remaining negatively fixated on their opponents). Obviously in countries with weak or no explicit state traditions (or in countries where ideals of *Rechtsstaatlichkeit* or the rule of law are more controversial and politicized, such as France) these debates can seem very particular, arcane, or outright meaningless (compare Dyson 1979).

Germany now has less 'Euro-fundamentalism', or what Karl Heinz Bohrer once called *Europaprovinzialismus* (Euro-provincialism), than it used to exhibit – that is, a starry-eyed, slightly too loud enthusiasm for a 'Europe' about whose particularities one does not necessarily know too much. More realistic and hard-nosed arguments justifying European integration have come to replace the evocation of ideals and memories which still dominated in the 1980s and 1990s. In general, this has made German debates more compatible with conversations and arguments elsewhere – especially, one would think, in Central and Eastern Europe, where the sensitivity to Germany pursuing its interests 'in Europe's name' is probably even higher than in the western part of the continent. What German thinkers have to offer now is a set of highly developed and subtle claims about the nature of the future of the EU, which, despite their inevitable particularity, might be better equipped to travel than arguments from, say, Britain or France. This is not to say that even with much increased travel they will ever converge on a common destination.

---

[26] In particular Hans Ulrich Wehler and Heinrich August Winkler. It is unclear in what sense a historian of the German Second Empire and the Weimar Republic respectively have any particular expertise on the borders of Europe. See Leggewie 2004.

5

'Borderline Europe'

French Visions of the European Union*

Justine Lacroix

The Community weakens the feeling that people may have of their own citizenship. Ordinary citizens are less and less sure of who makes decisions. They have no easy means to know if a specific decision was made in Brussels or in the capital of their country of origin. Even though the European Community tends to grant the same social and economic rights to all the citizens of the Member States, there is no such thing as a European citizen. There are only French, German or Italian citizens.

(Aron 1974: 638)

Introduction

Over the last three decades, French political doctrine has remained remarkably unchanged in its approach to the evolving European integration process. The institutional reforms undertaken since Raymond Aron wrote these lines have not in the least muted French critiques of the elitism of European construction, a 'Europe for the peoples, without the peoples' (Gauchet 2005a: 492). Aron had criticized the lack of parliamentary control over the European Community, given the purely advisory role of the Assembly in Strasbourg. While the European institutions may since then have acquired more formal legitimacy, not least with the Parliament's direct election since 1979, radical criticism of the European model has, if anything, been on the rise among contemporary French political thinkers. In many respects, their striking disillusionment with the EU

* For suggestions and comments on presentations of variants of this chapter, I am indebted to Kalypso Nicolaïdis, Jan-Werner Müller, Jan Zielonka, José Cao Rosas, Claudia Schrag, Agustin Menendez, and the seminar participants at the Centre for Political Ideologies, Oxford University, and at ARENA, Oslo University.

mirrors the progressive disenchantment of French public opinion with Europe. The proportion of Frenchmen who view Europe as 'a good thing' dropped by 17 per cent between 1991 and 2004. In spring 2004, one year before the failed referendum on the European Constitution, the EU evoked 'a positive image' for only 44 per cent (Cautrès 2005). Of course this does not necessarily imply outright opposition to the principle itself of integration between the nations of Europe. In its present form, however, the European Union is subject to severe and contradictory criticism, both among large segments of the French public and in the intellectual sphere.

A vast majority of those who have recently expressed an opinion on the European process are, or were, professors in political philosophy either in one of the Parisian universities, at *Sciences-Po* or in the *Ecole des Hautes Etudes en Sciences Sociales*. This confirms the conclusions drawn by Tony Judt in his study of French intellectuals between 1944 and 1956. At the end of *Past Imperfect*, Judt underlines that the decline of the great public intellectuals – whose renown and income largely derived from their journalistic and book-writing activities – coincides with the resurrection of the university professors. Whereas the former were free from any constraints whatsoever, the latter 'may publish and appear in a variety of media, but their credibility (and initial status) remain firmly grounded in an academic discipline, its rule and its material' (Judt 1992: 296). Consequently, 'these figures enter the intellectual arena as experts, even if they are then free to express an opinion on matters well beyond their professional range, most commonly in the pages of *Commentaire* or *Le Débat*' (Judt 1992: 296). This shift has in turn contributed to grounding French intellectual debates about Europe more firmly in the discipline of political theory.

An analysis of the various positions adopted on the European issue has the merit of qualifying some commonly held ideas about France's recent intellectual history. Most observers, particularly British and American scholars, agree on two specific features of the French intellectual scene, namely a return to 'liberalism' since the 1980s (Lilla 1994; Wolin 2004) and a rejection of revolutionary utopianism along with a decline of the figure of the *'intellectuel engagé'* (Drake 2002; Jennings 1993). The French theoretical debates on Europe reveal a more complex picture. In this chapter I show that the approach to political liberalism adopted by so-called 'liberal' French intellectuals is much more ambivalent than is commonly thought, and that the figure of the 'radical intellectual', inspired by the emancipatory ideal, is still present.

Since the hard-won ratification of the Treaty of Maastricht in 1992, the European issue has emerged as a bone of contention among French political thinkers. The French debate over the EU's democratic legitimacy has revolved around the connection between rights and boundaries, and around the appropriate locus of democracy. As for the meaning attached to 'rights' in democratic politics, Europe is conceived either as the symptom of 'a religion of law', which supposedly undermines democracy, or conversely blamed for its incapacity to effectively implement the human rights it endlessly claims to represent. To be sure, the different perceptions of Europe, seen either as an 'undefined' and 'open' space or an 'exclusive' entity centred on its own particularities, are in total contradiction. The title of this chapter, 'Borderline Europe',[1] refers to an object that lends itself to such starkly contrasting representations.

My main argument in this chapter is that the current French intellectual controversy over Europe is embedded in an even more salient debate on the very nature of democracy, and more specifically over the relationship between human rights and politics (Lacroix 2008). This controversy has spanned the last three decades. I proceed in three steps. First, after providing some basic historical context on the period before 1992, I analyse the debates that followed the 'turning point' of the Maastricht Treaty. In this first section I focus on representations of the relationship between human rights and politics. I then identify two main paradigms that structure current intellectual reflections on Europe: the 'neo-Tocquevillian' paradigm, discussed in the second section of this chapter, and the 'liberal-revolutionary' paradigm, discussed in the third section.

Europe, the nation, and the nature of democracy

Thinking about Europe is not everybody's favourite pastime (Díez Medrano 2003: 22). This also holds for contemporary intellectuals, and is especially true in France, where most authors turned their attention to this topic only recently (in particular after the referenda of 1992 and 2005). This is quite a paradox given that, as shown in the introduction to this volume, French thinkers significantly contributed in the past to reflection on European political identity. Between 1919 and 1939, two-thirds of the writings published on the unification of Europe were written in French (Chabot 2005). After the Second World War, a number of highly considered French intellectuals participated directly in the European construct, but they did so as French civil servants or as advisors to the European Communities' founding fathers. An example is the philosopher Alexandre Kojève, whose Hegel seminar of the 1930s had influenced Sartre, Aron, Bataille, and Lacan. In 1945 he joined the French Ministry of Economics, where he was involved in designing the ECSC and later the launch of GATT. Another French intellectual, François Duchêne, whose academic career developed in Britain, was Jean Monnet's advisor in the ECSC from 1952 to 1955, before chairing the Action Committee of the United States of Europe. Nevertheless, in the intellectual sphere in the narrow sense of the term, the great figures of French political thought hardly ever commented on

[1] A 'borderline' personality is characterized by changing moods. Psychoanalysts also use the term 'borderline states' to describe ambivalent identities and brutal shifts from love to hate.

European integration in the period between the Treaty of Rome in 1957 and the Treaty of Maastricht in 1992. Three explanations can be advanced for this indifference towards Europe among French intellectuals in the post-war period.

First, after the defeat in France in 1940, some of the former French 'Europe-ists' of the 1920/30s – such as Gaston Riou, Francis Delaisi, Georges Suarez, Drieu la Rochelle – had drifted into 'collaborationism', thinking that Hitler could achieve the unity of Europe (Frank 2002: 318). Consequently, many French intellectuals in the post-war period were suspicious of an idea of Europe that seemed contaminated by collaboration with the Nazis.

Second, at the time of the East–West conflict and of decolonization, many intellectuals of the left identified Europe with the scourge of colonial oppression, or considered it a simple vassal of American interests. Jean Paul Sartre's example is telling. In his 1961 preface to Frantz Fanon's *The Wretched of the Earth*, Sartre goes as far as to say of Europe that 'she's done for' (Sartre 1978: 8). Europe, to Sartre's mind, was 'at death's door' as she was facing the 'strip-tease' of her humanism, which had been nothing but an ideology of lies, 'a perfect justification for pillage' (Sartre 1978: 21). This is also the reason the sociologist Edgar Morin gives for having long been an 'anti-European'. To Morin, who had participated in the resistance as a communist, Europe in the wake of the war was 'a word that lied' (Morin 1987: 9). He perceived Europe as the home of imperialism and domination rather than democracy and liberty.

In addition to these explanations, which may also apply to other European countries, the indifference of French intellectuals towards European integration has to do with a more fundamental feature of the French political imaginary: the incapacity to accept that there might be politics beyond the nation-state. This 'mimetic obsession' (Nicolaïdis 2005: 502) boils down to the notion that politics could only happen at the European level if there were a European federal state. It is the origin of an almost systematic underestimation of the truly political importance of the European Community's economic and legal advances. In this regard, the example of Raymond Aron, and his well-known reservations about European integration, is revealing. According to Pierre Kende, Aron's sceptical position was probably only 'the expression of [his] disappointment, the consequence of [his] immense emotional investment' (Kende 2001). This interpretation is confirmed by Aron's profession of faith in a speech delivered to German students in 1952: 'the European Community cannot be a short-lived source of enthusiasm, it is the completion of a long process which gives meaning to life or sets an objective for a whole generation' (Aron, quoted in Kende 2001). Aron's initial affective commitment may explain why the history of European institutions, which during Aron's life took a mainly economic turn, could only lead to 'furthering his scepticism'. It eluded what he regarded as essential, i.e. the 'political and military dimension' (Kende 2001: 214).

More precisely, sociological considerations seem to account for Aron's sceptical stance on the European issue. As early as 1962, he wrote in *Peace and War* that the creation of a Common Market would not lead, either by juridical or historical necessity, to an authentic federation (see English translation, Aron 1966: 746). In his view, the idea that economic integration would give birth to a European federation 'by the tap of a magic wand' was based either on the assumption that economics controls and encompasses politics, or the assumption that the fall of tariff barriers would, in and of itself, cause the fall of political and military ones. For Aron, these 'two suppositions [were] false' (Aron 1966: 747). The hypothesis of a 'clandestine federalism' or a 'federalism without tears' disregarded something essential, namely 'the community power animated by a community of desire, the state and the nation, the human collectivity, conscious of its uniqueness and determined to assert it and to affirm it in face of other collectivities' (Aron 1966: 747). In other words, the 'system of obligations' established by European institutions was not sufficient to create, among the French, the Germans, and the Italians, a shared sense that they were 'autonomous as Europeans and no longer as members of historical nations' (Aron 1966: 748).

A few years later, Aron enriched his initial sociological analysis and adopted a normative perspective to address the necessary conditions for the emergence of multinational citizenship. In an article originally published in English (Aron 1974), Aron doubted the potential advent of a form of citizenship that would extend beyond the borders of the nation-state. In his view, the full exercise of citizenship implied the existence of an institution endowed with all the necessary means to assert its authority over all the actors concerned. As a result, he argued, the potential extension of such a political authority would only lead to a transfer, not a transformation, of citizenship. There were thus only two logical alternatives: the emergence of a new federal state in Europe or the persistence of some basic form of functional cooperation without any real political dimension. In many respects, this analytical dichotomy still prevails in France today, some thirty years later. Many French thinkers still struggle to wrap their mind around what Olivier Beaud calls the 'dualism of political existence': the simultaneous presence of a new political form *and* sovereign states (Beaud 2007).

Since Aron's death in 1983, the referenda on Maastricht (1992) and the Constitutional Treaty (2005) reignited the normative controversies about Europe among French political thinkers. Two different periods should be distinguished. Following the ratification of the Maastricht Treaty, the European issue served as a catalyst for the rehabilitation of cultural nationalism in republican discourse (Laborde 2001; Lacroix 2004b). Authors who defined themselves as 'republicans' reinvested the concept of 'nation', which had been left to the conservatives since the end of the nineteenth century (Debray 1999; Taguieff 2001; Thibaud 1992, 2006; Todd 1995).[2] These 'national-republicans'

---

[2] It was from the 1880s onwards that the republicans of the left began to speak of 'patriots' and 'patriotism' rather than 'nations' and 'nationalism'.

opposed both the political liberalism of left- and right-wing *démocrates* and the 'closed' nationalism of the extreme right, which reneges on republican values (Winock 1982: 11–40). The label 'national-republicans' harks back to the 'first' nationalism, which emerged at the end of the eighteenth century in close connection with republican ideals.[3]

The national-republican argument is twofold. First, its proponents hold that the democratic ideal cannot be disentangled from national identity, as suggested by the German philosopher Jürgen Habermas, the best-known proponent of constitutional patriotism on a European scale. Second, national-republicans maintain that the move towards a post-national entity is undermining democracy within the borders of existing nation-states. For it exacerbates the twin dangers facing contemporary democracies: the growing autonomy of individuals and their disinterest in public affairs (Lacroix 2002 and 2004b). In this perspective, every nation is characterized by a tension between the rational, formal, and abstract principles of citizenship on the one hand, and on the other the communitarian and ethnic reality of civil society. Consequently, national-republicans claim, universal principles alone cannot sustain a particular polity. If democracy is to survive, it needs to be reinforced with the strong feelings and emotions involved in a national tradition.

This tension between the universal and the particular already marks the classical French republican model. While its ambition is universal and it conceives of the national as political, it also confines the Republic to the territory of the French nation-state (Schrag 2008: 115). Granting the active and passive vote in municipal and European elections to European Union nationals in their country of residence, as foreseen by the Maastricht Treaty, clearly works against the grain of the French conception of citizenship. As Pierre Rosanvallon points out, giving non-nationals the vote in local elections is coherent with the 'civil' conception of municipal administration as it prevails in the United Kingdom and Northern Europe. In contrast, 'a universalism of the French type can envisage citizenship only in the form of one bloc' (Rosanvallon 1992: 441). Consequently, to many French thinkers the creation of a European citizenship would only make sense if it went hand in hand with the creation of a real federal state. If no European nation comes into existence, the European political project will never lead to a European democratic state, and therefore one need not speak of European citizenship (Dimier 2004: 895).

However, if the national-republicans were relatively active during the 1990s, they had almost vanished from the heart of the intellectual debate by the mid-2000s, when the referendum on the Constitutional Treaty took place. While

---

[3] This 'first nationalism' was that of the revolutionaries and the patriots. The Paris Commune can be considered its last manifestation, before a conservative nationalism emerged (Winock 1982: 13–15).

many economists and some constitutionalists actively participated in this new campaign, political thinkers remained conspicuously silent or deliberately refused to propose a clear yes-or-no answer.[4] Still, the months following the referendum led to contributions from some prominent political thinkers who had almost never intervened on the European issue previously (Gauchet 2005a, 2005b; Manent 2006a). A careful reading of these writings reveals that the vintage mix of nationalism and republicanism incarnated for a while by the 'national-republicans' might have concealed a deeper French controversy on the very nature of democracy. More precisely, the diverging conceptions of Europe that prevail today among French thinkers should be linked to the relation between human rights and politics. To elucidate this point, it will be helpful briefly to recall the evolution of French thinking on these matters over the last three decades.

In the 1970s, the philosopher Claude Lefort was among the first French authors to analyse the changing nature of contemporary politics as refracted through the prism of the Cold War. In contrast to totalitarian regimes in the Soviet bloc, he argued, Western liberal democracy was premised on social pluralism, the eroding power of fundamental rights, and disembodied politics (Lefort 1980). Hence, democracy not only afforded the greatest freedom of all regimes, but it was also the only regime that was truly human. For it alone could encompass the fundamentally divided and undetermined nature of society, and actively protect it through a number of institutions. The affirmation that human rights were inviolable and inalienable paved the way for the expression of social plurality in politics. In his criticism of the excessively restrictive nature of the Marxist vision of human rights, Lefort emphasized their social character and thus their essentially political nature. Fundamental rights kept the locus of power symbolically open because they officially allowed citizens to question existing hierarchies and resist oppression. In other words, human rights recognized 'the conflicting nature of human relations and the lack of certainty underlying every possible way of ordering society' (Geenens 2008: 278). These themes have remained predominant in theoretical debates on contemporary democracy in France until the present day. From this common critical stance two distinctive intellectual strands have emerged which approach the European model from diametrically opposed angles.

---

[4] Etienne Balibar published an article in *Libération* four days before the referendum. It was entitled 'Oui mais...Non car...' (Yes, but... No because...). He declared himself inclined to vote No, but admitted 'his acute awareness of the risks implied by such a choice' (*Libération*, 25 May 2005). Marcel Gauchet and Pierre Manent's works on Europe were published *after* the referendum.

Undefined Europe or the utopia of law

The first strand of thought is characterized by its critical stance on a political approach to human rights. According to authors such as Marcel Gauchet and Pierre Manent,[5] the dynamism of pluralist society as praised in *L'invention démocratique* might eventually undermine democracy itself. In fact, they argue, democracy exhausts itself in its efforts to promote human rights; the implementation of democratic principles thus effectively leads to 'weakening democracy, or even more fundamentally, [to] dissolving its framework and instruments' (Gauchet 2005a: 536). From this point of view, Lefort had placed too much emphasis on individual rights, and thus blurred the political references that shaped the modern democratic process. This school of thinkers can be called 'neo-Tocquevillian' as they are predominantly interested in the dynamics, and dangers, of individualization. Moreover, they mistrust a certain form of 'democratic fundamentalism' and its corollary of extolling the law as the ultimate regulator of social life. Their musings on democracy have obvious bearings on their views about the European integration process. They see integration as an illustration of 'the dissolving power of human rights' and of the pernicious effects of exacerbated individualism.

For the neo-Tocquevillian authors, the 'problem with Europe' is that it lacks any real substance. Europe is 'disembodied' because it lacks the very core of any effective political community, which is the collective sense of being part of a common political project and of sharing a common identity with fellow citizens. If there is such a thing as a feeling of belonging to the EU, it is confined to the happy few, who have been unable so far to formalize or spread this notion (Gauchet 2005b: 11). In effect, Europe has been unable to emerge as a new political entity. What is more, it even revels in its inherently undefined nature, supposedly marking the ultimate stage of a democracy that has relinquished the 'old rags' of a people, a territory, or particular national customs (Manent 2006b).

In this way, these authors argue, the widespread emphasis on the concepts of 'individual universalism' and 'passion for similarities' has effectively emasculated all attempts at defining a new federal nation in a clearly bounded territory. This 'implacable lever' has decisively contributed to imposing eastwards enlargement and accession negotiations with Turkey, two developments that underscore Europe's blind pursuit of 'a dissolution of political bodies' (Gauchet 2005a: 489). Manent regards the European model as only one aspect of a larger individualization trend, by which 'no group, no communion, no people is any

[5] Although I focus on Manent and Gauchet, the conceptions analysed in this part of the chapter are shared by many other authors – most of whom are regular contributors to *Le Débat* and *Commentaire*. See Crapez 2005, Finkielkraut 2007, Lazorthes 2005, Le Goff 2005, Thibaud 1992 and 2006.

longer legitimate' (Manent 2006a: 18). By opening up to the whole of mankind, he maintains, Europe has forfeited its existence as a proper, particular entity.

A comparably radical opinion is advanced by linguist Jean-Claude Milner in his 2003 book *Les penchants criminels de l'Europe démocratique*. In Milner's view, a Europe without borders implies the dissolution of politics – which requires a limited totality – into 'society', the key principle of which is limitlessness. Such a Europe embodies the dream of a totally new political form, just as unlimited as society, in which powers can be multiplied infinitely and borders are no longer meaningful. Like Manent, Milner emphasizes the 'Turkish question'. Whether or not Turkey eventually joins the EU, 'the very fact that this is conceivable proves one thing: Europe today acknowledges no geographical or historical limits...The only thing that matters is the homogeneity of society' (Milner 2003: 96). With more nuance, Gauchet underlines that European universalism, unlike American universalism, is 'polycentric'; it stems from the unification of various nations that have not merged into a single nation or a homogeneous whole. 'This is both its strength and its weakness' (Gauchet 2005a: 467). It is a strength because the European project is non-exclusive and open. It is a weakness in that its 'unencumbered' nature favours the perverse effects of the European model, in particular the loss of real representation (1), the displacement and transcendence of self-government beyond public debate (2), and the deteriorating protection of the most disadvantaged members of society (3).

First, as to the future of the representative model, Manent's conception is straightforward: there can be no political equality without a sovereign state and a well-defined people. Only because a state is more legitimate than any other entity can it create political equality between individuals (Manent 2006a: 18). Attached as Europeans may be to democracy, this principle will never be sufficient to bring about a political body on which citizens may exert influence. This criticism of the European model cannot be subsumed under the typical denunciation of the European institutions' 'democratic deficit'. For, far from suffering from a lack of formal democracy, the European model is criticized here as the embodiment of an extravagant dream of 'pure democracy', based on the idea that universal principles need not necessarily be limited to a clearly defined territory and population (Manent 2006b: 92). Europe, according to this criticism, has transformed the people into an unhappy but docile herd, submitted to multiple levels of governance whose main objective is to stifle any collective action other than blind obedience to the rule of law. European integration has replaced the nation with a 'central human agency' intent on gradually expanding the area of pure democracy, respectful of human rights, but with no collective foundation. It has produced a democracy, without the people, 'a *kratos* without a *demos*' (Manent 2006a: 16).

This remark leads on to the second perverse effect allegedly induced by the European model, which is the reintroduction of a certain prevalence of norms over political debate. This critique is not limited to the commonplace condemnation of the power of judges and experts in EU decision-making. Rather, it aims at a much broader gradual shift of balance between 'law' and 'power', in favour of autonomous legal power. This analysis sees the prevalence of norms in the European model as the expression of an 'ethical radicalism', which, like religious fundamentalism, determines 'the right course to follow' by conformity with the rule of law. Both ethical radicalism and religious fundamentalism strip political debate of its legitimacy and its *raison d'être*.

Third, with Europe's constant expansion, its contours have become so blurred that it is no longer a political object, i.e. an object that can meet the fundamental expectations that citizens place in a political community, especially if they are weak and deprived (Gauchet 2005a: 18). Europe 'does not protect'. This is true less in the technical sense of the word than in the sense that it does not constitute a coherent particular entity 'that offers the shelter of collective density to the vulnerable' (Gauchet 2005a: 499). The question of the political 'body' is at the very core of the divide between deterritorialized elites and a broader public in search of territorial roots.

The motif of a 'disembodied' Europe echoes the various and numerous fears expressed by the French public about Europe. The question of 'territory' was a prevailing topic in the spring of 2005, when fears about outsourcing were channelled against the 'Polish plumber' and the 'Bolkestein directive' on the liberalization of services. The No-vote reflected feelings of apprehension towards European integration seen as part and parcel of globalization, as well as the common call for protective borders at either the national or at the European level (Sauger, Brouard, and Grossman 2007). Seen from a republican perspective that links social and political issues through the action of a homogeneous state acting within intangible borders, a heterogeneous, multi-polar Europe with ever-evolving frontiers appeared increasingly threatening (Mergier 2005: 19). The EU's recent and imminent enlargements nurtured feelings that the French state was losing its homogeneity and coherence, while protective frontiers were also progressively disappearing. This is confirmed by surveys that link social anxiety and the French No-vote (Sauger, Brouard, and Grossman 2007). Since both Gauchet and Manent wrote the relevant pieces *after* the referendum, they cannot have influenced the vote. Rather, the neo-Tocquevillian intellectuals seem to have voiced widespread anxieties about Europe that were already present in the French social fabric; they theorized these fears as pertaining to the dissolution of political forms of belonging.

Moreover, there are striking similarities between the above critiques of European integration on one hand, and the reservations increasingly expressed by the same authors since the early 1980s about the rhetoric of 'human rights' on the other. In fact, they analyse the European question not as an object per se, but rather as a continuation of the debate on 'the dissolving power of human rights'. This is illustrated by the critical discourse, central in both contexts, on the pernicious effects of exacerbated individualism. In this line of argument, the 'silent cosmopolitan revolution' engendered by the cooperation between European states has contributed 'to reinforcing the reign of legal universalism by furthering the mirage of a common space for individuals, based on nations but existing beyond them' (Gauchet 2005a: 501). Some twenty-five years earlier, the same optical illusion had been ascribed not to Europe but to 'the politics of human rights', which was deemed responsible for 'the return of old ways, the dead end of a vision of man as opposed to society, the old illusion that the individual is the foundation stone, that we can start from the individual, his demands and his rights and arrive, all the way up, at the idea of society' (Gauchet 2002: 17).

Paradoxically, the thinkers discussed in this section are often considered as 'liberal' in the Anglo-American world. This interpretation was introduced notably by Mark Lilla's *New French Thought* (1994), which identified a French return to liberalism after decades dominated by Marxism and structuralism.[6] As far as Gauchet or Manent are concerned, this is misleading. These authors have indeed contributed to the rediscovery of some major liberal thinkers such as Constant or Tocqueville. However, they do not define themselves as liberal. In addition, their works reveal the difficult relationship of French political thought with some of the central premises and building blocks of political liberalism, in particular the commitment to rights-based individualism, the openness and the untidy compromise that lie at the heart of a liberal political order. Ironically, where liberal ideas have made inroads into French political thought, it tends to be in the cases of radical left-wing thinkers such as Etienne Balibar.

Exclusive Europe or a failed revolution

In contrast to the first intellectual strand analysed above, the second school of thought has taken up and developed Lefort's theory of democracy. According to Jacques Rancière, democracy is 'the very principle of politics, the principle that establishes political power by founding "good government" on the very absence of its foundations' (Rancière 2005: 44). Democracy is 'anybody's government' (Rancière 2005: 103), in contrast to the totalitarian or oligarchic forms of government that appropriate power to the ends of a caste. Social plurality, which furthers resistance to domination by a self-proclaimed elite, engenders a democratic process. This process is conceived of as a permanent reconfiguration of social cleavages. Democracy is 'the action of citizens who, working on the borders of their specific identities, redefine the contours of what is private and what is public, what is universal and what is specific' (Rancière

---

[6] Judt equally considers Manent and Gauchet as members of a 'tiny minority' of liberal thinkers in his book on the French intellectuals (Judt 1992: 315).

2005: 69). This perpetual motion is the prime motor of democratic life. Consequently, human-rights rhetoric sits at the core of the democratic process.

Jacques Rancière has not written on Europe, but his radical views are shared by those whom I propose to call 'liberal-revolutionary' thinkers. Led by Etienne Balibar, these authors initially viewed European integration as an opportunity to rejuvenate the democratic ambition. For them, an 'ideal' Europe would contribute to the emergence of a universal right to move and settle everywhere. Hence their disenchantment when confronted with the EU's actual praxis characterized by continuing attachment to national identities and denial of the basic civic rights of European citizenship to European residents.

French liberal-revolutionary thinkers criticize Europe for exactly the opposite reasons from their neo-Tocquevillian compatriots. Far from denouncing the perverse consequences of 'pure democracy' founded on individual rights and abolished frontiers, these authors regard European integration as a historical opportunity to revive the radical views originally expressed in the 1789 Declaration of the Rights of Man and the Citizen. Whereas many radical leftist theorists still combine their revolutionary approach with a certain dose of anti-legalism, Etienne Balibar proposes what may appear to be 'the most accomplished theory of democracy which partly acknowledges the liberal heritage while at the same time incorporating the legacy of Marx' (Raynaud 2006: 171). In this respect, Balibar agrees with Lefort that the prevalence of human rights is not solipsistic per se insofar as individual rights inherently bind the subject to his community.

It may seem ironic in this regard that the most fervent proponents of human rights in France were early Marxists. There is a connection, however. In the era of global capitalism, Balibar considers human-rights rhetoric as the major instrument for democratic struggle, since it both opposes social violence and challenges the limits of the constitutional state. In *Les frontières de la démocratie*, Balibar implicitly responds to Gauchet by stating: 'without human-rights politics there can be no democratic politics' (Balibar 1992). For Balibar, speaking out for human rights is a radical discursive act of political deconstruction and reconstruction through the affirmation of 'a universal right to activism and political recognition, in all matters relating to the question of the collective distribution of wealth, power and knowledge' (Balibar 1992: 247). As Philippe Raynaud argues, a radical version of classical liberalism may be discernible here, notably in the reference to the Anglo-American concept of civil disobedience (Raynaud 2006: 183). Even the strategic objectives of human-rights politics are expressed in a liberal language; they consist in creating new counter-powers adapted to the changes brought about by economic globalization, and extending modes of representation so as to include the deprived and most disadvantaged (Raynaud 2006: 183).

Such an ambitious goal, which Balibar calls 'equaliberty', implies universalism. In principle, democracy is limitless, insofar as it encompasses not only the rule of law but also a historical process extending rights to the whole of mankind. This is why, from the liberal-revolutionary perspective, the main obstacle to democracy is not capitalism but nationalism. Nationalism in its exclusionary sense implies a 'violence pertaining to the defence of an identity' or to the sovereign law of the state, which despotically integrates or expels people and reduces the community of equal citizens to nationals entitled to social benefits (Chemillier-Gendreau 2005: 168). Liberal-revolutionary thought thus rests on the founding principle of some form of 'pure' citizenship, which seeks to reverse the progressive confusion of citizenship and nationality.

However, it should be stressed that Balibar has never envisaged the possible disappearance of the nation-state or of national borders. This sets him apart from other more radical leftist thinkers such as Toni Negri. Even though the very foundations of the citizenship-nationality pattern are 'shaken' today, Balibar holds that it would be 'thoughtless' to draw the conclusion that nations will eventually disappear. He does not believe in the end of the concept of nationality, in the progressive dissolution of the links between nationality and citizenship, or in their transfer to the supranational level. He does not call for an abolition of the distinction between nationals and foreigners, but for making frontiers more 'democratic' according to the principle of reciprocity rather than discrimination. This new conception of citizenship is neither anti-national nor supranational, but transnational. It does not run counter to the concept of the state, but does imply the redefinition and reappraisal of the myth of the sovereign nation-state (Balibar 2002: 11).

This radical democratic promise is why Europe was originally regarded as a potential testing ground for a new form of citizenship. In his earlier work of the 1990s, Balibar considers Europe the ideal locus for radical democratic ambitions to be realized and for frontiers to become relative. Europe is a motor for the historical transformation of the notion of citizenship, in content as well in form. In fact, European integration only makes sense as the beginning of a new phase in the history of democracy, a 'democratic invention' *à la* Lefort. Conceived as a 'space' rather than a 'body', Europe's democratized frontiers will give rise to a universal right to free circulation and residence (Balibar 2002: 176). A conception of frontiers of this type implies that Europe needs to relinquish the old myth of closure and exclusive identity. Balibar conceives of Europe itself as a 'Borderland', or more precisely a juxtaposition of frontiers, cultures, and histories of the world (Balibar 2003: 33). Against 'the substantialist obsession' (Ogilvie in Balibar 2003: 64), the idea of Europe as a historical, cultural, or economic fact has to be refuted. The question of European identity is a false problem insofar as it should only be about extending the concept of citizenship (Balibar 2001: 12).

This is reminiscent of Jacques Derrida's idea of a European identity, 'open' to everything non-European by nature. In *The Other Heading*, Derrida insists on the necessity of 'making ourselves the guardian of an idea of Europe that consists precisely in not isolating itself in its own identity, and in advancing itself in an exemplary way towards what it is not, towards the other heading and the heading of the other' (Derrida 1992: 29). This entails (implies) a 'duty' to open Europe onto what 'is not, never was and never will be Europe', and to welcome foreigners 'in order not only to integrate them but also to recognize and accept their Otherness' (Derrida 1992: 77).

This conception of European citizenship resounds with some of the arguments developed by the neo-Kantian school. I have chosen not to delve into this strand of thought as it does not occupy a central place in French public debate.[7] Drawing largely on German sources, this school's leading representatives live in Belgium (Ferry 2000 and 2005) or in Switzerland (Cheneval 2005). I shall just mention here that these authors focus on European law, conceived of as the medium for mutual recognition among European peoples, rather than on individual rights. They envisage Europe as a regulating concept which might eventually lead to the first effective form of cosmopolitanism based on mediation between nations. According to this approach, the cosmopolitan paradigm does not downplay the role of the nation-state as it is precisely through the nation that the cosmopolitan dimension of law can be envisaged and realized (Cheneval 2005: 276). A cosmopolitan process thus understood respects the rights of peoples and does not call for the creation of a global state *ex nihilo*. It is thought of rather as a regulating or civilizing principle (Cheneval 2005: 256). Cosmopolitanism in this sense is a form of legal integration of free states, based on regular and organized deliberation, and not on their subordination to a higher authority.

Although Balibar does not refer explicitly to Kantian cosmopolitanism, he shares several of its postulates, admitting that his own intellectual approach 'is not incompatible with the "cosmopolitanism" reintroduced today by Habermas and his disciples' (Balibar 2001: 311). However, Balibar objects to the purely ethical approach of these thinkers. He points out that the idea of substantial transnational citizenship implies defining some 'democratic building sites' as potential loci for the transnational politicization of the European Union. This politicization could include the democratization of the legal system, transnational labour movements, the fight against discrimination exercised against non-member-state nationals, etc. These 'determined issues' could serve as focal points for transnational European social and political movements, and thereby open up 'the circle of ideal-type Europe to reality'.

Balibar and his followers further differ from the neo-Kantians insofar as the latter promote a somewhat idealized conception of the European Union. Conversely, liberal-revolutionary thinkers have increasingly criticized the Union's polity. Since the mid-2000s, they have become increasingly disenchanted with

---

[7] For more details on the neo-Kantians, see Lacroix and Magnette 2009.

integration's capacity to change traditional political categories significantly. While neo-Tocquevillians regard European integration as an expression of the prevalence of individual rights and the withering of the nation-state, 'liberal-revolutionary' thinkers find the 'real' Europe disappointing because it has failed to guarantee human rights as 'fundamental' rights and subvert the logic of the nation-state. Instead, nationality remains at the core of European citizenship. The Maastricht Treaty's definition of European citizenship, taken up verbatim in the Constitutional Treaty, is essentially national. Hence, liberal revolution-aries point out, the citizenship=nationality equation has merely shifted from the national to the supranational level.

Balibar reads this as a sign of the emergence of a new and dangerous phe-nomenon, a European 'racism' or 'apartheid' that introduces in each national space a discrimination between two types of foreigners: 'intra-' and 'extra-' Community nationals. It therefore introduces a new kind of 'Otherness' at a time when the EU proclaims its defence of universalism (Balibar 2001: 83). As a result, social exclusion is no longer a matter of sociological differences, but a truly institutional process: millions of third-country nationals are becoming an undefined mass of 'second-class' citizens or 'subjugated residents' at the service of fully-fledged Europeans (Balibar 2001: 85).

The use of the word 'apartheid' is justified here, according to Balibar, by the gradual emergence of a new inferior population. Inferior in rights as well as dignity, this population is ever more subjected to violent forms of security controls, and forced to live permanently on the 'borderline', not totally within or without the frontiers of Europe. This peculiarly European form of 'racism' against all those who are not 'white, secular, or Christian' (Balibar 2001: 85), and the 'denial' of the right of residence for the populations which do not belong to the founding European nations, is at the heart of Balibar's reserva-tions about the Constitutional Treaty (Balibar 2005b).

Of course, Balibar elaborates, the fate of non-Europeans includes not only residents within the EU, but starts with violence at its borders, further increased since the implementation of the Schengen agreement. Far from conferring a transnational dimension on Europe, the establishment of a 'Europe of police forces' has progressively given the European space all the characteristics of a 'territory' to be defended against a new enemy, both within and without: refugees and migrant workers. The new aporia of this 'provincial cosmopolitan-ism' leads Europe to consider itself the guardian of international legal princi-ples, while in reality it is often unable to implement them on its own territory. Europe is incapable of exerting its civilizing influence at home, Balibar con-tends. Consequently it has given up any active role in the establishment of a 'global citizenship'; at its own frontiers as well as in Palestine, Chechnya, or Algeria, it no longer acts to reduce 'the anti-political combination of militarism and humanitarian action, thus repeating the same mistake and showing the same powerlessness as in ex-Yugoslavia' (Balibar 2005a: 90). Europe, Balibar concludes, fails to play the role of 'mediator' or 'translator' that its own history and openness to the world would suggest.

In contrast to the motif of the disembodied Europe, the denunciation of an 'exclusive' European entity has found very little resonance among the general public. However, this 'progressive' type of opposition to the European Union's policies has significantly influenced the anti-globalization left (including groups like ATTAC-France),[8] whose fight for the regularization of illegal immigrants effectively turned into a principled opposition to Europe's immigration policies, as illustrated by the mobilization movement against the European directives on the return of illegal immigrants, adopted in June 2008.

Conclusion

I have argued that the visions of Europe found in France are ultimately linked to distinct ways of considering the relation between law and politics. For the 'neo-Tocquevillians', European integration presents itself as the symptom of a broader and longer-term process of depoliticization as opposed to an original phenomenon. The EU is merely the ultimate expression of the dissolution of politics, spurred by the dominant role given to individual rights. By contrast, the liberal-revolutionary thinkers acknowledge the innovative potential of European integration. They criticize its failure to implement true human-rights politics beyond the national paradigm.

Beyond these divergences, can one speak of a 'French specificity' in the theoretical debates over the European project? If there is one, it may be more accurately described in negative terms. There is no equivalent in French political thought to the model of 'federal supranationalism' advocated in Germany (Habermas 2001b), in the Nordic countries, or even in the United Kingdom (Hix and Føllesdal 2005; Morgan 2005). In the two main paradigms I have identified in this chapter, the concept of a European federal state is conspicuously absent or refuted. Either it is deemed coherent from a purely logical perspective, but is unlikely for historical reasons – which seems to be Pierre Manent's conclusion – or it is judged undesirable because it reinforces exclusionary borders at the European level – which would be the 'liberal-revolutionary' caveat. The absence of the 'European federal state' model might seem paradoxal if one considers the prevalence of the 'Europe sociale' topic in the 2005 campaign for the ratification of the Constitutional Treaty. However, a closer look reveals that the main objective of the leftist opponents to the

---

[8] ATTAC-France is an interesting case study since it differs from many other protest groups in that it enjoys the backing of numerous intellectuals. On ATTAC-France and the intellectuals, see Waters 2004. For more details on ATTAC-France's arguments during the campaign for the ratification of the Constitutional Treaty, see Heine 2009.

European Constitution was not so much a 'social Europe' – which would suppose mass transfers of resources from richer to poorer member states or the suppression of any barriers to free movement of workers from the 'new' countries – but rather the protection of the *national* social models from what is perceived as a 'neo-liberal' Europe (Moravcsik 2006).

Put differently, even though opinions on the evolution and functioning of the European Union diverge significantly, no French political thinker has upheld the idea that the national frame of reference should be abolished in the short or medium term. Rather, theoretical debates in France are marked by their refusal to envisage European integration as the mere 'transposition' of the mechanisms of national democracy to a supranational level. As Pierre Rosanvallon underscores, if the nation is defined as a 'distributive community', it follows that we are not progressing towards a European demos. With only 1.27 per cent of GNP devoted to social redistribution, Europe is much closer to 'the solidarity of humanity' than 'the solidarity of citizenship' (Rosanvallon 2003: 433). According to this author, this is why a unified Europe cannot be a substitute for re-foundation of nations.

Put differently, French political thinkers writing on Europe unanimously insist on the nation as the main locus for political socialization. In contrast, they disagree on whether an EU based on the laws of the market and the rule of law constitutes a powerful (and unwelcome) motor for the dissolution of national communities, or whether the EU's propensity to go beyond the nation-state framework constitutes a promise, even if one that is as yet unfulfilled.

6

Italy and the Idea of Europe

Mario Telò

This chapter focuses on the intellectual impetus for, and roots of, the rise of the large domestic consensus in favour of a federal European Union achieved in Italy during the so-called First Republic (1948–1992). It notably addresses the role of intellectuals in explaining the continuities and discontinuities found in ideas about Europe between the First and Second Republic (1992–).

The main argument made is that the current normalization of a pro-European intellectual presence in Italy maintains national particularities and distinctive features which cannot be explained without what the French historian Fernand Braudel called a *longue durée* approach. The intellectual debate, combined with sixty years of the process of Italian integration into Western Europe, is understood as part of long-term trends within national cultural history; this historical construction is powerful enough to counterbalance both past and recent tendencies of discontinuity.

Consistent with the general theme of the book, this chapter does not address Italy's role within the EU decision-making system, nor the impact of European policy in Italy. The political background and the policy dimension are taken into consideration only to the extent that they demonstrate how the intellectual perception of national interests and Italy's role in Europe – notably the debates shaping Italian ideas about Europe – are historically relevant. However the methodological challenge is to combine a horizontal comparative politics approach with the history of political ideas, which requires attention to the *longue durée* dimension of the Italian story.

The European Referendum of 1989: A symbolic event of the First Italian Republic

According to a *longue durée* approach, events only provide a superficial manifestation of deeper tendencies and historical trends rooted in persistent features of the social formation process. However, historians of the European Italian narrative often neglect the relevance of the symbolic event that occurred in 1989 within the Italian public sphere. Initially proposed by the left-liberal founding father of the EC/EU, Altiero Spinelli (1907–1986),[1] a consultative ad hoc referendum was held in Italy (and only in Italy) on 18 June 1989 – in conjunction with the third European direct elections – asking citizens whether they wanted the European Parliament to be endowed with constitutional powers.

The referendum of 1989 resulted in a landslide: 89.1 per cent voted 'yes' and 10.9 per cent 'no', with an 81 per cent participation rate. The yes-vote was supported not only by all the Italian parties belonging to the so-called 'constitutional arch', the anti-fascist coalition underpinning both the multi-party Resistance movement and the new Republican Constitution of 1947, but also by all the most relevant intellectual factions.[2] This rare intellectual convergence represents the European consensus during the first Italian Republic. Among other things, it legitimized the new European Parliament by again favouring a federal European Constitution (though there were controversies over the so-called 'Spinelli draft Treaty' voted for by the EP in 1984),[3] which the EP later supported twice more, in 1993 ('Fernand Hermann draft') and in 2003–5 ('Constitutional Treaty'). Such a consistent development of a Hamiltonian idea of a federal European constitution, on the one hand, and concrete national politics, on the other, has not been seen in any other European member state during the sixty years of European integration, including the most pro-European countries.

Diverging from contingent analyses, this chapter aims to help explain the intellectual dimension and background of the development of such a broad pro-European consensus, as well as its long-lasting impact on the public sphere (confirmed by Euro-barometer, until the mid-1990s). This analysis would be impossible without taking into account both the history of the European idea during the First Italian Republic and some of the main cleavages present in Italian modern history, notably the particular weakness of the idea of the nation underpinning the formation of the state and the national modernization process. The hypothesis of this chapter is that continuity prevails over discontinuity within the history of ideas: beyond superficial breaks, intellectual continuity is significant, rooted as it is in the secular *longue durée* of Italian ideas of Europe.

---

[1] See Spinelli 1975, 1986, and 1989.

[2] These ranged from the Christian Democrats (DC) to the Italian Communist Party (PCI) and from Socialists to Liberals and Republicans.

[3] The 'Treaty for a European Union', elaborated by the informal 'Club du crocodile' between 1981 and 1984, was voted for by an overwhelming majority in the first elected European Parliament in 1984, but rejected by the European Council (which adopted the Single European Act in 1986).

The First Republic and the 'Italian European ideology'

Despite the effects of the Cold War on the domestic level, including on Italian intellectuals, during the First Italian Republic founded on 1 January 1948, the evolution of European integration shifted from an early internal division to a 'constitutional' convergence between left and centre-right. When looking at *histoire événementielle*, the historian has little option but to focus on instability and divergence, such as the political conflict seen in the mass demonstrations and parliamentary opposition promoted by communists and socialists between 1950 and 1954 against the European Community for Steel and Coal and especially against the European Defence Community. However, this hard internal cleavage between pro-EC and anti-EC camps proved to be temporary and superficial, whereas the centripetal convergence on a federal idea of an internationally autonomous Europe gradually emerged as the central feature of what we call the ideology of the First Italian Republic.

The bipolar international context of the Cold War, which pitted the forces of communism versus capitalism as well as those of democracy versus dictatorship against each other, had a significant domestic impact in Italy, even more so than in France. Although the changing international framework and the rise of peaceful coexistence had a positive effect on the support for integration, several socialist intellectuals had already moved to pro-EC positions in 1957 when the Treaty of Rome was signed and ratified, and were able to attract notable ex-communist and pro-EC intellectuals such as Antonio Giolitti after the Budapest revolt against Soviet repression. External factors were thus only one of the relevant causes of this domestic evolution. For the Italian Communist Party (which conquered the main force of the Italian left under Palmiro Togliatti between 1945 and 1964) and its related intellectual movement, the evolution from a vague pro-European attitude to an explicit pro-EC position took two more decades. The new Eurocommunist leadership of Enrico Berlinguer (1973–84) and, later on, the crypto-social-democratic orientation of Giorgio Napolitano (elected in 2006 as president of the Republic) played a crucial role in overcoming post-war ideological ambiguity: not only (as in the case of the French Communist Party) was there a shared fidelity to the 'communist camp' and to 'socialism with national colours', but also notably a coexistence of communist orthodoxy and national intellectual hegemony, thanks to a distinctive anti-Stalinist intellectual legacy embodied in the theories of Antonio Gramsci.[4]

On the one hand, there was the political use of Gramsci seen through the work edited by Togliatti and produced by the prestigious publisher Einaudi in

---

[4] See Gramsci 1971 and 1978. The *Quaderni del carcere*, written in a fascist prison between 1929 and 1935, openly associate with the idealistic tradition of liberal thought: the notions of civil society, hegemony, and historical bloc evidently originate in the thought of G. W. F. Hegel, as underlined in Bobbio 1990. See also Showstack Sassoon 1987.

1947, which was evoked throughout the first international Gramsci conference in Rome in 1958; the work's explicit and largely successful purpose was to connect with the great intellectual tradition symbolized by Benedetto Croce and secularized Italian idealism.[5] On the other hand, Gramsci also became a shared intellectual reference between liberal, Catholic, and left-leaning intellectuals, as the introductory speech by Norberto Bobbio at the Cagliari conference of 1967 clearly shows. The debates about Gramscian thought largely paved the way to the Westernization of the Italian left, and allowed for a dialogue with the pluralist traditions of national and European culture. This historical background explains why, in the decades of competition between two universalist schools of thought, the Catholic and the Gramscian branches of communism, the left achieved ideological hegemony among intellectuals, universities, and publishing houses.

However, the increasingly reliable connection between universalist ideas, such as peace or a united Europe, and concrete steps towards European integration provided the Catholic-liberal leading group with a strategic advantage. This is significant in explaining the actions of left-wing intellectuals and the political leadership of the 1970s and 1980s. Twenty years of EC progress coupled with the growing intellectual and political criticism of the Soviet model gave birth to the intermediary stage known as 'Eurocommunism'. It was for many left-wing intellectuals a step towards full Europeanization,[6] even if it consisted of a patchwork of utopian and practical elements. However, a large international literature recognizes the political necessity of somehow filling the political vacuum perceived by the representatives of a strong teleological tradition, openly rejecting the communist orthodoxy. An identity crisis was about to emerge, highlighting the pressing need to look for an alternative way, namely a European one, to combine national intellectual history with a revised and innovative universalist perspective.

Elaborating the idea of a politically united Europe gradually became the main way of bringing not only the PCI but also the Italian intellectual left out of the past towards a new intellectual development, which was, however, rife with the conceptual ambiguities inherent in the search for a 'European third way' between socialism and capitalism, East and West. Thus for several decades the Europeanization of the Italian left was not limited to mere functional adaptation to an ongoing economic and institutional process, but also involved an intellectual evolution which created high cultural, social, political, and international expectations of a united Europe. From the late 1970s to the

---

[5] A few days before his death in 1964, Togliatti wrote the famous 'Yalta memorial', opening the door to the public criticism of the Soviet Union and to the re-actualization of Gramsci's 1926 break with Stalin.

[6] The consciousness of the strategic relevance of European integration grew in those years: see Napolitano and Hobsbawm 1976; Ranney and Sartori 1978; Urban 1978.

mid-1980s, the federalist ideas of Altiero Spinelli became an openly shared ideal and reference, replacing the alternative traditional ideals that had previously dominated: thus the Italian European ideology was gradually constructed.

Generally speaking, there is empirical evidence to show that ideas matter in the Italian case. We employ the concept of 'ideology' not in the Marxist understanding of a false perception of reality, but as an increasingly coherent intellectual framework through historical evolution. The European debate in Italy was both pluralistic and centripetal in the sense that convergence among several national intellectual schools was eventually possible, contrary to the French experience. In this chapter, we examine whether this debate was an intrinsic part of Italian intellectual history.

Advocating this interpretation requires several steps: firstly, we need to examine the historical context, that is to say the role of intellectuals in the constitutional foundation of the Italian Republic between 1945 and 1948. To what extent does this period clearly indicate the possible evolution of the intellectual paths in the coming decades? As mentioned above, the European intellectual narrative after the Second World War started with a serious internal rupture, provoked by both the international and domestic collapse of the former anti-Nazi and anti-fascist coalition (1947/8). However, early convergences began to emerge between the large array of anti-fascist movements, notably on three main issues: the Republican Constitution, the Peace Treaty, and the Marshall Plan.

The text of the Republican Constitution of 1 January 1948 itself is a significant indication of such intellectual convergences: in spite of huge differences, the Christian Democrats and the Italian Communists both held positions characterized by anti-nationalist, pacifist, and universalistic traditions of political thought. During the long debates of the Constituent Assembly of 1947, these parties as well as socialists, liberals, and republicans were represented by outstanding intellectuals, making the constitutional consensus particularly interesting for the history of ideas. The near unanimous approval of the Constitutional Charter at the end of 1947 is very significant for the future European intellectual and political convergence for two main reasons.

Firstly, the new Constitution of 1948 includes the famous article 11, which transformed traumatic memories of war into an intellectual advantage, anticipating the post-modern concept of sovereignty pooling:

Italy rejects war as an offence to the liberty of other peoples and as a means for international conflict resolution. Italy welcomes, on the condition of equality with other states, limitations of national sovereignty, which are necessary for building an order ensuring peace and justice among nations. Italy promotes and favours international organizations supporting these ends.[7]

---

[7] *Costituzione della Repubblica Italiana*, Art. 11, Rome 2007. Rusconi 2003 proposes a comparative study of EU practices and concepts of 'civilian power' in Italy and Germany after 1945, based on similar constitutional provisions.

To some extent, this provision recalls semi-sovereign features of the post-war constitutions of defeated countries. However, contrary to Germany and Japan, the Italian constitutional debate was free while dominated by universalistic political cultures. This legal provision was initially supported by Catholic and Italian communist intellectuals with reference to the newly formed United Nations and to the cosmopolitan values of universal peace. However, it was also instrumental in allowing the introduction of EC/EU treaties into the Italian legal and institutional system over the next sixty years without any constitutional amendments (which is very relevant for this book, because in Italy events such as European treaties and referenda affect the intellectual debate less than they do in France and other European countries).

Despite the differences between universal cosmopolitanism and Europeanism, underlined by the European federalist Luigi Einaudi in 1919, the two ideas proved coherent enough to limit national sovereignty. This new attitude was reflected not only in a positive reception to and support of the foundation of the UN, but notably also in support of the EC/EU practice of pooling national sovereignties in crucial fields of social life, including some of the more sensitive competences of the state.

Secondly, two further fundamental debates emerged during the crucial years of constitutional convergence: the controversial debate over the 1947 Peace Treaty with the victors of the Second World War, and the common interest in the Marshall Plan launched by the US in the same year. Both debates had European and international implications, and confirm that the understanding of and near unanimous support for the Constitution's text was not episodic but rather profound and visionary. The Peace Treaty was criticized by leading liberal nationalists, including members of the old pre-fascist political class represented by Vittorio Emanuele Orlando, or the great philosopher Benedetto Croce who rejected the humiliation involved in signing the Peace Treaty. Croce was isolated in defending the thesis that fascism was a parenthesis in Italian history and that there was continuity with pre-fascist Italian liberal thought and state. The support for the Peace Treaty, shared by such opposed leaders as the Catholic Prime Minister Alcide De Gasperi and leader of the Communist Party Palmiro Togliatti, was due both to the anti-nationalist political culture and to the consciousness of the importance of reconciliation with France, Britain, the US, and other members of the international anti-Nazi coalition (Santoro 1991). The widespread interest in the Marshall Plan shared by leading Catholic intellectual personalities such as Amintore Fanfani and intellectual representatives of the left such as the economists Claudio Napoleoni and Giorgio Napolitano was also based on the prevalent acceptance of Keynesian ideas and the possibility of a constructive relationship with democratic America.

From domestic cleavage to national convergence: Catholic and secular intellectual actors in Europe

The Catholic Church maintained a strong political weight during the first two decades of European construction. Alcide De Gasperi was one of the three influential Catholic (and German-speaking) founding fathers of the small but farsighted Community of Six (with Adenauer and Schuman). Was the idea of a 'Vatican Europe' complementary to the vision of European integration? International literature has emphasized the importance of the commitment to an integrated Europe held by one of the most influential Italian intellectuals during these hard times: the Pope Pacelli, alias Pius XII. Pope Pacelli is still surrounded by international controversy due to his silence when faced with Nazi crimes. However, after the war he gave many public speeches in favour of a united Europe and organized meetings in Rome for Catholic leaders. In his mind, 'Vatican Europe' firstly meant the '*esprit de revanche*' of supranationalism, like that of the Middle Ages, against the secularized nation-state; secondly, it symbolized a Europe that was both an anti-communist fortress and an independent entity from the US; thirdly, it would adhere to a 'Charlemagne model', excluding Protestant countries such as the UK and those in Scandinavia.

The influence of both this historical legacy and geographical proximity was very strong in Italy. However, the weight of a Catholic vision of Europe was not exclusive, but rather balanced with liberal and even socialist ideas as seen in the other five partners of the first communities. Even the Catholic Prime Minister De Gasperi, leader of the main Italian decisions in European policy between 1950 and 1954, asserted his autonomous profile, not only by championing the idea of a federalist Europe early on and taking concrete steps towards the EC at the time of the Cold War, but also by defending a liberal understanding of Europe in alliance with liberals, republicans, and social democrats led by Luigi Einaudi (president of the Republic), Giorgio La Malfa, and Giuseppe Saragat (Scoppola 1977). However, this pluralist leadership was confronted with the risk of isolation: for various and sometimes contradictory reasons, the business community (except the stream led by Giovanni Agnelli, the founder of FIAT and author of several pro-European essays), the trade unions, and the Catholic party were all sceptical of the decisions regarding the ECSC and the EDC, on the one hand based on inward-looking visions, parochialism, and protectionism, on the other in the name of a leftist critique of European communities perceived as too liberal, capitalist, and US-dependent.

De Gasperi's intellectual vision was strongly influenced by his experiences in the Austro-Hungarian parliament of Vienna before the First World War (as the elected representative of the Austrian province of Trento) and further developed by his daily analysis of the German Weimar democracy, as well as Belgian, French, and Dutch intellectual and political life of the 1920s and 1930s. His work reveals an evident hostility to nationalism due to his own experience living in border regions, sentiments shared by major European Catholic leaders such as founding fathers Schuman, Adenauer, and the Belgian Van Zeeland among others. After his death in 1954, De Gasperi's main decisions and ideas gradually became more popular in Italy and were shared by defenders of national interests and by much of the public, including his political and intellectual competitors.

What has not yet been sufficiently underlined is that, notwithstanding the fraught domestic and international climate of the years 1947–54, the first relevant ideal contribution of Italy to European construction took place in this period, anticipating a long-term convergent and distinctive approach to the primacy of European institution-building. This happened thanks to the intellectual cooperation between De Gasperi and his European policy advisor, Altiero Spinelli. Together they advocated a European political union as a necessary framework for a European army, the heart of the EDC Treaty of 1952 (conceived by Jean Monnet and proposed by the French Minister Pleven). After discussions with Adenauer and Schuman, De Gasperi himself formalized this amendment in the first version of the Treaty, through the famous article 38. The failure of the EDC due to the negative vote by the French *Assemblée nationale* in 1954 led to the abandonment of this political demand for thirty years. When the author of the EDC article 38, Altiero Spinelli, re-emerged with his idea of a European political union in 1981–4, he was able to unite a diverse array of national and European forces under this flag. With the public support of François Mitterrand, the first democratically elected European Parliament discussed and finally voted by an overwhelming majority in 1984 to establish the 'Draft Treaty for a European Union'. In addition, these ideas of De Gasperi and Spinelli gradually became the common language of all anti-fascist political parties in Italy including socialist and communist intellectuals.

How can we explain this relatively quick process of the 'Europeanization' of communist intellectuals? Italian communism is an expression of the traditional radicalism of the Italian left, a radical tradition which however never produced a revolution, instead evolving into the leading left-wing party by supporting republican and reformist demands (Ginzborg 1989; La Palombara 1987; Salvadori 1999; Sassoon 1986). The growing European consensus between the 1970s and 1990s had three main functional drivers: firstly, the large majority of the population gradually considered Europe as not only the road to economic recovery after the war, but also as a market for Italy's booming exports, and as a promise of enhanced prosperity. Nevertheless, the majority of the business community, weakened by twenty years of national protectionism and fascist autarchy, took some time to realize that the EC was an excellent market for Italian goods and an opportunity for economic growth. Secondly, for many the EC was an anchor of democratic consolidation in times of uncertainty: hard bipolar cleavages in the context of international politics, domestic political terrorism, and illegality in southern regions because of the revival of the mafia.

Thirdly, as far as the Europeanization and democratization process of the communist movement is concerned, its early commitment to the Republican Constitution was gradually complemented by a new European consciousness: on the one hand, the impact of proximity to the large social-democratic and Labour parties within the European parliamentary assembly, and on the other the belief that Europe offered the best framework for a 'third way' in international politics, or more precisely a strong European identity within the Western alliance, during the period of coexistence within the bipolar world.[8]

Despite domestic instability, there is evidence that by fostering a centripetal convergence of opposing leaders such as the Catholic intellectuals and political leaders Amintore Fanfani and Aldo Moro, the Italian communist movement, and the socialist camp among others played a major role in supporting European economic, social, monetary, and political integration – even before 1989 – as the best framework for both the modernization of domestic politics and economic prosperity.

Influential Italian intellectual thought underpinned this exceptionally large European consensus. The enthusiasm for Europe was so extensive that most Italians shared Spinelli's criticism of the Single European Act of 1986 as being apolitical and functionalist. The intellectual driving forces behind these events are important to note. Firstly, the influence of European federalist thought within universities (notably in Turin, Pavia, and Siena) and civil society remains significant, thanks to the activists of an organized pro-European federalist movement led by Altiero Spinelli, Mario Albertini, and others, who were able to influence almost all the political party leaders.

Secondly, the commitment to a deeper and broader European idea held by leading intellectuals often played a major role in national public opinion during this 'Habermasian' epoch (1981–2005) which, expanding on the book's introduction, should be defined as a 'third golden age' of the European debate (after the 1920s and 1950s). These intellectuals ranged from Umberto Eco to Massimo Cacciari, and from Claudio Magris to Biagio de Giovanni, among others, and were influential through their books and media presence (see for example Cacciari 1994; Eco 1994; Magris 1986; or, later on, De Giovanni 1992). Their opinions converge on the question of a European identity and public sphere, while they diverge on the issues of the relevance of the European

---

[8] See the famous Enrico Berlinguer interview to the *Corriere della sera* about 'NATO as a protecting shield for the PCI reformist way' followed by the parliamentary joint resolution of 1978, signed by Giorgio Napolitano on behalf of the PCI and supporting both the EC and NATO (the PCI belonged for the first time after 1947 to the majority coalition with DC and other democratic parties).

Greco-Roman cultural past and its interplay with national identities. Cacciari and Eco emphasize the uniqueness of Europe as a continent of linguistic and cultural diversity. Although they all converge in supporting the political union and the Central and Eastern enlargement of the EU (even before the fall of the Berlin wall in the case of Magris, as is clear in his elaboration of the concept of *Mitteleuropa*), they disagree about the relevance of the federalist idea in framing the new era of European construction.

Thirdly, in terms of the institutionalization of European research, and independently from any Euro-enthusiasm, Italy has witnessed the increasing legitimization of European integration studies within the academic disciplines of Social Sciences and Humanities, beyond the narrow perspective of pro-EC clubs, from History to Political Science, and from Philosophy to Law and Economics.

All in all, contributing to an innovative process of uniting Europe was understood by Italian anti-fascist political elites, as well as by the major intellectual factions and leading personalities, as the best framework for implementing Italian modernization and the values of democracy and social progress; and for developing a shared European identity, seen as both the achievement of the highest European cultural tradition and the destiny of the Italian nation. Why and how was such an emphasis possible?

Ideas matter: Five historical reasons explaining the weak roots of Italian nationalism

A large comparative literature stresses the inconsistencies in Italy between positive reception of European rhetoric or ideology on the one hand, and, on the other, the slow and partial transfer of European Community directives within the national legal system. In other words, Italy represents in this respect the antithesis of the UK, where the high level of EU policy implementation conflicts with a widespread Eurosceptical discourse. Nevertheless, rhetoric and discourse are also significant in Italy, and the overwhelming popular and parliamentary consensus has allowed for the acceleration of policy implementation on several occasions. The famous 'Della Pergola law' of 1989 is the first example. The aptitude of the first Prodi government (1996–8) in coping with the Maastricht Treaty convergence criteria for the monetary union – contrary to general European and notably German expectations – is a second and better example: it would be impossible to explain this without pointing to the material weight of 'Italian European ideology'. Moreover, this ideological and practical success by the Europhiles was even able to stem the secessionist movement (*Lega Nord*) growing in Lombardy and Northern Italy in the 1980s and 1990s, and to transform it into a reformist pressure for a federal Italy. One could assert that the European consensus combined with the successful process of European construction contributed to the preservation of national unity.[9]

Fostering popular support for European integration and even acceptance of several disadvantages of external European constraints required very specific circumstances. The relative disrepute of the Italian state within public opinion is not the only explanation: for example, this could have just as easily provoked an internal fragmentation. Behind Italian discourse and rhetoric about Europe, long-term trends rooted in national cultural history made it possible for fundamental and consensual decisions gradually to be taken, moving Italy towards a concrete European integration process. The weakness of the Italian nationalist tradition provides the main explanation for, and the common theme in, five national intellectual accounts: pre-Renaissance European supranationalism, twofold cosmopolitanism of Italian intellectuals, a late and elitist national unification, the fascist degradation of nationalism, and European unity as pluralist anti-fascist idea.

Pre-Renaissance European supranationalism

The idea of a culturally and politically united Europe was born in Italy before the era of the modern nation-state in Europe. More than the vague and controversial reference to the legacy of the Roman Empire, what is significant is its revival in pre-Renaissance times. Notably, in the early fourteenth century, Dante Alighieri's contribution to Italian identity situated the tradition of Italy as a cultural nation (*'il dolce paese dove il si' suona'*) within a distinctive vision of the global order (that is, a European order).[10] At first glance, this order appears to be an updated version of the supranational *Reppublica Christiana*, which includes the famous 'two suns', the Empire and the Church, each one shaping the European continent through its respective competences and roles. However, Dante's political reference to Augustine's Empire made it possible to overcome medieval limitations, and Dante could imagine a European power even in the absence of the Catholic Church (*'Ecclesia non existente aut non virtuante'*).

Simon de Sismondi and Fernand Braudel underline the Italian link between the end of the Middle Age (the 'See Republics' of Genoa, Venice, Pisa, and Amalfi) and modernity: the decentralized country of one hundred cities and early capitalist and civilian development. Henri Pirenne and, recently, R. Putnam also emphasize the role of cities and their civic culture, rather than the process of nation-building. Francesco Petrarca and other humanist and

---

[9] This interpretation fits with the famous approach of Alan Milward to the early years of European integration: see Milward 1992.

[10] We are thinking of the development of Dante's political thought from *De Monarchia* to the *Divine Comedy*: for a critical presentation see Cheneval 1995: 1–7. Cheneval rightly underlines Dante's relevance and influence beyond his immediate impact.

Renaissance Italian intellectuals, from Leonardo to Michelangelo, shared Dante's vision of Italy as an open cultural nation and emphasized her implications in the vision of a united Europe. In this context, Europe was not seen as a battlefield between competing national political hegemonies, but rather as a complex 'container' (in the sense of Ortega y Gasset, as quoted by Brague 1992) of multiple cultural communication flows, and a network of traders, dialogues, roads, universities, and monasteries, based on the common background of a shared legal Greco-Roman cultural legacy (notably in Roman law), and a lingua franca (Latin).

Twofold cosmopolitanism of Italian intellectuals

This 'cosmopolitanism' (as opposed to nationalism) of the Italian intellectuals took two new forms after the defeat of the precocious traders and bourgeoisie of the northern and central Italian cities, notably after the decline of their political and economic hegemony and the French, Imperial, and Spanish invasions that followed (events which consolidated internal fragmentation and political backwardness for the next three centuries). In a sense, the secularized cosmopolitanism of many Renaissance intellectuals emerged first, because the previous cultural Italian influence lasted for a further century. For example, Machiavelli's famous theory of the modern state was the expression of a contemporary non-Italian (but European) movement of ideas, and the building of sovereign nation-states.

Machiavelli's theory provided a relevant even if fragile Italian blueprint for a diplomatic road to future Westphalian European stability (cf. *Arte della Guerra*). During the three post-Renaissance centuries of Italian political division, Giordano Bruno, Paolo Sarpi, Galileo Galilei, Giambattista Vico, the Verri brothers, Cesare Beccaria, and Francesco De Sanctis among others founded the classical and modern secularized tradition (*la laicità*) that persisted up to the nineteenth century and beyond, in spite of the extraordinary influence of the Catholic Church (Ciliberto 2008). However, during the centuries following the Renaissance, a second kind of cosmopolitan intellectual, the conservative and reactionary wing, emerged from Italy. This branch represented the large international Counter-Reform movement started by the Catholic Council of Trent that quickly spread around the word (notably in Europe and in Latin America). Neither of these major intellectual cosmopolitan philosophies was committed to the construction of Italian nationalism (Gramsci 1975).

A late and elitist national unification

The fragility of the nation-state could only have a negative impact on the Italian role within the European Westphalian balance of power, which subsequently affected Italian ideas of Europe. In the early nineteenth century Giacomo Leopardi drew pessimistic conclusions in his *Le Rimembranze* (1816), due to past failures and the marginal impact of the Enlightenment, about Italy's capacity to increase its European presence to the level of two historical moments: classical Rome and period of the See Republics and Medieval communes. National unity and independence were eventually achieved only very late, through a three-stage, elitist process: from 1861 (Kingdom of Italy), to 1866/70 (Venice and Rome), and eventually through the First World War (Trento and Trieste). Based on the imported French model, a weak nation-state construction was made possible by the refined diplomatic action of Piedmont Prime Minister Camillo Benso, Count of Cavour, within the European concert of powers, rather than by various minority popular national movements. Notably, the Italian secularized republicanism led by Giuseppe Mazzini and Giuseppe Garibaldi was eventually dominated by the hegemony of moderates, although its avant-garde role and symbolism remained important. This was both the effect and the cause of the above-mentioned domestic legitimacy deficit, but it also represented the failure to associate the national independence process with an innovative idea of Europe. Two failed intellectual attempts need to be mentioned here.

Both of the complementary movements led by Mazzini, *Giovane Italia* and *Giovane Europa*, rejected on the one hand the traditional diplomatic approach of Cavour and, on the other, the cosmopolitan dream of Victor Hugo of a United States of Europe (1848): at the Paris Conference of 1848, Mazzini openly criticized Hugo by proposing a 'Europe of nations' as a third alternative to the utopia of importing the American federal model and the reality of the existing European Concert (Mazzini 2001). Even the Catholic ambition of leading the movement of independence represented by Vincenzo Gioberti and the 'Neo-Guelph movement', focusing on the Catholic role within national unity and asserting the idea of an 'Italian primacy' in Europe on the basis of its cultural and religious civilization, was completely marginalized by the reactionary stance of Pope Pius IX after 1850.

The rise of the liberal nation-state (from Cavour to the next prime ministers Francesco Crispi and Giovanni Giolitti) benefited from limited intellectual support inspired by personalities like Francesco De Sanctis and Giosuè Carducci, among others. Italy's new place within the Concert of Europe also did not help to overcome the fragility of the victorious political and intellectual ruling class of the 'Risorgimento'. All in all, the new Italian Kingdom suffered dramatically on one hand from the failed combination of the process of national unity-building with a revised European governance system, and on the other from the failures of both Catholic and liberal/republican attempts to change it.

The fascist degradation of nationalism

The collapse of the liberal state and of the liberal idea of nationalism with the victory of fascism in 1922 were anticipated by their joint failure to 'nationalize the masses', according to the concept of the German historian George Mosse (1974) which became urgent during the social and political crisis following the First World War. Fascism won out as a promised remedy to the failure of liberal elites by providing the state with the support of national emotion, popular legitimacy, and organization of the masses. However, despite the pluralist nationalist intellectual trends of the second decade of the century (including democratic and republican nationalism, D'Annunzio, futurists, etc.), the remedy eventually proved worse than the problem. The disastrous experience of the fascist regime (1922–43) emphasized nationalism by force, as never before in Italian history, constructing a national rhetoric and ideology that drew on Italian experiences as far back as the Roman Empire. Astonishingly, the regime combined several hyper-nationalist traditions of thought (Enrico Corradini, Gioacchino Volpe) with 'state ideologies' such as those of Giovanni Gentile and Alfredo Rocco, together with a rhetorical fascist understanding of European unity as opposed to both Russia and America (Ugo Spirito and Bruno Bottai, among others). The regime's collapse in 1943 at the national level, and in 1945 in the Northern Republic of Salò, discredited the nationalist idea and centralized 'state ideologies' in Italy for many decades.

The problem of continuity and discontinuity in the Italian history of the nineteenth and twentieth centuries is very complex. Several tentative reconstructions exist among liberal historians: for example, on the one hand, Federico Chabod's 'History of the idea of Europe', influenced by Guizot, stresses the process of the gradual civilization of the Concert of European states and the possible creation of a European 'society of states' (Chabod 1961). On the other hand, there is Benedetto Croce's thesis of the two stages of the history of the national idea in Europe: the progressive one, followed by the aggressive and reactionary one. Both Chabod and Croce (1932) fall short of a convincing explanation for the fascist regime. However, both highlight European unity as the best political framework for a post-fascist Italy to achieve reconciliation with its national history and move towards peace. For many decades, Croce's writings emphasized Europe as the place for political liberalism and the 'religion of liberty' to flourish, condemning fascist nationalism as a parenthesis of Italian history.

European unity as a pluralist antifascist idea

A fifth historical element explains why European unity was seen as an antifascist idea, or rather as a pluralist collection of anti-fascist ideas. Of course, it would be wrong to deny and ignore the various local, social, religious, and national motivations that coexisted within Resistance movements (Bobbio 1975; Pistone 1975). However, at least four intellectual streams could be qualified as anti-fascist. Firstly, the European liberal-democratic federalism, with the famous '*Ventotene Manifesto*' written by Altiero Spinelli, Eugenio Colorni, and Ernesto Rossi in 1941, held significant political weight (if compared with British, French, and German federalist thinkers) by combining federalism with the idea of Europe. The European Manifesto corresponds to a tragic idea of history, where firstly a catastrophic vision of the future replaces the optimistic view of the Enlightenment, and secondly, an active pacifism is asserted as a counterpart to a radically negative understanding of the modern sovereign state as a potential cause of 'total war'. Because the Second World War was considered as having put an end to the rules characterizing the *jus publicum europeum* described by Carl Schmitt, a new political theory was required that would combine the decentralization of the state with the supranational unity of states through a federalist construction. The Manifesto focuses on the need to pool state sovereignties within a US-styled federal structure (similarly to the Hamiltonian thought in *The Federalist* and to British federalist thought of the 1930s), against the dangerous fusion of absolute sovereignty and nationalism, typical of Europe and notably (in its extreme form) also of fascist European states.

The project of a European federation is original: on the one hand, federalism could be implemented on a European scale or context, and on the other the European idea could be based on alternative institutional paths. Furthermore, after 1945 and until his death, Spinelli was very active in emphasizing the need for legitimacy from the people, by arguing in favour of a democratic European federation. With regard to the economy, he was also a convinced liberal in the mould of the Richard Cobden tradition.

Secondly, the influence of economic liberalism on Italian intellectuals in favour of European integration after the First World War should also be stressed. In the name of economic liberalism, free trade, and the fight against mercantilism, both Luigi Einaudi, the future president of the Republic (Einaudi 1950; Pistone 1975), and Giovanni Agnelli, the founder of FIAT, championed the European federalist model. They consistently argued against the League of Nations model, accusing it of preserving the national sovereignties of its member states (Agnelli and Cabiati 1918).

Thirdly, liberalism was also combined with an emphasis on social justice within the left-wing tradition, from Piero Gobetti to the Rosselli brothers, killed in France in the 1930s by agents of the fascist secret police but very influential through their intellectual legacy in the anti-Nazi and anti-fascist resistance movement the *Partito d'azione*. This was a liberal-socialist elite formation of prominent intellectuals including Noberto Bobbio, Vittorio Foa, Duccio Galimberti, Ugo La Malfa, and Silvio and Bruno Trentin among others. The secularized Italian legacy of the Risorgimento was able to join forces with European federalism in line with Spinelli's approach, despite significant differences.

What remains to be mentioned, as underlined by the major political philosopher Norberto Bobbio, is that several intellectual ambassadors of a secularized and anti-fascist vision of Europe (Silvio Trentin and Umberto Campagnolo among them) stressed the need for a strong link between federalism at the European (supranational) level and sub-national federalism at the Italian (national) level, as elaborated for example by the legacy of the minority faction of the Risorgimento led by Carlo Cattaneo (Bobbio 1975; Cattaneo 1991). By emphasizing regional and local autonomy, they viewed the project for a federal Italian Republic as part of a federal European Republic. Addressing internal sovereignty and not only its external form both strengthens theoretical consistency and fits with the distinctive (and already mentioned) features of the complex Italian nation. Eventually, the two legacies of centralized Napoleonic culture, imported by the ruling intellectual and political forces of the Risorgimento, and on the other side memories of the authoritarian fascist regime, entered into a final phase of crisis at the end of the twentieth century, even provoking secessionist tendencies in Northern Italy and explaining the late revival of Cattaneo's federalist thought.

A similar emphasis on both sub-national/local authority and supranational European power was shared (albeit in different forms) by Luigi Sturzo, Alcide De Gasperi, and other leaders of the Christian Democrats. In the 1940s and 1950s, Italy witnessed the political and intellectual rebirth of the Christian idea of European unity; however, this medieval legacy was presented in a new liberal-democratic understanding. This Catholic influence has been very relevant, even decisive, in Italy and elsewhere by providing legitimacy for European construction as well as a distinctive intellectual contribution to the concepts of 'subsidiarity' and 'supranationality'. This development has taken on distinctive characteristics, as we shall see below.

The Italian ideology of Europe

These five historical accounts converge in explaining the strength of the Italian commitment to European integration during the First Republic. Was it an alternative identity elaborated by various intellectual movements due to the Italian state's lack of an 'emotional hard core' (Duggan 2008)? It is undeniable that the historical weaknesses of the Italian state are significant, as is the fact that Italian intellectuals were and still are profoundly divided by open controversies regarding crucial aspects of national memory: the North–South division, or the roles of the Counter-Reform movement, the Risorgimento, the fascist regime, and the Resistance. One cannot find the close links present between state and nation in French and English intellectual elites; similarities lie rather with Belgium and the German *Bonner Republik* (albeit for differing reasons). Evidently, there is not a single paradigm for nation-building and diversity prevails in this field, according to the various national cultural contexts.

As far as Italy is concerned, what several historians fail to capture is that these internal controversies and weaknesses paradoxically provided, and to some extent still provide, a distinctive and dynamic balance between the traditions of localism, nationalism, regionalism, and supranationalism (in the form of Europe). Several intellectual philosophies eventually supported the European post-national unity in the framework of the search for a complex political identity.[11] Their impact was exceptionally important and is part of the explanation for why the Italian intellectuals were, to a minor extent after the First World War and especially after the Second World War, more ready than others to support a European political community as a part of a multilevel identity rising from the municipality to the region, the nation, and Europe.

The 'Second Republic' (1992–2008): The limits of the European consensus and the changing intellectual debate

To what extent did the dramatic change of Italian domestic politics occurring in 1992–3 shake the European intellectual consensus achieved throughout the previous decades? At first glance, it appeared that Eurosceptical intellectuals were gaining ground in Italy as they were supported by the emerging and three-time election-winning coalition (1994, 2001, 2008) of centre-right parties led by Silvio Berlusconi. The magnitude of the so-called 'Berlusconian revolution', which transformed the Italian political system from a centripetal and parliamentarian one to a bipolar democracy, and has dominated Italian political, media, and cultural debates for at least twenty years, pulling all the previous republican political cultures out of government, reveals the importance of this question (Tremonti 2008; Tuccari and Armao 2002).

The commitment to the process of further European integration was considered negatively by the centre-right as a consensual pillar of the First Republic's intellectual and political elites, while factual evidence of its shortcomings were strengthening a new approach, to some extent ideologically inspired by the model of mixing extreme economic liberalism with traditionalist values typical of the Anglo-American neo-conservatism of the 1980s.[12] To what extent did this domestic change affect the European debate? While the profile of Italian intellectuals during the First Republic was marked by repeated expressions of disappointment at the insufficient European integration agreed by the Single European Act (1986) and the Maastricht Treaty (1991), the climate changed with the emergence and the victory out of the ruins of the First Republic

---

[11] For a conceptual foundation of this post-national research beyond narrow understandings of sovereignty, see Lacroix 2004b.

[12] See for example the ideological manifesto by the Minister of Foreign Affairs in Martino 1994.

(after the judicial 'Clean Hands enquiry' of 1991–2) of new political and intellectual movements which were to some extent framed by centre-right political waves.[13]

Exploiting Eurosceptical intellectual traditions was also possible because of two practical developments with regard to Italy's role in Europe (Fabbrini and Piattoni 2008). On one hand, the numerous Italian inconsistencies with EC/EU norm-making, as well as the frequent delays in top-down implementation of EC/EU directives at the national level, pointed to the existence of a real problem: behind the ideal consensus was a tangible and growing implementation gap caused by typical deficits of the nation-state. On the other hand, the lack of a bottom-up influence of Italian ideas (and interests) on the EU level provoked frustrations and irrational reactions instead of an analysis of the insufficient coordination, administrative limits, and ineffective state bureaucracy hampering Italy's ability to influence the EC/EU decision-making process. Thus, when passing from discourse to implementation, the perception of superfluous regulations in an increasingly wide range of areas made it possible for several intellectual groups to present the EU as a constraint rather than as a resource, and also as a threat to local, national, and regional interests and traditions – particularly in a decade revealing the negative impact of globalization on Italian interests.

Consequently, a dramatic shift of internal intellectual and political cleavages occurred, to some extent similar to those in the UK: a new Eurosceptical centre-right movement in opposition to a pro-European centre-left coalition emerged. Romano Prodi, the Catholic intellectual and state industry manager, led the centre-left coalition over a period of thirteen years. He benefited from the co-operation of a qualified group of committed political intellectuals of the first federalist Europhile generation, such as Carlo Azeglio Ciampi, Giorgio Napolitano, Giuliano Amato, and Tommaso Padoa Schioppa. This group supported Prodi in his staunch defence of European 'federal orthodoxy' (the Euro and the convergence criteria, the political Union, the process of strengthening and 'communitarizing' the third pillar, etc.).[14] With the support of the Mazzinian president of the Republic, Carlo Azeglio Ciampi, the group obtained an initially positive record by playing the Europe 'card' on the question of Italy joining the common currency, and by reviving the idea and symbols of national unity in the framework of EU unity.

The early intellectual centre-right profile was a true break with the past, putting in question both the Euro and the political Union: the Friedman-oriented

---

[13] Forza Italia, Alleanza Nazionale, and Lega Nord.

[14] Among their books: by R. Prodi and G. Napolitano, president of the Republic since 2006, see Prodi 2000, Napolitano 2002; by Giuliano Amato, internationally renowned professor of constitutional law, twice prime minister and vice-president of the European Convention, Amato 2007; and Padoa Schioppa 2004 for the view of an economist and finance minister.

economist Antonio Martino, an intellectual appointed to the post of foreign minister in the first Berlusconi government (1994), took a strong position against the Euro; the 'Northern League' intellectual and constitutionalist Gianfranco Miglio campaigned against a centralized EU 'superstate' and in favour of a Northern secession from the Italian Republic; the political scientist Domenico Fisichella, a founding member of the post-fascist party (*Alleanza Nazionale*), is the author of publications in favour of a new, more realistic balance of power between national interests and the European Union, as is the right-wing intellectual Marcello Veneziani (2002).

In general, the era of the so-called 'Berlusconian revolution' was characterized early on by combining domestic political transformation with the support of new and various Eurosceptical factions within the broader public, from universities to publishing houses and the media. Important intellectual leaders supported the government by implementing on the one hand a pro-Atlanticist shift within the traditional Italian balance between national interests, European solidarity, and their alliance with the US, and on the other a moderate renationalization of Italian policy-making and of its approach to the EU ('normalization').

International and internal factors explain these developments. The two decades after 1989 witnessed multiple calls for a reconsideration of the place of Italy in Europe, starting with the revision of contemporary history. For example, Ernesto Galli della Loggia founded the 'Il Mulino' book series: *L'identità italiana*. A new revisionism emerged, emphasizing the distinction between the 'hard' German Nazi regime and 'soft' Italian fascism, the need for reconciliation between the two sides of the Italian 'civil war' of 1943–5, the call for commemoration of Tito's persecution of Italians in Yugoslavia in 1945, and rewriting the relevant pages of school textbooks. Leading newspapers such as the *Corriere della sera* engaged openly Eurosceptical columnists. New journals (e.g. *Limes*) revived the nationalist tradition of geopolitics, asserting Italy's interest in the Mediterranean region as opposed to a European commitment, although without any nostalgia for Italian colonialism.

These oscillations were, however, not just a superficial trend combining internal frustrations and imported Euroscepticism. The official discourse about European unity has hardly been challenged, certainly not enough to propel an abstract substitutive identity but to become more mature and less idealistic. In this context, several intellectuals advocated a new kind of Italian republicanism, able to cope both with Northern demands of autonomy and even secession, and the Southern swing towards illegality. This new republicanism was not perceived as necessarily opposed to European unity, but as a means of fostering a new balance between the recognition of regional and national identity and the European perspective (Bodei 1998; Rusconi 1993).

In this context, the notion of Europe in the world as a civilian power assumes a new realistic understanding in the hands of Italian authors, as far from the previous Eurocentric optimist vision of 'gentle power' or civilizing power as it is from the French concept of 'puissance' or the Scandinavian notion of 'normative power'.[15] Civilian power is the expression of historical legacies and internal structural limits (constitutional and military capacity, priority of welfare state) combined with ambiguous international identity needs.

In this context, the Catholic Church (Pope Woytila and notably Cardinal Ratzinger, the future Pope Benedict XVI) attempted to influence directly the cultural debate in Europe by taking hard positions against the European 'Charter of Fundamental Rights' of 2000 and the preamble of the EU Constitutional Treaty of 2004, and by launching a large campaign for a 'Christian Europe', surprisingly supported by J. H. H. Weiler in a book published in Italian (Weiler 2003b). These multiple pressures were able to gain unexpected support even within secularized groups due to a shared perception that European cultural identity was increasingly exposed to internal and external threats because of immigration, Islamic terrorism, and the 'clash of civilizations'.

Finally, on the opposite side of the intellectual spectrum, the extreme left and neo-Marxists (the most renowned being Rossana Rossanda, Danilo Zolo, and Luciano Canfora, among others) were, unlike the French, unable to capitalize on the public's disillusionment with the EU. They were active in criticizing what was perceived as an overly bureaucratic and pro-American European Union with little emphasis on social needs, and in calling for a rejection of the Constitutional Treaty. However, their anti-EU impetus was diminished when Antonio Negri, internationally renowned as an intellectual leader of the anti-global movement (Negri and Hart 2000), openly supported the European Constitutional Treaty in *Le Monde* precisely on the grounds that it was a possible framework for an 'anti-Empire' EU. In this milieu, an alternative and old idea of Europe was also revived, that of a 'Mediterranean Europe' opposed to the current 'Atlanticist Europe' and providing a synthesis of European and Arab culture, evident in shared cultural roots from the 'Alger School' to Southern Europe (Horciani, Zolo, and Giolo 2005).

In concluding the evaluation of the so-called 'Berlusconian Era', the process of 'normalization' of the Italian approach to the EU has shown clear limits, which make it very difficult to compare Italy with the UK and France. In order to explain the centripetal tendencies eventually prevailing after fifteen years of bipolarization of the Italian intellectual and political debate, it is worth mentioning two elements. On the one hand, there is no doubt that the Italian idea of Europe has been challenged and subsequently further developed to cope with the new post-Cold War perception of national interests. On the other, it is widely accepted that Italy is a success story within the EU, as proved by several conclusions of historical and political research. Participation in the integration

---

[15] De Giovanni 2002, Manners 2002, Padoa Schioppa 2004, Rusconi 2003, Telò 2004.

process has been compatible with the predominant Italian preferences and interests, including post-fascist and democratic consolidation (despite the opposition of terrorist groups, several attempts to overturn the governing coalition, and the proliferation of the Southern mafia); unprecedented socio-economic prosperity; and peace and international influence, in spite of the Second World War and the unstable global order.

Moreover, beyond the oscillating ideological and superficial debate of politicians, European integration studies are increasingly established within academic disciplines and multidisciplinary research institutes. The Spinelli tradition of federalist thought endures, while becoming a lasting presence within the scientific and cultural community (Centro Studi sul Federalismo in Turin, AUSE in Pavia, Parma College, Siena University, etc.). Consolidated European think tanks (e.g. Istituto Affari Internazionali, Istituto per gli Studi di Politica Internazionale) actively interact with the national public sphere, especially at decentralized and local levels. Private enterprises and foundations provide more funding for European studies than in many other countries. Moreover, new multidisciplinary approaches within the main academic fields are showing more vitality and maturity for EU integration studies within university institutions than before.[16]

From an Italian perspective, the intellectual debate is an active part of a national complex: after sixty years, the EU system and the achieved consensus look able to constrain extreme domestic changes, hard stances, and unexpected national options by framing them within common EU orientations, provided that they are supported by long-term national tendencies. For example, in 2008, the press and opinion leaders emphasized a trivial opposition between the EU institutions of Brussels (Commission) and Luxembourg (Court of Justice) on the one hand, and, on the other, some of the main decisions taken by the new Berlusconi-led government and its intellectual representatives. Cultural discontinuity was highlighted through phenomena such as Giulio Tremonti's book (Tremonti 2008), which focused on a critical approach to globalization and proposed increased state interventionism (and some trade protectionism), while, as Minister of Economy the same intellectual leader symbolizes the EU-stability; the Lombard temptation of channelling populist pressures against illegal immigration and gypsies, becoming a diffused theme in domestic European politics; the drive to curb the French leadership's power through a preferential relationship with new member states; Emma Marcegaglia's demand, on behalf of Italian industry, to restrain the European role in environmental protection and climate change, which was eventually included in the European

---

[16] For example, in literature: C. Magris; in political philosophy: F. Cerutti, B. De Giovanni, S. Maffettone; in constitutional law: G. Amato, A. Cassese, G. Zagrebelsky; in international political economy:. Paganetto, R. Rovelli, P. Bianchi; in political sciences: S. Fabbrini, F. Attinà, P. Portinaro; in social sciences: M. Ferrera, L. Balbo; in history, A. Landuyt, G. Laschi, among many others.

Council compromise of December 2008. All in all, these trends are compatible with Italian support for the innovative French Presidency in 2008 (Georgia war, financial crisis), opening the EU to further enlargements while maintaining a good relation with Russia, and other developments. The picture of European institutions in Brussels and Luxembourg leading a cultural struggle against a centre-right and Eurosceptical mood coming from Rome would be a wrong conclusion indeed.

Combined with the weight of the EU institutional framework, the legacy of the long-term tendencies and ideas mentioned above was strong enough to provoke a step-by-step Europeanization of extremes, including right-wing parties and intellectuals, and to mitigate previous nationalism and ethnocentric regionalism as well as involving new Eurosceptical factions. The national consensus explains the quickly achieved unanimous support for the parliamentary ratification of the Lisbon Treaty in 2008, and for further enlargement to the Western Balkans and Turkey (with the marginal exception of the Northern League). The serious deficit in implementing the 'Lisbon strategy for a European knowledge society' and the poor funding of universities and research, in line with the low rate of investment by the centre-left government dominated by convinced Europhiles, indicate the chronic limits of the real impact intellectuals can have on the decision-making process.

Conclusion

What is contingent and what is structural within the Italian intellectual debate about the idea of Europe? The Europeanization process in Italy has proved consistent with long-term trends in national intellectual history. According to many scholars, the central reference to the building of a new united Europe after 1945 proved to be the best framework to cope with national interests, in combining the Western alliance with the geopolitical implications of the Mediterranean tradition, as well as socio-economic prosperity with the consolidation of domestic democratic institutions. This largely explains the convergent commitment of many intellectual streams to an imagined Europe over several decades. A lot of evidence shows that the ideal legacies and the complex European intellectual debate are useful not only in explaining the rise of a consensual Italian European ideology, but also in analysing its significant and long-lasting impact in spite of political and institutional discontinuities.

The dramatic changes of 1992–2008 could have jeopardized the continuity of the Italian federalist idea of Europe and, to some extent, opened a new epoch of dilemmas and alternative scenarios, including a second phase of detachment from Europe similar – *mutatis mutandis* – to the analogous moment of the Counter-Reform era denounced by historians such as Ginzburg and Prosperi. A deep ideological crisis cannot be totally excluded. However, in spite of the emergence of new cleavages between governmental policies (environment, immigration, media regulation, etc.) and EU norms, the intellectual legacy of the past still appears to be consolidated and effective in mitigating these cleavages. Similarly to Germany and other countries,[17] Eurosceptical trends were not strong enough to provide an alternative to traditional Europhile approaches. As a consequence, no fundamental discontinuity is taking place: the Italian narrative about Europe is arguably becoming more mature and 'normal', less idealistic and more apt to cope with a dramatically changing European project.

Contrary to the UK (1688), France (1789), and other countries, Italy is a country that has never experienced a revolution, and is a symbol of historical continuity. This does not necessarily mean that the Sicilian novel-writer Tomasi di Lampedusa was still right in asserting that everything changes in order to change nothing. As far as the European narrative is concerned, in the words of Italians, what we are witnessing is a kind of 'passive revolution' (or 'revolution-restoration', according to the suggestion by Edgar Quinet, quoted by Antonio Gramsci with reference to the break of 1789 and – in spite of serious oscillations – its long-term impact on French and European history in the nineteenth century). By 'passive revolution' we mean that a process of conservative 'restoration' can never be a mere retreat (in this case to nationalism), but a new synthesis between innovation and restoration.

The period of 1945–50 remains a fundamental reference for Italy, notably representing both an historical break with nationalism and the revival of a *longue durée* European vocation, where intellectual history is concerned. The recent controversial process of 'normalization' of the Italian intellectual tradition, championing a European united political community, looks set to consolidate a more mature compromise between the ideal legacy and the multiple common challenges of the new century, where the European project is dramatically changing far beyond the early federalist idea of the United States of Europe towards new transnational visions, better fit to cope with a more complex and globalizing world.[18]

---

[17] See the Müller chapter in this volume.

[18] Regarding the new common challenges of a transnational Idea of Europe beyond the federal state and the confederal path, see the first chapter by Nicolaïdis and Lacroix in this book. See also Pagden 2002 and De Giovanni 2004.

Part III

Joiners

7

Mid-Atlantic Musings

The 'Question of Europe' in British Intellectual Debates, 1961–2008*

Georgios Varouxakis

> *'What do they know of Europe who only Europe know?'*
> (Pocock 2005: 288)

Introduction: Stereotypes, myths, and definitions

Michael Oakeshott was asked in the early 1960s at a public lecture at the LSE on British entry to the European Community, 'where he personally stood on the matter'. He is reported to have replied: 'I do not find it necessary to hold opinions on such matters.' The questioner 'thought such Olympian detachment on the part of a professor of political science excessive' (Annan 1990: 400). One of the twentieth century's most eminent political philosophers was, in that instance, either refusing to play the role of an 'intellectual' and pronounce on 'such matters'; or he was not sufficiently interested in the particular question of his country's potential membership of the EEC; or both. The story might at first seem to confirm the two main stereotypes about British intellectuals and Europe. British men and women of letters and academia are habitually thought to be reluctant to pronounce on political issues and be 'intellectuals'. And the British in general are supposed to be – at best – ambivalent about 'Europe' and their relation to it.

* I am grateful to Justine Lacroix and Kalypso Nicolaïdis for their patience and extremely valuable advice. For generously provided help and advice at various stages I am also most grateful to Vernon Bogdanor, Madeleine Davis, Ilaria Favretto, Michael Sutton, Bella Thomas, and Hugh Thomas (Lord Thomas of Swynnerton). None of them is in any way responsible for the shortcomings of this article of course.

But then, like most stereotypes, these two do not stand up to critical scrutiny. Oakeshott's comments were, in fact, idiosyncratic – he was, after all, 'a deviant' (Annan 1990: 387–401). On the first point, Stefan Collini recently challenged the cliché that there are no intellectuals in Britain, or at least (as the argument immediately collapses when challenged) that there are no 'real' intellectuals in Britain, or that, if there are any, they are insignificant and powerless compared to those in other countries. Collini (2006: 45–65 and *passim*) demolishes this 'absence thesis' by showing that there has existed – and still exists – a thriving culture of intellectuals and intellectual activity in a country that sees itself as uniquely inimical to them.

As to the second point, it is not true that the British *tout court* are not interested in their relationship with 'Europe'. Of course there is no gainsaying that 'popular enthusiasm on European matters has been noticeable in Britain only by its absence' (Bogdanor 2005: 700). But things are more complicated as far as the elites (political and intellectual) are concerned. What has generated the perception of lack of interest in 'Europe' is the relative decline of passionate debate on 'the European issue' in British public life in the last decade or so. 'Intellectuals' tend to discuss publicly the issues that are on the political and media agenda, and Europe has been taken off the agenda in recent years.[1] This relative quiet has been the result of an unspoken 'moratorium' which the leaderships of the two main political parties (not least due to pressure from Australian- or Canadian-born press magnates) have been trying to impose on debates on Europe. But that moratorium is, if anything, proof of the strong passions generated by 'the European question' in the UK. It is the fact that debates and divisions on Europe became so sharp, tribal, and vicious in the late 1980s and 1990s, especially within the Conservative Party (Labour had their fair share in earlier decades) that has led to the attempt 'not to talk about Europe'.[2] Things were not so 'quiet' from the 1960s to the 1990s, however, and apparently dormant passions may resurface in the future.

There is no doubting the paramount role that perceptions of the past and certain understandings of the country's history have played in generating the difficulty the British political class have displayed in reconciling themselves with the idea of Britain being – or becoming – just one more 'European' country (Peter Anderson 2004; Daddow 2006; Holmes 1996; Young 1998: 1–2 and

---

[1] At this point we should define the term 'intellectual' itself. Collini (2006: 45–65) has distinguished at least three different senses in which the term 'intellectual' is used. The third is what he calls the cultural sense. The intellectual in the 'cultural' sense is someone who has attained to a position of acknowledged expertise or achievement in some specialized field which gives him or her a degree of cultural authority, a claim to be recognized, and who then capitalizes on this degree of deference or recognition he or she has earned by addressing a broader (non-specialist) public eager for general guidance – addresses them, that is, on issues beyond his or her expertise.

[2] On the bitterness of divisions on Europe within the Conservative camp see, for example, Marquand 2008: 310–15, 323–8; Young 1998: 400–1, 412–71.

passim). The Reformation (and the particular way in which it happened in England) has been seen as a crucial turning point, but the antiquity of British/ English isolationism should not be exaggerated. England (to say nothing of Scotland) was very much part of European movements, developments, and networks in the seventeenth and eighteenth centuries. It was in the nineteenth century particularly that the attitude of isolationism and complacent superiority syndromes became most pronounced. Several factors may be adduced to account for that, including Britain's prosperity and strength at the time, repulsion at the excesses of the French Revolution after 1792, the sometimes overweening pride that resulted from the British role in the defeat of Napoleon, repeated invasion scares, and, far from least, the magnitude of Britain's global empire during the Victorian era.

But besides the consciousness of Britain's power and prosperity, there was, among the Victorian intellectual elite, a particularly *political* source for their sense of uniqueness and complacency. The vast majority of nineteenth-century British liberals were (or became, not least after 1848) convinced that Continental Europeans were not sufficiently liberal, and indeed could not understand what real liberty consisted in (Parry 2006; Porter 1983; Varouxakis 2002). The belief that Britain (or, more often, 'England') was the quintessentially liberal nation surrounded by illiberal Continental nations who were obsessed with uniformity was almost unanimously held in the nineteenth century – and has not yet lost its grip on British imaginations, if one is to judge from the pronouncements of some British Eurosceptics (Scruton 2006: 30).[3]

Such historically formed attitudes were considerably reinforced by the experiences of the Second World War. Not only did Britain resist being invaded. She also played an indisputably major role in defeating the Nazis. And she did so in cooperation with the Americans. Finally, the fact that Britain has not undergone any major constitutional shake-up as a result of violent upheaval since the seventeenth century has had profound effects both on British self-identification as a paragon of political stability and on British attitudes towards constitutional arrangements and constitutional change.

In the following pages I begin by offering a brief historical overview of the attitudes of British intellectuals from the time the debate on 'Europe' began in earnest, in 1961 (when the UK first applied to join the EEC), to the time when Britain's continued membership was confirmed by the result of the referendum of 5 June 1975. Following this, I proceed to examine more recent debates, once British membership itself was an established reality, but the shape and future of

---

[3] In that context, historian Andrew Roberts produced what might be called the 'intellectual' equivalent of 'Up Yours Delors', when he published, in 1994, *The Aachen Memorandum*, a futuristic novel about the British Resistance Movement, fighting against the new Nazi-like Reich which the United States of Europe has recreated. Set in 2045, the novel was (as its author has put it later) 'a dystopian vision of what Britain might turn into if it became a minor satrapy of a vast protectionist, illiberal anti-American, politically correct EU'.

the European entity was at issue. This examination begins with different strands of Euro-federalism represented in British debates by academic political theorists such as Larry Siedentop and Glyn Morgan. This is followed by a brief account of the trajectory on the European issue of early participants in these debates who are still active today (Perry Anderson and Tom Nairn), who turned from major advocates of the EEC into stringent critics, due to the direction it has been taking in the last decade or two. The paper then moves on to consider a completely different strand of 'Euroscepticism', that represented by the long-standing animosity towards the EEC/EU among British conservative intellectuals (Noel Malcolm, Roger Scruton, and – more recently – Niall Ferguson). The longest section is dedicated to British attempts to find 'third ways', as it were, between diverse competing conceptions of Europe. Though very different from one another in what exactly they propose, several participants in British debates fit such a description, including Anthony Giddens, Richard Bellamy, Kalypso Nicolaïdis, Robert Cooper, and Timothy Garton Ash. Finally, in the concluding section, I advance some overall claims about issues such as the role of historians in British intellectual debates on Europe, the convergence of right- and left-leaning intellectuals in defence of the nation, the peculiar position of the UK in relation to the United States, and the relevance of British political traditions and thought to the European Union as it stands today and as it is likely to be in the foreseeable future.

Debates prior to the 1975 referendum

Ideas and projects by political thinkers or 'intellectuals' aiming at different forms of federation, supranationalism, or European unity of one form or another have a long history, and British thinkers have had their fair share of attempts. Some British intellectuals played their part in federalist plans in the interwar period.[4] But I want to focus in this paper on intellectuals' responses to 'the European idea' once a concrete and real prospect of European unity of some form was on the political agenda. This happened with the creation of the EEC following the Treaties of Rome of 1957. Britain did not join the 'Six' then (Ellison 2000). But soon second thoughts started to gain ground. The context was one of deep anxiety about Britain's place in the world (Hennessy 2006: 613–20). The victors of the Second World War came very soon to realize that they had emerged from it an

[4] It has to be noted, however, that some prominent strands of federalist thinking in Britain in the nineteenth and early twentieth centuries were not necessarily in the direction of a European federation, but rather preoccupied with ways in which some form of imperial federation (either of the English-speaking part of the British Empire or broader) would preserve Britain's influence in the world and keep it on the first rank of powers. See, for instance Bell 2007 or Mazower 2009: 66–103; Bosco 1991.

impoverished and visibly diminished power, which had recently lost its empire in a rapid succession of developments.[5] The late 1950s was the time of 'angry young men'; when John Osborne's *Look Back in Anger* and *The Entertainer* were great hits, and when young intellectuals and academics began castigating and sending up 'the Establishment' (Annan 1990: 402–5; Collini 2006: 155–69; Hennessy 2006: 502–5; Marquand 2008: 164–6, 185–6; Thomas 1959). The Suez debacle of 1956 had further accentuated the sense of crisis – and finally brought home the message that it was the US that was now in charge (Hennessy 2006: 458–63). Britain had arguably been in decline since at least the 1890s, and the US had been steadily emerging as a major power since before then, but it was after Suez that it was no longer possible to make believe that Britain remained a leading power. The country was in shock and began to look for a new role (Harrison 2009: 70–122). The British Conservative government of Harold Macmillan decided to request the beginning of negotiations on joining the EEC in the summer of 1961. The application was negotiated in 1961–2 and British entry was eventually vetoed by Charles de Gaulle in January 1963.

What did British intellectuals think of the question of EEC membership? Even before the government's decision was taken, the declaration of the Campaign for the Common Market, chaired by Lord Gladwyn [Jebb], which called on the British Government 'formally and explicitly to declare their readiness in principle' to join the European Common Market, was signed by several academics and writers. Isaiah Berlin, Noel Annan, Maurice Bowra, T. S. Eliot, Rebecca West, A. J. Ayer, Max Beloff, and Hugh Trevor-Roper were among them.[6]

An altogether different kind of response came from intellectuals of the (first) New Left. Stuart Hall and Perry Anderson (1961: 1) undertook to offer the British left guidance on the question in the summer of 1961. They emphasized the close links of the creation of the EEC with American involvement in Europe and with the Cold War and highlighted the very small representation of socialist political forces in the European Parliament and the Commission. The issue of Britain's entry was not purely economic, it was political: a Labour government would not be able to withstand the pressure coming from six other countries that were orientated against the left and therefore would not be able to implement the socialist policies of the Labour manifesto (ibid.: 9–10). They also predicted negative consequences for the Cold War, fearing that 'the harmonisation of foreign policy, will make possible, at least, a single European riposte to any international crisis'. And they took for granted that the single European riposte would coincide with that of America, thereby

---

[5] The mood is described succinctly in Mount 2001.
[6] *The Times*, 26 May 1961. See also Greenwood 2008: 409–12. Lord Gladwyn had been asked to chair the 'Campaign' by the prominent pro-European statesman (later to become President of the European Commission) Roy Jenkins (see Gladwyn 1972: 338).

creating a 'Euro-America' pitted in deadly confrontation with the Eastern bloc (Comecon). But the Common Market would have 'its most far-reaching impact upon the under-developed territories'. Incentives provided by EEC development funds were most likely to lead African regimes to choose 'the path of free-trade and private investment' rather than 'policies of planned investment and controlled industrialisation' (ibid.: 11–13). In the final section, Anderson and Hall discussed potential alternatives to turning to Europe 'as a desperate relief from stagnation'. They proposed to look again at EFTA (all of whose members, except Britain, were neutrals) and, even more, the Commonwealth. They preferred the 'more radical alternative', which 'would certainly involve a realignment of Britain in the world political system...and a turn towards non-alignment in the military and international power struggle' (ibid.: 13–14).[7] This position was in conformity with the 'positive neutralism' advocated by the first New Left.[8]

But there was no complete unanimity in the New Left even then. As early as 1962, the Scottish political philosopher Alasdair MacIntyre (who had not yet left Britain for good and was in his New Left phase) took a position that anticipated the one Tom Nairn (and Perry Anderson) would come to defend in the early 1970s. He thought that it was sad that Gaitskell and the Labour Party were adopting Stalin's 'Socialism In One Country' slogan. Socialism was international. The revolutionary changes involved in the ends of socialism could not be insulated from the outside world. 'Either, as Lenin saw, they expand to an international scale, or they regress.' In a sentence characteristic of the strategy he was proposing MacIntyre wrote:

The last intention of the fathers of 19th-century capitalism was to lay the foundations for the Labour movement; but they did. The last intention of the founders of the Common Market is to pave the way for a United Socialist States of Europe. But I am all for taking them by the hand as a preliminary to taking them by...But that would be tactless. ('Going into Europe: Symposium III', *Encounter*, Vol. xx, No. 2 (February 1963), p. 65).

Another interesting New Left case is that of Raymond Williams. Initially he was equally opposed to both the EEC (as a form of capitalist integration) and the right-wing defence of national sovereignty (Chun 1993: 141; 'Going into Europe: Symposium III', *Encounter*, Vol. xx, No. 2 (February 1963), p. 65). But by 1971 he had come round to preferring ('marginally') the Common Market choice to what he saw as the alternative ('an economic assent to increasing subordination to United States capitalism': 'Going into Europe: Symposium III', *Encounter*, Vol. xx, No. 2 (February 1963), p. 65). By the mid-1970s he had come

---

[7] Given how negative the article was towards EEC membership, it is surprising to read Paul Blackledge (2004: 141) claiming: 'I have already shown that as early as 1961 Anderson had supported European integration as the lesser evil compared to British isolationism.'

[8] See also: Barratt Brown 1961; Chun 1993: 55–6; Kenny 1995: 168–94.

to choose a 'Western European identity' against 'the economic nationalism of the Labour Left' (Perry Anderson 1980: 156; Chun 1993: 141).

But the most sustained treatment of the question came from some of the younger generation of thinkers of the (second) New Left, led in this respect by Tom Nairn and Perry Anderson. They were soon to look at the EEC much more favourably, for instrumental reasons. This was in the context of their belief that Britain was so archaic ('Ukania' was the name Nairn coined to convey this) that Europe would be a better terrain for radical reform.[9] The most comprehensive and straightforward analyses at the time were contributed by Tom Nairn in articles in the *New Left Review* in 1971 and 1972, and a book in 1973 (see references).

On the other hand, at the time of the actual British entry in 1973 and the subsequent referendum on continued British membership (1975), the EEC was still vehemently opposed by some of the old guard of the New Left, notably historian E. P. Thompson and the British section of the Fourth International. Thompson argued in a newspaper article a few weeks before the referendum that he perceived 'a time of unparalleled socialist opportunity' in Britain, if the country stayed out of the EEC. Thompson could glimpse, in England, 'the possibility that we could effect here, a peaceful transition – for the first time in the world – to a democratic socialist society. I mean that we could do this in the next five years, not in the next century.'[10] But others on the New Left had decided, after the failures of the Labour governments of 1964–70 to implement radical change, that 'socialism in one country' would not do and castigated what they saw as the Labour Party's nationalism (Nairn 1973: 97).

A major forum where intellectual debate on Britain's relationship with the EEC was conducted was the monthly magazine *Encounter*. Founded in 1953, *Encounter* 'was for a while a principal medium through which British intellectuals could reach an educated but non-specialist public'.[11] Symposia dedicated to the question of 'Going into Europe' featured in successive issues of *Encounter* (1962–3 and 1971).[12] Most respondents were in favour of entry.[13] There

[9] For an early example see Perry Anderson 1992a [1964].

[10] Thompson's article was published in *The Sunday Times*, 27 April 1975. The issue of Thompson's 'patriotism' has vexed relations among New Left members. See Perry Anderson 1980: 112, 156, 193; Kenny 1995: 180–5.

[11] It was also 'supported by the Congress for Cultural Freedom, an American-funded anti-Communist cultural organization, based in Paris; only in 1967 did it become widely known that the source of funds was in fact the CIA' (Collini 2006: 145–52).

[12] 'Going into Europe: A Symposium': *Encounter* XIX (6) (December 1962), 56–65; XX (1) (January 1963), 53–64; XX (2) (February 1963), 64–74; XX (3) (March 1963), 68–78. The responses published in *Encounter* were all written before the new year and the veto (even those published in February and March 1963). 'Going into Europe – Again?: A Symposium', XXXVI (6) (June 1971), 3–17; XXXVII (1) (July 1971), 18–32; XXXVII (2) (August 1971), 28–42.

[13] According to the calculations of the Editor as stated in the fourth instalment of the 1962–3 Symposium the results were: 'FOR (including 7 tentatively 'for, on balance . . . '): 77. AGAINST: 17. INDIFFERENT, UNDECIDED (etc.): 16' (*Encounter* 1963: 68).

emerged some noteworthy convergences. There was near-consensus that the question was not primarily economic, but rather *political* (and the New Left thinkers discussed earlier agreed on that). Another view that was expressed by many was that, on the issue of Europe, reasons and rational explanations were simply ways of justifying one's prejudices, cultural biases, and gut reactions. It was the latter that ultimately determined people's attitudes. Among those who were in favour, a considerable number agreed that one of the key reasons (and *the* main reason for some of them) was the prospect of entry into the EEC ending British stuffy parochialism. A concern raised by many was that the EEC should not become a protectionist and isolationist club, because in that case entry would damage Britain's links with the non-developed world and not least the countries of the Commonwealth. But the Commonwealth was seen as a real viable alternative to the EEC by precious few (e.g. Iris Murdoch or the economist Nicholas Kaldor). Most thought that Britain had to digest that it was no longer a world empire and that the Commonwealth was 'no more than a social club'. On the other hand, the alternative that was raised as real and serious was that of Britain opting for a closer relationship with the USA rather than joining the EEC (the term '51st Stater' was used a lot in these debates).

The responses in 1971, when Britain had applied for the third time, were no less interesting. Most of those who had already been asked in 1962 had not changed their mind. A noteworthy response came from Ernest Gellner, who (clearly influenced by arguments in *The Federalist Papers*, No. 10) maintained that 'a Western [European] federal union would probably favour liberal stability, by making it that much harder for colonels, generals, saviours, and Guevara-impersonators to seize the centre of power. Federalism adds a dimension to pluralism, it multiplies the countervailing forces.'[14]

A major contributor to the overall debates in 1971 was the Budapest-born Cambridge economist Nicholas Kaldor, who became an influential figure of 'the case against' in the (second) 'great debate' in 1971, not least thanks to his article 'The truth about the dynamic effects', in the *New Statesman* (12 March 1971). Kaldor made an economic case against Britain joining the EEC, arguing, among other things, against the CAP, and predicting that Britain would be unable to compete with the industries of the 'Six' and would be relegated to a kind of northern Sicily dependent on structural funds. Those on the left who argued in favour of Britain's EEC membership had to reckon with and refute 'Professor Kaldor's' arguments (Thomas 1973: 106–7, 145, 184–5; Nairn 1973: 97–8).

The European question stirred passions sufficiently among many British intellectuals and writers to lead to a public intervention in the press *à la française* shortly before the referendum of 5 June 1975. Writers for Europe was

---

[14] The second time round, the result was: 'Of the 67 published replies, a tabulation reveals: FOR (including those tentatively 'FOR,' on balance): 46. AGAINST: 17. INDIFFERENT, UNDECIDED (etc.): 4.'

a campaign in favour of 'yes' organized and chaired by the historian Hugh Thomas and signed by more than two hundred authors and academics.[15]

Post-Maastricht federalist solutions

Once the UK was in the EEC (and decided to remain so as a result of the referendum), the Community (later Union) evolved considerably over the years, and so did British intellectual responses to it. The most widely discussed contribution to debates on 'Europe' by an academic political theorist in the UK to date has been that of Larry Siedentop. An American-born Oxford don, with a particular interest in the political thought of Alexis de Tocqueville (Siedentop 1994), Siedentop made his major foray into debates on the EU with the book *Democracy in Europe* (2000). The very title of the book was Tocquevillian, as was the ambition implied in the undertaking. No less Tocquevillian was the book's claim that there was a great and imminent danger of bureaucratic despotism in Brussels. Siedentop recommended a federal constitution as an antidote against the danger of such despotism. The book was received enthusiastically by reviewers and commentators in Britain, hailed as, at last, 'a proper book on Europe' and the like. It was, however, quite severely criticized by some academic specialists on the EU. Andrew Moravcsik (2001) was especially condemning: 'Despite its factual inaccuracy and political romanticism, Siedentop's anachronistic philosophical purity appeals to many British critics.' That Siedentop's book was received so positively by the British press, politicians, and political pundits, against the judgement of many academics conversant with the EU and how it had developed by the time the book was published, may be accounted for by the fact that there was *so little* of any seriousness at the time to have been written in an accessible register of political thought.

Now, given Europe's striking dependence on the United States (as noted also by Perry Anderson and Tom Nairn – see below, next section), it is not surprising that there are thinkers who put security at the forefront of their discussions of the question of Europe. Glyn Morgan is a Welsh-born political theorist based in the US. Besides being the author of the book *The Idea of a European Superstate* (2005), Morgan (a former journalist) sometimes contributes to the British press (particularly in *The Independent*) on topical issues related to the EU. Morgan's major argument is that justification debates are misplaced, and that security should be more seriously considered as far as the EU's role is concerned. Unless

---

[15] *The Times*, 2 June 1975: 24. See also *The Times*, 3 June 1975: 12. Other members of the Committee of Writers for Europe included Asa Briggs, Anthony Sampson, C. P. Snow, John Gross, Stephen Spender et al., and signatories included Noel Annan, Isaiah Berlin, Herbert Butterfield, Bernard Crick, A. J. Ayer, Max Beloff, Stuart Hampshire, W. G. Runciman, Ferdinand Mount, Harold Pinter, J. H. Plumb, Philip Ziegler, J. B. Priestley, Karl Popper et al.

Europe becomes a unitary sovereign state, it will remain, insists Morgan, weak and too dependent for its security on the United States. Morgan stresses the importance of the notion of non-dependence and professes himself influenced in this respect by neo-republican political theorists, most notably Richard Bellamy.[16]

Eurosceptics of the marxisant left

It may not be particularly surprising that the most vociferous Eurosceptics on the intellectual left today are people who had endorsed Britain's membership of the EEC as a vehicle for socialist reform. These hopes having been frustrated, their support for 'Europe' has turned to bitterness. As we have seen, Perry Anderson, one of the leaders of the 'second' New Left (after 1962) has displayed a long-standing interest in European integration (Perry Anderson 2009). We saw his critical stance in 1961. But at least as of the early 1970s he shared the same analysis as Nairn on EEC membership. In a variety of writings Anderson attacked the unreformed and archaic nature of Britain's institutions and state and predicted that things might change only in a European federation of one shape or another (Perry Anderson 1992b: 351–3). In two essays in 1996, Anderson discussed how the EEC (recently subsumed into the newly created EU) had emerged and what could be surmised about its future by an analysis of its history.[17] He construed the (then) forthcoming monetary union as an implementation of Friedrich Hayek's vision of how a federal Europe could 'mean not a super-state – as Conservatives in Britain fear – but *less* state' (Gowan and Anderson 1997: 130–1). But then, he thought, maybe there was a hidden agenda at least in the mind of Jacques Delors. It was precisely 'the extremity' of the prospect of a deregulated, Hayekian Europe, which

poses the question of whether in practice it might not unleash the contrary logic. Confronted with the drastic consequences of dismantling previous social controls over economic transactions at the national level, would there not soon...be overwhelming pressure to reinstitute them at supranational level...? That is, to create a European political authority capable of re-regulating what the single currency and single-minded bank have deregulated? (Gowan and Anderson 1997: 131).

Anderson was not sure which way things would go in 1996. He was worried, but could still then see reasons to hope that a centralized, supranational Europe might emerge to regulate the market on a grand scale, confounding the hopes

---

[16] This does not mean that Morgan shares the same approach to the EU and its future with Bellamy.

[17] The articles ('Under the Sign of the Interim' and 'The Europe to Come') were published in the *London Review of Books* on 4 January 1996 and 26 January 1996 respectively. They were both included in a volume on 'The Question of Europe' (Gowan and Anderson 1997: 51–71, 126–45).

of British Conservatives. But he seems to have lost hope by the developments of the ensuing decade. Thus in 2007 he came to take issue with recently expressed optimism about the EU, the 'European social model' or the future global role of Europe (Perry Anderson 2007). He had now come to call the EU an 'oligarchic structure', and 'a cartel of self-protective elites'. The hopes of adversaries of European federalism 'that the more extended the Community became, the less chance there was of any deepening of its institutions in a democratic direction, for the more impractical any conception of popular sovereignty in a supranational union would become', had 'come to pass' (ibid.: 7, 16). It was the Hayekian inspiration that had prevailed. Hayek had envisaged 'a constitutional structure raised sufficiently high above the nations composing it to exclude the danger of any popular sovereignty below impinging on it'. For Hayek, electorates in the nation-state 'were perpetually subject to dirigiste and redistributive temptations, encroaching on the rights of property in the name of democracy'. However, 'once heterogeneous populations were assembled in an inter-state federation', as Hayek called it, 'they would not be able to re-create the united will that was prone to such ruinous interventions. Under an impartial authority, beyond the reach of political ignorance or envy, the spontaneous order of a market economy could finally unfold without interference.' According to Anderson, the European Central Bank in Frankfurt 'conformed perfectly with Hayek's prewar prescriptions' (ibid.: 18).

Turning his critical glare to recent tributes to the 'unique role and prestige of the EU on the world's stage', Anderson was even more scathing: 'How independent of the United States is it? The answer is cruel, as even a cursory glance at the record shows. Perhaps at no time since 1950 has it been less so.' After an exposition of what had recently become known regarding European involvement in US 'rendition' practices, Anderson commented: 'What has been delivered in these practices are not just the hooded or chained bodies, but the deliverers themselves: Europe surrendered to the United States' (ibid.: 19–21). A similar attitude has been displayed by Tom Nairn (2004), who vehemently attacked Timothy Garton Ash's arguments and proposals for European–American partnership in his book *Free World* of the same year: 'What Garton Ash is pointing to can be described . . . as a process of general "self-colonisation", the willed prostration of the non-great-power world to the great power.'

Eurosceptics of the right: defining sovereignty, defending the nation

Although 'Euroscepticism' is by no means confined to one particular political camp or party, it is more common today to find the most vociferous critics of the European project among British conservatives. A recent diatribe came from the pen of Scottish Harvard-based historian Niall Ferguson, who, in 2004, predicted the complete collapse of the EU at some point in the not too distant future. According to him, the EU 'is an entity on the brink of decline and perhaps ultimately even of destruction'. Like organizations such as the OECD, one day the EU may 'be no more than a humble data-gathering agency with expensive but impotent officials in the city of Brussels or elsewhere' (Ferguson 2004).

Another Eurosceptic historian who deserves our attention is Noel Malcolm. A highly respected specialist on Thomas Hobbes, Malcolm is also an astonishing polyglot and has written acclaimed histories of Bosnia and Kosovo. As political correspondent and then Foreign Editor of the magazine *The Spectator*, and as a frequent contributor to the *Daily Telegraph*, Malcolm has not lacked opportunities to air his views. His most significant contribution to Euro-debates to date has been the pamphlet *Sense on Sovereignty*, which he wrote in 1991 for the Conservative think tank the Centre for Policy Studies. According to Malcolm's definition: 'Sovereignty means constitutional independence, the exercise of plenary and exclusive political authority in a legal order' (Malcolm 1991). As a corollary of this, '[t]he idea that constitutional independence can be "pooled" is therefore an evident absurdity'. Insisting on the importance of the classic distinction between 'power' and 'authority', Malcolm argued that power could be 'pooled', but authority could not. Rather, '[w]hen the sovereign authority of the United Kingdom is "pooled" in Europe, the sovereign authority of the United Kingdom will cease to exist, because the United Kingdom will have become subject to a higher authority' (Malcolm 1991, 25–6). Malcolm argued that the fundamental change in 'legal authority' had already taken place, with the famous European Court ruling in the case of *Costa* v. *E.N.E.L.*, which established the supremacy of EEC law over national law. What was still left to the states was 'political authority'. If that were transferred to the European level, then the nation-states would no longer be sovereign states.

Malcolm had 'a fundamental objection to the creation of a federal European state'. But that objection was not directly relevant to anything he had said in the pamphlet about the nature of sovereignty. Rather, it concerned 'the nature of a political community'. Winding up with a version of the 'no demos' thesis, Malcolm argued that a European federal state would need to have representative politics on a Europe-wide scale, including European parties, functioning across Europe, for the kind of democratic political institutions achieved in some European nation-states 'over the last hundred years or so' to work. That democratic politics worked very well 'in an established political community, where people share the same customs, political traditions, and, above all, the same language'. But could one really imagine that kind of politics writ large in Europe? 'Can we imagine a London housewife during a Euro-general election watching the leader of her preferred Euro-party on television – a Greek, perhaps, making a rousing speech in Greek?' (Malcolm 1991: 27–30).

Malcolm continued to argue 'The case against "Europe"' (Malcolm 1995). His worst fears were confirmed by the proposed EU Constitution, which he attacked in the press in 2003. His first objection to the Constitution was that it did not settle the question of the respective powers and competences of the Union and the member states once and for all as constitutions are supposed to do. Rather, it read more like a manifesto, a statement of political principles and aspirations ('one of the most disturbingly untypical constitutions ever written'), with the old incrementalism of previous treaties still there. But that was its minor defect. What really exercised Malcolm was an issue he had already raised in *Sense on Sovereignty*: 'The fundamental change here is the very fact that the powers of the European Union, which were previously based on treaties, will now be based on a "constitution". With this change, the EU crosses the Rubicon, from something that could not legally be considered as a state to something that most definitely can.' The authority of the EU would thenceforth be located in its own governing document. Any disputes about that authority would have to be dealt with 'not under international law, but by the EU's own constitutional court – whose powers will themselves be derived from the EU's own authority'. Thus, '[t]he central problem is the sheer fact of its being a constitution. For, in the political realm, only states have constitutions – and the definition of a sovereign state is that its own constitution is not subject to the authority of any higher constitution' (Malcolm 2003).

The philosopher Roger Scruton has been a consistent defender of the nation in general and of England in particular (Scruton 2004; also 1980, 1990, 2005, 2006; Dooley 2009: 149–78). He stands for what David Miller (2000: 103–4) calls 'communitarianism of the right'. Scruton has always been vigilant against England-bashing. He has coined the term 'Oikophobia' to describe the condition ('oikos' in Greek means home: an 'oikophobe' is the opposite of the 'xenophobe', in Scruton's register). He does not avoid using some spurious arguments, including the classic one of – at least implicitly – talking of the European Convention of Human Rights and the Strasbourg Court as if they were EU-related or imposed on Britain by the EU, thus confounding institutions and documents emanating from the Council of Europe with those of the EU (Scruton 2004: 31–2).

Although I classified them under the same section, I do not mean to lump Malcolm and Scruton together. Scruton's emphasis is on the need to preserve – or rather, reclaim – *England* and its way of life (Scruton 2000; 2004: 19–21). The arguments against the EU, the UN, the WTO, and other forms of 'transnational legislation' are enlisted in the battle against 'the undoing of England' that he fears has been the main aim of various 'oikophobes' (Scruton 2004: 34). Where there is convergence between the two thinkers is in the argument that we need nation-states, that political authority should reside with them and not be handed over to transnational or supranational organizations and that any alternatives to the nation-state are dangerous.[18]

Third (and fourth) ways on Europe

The most densely populated category in British debates is what could be called 'third ways' of one sort or another. What is meant by 'third ways' in this section is attempts to find the right balance and combination of merits between competing conceptions of Europe, be they (these latter) federalist versus nationalist, cosmopolitan versus nationalist, or Euro-Gaullist versus Euro-Atlanticist. To start with the intellectual most associated with the very term 'third way', Anthony Giddens has displayed a strong interest in Europe. A renowned academic sociologist, for many years Professor in Cambridge and then concluding his academic career as Director of the LSE, he has also been highly active in public interventions, think tank activity, writing for the press (in several countries), and advising prime ministers. He was considered Tony Blair's guru, as the main advocate of the 'Third Way' set of ideas. Currently Giddens is heavily involved in the activities of the think tank Policy Network. Europe and matters European loom large in Policy Network's concerns and activities. Giddens sometimes makes public interventions à la Habermas, such as the articles he co-signed with Ulrich Beck (Giddens and Beck 2005). And in 2007 he published *Europe in the Global Age*.[19]

Giddens defines the EU 'as a democratic association (or community) of semi-sovereign nations' and describes Europe as 'a new type of cosmopolitan project'. In the spirit of his earlier book *The Third Way*, where a chapter was dedicated to the idea of 'cosmopolitan nationalism', he is reluctant to do away with the nation: 'The perspective of the nation is the condition of a cosmopolitan Europe', according to Giddens. He argues for the importance of diversity in Europe and wants Turkey in. Rehearsing the proposals of the Third Way, he wishes to see combined economic performance leading to economic growth with high levels of social protection and equality (as exemplified by the Nordic nations).[20] One might comment that all this sounds good and well, but that not

---

[18] Having said this, Scruton's concern is not, strictly speaking, with a nation-state, but rather with a nation (England). He makes no secret of his understanding of Britain as an extension of England (or, to put it differently, of England as the core nation of the UK).

[19] Giddens 2007: 199–230. See also Giddens, Diamond, and Liddle 2006.

[20] Without wishing to imply any other similarities with Giddens' views, another defender of the 'European social model' should be mentioned here. I am referring to the British-born historian Tony Judt – Professor at New York University and Director of the Remarque Institute. Besides being a distinguished historian of France, Judt developed a strong interest in Central and Eastern Europe. In 1996 he published the widely commented-upon short book *A Grand Illusion? An Essay on Europe*, where he warned against exaggerated expectations on the part of (recently post-communist) Central and Eastern European countries in terms of what they

much original or concrete intellectual substance has so far been put into these rather vague proposals.

A third way between the nation-state and federalist models is also propounded by the most prolific British academic political theorist working on normative political theory on the EU in recent years, Richard Bellamy. Bellamy has argued (with Dario Castiglione) that the best way forward for Europe is neither a universalistic 'cosmopolitan patriotism' model nor a communitarian-nationalist model but rather what they call a 'cosmopolitan communitarianism' (a Civic Europe of multiple communities involving variable geometry).[21] Drawing on the neo-Roman republican tradition rediscovered by Quentin Skinner and Philip Pettit, Bellamy and Castiglione 'emphasise structural as opposed to legal mechanisms as the key factor of European constitutionalism – most particularly the balance and separation of powers produced by the European Union's unique mix of intergovernmental, supranational and transnational decision-making mechanisms'. They argued that it is 'the plurality of demoi and legal systems that have both legitimized and fostered European integration' (Bellamy and Castiglione 2004: 190). Bellamy has also argued that rather than either a rights-based model or a popular sovereignty model, the best model of constitutionalism for the European Union is a third, common-law model that employs elements of each. Before the proposed European Constitution was rejected by French and Dutch voters Bellamy was arguing that Europe needed not a constitution, but 'an evolving system of mixed government that gives voice to the various interests and values found within the Union and fosters their working together to identify common, public interests' (Bellamy 2004).

After the rejection of the Constitution, Bellamy criticized the analyses both of 'strong advocates' of the Constitution (and the idea of demos formation through 'constitutional patriotism') and of weak proponents who portrayed the Constitutional Treaty as a mere tidying-up exercise. What he proposed instead was 'bringing the Constitution back home' in the sense of increasing accountability to *national parliaments* (Bellamy 2006a, 2006b). Another contributor to British debates who has advocated a 'third way' (explicitly) has been the Oxford-based academic Kalypso Nicolaïdis, not least with her advocacy of the notion of a European 'demoi-cracy' (Nicolaïdis 2003a, 2003b).

---

could expect from a 'return to Europe' based on a historical comparison with the circumstances of Western Europe after the Second World War. Judt continued to reflect on Europe's past, present, and future in his major book *Postwar: A History of Europe since 1945* (2005). And, not least, he has made some original and distinctive contributions to discussions on Europe in various shorter essays in recent years (see, for instance Judt 2008). One of the features of his most recent contributions was a defence of – and optimism about the viability of – the 'European social model' as compared to the American.

[21] For a criticism of this position see Lacroix 2002. For the debate that followed see Bellamy and Castiglione 2004; Lacroix 2004a.

Some original contributions to British debates have been made by the senior diplomat and strategist Robert Cooper. Cooper was a British diplomat until 2002. After that he became Director-General for External and Politico-Military Affairs at the General Secretariat of the Council of the European Union (an insider, that is, working for Javier Solana, High Representative of the EU's Common Foreign and Security Policy). Cooper meanwhile has been performing the role of public intellectual, writing (in a strictly personal capacity) articles in newspapers and magazines (such as *Prospect*), producing interviews, lectures, and books. According to him, Europe could be seen as a 'voluntary empire'. He has used this expression in order to challenge people out of conventional assumptions about nation-states and supranational entities. If nations arose out of the break-up of the European empires, the nation-states of Europe are now assembling themselves in a new non-national framework that is comparable to an empire, the difference being that Europe is a non-coercive construct. Rather, it is a voluntary empire which each of the nations chooses to join. This is a teasing way of getting people to think about the post-national framework. For one of Cooper's main contributions has been to come up with a division of the contemporary world into three categories of states: pre-modern, modern, and post-modern states. Pre-modern states are what some might call 'failed states' like Afghanistan before 2001 (and, alas, perhaps still) or Somalia today, many fear. Modern states are states that still think and behave in traditional terms of power and *raison d'état*, such as the US or Russia for instance. The states of the EU exemplify and in many ways define the third category: 'post-modern states' are those states that have embraced as their guiding principles: cooperation; mutual interference; and a heightened sense of morality in international affairs.

Cooper rejects the idea of a European super state. 'It is curious', he writes, 'that having created a structure that is ideally adapted to the post-modern state, there are still enthusiasts who want to destroy it in favour of an idea which is essentially more old-fashioned' (i.e. the 'modern' state, in his terminology). But Cooper is fairly convinced that Europe *can* and *must* lead the way in terms of dealing with the new threats of the contemporary world. He is credited with having convinced Tony Blair to push for a European military capability. He advocated the need for a European army, as post-modern nations need muscle to defend themselves when they deal with 'pre-modern' (or 'modern') states. In this context, Cooper advised Europeans to get used to the idea of 'double standards' in international dealings, depending on who one is dealing with. We keep the law amongst ourselves, but when in the jungle, we may have to use different standards, is the idea (Cooper 2000, 2003).

A major contributor to British Euro-debates is Timothy Garton Ash, who describes himself as a *'spectateur engagé'* and a 'historian of the present'. He is Professor of European Studies at Oxford University and also writes frequently in the mainstream press (he has a widely syndicated weekly column in *The*

Guardian). His books on Germany and Central Europe in the 1980s and 1990s have received ample praise even by ideologically inclined critics.[22] He is often in the company of politicians both in Europe and in the US and declares himself 'a genuine liberal internationalist'.[23] His book *Free World* (Garton Ash 2004) made him appear to many as 'one of the most authoritative voices of Atlanticism, an ardent advocate for the enlargement of Nato and the European Union alike'.[24] He has said that in his book and overall work he wanted to give 'a warning against a definition of Europe as not-America or America as not-Europe (both serious contenders during some of the George W. Bush presidency years). The new common strategy that we need should be based on an analysis of common interests.'[25] He insisted that he did not preach the traditional 'special relationship' between Britain and the US but argued that '[f]ar from nursing the treasured exclusivity of our Special Relationship ... we should want every country in Europe to have a relationship with the United States as close as ours'. Thus 'the bridge we need is one between the *whole* of Europe and America' (Garton Ash 2004: 199). Discussing Britain's strategic options he identified four: '1. regain independence; 2. choose America; 3. choose Europe; and 4. try to make the best of our intimate relations with both America and Europe' (ibid.: 34–5). He made no secret of his preference for the fourth option: 'to try to preserve what can still be preserved of British independence in an increasingly interdependent world, maintain close ties with America *and* be fully in Europe'. He wrote that he 'might be tempted to call this the fourth way, were it not for the fact that the idea of a "third way", as revived by ideologists of the post-Cold War liberal left and popularized by Tony Blair, has met such widespread scepticism, mounting to derision'. Garton Ash added that, '[u]nlike the "third way" this fourth option is not some vague ideological construct. It is what most British governments have in practice more or less continuously attempted to do since, in 1961, Harold Macmillan made what he called the "grim choice" to apply to join the European Economic Community' (ibid.: 34–5).

During the year 2007 – marking the fiftieth anniversary of the signing of the Treaty of Rome – Garton Ash wrote extensively in *The Guardian* and elsewhere of the need for the EU to have an 'overall story that Europe wants to tell' and new ways of telling it (Garton Ash 2007a). The gist of Garton Ash's proposed narrative for Europe as it emerged in 2007 was that Europeans should not pretend to have the same past, on the model of mythopoeic historical constructions of nineteenth-century nationalism. Such teleological mythologies would not work, as the pasts of different European nations as well as their

---

[22] Anderson 2005: 60–100. Garton Ash's earlier books include *The Polish Revolution* (1984), *The Uses of Adversity: Essays on the Fate of Central Europe* (1989), *We the People* (1990), *In Europe's Name: Germany and the Divided Continent* (1993), *The File* (1997), *History of the Present: Essays, Sketches and Dispatches from Europe in the 1990s* (1999).
[23] Hilton 2005.   [24] Krastev 2004.   [25] Hilton 2005.

respective paths to 'Europe' were very different. Equally he rejected the other major component of nationalism-building narratives of the past, hatred of an 'other' – be it Islam or the United States, in Europe's case. Rather than taking any of these routes to 'Euronationalism', he argued that Europeans do aspire to some shared goals and that they 'can construct a common political narrative in terms of our progress towards those shared goals and the distance we still have to go'. The six goals he (and his website) proposed are: Freedom, Peace, Law, Prosperity, Diversity, and Solidarity (Garton Ash 2007b, 2007c). He conceded that they were not goals peculiar or exclusive to Europe but argued that most Europeans would agree on them. The question some may want to ask here (I can well imagine Roger Scruton raising it) is, would most Europeans be prepared to die for them?[26]

Conclusion

A number of conclusions can be drawn. Firstly, it is striking how many of the most vociferous participants in British debates on Europe are historians. This – besides possibly reflecting my own biases – may not be unrelated to the role of history in British culture in general and in British elite culture in particular.[27]

Secondly, there is a clear convergence in recent British debates on the question of the need to preserve the nation between conservative thinkers such as Malcolm and Scruton on the one hand, and left or centre-left thinkers and writers on the other. The most sophisticated and sustained defence of nationhood by a political theorist in Britain since the 1990s has been contributed by David Miller (1995, 2000, 2007), from the social-democratic left of the political spectrum. And a similar argument generated major discussions in the periodical and newspaper press when it was made by the Editor of *Prospect* magazine, David Goodhart (2004, 2006, 2008), who came out in defence of what he called 'progressive nationalism'. The theses of both Miller and Goodhart boil down to the argument that national allegiance is indispensable to progressive, left-wing politics of welfare and redistribution, because people will not accept the burdens of taxation and welfare if they do not feel a strong identification with those who might be the beneficiaries of such schemes. The difference between left and right in this respect is that the arguments coming from the left that I am referring to are not directed against the EU, but rather against cosmopolitan arguments more generally. On the other hand conservative authors, while

---

[26] For a selection of articles on Europe written during the last decade see Garton Ash 2009: 53–148.

[27] I am grateful for this idea to Richard Bellamy who raised this issue during the session at which my paper was presented at the first European Stories conference in Brussels.

rejecting cosmopolitanism in general, raise vociferous objections against the EU in particular.

Thirdly, the historical examination of debates among intellectuals on Europe and Britain's relationship with the EEC/EU proves particularly revealing as far as one major issue is concerned, namely Britain's position vis-à-vis (or between) America and Europe. When the debate began seriously in 1961–2, Britain was a country in a deep crisis of confidence, bewildered about its 'role' in the world. The loss of Empire was too recent for it not to loom large in public consciousness. Although the vast majority of the intellectuals who publicly expressed views on Britain's application were not strategists or specialists in geopolitics, it is striking how many of them discussed Britain's need for a new international role or for a wider domain where Britons could act and flourish, as a replacement for the Empire. 'After contracting for so long, our immediate world may begin to enlarge. There may again be a larger stage on which Englishmen could play their parts', as Michael Young put it (*Encounter* 1962: 61).

Thus, Europe was seen as a necessary substitute for the lost empire by some. But others saw another option. It has been the so-called 'special relationship' with the United States (so special that only one of the two sides knows it exists, as Helmut Schmitt is reported to have said of it: see Garton Ash 2004: 199) that has decisively shaped British debates and attitudes. And there has been much talk of 'the English-speaking peoples' or the 'Anglosphere' in Britain throughout the period under consideration.[28] As the historian Max Beloff put it at the beginning of these debates, it was ultimately a matter of one's 'aesthetic preferences', and the options were clear: 'There are extremists on the one side who would presumably prefer to see Britain engulfed in some kind of extended Communist world empire; there are extremists on the other wing who cherish a nostalgia for the imperial Britain of the past. But for the broad middle band of British intellectuals I suppose the real choice is between a European and an American orientation' (*Encounter* 1962: 63). The dilemma has not gone away. As Garton Ash has recently reminded us, it is not an issue only for Britain, but for all European countries. They all have to decide what they want their relationship with the *hyperpuissance* to be.[29] In Britain, however, this dilemma is more acute and complicated due to the lures of the alleged 'special relationship' and the temptation to play Greeks to the American Romans, as a source of 'vicarious greatness'.

Finally, there is a curious irony in the perception of Britain as a reluctant European and 'an awkward partner', and of British intellectuals as being

[28] For more on 'Anglospherism' see Garton Ash 2004: 15–53 and *passim*. One cannot help remembering what Matthew Arnold was castigating in the late nineteenth century as 'plans of vicarious greatness' on the part of the 'devotee[s] on Anglo-saxonism – those who thought that it did not matter if Britain were to decline because her offspring in America would take over the leadership of the world (cf. Arnold 1960–77, Vol. V: 27).

[29] For the US as *hyperpuissance* see Védrine and Moïsi 2001: 6.

ambiguous about Europe. British intellectual debates on Europe since 1961 have in fact been rich and stimulating. I would also argue that they are especially pertinent to the future of Europe. If there is such a thing as a British intellectual tradition (or if there is anything peculiarly British about British intellectual debates and political thought), it is widely said to be a willingness to compromise, a refusal to push all ideas, values, and principles to the extremes of their logical conclusions without regard for competing ideas, values, and principles that might have to be taken into account and combined with them. Already in the nineteenth century, John Morley (1874) complained that there was a danger that the English might overrate the value of 'compromise'. But a mindset used to compromise and intellectual untidiness may be an invaluable asset in dealing with the European Union of twenty-seven (or more) member states, including countries as different as Britain, Sweden, Bulgaria, and Cyprus. In the intellectually fertile decade of the 1820s, the French historian (and later statesman) François Guizot argued most emphatically that the source of what he saw as the greatest asset of European civilization (its progressiveness) was its irreducible diversity and messiness (its being 'variée, confuse, orageuse': see Guizot 1985: 73–93; Varouxakis 2000: 27–39). Among all the attempts to identify a distinctly 'European' way, intellectuals and politicians would do well to take note of Guizot's insight in this respect. And it is here that the British might have more to offer than other countries or intellectual traditions.

For the political thought and intellectual and constitutional traditions of a country that tolerates diversity, untidiness, and flexibility as much as Britain may hold important answers for today's Europe. A country that professes to be simultaneously one nation as well as four nations as well as a model multicultural society; which has different legal systems and educational arrangements applied to different parts of its territory; which has both a unitary parliament and government as well as three separate regional/national parliaments (in Scotland, Wales, and Northern Ireland) – to say nothing of peculiar jurisdictions such as the Channel Islands; which ultimately refuses to 'choose' between America and Europe but prefers to be both European and Atlanticist; in which multiple identities (Scottish-British, English-British) are common and encouraged; in which several flags and football teams are 'national'; which is known by different and disputed names;[30] such a country is either deeply troubled and about to break up, or a model for the future of an ever more complex and irreducibly diverse Europe. Straddling such a fractured state of affairs is a British specialism. To that extent, the inconclusiveness, messiness, ambivalence, willingness to combine and compromise, and flexibility that characterize British political culture in general and British intellectual debates on Europe in particular, might be not a marginal and idiosyncratic case, but rather the way forward.

---

[30] The list of such peculiarities could go on if it were not for the word limit!

8

European Stories as National Narratives
Irish Intellectuals on Europe

Katy Hayward

The 'European stories' told by public intellectuals in Ireland commonly share a defining trait: they have the Irish nation at their beginning, at their centre, and at their conclusion. In these discourses, 'Europe' is at times a concept and other times a context, but in all cases it serves to validate a *national* narrative or project. This was evident in the utopian ideals propounded by independence movements prior to the foundation of the Irish state in 1922, it was so in the campaigns around the referendum on EEC accession fifty years later, and it is still the case in all discussions on Ireland's EU membership broadcast from the studios of RTÉ.[1] The nature of intellectual debate about Europe in Ireland has thus been largely determined by the predominant concerns of building and developing the Irish nation-state. In Ireland, such concerns emanated from a desire to shake off the mantle of post-colonialism, with its patchwork pieces of economic dependence, territorial partition, and cultural vulnerability. Thus, to investigate the nature of Irish intellectual debate about Europe is, by necessity, to trace the path of maturation in official national discourses.

As building the nation-state has been the priority, so Irish intellectuals' approach to and, in the main, support for European integration have been mediated through national(ist) discourses. All debates about EU membership, from all quarters, have been conducted around particular readings of national identity, integrity, and interests, and correlated claims as to how these would be best preserved. As a consequence, the need to protect Irish military neutrality, for example, has featured in 'No' campaigns in every Irish referendum on an EU treaty, regardless of the actual remit of the treaty for European foreign and security policy. For the 'Yes' side, which has enjoyed the support of the largest political parties and the majority of public (specialized) intellectuals, the

---

[1] Radio Telefís Éireann, the national broadcaster.

nationalist rationale behind pro-Europeanism is best summarized under the slogan that has adorned many a referendum poster: 'Europe is good for Ireland'. Indeed, much of the warmth bestowed on the popular image of a Europe in which Ireland 'belongs' was fostered through bipartisan political discourse which brought together fundamental tenets of Irish official nationalism with an integrationist agenda. This extension of national narratives into European stories by Irish intellectuals in particular constitutes the focus of this chapter. Before considering the details of these discourses, it is necessary to outline the position and nature of public intellectualism in Ireland.

Intellectuals in Ireland

Disparate and disappearing

There are two crucial qualities of Irish intellectualism that differ from common experience in continental Europe and which have had a profound effect on the public role played by intellectuals in national debate. First, it is not possible or even useful, on the whole, to identify distinct and classic 'schools of thought' in Irish intellectual debate. Whilst some intellectuals may be loosely associated with others in terms of their generational peers or political 'leanings' (a phrase, in its ambiguity, that is generally more apt in the Irish case than the term 'ideology'), their role is not generally considered in the context of a philosophical tradition as it might be recognized elsewhere in Europe (Meagher 2001). This is, in part, due to the predominance of the 'national question' in Irish intellectual debate. For example, in her overview of Irish intellectual thought in Ireland, Denise Meagher (2001) categorizes the contributions of individual scholars under the headings 'post-colonialism', 'revisionism', and 'feminism'. Given the nature of intellectual debate in Ireland, even feminist critiques have concentrated on reinterpreting and rebalancing Irish national stories rather than on turning the focus around to the wider context. The other reason for the absence of intellectual traditions with clear European parallels is that scholarly contributions to national debates tend to be recalled and assessed in terms of key personalities. This is also true in intellectual positions on European integration, the array of which would be better represented by a brief list of names (including Anthony Coughlan, Desmond Fennell, and Garret FitzGerald, for example) than a philosophical spectrum. Maurice Goldring (1987) has described this phenomenon as 'personalised intellectualism'. This may be in part due to changes of opinion on the part of the individual thinker over time,[2] a corollary of

---

[2] As is famously so in the case of Cruise O'Brien, the left-wing intellectual-cum-Irish-diplomat whose distaste for Irish nationalism led him to become a member of the United Kingdom Unionist Party in 1996 only to resign and rejoin the Irish Labour Party ten years later.

being a relatively small country with tight and overlapping social networks, or because of a certain amount of anti-intellectualism that lingers in Irish political culture.[3]

The second distinguishing characteristic of Irish intellectualism is that a significant proportion of those most critical and/or visionary about the Irish nation in its wider context leave Irish shores and speak to it and its needs from abroad, following in the footsteps of predecessors such as Shaw, Wilde, Joyce, and Beckett, to name but a few. It is curious that the reversal in migration flows that Ireland experienced in the late 1990s did not appear to extend so far as to the intellectual 'community'. Indeed, some departed Ireland as the Celtic Tiger arrived. Many of the most notable Irish intellectuals, particularly those who directly and conscientiously challenge dominant Irish nationalist discourses, make their contribution from a position outside the island of Ireland. Today this includes academic scholars from various disciplines, such as the historians R. F. Foster and Joseph Lee, the political theorist Philip Pettit, the sociologist Gerard Delanty, the literary critics Seamus Deane, Luke Gibbons, and John Wilson Foster, and the philosopher Richard Kearney.[4] The audiences and readership they address are, as a consequence, rather less likely to be Irish policymakers or voters than students and scholars of Irish Studies in universities in Uppsala, Notre Dame, Liverpool, or Melbourne. Of those intellectuals who have stayed in Ireland, it is notable how few have instigated, or even directly engaged with, public debate about the European Union (especially as one of twenty-seven member states) and Ireland's place within it.

Cultural authority and the communication of 'Europe'

If public intellectuals by definition possess 'cultural authority' (Collini 2006),[5] intellectuals in Ireland have been granted their status due to particular priorities and conceptions of nation-building in the twentieth century.[6] Intellectuals' engagement with nation-building was as much a cultural as a political affair

[3] For example, Joe Lee (one of many Irish intellectuals who have made a remarkable contribution to Irish Studies despite having made the decision to emigrate) has identified in Ireland 'a feeling that there is something suspicious about the person that . . . seeks to transcend the boundaries of conventional specialization, so reassuring to the dependent psyche' (Lee 1989: 636).

[4] Before he himself emigrated to Boston, Kearney mused that, although James Joyce left Ireland to live on the Continent and had his literary alter ego Stephen Dedalus chiding nationalism as a mere 'afterthought of Europe', Joyce remained proud to be an Irishman in foreign company (Kearney 1984: 11).

[5] In a similar vein, Richard Posner describes intellectuals as 'cultural critics who write with a political edge and aim at a non-specialist audience' (Posner 2003: 20, n. 6).

[6] Liam O'Dowd has put it even more strongly, arguing that, in the Irish case, 'the socio-political role of the intelligentsia continues to be structured fundamentally by the lack of co-incidence between state and nation, in other words, by the problem of nationalism' (see O'Dowd 1996: 15–16).

169

for these elites (Hutchinson 1987). In the Irish case, this has meant an emphasis on the Irish 'imagination',[7] an emphasis on Catholicism, and an emphasis on national interests and state-building. Thus, intellectuals valued in Irish national culture traditionally included poets and writers, priests and theologians, policy-makers and scholars. The contributors and the contributions to intellectual discussion have altered according to the priorities of the national political leadership and dominant social culture. O'Dowd's analysis of this connection led him to contend (after the study of modern French intellectuals by Debray 1981) that the key institutional arena for intellectual activity in Ireland shifted from church to state in the 1960s, only for both to be replaced within a generation by the media as the dominant cultural apparatus (O'Dowd 1985, 1996: 14).

Certainly, under Eamon de Valera's premiership (from the 1930s through to the 1960s) the ecclesiastical influence on policy-making affected most intellectual contributions, be it by those speaking from within the Church (including the numerous humanities and social science professors in the National University of Ireland who were ordained Catholic priests) or by those who were reacting (either positively or critically) to its precepts (Garvin 2005). By the turn of the twenty-first century, the Celtic Tiger had replaced Mother Church as the source of ideals to be embraced and practices to be adhered to. As Fanning (2008: 226) puts it, 'the pursuit of economic growth became the defining nation-building project'. Economic transformation in Ireland further reduced the prominence and acceptance of intellectual paradigms (particularly from left-wing or Catholic quarters) and, indeed, of public intellectualism in general. Today, representatives of the Catholic Church are rarely invited to contribute to national debates, civil servants are not expected to perform a role that is either public or intellectual,[8] and most Irish politicians who might befit the label of 'intellectual' now speak from the position (or age, as in the case of the inimitable Michael D. Higgins) of official (if not actual) retirement. The common – perhaps defining – characteristic of most public intellectuals in contemporary Ireland is that they are (or at least have been) academics by profession.

Furthermore, the public role of 'intellectual' has been replaced by that of 'commentator' (usually journalists, former politicians, business leaders) or 'expert' (most frequently, economists and historians, with the occasional political scientist). The assortment of commentators and experts who speak on 'Europe' is particularly slim and the scope for their analysis is tightly confined. Individuals with the knowledge and capacity to debate the subject of EU integration

---

[7] Kearney 1984 argues that a preoccupation with the 'Irish imagination' has led to a neglect of the important, deep-rooted intellectual traditions in Ireland and their European heritage.

[8] In contrast to the innovative contributions by individuals such as T. J. Barrington of the Institute of Public Administration, T. K. Whitaker in the Department of Finance, and Noel Dorr in the Department of Foreign Affairs in the latter half of the twentieth century.

rarely get the opportunity to do so in a public realm, and when they do it is invariably in the context of a referendum on an EU treaty (either forthcoming or failed – there is little discussion *after* ratification). At such times, all broadcast contributions to the debate are categorized as being on one side or another[9] – there is no room for ambiguity or what Posner (2003: 5) describes as a 'respect for the complexity of problems'. As a consequence, specialized intellectuals invited to speak on 'Europe' must decide which position, either 'Yes' or 'No', they will speak from. The lack of deliberation in, and even detailed telling of, 'European stories' in today's public sphere belies the rich European dimensions of Ireland's intellectual heritage.

European dimensions of Ireland's intellectual heritage

Many of Ireland's most influential thinkers and national story-tellers have been shaped by practice and ideas on the Continent. Direct experience of 'Europe' was common in times past; many Irish 'saints and scholars' who lived and studied on the Continent did so as a result of British colonial rule in Ireland – for example, the impact of penal laws on Catholic education (Kearney 1984: 14). Interestingly, this movement was not only one way, and one of the first scholars to write on the subject of Irish society and the devastating effects of British policy was the French social reformer, Gustave de Beaumont (2007 [1839]). More recently, the philosopher Richard Kearney was influenced by contemporary continental philosophy, particularly that of Paul Ricoeur. He studied in Paris before returning to Dublin to become the public intellectual who engaged most directly with the need to define European values and to respond to their implications for Irish national culture and politics.[10] His co-founder of *The Crane Bag*, the Benedictine monk Mark Patrick Hederman, also studied philosophy in Paris under Emmanuel Levinas. In the present day, a survey of the biographies of many of the most eminent Irish novelists and poets would reveal that emigration, be it a consequence of necessity or curiosity, has meant that continental Europe has been a home and inspiration to many and this has been reflected in their writings (cf. O'Grady 2001; Sweeney 2007; Tóibín 1994).

In more circuitous ways, the intellectuals behind many Irish nationalist organizations were also apparently inspired and influenced by similar

---

[9] This is in part a consequence of the judgment of the High Court in the case of *Coughlan* v. *Broadcasting Complaints Commission* in April 1998 (confirmed by the Supreme Court in January 2000) which ruled that 'Yes' and 'No' positions in referendum campaigns would have to be given equal time and fair presentation in the national media (see O'Mahony 2010: 19).

[10] Richard Kearney's collaboration with RTÉ in making television series based on debates with contemporary European thinkers (including one specifically about 'Visions of Europe'), their publication as edited collections, and his later attempts to define a 'postnationalist Ireland' exemplify his efforts in this regard. See Kearney 1995, 1997.

movements on the Continent. For example, *The Nation* (an Irish nationalist newspaper of the Young Ireland movement in the 1840s) was, according to Oliver MacDonagh (1983), a mouthpiece of 'romantic nationalism of the German and more specifically Prussian type'. In fact, Richard Kearney traces most tendencies in Irish political thought back to 'an inclination to readapt foreign, usually French, ideological precedents'; he gives as examples Edmund Burke's liberal adaptation of Montesquieu, Wolfe Tone's republican adaptation of Robespierre and Voltaire, and James Connolly's socialist adaptation of Marx and Fourier (Kearney 1984: 25).

In terms of twentieth-century Irish political thought, the intellectual preoccupations of Conor Cruise O'Brien, the former diplomat identified by some as the leading Irish political thinker of his time – arguably because his views were often as provocative as they were erudite (English and Skelly 1998) – have been said to originate from the 'colossal moment' of the Second World War (McNally 2008). O'Brien, like many of his peers (such as Owen Sheehy Skeffington) and forebears (such as Peadar O'Donnell), was appalled by the similarities between the dominant political culture in Catholic Ireland and the anti-modernism and authoritarianism in much of the Catholic part of Western and Central Europe (including Italy, Spain, Portugal, Hungary) in the first part of the twentieth century (Pašeta 1999). It was the causes and consequences of untrammelled nationalism, rather than the political means to temper it (such as European integration), that concerned O'Brien. He drew direct connections between Irish and European history in a negative sense (in contrast to most of his fellow intellectuals), blaming medieval Europe for the early origins of the 'sacral nationalism' that he despised so much in its modern form of religious nationalism (O'Brien 1988). Such examples illustrate the point that the focus of Irish intellectual contributions on Europe is the nation, or Irish nationalism, itself. Myths of Europe serve to reinforce particular normative conceptions, *be they positive or pejorative*, of the past, present, and future of the Irish nation.

Myths of Ireland's European legacy

> There is an enormous possibility here of projecting a stronger sense of the antiquity of our culture, of the different strands of it . . . there is an opportunity in Europe for Ireland to project its culture . . . We have a much broader spectrum [in the EU] to reassess Irish culture and reinforce the linkages with other European countries.
>
> (Robinson 1992)

Pro-European intellectuals have frequently sought to emphasize the historical legacy of Ireland's relationship with the Continent – thus EEC/EU membership, rather than creating new partnerships, merely 'reinforced linkages' long-held with fellow Europeans, as President Robinson argued. In outlining such discourses, intellectuals sought above all else to quash the post-colonial notion that Ireland is an insignificant country hidden behind another on the margins of Europe. Hence the allusions to myths about the role of Irish saints and scholars in preserving Latin and Christianity whilst the rest of Europe wallowed in the Dark Ages, the stories about the earls from Ulster finding refuge in European colleges when in flight following the Tudor re-conquest of Ireland, the tales about the interventions of the Spanish Armada in support of Irish rebels...these are still recounted today much as they were one hundred years ago, and still with the same intention: a nationalist desire to write Ireland into the European story and, in so doing, to erase the remnants of a history of oppression and internal division. In fact, mythical conceptions of Europe in post-accession Ireland have retained a remarkable degree of consistency with key themes of the romantic nationalist movements of the nineteenth century. Such myths centre on a loose interpretation of the Celts as a 'European people' and of implications drawn from this for 'ancient connections' between the Irish and the Continent (typically in patterns that may include Scotland or Wales but, of course, bypass England). Mary Robinson, when President of Ireland, spoke in a manner representative of official discourse on the subject when she said: 'the Celtic heritage is really the pan-European one. It's the strongest pan-European basic culture and we in Ireland have a unique role in that Celtic culture' (Robinson 1992).

This emphasis on Celtic heritage as a connecting point among European countries, and between contemporary Europe and its 'shared past', experienced a revival in popularity across the Continent in the late twentieth century.[11] Ireland benefited from and contributed to this resurgence, not least through the 'Riverdance' phenomenon that embodied a new vibrant confidence in Irish culture.[12] Its geographical location on the periphery of Europe gave an additional air of plausibility to national stories that presented Irish culture as a sanctuary of such unspoiled 'European heritage'.

Drawing a connection between EEC/EU membership and the revival of Ireland's cultural integrity and identity is a common feature in intellectual discourse on the subject. See, for example, Tarlach Ó Raifeartaigh's claim in a pamphlet published prior to the 1972 referendum on EEC accession:

It is the most natural thing in the world that we should strengthen our links with the continent. It was when we were most Irish, that is, from the fifth century to the French Revolution, that these links were strongest. In the early days, our missionaries, some of them martyrs, saw to that. (Ó Raifeartaigh 1972: 4)

---

[11] As Mackey observed in the early 1990s: 'it has become fashionable quite recently in conferences and exhibitions devoted to their memory throughout Europe to describe the Celts as the first Europeans (e.g. "I Celti: La Prima Europa" exhibition at the Palazzo Grassi, Venice, 1991) (Mackey 1994: 2).

[12] It is notable that the supposedly 'Celtic' dimensions of Irish identity feature far more prominently than 'European' ones in this 'commodification' of Irish culture. For a sociological critique of this trend, see Kuhling and Keohane 2007.

The historical narrative of Irish pilgrims in Europe not only reinforces 'bonds' with the Continent even to this day,[13] it is also a literary trope familiar in other European countries, particularly with the emphasis on specific places of shared significance.[14] The fact that Ireland's mythological relationship with Europe has a strongly religious theme and a fairly ephemeral quality is admittedly useful to Irish elites seeking to embellish Ireland's historical role. President de Valera's 1933 speech on 'The Values of the Spirit' is a classic example of this grandiose narrative:

The Irish genius has always stressed spiritual values and intellectual rather than material values. That is the characteristic that prepared the Irish people in a special manner for the task ... of *helping to save western civilisation*. (Moynihan 1980: 233; emphasis added)

This notion was revived and given a new significance in response to the prospect of European integration, not so much to put the case for Irish accession as to reaffirm the unique importance of historical Irish *nationhood* in a European context. This narrative can only be fully explained in relation to the principal assumption of Irish intellectual discourse on 'Europe' in the 1950s–1960s (the period of the EEC's formation and Ireland's application to it), namely that its 'common civilization' is based on Christian heritage. Recalling the point made earlier, i.e. that the Catholic Church was the dominant cultural apparatus at this time, we understand why Irish intellectuals welcomed the development of European political cooperation on the grounds of preserving this civilization against totalitarianism (be it under the pretext of fascism or communism). Support for the creation of the European Defence Community, for example, was framed in terms of building on a history in which 'men of European loyalties and the European spirit have defended Europe' (Murray 1952: 277). In such Irish narratives, this European spirit and heritage is specifically identified as a Catholic one. One of the most prolific Irish writers on developments in Europe at this time, John Murray (a Jesuit priest), was quite clear about why Ireland had nothing to fear from European cooperation and, indeed, should welcome it:

[13] For example, the Mícheál Ó Cléirigh Institute is named after a Franciscan friar who fled Ireland in the early seventeenth century, and chronicled Irish history and literature from what became the Irish College in Louvain. This Institute, based in University College Dublin, was engaged in a project in 2007, with the support of Irish government funding, to commemorate the 400-year anniversary of the College in Louvain. The foundation of the College by the Franciscans, and its role in providing sanctuary for Gaelic chieftains heading to Rome in the 'Flight of the Earls', were described by a researcher in the Institute as having 'a profound effect on Ireland'; indeed, 'they still inform the profile of the Irish in Europe and our own sense of nationhood' (Breathnach 2007).

[14] For example, the Marian shrine at Mariazell has its origins in a Benedictine cell but developed as a place of pilgrimage as benefactors from across Central Europe worshipped the Madonna there as Magna Mater Austriae (Great Mother of Austria), Magna Domina Hungarorum (Great Lady of Hungary), or Mater Gentium Slavorum (Mother of the Slav Peoples) (Feuerstein 2007).

the Catholic can remember that what we know to-day as Europe is largely the creation of the Catholic Church ... For the Catholic the proposal of a United Europe is, so to say, only putting the clock back ... That a Catholic should welcome closer collaboration between European countries and should look with understanding and sympathy upon a properly balanced attempt to recreate unity in Europe is reasonably to be expected. (Murray 1952: 273)

Murray goes on to note, with approval, the Catholic faith of architects of integration, including Schuman, Adenauer, and De Gasperi.

The assertion that the saving and uniting of Europe is, above all, a spiritual quest is typical of the 'European stories' that set the stage for Ireland's *continued* contribution to what Murray referred to as the European 'community of peoples'. The style of Irish narratives that built upon this foundation is sampled in the pamphlet written by a civil servant, Tarlach Ó Raifeartaigh, on 'Ireland and the EEC' in preparation for the 1972 referendum on accession:

In the economic field we Irish have not much to contribute ... On the cultural side, however, we can fairly claim to be foundation members of that post-Roman civilisation which has evolved into the Europe of to-day. We are in fact among the very oldest identifiable peoples of the Ten [this was written a few months before Norway's referendum vote against EEC membership]. At that early beginning time, *we played our fair part in the Christianising and civilising of the barbarian hordes, whose posterity was destined to mould the European heritage* into its present context and form. (Ó Raifeartaigh 1972: 6; emphasis added)

So, even in purportedly 'European' stories, the central character is the Irish nation, playing – perhaps beyond the notice of its fellow Europeans – a discreet but nonetheless pivotal role.

Pro-European narratives in Irish nationalism

Many Irish politicians have propounded the view that 'Europe' is not 'them' but 'us' – an argument premised on the notion that Irish sovereign identity has been enhanced through membership.[15] The extent of this shared European identity is rarely articulated and, when it is, the matter of what Europe is not (i.e. a colonial power or empire) is as important as what it is (i.e. a 'great community of nations', at least according to Irish national discourse).[16] In a

---

[15] For example, Bertie Ahern described this reciprocal relationship thus: 'While Ireland belongs to the Union, *through our shaping of the Union over the last quarter of a century, the people of Ireland can genuinely claim that the Union belongs to them*' (Ahern 2000; emphasis added).
[16] Phrase used to describe contemporary Europe in a speech given by Taoiseach Charles Haughey in his famous 'Spirit of the Nation' address to the fiftieth Fianna Fáil Ardfheis (party conference), 11 April 1981 (cited in Hayward 2009: 123). It is a delectable (and, perhaps, on the part of Haughey's principal speech writer, Martin Mansergh, deliberate) irony that this same description was used of the British Empire in the divisive Anglo-Irish Treaty of 1921.

similar way, the advocacy of nationalism by Irish leaders and intellectuals in the nineteenth and twentieth centuries was not considered to be in opposition to other nationalisms in Europe but in fellowship with them in promoting shared national values and ideals above the divisions of creed and class.[17] Irish nationalism, therefore, was not conceived by its proponents as pulling Ireland apart from other European countries or movements, with the deliberate and crucial exception of its British neighbour.

This same nationalist logic persisted into the reasoning behind accession to the EEC in 1973. Indeed, in a pamphlet setting out the 'cultural aspects' of the prospective accession and their expected benefits, Tarlach Ó Raifeartaigh quotes liberally from Douglas Hyde (founder of the Gaelic League in 1893). He draws direct parallels between Hyde's arguments for Gaelicization in response to the threat from Britain and his own argument for what might now be termed Europeanization in response to the threat from Anglo-American culture. Ó Raifeartaigh argues that Hyde recognized 'the importance of being ourselves and not an inferior version of somebody else' (Ó Raifeartaigh 1972: 4). Kearney describes Hyde's Gaelic League as primarily an 'intellectual movement' to 'repossess Ireland's dispossessed culture', and it is apparent that many Irish intellectuals who supported accession to the EEC did so for similar reasons, albeit in a different context and in response to an even more broadly defined threat (Kearney 1984: 8).

This leaflet by Ó Raifeartaigh, the first Chairman of the Higher Education Authority in Ireland, exemplifies core arguments made by intellectuals for European integration, aside from the 'economic issue', which he acknowledges to be 'the deciding factor' (Ó Raifeartaigh 1972: 1). First, in notable contrast to the arguments made in some other EU member states about the effects of integration, EEC membership was not seen as a threat to Irish cultural integrity but rather as a means to its preservation (this theme has continued to be sustained among pro-EU elites in Ireland). Indeed, Ó Raifeartaigh comments that 'it is open to surmise that the original creation of the Common Market was an instinctive reaction against the menace of cultural submission'. The source of this menace (generally implied rather than stated) was 'the American challenge' (Ó Raifeartaigh 1972: 3–4).

Anti-Americanism was also a shared feature in the new wave of left-wing Irish intellectuals who emerged in the 1950s, including Conor Cruise O'Brien, Hubert Butler, Valentin Iremonger, and Owen Sheehy Skeffington (Whelan 2005). Not all of them were overly enamoured with the EEC; indeed, the 1972 referendum on accession to the EEC was one of the few points in modern Irish history at which a clear and distinct 'left-wing' position could be detected in Irish politics. On the matter of EEC membership, the Irish Labour Party and the

---

[17] As argued by Dwan 2009.

Irish Congress of Trade Unions agreed with the position of their British counter-parts and opposed EEC entry on the grounds of the threat to native industry. Yet, as in Britain, this left-wing opposition to European integration did not endure (see Varouxakis, this volume); moreover, in contrast to Britain, Europe came to be presented by many such intellectuals as a benign alternative to 'our own way of life . . . being greyed out against the background of the mighty mid-Atlantic civilisation' (Ó Raifeartaigh 1972: 13). This discourse follows the trad-itional path of Irish intellectual thought on Europe in the twentieth century. Twenty years previously, John Murray had also argued in apocalyptic terms about the saving of Europe, and about the potential of this community in a global context:

Europe will be saved, if saved it is to be, not in the order of economics and production, not through the advance of science and technique but through a widening and deepening understanding of those ideas and values which have made Europe what Europe was and is and, once incorporated in Continental Europe, have given Western culture and civiliza-tion to the world. (Murray 1952: 280)

When this narrative turned to the specific question of Ireland's accession, EEC membership came to be seen as offering 'abatement' to the situation of 'the decline and eventual disappearance of whatever is natural to our way of life', on the grounds that 'in a plurality of cultures a small country can confidently hope to preserve its national being and identity'. Given this chance to escape from American cultural dominance, 'if we fail to join hands with the Continent', Ó Raifeartaigh warns most ominously, 'we face eventual total assimilation' (Ó Raifeartaigh 1972: 4).

Other elements of Ó Raifeartaigh's argument include: the opportunity to 'end provincialism and insularity'; the means to escape 'being in various ways at the mercy of our nearest neighbour'; the claim that 'a united Ireland could find a better background than is available at present' due to the total population of the European Community being 'about half and half' Catholic and Protestant; intriguingly, the expectation that 'close contact with Continental peoples must add to our intellectual stock'; and, in sum, the chance to no longer appear 'as that charming but sometimes troublesome little country' (Ó Raifeartaigh 1972: 6–13). He concludes his call with a flourish, and a wink to his sceptical, left-wing intellectual friends:

Within [the EEC] we could legitimately combine affection for our own Country with a feeling for the wider heritage in which we also share – and at the same time enjoy the bonus of a partial escape from the present economic and cultural near-monopoly which holds us in its whim. Culturally, at least, in becoming a member of EEC [sic] we could have nothing to lose but our chains. (Ó Raifeartaigh 1972: 13)

These arguments – all of which are representative of the key elements of Irish intellectual discourses on European integration over the course of EU membership since 1973 – can be summarized in one word: *sovereignty*. This is yet another distinctive and defining feature in the Irish case: Ireland's accession to the EEC in 1973 was presented as the fulfilment and enrichment of Irish national sovereignty. This was due to prevalent contemporary concerns about the incompletion of the 'project' of Irish nation-statehood, which in turn were inseparable from a collective preoccupation with the legacy of colonialism. As Ó Raifeartaigh's comments illustrate, the most pressing issues for national debate about Irish sovereignty were the ones that any debate about Irish membership of the EEC focused on: dependence on Great Britain, the unsettled existence of Northern Ireland, the threat to 'native' Irish culture posed by Americanization, and the poor state of the Irish economy. It was these four issues – against which the realization of Irish sovereignty and the integrity of Irish nationhood would be measured – that dominated the reasoning behind support for European integration.[18] Since the late 1990s, however, all of these issues have been removed as threats to national well-being: the Irish economy was a global exemplar, the position of Northern Ireland was 'agreed', what Mary Robinson describes as 'the shadow of Big Brother' (i.e. Britain) was no longer relevant, or at least not a source of anxiety.[19] On the matter of Americanization, the United States came to be more powerful in economic and cultural terms than any commentator in the 1960s could have envisaged – but this was interpreted as part of the experience of globalization and was welcomed largely in conjunction with, rather than in opposition to, Ireland's European role.[20]

Critiquing European story-telling in Ireland

The nature and substance of historical 'European stories' in Ireland have been shaped by the three types of intellectual contribution to Irish national debate, namely literary (i.e. the writers), spiritual (i.e. the theologians), and structural (i.e. the policy-makers). These correspond (not coincidentally) to the three aspects of 'European culture' to which Ireland is said to have made a crucial

---

[18] Perhaps it is no coincidence, therefore, that it was this theme that Richard Kearney decided to explore, some twenty years after accession, as the means by which 'the newly emerging Europe' could become 'truly democratic', namely through 'fostering notions of sovereignty that are inclusive rather than absolute, shared rather than insular, disseminated rather than closed in upon some bureaucratic centre' (in Kearney 1995: 10–11).

[19] Robinson, in Kearney 1995: 140.

[20] The juxtaposition of 'Boston' and 'Berlin' posed by the Tánaiste (deputy prime minister) Mary Harney in a speech to the American Chamber of Commerce in Dublin, July 2000, generated such interest precisely because it diverged so greatly from the usual official discourse which saw Ireland as bridging, not falling in between, the United States and the European Union (see Hayward 2009: 139).

contribution: literary culture, religion, and education.[21] It is revealing to consider, however, what elements of Irish intellectual thought have been excluded or heavily reinterpreted by official political discourses on 'Europe'. The analytical tradition of post-colonialism among intellectuals in late twentieth-century Ireland, for example, had direct implications for Irish conceptualization of the EU. In this vein, Declan Kiberd highlighted the 'invented' nature of 'Europe' itself, and suggested that, 'as a post-colonial country sharing the EEC with some post-imperial countries', Ireland can 'tell other Europeans about the barbarism as well as the beauty of the traditions that have made us what we are' (quoted by Mackey 1994: 6). However, what actually happened was that Irish official discourses have highlighted the benefits of European integration as a means of *overcoming* the legacy of colonialism. For example, when addressing audiences in accession states prior to the enlargement of the EU in 2004, the then-Taoiseach, Bertie Ahern, made an effort to draw parallels between Irish experience and that of Malta and Cyprus – a tactic intended to bolster the government's claim that Ireland was a 'model' member state.[22] Beyond such a blend of pragmatism and bluster, the Irish political elites have not widely perceived EU membership to necessitate or influence 'a fundamental re-thinking of historically legitimated identity patterns' (O'Mahony and Delanty 1998: 175). In actual fact, dominant national discourses have presented EU membership in such a positive light by claiming that it doesn't challenge Irish identity patterns but actually reinforces them. President Robinson's comments on this subject are, again, representative of typical discourses among the Irish intellectual and political elite:

Since we joined in 1973, our participation in Europe has been very good psychologically. It is hard to define precisely what is meant by that, but it has been good for Ireland to be one among . . . twelve member states . . . That, I think, has reinforced our sense of nationhood, our psychological sense of identity. (Robinson, in Kearney 1995: 140)

---

[21] Gwenaël Le Duc contends, in the interests of accuracy, that Ireland's contribution to European culture was 'mainly to acquire or receive a lot from the continent, select it, and afterwards to give back the deposit – with interest' (Le Duc 1994: 21).

[22] The Taoiseach's speech in Malta before its accession to the EU (notably similar to one presented in Cyprus around the same time) exemplifies this discourse which blends the prospect of European integration with post-colonial sensitivities and national pride: 'As island peoples, the Irish and the Maltese are both proud of our rich historical inheritances and our distinctive traditions. We cherish our independence . . . We have both had long, complex, at times difficult relationships with Britain . . . In reflecting on our European experience today . . . Malta and Ireland, as two neutral and independent-minded countries, continue to have much in common . . . we each have our own values and our own distinctive approaches. We are both on the periphery of Europe, and both have to work hard for a living. However, both Ireland and Malta have shown through past adversity and present challenge that our people are capable of using their natural talents to achieve a success and influence greater than their numbers alone would suggest' ('Ireland's experience of EU membership', speech by the Taoiseach to the Malta Chamber of Commerce, Valletta, 8 January 2001, quoted in Hayward 2009: 125).

179

The crucial question now, however, is whether and how this 'reinforced' Irish identity can be sustained in a changing European Union.

The perennial features of Irish national discourses outlined above (identity, integrity, interests) were convincingly made by pro-European Irish intellectuals into motivating factors for enthusiastic support for European union. However, as the urgency and insecurity surrounding these nationalist preoccupations have dissipated (in part through EU membership), the lack of responsive adjustment in Irish official discourse about the EU has become apparent. Indeed, this withering of intellectual engagement with Europe arguably contributed to 'No to Nice' (2001) and 'No to Lisbon' (2008).[23] The debate about the causes of these 'No' votes is beyond the remit of this chapter; nevertheless, it is important to note that few academics identify a growing trend of Euroscepticism in Ireland (the wholesale defeat of the Libertas party in the 2009 European Parliament elections confirms this). Moreover, Irish satisfaction with the EU, although not unqualified, remains high in comparison with other member states despite a collapse of trust in Ireland's economic and political institutions.[24] The general public are also familiar with the pro-European rationale of the main political parties, although the political conviction that Irish nationalism and European integration are complementary has not been taken to heart by all.[25] Perhaps the Irish public are *too* familiar with the arguments put forward by the Irish elite in favour of strong European union, as they have not altered in line with the major domestic and European changes that have occurred in recent times. This is not to say that Irish voters now reject the fundamental tenets of the European 'stories' outlined above or that these concepts are no longer appropriate. Yet the absence of a clearly defined, ambitious, and specific vision of Ireland's place in a Europe of twenty-seven or more, plus the dearth of knowledge about the actualities of EU activity and policy (Laffan and O'Mahony 2008: 128–30), no doubt contributed to the mixture of apathy and hesitation that characterized Irish popular reaction to the Lisbon Treaty in 2008. Brigid Laffan and Jane O'Mahony summarize the mismatch between new public questioning of a future EU and tired pro-EU narratives in Ireland thus:

[23] The first Irish referendum to ratify the Treaty of Nice was rejected by 53.9 per cent of voters, on a turnout of 34.8 per cent, in June 2001 (it was passed in a second referendum the following year). The first referendum on the Treaty of Lisbon, held in June 2008, was rejected by 53.4 per cent (on a turnout of 53.1 per cent) (it was passed in a second referendum in 2009).

[24] According to Eurobarometer no. 70 (December 2008), 67 per cent of Irish respondents consider EU membership to be a good thing (third only behind the Netherlands and Luxembourg). Notably, however, there was a decline (by 8 per cent) of trust in EU institutions and a dramatic increase (by 19 per cent up to 35 per cent compared to a Eurobarometer survey six months' previously) of respondents saying the EU is going 'in the wrong direction'. But this is still significantly better than the 60 per cent (up by 24 per cent on spring 2008) who perceive that *Ireland* itself is going 'in the wrong direction'.

[25] Unsurprisingly, research suggests those who identify exclusively with the Irish nation are more likely than those with some sense of European identity to think that EU membership is a bad thing (Kennedy and Sinnott 2007: 72).

while the Irish electorate may be positively predisposed towards membership of the EU, reservations regarding the future trajectory of integration do exist and there is no longer a consensus on Europe in Ireland. The localism and personalism of Ireland's political culture militates against meaningful and sustained public debate on Ireland's relationship with the EU. The old narrative based on modernization has no resonance in post-Celtic tiger Ireland. It has not been replaced with a new narrative. (Laffan and O'Mahony 2008: 131)

Discursive elements shared with other European countries

Are the challenges now faced by the Irish intellectual and political elite unique in Europe? Certainly, the degree of success that they had in the past in constructing a notion of European integration that complemented popular nationalist narratives was quite remarkable. Although all EU member states have had to present the pooling of sovereignty as an act of national interest, the internal 'productive paradox' in the predominant Irish intellectual discourses – one which enables pro-Europeanism to be presented as a natural extension of proud Irish nationalism – is not common in other member states. For example, in contrast to the parallels drawn between Ireland's post-colonial experience and that of post-communist states by some Irish commentators,[26] pro-nationalist movements and intellectuals in such countries may regard Europe as a danger or cultural threat (see Blaive and Maslowski, this volume). As exemplified in the discourse of Czech President Václav Klaus, staunchly nationalist discourses in these countries can draw negative analogies between the European Union and the Soviet Union.

Nonetheless, there are many strong similarities between dimensions of Irish discourses on Europe and those in other member states. The idea of *regaining* independence through integration with Europe, thereby weakening the clutches of a former colonizing neighbour, also underpins some pro-European discourses in Poland (Góra and Mach, this volume), for example. Similarly, the notion that European integration will enable a return to an integral, pre-colonial national identity is shared by intellectuals in Romania (Barbu, this volume). Other parallels between the European stories of intellectuals in Ireland and elsewhere can be found in the notion of 'balancing' a powerful member state through European integration. Just as Irish intellectuals looked to the EEC to offset some of the influence of Britain, so British intellectuals offered support to integration on the grounds that it was the best chance of 'neutralizing'

---

[26] Such as in the opinion piece by the Deputy Editor of the *Irish Times*, Paul Gillespie, 'Parallels of accession states and Ireland' (2 May 2009), in which he elaborates Tom Garvin's contention that 'Europe symbolizes the end of empire and, therefore, the obsolescence of the ancient English-Irish quarrel' in relation to the post-communist member states' approaches to and experiences of European union.

German power. Another common feature between Irish and British pro-European discourses is their traversing of the cultural tension that arises from their geographical and historical closeness to *both* the United States and the European Union (Varouxakis, this volume). Greece's experience of the EU has similarly been affected by its relatively 'peripheral' geographical position. Indeed, although Greek intellectual discourses on European integration are, like Ireland's, constructed from a position on Europe's periphery, both claim to have had a core role in the making of European civilization. Most notably, it is evident Irish intellectuals' conceptions of 'Europe' have little in common with those among the 'founders' of the European Community. In fact, Irish discourses appear to bear most resemblance to those among 'outliers' of the current EU, in their overtly nationalist construct of 'Europe' (note Onar and Evin's analysis of the Turkish debate, this volume) and their dominant obsession with 'the national issue' (as Fossum and Holst identify in Norway, this volume). If, despite Ireland's commitment and experience as a member state, analysis would suggest it is still an 'outlier' at heart, the task now faced by Ireland's pro-European thinkers and leaders is exceptional in its magnitude.

Conclusion

What is emerging from the ashes of economic crisis and the failure of the first referendum on the Lisbon Treaty in 2008 are not propositions for preparing for the future but instead speculations as to how best to rediscover Ireland's glorious past. This is perhaps to be expected, given the patterns of Irish public intellectual discourses outlined above. Maurice Goldring's comment that 'the dream of a Gaelic Ireland has been used *ad nauseam* to fill the vacuum and revive popular enthusiasm... it even works today' remains true even in the post-Celtic Tiger era (Goldring 1993). When Irish intellectuals now attempt 'to think and act outside the consumer capitalist box which shapes our existing mentalities', the most radical plan they devise is to 'capitalise on culture': 'To go forward, they argue, we must go back, back to our Irish cultural roots, to all those things that made us different in the past' (Inglis 2009). Although membership of the European Union enabled a reinterpretation (not to mention rejuvenation) of some elements of Irish nationalism, this did not incorporate the deletion or even deep-rooted revision of the principal tenets of nationalism itself (Hayward 2009). Now that Ireland is popularly viewed as having definitively moved beyond the post-colonial legacy, there is a need for a new type of intellectual engagement with Europe that is more forward-looking than the dreams of Gaelic Ireland and more outward-looking than the reverie of the Celtic Tiger. Ireland is now ready to contemplate a 'Europe' far greater than the national self writ large.

9

Europe Othered, Europe Enlisted, Europe Possessed

Greek Public Intellectuals and the European Union

George Pagoulatos and Xenophon A. Yataganas

Though their supposed 'absence' at times of societal crisis is stereotypically lamented, public intellectuals (academics, prominent journalists, artists, novelists, poets, and musicians) have always been influential in the Greek public sphere. During the post-war decades, when the left was politically repressed, left-wing intellectuals became the voice of the politically excluded. Through the *engagement* of its public intellectuals, the losing side of the civil war (1945–9) established an ideological hegemony in Greek society, which took its toll after the 1974 transition to democracy and lasted well into the late twentieth century – some would say into the twenty-first. Thus a societal practice of seeking the opinion of personalities holding some intellectual authority was nurtured – though selection criteria obviously varied. In a socio-political system typically characterized as statist and partitocratic (Mouzelis 2002; Mouzelis and Pagoulatos 2005), public intellectuals have developed symbiotic relations with the Greek state, close ties with political elites (often joining their ranks), and a tendency to declare political preferences. That said, it should also be stressed that the country's principal strategic and ideological choices are defined by the political, not intellectual, leadership. The national agenda-setters whenever it came to Greece's relations with 'Europe' (whether to pursue EC accession as with Constantine Karamanlis in the 1970s, or to criticize it as with Andreas Papandreou in the 1980s, or to fully embrace the EU as with Costas Simitis post-1996) have invariably been national political leaders.

Almost three decades since its 1981 accession to the EC, Greece as member-state has graduated from the 'reluctant partner' of the 1980s to becoming a more or less committed European. This development not only summarizes the country's socio-economic and political transformation, but also testifies to the EU's success in helping bring it about. Underlying this seemingly linear course, a less concordant domestic public debate over the EU and Greece's position in it has evolved, both actively framing public stances and profoundly affected by the country's ongoing 'Europeanization'. This chapter attempts to sketch some of the main features of this debate, tracing ideas to their principal public exponents (public intellectuals, as defined in this volume), and attempting conceptual taxonomies that will help us locate ideas and perceptions within their proper ideological and cultural universe.

Right versus left, independence versus integration: The cross-cutting cleavages

Following a standard comparative taxonomy (Hix 1999), we can locate ideas and conceptualizations of the EU on a two-dimensional space defined by two cross-cutting lines of cleavage. *First*, a horizontal axis, corresponding to the traditional left–right cleavage. While representative of the standard European left–right ideological division, this division in Greece has been particularly informed by the experience of the civil war, whose aftermath placed the left in the position of the defeated. Subject to varying degrees of political persecution through the post-war era, culminating with the 1967–74 dictatorship, the left emerged after the 1974 democratization as bearer of a legitimate claim to a higher moral ground and ideological hegemony over Greek society; especially so in the areas of academia, culture, and the mass media (Voulgaris 2008).

The left and its intellectuals have naturally viewed the EU through distinctly Marxist, anti-imperialist, anti-capitalist lenses (e.g. Psyroukis 1986). In the 1970s, such views were also represented by intellectuals close to or identified with the Panhellenic Socialist Movement (PASOK), which at that time subscribed to a *tiers-mondiste*, post-colonial, anti-imperialist, anti-capitalist worldview and rhetoric that sustained a negative image of the Common Market. Since around the mid-1980s, such reception of the EC went gradually out of fashion with PASOK, as will be later discussed. Today it is sustained by the communist and leftist pole of the ideological spectrum, whose intellectual appeal, however, re-baptized as it is in the current anti-globalization discourse, exceeds the sum of the electoral following of the Greek Communist Party (KKE) and the post-communist/post-Eurocommunist constituent of the Coalition of the Left party (SYRIZA). Indeed, anti-EU leftism is rampant within a minority but influential section of the Greek intelligentsia, who rarely miss an opportunity to decry the EU and its institutions for pandering to world capitalists, multinationals, and the United States.

The *second*, vertical axis and line of cleavage is that of nationalism versus cosmopolitanism, or independence versus integration (Hix 1999), or, to put it in the terms adopted in the introduction to this book, statist/national versus supranational or transnational. It makes sense, for the case of Greece, to present this ideological antithesis in binary terms since the third, 'transnational', school of thought, has been relatively underrepresented until recently and subsumed in the pro-integration 'Europeanist' or supranational section of the debate. That said, it is also the case that the reality of Greece's participation in the EU, and the obvious benefits derived, eventually turned some earlier exponents of the national/statist school of thought into 'transnationalists'. By the same token it can also be claimed that the Euro-pessimism following the rejection of the Constitutional Treaty has been encouraging earlier enthusiastic federalists towards 'transnationalist' realism. In both cases, transnationalism can be said to represent the middle, bridging ground between the two conflicting poles of independence versus integration or statist/national versus supranational.

This vertical cleavage in Greece gained renewed momentum and salience under the post-Cold War international environment of the 1990s and 2000s. Rather than an 'end of history', as had been frivolously proposed by the Fukuyamas of this world, the collapse of the former communist bloc and especially of the former Yugoslavia awakened dormant historical ethnic nationalisms, 're-Balkanizing' Greece's immediate neighbourhood. Thus, while the Cold War had resolved Greece's identity dilemma by placing her decisively with the Western camp, the post-communist Balkan implosion opened a can of worms, reviving nationalistic reflexes and Eastern orthodox cultural allegiances that the country's Europeanizing elites had often in the past sought to contain. As we shall see further on, this cleavage can be argued to run even deeper in Greek culture and society than the one between left and right. The left–right division (the left's intellectual capital notwithstanding) has experienced relative erosion during the last several decades (at least until the 2008–9 economic crisis) by the forces of dynamic socio-economic mobility in a Greek society largely composed of expanding middle-class and petty bourgeois strata. On the contrary, the tension between nationalism and cosmopolitanism has drawn both on deep cultural undercurrents of Greek society, and on a recent global context that tends to accentuate it.

The cultural undercurrents

The reception of Europe by Greek intellectuals and public opinion is framed by the main competing worldviews, serving as mental frameworks 'within which human beings can order and understand the entire world in which they live', frameworks that furnish 'abstract guidelines, a general outlook, a manner of thinking' (Berman 1998: 20). Scholars such as Diamandouros (1994 and 1997) and Kitromilidis (2000) have asserted the existence of two powerful and sharply conflicting cultural traditions. These originated from the highly contested process of Greek nineteenth-century state-building, in which Western European liberal political institutions were introduced and grafted onto the traditional pre-capitalist indigenous structures resulting from the Byzantine and Ottoman heritages (Diamandouros 1994: 8). The older culture originated from the traditions of the Eastern Orthodox Church, while parochial local structures were inherited from Ottoman state organization. This traditionalist ethnocentric, or (under current terms) nationalistic culture is characterized, amongst other things, by a pervasive anti-Western (and anti-Catholic) stance of suspicion and hostility towards the more advanced capitalist countries, and views Hellenism and Orthodoxy as subject to constant external threats (Kitromilidis 1995). This culture involves 'a siege mentality[1] combined with a distinctly defensive perception of the international environment', 'a pronounced sense of cultural inferiority towards the Western world, coupled with a hyperbolic and misguided sense of the importance of Greece in international affairs and, more generally, in the history of Western civilisation' (Diamandouros 1994: 13).

True, nationals of nearly every country in the world can assert the existence of certain features on the basis of which their country stands out as different from the others, as somehow 'exceptional'. National histories are often constructed as mythologies to accommodate a sense of national 'distinctness' or even 'uniqueness' through bold juxtapositions with 'the others' or through cultivating an ethnocentric understanding of the world. In that sense, a worldview of national exceptionalism (Pagoulatos 2004) is far from exceptional to Greece. Speaking of Greece, Spain, and Portugal, Malefakis (1995) noticed a deeply ingrained common culture of self-contempt originating from a rather miserable recent past and present, as painfully contrasted with a historically glorious farther past. Ethnocentrism tends to exaggerate both past glory and present misery.

Young pupils in Greece learn from the first classes of grammar school that they are direct descendants of ancient Greeks and, consequently, the heirs of the culture that discovered poetry, history, philosophy, theoretical mathematics, and physics and, above all, democracy (Davies 1993). They also learn that Greek civilization inspired the Renaissance and Enlightenment in the Western world, in other words that civilized humanity as a whole owes Greece almost everything (Varouxakis 1997: 33). Greek intellectuals, of course, are not solely responsible for these kinds of perceptions. European Romanticism and the humanistic tradition also enthusiastically embraced these views, which have been widely accepted by a plurality of European intellectuals from Lord Byron in the early nineteenth century to Jacqueline de Romilly (1992) today. Back in the late seventeenth and eighteenth century, West European travellers to

---

[1] This siege mentality is encapsulated in the phrase of an ex-President of the Republic, Christos Sartzetakis, in the 1980s: 'we are a brotherless nation'.

Greece 'discovered' Athens as the birthplace of European civilization (Giakovaki 2006). Geography and language support a perception of uninterrupted continuity, but history poses more complicated questions. From the classic period to the 1831 establishment of the modern Greek state, the geographical area of what was to develop as contemporary Greece became subject to the Roman conquest, the dominance of Christianity, eleven centuries of the Byzantine Empire, and – most damagingly – four hundred years of Ottoman occupation. Roman rule and Christianity were easily absorbed by the Greek classical tradition: Rome contributed to law and public administration, while Christianity brought a code of ethical values compatible and complementary – though not without tensions – with classical Greek civilization. In contrast, Byzantine theocratic despotism and the Ottoman Muslim multi-ethnic state meant fifteen centuries of continuous coexistence of the Greek people with modalities and principles that had very little to do with the classical tradition and values transmitted to the Western world. As Castoriadis (2006–8) has argued, ancient Greece represented an autonomous entity which shared constructed and changeable values, whereas Byzantine and Ottoman societies were heteronomous entities that believed in revealed and unmovable principles.

There were of course valiant intellectual efforts to establish the unbroken continuity of Hellenism. The direct heritage of the Eastern Roman Empire and the continuity of language and religion through the Ottoman occupation were the founding stones for the ideological construction of the so-called Helleno-Christian civilization. The great nineteenth-century historian Constantine Paparrigopoulos (1858) elaborated a powerful narrative concerning the unique, continuous, and unitary character of the Greek nation from ancient times to the modern era. This achievement was of great importance for the consolidation of the modern Greek state, and still constitutes the official ideology. More recent historiography, initiated by Nicos Svoronos (1973), brought some relativism to these artificially coherent stories, tracing the modern Greek nation back to the eleventh–fifteenth (Byzantine) centuries, and attributing the resistance and survival of Greeks during prolonged periods of occupation to the administrative skills of the Byzantine Empire and the vigour and persistence of the Hellenic Diaspora. Contemporary challengers of the 'axiomatic identification of progress with the West European canon' include the political science professor Georgios Kontogeorgis (2005), who contests that 'the Greek nation cosmosystem created the Greek nation-state' and not the other way round. Kontogeorgis defends the continuity of an anthropocentric Hellenism that spared Greece from Western feudalism, arguing that nineteenth-century Greece was a forerunner of the West in many ways, by introducing universal (male) suffrage in one of the first Constitutions (1844) of the independent Greek state at a time when (1832) only 7 per cent of the British people had the right to vote, or by launching non-class, non-ideological, catch-all political parties, a century or more before they were introduced in Western societies (Kontogeorgis 2005: 16).

The traditionalist, ethnocentric cultural stream overlaps heavily with what the introduction to this book identifies as statist/national school of thought. Diamandouros (1994) has coined the term 'culture of the underdog', juxtaposed to its opposite, Enlightenment-inspired, European-minded, liberal-leaning, reformist-driven culture. The 'culture of the underdog' carries a xenophobic and defensive view of the world, sees the state as protector of the weak and least competitive socio-economic strata and defender of traditional local structures from the opening of the economy and society to the forces of internationalization and change. This culture promotes a narrow particularistic allegiance (to family, close friends, and fellow-villagers) at the expense of universal values of citizenship, rights, and the rule of law. It contains values and stances that sustain Eurosceptic attitudes.

A sophisticated version of the traditionalist ideology is represented, among others, by the neo-Orthodox philosopher Christos Yannaras (1983, 1990, and 1992). This communitarian[2] intellectual tradition tends to oppose modern Western Enlightenment values by juxtaposing the egoistic individualism of the West to the warm collectivity of the Greek Orthodox tradition. The debate has been going on for over two centuries, beginning with the antithesis between the Greek Enlightenment scholar Koraïs and the military general Makriyannis at the turn of the nineteenth century;[3] continuing with the conflict between Western-leaning historians and philosophers such as Renieris, Rigopoulos, and Vrailas-Armenis on one side and Romantic intellectuals like Yannopoulos and Dragoumis on the other at the turn of the twentieth century; and culminating with the debate held by Psycharis and his followers in the first quarter of the twentieth century that opposed folk culture, demotic language, and the cult of Byzantium to European influences (Varouxakis 1995: 27). Some representatives of the traditionalist intellectual stream, once led by the professor of legal history in Thessaloniki N. Pantazopoulos (1967 and 1993) and C. Karavidas (1931), sought to defend the main values of Greek Christian community life; others, like the essayist Costas Zouraris (2009),[4] set out to embody the rebellious Greek soul and proud spirit. Viscerally anti-European, this school of thought is also a minority in Greek society. Today, the ultra-right-wing populist party LAOS (Popular Orthodox Rally) aspires to represent the Orthodox nationalist ideological tradition in political terms, although traditionalist culture still cohabits with more modernistic elements inside the

---

[2] Not to be associated with modern-day communitarians such as MacIntyre, Sandel, Taylor, Walzer, etc.

[3] The first, living essentially in Paris, was the most important representative of the Greek Enlightenment movement, the second was a military hero of the Greek revolution against the Ottomans (1821–8).

[4] Zouraris 2009: 'To hell with such liberty, where I will turn you into a pasha' (Να την χέσω τέτοια λευτεριά, όπου θα κάμω εγώ εσένα πασιά). The title is a phrase of General Makriyannis, meaning that liberty under Western European influence is no liberty at all.

New Democracy (ND) party, and even – to a far lesser extent today – inside PASOK.

It is worth noting here that the same conflict between an inward ethnocentric and an outward-looking cosmopolitan worldview is also present in Greek literature. There have always been writers who emphasized the peculiarities of Greek life, and others who used them in a more distant and relativistic manner. The pairs Stratis Myrivilis versus Cosmas Politis (*cosmopolitis* = 'cosmopolitan') or Alexandros Papadiamantis versus George Theotocas are, among many others, indicative. The contrast between indigenity/particularity on one side and modernization/cosmopolitanism on the other has always been present in the Greek literary tradition.[5] Writers of the younger generation seem to be relatively liberated from such polarization, but the conflict lurks in the background.

In its defence of the weak and non-competitive, in its hostility to the market and foreign powers, the underdog culture (representative of the most traditionalist and conservative elements of society) overlaps with left-wing anti-market, anti-globalization, and by extension anti-EU stances. Indeed, the rhetoric of the ultra-right populist LAOS in defence of the 'little man' or the 'small Greece' against the 'powerful Americans and Europeans' at times becomes almost undistinguishable from that of certain representatives of the Greek Communist Party (KKE), such as Liana Kanelli, a vocal formerly conservative journalist turned fiery communist MP. Needless to say, though instinctively opposed to any such Western-imposed taxonomies, the adherents of the ethnocentric, traditionalist culture ironically end up affirming the Huntingtonian thesis ('clash of civilizations') that places Greece in the Eastern-Orthodox-Slav civilization group – a thesis deeply disconcerting to Greece's Western-oriented, European Enlightenment-inspired elites.[6]

It becomes evident in the above analysis that Western-leaning, reform-minded elites and intellectuals have vitally relied on the European Union as the single most important strategic and ideological ally in their effort to promote the country's socio-political and institutional modernization, including the separation of church and state, the drive to provide more effective guarantees of civil and minority rights, and to overcome the deeply entrenched forces of parochialism. Their case represents one of 'Europe *enlisted*' in the purpose of advancing the country's overall modernization. Later in the chapter we will expand on pro-Western Europeanist intellectuals, the evolution of their stances and the EU-related public debate.

---

[5] We owe the argument of this paragraph to Maria Mexi.

[6] Revealingly, an initiative by the late Archbishop of Athens Mgr Christodoulos to oppose the 2001 decision of the Simitis government to remove from the identity cards the mention of religion, in accordance with the jurisprudence of the European Court of Human Rights, gathered three million signatures, including those of the later ND prime minister of 2004–9 Costas Karamanlis and his spouse.

What now makes the cultural cleavage (Greekness/Orthodoxy versus Europe/ the West) different and representative of the post-Cold War ideological universe is that increasingly, since the 1990s, it has demonstrated a rediscovered ideological affinity between conservative nationalists (including staunch advocates of the Greek Orthodox Church and intellectuals of the 'neo-Orthodox' stream) and certain intellectuals originating from the Greek pro-communist left. They share a common hostility to the EU, which they view as part and parcel of the forces of cultural globalization and 'homogenization' that are a great contemporary 'threat to Hellenism' and national identity, and a danger to Greek national interests (e.g. by supporting Turkey's European accession course, and by imposing a mutual compromise over the Greco-Turkish and 'Macedonian' dispute and the Cyprus issue). Moreover, in a world of globalization, the nation-state is regarded by nationalists as the last line of defence not just against the loss of national tradition and identity (for the conservatives) but also against the triumph of global markets and 'Americanization' (for the left). Thus, both the conservative right and the communist or post-communist left converge in an anti-EU nationalistic discourse.

Though analytically distinct, the two lines of cleavage explained in the previous section converge in juxtaposing two opposed images of the EU. On one side are those who view the EU as a force of far-reaching socio-economic, political, and institutional modernization ('Europeanization of Greece'). The other camp unites defenders of a nostalgic version of Greek tradition – communal values, life as it used to be, a slower, less hectic, Greek/Mediterranean way of living. This tendency struggles against the vulgarization and de-humanization imposed by the 'modernizers', whom it accuses of seeking to import a model of anxious lifestyles, cut-throat competition, job insecurity (the Greek 'precariato') brought about by the aggressive globalized capitalism of the EU, and the foreign patterns and values that are eroding Greek communal norms and lifestyles. Unsurprisingly, such versions of Eurosceptic, anti-market discourse grew stronger in the 1990s, following the implementation of the single market, the effects of globalization, and the reverberation of the 2000s 'Polish plumber' debate in Greece.

To generalize the point on our two cross-cutting cleavages, at times they appear to merge: anti-capitalism is also very often nationalistic or anti-cosmopolitan; pro-market stances are also often informed by cultural cosmopolitanism and universal Enlightenment values. But not necessarily: pro-market conservatives espouse the EU for the guarantees it offers to Greece's capitalist institutions, but resent the surrender of sovereignty to Brussels or what they may consider as erosion of national identity. And anti-capitalist opponents of economic globalization may dislike the EU as a triumph of free markets but aspire to internationalization and the opportunity to overcome national socio-cultural and institutional parochialism that it brings (e.g. Tsakalotos 2005). In other words, all four quadrants in our two-dimensional space are important and relevant in locating public stances and utterances towards the EU. That said, the heaviest 'traffic', so to speak, occurs around the centre of both the vertical and horizontal axes. In other words, at normal times, public EU-related intellectual debate tends to be centripetal on both axes (centripetal not in terms of ideological span, which remains wide, but in terms of public influence). This is not the case during special conjunctures that have made the EU either particularly unpopular (e.g. the 1999 NATO war on Yugoslavia or an EU decision contravening Greek public sentiment, e.g. over the 'Macedonian' issue) or particularly popular (e.g. accession to the Euro or Community solidarity to Greek foreign policy) with the Greek public. Such occasions tend to privilege the respective polarized views (rather than the centre), placing their exponents at a position of relative advantage – or the opposite.

Public exponents and political elites

Though nationalist traditionalism and the 'culture of the underdog' represent a powerful undercurrent in Greek society, it is also true that the entire two-party system of ND and PASOK, the two parties alternating in power since 1974, has been almost without exception led by politicians of a decisively Europeanist orientation. When in government, ND and PASOK have promoted Greece's participation in European institutions. They have of course sought to accommodate the anti-Western, parochial, nationalistic elements in their parties through various concessions, without however putting into question the country's fundamental strategic European orientation. This defence of the country's EU membership by the mainstream party system has carried public opinion in a top-down manner, crucially transforming Greek society (with the crucial assistance of EC inflows, it should be noted) into one of the most supportive of the EU, as recorded diachronically in the Eurobarometer studies. We attach particular importance here to the role of the party system, as the parties' public positions tend to override those of individual independent intellectuals in terms of societal influence.

In its history as an independent state, Greece has oscillated between governments and leaders representing the forces of parochialism and others with a strong reform-minded, Western orientation. Greece's historical leaders of the reformist tradition, and a source of inspiration for the country's Europeanizing modernizers, were Ioannis Capodistrias and Harilaos Trikoupis in the nineteenth century and Eleftherios Venizelos in the early twentieth. This pro-European tradition was followed, in terms of the country's external orientation, by all of the country's post-dictatorship prime ministers from 1974 until the present, though with varying degrees of commitment and efficiency. The most ardent and prominent pro-European prime ministers of the last thirty-five years have been particularly Constantine Karamanlis (1974–81) and Costas Simitis

(1996–2004), who take the historical credit for Greece's accession to the EC and the EMU respectively. Both went to great lengths in pursuing the Europeanization of Greece as well as that of their respective political parties. All other prime ministers of the last three decades have also been pro-European. This can be said to include Andreas Papandreou, founder of the socialist PASOK, who started out with a strong anti-EEC stance, but gradually over the 1980s shifted to accepting the EC and championing its benefits.

A prominent US academic turned charismatic politician himself, Andreas Papandreou came to power in 1981 with a *tiers-mondiste* nationalistic discourse, proclaiming national independence to be the supreme priority, denouncing social democracy as the 'genteel mask' of capitalism, and condemning EC membership as a subjugation to imperialism (Koliopoulos and Veremis 2010: 159ff.; Verney 1996: 174–5). Eurosceptics of the 1970s and 1980s stressed, among other things, a pessimistic interpretation of Greece's economic underdevelopment compared to the advanced EC-9, pointing out that if subjected to market opening without developmental policies the Greek economy would never survive European competition. Soon after, in 1982–3, Papandreou's position evolved more constructively into a successful bargaining effort of his government with the EC, which led to the Integrated Mediterranean Programs. As prime minister, Andreas Papandreou (father of the later prime minister George Papandreou) accepted the single market and supported Greece's accession to the EMU. The gradual but steady European transformation of PASOK was critical in turning the Greek public towards a strong pro-EU stance.

For its part, Constantine Karamanlis' ND of the 1970s also realized Greece's structural-economic backwardness compared to 'Europe' and its 'exceptional' geopolitical standing: no common borders with any country of the EC; the only current or prospective EC country facing a serious and imminent security problem (with Turkey); the only consolidated democracy in the Balkans, and so on. But it stressed the superior political benefits of irreversibly anchoring Greece in the advanced club of Western European democracies and market economies, and providing vital political insurance for its fledgling Republic and external security. Karamanlis' Europeanist doctrine was that 'Greece belongs to the West' – to which Papandreou once famously retorted 'Greece belongs to the Greeks'. In other words, in political terms, the pro-EC camp of the 1970s and early 1980s coincided with the nationalist-leaning early socialist one in perceiving 'Europe' as 'othered'. But it differed from the socialists in pursuing a strategy of Europe 'possessed' (proclaiming that 'on account of its ancient history, Greece has always belonged to Europe'). It 'enlisted' Europe in the purpose of the country's modernization, in order to bridge the historical, structural, cultural, and geopolitical distance.

This sense of Greek exceptionalism so prevalent pre-accession and in the early period of Greece's membership was weakened as a result of the country's gradually deepening integration. While Greece during the 1980s, in economic terms, lost ground by further diverging from the EC, its institutional and cultural distance from the Community was narrowed. National exceptionalism was eroded as a result of the expanding institutional and cultural Westernization and Europeanization of Greece. A related contributing factor was the increasing transnationalization and technocratization of policy, particularly from the second half of the 1980s, when the single market process was launched. As a result of growing interdependence and functional spillovers within the EC/EU, national political and administrative elites were increasingly integrated within European policy milieus and increasingly influenced by the views of their international peers.

This is far from saying that ethnocentric cultural undercurrents and a difficult course in Europe have not left their marks on the structure of EU-related public debate. Very limited in terms of participation and at the margins of public interest when it comes to European integration per se, EU-related debate carries a discernible 'provincial' syndrome visible across the ideological and political spectrum. Greece is widely perceived as a small country which cannot influence the main EU trends – thus, little use in even trying to engage Greece in the EU-wide debate. Hence the debate is mostly if not exclusively limited to matters of Greek interest. This tendency is somewhat counterbalanced by the pro-Europeanism of mainstream 'status quo' intellectual elites, but it does remain a key feature of the public debate.

An additional related feature is the attribution of difficult and unpleasant political decisions to 'Brussels' in order to eschew responsibility and deflect domestic opposition. This situation conceals the real functioning of EU institutions and reduces consciousness about the necessity of respecting the rules of the game. This implicit scapegoating tendency has been expressed recently with regard to unpopular policies such as the mutual recognition of diplomas and exercise of professional qualifications, the privatization of public enterprises, and the ECJ ruling to equalize pensionable age between women and men. None of these patterns of course are unique to Greece, but can be observed throughout the EU.

As is the case with other EU countries, Greece's natural and most ardent pro-EU constituency is located in the middle of the right–left ideological and political spectrum, in the centre-right and the centre-left. The bourgeois, middle-class vote usually oscillates between ND and PASOK, defining the electoral outcome. The centre space espouses a pragmatic, moderate, non-ideological view of material day-to-day problems. It constitutes the mainstream of rational utilitarian citizens, who, despite being occasionally disappointed by the EU adopting policies with which they might disagree or by the neglect of Greek interests and aspirations, remain committed to accepting in general terms the European destiny of the country. The gradual transformation of PASOK into a strongly pro-European party over the 1980s and especially 1990s has cemented the centre-left constituent of the country's pro-EU public opinion majority.

At the level of print media, the two main pillars of the pro-EU camp are the centrist daily newspaper *Kathimerini* and the centre-left *To Vima*.

By the same token and for reasons already elaborated, the two ideological extremes, both left- and right-wing, are the pool of the country's various anti-Europeanists and Eurosceptics, mostly nationalists on the extreme right and mostly anti-capitalists on the extreme left. Earlier we mentioned the extreme traditionalist right. On the opposite side of the spectrum, the radical socialists, including the former Eurocommunist party that has evolved today into the constellation of the Left Coalition and other social movements (SYRIZA), believe in the non-negotiable character of national sovereignty and consider that democracy is only practicable in the framework of the nation-state, which they view as the last defence against the expanding realm of globalized markets. They regard the EU as having yielded to the most aggressive version of market globalization – on the basis of which they opposed both Maastricht and the Constitutional Treaty – and are doubtful about the extension and further development of European integration. This position is elaborated by, among others, the law professor at the University of Thessaloniki Antonis Manitakis (Manitakis 2004, 2007). Similar voices, such as Costas Vergopoulos (2008) of Panteion University, support intergovernmental cooperation and oppose participation in supranational entities on similar grounds of opposition to liberal globalization and advocacy of extensive economic intervention and redistribution.

Finally, the communist left (KKE), whose electoral support is still around the 7–8 per cent level, remains attached to the Soviet model, considers destalinization as a political error, draws moral vindication from its strong working class social roots and splendid isolation from any exercise of power. The Greek communist party and its intellectuals have never wavered from their adamant opposition to everything the EU stands for, i.e. exploitation of the working class, capitalism, and imperialism. In the 1990s, the Greek communists also began to flirt with tradition, religion, and nationalism as the last bastions of resistance against capitalist and American-led globalization, as already mentioned.

It seems that the most vigorous and convincing opposition to the EU articulated over the last ten to fifteen years results from its being identified with globalization. Both in its traditionalist conservative and left-wing radical versions, the anti-globalization/anti-EU discourse has been a compelling one, nurtured by socio-economic insecurities and existential anxieties brought about by societal transformation under the force of opening borders to immigration and trade. However, even anti-EU, anti-global social movements and discourse are an affirmation of societal Europeanization and openness, not only by virtue of forming an anti-globalization reaction but also in the sense of adopting the 'globalized' language and repertoire of 'anti-globalization'. Indeed this tendency arguably constitutes proof of socio-cultural Europeanization and internationalization for a country which only a few decades ago was still a developing economy and a fragile democracy.

It is an indication of the limitations of EU-related public debate that the obvious progressive counterargument to the anti-globalization/anti-EU narrative (i.e. the argument for a stronger Europe, global power) has probably failed to gain prominence and capture the hearts and minds of the Greek public. While Greek public opinion is formally in support of European political integration by one of the highest percentages in Europe, much of its pro-European section remains captive to an instrumental approach to the EU that can locate Greece's benefits from the EU as the main, if not exclusive reason, for supporting the latter. This approach probably fails to go as far as perceiving a powerful Europe defining the terms and mediating the negative effects of globalization (the provincialism we mentioned above). The argument of a powerful EU making possible a progressive governance of globalization – which has failed to convince the Left Coalition (SYRIZA) to support the Lisbon Treaty – is mostly articulated by PASOK and centrist and social democratic-leaning pro-European intellectuals (e.g. Mouzelis 2002; Pagoulatos 2007; Tsoukalis 2006 and 2009; Tsoukas 2007; Yataganas and Kaloudiotis 2009).

This progressive 'stronger Europe, global power' argument has found its most prominent exponent in former prime minister Costas Simitis. An erstwhile professor of law with a distinguished anti-dictatorship record, Simitis was one of PASOK's few conscious Europhiles, a public intellectual himself, leading figure of a group of academics and intellectuals who championed Greece's modernization (*eksynghronismos*) and identified it with Europeanization and a full participation of the country in the core processes of European integration. From the 1970s and 1980s, given the nationalistic origins of PASOK, Simitis consistently sought to push his party closer to Europe, arguing, e.g. that 'our nationalism will exist as a creative element only if it becomes connected with supranationalism. This is the only way it can help the country progress and integrate into broader totalities' (Simitis 1992: 116). Simitis (2002: 108–15) advocates a rapid transformation of the EU into a political union that will be able as a union to achieve what its constituent parts alone cannot, that is a progressive re-regulation of globalization. In a recent book on the 2008 global financial crisis, Simitis (2008) embraces differentiated integration, enhanced cooperation, as a realistic strategy for achieving a necessary deepening of economic governance in the Eurozone.

The Europeanist discourse and its evolution

Twentieth-century Greek intellectual discourse about Europe was dominated by what we could call the 'canonical' perception of Europe, in terms of a civilization that partly owes its existence to the ancient Athenian democracy, and to which Greece organically belongs. This certain idea of Europe is identical to that held by a plurality of West European 'philhellenes' – mostly but not exclusively bearers of an education in classics. That was the exact story (coupled with Greece's large toll of sacrifice during the war) stressed by the Karamanlis government in the 1970s during the difficult negotiations for Greece's EEC accession, and was largely the story adopted by Greece's crucial political allies of that time (most notably French President Giscard d'Estaing) in order to curb EC opposition to Greece's entry. More precisely, the story was a combination of past historical contribution with current economic and political weakness, suggesting that the idealistic prospect of accession of this erstwhile birthplace of democracy and European civilization would not disrupt EC balances and would absorb only a negligible share of agricultural subsidies.

We can locate this canonical perception of Europe in the writings of some of Greece's most notable twentieth-century pro-European public intellectuals prominent in the 1950s, 1960s, and 1970s, such as George Theotokas (a leading novelist of the so-called '1930s generation') and the scholars/politicians Panagiotis Kanellopoulos,[7] Constantine Tsatsos (1977 and 1982) and Ioannis Pesmazoglu (1962 and 1964). The following excerpt from Theotokas (1976; from a speech in 1958) is representative of the canonical perception of Europe still dominant in Greek society: 'Europe is more than a geographical and economic unity. It is above all a spiritual and cultural community. It is the civilization born by the union of ancient Greek and Roman world with Christianity.' Greeks being Europeans, continues Theotokas, means that 'our tradition, our character, our mentality, the whole of our collective being, have been formed by the same basic elements that compose the European civilization'. Furthermore, reversing traditional irredentist nationalism, Theotokas proposes that, for the younger generation, 'for those who feel the lack of a fertile contemporary ideal...Europe could be the new Great Idea (*Megali Idea*)'.[8]

These influential pro-European public intellectuals of the post-war decades were followed, post-accession, by a younger generation of Europeanist scholars,[9] whose ranks were joined by some earlier Eurosceptic (mostly socialist) economists of the 1970s who finally acceded to the pro-EC camp, convinced by the force of events and the modernizing vigour of membership.[10] For the reformist, Europeanist school of thought, the EU has been the vital anchor,

[7] Panagiotis Kanellopoulos, a sociology professor and leading twentieth-century conservative politician, was a prolific public intellectual, who authored an eleven-volume *History of the European Spirit*.

[8] 'Megali Idea' was the nineteenth- and twentieth-century irredentist concept of Greek nationalism that expressed the goal of establishing a Greek state that would encompass all ethnic Greeks living outside the present national borders.

[9] Such as Loukas Tsoukalis, Panayiotis Ioakimidis (1998, 2007a, and 2007b), George Papadimitriou (1995, 1996), Constantine Stefanou (1996), and others.

[10] E.g. Constantine Vaitsos, Tassos Yannitsis, Panos Kazakos, Yannos Papantoniou, and others.

the reliable compass or Ulysses' proverbial mast (one may choose among various marine metaphors) that has managed to keep the Greek boat afloat and on the right tack. The pro-Western, pro-European, reformist tradition has historically viewed Europe as Greece's final destination, and commitment to European institutions as the most important defence mechanism against the country's main forces of structural backwardness and political entropy: political clientelism, partitocracy and corruption, excessively high influence of the church on state affairs, a large but inefficient public sector, chronic fiscal deficits, a protected and largely uncompetitive business sector, a cachectic and party-dominated civil society. The passion with which pro-European Greek intellectuals embraced the EU (which earned them the mocking appellation '*Euroligourides*' – roughly translated as those who salivate with Europe!) was proportionate to the risks the country faced if it failed to catch up with Europe. The dilemma was summarized by the Athens professor Panos Kazakos (1991) as 'adjustment or marginalization'.

The Europeanist discourse has evolved over time. In the 1960s and 1970s (with the parenthesis of the 1967–74 dictatorship) it emphasized the benefits of Greece's participation in the EEC, seeking to win the economic argument.[11] This was not an evident case for an economy that was just graduating from developing to middle-income status, and whose protected enterprise sector had a lot to fear from a highly developed EC with as yet no substantial redistributive instruments (the structural and cohesion funds came later) aside from the CAP. The truth was that socialist-leaning Eurosceptics of the time were right to point out the competitive risks of the common market for the Greek private sector, but they were wrong in failing to grasp the dynamic dimension of integration. In either case, the Community's main virtues at that time were mostly political and institutional (the EC underwriting Greece's fragile Republic) rather than economic.

In the 1980s, and with the completion of the Mediterranean enlargement, the emergence of a Southern pole in the EC absorbed much of the attention of both scholars and public intellectuals. In the first half of the decade much intellectual capital was invested in the effort to demonstrate why Greece deserved special treatment in the EC, which to some extent was obtained through the Mediterranean Integrated Programs. In the second half of the decade, the '1992 program' revived fears of Greece being left behind. Pessimism reached its darkest depths at the end of the 1980s and early 1990s, when soaring deficits and public debt popularized the conception of a 'lost decade'. The EU-related literature from the late 1980s until the mid-1990s was deeply pessimistic, as the gap between promise/desire and actual performance was widening (Allison and Nikolaïdis 1997). In the variable-geometry, multiple-speed Europe that was

---

[11] E.g. Xenophon Zolotas (1976) and Ioannis Pesmazoglu (1962 and 1964), respectively governor and deputy governor of the Bank of Greece.

apparently emerging in the mid-1990s, Greece's future appeared to be stuck at the back of the train. Publications and op-eds during this period are imbued with a sense of despair over Greece's European vocation slipping away (e.g. Someritis 1996). Authors like Kazakos (1991), Mouzelis (2002), Tsoukalis (1995), Veremis (2006), and others identify Greece's modernization imperative with Europeanization, and lament the growing gap and missed opportunities of socio-economic and institutional adjustment.

The climate was bound to shift after 1996, with the rise of Costas Simitis to the premiership and the PASOK leadership. Probably for the first time since its 1981 accession, official Greece was finally in full mental and political accord with the European Union, seeing eye-to-eye with its integrationist core.[12] The Europeanization strategy hinged upon what became the country's major national challenge of the 1990s, i.e. the successful fulfilment of the nominal convergence criteria and accession to the EMU. This was finally clinched in 1999, and Greece joined the single currency in 2001. Throughout the 1990s, the macroeconomic austerity policies necessitated by the Maastricht nominal convergence criteria provoked some opposition from the left (Vergopoulos 1997); in that regard, Greece had much in common with other EU countries. EMU accession, however, generated a wave of optimism for Greece's European prospects, which was further enhanced by the successful (though massively overspent) hosting of the 2004 Olympic Games. The national psyche was filled with confidence and a sense of achievement, which boosted the most extrovert and cosmopolitan elements of Greek society. The year 2004 represented probably the highest moment in the Greek population's collective self-esteem; it has been in decline since then, under an avalanche of economic deterioration, political corruption scandals, and a widespread feeling of socio-political and institutional crisis. Following the 2008–9 global economic crisis, in an atmosphere of political corruption (2004–9), Greece's sliding economic competitiveness and soaring public debt and deficits have revived the threat of marginalization within the Eurozone. The gradual deterioration of Greece's socio-economic conditions unfolded against the parallel background of a severe political crisis of integration, following the ratification failure of the Constitutional Treaty. The new climate of lowered expectations affected the pronouncements of Greek Europeanists, tempering earlier optimism and imposing a new realism about the future of European integration (Ioakimidis 2007b; Tsoukalis 2009).

Indicative of the short-lived 'era of optimism' (late 1990s to mid-2000s) in Greece's national prospects and European vocation, public pronouncements during that period of extroversion revolve not only around the role Greece pursued in the integrationist avant-garde of the EU, but also around the future

---

[12] Prime Minister Constantine Mitsotakis of 1990–3 was also a convinced Europhile, but Greece's relationship with the EU was strained by the emergence of the 'Macedonian' dispute.

of Europe itself (in the framework of the Future of Europe debate), as well as Greece's leading role in the Europeanization of the Balkan neighbourhood.[13] Some Greek Europeanists articulate their vision for the transformation of the EU: Loukas Tsoukalis, one of the country's foremost European scholars with an international standing, sees it in the direction of a more democratic Europe politicized along the left/right axis (Tsoukalis 2006). Athens professor P. C. Ioakimidis (2002) favours a European federation. Others, like former MEP Costas Botopoulos (2007) of the European Socialist Party, advocate a constitutional political union and 'social Europe'.

Perhaps the leading representative of what this volume identifies as a 'transnational' normative vision of Europe is constitutional scholar and former MEP Dimitris Tsatsos (2007a and 2007b), who played a significant role in the European Convention and Constitution-building process. His publications elaborate the concept of a 'European Sympolity' of states and peoples, stressing its fundamentally transnational nature, in contrast to a federation which would presuppose a unitary demos or nation that does not currently exist in the EU. The younger scholars Dimitris Chryssochoou and Kostas Lavdas are also representative of a transnationalist school of thought. Chryssochoou's understanding of an 'organized synarchy' conceptualizes the EU as 'a system of political co-determination based on mutually reinforcing norms of "co-governance" ... being constituted on the basis of co-determining state sovereignties' (Chryssochoou 2009: 131). Lavdas invokes republicanism as a means of disentangling the issue of participation in an emerging polity from the cultural and emotional dimensions of citizenship; he argues for a Europe that would embrace what he calls 'civic polyculturalism': a condition in which multiple allegiances coexist without denying the basic adherence to certain minimal but commonly shared political values (Lavdas 2001 and 2009).

Revealing of the growth of national self-confidence regarding Greece's prospects in the EU was the evolution of the country's official stance towards EU institutional reform. During the first half of the 1990s, Greece opposed variable geometry, or what was finally stipulated in the 'closer cooperation' provisions of the Amsterdam Treaty. Willing but not able to participate in the EU core, Greece feared that variable geometry would seal its marginalization within the EU (Ioakimidis 2007a). However, having earned the right to participation in the prospective EU/EMU core, Greek governments shifted to become proponents of 'closer' or 'enhanced cooperation'. Similarly, Greece's erstwhile defence of the unanimity rule as a last refuge against larger core countries of the EU has matured into support for a federalist-oriented, consensus-seeking stance, attempting to define national interest proactively in conjunction with a common European interest. These positions have been expressed by the two major

[13] See various contributions in Ioakimidis 2002.

parties, ND and PASOK, and articulated by scholars such as Ioakimidis (amongst others). In the constitutional debate, the two main political parties supported the transformation of the EU into a political Union, a federalist system based on the Community model and the Community method of integration. Thus Greece officially espouses a supranational and decentralized federation of national states in which national sovereignty would coexist with the political authorities of the Union (Pagoulatos 2002; Yataganas and Kaloudiotis 2009).

The implosion of the former Yugoslavia in the 1990s re-energized anti-Western, anti-European reflexes. A large section of the Greek public felt a sense of brotherhood with the fellow-Orthodox Serbs, who had suffered at the hands of common enemies under Ottoman rule and, later, the Axis invasion. Sympathy persisted despite the war crimes committed by the Milosevic regime in Bosnia, and a section of the Greek public (subscribing to what we have identified as the underdog culture) regarded Karadzic and Mladic as Christian-Orthodox heroes recalling the Greek war of independence against the Ottomans. Consequently, the majority of the Greek public viewed with hostility what they perceived as unfair treatment of the Serbs by the EU and the US, culminating with the 1999 NATO bombardment of Serbia over the Kosovo issue. Unanimously supported by the EU governments, and opposed by neither the Simitis government nor the ND opposition party, the NATO-Yugoslav conflict increased the EU's unpopularity with Greek public opinion. The prosecution of Milosevic and Karadzic by the Hague tribunal was perceived by the same section of the Greek public and opinion leaders as a case of Western double standards (Lygeros 2008). The Yugoslav and Kosovo crises demonstrated the tenuous grounds upon which Greek pro-EU sentiment has been built.

Though the unresolved bilateral dispute over the name of the neighbouring country officially called the Former Yugoslav Republic of Macedonia continues to burden Greek foreign policy, the improvement of Greco-Turkish relations following Greek support for Turkey's EU accession process in 1999[14] allowed Greece to develop a strong Southern European policy, and to emerge as a protagonist of regional Europeanization. In the framework of Greece's Balkan corporate 'expansion', the EU was viewed through Greek eyes as a force of regionalization. At the forefront of the EU's expansion in South Eastern Europe, Greece became pivotal for the transformation of the region towards greater interdependence and the deepening of democratic and market institutions, much as the EU had helped transform the political and economic institutions of Greece in the 1980s and 1990s. Such views were expressed by several prominent Greek public intellectuals, such as international relations scholars Theodore Couloumbis (2007) and Thanos Veremis (2006).

---

[14] For an extended analysis of Greco-Turkish relations in the framework of European politics, see Anastasakis, Nicolaïdis, and Öktem 2009.

Conclusion

Thinking on Europe has been interwoven with the Greek nation-building process. The idea of Europe has been inextricable from the Greek project of national self-consciousness, the kind of Europe that was viewed by West European classicists and humanists as having originated in classical Athens. Acceding to this Europe, which ancient Greece had helped create, was viewed by Greek public intellectuals and political elites as a natural return to origins, or a long-postponed European family reunion. Europe is 'possessed' in the public pronouncements of many Western-oriented Greek public intellectuals, but this is so largely as a result of awareness of the distance created by successive historical layers of Byzantine and especially Ottoman rule between Greece and Western Europe. It is a Europe officially 'possessed' in national fear of being 'othered', politically revered for fear of being culturally relinquished.

The prevalent European story among Greek public intellectuals has equated Europe with progress, identifying the country's modernization challenge with catching up with Europe. Pro-European reformist political and intellectual elites, of the centre-right and the centre-left or even the non-communist left, have thus repeatedly enlisted the EU in the service of promoting Greece's modernization. This 'enlisted' Europe can only operate as an effective external constraint and driving force for national progress if it is integrated enough to generate rules and norms that can be internalized by the national socio-economic and political order. Hence this pro-European school of thought has naturally gravitated towards an (occasionally even simplistic) 'supranational' idea of Europe. Pro-European supranationalism has been the most vocal opposition pole of the debate, struggling against a long tradition of cultural gravitation towards Eastern Orthodoxy, ethnocentrism, a nostalgic communitarian vision of an unadulterated past, a 'culture of the underdog', or – to follow a more systematic typology – the statist/national school of thought. The independence versus integration, nationalism versus supranationalism divide has been the most salient one in the Greek public intellectual debate. Such ideological polarization, however, has been mitigated by the emergence of a 'third pole', a middle of the road 'transnational' school of thought, which was given impetus by the increasing complexity and mishaps of the European integration project, and especially the disenchantment following the rejection of the European Constitutional Treaty. This transnational school of thought is gathering pace among Greek intellectuals who are principally European scholars.

Public intellectuals have had a significant influence in the Greek debate on Europe, but most crucial has been the impact of political leaders. Some of these (from Panagiotis Kanellopoulos and Constantine Tsatsos to Costas Simitis) have been public intellectuals in their own right. The gradual development of the socialist PASOK to pro-EU orthodoxy in the course of the 1980s and 1990s has sealed a bipartisan majority of Greek public opinion solidly in support of the EU – though not without the occasional wavering and setback. The mainstream pro-European story of Europe, which has become dominant with public opinion, has emphasized the crucially stabilizing role of the EU in underwriting the Hellenic Republic in the late 1970s and 1980s, supporting Greek farmers and the periphery in the 1980s, and vitally anchoring the unstable Greek economy of the 1990s and 2000s to the EMU. For Westernizing Europhiles, the EU has been the single most important ally in the far-reaching modernization of Greece. For its opponents and critics, the EU provides a convergence point of both conservative traditionalists and nationalists close to the worldviews of the Orthodox Church on one hand, and left-wing Marxists militating against the foreign imperialist, global-capitalist *directoire* allegedly represented by the EU on the other. For both the left- and right-wing extremes, the nation becomes a last bastion of defence against the pervasive forces of globalization allegedly represented by the EU. But this, too, is a very typical 'European' Eurosceptic reaction . . .

10

Consensus, Benign Neglect, and Specialized Knowledge
Spanish Intellectuals and Europe*

Carlos Closa and Antonio Barroso

Introduction

Spanish intellectuals (in the words of Collini 2006: 47, those possessing some kind of 'cultural authority', that is who deploy an acknowledged intellectual position or achievement in addressing a broader, non-specialized public) have been very actively involved in various political issues and topics on the Spanish agenda. Intellectuals were highly engaged in debates during the transition and beyond on issues such as terrorism (with leaders such as philosopher Fernando Savater acting as mobilizers of civil society); nationalism (on which intellectuals have followed the same polarized pattern as public opinion and political parties); or, more recently, in debates on the politics of memory and transitional justice. Moreover, there are cases of intense intellectual mobilization, for example the public position adopted in relation to the Iraq war in 2003.

In contrast, however, intellectuals have shown a relative lack of concern, or a benign neglect, towards the EU and European integration. The reasons for this attitude are to be found in the Spanish historical trajectory since 1898 and the place that Europe has played in the collective imaginary. As a result of the struggle for democratization and the almost automatic link between this and Europe, the latter occupied an almost totally uncontroversial position; hence, public intellectuals did not show much interest in debating it. This provoked a vacuum which more specialized intellectuals (i.e. academics) tried to fill in.

* Support for this research has been provided by RECON Project VI Framework Programme. We are grateful to the participants in the Brussels and Oxford Workshop for their very valuable comments. In particular, Jan Zielonka discussed the paper intensively, and Julio Crespo MacLennan and Juan Díez Medrano provided useful insights.

However, the more technical character of their approach meant that they came to the forefront only when a large and significant issue (such as treaties) was on the line. In this situation, and equipped with their expertise, they provided a more technical and specialized discussion whose effect has probably been that the general broader public has remained aloof from them. The third section below includes two brief case studies (the ratification of the Maastricht Treaty and the debate around the European Constitution) which aim to illustrate both propositions. Given the restricted amount of categorical information that is available on these events, the chronological scope of the analysis will be broadened in order to include any academic contribution with relevant normative implications. Finally, the conclusions describe the normative framework that emerges from the study, and speculate on the possible specificity of Spanish academia in the area of EU studies.

The historical evolution of Spanish intellectual debates on Europe: The sources of consensus

The roots of contemporary Spanish intellectual debate on Europe date back to the last years of the nineteenth century. Following the loss of Spain's last colonial possessions and the subsequent crisis of national identity, a group of intellectuals (the 'Generation of 98') examined the existing political, cultural, and economic deficiencies of the state and sought to provide solutions. Two contrasting perspectives on Spain's position in the international milieu emerged, and these approaches permeated Spanish stances towards Europe throughout much of the twentieth century (Closa and Heywood 2004: 6).[1] On the one hand was an 'introspective' view, promoted by thinkers such as Miguel de Unamuno who underlined the country's distinctive values and principles, and advocated its protection from external influences. Europe, in this view, was 'othered'. On the other hand, there existed a 'Europeanist' perspective, which perceived European values and principles as the best solutions to Spanish problems, its main proponents being the economist Joaquín Costa and the philosopher José Ortega y Gasset. The first coined the word 'Europeanization' in 1900, and the word transformed Europe into the symbol of the agenda of reform and modernization of the country (Costa 1981). Ortega, meanwhile, theorized the idea that 'Spain is only feasible if viewed from Europe' (Ortega y Gasset 1910). Rather than a call for a federal Europe, the motto meant that the country would be strengthened through a more determined incorporation into the European arena. Europe, in this view, was invented or aspired to.

---

[1] For a comprehensive overview of Spanish political thought on Europe in the twentieth century, see Beneyto 1999, and for a broader view, Díaz 1974.

To some extent, the history of Spain during the twentieth century can be portrayed as the struggle between these two opposed tendencies. The instauration of Franco's dictatorship in 1939 meant not only the consolidation of the introspective view; it also practically erased any discussion about the place of the country in Europe. From a political perspective, both the authoritarian character of the new regime and the non-participation of Spain in the two world wars (as well as in post-war reconstruction) helped to reinforce the political seclusion of the country from European states.[2] Indeed, Spain's relationship with Europe has to be comprehended in the framework of its isolation from the original institutional development of the European project (Closa and Heywood 2004: 7). Francoism produced its own view of Europe by means of its organic intellectuals: a Christian continent corrupted by the excesses of democracy and political parties, and threatened by Soviet communism.

Nonetheless, the power of a Europe imagined or aspired to did not fade, and opposing intellectuals articulated an alternative view of Europe to the official one. With the start of economic recovery and development in the early 1960s, a group of individuals gathered in a collective volume entitled *Libertad y organización* (Freedom and Organization)[3] to endorse the thesis synthesized by philosopher José Luis López Aranguren in the introduction: the legal and political need for Spain to adapt to a transforming society and culture. The model for this transformation was Europe. However, the 1960s also saw the appearance of tendencies favouring non-alignment and even third-worldism as an alternative to Europeanism, moving in parallel with contemporary issues of decolonization and third world revolution. This position was articulated by writer Juan Goytisolo in the French journal *Les Temps Modernes*. Goytisolo proposed the Africanization of Spain: 'nowadays, our views must turn towards Cuba and the peoples of America, Africa and Asia that fight for their independence and freedom. Europe symbolises the past, immobilism. It is time to Africanise' (Goytisolo 1962). This minority position influenced some positioning alongside non-aligned countries until Spanish accession to Western European organizations.

In parallel with these internal debates, Spanish intellectuals in exile (together with some internal ones) played an important role as mobilizers of Europe and the nascent European Communities against Francoism. Led by writer and diplomat Salvador de Madariaga (founder of the College of Europe), they gathered in Munich in June 1962 at the fourth Congress of the European

---

[2] It should be noted that despite the autarchic character of the Franco regime, in 1957 the six founding countries of the European Community were buying 30 per cent of Spanish exports and selling 23 per cent of its imports (Powell 2007: 44).

[3] AAVV 1963. Among the authors were Pedro Laín Entralgo, José Ferrater Mora, Fernando Lázaro Carreter, Francisco Ayala, Julián Marías, Juan Marichal, Carlos María Bru, Carlos Castilla del Pino, and Luis Ángel Rojo.

Movement.[4] Communist intellectuals were not invited and radical leftists did not attend; centre-right intellectuals therefore dominated. The Congress approved a resolution stating that European integration required participating countries to have democratic institutions and respect human rights. These intellectuals, some of whom would reappear as key figures and politicians during the transition to democracy, were imprisoned and confined in internal exile upon their return to Spain. However, the Congress (known among Francoist circles as the *Contubernio de Munich*) successfully convinced the EP and EU member states to reject the Franco regime's application for the status of associated member. In 1963, the EP approved the Birkelback report which, albeit without explicitly mentioning Spain, nevertheless established the democratic requirement for associated membership status.

This result firmly re-established the old perception that mechanically linked Europe and modernization, but now the link was enriched with additional meanings: democratization and respect for political pluralism and human rights. In parallel, the US support for the Franco regime provided a negative referent or antagonism to the idea of Europe in a way seldom seen in post-Second World War European countries (although the traditional anti-Americanism of sectors of the Spanish left progressively faded away to become a marginal feature of radical left positions). These two ideas provided a basic consensus which public opinion and intellectuals largely shared. In 1974, lawyer and philosopher Elías Díaz summarized the consensus: the incorporation of Spain in Europe is nowadays accepted as a positive fact supported by a large consensus including the most progressive tendencies and positions, even if they propose a profound transformation of European capitalist systems. Only the most reactionary tendencies are nowadays coherently anti-European (Díaz 1974).

The transition to democracy sanctioned this basic consensus among elites about the relevance of Europe for the political and economic development of Spain.[5] Specifically, Europe represented not only the possibility of improving the country's dire economic situation, but also the opportunity of putting an end to Spanish international (political) isolation through democratic 'anchorage' (Álvarez Miranda 1996; Closa and Heywood 2004; Morata 1998). The rigorous Community application of the democratic clause (in contrast with other international organizations) reinforced this 'homologating strength' of Europe (Powell 2007: 52). The diffusion of this attitude signified to a certain extent the return to the idea of 'Europe as solution' that had been formulated at

[4] Among these, Fernando Álvarez de Miranda, Jaime Miralles, Barros de Lis, Joaquín Satrústegui, Cavero, Ruiz-Navarro, Alfonso Prieto Prieto, Pons y Casals, José María Gil-Robles, Dionisio Ridruejo, Jesús Prados Arrarte, José Federico de Carvajal, José Vidal-Beneyto. According to the latter, eighty persons came from Spain and thirty-eight from exile: Vidal-Beneyto 2009.

[5] See Álvarez Miranda 1996 for a comprehensive analysis of Spanish elite consensus on European integration.

the beginning of the century. The democratization approach pervaded most subsequent (early) academic evaluations of Spanish membership to the EC/EU, which emphasized the characterization of Europe as an anchor for democratic consolidation (Barbé 1999; Ortega 1994).[6]

In fact, it can be argued that this view has eliminated the 'national/exceptional' approach in Spanish debates on Europe. Some scholars even assert that this might represent the end of the dialectic tension that has defined Spain–Europe relations in the twentieth century (Moreno Juste 2000). This absence contrasts with the vigorous involvement of public intellectuals in other issues of the contemporary Spanish political agenda, such as the Spanish autonomist state or the question of peripheral regionalisms;[7] some positions and episodes of Spanish foreign policy (e.g. participation in the invasion of Iraq in 2003); and, more recently, the heated debates on the politics of memory on the civil war, the Franco regime, and transitional justice measures. The 'European' theme appears only episodically in the public debate of intellectuals; moreover, those involved tend to be specialized academics rather than figures who could properly be considered as the most representative public intellectuals.

The academic configuration of Spanish intellectual contributions on Europe

One of the effects of the underlying consensus on Europe, European integration, and the EU among Spanish intellectuals is their absence from public debates. An additional effect relates to the kinds of issues discussed (or not): perhaps as a reaction to former 'essentialist' conceptions held by the Franco regime, cultural, religious, and spiritual approaches have not significantly defined debates. Thus, for instance, the issue of Turkish membership was not approached as a cultural/religious question.

In turn, specialized intellectuals from specific epistemic communities, i.e. those who have a professional interest in European integration, have filled this vacuum. Contrary to what could be expected, political scientists, philosophers, and even economists have not taken the central stage. It is public lawyers who have in fact played the most significant role, with the effect that discussions on the EU have turned into an arcane reserve of specialists. This, together with the underlying consensus, has arguably done a great deal to alienate public opinion from EU affairs. The prevailing presence of law in public discourse in turn derives from the traditional legal 'technification' policy processes in Spain.

---

[6] In fact, as Moreno Juste (2000) points out, 'the transition and the consolidation of democracy have entailed such an important change that it is considered to be the only process in Spanish contemporary history that has deserved a universally positive judgement'.

[7] See for example Fox 1997, Fusi 2000, Marías 2000, or Sánchez Prieto 2000.

The overall strength, expertise, and solid 'corporatist-networking' organization of legal scholars have favoured their predominant position in the study of EU affairs. Additionally, by speaking in legal terms even in public discourses, lawyers have been successful in fencing off other scholars, reinforcing the traditional reticence of the Spanish legal community towards interdisciplinary work (Closa 2005: 86). Finally, the late arrival of political scientists to EU studies has also contributed to the pre-eminence of lawyers in European integration debates. This scenario can be attributed to the evolution of Spanish 'modern' political science, since the Francoist regime severely limited its development (Vallés 1989). Indeed, the advent of democracy opened favourable perspectives for a 'normalization' of political studies (Jerez Mir 1999: 75). However, despite Spanish application for EC membership in 1977, scholars were mainly concerned with issues that had a direct impact on the political situation of the country. Consequently, they devoted most of their research to topics such as the political transition to democracy, the electoral system and electoral behaviour, or the political and administrative decentralization of the state (Pasquier and León 2001: 1053).

Other institutional factors, such as the lack of alternative platforms to universities, also explain the dominance of the legal perspective. Similarly to the German case (see Jan-Werner Müller's contribution in this volume), legal scholars also had a significant presence in the written press. Only at the beginning of the 2000s did the emergence of some think tanks provide alternative platforms both in terms of discourses and channels. In particular, the *Real Instituto Elcano*, created in 2001, stimulated a broader interdisciplinary discussion on EU affairs. But even so, themes and issues continued to be predominantly framed and defined as 'technically legal' ones; only circumstantial events, such as EP elections for instance, provide further opportunities for press discussion.[8]

These structural characteristics have framed intellectual debates. The evolution of debates has been contingent to the topics analysed by scholars. This has been especially the case in the discussions about the Constitutional Treaty, when lawyers primarily used notions generated in the domain of EU law such as Joseph Weiler's principle of 'constitutional tolerance' (Weiler 2003a). According to this view, the EU should be conceived as a structure of law that respects the legal systems of its constituent parts, that is, the member states. This conception would fit to a certain extent within the historical 'Europeanist' approach mentioned above: the enhancement of Spanish democracy through the imposition of a European constitutional discipline. However, this view

---

[8] As an example, after the 2009 EP elections, Vidal-Beneyto wrote that disaffection is provoked by the 'soft' consensus in EU decisions and behaviour, the re-nationalization of concerns (which he associates with the reluctant attitude of the UK towards integration), and the routine bureaucratic mode of business of EU institutions and personnel (Vidal-Beneyto 2009).

constitutes neither the sole nor the predominant theoretical approach in Spanish analysis of EU affairs. The study of the contributions made during recent 'critical moments' of European integration reveals how certain intellectuals have remained sceptical about the possibility of perfecting national democracies through supranational law.

The contribution of academic intellectuals to the debate on Europe

The contributions of Spanish intellectuals can be assessed in two key moments of European integration: the ratification of the Maastricht Treaty and the process of elaboration, discussion, and (failed) ratification of the treaty establishing a Constitution for Europe. It should be noted that the number of available contributions differs considerably between cases. For instance, the mobilization of intellectuals during the process of elaboration of the European Constitution was higher than during any other former round of EU reforms. Furthermore, the type of topics discussed during the drafting of the Constitutional Treaty favoured the extensive participation of scholars. Consequently, it is not surprising that a large number of contributions with substantial normative implications were made during the debates on the Constitutional Treaty.

The debate on the Maastricht Treaty (1992–1994)

The domestic public debate that took place during the elaboration and ratification of the Maastricht Treaty has been qualified as very poor, despite the Spanish government's efforts to inform the population (Closa 2005: 86; Gil Ibañez 1994: 136). Judging by public opinion data, this account seems more than reasonable: 92 per cent of Spanish citizens – the highest figure among the twelve member states – declared in December 1992[9] that they knew little or nothing about the text. It must be recalled that the national political and economic climate did not favour the development of public discussion. First, a strong economic recession had set in in 1992, causing support for EC membership to decline for the first time since Spanish accession to the Community. Besides, domestic political turmoil linked to corruption within the ruling Socialist Party and the upcoming general elections constrained the public agenda within the national frame of reference.

Two basic issues preoccupied intellectuals: the consequences of the ratification process in Spain and the implications of the new text for the future of the European project. As regards the first question, the debate focused mostly on

---

[9] Eurobarometer no. 38, December 1992.

technical questions, in particular the reform of the Spanish constitution that would be necessary in order to implement the new electoral provisions of the treaty, or the repercussions of the future monetary union for the Spanish economy. However, the prospects of constitutional modification did not stimulate a high degree of mobilization, and only lawyers seemed to be specifically concerned with the question. Considering the negligible changes finally introduced by the reform (just one additional word), it is hardly surprising that the discussion that accompanied it did not offer significant normative reflections.

In contrast, the debate on the future of Europe reflected a rich array of analysis of the changes that the new treaty brought about. Bearing in mind the magnitude of such modifications (i.e. the creation of the EU and monetary union), it is not surprising that intellectuals were especially concerned about the future of the European project. Two topics were particularly discussed: the repercussions stemming from the ratification process and the potential political consequences of the new legal framework provided by the treaty. Specifically, the debate surrounding the referendum in France – discussions on the possibility of convening a popular vote in Spain were practically absent – was followed and reproduced in Spain. Some authors analysed the outcome of the vote from an optimistic perspective, claiming that it had had a positive democratic effect: the promotion of public deliberation across Europe. For instance, constitutional lawyer López Garrido (1992) stated that the referendum had originated an 'unimaginable debate' that has produced the emergence of 'a European public opinion'. Other intellectuals used an 'inverse' reasoning, chastising those who asked for a revision of the treaty on the grounds that a 'large minority' had opposed the text (Vidal-Foch 1992). Finally, more cautious voices argued that the outcome of the referendum had built a ground for the debate about the democratic shortages of the European project, but at the same time criticized those who opposed the treaty for its lack of alternative proposals (Vilá Costa 1992).

Maastricht triggered for the first time a polemic on the EU and European integration. The different contributions to the debate adopted quite diverse interpretations of the political implications of the new text. For some, the treaty represented an unequivocal further step in the spillover process towards European unification. While acknowledging the intergovernmental dimension of the Treaty on European Union (TEU) and the democratic shortages emerging from the new scenario, they saw the text as a 'quasi-constitution' invested with federal elements and providing the Union with a solid ground for the advancement of its 'inherent political vocation' (Fonseca y Martín 1992). In a more nuanced approach, certain contributions asserted the constitutional character of the treaty but criticized it for falling short of political provisions. For instance, Cotarelo (1992) considered that the TEU was 'putting the cart before the horses' by giving priority to the Monetary Union over political union, and warned Maastricht supporters that 'their view [did not] provide them with the exclusive condition of pro-Europeans'. The author also expressed his fears that the treaty would establish a 'top-down' approach to European unity. Philosopher Julián Marías (1992) offered a similar – although somewhat more abstract – evaluation, advocating the search for a common European project and emphasizing the need for the mutual recognition of European nations:

The European Community was born under the sign of the economy...however, every economic element has the condition of being an instrument...which is necessary for the [constitution of] *aims* or *projects*. Neglect of the latter is the main cause for the discontent that invades us and comes symbolically with that geographic name, Maastricht...the reciprocal presence of nations, their mutual knowledge, must be achieved...we have to look for a historic European life project capable of attracting and bringing together the different nations.

Similarly, Berlin-based sociology professor Sotelo adhered to the familiar criticism of the lack of popular support. According to Sotelo's diagnosis (1992):

Maastricht opened a Pandora's Box, boosting an anti-Europeanism that had not been relevant until then and splitting the majority of supporters of the unification process between those who advocated a rapid pace and those who desired a slower one.[10]

In the sceptical camp, some authors talked about the 'exhaustion' of the integration process and expressed their doubts about the prospects for further integration (Remiro Brotons 1994). Rubio Llorente, a former chairman of the Constitutional Court and a leading constitutionalist, coined the term 'Euro-perplexity' when trying to describe the outcome of the reform process. The author upheld the view that the new provisions highlighted the contradictions between the technocratic dimension of the Community and the political aspirations of the treaty. While conceding that the traditional conception of sovereignty was outdated, he seemed to be doubtful about the prospects of endowing the Community with functions that could only be assumed by states:

The Community is simply a system that manages the common market and resolves its problems through coordinated action of the interested parties...I do not see how Europe could do without structures that allow for the use of force. It will be the United States of Europe or maybe the Divided States, but in any case, it will be the States, not managerial structures. (Rubio Llorente 1994: 85–6)

Criticism of the European Monetary Union appeared also from more leftist positions. Although the old communist thesis about a pure market or capitalist Europe was not fully recovered, arguments were addressed in particular at the social costs required for achieving nominal convergence (Montes 1993). Maastricht marked the start of a marginal criticism made by leftist intellectuals

---

[10] All the quotes are author's translations from Spanish unless otherwise noted.

and directed at the liberal and/or neoliberal dimension of the process of integration, often associated with a negative view of globalization (Taibo 2005).

Despite these criticisms, a clear-cut Eurosceptical stance in the Spanish intellectual arena did not appear. Put another way, although the TEU reforms were controversial, the perception that Spain should be an active part of Europe was almost pervasive. As one of the founding fathers of the Spanish constitution would proclaim with regard to the reform of the Maastricht Treaty, 'outside a united Europe there is no Spanish national interest' (Herrero de Miñón 1992).

Debating the European Constitution (2003–2005)[11]

Academic intellectuals made their voice heard during the elaboration, negotiation, and (failed) ratification of the treaty establishing a Constitution for Europe more than in any other former 'turning point' of European integration. This could be partly explained by the fact that the reform process involved, to a large extent, a scholarly exercise of definition of conceptual categories such as 'constitution', 'federation', or 'distribution of competences', rather than a mere analysis of the negotiations conducted by member states. Legal scholars (particularly international public, constitutional, and administrative lawyers) dominated the debate, with some input from political scientists.

Two features defined the debate (both political and intellectual) before the opening of the preparatory stage of the reform: a reactive approach and a defensive attitude. Spanish discussions reacted to proposals formulated by other European leaders and/or EU institutions. Comparatively speaking, Spanish academics produced a limited number of contributions to the discussions. In contrast, scholars were particularly active during the Convention, which acted as a catalyst for the debate and as an anchor reference that supplied researchers with both inputs and a wide target for their proposals.

Three of the topics discussed could be qualified as 'non-contentious', and therefore did not induce any significant debate. These were the Charter of Fundamental Rights (whose incorporation into the Constitutional Treaty academics and politicians alike largely endorsed), the simplification of the treaties, and the role of national parliaments. In contrast, the distribution of competences and the reform of institutions attracted significant attention from scholars. However, the approach to these questions was somewhat pragmatic and reactive. For instance, some intellectuals opposed the German proposal to include a clear definition of competences in the text, fearing that it would lead to a re-nationalization of Community *acquis* (for instance, Areilza Carvajal 2002; Beneyto 2002). As for the institutions, the debate focused on the modification of the system of qualified majority voting and the fairness of an eventual

---

[11] This section draws extensively on Closa 2005.

new weighting of votes.[12] Finally, religion was also a hot topic during the Convention, with scholars debating the inclusion of a reference to Europe's Christian roots in the draft text.[13]

The more remarkable contributions from a normative point of view were the reflections on the nature of an (eventual) Constitution for Europe. Two basic positions emerged with regard to the outcome of the Convention: the 'functional' position and the negative view of the 'EU constitution'. For the 'sceptical' scholars (mainly constitutional lawyers), it made sense to speak of a constitution only in the framework of a state. It should be noted that most constitutional lawyers in Spain (with significant exceptions) had, until the 'constitutional period', been unconcerned with the EU. Besides, rulings by the Spanish Constitutional Court have vehemently established the infra-constitutional status of EC law. In fact, the enormous symbolic connotation of the Spanish constitution as an instrument for democratic reconstitution and its iconic nature may have played a role in the cautious scepticism of part of the legal profession towards a supra-state constitution. Some of the scholars argued that the utilization of the term 'constitution' instead of 'treaty' was a cosmetic or even a misleading step, and cast doubt on the utility of the concept.

Rubio Llorente (2002) upheld the view that the proposal to equip the EU with a constitution was constructed as an unintelligible discourse because of the confusion of ideas. According to him, it was not easy to identify the material contents of the proposed constitution, what innovations it would bring, or the reasons for calling an international treaty a 'constitution'. Moreover, the mere simplification and systematization of the treaty were not sufficient to justify the new label. From a highly sceptical standpoint, he identified two problems: first, the judicial construction of a potential EU constitution was unstable, since it lacked firm grounding on national constitutions. More importantly, the debates on the constitution could be seen as a 'smokescreen to elude discussion of real problems'. Some scholars adopted a more moderate view on the constitutional status of the European legal architecture, but also criticized the use of the 'C' word. As constitutional lawyer López Castillo (2005) asked, 'if there are already Constitutional treaties, why a European Constitution?' These lawyers, together with Pedro Cruz, former president of the Constitutional Court, have a German influence in their education, which naturally conveys a strong influence of German debates (and constitutional doctrine) on Spanish ones.

The functional approach to the Constitution can be summarized by a statement made by Rodríguez Iglesias, former president of the European Court of Justice and professor of Public International Law: when the Court had

---

[12] See Torreblanca 2003 and Areilza Carvajal 2003 and 2005 for two diverging views on the institutional issues.

[13] See for instance the dialogue between Rubio Llorente and Joseph Weiler (2003) on the Christian roots of Europe.

previously designated the treaties as a constitutional charter, it had characterized them by analogy. In other words, the treaties function as a constitution in
the judicial system of Europe (Rodríguez Iglesias 2002). Most Spanish lawyers
seemed to share this view, although they pointed towards two substantial
restrictions on the full constitutional status of the treaties: (a) legitimacy should
remain indirect, channelled by member states; and (b) the future adoption of a
text called a constitution would not change the fact that it would be based on a
treaty agreed by member states. It should be noted that legal scholars who
advocate a 'functional' position on the Constitution are more open to the
international dimension of law. They are exposed to the influences of scholars
such as Joseph Weiler, and thus approached the process in the context of the
conceptual apparatus developed by the author around the notion of 'constitutional tolerance'. This notion understands the European Constitution as a
system of law that respects the legal systems of member states. For instance,
scholars such as Areilza Carvajal (2001) explicitly endorsed this view, stressing
the fact that it allowed member states to avoid deciding in a definitive form
what authority – national or European – should be predominant.

In addition to these contributions, some Spanish scholars also evaluated the
outcome of the Convention from the point of view of 'deliberative' constitution-making. Drawing on Habermas' notion of 'constitutional patriotism', they
sought to analyse whether the new text represented a value-based constitution
that might help create the basis for a European model of citizen allegiance and
loyalty. This type of research generated mixed impressions: while the Convention might have provided Europe with an ideal-type, rights-based structure for
political and legal legitimation (Menéndez 2004), it did not by itself imply the
automatic appearance of constitutional patriotism. According to Closa (2004a),
pragmatic mechanisms (e.g. the practice of rights) 'would have to mediate
between the Constitution and the underlying self in order to generate a feeling
of attachment and allegiance of citizens'.

Once the draft treaty was presented, public intellectual discussion on the
negotiations focused on the most controversial questions posed by the text. In
Spain, the debate was virtually limited to the issue of the voting system in the
Council, since the formula retained by the Convention did not satisfy the
Spanish government. In fact, the failed negotiations of the Brussels European
Council were interpreted as a direct consequence of the disagreement between
member states over the definition of 'qualified majority' in the new treaty. Some
scholars were particularly critical of the 'veto' position of the Spanish government, stating that the executive was conveying a 'nationalistic' message that
would jeopardize the subsequent ratification of the text (Closa 2004b). Certain
contributions even asked if the votes were so important, pointing at the con-
comitance of other decisive factors in the EU decision-making process (Estella
2004). The change of government after the March 2004 elections led certain
intellectuals to call for a more nuanced approach: votes were important, and

Spain should defend its national interests within the negotiations. However, the government should put forward a proposal that would be fair not only to Spain, but also to other Europeans. A proposed theoretical solution – which might have empirical implications – could be to adopt Rawls' 'original position' (Rawls 1999) in order to design a set of rules that would be just for all the actors (Torreblanca 2004).

Finally, the ratification process of the Constitutional Treaty offered an opportunity for further involvement. On the one hand, in its information campaign the government itself relied on 'celebrities' to diffuse the contents of the Constitution, through television advertisements for instance. The use of public celebrities (i.e. mainly television celebrities, actors, and sportspersons) shows clearly the relative lack of importance granted to intellectuals for conveying influence. On the other hand, the call for a referendum triggered a rich debate on the consequences of convening referenda both in Spain and in other member states. While some scholars warned about the perils of putting the ratification of the treaty to a popular vote (Closa 2004c), other contributions cast serious doubt on the motivations for organizing a referendum in the Spanish case (Rubio Llorente 2003; Sotelo 2004). After the French and Dutch referenda, Francisco Laporta criticized the false seduction of this method of decision-making: when such a complex question as the content of a constitution or a European Union treaty is submitted for consultation, democratic essences appear to prevail, yet in the background there remains a predominantly emotive fabric of fears and passions that are the province of opportunists and demagogues (Laporta 2005). However, the support for the 'yes' was almost unanimous. In general, even if the Constitution was not considered to be the best possible outcome, intellectuals saw it as a crucial advancement in the process of European integration (Aldecoa and Gil Robles 2005). Therefore, the positive vote for the ratification of the Constitutional Treaty should be considered as a 'patriotic act', a 'manifestation of support for Spanish integrity and solidarity' (Gil Robles 2005). The sceptical camp – which advocated a 'no' in the referendum – was limited to scholars traditionally associated with an extreme leftist view of Europe (for instance, Taibo 2005).

The debate on the Constitutional Treaty produced the greatest volume of reflections about Europe in the history of Spanish academia. From a normative perspective, the kinds of issues at stake generated comprehensive discussions about the legitimacy of the European project. Research work and commentaries reflected the wide range of different theoretical interpretations of the constitution-making process. However, a number of scholars have upheld the 'functional' view of the EU Constitution. Once again, this could be attributed to the fact that the notion of constitutional tolerance fits within the historical 'Europeanist' conception of Spanish intellectual reflections on Europe: the insertion of Spain within the European constitutional architecture as a way of perfecting national democracy. As Mangas Martín (2005) wrote in her analysis of the

Constitution, 'our national project, Spain's project as a sovereign and united nation ... depends on the European integration project'. This echoes earlier positions in the same direction; thus, Closa and Heywood (2004) conclude their analysis of Spain in the EU with a similar sentence.

Conclusions

This chapter has argued that Spanish intellectual debates on Europe have been shaped both by historical and organizational factors. The analysis of the contributions made during three milestones of European integration seems to confirm these patterns. First, Spanish intellectuals have traditionally shared a certain idea not only of Europe, but also of the place of Spain within the process of European integration. The 'Europeanist' conception seems to be more prominent in certain intellectual positions, and permeates most academic reflections. According to this view, Europe is conceived as Spain's national project and thus the consecutive advancement of the integration process would serve to strengthen the country. However, this idea should not be equated with the argument that Europe has rescued the nation-state (Milward 1992). On the contrary, the dominant perception among political and intellectual elites is that reinforcement of the state is indissolubly linked to EU membership and the parallel transformation of the notion of statehood. The existence of a robust pro-EU public opinion created a suitable environment for these dominant positions. Only later have some minor criticisms also appeared in connection with some small signs of disaffection among public opinion.

On the other hand, the predominance of certain professional profiles, mainly legal scholars, has defined the type of normative apparatus used in the study of EU affairs. This has been especially the case in intellectual discussions on the European Constitution, which generated a number of reflections that made extensive use of legal concepts and notions associated with the study of EU law. Nevertheless, these structural conditions seem gradually to be changing with the growing incorporation of political scientists in the debate on Europe.

From a theoretical standpoint, it can be argued that these two explanatory elements characterize a system of thinking that does not reflect a systematic normative conception of Europe, but rather a limited mix of approaches. This 'open' framework could be characterized by certain specific characteristics. First, the strong federalist discourses that were present in the 1970s and 1980s have progressively yielded to more nuanced accounts. This does not mean a rejection of federalist principles, but rather their subordination to more pragmatic attitudes.

Additionally, there is an increasing consensus in Spain around the idea that the European Union has a specific legal architecture, a kind of European 'constitutional arrangement' (Weiler 2003a) that respects the national constitutional traditions of its member states. This is coupled with a widespread agreement on the benefits of this European constitutional discipline for national democracy. Moreover, whilst some intellectuals have reflected specifically on the emergence of a European demos and the prospects of constitutional patriotism, recent contributions have explicitly endorsed Nicolaïdis' (2003a) view about the composition of Europe by different *demoi* and its democratic implications (for instance, Ortega 2007). However, the question of EU legitimation remains open to discussion: although several scholars uphold the view that the main source of legitimacy in the European project comes from the member states, some also highlight the inherent democratic value of supranational institutions (e.g. the European Parliament).

In sum, Spanish intellectual debates on Europe have specific qualities that can be attributed to the evolving idiosyncrasy of the country. In particular, the relative non-involvement of non-specialized intellectuals (such as novelists, painters, actors, musicians, etc.) in the debate means that Europe and European integration enjoy a large consensus. This benign neglect provoked a vacuum that specialized players have filled: the exploitation of more arcane EU debates offers a track towards public visibility that academics cannot easily renounce.

It remains to be seen whether Spain can be conceived as a singular case within the constellation of national academic debates on Europe, or if the aforementioned features are applicable to other EU member states. In any case, it can be expected that, given the increasing international exposure of Spanish scholars and the progressive 'normalization' of EU studies within certain disciplines (especially political science), normative discussions about the European issue will reflect a richer diversity of theoretical approaches in the future.

Part IV

Returners

11

Between Old Fears and New Challenges
The Polish Debate on Europe

Magdalena Góra and Zdzisław Mach

Introduction

The course of history has left Poles on the outside of reflections about the shape of political processes in Western Europe after the Second World War. Nevertheless, the origins of various Polish concepts and visions of the country's place in Europe can be traced back to the fifteenth and sixteenth centuries and the Jagiellonian Commonwealth, spreading from the Baltic almost to the Black Sea. This period was characterized by a wide, multi-ethnic and multi-religious composition of the state, ruled by a strong and vast gentry mostly identifying with Polishness and then transmitting further the crucial elements of the political culture. The most important element was the identification with Western European civilization versus that of the East. The idea of the *antemurale* – presented in religious terms – is based on the conviction that Poland as a Christian (Catholic) country defended other Christians from barbaric, Islamic, and other threats (Tazbir 2004).

It is worth mentioning that the founding period of European modernity, the Enlightenment, put a visible yet rather shallow imprint on Polish political culture. The period of the eighteenth-century state reforms initiated by Enlightenment politicians and reformers did not secure the country from internal devastation due to its inefficient political institutions and external threats. The significant changes – crucial as regards time and scope – were brought on by the difficult years for Polish statehood and Poles following the three partitions, starting from the end of the eighteenth century, made by three local powers: Tsarist Russia, the Habsburg Monarchy, and Prussia. In Europe, this was a crucial time for the creation and consolidation of modern nation-states and the modern version of national identification. This process did not pass over Polish soil, yet it took on a different form and, due to the lack of state institutions, it referred to the structures already available to Poles, such as the Catholic Church. It is often stressed, and is evident even today, that Polish national identification was developed not based on state institutions but in opposition to them, due to the fact that they were imposed on rather than supported by the Polish people (Mach 1993).

One of the crucial elements compensating for the lack of state structures was the intelligentsia. This distinct social stratum – urban, educated, and made up largely of professional categories such as teachers or doctors – developed in Poland in the eighteenth century, and was for a long time responsible for the well-being of Polish society and the preservation of national identity challenged by the partition powers. Moreover, in Polish political culture the role of this social stratum, in terms of cultural authority, has arguably been more significant than that of individual public intellectuals. During the difficult years Polish elites, especially the intelligentsia, referred to Western Europe as an important cultural source and civilization. It was clear for Poles that 'Europe existed not as a community of customs and traditions but as a common civilization. And the Polish intellectual elite has always belonged to this latter community since the Middle Ages' (Tazbir 1999: 59).[1]

Another characteristic element, since early times, was a strong political self-identification – albeit mostly among the Polish gentry – in relation to neighbouring Germany and Russia. The construction of Polish national identity was dominated by the interpretation of history as a process of continuous struggle against these two neighbours. Other neighbouring countries and peoples were mentioned only marginally, while the meaning of relations between Poles and their two large 'significant others', and the respective images of these countries in relation to Poland, dominated Polish national history as it was presented in literature, art, and school education as well as in numerous myths and certain elements of the public landscape such as historic buildings, monuments, or street names. The concept of history constructed around the dichotomy of 'us' versus 'them' made the development of the Polish nation meaningful, justified past victories, and gave hope for the future.

The years of the partitions, with frequent uprisings against the foreign powers, invested Polish political culture with another interesting notion, that of messianism. The messianic rhetoric depicted the suffering of the divided – yet chosen – nation thrown apart by powerful countries as a sacrifice for the well-being of other Western nations. This mythical concept, still present in the Polish national-historical memory, strengthens the image of Poland as a country always threatened and attacked by others. This implies an image in which defeat and suffering are elevated to the status of virtue and give to the nation a moral, if not practical, superiority over its enemies. This myth was, and still is,

---

[1] All translations from Polish are the author's unless stated otherwise.

very useful to Poles, offering a sense of self-importance and moral superiority even in times of political loss and economic failure. It is also often used as a justification for the claim of compensation which other nations allegedly owe to Poles for their historic suffering.

Such a belief, however, also means that Poles find it very difficult to see themselves as guilty of causing the suffering of others, of committing any historical injustice. Polish historical memory does not contain aggression against others. This mentality persists in spite of the fact that Poles may be seen differently from the outside (especially by their Eastern neighbours), and the historical experience of domination by others stands in paradoxical contrast to Polish attempts to dominate its own (less developed) neighbours. Poles read their history in such a way that all events which may be seen as aggressive or dominating are either eliminated or marginalized, or seen in a very particular, biased interpretation. This traditional self-perception, developed mostly during the romantic era – the founding period of Polish modern nationalism – is still recalled by Poles when justifying political decisions (Janion 2007).

'The East of the West or the West of the East'

Since the end of the nineteenth century, two major camps – although neither was internally unified or in possession of a monopoly of political choices – were clarified as regards the future of the projected independent state. After more than a hundred years of partitions, the fundamental questions were how Poland was to be built, on which territory, and with a citizenry made up of whom; and finally, how to secure its existence. Ideas therefore developed within these two groups – the first right-wing and the second more left-leaning – at least until the 1920s, determining the future shape of identity formation in the country as well as political decisions (before and after independence).

The first camp grouped around the ideas and thoughts of Roman Dmowski, a political writer and politician, favouring the ethnic Polish basis for the creation of the state with an essentialist vision of the nation and national identity. For this leader and his movement – National Democracy – the future independent state should be for and composed predominantly of Poles. This was followed by sceptical opinions on the possibility of coexisting with other peoples living in the same territory, especially Jews, and later contributed to the anti-Semitic rhetoric promoted by Dmowski's political movement (Dmowski 1903 [1996]; Kawalec and Kulak 1992: 125; Walicki 2000: 324–5). As Wandycz noted (1990: 454), 'Just as the state was subordinate to the nation, so was the individual transcended by it. In that sense one can call Dmowski the father of integral Polish nationalism.' The second camp, connected with the activities and ideas of another founding father of independent Poland – the politician and activist Józef Piłsudski – tended towards a multi-ethnic composition of the country referring to the heritage of the Jagiellonian Commonwealth, and merged the tradition of the Polish gentry with elements of social justice (Wandycz 1990: 453).

We can find most elements of Polish political culture in these two contrasting visions. One may stress Piłsudski's activism and realism in foreign policy, orientation towards the West coupled with a cautious position towards Germany, and the strongly anti-Russian stance (initially perceiving Tsarist Russia as the greatest threat, and later seeing the Bolshevik regime as an even larger threat). On the other hand, Dmowski emphasized the necessity of a more homogeneous ethnic composition of the state, with ethnic Poles predominating; he was aware of the geopolitics of Poland's location in Europe, but perceived threats as coming more from the German side than from Slavic countries (Longhurst and Zaborowski 2007; Wandycz 1990). The threat from both Germany and the Soviet Union proved both of them right as regards the outcome of Polish geopolitics. Finally one can say that their ideas flourished in Polish political life in the decades after their lifetimes (Kuźniar 2008; Longhurst and Zaborowski 2007; Michnik 1985).

One of the major topics of the intellectuals' reflection for centuries in Poland – closely interrelated with Europe – was the modernization of the country. For both groups mentioned above, the source of modernity lay in Western Europe. It is somewhat paradoxical that imperial tendencies, especially in Germany, made the absorption of this country's cultural influence difficult for Poles in practice. This resulted in 'the glorification of distant civilizations, treated as a political chance and ally. For a long period of time, this referred to the high perception of French culture, and, beginning with World War II – the American one' (Dobroczyński 2003: 133). It is visible too in the political choices of Piłsudski, who once said: 'the bright side of our external relations is our particularly close relations with the states of the *Entente*. Deep sympathy linked Poland even earlier with the world of democratic countries of Europe and America, which did not seek glory in conquering and oppressing other nations, but were willing to organize these relations according to the rules of justice and rightness' (Piłsudski 1919 [1999]: 185).

The concepts of leading personalities of the right-wing National Democracy demonstrate acknowledgement of patterns of modernization in the West, even (in one sense) in the ways in which they were imitated. At the same time, they betray a parallel fear of the effects of modernization in the sphere of morality and tradition (Kawalec 2006: 70; Koryś 2006: 83). The second group of modernizers came from leftist circles, including writer and philosopher Stanisław Brzozowski, philosopher and socialist politician Edward Abramowski, thinker and socialist politician Bolesław Limanowski, and others (Cywiński 1985; Kawalec 2000; Michnik 1985). Their major concern was to condemn the romantic tradition and promote modernism, concentrating on progress and spreading socialist ideals in the country. The reflection of the entire group of leftist intellectuals on the necessity of modernizing the country from the beginning of the twentieth century was based on European ideas coming to the country from outside.

Post-Second World War Poland was different, in almost all dimensions, from the country invaded by the Third Reich and the Soviet Union in September 1939. The new borders of the country decided at Yalta and Potsdam decreased the territory and shifted the country to the west. As a result, the population structure changed. From the pre-war multinational society with an almost 30 per cent minority population, post-war Polish society was composed almost entirely of ethnic Poles. Germans were expelled to the west, Ukrainians and Byelorussians stayed in the eastern territories attached to the USSR, and, last but not least, the Jews constituted approximately 10 per cent of the population of Poland before the war, which declined to 0.4 per cent after 1945 due to the horrors of the Holocaust (Hurwic-Nowakowska 1996: 25). Finally, a new communist regime settled in the country, establishing a non-democratic, socialist system in Poland with a state monopoly in almost all areas of social activities.

The communist regime, enforced by the Soviet Army and lacking public support, tried to obtain at least partial support from the public via a brutal ideologization (even falsification) of collective memory and social and political life. The desire to legitimate the new regime in Poland incited communists to nationalize wider communist rhetoric (Zaremba 2001). In explaining these processes, historian Krystyna Kersten (1993: 11) stresses that the war brought national divisions to the surface and strengthened the nation as the dominant category. It was thus useful after the war to refer to these structures in justifying the communist regime. The peak of this approach was reached during the anti-Semitic campaign of 1968 followed by the purge of the remnants of the Jewish population from the country, and the nationalization – in contrast to the 'cosmopolitan' Jewish communists – of the regime in Poland (Eisler 1991; Zaremba 2001). Paradoxically, the period of communism in Poland contributed to the development of forms of national ideology based on anti-German, anti-Semitic feelings skilfully fuelled to maintain control over society.

Cold War rhetoric and communist control over the country set a crucial mark in relations with Europe. The initial intention (blocked by Moscow) to participate in the Paris Conference (which debated the generous offer of the USA presented by Secretary of State George Marshall) was the last attempt made by Poles to participate actively in the course of events (Borodziej 1990). The Western part was subsequently left on the other side of the Iron Curtain, on the enemy side. However, the perception of Western Europe during communism must be nuanced, and not presented in black and white categories. There was no single option within the communist movement in the country: opinions on Europe varied, and the 'openness' – even if partial – towards the West was different in the various periods of the communist era in Poland. Not all countries were perceived as equally 'hostile', and specifically France and Italy received (especially after the 1956 thaw) the status of semi-friendly countries. The major propagandist effort was directed against the Federal Republic of Germany – mostly to play on negative Polish sentiments from the partition years and the still fresh memories of the horrendous Nazi occupation. The nationalization of communist rhetoric from the 1960s onwards brought with it the concept of 'rotten West' used by communist leader Władysław Gomułka, referring to the moral inferiority of Western liberal systems in comparison to the high moral stance represented by the working and peasant class – using socialist categories.

The communists did not, however, manage to achieve complete domination and control over Polish political thought. The important contribution to the contemporary development of the Polish visions of Europe came from émigré circles in Paris, London, and the USA. The most important and novel ideas were drafted and later also spread in the country, via democratic opposition circles in Poland, in Jerzy Giedroyc's *Kultura* – a literary and political journal published from 1947 in Paris. The major ideas developed by Giedroyc and his main political publicist – Juliusz Mieroszewski – contained several core elements. Their stance was predominantly pro-European in the sense that the only future for post-Cold War, independent Poland could be imagined with a democratic Germany on the western border. Both Giedroyc and Mieroszewski noticed very early on that the only escape from the geopolitical trap, lethal for Poles, was via a democratic and pro-European Germany deeply embedded in European structures of political, economic, and cultural integration. They bravely stood for the position of reconciliation with the democratic German government and participated in various initiatives (Giedroyc and Mieroszewski 1999). In their political journalism they supported the Polish gestures initiating Polish–German reconciliation (Pomian 1999; Terry 2000). The second crucial element of *Kultura*'s influence is actually a continuation of the debate on the shape of the country that the Poles were already witnessing at the beginning of the twentieth century. This was the position that a return to the pre-war Polish borders was not only impossible, but also undesirable for Poles, who stood up for and were again actively involved in the support of the Ukrainian independence movement. These two concepts of a democratic, friendly Germany and strong, independent Slavic nation-states to the east of Poland were connected with the third element – a strong concentration on Europe and its integration project, starting in the 1940s with special emphasis on federal concepts (Wolański 1996). This was also due to the fact that democratic Germany, located in the centre of strong European institutions, brought Europe closer to Poland (Giedroyc and Mieroszewski 1999).

The ideas developed in Paris had a significant impact on the major intellectuals of the democratic opposition in Poland. They also contributed to the redefinition of ideas regarding the future foreign policy of the independent country in the Solidarity circles of the 1980s (Rotfeld 2008). Thus Polish opposition circles, who took power in the country after the Round Table discussions, faced tremendous challenges resulting from the recreation of the entire international system after the Cold War as well as from the dramatic internal situation and the collapse of the domestic economic and political system. They were, however, equipped with various concepts as regards possible post-Cold War scenarios. In this pivotal moment in the course of Polish history the overarching, general question was what could be expected from Europe during transformation. The legacy of the intellectuals who dominated the debate in this formative period is crucial for understanding the framework in which the contemporary debate on Europe is located.

'We return to where we belong'

The initial years of Polish statehood after 1989 witnessed a multitude of challenges. The international system went through fundamental changes, pushing Poland into the 'security vacuum' which emerged in Central and Eastern Europe at the beginning of the 1990s (Kuźniar 2008). While the Soviet sphere of influence and polity itself was undergoing dissolution and decomposition, Western Europe – to some extent as a reaction to what was going on in the East – was enforcing integration and heading towards a new stage of integration, introduced in the Maastricht Treaty, namely the European Union. On the other hand, the internal situation in Poland was also dramatically unknown, with a ruined and rapidly deteriorating economic situation, devastated societal institutions, lack of local self-government, and the malfunctioning of centralized over-bureaucratic institutions. In this context, the new political order was recreated with reference to previous historical experience, culture, and dominant identity discourse.

The major – and hardly contested – decision of most elites was to integrate with the Western European structures. Generally speaking this pro-Western shift was motivated by the strong conviction that Poland had always belonged to Western civilization. What is important here is that elites and leaders in Poland – and many other countries in the region – stressed that 'they are not conforming to but rather re-adopting practices and values that they share but to which they historically contributed' (Fawn 2003: 32). This perspective was also helpful in justifying the high costs of compliance with the norms and standards imposed during the EU enlargement process. The Western structures, and especially the EU and NATO, were treated as the institutional design helping to strengthen the Polish nation-state. The final fulfilment of these goals was reached in 1999, when Poland entered NATO, and five years later, when in May 2004 the country finally became a member of the EU.

During this period security guarantees were of major importance. All Polish political parties joined in the common effort to enter NATO. This unity, very unusual in Poland, can only be explained by the rare importance of security for Poles – a sensitivity well justified by Polish history and the country's difficult geopolitical location. At the time of NATO accession, the EU was perceived predominantly as a means of improving economic conditions in the country; but since membership in the EU was more demanding and since the EU was also seen as having a political and cultural significance, Polish accession to the EU was more controversial. At the same time it seems that EU accession became a catalyst which revealed with double strength the main lines of political and axiological divisions among Polish political elites originating from at least the beginning of the twentieth century. The reflections on Europe, the role and place of Poland in the integration project, and the future vision of the EU elevate the hidden, deep differences of the worldviews presented by Polish intellectuals.

The end of the Cold War exposed the problem of a newly united continent which needed to reinvent itself after communism. The topics of freedom often return in the debate on Europe, and thus a new common identity. The lack of divisions and the requirement of redefining identity posed one of the most important questions for both Western and Eastern Europe (Michnik 1995: 231; Porębski 2000: 168). This concept of redefinition of a finally united, complete Europe was also spread by the late professor Bronisław Geremek – another leader of the democratic opposition, historian, and politician – who said 'we are bringing the need of a positive self-defining to all of Europe, because we are entering [the EU] based on the principle that this is the real end of World War II and the Cold War. The entry of our countries ends the era of a divided world' (Geremek 2004: 26).

In this context the first major topic of discussion was around the conditions of Polish democracy, which concerned most of the leading intellectuals after the breakthrough. To paraphrase the Spanish philosopher José Ortega y Gasset, commenting on Spanish politics, one can coin the slogan 'Poland is the problem, Europe is the solution' as depicting the dominant way of thinking. In the debate on Polish problems, the major negative experiences from the short period of the interwar democratic state have returned: the assassination of the first democratically elected president of the Republic of Poland Gabriel Naruto-wicz by a right-wing activist in 1922, the coup in May 1926 organized by Józef Piłsudski, the persecution of the opposition in the Bereza camp in 1930s, and last but not least the eruption of vicious anti-Semitism in 1930s and the activities of far-right political organizations of fascist origin (Michnik 2005; Michnik, Tischner, and Żakowski 1995: 581; Walicki 2000). Europe was perceived as a guarantor of democratic changes, protecting the newly established democracy. One of the most visible fears was the 'Balkanization of Central and Eastern Europe' in the sense of the rise of a multitude of hidden and visible ethnic conflicts on almost all borders (Michnik 1990). For Michnik and many others, Europe was the only option securing democracy in Poland. Polish intellectuals perceived and still perceive the return of vicious, aggressive forms of nationalism as a major threat for the fragile democracies in this part of Europe or in Europe in general (Michnik 1995, 2005; Pomian 2006; Walicki 2000).

Another topic which returns persistently in the debate on Poland and Europe is the de-falsification of the collective memory of the nation after decades of communism. One of the most profound tasks was to deal with the normalization in the debate on Polish–Jewish relations, especially in the context of the Holocaust (Gross 2000; Michlic 2004; Michnik 2005). The visible trait was the stance that the normalization of political life in Poland should be completed before the return to Europe. The debates about the past – about 'skeletons hidden in the closet' – brought with them troubling emotions. Michnik wrote: 'There is no other option – we need to absorb this past. We must learn how to understand the hidden meanings. One must defend the right to different experiences – because we are different. Poland is our only common concern' (Michnik 2005: 144). There was, however, no consensus on how to deal with the troubled past and questions such as de-communization and lustration; Polish–Jewish, Polish–German, or Polish–Ukrainian relations evoked vigorous and long-lasting debates. The axiomatic divide is clearly visible in those disputes on democracy or approach to collective memory. Right-wing groups of intellectuals have been rather critical of the changes in Poland since 1989, accusing them of being too liberal and forgetting the Polish interest.

For many Polish intellectuals Poland is located in the periphery, on the crossroads, on the borderland; Europe is at the centre. Jerzy Jedlicki – historian and essayist – presented a vision of transmitting cultural patterns from the centre to the periphery where he located Poland, and explained the difficulties of overcoming these patterns:

The ideology of 'combating the foreign fashions'-type aversion to the West and to modern civilization – experienced as alien, heartless and cosmopolitan – was reborn many times in all politically and culturally dependent nations, which bitterly felt their own secondary importance. A similar ideology clearly fulfils compensation functions, and also easily transforms either into national megalomania, or into the romantic belief in a specifically messianic national mission. (Jedlicki 2007)

Another reflection of the complexes which affect Poles in the wake of EU enlargement and later is presented in an analysis by Maria Janion – a literary critic and feminist. She employs post-colonial theories to analyse Polish relations with both Western Europe and Russia and the rest of Eastern Europe. As a motto of the research she selects a passage by Jacques Maritain written to Józef Czapski, Polish writer, thinker, and painter: 'You claim that you are the *antemurale* of Christianity, but on the other hand you think that Russians are half-people and you hold them in deep contempt' (quoted in Janion 2007: 323). This results in an inferiority complex towards Latin culture or civilization, and simultaneously a dispossession from Slavic heritage which is also connected with a superiority complex (yet also fear) towards Russia – as she points out 'In a word, being colonised in the nineteenth century by the partition powers, we could be proud of the fact that we were once colonizers [of the eastern part of Poland known as *Kresy*]' (Janion 2007: 170). The author notes that actually being both the West and the East – the 'western Easternness or eastern Westernness' is characteristic of Polish culture (Janion 2007: 177). This debate about being in between is connected with the older reflection on the idea of Central Europe developed by leading intellectuals in the region, for example the Czech writer Milan Kundera or in Poland the poet Czesław Miłosz (1994).

Some intellectuals notice the differences between the West and the East as regards the visions and philosophical foundations of concepts such as the state, law, and social order (Pomian 2006; Staniszkis 2006). Poland has remained for centuries outside the major European intellectual trends, and has had its distinctive historical experience which contributed to 'contemporary misunderstandings as regards the essence of the social order and the distinctness of the assumption as to what power is' between itself and Europe (Staniszkis 2006: 69). The opinion of Andrzej Walicki, a historian and philosopher who perceives the Enlightened traditions in Poland as forgotten rather than absent, is slightly different. He argues that 'the pro-European tradition in Poland is indeed very rich', and especially visible during the period of the Enlightenment when 'Poles sought to save themselves and gave the guarantees for the existence of the country via a pan-European, all-European order' which recognized the rights of all nations (Walicki 2000: 308). As regards the potential threats to Polish identity in the process of integration, he clearly stresses that 'in the Polish tradition there are – as mentioned already – many elements allowing for our Europeanization without betraying our own values' (Walicki 2000: 313).

The question of European and/or Polish values highlights deep axiological divisions among intellectuals in Poland. For some right-wing, orthodox Catholic, conservative Poles, and their political representatives, Poland has always been in Europe understood as a moral entity, the essence of which has always been Christian values and the Catholic religion. In this view, not only has Poland always been in Europe, but it has represented the core of Europe, being more European than other countries where decadent peoples have forgotten the Christian essence of their heritage. The contemporary Europe in the West, organized in the EU, is in this view very far from the original and authentic European Christian civilization. It is, as has sometimes been expressed, dominated by the 'culture of death', allegedly propagating euthanasia, abortion, drugs, and sexual perversions. This moral decay, Polish right-wing activists say, presents a grave danger to Poles, whose moral integrity and cultural purity is threatened. Only isolation can protect them. Therefore Poland should not join the EU. Now that this has already happened, and Poland is a member of the EU, it is its duty to bring Christianity back to Europe, to play once again the role of the saviour of Europe, to protect itself this time not from Eastern barbarians, but from the internal danger of atheism and liberalism. This is a new version of the old *ante-murale* concept.

Right-wing intellectuals have also stressed the significant difference between Christian (and as such mostly widespread and protected in Poland) and Western, liberal values originating in the Enlightenment. Catholic publicist and politician Jan Maria Jackowski, in his *Bitwa o Polskę*, 'contends that Poland should return to the ideas of *Civitas Christiana*, whereby the nation was a medium between the citizenry and the Absolute, supporting the individual on his way to salvation by means of an educational system, laws based on those of the Roman system, a ruling morality consolidated by faith, and a political system which accorded with the Ten Commandments' (Sokolewicz 2003: 364). Most of the voices in this group reclaimed the heritage of Roman Dmowski and his integral nationalism. In contrast, Catholic liberal circles stress the profits of European integration. One of the intellectuals most representative of this group is Jerzy Kłoczowski – historian and essayist. He perceives Poland as having been part of Europe since at least medieval times, and perceives Europe as a mechanism to strengthen Polishness: 'We must clearly join in the great, contemporary debate on Europe and its culture and in this kind of frame of reference also perceive our culture and national identity – not isolated, alienated and as such weakened and doomed to failure from the start, but anchored strongly in its own civilization for 1,000 years' (Kłoczowski 2002: 6). This provides a chance for Poland to protect its own values and traditions yet profit from the benefits of integration.

Since the 1990s the Polish debate on European integration has been predominantly organized along the axis of the first-order debate between the supporters of integration and those who wanted to protect the Polish nation-state and national identity. Centre- and left-oriented intellectuals favour at least the recreation and redefinition of national identification, arguing that the selfish and self-oriented Polish activities will undermine the common European project which is needed and favoured by Poles. These figures mostly represent traditions in Polish political thought open towards Europe and not afraid of it, combating Polish complexes and promoting instead a more pragmatic, future-oriented stance. On the other hand we have the second stream of argumentation, preferring the adjustment of actions to a rethinking of Polish identity itself. One of these voices warns (also describing the assessment of the negotiation period): 'we were entrusted to be taken care of like well-behaved children at the kindergarten. Meanwhile, our relationship with Europe is more like a marriage, and we must accept each other... [However] Project Europe is not ready-made and we do not have to accept it, Polishness is not something to be destroyed' (Bryk et al. 2007). This is a rather typical position stressing Polish uniqueness, the Polish vision of various values and human rights (not always complying with their European equivalents), which must at least be taken into account in the EU. Between the lines, one can read the fear that integration will damage Polish national identity, shared values, and so on.

Another major axis of the intellectual debate in Poland is focused on assessment of the democratic transformation after 1989. Since the beginning of the 2000s this has been an exchange of arguments between proponents of the changes introduced in the Third Republic of Poland and those critics connected with the ideology of the 'restoration' of the Fourth Republic of Poland who support the general idea that Poles need to have and cultivate their own history, tradition, ideas which could serve as a contribution to a common Europe. This controversy is also connected with the assessment of the role of Europe as a guarantor of democracy in Poland and provider of the model to be followed. 'Polish liberalism' – the name Zdzisław Krasnodębski, philosopher and thinker, used to describe a project of reforms and the meaning of democracy which have, in his opinion, totally dominated the Polish political scene since the 'Solidarity' years – deserves critical assessment.

This project consisted of several clear elements: from the idea of moral pluralism and the neutrality of the state, with the conviction of the imitative nature of the Polish transformation, the recognition of a fast modernization as a major goal (including cultural modernization), stemming from the lack of trust and reluctance to the national tradition, the ban on de-communization and so on . . . It did not pay much attention to the question of the affirmative sharpening of identity and collective memory. It idealized the relations between states in the Western world, in the EU, and was not able to draw proper conclusions from the peripheral location of Poland. (Krasnodębski 2005: 8)

As a result of this critical opinion about the transformation, Krasnodębski also has a contradictory stance to the major trends in the Polish debate on Europe which dominated in the 1990s. He calls for a more nuanced vision of integration – not as a naïve, unreflective move towards a better world, but rather as moving to the centre from the periphery where the country – no matter whether outside or inside the EU – is located (Krasnodębski 2005: 198). He changes the perspective of the analysis and looks from the West (Germany predominantly) towards Central and Eastern Europe, which in such a perspective 'is a worse Europe, which is supposed to be lifted from backwardness' (ibid.: 198). He denounces the division, popular in Western Europe, into the 'civilised West and backward East' (ibid.: 200). What he condemns in the Polish path towards Europe is an imitation of the Western model of development without criticism of either economic or moral terms. He protests against the contrasting of the 'mature, normal and rational West' and the 'poor and sluggish incompetence of the East' (ibid.: 205). This kind of linear thinking is in his opinion a remnant of Marxism – as 'modernization was a legitimization of Marxism' (ibid.: 206). However, in the place of Marxism a new ideology has appeared: a linear tendency towards Western modernity with its 'rationalism, Enlightenment and cosmopolitism' (ibid.: 207). He concludes that the project of

European modernity is not 'finished' and is not uncontroversial. He asks the question whether the merger of Polish native traditions and Western political culture is impossible, concluding 'of course not, because despite our complaints, despite the mud and storks, Polish culture is Western culture' (ibid.: 224). Such views have become popular, and widely accepted by the emerging group of moderate Eurosceptics locating themselves in contrast to the present, yet much less popular among Polish Euro-enemies or Euro-rejects.

Leftist thinkers – also critical towards the Polish liberal 'project' – stress the paradox that the project of Polish transformation was fuelled more by the American version of liberalism than the European one. For the late Jacek Kuroń, one of the main figures of the Polish democratic opposition, transformation lacked sensitivity towards the disadvantaged, leading him to turn to the European welfare model. Today this group's criticism is predominantly directed against the economic neoliberal doctrine in the country as presented by publicist Jacek Żakowski (2007), the milieu of the *Krytyka Polityczna* journal, or feminist circles. They are trying to reinvent old Polish traditions of the democratic left supplemented with new topics and concepts developed on the European left such as tolerance for diversity, gender equality, homosexual rights, multiculturalism, and so on. (Bikont 2007; *Krytyki Politycznej Przewodnik Lewicy* 2007; Szczuka 2007). This renaissance of the New Left in Poland is slow, and this perspective is not the most visible especially in the debate on Europe. Yet it has an interesting dimension, bringing a greater focus on European welfare in various versions in contrast to the American neoliberal system, stressing European diversity, tolerance, and environmental protection (*Krytyki Politycznej Przewodnik Lewicy* 2007; Żakowski 2007).

This is connected not only with the reflection on what kind of Europe we imitate, but also what in reality these European affairs look like. Such topics are evoked in the context of relations with two neighbours – Germany and Russia – and that of security issues. As was mentioned above, for centuries relations with these two countries determined the fate of Poles. The end of the Cold War changed the relationship with both, yet directed them to opposite extremes. Germany became, especially during the process of EU enlargement, one of the most important allies; Russia – quite the opposite – became the country which posed numerous problems for Polish foreign policy. There is a widespread conviction, often presented in the debate, that Germany should be embedded in the European project. Former Polish Minister of Foreign Affairs Stefan Meller (2007a) stated that the best keyword for Polish–German relations is 'together', because without good relations between these two countries 'there will be no truly good climate in Europe'. However, voices are also audible warning against such an optimistic tone and advising more careful relations with Germany, balancing the influences of the 'Franco-German Latin empire' with special relations with the United States (Cichocki 2004: 28).

The debate on the model of relations with the West and within the West – Europe and the US – was especially acute in 2003 and 2004 following the controversies around the invasion of Iraq. This was a result of the necessity of confronting the Europe imagined with the Europe approached. Marek Cichocki – historian, political thinker, and conservative publicist – depicted the Polish problem in the context of the crisis within the West:

> This dilemma for many Poles seems to be a special malicious fate, because it appears exactly at the moment when they should rather celebrate the integration of their country with the structures of the desired West. This authentic desire to be a part of the West, Western Europe, Western civilization, the normal, free world was a very strong – if not the principal – motive of Poland's transitions in the 1990s . . . we wanted to sneak in to the 'post-national paradise', whose gates were closed to us for so long. (Cichocki 2004: 50)

But the reality to which Poles were heading was not unified, and even though they wanted to reach the safe, organized, wealthy world, this world was and is going through major changes. It requires a stance to be taken in the vigorous debates on the shape of the European project. It seems that Poles were not ready for the fact that the project they wanted to be a part of was not ready-made, final, or decided. One might say that the question of what kind of Europe is desired is the most difficult for Poles to answer. They had more of a tendency to fight for their state and die for its survival and independence than to deal with the everyday, pragmatic, task-oriented building of the wealth of the nation and continent. Paraphrasing the nineteenth-century Polish poet Cyprian Norwid, Andrzej Walicki (2000: 314) says, 'The differentiation between insurgent deeds and work – deeds are a contradiction of work as Norwid said – is a Polish problem.'

What kind of Europe?

The year 2004 is widely perceived as another breakthrough in Polish history. Since entering the EU Poles have started – still with shyness and uncertainty – to discuss the meaning of the integrated union and the possible future models of integration. This debate is still predominantly between the nationalist (still more dominant in the Polish landscape) and the supranational school.

The first major topic was the question of whether Poles would utilize the chances offered by integration. Jerzy Jedlicki (2007) noted that 'as of this moment we are responsible for what we do with our membership, not the results of the thousands of years of the history of Europe, which we cannot change'. The discourse of opportunity appears in Michnik's writings as well. He has condemned Polish faults and political discourse in the country, stressing that after EU enlargement:

everyone will bring their own distinctness, their own different way of thinking about history, about values, about today... We have a free Poland and free people in Poland. This is a great Polish chance. And a democratic Poland, wealthy, just and present in the structures of the EU is within reach. It depends on us whether we take advantage of this historical chance, the chance which our country, our nation did not have for the last three hundred years. It is a historic chance for our children and our grandchildren. Once Churchill said that Poles are excellent in defeat and deplorable in victory. Today the answer to the question whether Winston Churchill was right depends on us. (Michnik 2005: 288–93)

Some of the voices in the debate sound strong and direct in combating Polish cowardice, calculating EU membership along with Poland's self-centred interests. Maria Janion, for instance, traces the traits of typical Polish romantic discourse, which she describes as 'spoiled post-romantic speech', in the debate in Poland on the EU. In the analysis of the campaign for the European Parliament in 2004 she found

the most popular romantic motifs – national uprising, messianism, martyrdom, the Christian crusade. This is characteristic, even though they do not suit the situation at all – for working as a deputy in the European Parliament is not taking part in a national uprising with all its accessories and justifications, nor the tribune for messianistic fantasies – yet they are broadly used with great ease by various political orientations. What is revealed here is that the set of romantic stereotypes is recognized as the cornerstone of Polishness. (Janion 2007: 305–6)

The results of the shallow rhetoric are disastrous, as she writes: 'it was no coincidence that the reduction of European ideas and lack of broad discussion on its sense and nature were in parallel (accompanied by the other social events) with the disclosure of distinctive changes, specifically in the patriotic consciousness of young people... For many of them decided – to put it bluntly – to say goodbye to Poland' (Janion 2007: 304). She also points out that there is no language in Poland for debating on Europe; instead several over-used phrases dominate, not accepted by the young generation of Poles (Janion 2007: 307).

The language in which the EU and its future shape is described and debated is under construction in Poland. Many intellectuals have tried to translate this European experience for Poles. For the historian and philosopher Krzysztof Pomian (2006: 221) the 'essence' of Europe is 'a consensus – with a full awareness of the differences'. For Michnik the EU is based on one founding myth – anti-fascism:

It is the defeat of Hitler from which the idea of European integration arose... Today's Europe is searching for its own new identity among the complicated conflicts and political inconsistencies. It is looking for an axiology, which will allow for the solid foundations of democracy to be built – between cynicism and despair. The debate on the tolerant and multinational state, which at the same time cultivates national identity and its own historical tradition, is ongoing. European democracy rises from two currents – one of human rights, from which parliamentarian democracy and tolerance for minorities arose, and the second current of the market economy from which the middle class, the guarantee of social stability, arose. (Michnik 2005: 275)

In another publication he stressed – relating himself to the ideas of Jürgen Habermas – that 'the spirit of European democracy needs what is relative, because this spirit is dubiety and quest. It also needs what is absolute, because this spirit is faithfulness and mercy. Only when approached from this perspective on European democracy will we notice what radically differentiates it from every form of dictatorship and a world based on intolerance' (Michnik 2005: 284). Somehow similarly, in the heart of the definition of Europe the sociologist and political scientist Jadwiga Staniszkis locates the notion of auto-reflectivity or 'even the tendency to theorize about itself' (Staniszkis 2006: 51). Geremek stressed that Europe is not merely an economic project, but rather a community of values. In reply to the question of why Europeans want to be together, he explained that the goal is: 'to fulfil our future aspirations, that the values to which we are attached will be fulfilled and as a result that we have a community of feelings and fundamental values' (Geremek 2004: 28). Commenting on the eruption of national egoisms and Euroscepticism in 'old' Europe in the wake of enlargement, he said: 'The reasoning in terms of community interest must be initiated. The common interest is characterized by the fact that it cannot be described in the language of accountants, but a certain reflection on the meaning of Europe, the sense of European unity, on its historical foundations, because then this feeling that we have a common interest appears' (Geremek 2004: 46). Very similar opinions are given by Władysław Bartoszewski – historian, writer, activist, and politician:

Europe must show solidarity most of all with itself. I am thinking here about the solidarity that results from a sense of belonging to a specific community and far-sighted awareness of common interest. It is rooted in the past but oriented towards the future. There is no way of building a permanent peace other than by bridging the development gap and reducing the area of poverty. That is why solidarity should cement Europe and could give Europe a new dimension, not limiting it to being one large common market. (Bartoszewski 2001: 34)

For Marek Safjan – former judge and president of the Constitutional Tribunal in Poland and since 2009 Polish judge in the European Court of Justice – the reforms of the EU are

not only concrete, detailed legal solutions, but predominantly are about what Europe is supposed to be in the future: only an area of free economic exchange or a union of states respecting common values, which were shaped as a result of common historical and civilizational experience . . . One thing is clear: the controversy about the vision of Europe is today also a dispute about the Polishness which we want to promote in Europe. (Safjan 2007)

The nature of the Polish debate on the EU is exemplified by the discussion on the Charter of Fundamental Rights, which the Polish government decided not to accept, in spite of earlier promises to the contrary. The main objection was that the Charter may force Poland to introduce laws which would undermine the Catholic principles of Polish traditional identity. Abortion, euthanasia, and the legalization of same-sex marriages were the main issues in question. In fact, the same fears were expressed even earlier, when Poles discussed their membership in the EU, and when the Constitutional Treaty was to be signed and ratified. Hardly anyone spoke about the need to make Europe more effective, to improve its functioning, or about European cultural pluralism. The only question was whether these documents would, if accepted, destroy the Polish traditional way of life and national identity. One of the voices which spoke directly about Europe came from the Catholic Church. Bishop Henryk Muszyński, himself enjoying a reputation as a Church liberal, expressed his deep regret that there was no direct reference to God or Christianity in the Charter or in the Lisbon Treaty (Muszyński 2007). He also expressed concern that the lack of the definition of marriage as a union of a man and a woman might open the possibility for the legal recognition of homosexual marriages.

In his comment about the Charter, another right-wing intellectual, Bronisław Wildstein, spoke against the need for establishing a common axiological foundation of Europe, which in his view would increase the power of Euro-bureaucracy against the independence of nations (Wildstein 2007). Even those authors who had exceptionally high competence in European matters, such as Jacek Saryusz-Wolski, himself a prominent MEP, spoke about the Treaty and the Charter only in the context of the threats and benefits for Poland. Saryusz-Wolski supported the Charter, because he believed that it would not impose any unwanted consequences on Poland, while Poland needed to be in the mainstream of EU politics in order to build its position and prestige (Saryusz-Wolski 2007).

This debate showed that twenty years after the 1989 revolution and five years after joining the EU, the European debate in Poland is still almost exclusively focused on the question of the losses and benefits, or challenges and chances, brought about by membership. What is almost completely absent is a reflection about the EU as such, and about Europe as a whole. Poles do not identify with Europe, the EU is not 'us', even if an overwhelming majority of Poles value membership very highly and see much more positive than negative consequences of the accession. 'Relations between Poland and the EU' is an expression commonly heard in the Polish media, as if Poland was not a member state. This external approach – stressing the distinction between the Polish nation-state and the EU – characterizes both those who are positive and those who are critical of the EU (Bielecki 2007; Meller 2007b). This is probably the result of the way Polish national identity was constructed, with the complex of always being attacked by others, never thinking in terms of either attacking others or acting in concert with them. In the Polish national culture and collective memory there is no concept of a joint, international enterprise.

Even if there is a reflection on the future of the EU it is again focused on Polish interest. The commentator and politician Jan Maria Rokita emphasized that the Polish national interest would be best encapsulated in a federal Europe, even though this means rather quasi-federalism. He argues that after two occupations in the twentieth century, Poland will for many years not be able to compete with other European nations – thus it is better for it to accept the federation (Bryk et al. 2007). This idea – that dialogue with other nation-states via Brussels and supranational institutions is easier for Poland than without the EU – also appears elsewhere, and is becoming the argument for the Constitutional Treaty. It shows that the European institutions are rather perceived as the facilitators of cooperation blocking other states from taking selfish decisions, especially when the decisions are against the presumed interest of Poland.

The third school of thought about European integration – the transnational one – is rather weak in Poland. Very rarely can intellectuals move beyond the perspective of the nation-state. One attempt to think about Europe in novel terms and to lead a reflection on the possible future scenarios for Europe is the following one presented by Staniszkis. She introduces in her review of models of European integration three possible roads for Europe: a union of sovereign states, a federation, or a 'de-politicised and a-hierarchical Union with substantially changed decision-making' (Staniszkis 2006: 201). The third model draws much of her attention, as she writes: 'The advantages of the third model would be a new quality of problem-solving, deep integration of the public management on a European scale and removing the dangerous (for us) possibility of creating a European "avant-garde" without us' (Staniszkis 2006: 203). Even though she perceives the new model as a new version of governance – a 'unique mixture of a multi-subject structure (of "homelands") with the capability – acquired by an individual act of recognition, not as a uniform matter – to act in certain situations as one subject' – it would be up to nation-states and societies to reach this solution. She perceives Polish participation as highlighting that 'If we Poles are not able to participate in these mostly institutional processes in a creative way (and promoting ourselves), we will remain in the peripheries of Europe, with an immobile society with a low level of activism and with the young generation searching for chances and intellectual opportunities abroad' (Staniszkis 2006: 206–7). Staniszkis' reflection on the future of the nation-state concludes with the opinion that the structure will not survive – in contrast to the politicians' desires – in a form known since the sixteenth century (Staniszkis 2006: 213). As a result, she demands the Europeanization of the Polish state as being the only option for participating in the profits of integration, even if society does not comprehend some of those novel solutions.

Conclusion

The major reflection stemming from the analysis of the debate on Europe in Poland is that it is tremendously historically determined. Certain ideas return endlessly, century after century, in the Polish reflection on the world. These are the concepts of the *ante-murale*, peripheral location, or the geopolitically determined perspective. For instance one can say that the modern variation of the *ante-murale* is visible in the question of Ukraine and the place of this country in Polish efforts in the EU (which is probably a major positive, constructive element in Polish European policy). The Polish Eastern policy (or Eastern dimension) contains similar elements – as in the previous versions – of enforcing the Eastern frontier of Europe and its protection as a transmission line of Western European values and modernization to the East, as well as an agent of Europeanization. Poles once again seem responsible for European safety against the threat from the East. A similar element which is frequently historically motivated is the fear of both great neighbours: Germany and Russia. This concept returned in the debate on the institutional reforms of the EU and on the goals of European foreign policy. These are examples of the historical background of many Polish contemporary political preferences and actions in the EU.

The second characteristic element of the Polish debate is that it seems very difficult for Polish public intellectuals to think in the categories of the common, European 'we'. It is a rather rare case that invokes European interests as equal with the Polish interest or of solidarity going beyond the national borders. This results in tremendous difficulties in ceasing to think about Europe in the categories of particularism, national interest, counting only one's own short-term costs and profits. Generally speaking the arguments stressing the utility of the project for Poland are the major measurement, and dominate in the debate. This not only makes the debate on Europe egoistic, but also prevents Poles from cooperating within European structures. Arguments which use the notion of European interest are almost automatically accused of betraying Polishness and of cosmopolitanism – perceived by the majority as a synonym of treason.

The last element is the division between the Catholic and the liberal, individualistic values, originating from the Enlightenment. For the proponents of the former, Poland is good as long as it is Catholic, and Europe is good as long as it allows Poland to be Catholic. For the latter, Europe is the ultimate guarantor of the protection of individuals, human rights, democracy, the rule of law, diversity, equality, and freedom.

The debate on Europe in Poland is reaching three levels. The first one is economic. In this dimension the EU is perceived as good for Poland, and only some radicals have depicted a negative picture of being exploited by Western imperialism. Taking the economic perspective into account, the majority of intellectuals and society as a whole perceive the benefits of European integration. The second dimension is concentrated on democracy – liberal circles are looking for guarantees of Polish democracy in Europe. On the other hand, those with nationalistic and authoritarian tendencies perceive the European criteria of democratization as the price to be paid for the economic profits of integration and modernization. The third level of the reflection on Europe is axiological. In this dimension there is extremely strong polarization visible in Poland. On the one hand the EU is the embodiment of the Enlightenment, human rights, liberalism, and individualistic values. On the other, there are nationalists and conservatives, mainly of Catholic denomination, for whom Europe only makes sense when it is Catholic, or at least Christian, and for whom liberal values and the legacy of the Enlightenment mean danger and destruction for Europe and for Poland. These people can only justify the membership of Poland in Europe through the reintroduction of Christianity to Europe.

However, noticing the deep divisions in the Polish debate on Europe, one must also stress that Polish society is constantly becoming more pro-European than it was. It has gone through remarkably deep social, political, and economic changes. Poles have recently started to take the reality of being in Europe with all its benefits for granted: free mobility, the free flow of ideas, and pluralism. One can expect that the tone of public debate will also develop to meet the social demands. One important voice on the desired Poland in the desired Europe is worth mentioning at the end of this brief review of the Polish debate about Europe. Geremek (2004: 97) once said, 'I wish the Polish voice were the ecumenical voice, in other words open in its essence to others, accepting European pluralism.' He predicted that the role of Europe in the world 'depends on the realization of what Karl Jaspers referred to as the "European spirit", and what is called the spiritual dimension of European integration in contemporary debates' (Geremek 2004: 111). This European spirit is gradually becoming more and more important for Poles, but it will takes years to overcome the historically determined way of thinking on Europe that still dominates Polish debate.

12

The Geopolitics of the European Spirit in Post-Secular Romania

Daniel Barbu

Once communism finally collapsed in 1989, 'the time has come, as predicted by Constantin Noica, for Western Europe to recognize its own spirit rather in its keepers from the East than in its everyday present' (Patapievici 2009: 245). Taken from an essay on the values of Europe published by a successful Romanian public intellectual in praise of another leading public intellectual, this phrase provides a reliable insight into who the mainstream Romanian intellectuals of today think they are, into where they are coming from in terms of intellectual genealogy, and especially into what they believe when European integration is under debate. As in most national settings, post-communist Romanian intellectuals make up a very diverse population of individuals who have in common – in the eyes of the media and for the benefit of a wider audience – a generic, implicit, and usually undisputed cultural authority related to some form of supposed or actual achievement in philosophy, literature, and, to a lesser extent, the social sciences.[1] Among them there is probably an authoritative, albeit loose, group of intellectuals who trace the source of their theoretical positions back to the 1930s. They tend to accept as true that there is, beyond individual reason and the social production of knowledge, a 'European spirit' of which they should be deemed natural shareholders.

The recent history of this spirit is paradoxical: during the Cold War, it almost vanished from the 'well-to-do' Western Europe, where genuine thinkers were marginalized if not suffocated by a politically oriented society in pursuit of welfare and equality; in contrast, it thrived – in a prophetic, covert, and non-political manner – in the dark times of communism. The dismissal of the regime has supposedly unveiled the continued existence of this spirit with a built-in

---

[1] I follow the broad definition proposed in the introduction to this volume by Justine Lacroix and Kalypso Nicolaïdis.

241

mission: to radiate again from the East to the spiritually depleted West. Unlike Polish or Czech intellectuals, who addressed communism in the idiom of political dissent, Romanian intellectuals were simultaneously public and silent. They were public because they published books and essays, went on conference tours, paid long visits to major European universities, and were, albeit not often, invited to radio and television broadcasts. In all circumstances, they remained utterly silent on political and human rights issues. They spoke the language of culture, of high European culture. They intimated that discussing Plato or quoting from Heidegger were, in the intellectual order, more damaging acts for the regime than any political remonstration.

If such is the *raccourci* of the intellectual landscape of post-communist Romania, where do intellectuals position themselves with respect to the process of accession to the European Union? Drawing on a mainstream literature rooted in the works of two iconic figures of Romanian culture, Mircea Eliade and Constantin Noica, this chapter argues that Europe was, and still is, almost canonically regarded in Romania by those who speak out in the public space as both a convenience in terms of free trade and freedom of movement, and as an ethical hazard. According to this line of thinking, echoed also – though not without some particular nuances – by spokesmen of the culturally dominant and (semi-)established Greek Orthodox Church through the language of con-stitutionalism, democracy, and human rights, Europe would tend to sponsor the emergence of a ready-made 'recent man', just as the ideology of state socialism used to enforce the model of a standardized collectivism.

European integration – expected to promote such social goods as welfare and political pluralism – was mainly described as a historical technique marshalled from above, as a political device of extracting consent from a national society characterized not only by a backward and unregulated economy in need of assistance, but also by a collective identity deemed to be unhistorical and European in its remote origin, as its 'spirit' appears to have remained unmoved by the secularist exertions of the liberal regime of the nineteenth century and of twentieth-century communism alike. Looking back from the moment of the merger of the aspiring Romanian post-communist democracy with the self-aware Western ones into an enlarged European Union, this chapter will try to highlight, and hopefully deconstruct, some of the transformations undergone by the language and enactment of intellectual assent given to the progression of Europeanization by Romanian public intellectuals.

Europe at hand: A short history of the present

In the aftermath of the demise of state socialism, Romanian experts, intellec-tuals, social scientists, and theorists – who, during the Cold War, developed the habit of qualifying the communist system as the exact opposite of European democracy based on constitutionalism, citizenship, and human rights – thought that their past experience of ideological competition and political confrontation was immaterial for the present transformation of democracy envisaged rather as a range of institutional and discursive expectations (Barbu 2007). Europe was the immediate present, as communism was a happenstance of the recent past. As such, it deserved an instant history. Therefore, a topical literature on Europe thrived as naturally as the writings on 'scientific socialism' and related issues once had, and more often than not the authors remained, if not the same, then at least of the same intellectual breed. For that reason, Europe was conceived more as a mere source of literal regulations that had to be formally observed by the prose of the national legislation (*acquis communautaire*) than as a new type of polity that Romanians had to join, make their own, and eventually help advance.[2]

By way of consequence, and in an uncritical and consensual approach comparable perhaps to that practised by Spanish intellectuals,[3] most of the Romanian academic literature on European politics and policy is purely descriptive, and embraces either an international relations perspective treating the Union as something close to an intergovernmental organization, or a comparative approach explaining it as a supranational body with some federalist features. Scores of handbooks and essays on European construction, enlargement, law, and policy should be counted for the record, although they typically include very little original wisdom. And when they do, as in the proposal for a federalist reform of the European institutions authored by a former social-democrat foreign minister and a leading human rights activist (Andreescu and Severin 2001), such pieces of literature ignore that European federalism has quite significant intellectual roots in Romania, summed up by George Ciorănescu (2005),[4] active member of the European Movement and the *Nouvelles Equipes Internationales* (Delureanu 2006: 181–240) and erstwhile marginal participant in the foundation of the European Communities alongside other prominent politicians, academics, and intellectuals in exile and harboured by the Christian Democratic circles (Delureanu 2007).

Under the overarching principle of federalism, many Romanian politicians and academics worked in the first half of the twentieth century towards a normative grand political theory on Europe. But this legacy remains exterior to the mainstream political and intellectual discourse. Indeed, in the 1990s, the interest in the European Union shown by most Romanian politicians and academics was related mainly to the hope that close association with the

---

[2] The Romanian chief negotiator avows that he was interested exclusively in the 'formal aspect' of the negotiations: see Puşcaş 2007: 7.

[3] See the analysis of Carlos Closa and Antonio Barroso in Chapter 10, this volume.

[4] This volume combines a reprint of Ciorănescu's 1946 dissertation *Les Roumains et l'idée fédéraliste* with an edition of ensuing articles and studies written in exile.

Communities might bolster economic growth and improve the rule of law in a post-socialist country that was striving for international political and financial recognition. If Europe is an entity which has a patent and undisputed character, that would be none other than *affluence* in the eyes of Romanians: 'This structure [the European Union] warrants one of the highest standards of living in the world and is doing that, most importantly, in a democratic and open world. For a country that knew only distress and strived to make ends meet, the abundance of the European Union may come as a cultural and material shock,' as observed in 2004 by Prime Minister Adrian Năstase (2004: 114), a professor of international law and (when not in high office) a noteworthy editorialist, while negotiating the roadmap of Romanian integration with the Commission.

Seduced at first by the promise of prosperity, Romanian informed opinion on Europe slowly became aware of the dangers presumed to lie underneath it. A study on the Romanian public debates on Europe (Beciu 2006), notably as reflected in the media, found that the Union was initially approached as a know-how issue, then as an identity problem, and more recently as a question of national standing. At the beginning, in the 1990s, the word was with the experts, policy-makers, and politicians who pictured Europe exactly as most citizens had dreamed about it: an *affluent society*, a 'giant supermarket', as one public intellectual ironically summarized the general view (Marino 2005: 134), where Romanians might one day go shopping if some highly complex procedural prerequisites could be satisfied. When, in 2000, the Parliament decided to decriminalize homosexuality in the process of Europeanization of the penal culture inherited from state socialism, the floor was open to the first coherent debate on what it might mean to be European in terms of forfeiting something that many tended to believe was an incontrovertible collective identity. The discursive contours of this identity were authoritatively pencilled in by the elderly Orthodox Archbishop Bartolomeu Anania of Cluj. The learned bishop disrupted his labours of giving the Bible a new Romanian version to warn that 'Europe asks us to accept sex, homosexuality, vices, drugs, abortions, and genetic engineering' and to remind his flock that '[spiritually] impoverished Europe [is] built exclusively on politics and economics, lacking any trace of spirituality, culture, or religion' (cited by Stan and Turcescu 2007: 177).[5] Given that the riches of Europe could be but a cover-up for spiritual poverty, Romanian theologians have chosen to work extensively and admonitorily on what looks to them like a 'European amnesia' (Preda 2004) – that is, on relativism, secularism, and estrangement from tradition – as diseases ingrained in the make-up of a Union designed to make sure that oblivion of tradition and political neutrality prevail over particular cultures and identities (Preda 2008: 296). In so doing, they reduced the issue, for the use of their public, to the

---

[5] The fate of this debate is narrated in Stan and Turcescu 2007: 171–98.

failure of the Constitutional Treaty to account for the 'Christian roots of Europe', and disregarded the complexity of other national debates on both collective memory and secular reason.

Ever since, the country's integration into the European Union has been pondered not only as a matter of bureaucratic and technical expertise, but also as a choice of civilization, or, in the words of a distinguished conservative scholar, as a tension between two ideal types of society: one grounded in the 'organic solidarities' of the private life that hold together families and small communities, and the other structured by the 'organized solidarities' steered by political power (Duţu 1999: 9). Of course, the community model is not only better suited to Romanian society, but is also more apt to give a new shape to Europe at large than liberal individualism, understood as the primary driving force behind the rise of the Union (Duţu 1999: 138). Philosophers and public intellectuals, not necessarily always of Christian persuasion but doubtful about the autonomy of politics when grounded exclusively in reason, share a similar position. The thrust of such an appraisal is not so much directed against Europe itself as aimed at establishing where Romania stands in the wake of its accession to membership; and, more importantly, at determining *who* is intellectually entitled to report its position. These strictures serve to put in context a story that might unveil the 'cultural authority' from which the tale of Europe is told on behalf of Romanian society.

Backwards into Europe: The present of history

The narrative power of Romanian national history in the face of the short chronicle of European integration was manifest on 11 May 2008, when a dozen bishops of the Romanian Orthodox Church held a grand outdoors ceremony on a field in north-eastern Transylvania. The prelates went there to convey to a crowd of tens of thousands and celebrate with a solemn liturgy the decision of the Holy Synod to canonize four Romanian peasants put to death on the same ground in 1763. They were earnestly decreed martyrs of the ancestral faith of the nation. Who were the four newly proclaimed saints, what did they do to deserve such an appreciation, and why had the Church waited so long to recognize their extraordinary merits? Except for their leader, aged 100 and travelled abroad as far as Russia in his double capacity of soldier of fortune and (perhaps) self-styled monk, they were illiterate local serfs who vigorously opposed the transformation of their home country into a militarized border zone. The operation, part of a comprehensive process of state-building (*Einrichtungswerk*), included the enfranchisement of the peasants of the villages set on the boundary with Ottoman Moldavia: in exchange for their new social status, they had to become freeholders under arms, employed by the Austrian military as full-time border patrols. However, as the highest-ranking bureaucrat of the province maintained,[6] to guarantee the safety of the territory entrusted to them was not the primary concern of the imperial authorities: their foremost assignment was to aggrandize 'the effective power of the state' by their *Umbildung*, by the transformation of their social behaviour, function, and utility. The government provided civil rights, equipment, elementary schools run by German- and Latin-speaking teachers, and a clear prospective of upward social mobility. Freed from most feudal bonds, the peasants had to agree to serve the emperor and apostolic king and were strongly encouraged (though not obliged) to join his Church, the Catholic, preserving nevertheless their old rite, the Byzantine.

A fair deal, one would say, at least as far as the enlightened *Staatswissenschaften* of the late eighteenth century were reasonably inclined to go. The four (retroactively nominated) saints would not accept this arrangement, and stirred their fellow peasants to refuse to be unbound from feudal duties, to bear arms, to behave as loyal and useful subjects, to go to school and to learn foreign tongues, to take communion in churches acknowledging the primacy of the Pope in Rome. The villagers were enthused by them to remain faithful to their traditional customs and hierarchies. Insulated in a popular religion that was remotely protected by the sovereign of all Russia and all Orthodox believers, they were enclosed in a backward, illiterate, and self-sufficient rural micro-universe ruled by natural oligarchies, and ignorant of any rudiments of the legal culture of their age. Found guilty of sedition and incitement to rebellion against the state, they were sentenced to capital punishment and executed on the very premises of their mutiny. Carefully documented by the bureaucrats of the administrative monarchy[7] – which tended to articulate itself as a paper power (*eine papierne Gewalt*), to use the choice of words of a contemporary Transylvanian observer (Bernath 1972: 45) – the whole incident was eventually forgotten by all interested parties until Romania signed the papers of its accession to the European Union.

This may be a rather long-winded tale, apparently disconnected from contemporary debates. Still, my contention is that this account is quite telling for the topic at hand. The events may have taken place in the eighteenth century, but the story should be dated politically to 2008. Indeed, why would the dominant church of a European state choose to sanctify a reaction against modernization and Westernization that went unnoticed for almost two and a half centuries even by the most devout of believers? And for a good reason: the religious dimension of the social movement of 1762–3 was rather inconspicuous. The well-trained military officials and civil servants that dealt with the matter considered it a mere manifestation of popular yet reactionary

---

[6] Report of Baron von Brukenthal quoted by Göllner 1973: 26, 196.
[7] The minute accounts of the events and the acts of the trial undusted in the imperial archives by Mathias Bernath 1972: 158–60 and Göllner 1973: 44–6.

conservatism, fuelled by ignorance, fanaticism, and xenophobia, and opposing a measure of enlightened reformism. The resistance of the four peasants to the impersonal, paper power of the modern state in its Austrian version was barely noticed either by nineteenth-century romantic or twentieth-century communist historiographies, both equally disposed to value national uprisings against foreign rule. They had to wait until 2008 to be officially recognized as holy confessing martyrs. Their silhouettes emerge as the backdrop of a calculated response given less than one year later by the national Orthodox Church to the European membership of the Romanian nation-state.

What kind of faith, after all, was confessed by these eighteenth-century villagers from a secluded corner of an empire that stretched across Europe from Transylvania to Brussels? Whatever their intentions, any educated witness from the twenty-first century, regardless of his or her personal beliefs and political outlook, would probably find what was already obvious for the Austrian bureaucrats – that the villagers stood up for and finally died in defence of a local and rural tradition entrenched in illiteracy, localism, superstition, distrust of strangers, and disbelief in the social productivity of the written law, as well as in the aptitude of a public administration to connect people and things in a rational and impersonal way. If that is reasonably true, it means that the Church provided its 2008 followers with an official counter-narrative of European integration, with a normative script of how Orthodox Romanians should behave in front of Europe, understood as a political unit that once again encompassed Transylvania and Brussels.

Should we take this event seriously? Is it not perhaps a merely anecdotal endeavour of a religious organization, with no real bearing on a public opinion whose values are fashioned by the secular age that unified and enlarged Europe? The right answer to this question should take careful account of the political and cultural weight of the Church in Romanian public life and, consequently, its possible role in framing an influential image of Europe and the fate of Romanians in the Union. The post-communist censuses indicate that 86 per cent of Romanians identify themselves as belonging to the Orthodox Church. In all surveys, the Church enjoys a higher level of trust than institutions such as the military, the government, parliament, or the media (Sandu 1999: 74–84); it also had sufficient political influence to determine the Ministry of Education's decision, in 2007, to ban any reference to the theory of evolution from high-school textbooks. In spite of this, the proportion of regular church-goers may not exceed the European average. In all probability and in terms of individual behaviour, Romanians are statistically living in secular times.

Therefore, the influence of the Church in the public sphere may be best understood by using the concept of 'vicarious religion', coined by Grace Davie (2007) in order to describe a situation where a minority of organized professionals perform religious acts in the name and place of a majority that does not necessarily behave as instructed by these 'qualified practitioners', but is aware of and agrees upon what they are doing on behalf of the community. In such a conceptual pattern, personal commitment to religious values and practices may be scarce, loose, and socially inconspicuous. Indeed, it is not to the institution as such that public opinions look up for explicit political direction.[8] Instead, most aspects of the current political culture seem to be firmly encoded by the Orthodox ethos. Or, in the language of one influential essayist and cultural administrator, 'If the Church means the institution and its clergy... I have few connections with the Church... but if the Church is the community of believers gathered around the sacraments and with the view of keeping up the tradition... I am within' (Patapievici 1996: 241). The style and sometimes even the content of the post-communist intellectual debates on political issues, the common understanding of personal and institutional accountability, the model of family life still benchmarked by baptism, marriage in church, and religious funerals, the perception of the functional divisions cutting across society, have all taken shape in a religious context that is still at work and has not lost its authority even under state socialism.[9]

Europe possessed: The present of a paper power

Romanian society appears to be rather culturally homogeneous after the collective historical experience of communism (Barbu 2002), and seems to have remained cohesive and consensual in its opinions throughout the process of European integration. It seems that the fall of a unanimous and publicly unchallenged ideology (that of communism) called for another form of collective consent with respect to values and moral norms. By its mere but monumental social presence (in the media, in the army, in hospitals and prisons, in public schools, during all major political events), legally or tacitly approved by the state, the dominant Church provided such an opportunity for consensus and was perhaps able to fulfil the need for a substitutive cultural authority. Romanian politicians and experts may have been the leading actors of the country's European integration, but they were not compelled by academics and public intellectuals to perform their political assignment as self-conscious subjects of their own actions. They had to articulate (in speech, in writing, and in decision-making) what they were neither trained nor bound to think. That is why the national Orthodox Church, widely regarded as a cultural repository of

---

[8] In the 2000 presidential elections, the candidate overtly endorsed by the Orthodox hierarchy received only 9 per cent of the votes, and the candidate who won the 2004 ballot was known for his blatant, if brief, support of the homosexual minority and for opposing (once again not for long) the project of building the new grand cathedral 'of the Redemption of the Nation' in Bucharest.

[9] The clearest insight into the ambiguous church–state relations under communism is provided by Gillet 1997.

meanings, as well as the intellectual legatees of Mircea Eliade, Emil Cioran, and Constantin Noica, reactionary anti-modern and (at least for a time) nationalist thinkers, almost naturally joined forces in order to take control over the authoritative dicta of public life.

How could that be? There are of course several reasons, but I will highlight here only one. The ongoing process of rationalization of the public sphere considered by Max Weber as the main avenue of social transformation in modern times can hardly be grasped in Romania even by the thickest of historical descriptions. Political equality was not only established in Romania on imported normative qualifications, which the ruling elites were not intellectually proficient enough to explain and warrant, but the very surfacing of electoral democracy in the 1920s and 1930s was first deferred and then conditioned by a liberal state unable to imagine how the equal representation of politically incompetent (because illiterate) citizens should be organized (Barbu and Preda 2006). Moreover, a moderately original Romanian cultural life was able to take shape in the interwar period only as a multiple critique of secularism, democracy, Western culture, enlightenment, Europeanization, and majority rule.[10] Since the late 1930s, Mircea Eliade has been definitely considered not only the privileged witness of this golden period, but also the most influential Romanian public intellectual of all time.[11] His work, and most significantly his theoretical approach to the issue of the autonomy of the political, is still setting the tone, either directly or through a profusion of restatements and reinstatements of his assumptions.

'Where does the mission of Romania begin?' An article published by Mircea Eliade (1937) lays down the terms of a debate that is still unfolding: the historian of religions and right-wing journalist observes that the process of modernization could be deemed a failure precisely because it was conducted from a political standpoint: 'the primacy of politics' in liberal and democratic societies and, by imitation, in the Romanian one also, proved to be ineffective because the country is doomed to remain a periphery of secularized Catholic and Protestant Europe, an insignificant nation fostering a minor culture; only through 'a primacy of the spiritual', both anti-democratic and religious, could Orthodoxy and Romania 'dominate the whole Europe', that is, reverse the centre/periphery axis of modernity in order to wield its spiritual influence over the continent. Romanians, inhabited by a 'collective thirst for holiness', will create a 'new man', but not in order to 'make politics, but to make history by means of supra-historical values'.

---

[10] A solid introduction to this topic is offered by Livezeanu 1995.
[11] In capturing the significance of Mircea Eliade for the Romanian contemporary intellectual tradition and his stands on various issues addressed in this chapter, I follow Turcanu 2005.

When he first entered the public arena, Mircea Eliade used to style himself as a disciple of René Guénon.[12] The Western world had for him obscured the real inner identity of any society, which resides in tradition. The autonomy of politics and the invention of the self perverted human nature as such, best and originally defined by the *homo religios*, a man not only organically attached to his community, but also naturally tied to a superior authority, normative and explicative at the same time. Both the project of Enlightenment and the enduring triumph of Hobbesian political science are therefore to be considered intellectual operations far removed from a genuine science of the spirit, which cannot be experienced on a private basis and in conditions of equality of the individuals involved, but has to be embodied by unified, purified, and hierarchically organized national communities animated by the vocation of spiritual primacy. Hence, nations have missions. They either dominate or are dominated. For obvious reasons, Eliade fostered his ideology as of the 1950s in the academic discipline of the history of religions, which helped him achieve international recognition. But many a Romanian intellectual at home remained constantly alive to the holistic and political purpose of Eliade's theoretical endeavour.

Europe othered: The history of a disillusion

In 1988, a member of Mircea Eliade's generation, the philosopher Constantin Noica,[13] issued in German, at a local publishing house, a collection of essays that were translated into Romanian five years later (Noica 1988, 1993). The volume opens with a widely read and still commented upon 'Letter to a Western intellectual', which comprises, among other considerations, a seminal assessment of Europe as a 'bye-bye society' (Noica 1993: in English in the Romanian text), as a civilization characterized by total disconnections and multiple partitions. In 2003, when the imminence of European integration was an acquired political conviction, Archbishop Anania rephrased this topic of separation as such: 'We find that the New Europe has only two dimensions, political and economic ... very important, but insufficient. Both politics and economics can divide the people. The New Europe lacks two vital dimensions: religious and cultural' (cited in Stan and Turcescu 2007: 207). As for Noica, he continued his search for an original, supposedly authentic Europe and pursued his research into an ideal-type 'European cultural model' by drafting a kind of historical

---

[12] Guénon's *La crise du monde moderne* was printed in 2008 in Romanian translation, alongside other writings in several editions of the French author, by the Humanitas Publishing House, whose CEO and main shareholder is Gabriel Liiceanu, a trustee of Mircea Eliade's intellectual heritage; the preface states that 'the work [of René Guénon] has today not only a doctrinaire value, but also a prophetic one' (Guénon 2008: 18).

[13] The most useful monograph on Noica's philosophy is Pamfil 2007.

grammar of the European spirit: the Middle Ages were a period of the *noun*, interested in naming the substances of being; from the Reformation to nineteenth-century Romanticism, Europe turned from an *adverbial* to a *pronominal* culture, exploring first the moods and modalities rather than the essences and ending up in coining the self, the *I* of the individual; contemporary Europe is for Noica an era of the *conjunction*, concerned with ascertaining relations on the 'and, or, if, then' mode; yet to come, if longed for and properly prepared by competent heralds, is the time of the *preposition* (of the 'with', 'amid', 'into', or 'like'), an era of a renewed correlation between men, and between men and things (Noica 1993: 92 and *passim*). Whatever happened in Europe in recent times, including the period of European construction, could be considered in the view of Constantin Noica as a process of incremental alienation from metaphysics.

Hence, an effort of de-rationalization, a guided tour into the 'religious roots' of the modern man, an almost wished-for attempt to re-enchant the world (*Wiederverzauberung der Welt*) (Patapievici 2008: 7; in German in the text) is what Noica's followers would recommend as a cure for this metaphysical disaffection. For instance, Horia-Roman Patapievici, probably the most widely published Romanian non-fiction author of the early 2000s, calls for a restatement, and possibly a reinstatement, of the pre-modern exploitation of *space*, dislodged by the modern experience of *time*: drawing on a somehow shallow and oblique reading of Carl Schmitt, he believes that Christian tradition is dependent on solid land and other essential substances,[14] whilst 'errant centre-less Judaism' relies on time and the fluid span of the sea, and as such it perfectly befits modernity, which understands existence not as a noun, an object and a presence, but as verbal mood, a passage, a loss, and a gap (Patapievici 2008: 196–7). If enthusiasts of the return of metaphysics had hoped to 'make history' in the 1930s by taking part in the actions of the fascist movement and sharing its plans for a unified European *Raum*, during communism and beyond 1989, their only prospect was to engage in a critique of the predicament of modern political history in the name of 'supra-historical values', to escape the restraints of the age of democracy by cultural action. 'Universal suffrage should therefore be limited, not by disenfranchisement but by the qualification of the vote' (Patapievici 2008: 390), more precisely by a hierarchical classification of the ballots based on the cultural proficiency of the voters, concludes Patapievici.

---

[14] Patapievici is far from being alone in his construing of space as a more important dimension than time in the fabric of national identity: Horia Bernea, acclaimed visual artist and founding director of the Museum of the Romanian Peasant in 1990, not only painted over and over again the same mystic hill and paradisiacal garden, but also conceived the museum entrusted to him by the government as a recreation of an atemporal, homogeneous, continuous, and religion-oriented traditional space populated by artefacts extracted from their original timeframe and initial use.

Culture alone becomes the remedy to this drifting apart of Europe with respect to its own original and atemporal spirit, far removed from the praxis of equality. But why culture and, moreover, whose culture? Unequivocally inspired by Mircea Eliade, a prominent member of Noica's circle defined culture as the best conceivable way to something beyond it and otherwise unattainable, as the optimal method to subsist in time, to stand in the right position between real life and the sacred (Pleşu 1988: 107–10). Vicarious by nature, culture logically calls for vicars. Pointing to an answer already advanced in 1937 by Eliade, the philosopher and essayist Emil Cioran[15] tells Constantin Noica in a letter of August 1980 who those may be: 'The fading of the West is an unquestionable and irremediable phenomenon', whereas south-east Europe (as Latin America) is more 'interesting, complex, surprising and has more vitality' (Cioran 1995: 311). Despite, if not thanks to, its communist experience, Romania may be one of the refuges of the essential European culture, almost vanished from today's standard Western Europe. Under state socialism, the Romanian intellectuals grouped around Constantin Noica claimed, in a language uttered in 1986 in the face of a totalitarian ideology, to be themselves the advocates of a 'cultural totalitarianism', that is of a 'totalitarianism of the values, [which] is the ideology of the thing-well-done'.[16]

It may seem astounding that in the decade preceding the demise of communism the central position of the intellectual stage was occupied by a philosopher trained in the 1930s, marked by a history of personal association with the national fascist movement and theorizing in the 1980s the contrast between the *realm of the spirit*, of which he assumed Romania was still a witness, and the European *realm of the butter*.[17] In a discussion reported in 1983, Constantin Noica purportedly asked someone who shared with him the intention of defecting to Germany, 'to what Germany do you intend to go, to the Germany of the butter or to the Germany of the culture?' immediately adding that 'paradoxically, [the Germany] of culture could be found more easily right here [i.e. in socialist Romania]' (Liiceanu 1983: 136). By an intended and finely tuned later distortion of this carefully worded statement, the historicist allusion of Noica to a famous cliché of the 1930s passed immediately into the common intellectual idiom under the canonical form 'the Europe of the butter', interpreted as a current description of the ambition of the Western member states of the European Union to be affluent societies. The saying would be used as such indistinctly by self-appointed cosmopolitan proponents of Western values (e.g. Marino 2005: 135) and by traditionalists close to the Orthodox hierarchy.[18]

---

[15] An appraisal of the Romanian work of Emil Cioran in Petreu 2005.

[16] Letter of Gabriel Liiceanu to Ion Ianoşi from November 1986, in Liiceanu 1987: 291.

[17] A partial explanation of this strange case in Verdery 1991: 256–301.

[18] E.g. the intervention of the theologian Costion Nicolescu, public relations director of the Museum of the Romanian Peasant, at a summer university organized by the governmental

By the time of his death in 1987, Constantin Noica had become, according to the philosopher – and, after 1989, major publisher – Gabriel Liiceanu, his chief disciple, a 'national institution' or, as another notable devotee put it, 'a representative of culture itself' (Pleşu 1988: 97). The tale of how an individual, albeit unusually learned and cogent, turned out to become an institution grew up in the expounding of his teachings in unrelenting successive editions of the *Păltiniş Diary* (Liiceanu 1991), first published in 1983 with the approval of communist officials. Liiceanu would eventually recount that, in the winter when this narrative of a sage isolated on a mountain and imparting metaphysics to younger followers was first released, consumption goods were scarce and hard to come by. Still, a copy of the book was exchanged on the black market for four packages of butter. One may comment that under communism, unadulterated culture was considered to be worth four times its own printed amount in dubious butter. In real life, reasons Liiceanu, totalitarian societies are unpolitical. Accordingly, culture (if well expounded by carefully selected and properly taught people) may break the monopoly held by a thin minority over politics. In fact, compared to the certified ideology of scientific socialism, European high culture was an 'alternative script' and as such had a political meaning as a venue of political resistance. Through culture, well-educated, insulated individuals tried less to evade on their own account the absurdity and paucity of the public discourse than to 'participate from the shadows' in the destiny of the community, in a cultural timelessness incarnated by their nation.

Europe imagined: The sovereignty of culture

As far as a core Romanian cultural public is concerned, Mircea Eliade has said it once and for all: nations do have missions. And in order to accomplish them, they are in need of intellectual guidance, as they were in the 1930s and again in the 1980s, when Eliade, Cioran, and Noica acted as authoritative 'national institutions' proclaiming the poverty of the political (of democratic politics in particular) and announcing the primacy of the spiritual and the cultural. Today, it is precisely the lack of such 'legitimate authority' based on pre-political normative premises that may be considered the cause of the 'radical powerlessness of democracy', based on rights and neglectful of duties, insists Patapievici (2008: 94–5), president of the Romanian Cultural Institute, a government-sponsored organization designed to disseminate abroad the excellence of Romanian culture. Culture, he argues, is by definition a form of inequality embedded in the old European tradition of the hierarchy of values; hence culture runs the risk of being destroyed by the emerging figure of the 'recent

Department for the Romanian Diaspora reported by the local paper *Adevărul Harghitei* XX, no. 2501, 23 August 2000, p. 4.

man', construed as a combination of Chinese collectivism and American political correctness, as a product of a politically empowered egalitarianism (ibid.: 254–6). Unlike Eliade's 'new man' of the spirit, thirsting for Orthodox holiness, the Western *recent man*'s only value is material prosperity appraised at the expense of both freedom and culture (ibid.: 216).

Set in motion by politics and economics, Europe is not only divisive, as Noica or Anania observed, but also alien to both religion and culture construed as expressions of an unpolitical truth, Patapievici stresses. If that is the case, how should Romanians fit into Europe? Theodor Baconsky, theologian by training and senior political advisor and diplomat by trade, admits (without quoting him by name) that Eliade's vision of 'Orthodoxy as a spiritual alternative to an excessively secularized West' still survives as an 'inner dream', an ideal or a positive utopia shared by the Orthodox believer (Baconsky 2002: 355). This geopolitics of the spirit, contrasting a secularized and political Europe on the one hand, and a passionately Orthodox and highly cultured Romania on the other, represents the meeting point of the historicist counter-narrative of Europe created by the Church authorities around four eighteenth-century martyrs and the revival of metaphysics propped up by the mainstream intellectuals who perpetuate the legacy of Noica without espousing an explicit confessional – or even Christian – position.[19] Given that in the European template post-secularism and post-metaphysical thinking are normatively entwined, as Jürgen Habermas (2006a) believes, Romania should be regarded as a deviant case.

The Church hierarchy may well be, and was often accused by its own enlightened supporters of being, engaged in anti-intellectual policies, among which figures the canonization of several saints decidedly unfamiliar with the works of Plato or Augustine and unsuspecting of the possibility that thinkers such as Hegel or Heidegger might one day come out in favour of metaphysics. Public intellectuals, by definition 'men of culture', are there precisely so as to append what the clergy is ignoring or dismissing. Andrei Pleşu said in the immediate aftermath of the breakdown of state socialism: 'In normal societies, the Church has the charge of leading the consciousnesses, and culture feeds itself from the Church as from a secure foundation. With us the situation is now such that culture has to take up temporarily the role of influencing the Church in a positive manner and from a moral and intellectual point of view' (quoted by Ică Jr. 2002: 550). The alpine meadows of Salva, where four peasants rebutted the eighteenth-century European science of the state, and the mountain of Păltiniş, from where the philosopher Noica invalidated the twentieth-century 'Europe of the butter', ultimately belong to a complementary spiritual geography. Religion and culture are mobilized, either together or in turns, in order

---

[19] A theologian and frequent contributor to cultural magazines reproved Patapievici for not taking an unequivocal confessional stand: see Neamţu 2008. As for Constantin Noica, he was exceptionally discreet with respect to his personal Christian commitment.

to map the expanse of the pre-political spirit of a Europe that Romanian intellectuals manifest the intention of keeping alive.

Indeed, this tight interweaving of religion and culture in a civilizational order fusing a national church, a traditional sense of family, a cultural denial of modernity, and an unconcealed distrust in equality retrospectively resembles some of the traits of what Charles Taylor has dubbed as the 'Age of Mobilization', foregoing the Secular Age he extensively explored (Taylor 2007: 445–72). Indeed, if secularization implies that all individuals have equal entitlement to phrase or rephrase the public arguments used in a political space which does not admit any other resource than natural reason, Romanian political culture was never really secular, inasmuch as the autonomy of politics is hypothesized as a distinctive feature of secularism. The liberal parliamentarism of the nineteenth century and of the first part of the twentieth century believed that politics was contingent on the destiny of the nation, while state socialism treated politics as a dependent superstructure of an implacable meaning of history better explained by economic and social processes. Post-communism laid a comparable claim on politics. There was always something, a deeper and more significant essence, to look for beyond politics, although this something was not the same in all circumstances nor for all persuasions.

Thus, the Romanian public space may be considered a post-secular one inasmuch as mainstream intellectuals pivoted their career and achieved their cultural authority on the claim that European union may be a hazard for Europe itself. For them and their audiences, the union turned out to be, in the long process of its making, a post-modern political and bureaucratic venture estranged from the genuine European spirit that energized the early founders of the Communities, educated in a tradition of interlocked Christian and humanist values. In the meantime, 'the repudiation of humanism, the oblivion of Christianity and ideological relativism could kill Europe, not only in a cultural sense, but also in a political, economic, and military one' (Patapievici 2009: 259). Romanian intellectuals may not be entirely original in their disparagement of the European Union, though they tend to give a sharper edge to positions taken elsewhere, with delicate shades of meaning, by the few contemporary authors they accidentally care to quote (among them Pierre Manent, Roger Scruton, or Joseph Weiler). This stern approach to the European political project is perhaps no more than a method of explaining away the enduring unlikeness of Romanian polity and the European Union.

There appears to be no doubt that the ideal-type narrative of European integration manufactured by Romanian intellectuals could be summarized as follows: in the realm of the spirit, Europe survives mainly in the East, shepherded by such intellectuals as the Romanian ones; in political and economic terms, meanwhile, the European Union is monitored according to secularist and relativist guidelines by the bureaucracy in Brussels. Whatever the latter, together with their Romanian counterparts, may have realized in the course of European enlargement is of little concern for the former. As public (but silent) intellectuals they were middle-class professionals even before 1989, and they got anyhow their freedom of speech and freedom of movement after the fall of state socialism. They are engaged now in an operation that should have defined them as critical intellectuals long before the fall: to boost intellectual non-conformity with respect to the politically dominant discourse as a way of refusing the debate by taking it seriously. And they do it by means of the same narrative device that kept them silent under communism: they tell the story of the prevalence of culture and the spiritual over everything political.

13

The World of the Two Václavs

European-Minded vs. National(ist)
Intellectuals in Czechia

Muriel Blaive and Nicolas Maslowski

After the fall of the Iron Curtain in 1989, issues relating to post-communism, both on a political and economic level, took precedence in Czech intellectual and political life over every other topic. Paradoxically for a revolution undertaken in the name of the 'return to Europe', even Europe could not compete with post-communist issues for centre stage.[1] However, most observers have distinguished two currents of political thought on the European topic, generally considered to be represented by the 'two Václavs': Václav Havel and Václav Klaus,[2] two individuals who make no secret of their antipathy towards one another.[3]

The former is one of the leading Czech intellectuals: a famous dissident under the communist regime and subsequently the inspired leader of the Velvet Revolution in November 1989, Havel was also the first president of free Czechoslovakia and of the independent Czech Republic. His humanist and ethical views are well-known; as a dissident and founder of Charter 77, he promoted 'apoliticism', solidarity, reconciliation, and effortlessly sustained the Czech tradition of 'truth' and 'love' during the Velvet Revolution (Ducreux 1990).

---

[1] If we consider contemporary historians to be intellectuals in the best Czech tradition, it is remarkable to notice how little Europe has structured, permeated, or even simply featured in their issues of concern: see the rare analysis of post-communist debates in Mayer 2003, where Europe is barely mentioned.

[2] See for instance Bugge 2000. Some even see *three* Václavs if they take into account Prince Václav or the 'Good King Wenceslas' (907–35), the patron saint of Bohemia who symbolizes the greatness of the Czech nation. See Stroehlein 1999.

[3] See the film directed by Pavel Koutecký, *Citizen Havel* (Prague, Film et sociologie, January 2008). The crew filmed forty-five hours of images and recorded ninety hours of sound material over the course of thirteen years. Both Václavs are represented in all the depth of their mutual dislike.

Klaus, meanwhile, takes pride in his role as a technocrat, avoiding any political commitment before 1989 while rapidly shaping and taking control of the Czech conservative party (ODS) after 1990. Klaus became the emblematic prime minister of post-1989 privatizations and decommunization, and eventually succeeded Václav Havel as president of the country in 2003.

We will attempt here to describe the different worlds in which these two figures and their supporters position themselves in relation to Europe,[4] starting with an emblematic regional outpost of the European idea: the concept of Central Europe. Although it might seem irrelevant and distinct from 'Europe' as seen from the West, the concept of Central Europe carries a crucial, symbolic value on the Czech intellectual scene, without which the wider European debate would take a completely different shape. Central Europe is an intellectual gate which cannot be ignored since, as we will see, individual and collective answers to the geopolitical, strategic, historical, and philosophical issues that it raises always predetermine attitudes to Europe as a whole.

Czech intellectuals and Central Europe

Václav Havel's vision of Central Europe had already been promoted by the first president of the Czechoslovak Republic (1918–35), the philosopher Tomáš Masaryk. Because Masaryk supported a European federation and a political integration of Central Europe, the pro-(Central) European stance in Czechoslovakia became retrospectively associated, under communist rule, not only with centre-left democracy but with the democratic era as a whole. The debate on the position of Czechs in Europe and, simultaneously, on the identity of a real or imagined Central Europe, came to represent the opposition between the democratic and the communist camps. Between Germany and Russia, where did the Czech Lands stand (Rupnik 1988: 3–23)? Was Central Europe East of the West, or West of the East? Did Central Europe exist at all, or was Czechoslovakia part of Eastern Europe only?

The Cold War, the Iron Curtain, and the East/West divide seemed to impose an answer to this question.[5] However, Czech intellectuals were unhappy with this forceful geopolitical 'solution', and tried to bring the question back to the fore first of all during the Prague Spring in 1968, and later as dissidents or exiles between 1969 and 1989. Czech dissidents, like their counterparts in the other

---

[4] By 'position', we are referring to the concept defined in Boltanski and Thévenot 1991: 69. The dissidents created their own world and justified its existence through important texts, references, and people. Havel's high position can be called an *estate*, as it is constitutive of this world and as he participates in its very construction.

[5] For a good analysis at the time, see Halecki and Simon 2000 [1952]. For a recent update, see Horel 2009, a valuable reflection on Central Europe, self-consciousness, and history, although the author regrettably does not include Poland in her definition of Central Europe.

'satellite' countries, were strong supporters of Central-Europeanness (Faraldo, Gulińska-Jurgiel, and Domnitz 2008; Laignel-Lavastine 2005; Miłosz 1964; Rupnik 1988). Their Homeric efforts to meet with Polish dissidents over the Polish–Czech border in the vicinity of Havel's country house became legendary, while one of the biggest Czech *samizdat* reviews was called *Střední Evropa* (Central Europe).

Rehabilitating Central Europe was a way of asserting these countries' moral superiority over occupying Russian forces, and of grappling with the threat of a disappearing cultural heritage (Blaive 2006). Milan Kundera should of course be singled out here for his 'Tragedy of Central Europe' (the telling original French subtitle being, 'L'Occident kidnappé' [The Kidnapped West]: Kundera 1983), a text written in exile in 1983 but largely rooted in his essays from the end of the 1960s, and in particular from his much debated 'Czech Fate' essay of 1968.[6] By defining Central Europe as something 'culturally in the West, geographically in the centre and politically in the East', his intention was of course to reposition Czechoslovakia in the West and to show how alien the Soviet dictatorship was to its political tradition (Nilsson 2000).

From Central Europe to Europe

The fight over the legitimacy of Central Europe in fact hides a wider controversy over the legitimacy of Europe and the position Czechoslovakia should play within it. Through his dissident political activity, Václav Havel took a clearly favourable position on Europe as an intellectual concept (Kopeček 2005). The Charter 77 manifesto, which he largely inspired, repeatedly emphasized the importance for the Czechs of belonging to Europe (Skilling 1981). In its 1985 'Prague Appeal', for instance, the Charter pleaded for an end to a divided Europe and for its reunification – including that of Germany.[7] Havel also insisted in all his political essays – implicitly or explicitly – on Czech 'Europeanness' (Havel 1989); as, of course, did the most important Czech philosopher of the twentieth century Jan Patočka, another key opponent of communist rule and a proponent of an inherent Czech 'Europeanness'.[8]

---

[6] See Michal Kopeček, 'Polemika Milan Kundera – Václav Havel. Spory o českou otázku v letech 1967–1969' [The debate between Milan Kundera and Václav Havel. Controversies over the Czech question in the years 1967–1969], presentation at the conference *Pražské jaro 1968: literatura, média, film* [Prague Spring 1968: literature, media, film], Prague, City Library, 20–22 May 2008, organized by Petr Cornej.

[7] See the document 'Pražská výzva' (Prague Call) in Prečan 1990: 423. This statement was in line with the Charter's long-standing positions, but it certainly did not contribute to the dissident movement's popularity among the wider Czechoslovak audience which was, and remains, fiercely anti-German – not least thanks to communist propaganda.

[8] For instance in his famous essay *Evropa a doba poevropská* (Europe and the post-European era), Patočka 1992. For an excellent analysis of Patočka's work, see Laignel-Lavastine 2005.

At the opposite end of the political spectrum, the regime ideologist Zdeněk Nejedlý denied that Western Europe had held any cultural legitimacy during the era of European construction, which he saw as a 'dollar-driven American project'; he considered the Soviet Union as the only 'true Europe' (Reijnen 2008: 111–12, 116). It must be underlined that after the Second World War, Czech society was largely ripe for the advent of communism. As historian Carlos Reijnen (2008: 112) explains: 'The post-war Czech communist perception of Europe and the West and the need to formulate new positions in "national" questions were deeply entangled. Rethinking the future was also rethinking the past', not least concerning the national relationship to the vanquished and victorious regional powers of the Second World War, Germany and the Soviet Union, in a process of respective demonization and glorification.

The 'East' represented not only a sought-after geopolitical security but also socialism, a societal project which suited a Czech political and social practice imbued with egalitarianism. The communist regime also revived and promoted pan-Slavism, which had taken root in Czech culture as early as the nineteenth century.[9] All in all – and this explains its long-lasting success – the anti-European and pro-Russian mindset of Czech communist propaganda did more than match Stalinist standards: it took up its 'self-evident place in the intellectual history' of Czechoslovakia, while addressing the widely shared concern among the Czech population that Nazism and fascism were 'inherently linked to a deep crisis of Europe itself' (Reijnen 2008: 111, 115). European references disappeared from the Czech public sphere after the war; while Czechoslovakia, which had featured so prominently in all debates on the European idea after 1918, simultaneously disappeared from a European meta-narrative which increasingly came to resonate with the successful history of the (Western) European institutions (Schulz-Forberg 2008: 41).

What is important to understand is that the intellectual attitude to Europe has been historically 'politicized' by the fact that the pro-European discourse was carried on only by exiles[10] and dissident circles. In the Cold War context, being in favour of 'Central Europe' and then of 'Europe' was akin to positioning oneself against the communist regime. By contrast, the famous 'return to Europe' advocated by Václav Havel as newly elected president of free Czechoslovakia in December 1989 was meant to represent the antinomy of everything noxious that was represented by real existing socialism.

The politicization and simultaneous de-intellectualization of the European issue today in the Czech Republic is in large part an outcome of this particular

---

[9] See the main works of ideologue Zdeněk Nejedlý, for instance *Komunisté: Dědici velkých tradic českého národa* [The communists: The great inheritors of the Czech nation's tradition] (1950), first published in 1946.

[10] Whom the communist propaganda depicted as 'servants of American imperialism': see Reijnen 2008: 120. Yet they thought of themselves as speaking in the name of Europe, which was exemplified by their engagement in Radio Free Europe; see Lane 2008: 301.

historical path and conceptual confrontation. It explains why the pro-European stance, both past and present, is not only a primary political issue, but is also closely linked to certain attitudes on the domestic front relating to decentralization and civil society. Because themes such as Central Europe, Europe, humanism, human rights, civil society, or ecology were historically shaped as one and the same ethical weapon against the communist regime, they still go hand in hand today. After the fall of communism, the issue of 'Europe' was additionally politicized by the fact that many Czech politicians are intellectuals and former dissidents, and that they have brought their previously philosophical debate onto the political scene.

Intellectual conceptions of Europe

Accepting a decentralized power shared between Brussels, the central government, and local governments or authorities is tantamount to a 'democratic approach',[11] recognizing an intermediary between the state and the citizen in the form of trade unions, confessions, associations, and so on. Groups who accept this view tend to support 'Europe'. They range from the centre-left (Vladimír Špidla, former right-wing social-democratic prime minister) to the centre-right, from social-democrats to conservative Christians (journalist Petruška Šustrová, adherents of the review *Střední Evropa*, which is still published today) and of course to the centre: Greens (Jakub Patočka, who also for a long time published the literary weekly *Literární noviny*), Christian-Democrats (former dissident and university professor Petr Pithart), and social liberals.[12]

These intellectuals sometimes disagree with Václav Havel's views, but pay him tribute and respect. The Greens, for instance, are opposed to the state negotiating with organized religion; conservative liberal Christians are not supportive of trade unions, and so on. All of them, however, support the existence of these intermediary bodies with whom the state should negotiate, what Havel calls *civil society*. Some NGOs, conceived almost structurally in the Czech Republic as heirs to the former dissident movement for the historical reasons explained above – which tightly associate civic society, Europe, and

---

[11] Sociologist Michel Wieviorka pointed out that such an opposition also exists in France and uses the definition of conservative (French) politician Michel Debré: in France, 'Republicans' consider that there should be no intermediate body between the state and citizens, whereas 'Democrats' value intermediary bodies like confessions, associations, or other civil society organizations. See Maslowski 2008: 1.

[12] Here we can draw an interesting parallel with Justine Lacroix's analysis (Chapter 5, this volume) concerning the definition of democracy and of republicanism in France. The Czech debate can also be compared with that prevailing in intellectual circles in the UK. The intellectuals classified by Georgios Varouxakis (Chapter 7, this volume) as choosing the 'third way' are participating in what we call the 'democratic approach'. They are clearly opposed both to nationally centralized Marxist Eurosceptics and to right-wing Eurosceptics.

intellectuals – also lead reflection on Europe and its importance, but their representativeness is as limited as was that of the dissident movement under communism.[13] In comparison with a country like France, these NGOs and 'civil society' in general represent only a tiny portion of the population.

Among the most prominent intellectuals reflecting positively on Europe, we can cite Petr Pithart and Jan Křen. In the best 'Havel spirit', Petr Pithart – a major Czech intellectual and former dissident, last prime minister of the federal Czech Republic before the dissolution of Czechoslovakia and today vice-president of the Czech Senate – defends European integration because he is convinced that it is a 'story without ending', without a definite and quantifiable shape, where the process of construction constitutes a goal in itself. Referring to philosopher Karl Popper, Pithart expressed his belief that Europeans would correct and improve their mistakes in a continual process, rather than try to impose their conception of truth (Pithart 2006).

In a thinly veiled criticism of Václav Klaus, he warned against the tendency of Europeans, as opposed to Americans, to succumb at the least temptation to universalistic ideologies such as fascism, Nazism, communism – and now nationalism. It is true, he claimed, that the EU is hit hard by bureaucracy; but the case of the United States shows that federalism, self-management, and the most developed civil society in the world are the best weapons against this tendency. The third sector in the US, primarily churches and NGOs, takes over many tasks fulfilled by the state in Europe; this, claimed Pithart, should be our model (Pithart 2006).

As a prominent historian, specialist of the hotly debated Czech–German relations, and advocate of reconciliation (he has presided for years over the Czech–German Historical Commission), Jan Křen portrays Europe as a complicated superimposition of national narratives. Facing the quasi-impossibility of writing a 'European History', he proposes to take into account, as a first step, macro-regions. Indeed, he considers that regional grouping is not a danger but an asset for the European construction. That is where Central Europe reappears as a conceptual stage on the way to Europe as a whole.[14]

Other intellectuals consider themselves simultaneously as pro-European and enlightened Czech patriots, judging that commitment to European civilization and community is not incompatible with a deep love of the nation. We are

---

[13] Some think tanks, for example, make use of academic legitimacy to obtain subsidies from the EU, be it on a political or technical level (see for instance the association Europeum). Others, like Yes to Europe (*Ano pro Evropu*) use the intellectuals' and former dissidents' legitimacy. Others still, like AMO (Association for International Relations) make use of a mixture of political, academic, and dissident legitimacy – its current president, Antonín Berdych, is the head of staff for the deputy prime minister in charge of European affairs, Alexandr Vondra. A final example of the way 'dissident legitimacy' has been used is the new European Partnership for Democracy, a new international NGO whose patron is none other than Václav Havel.

[14] See the introduction to Křen's 2005 masterpiece (of 1,110 pages), *Dvě století střední Evropy* [Two centuries of Central Europe].

referring to the group of the so-called 'Bad Boys' (*Parta u Stinadel*), inflammatory intellectuals such as Bohumil Doležal, Emanuel Mandler, and Milan Churaň. Ever since 1968, those strongly anti-communist intellectuals have been publishing in the reviews *Tvář* and the above-mentioned *Střední Evropa* (Central Europe) – although Emanuel Mandler died in January 2009. Even though they hold or held different opinions on nearly every subject and do not always offer a coherent vision, this group of three strongly rejects close-minded Czech nationalism, especially the violent version which characterized the period 1945–8. Their motto is reconciliation with the Germans, a will to open the Czech intellectual scene to the world's ideas, and a rejection of isolationist nationalism.

Their commitment to and support for the dissident movement and Charter 77, meanwhile, paradoxically translates into an ever more radical criticism of former dissidents and a claim for pragmatism, as opposed to idealism. Although this is a generally pro-European group, the result sometimes and unexpectedly borders on anti-Europeanism – Bohumil Doležal was, for instance, an advisor to Václav Klaus at one time.

Doležal and Mandler have argued fiercely with Jan Křen on multiple occasions over a core issue for the European conception of Czech intellectuals: Czech–German relations, especially at the time (1997) when the joint Czech–German Historical Commission published its first results and its Declaration (Stroehlein 1997). On a parallel issue, the two 'ultras' (as Andrew Stroehlein calls them) deplored that the past was insufficiently represented in the media, while Křen claimed the contrary.[15]

Younger intellectuals led by Petr Placák around the satirical, artistic, and intellectual review *Babylon*, but accompanied by older figures such as former dissidents Ivan Jirous and Zdeněk Vašíček, have been influenced by the 'Bad Boys' ideas in their most scathing and provocative incarnation, to a point which could hardly be considered serious in Western Europe but which is not shocking on the Czech scene. For instance, even under communist rule Placák and his colleagues had gone so far as to create a semi-serious monarchist party [*sic*] in the name of their fight for maximum individual freedom. In a peculiar conception of Europe and to symbolize their rejection of Czech nationalism, they still call today for Emperor Franz Joseph's return to the Czech Crown, while organizing an annual rally to stage this demand (Placák 2009). The provocative dimension of this endeavour is of course proportional to the historical role played by Czech nationalism in bringing down the Austro-Hungarian empire. This group of intellectuals sees Europe as a Europe of Nations, even though some of them are not far from federalist conceptions. Interestingly, Petr Placák is now a recognized authority on Europe: he has been designated editor-in-chief of

---

[15] See their debate as printed in *Právo* (15 May 1997) and *Mladá fronta Dnes* (26 April 1997 and 2 May 1997).

<http://www.euroskop.cz>, the Czech government information webpage on European questions set up on the occasion of the Czech presidency of the EU.

Havel himself is federalist or confederalist.[16] Like his most famous political friends and allies (aside from Petr Pithart and Jan Křen) – Karel Schwarzenberg (former president of the Helsinski Committee for Human Rights, currently Minister of Foreign Affairs), Jiří Pehe (prominent political scientist) or Tomáš Halík (former dissident, university professor of sociology and theology, and much publicized priest) – he believes that Europe should be based on the values of human rights and democracy. He and his supporters believe that this humanist Europe has much in common with and owes its freedom to the United States of America, with which it should be strongly allied:[17] hence his consistent support of US policy (bombing of Yugoslavia, war in Iraq, radar installation on Czech soil). It should nevertheless be underlined that other personalities from Havel's 'camp', such as social-democratic politician Lubomír Zaorálek, evangelist and folk singer Svatopluk Karásek, poet Ivan Martin Jirous, sociologist and feminist leader Jiřina Šiklová, politician and intellectual Jiří Dienstbier, journalist Petr Uhl, and others, are not as clearly in favour of a strong partnership with the US, though they do share a positive image of the Americans. Their position is rather to support a 'strong Europe'.[18] As Šiklová expressed it, 'I prefer to be wrong with America, than to be right with Russia' (Kouřil 2008).

From the world of ideas to politics: The 'Klaus trend' and Europe

In the opposite camp on the European question – which does not necessarily overlap with the opposite side of the political spectrum in a general sense[19] – Václav Klaus has endeavoured to construct an alternative ideology. But is Klaus an intellectual in the strict sense? He claims not to be, precisely so as to distance

[16] See for instance his speech before the European Parliament on 16 February 2000, where he called for the creation of a second, federal chamber at the European Parliament where each European state, small or large, would have two deputies on the American model. This speech, or one with similar contents, delivered on 3 March 1999 in front of the French Senate, can be downloaded on the French Senate's website <http://www.senat.fr>.

[17] Karel Schwarzenberg even expressly denies that there are any 'European values'; in his famous speech 'European values? A notion which I dislike', he claimed that European values are only those shared with the United States. See the debate on the theme 'European values–Do they exist at all?' on the website of a prominent Czech think tank, Občanský Institut (Civic Institute) <http://www.obcinst.cz/cs>.

[18] See for instance Jiří Dienstbier's seminal speech 'Let us say yes to a strong Europe!', 19 June 2007, originally published in *Mladá Fronta Dnes* but also accessible on his webpage at <http://jiri.dienstbier.cz>. Dienstbier is also the author of the book *Dreaming About Europe* (Snění o Evropě) which came out in samizdat form in 1986.

[19] Current Prime Minister Mirek Topolánek, although a member of Václav Klaus' party (ODS), for instance, is very critical of the anti-European and pro-Russian attitude of his president. See Topolánek 2008. The attitude of 'EU dissident' President Klaus has also been qualified by commentators as akin to 'sabotaging his own government': see Verner 2008.

himself from Havel and his ideas. In a 2005 speech, he came up with a scathing criticism of what an 'intellectual' represented for him, quoting Friedrich Hayek: intellectuals are allegedly 'professional second-hand dealers in ideas', who are proud 'not to possess special knowledge of anything in particular', who do not take 'direct responsibility for practical affairs', and who need not 'even be particularly intelligent' to perform their so-called 'mission'.[20]

Moreover, this unflattering description of intellectuals is politically loaded: Václav Klaus argues that an intellectual is 'interested in visions and utopias, and because "socialist thought owes its appeal largely to its visionary character" (and I would add lack of realism and utopian nature), the intellectual tends to become a socialist'. This description, of course, smacks of communist intellectuals who – as Czechs know and remember well – enthusiastically led the country to communism between 1945 and 1948 and even to Stalinism after 1948, with the youthful poet Pavel Kohout, for instance, calling for a 'dog's death for the dogs' during the Slánský show-trial in 1952 (Rupnik 1988: 109).

However, although President Klaus does not consider himself a 'socialist', having built his reputation as an 'economic expert' after 1989 and during his rise to power, we consider that he should be credited with this effort at defining intellectuals. He did participate in the main academic discussions in the country's post-war history, writing articles under the common pseudonym 'Dalimil' with arch-intellectuals Antonín J. Liehm and Emanuel Mandler in 1968's *Literární noviny* (Hoppe 2004); and taking part, despite his claims to the contrary, in alternative dissident seminars in the 1980s.[21]

The European critics in Klaus' camp support a strong state in a 'republican' approach. Everything has to be decided centrally on the national level, and they consider any intermediary body as a danger to procedural democracy. Despite the professed anti-communism that they share with the social-democrats, they have largely remained in line with the main options followed by the communist regime and with its sources of legitimacy, and their political weapons remain essentially the same on nationality and identity.

The ODS (conservatives), the left wing of the ČSSD (social-democratic party) and, in fact, the KSČM (communist party) perpetuate a discourse that underlines the danger arising from European construction, a danger that allegedly comes from such neighbouring countries as Germany and Austria. In this sense, President Klaus' vision of Europe is a systematic and uninhibited counterpart to the 'Havel trend'. Even though it would be absurd and completely wrong to ascribe the defence of Soviet intervention in Czech affairs from 1948 to 1989 to Václav Klaus, it cannot be denied that his current political vision is largely heir

---

[20] See Klaus 2005. The following quotes are extracted from this same speech.
[21] See Daye 1999; also Suk 2003. However, by serving our own purposes and considering Klaus as an intellectual, we are adopting a different definition of intellectuals from that of Francis Cheneval (see Chapter 1, this volume).

to the old propaganda line which had made the success of the communist regime in its time: nationalism, anti-Germanism, rejection of intellectual dissidents, fear of Europe, refusal of Central European solidarity, to which Klaus added isolationism (Maslowski 2007: 15). This political stand allowed him to build the biggest post-1989 Czech party, retroactively – and unwittingly – illustrating the genuine support base which the communist regime had managed to build for itself.

The last general elections (2002) before the accession of the Czech Republic to the EU were the pretext for an orgy of nationalism and barely disguised xenophobia towards these German-speaking neighbours, notably around the issue of the infamous Beneš decrees (Blaive 2002; Blaive and Mink 2003). President Klaus was then elected by the Parliament in 2003 thanks to the combined votes of the conservatives and the communists, against intellectual and former dissident Jan Sokol, who was castigated for his alleged 'soft' position on the Sudeten German issue (Blaive 2007).

President Klaus' anti-European tendencies are rooted in this historical predetermination.[22] The 'danger' for the Czech nation would come from the West, an idea which was historically reinforced by the Munich Agreement in 1938, when France and Great Britain notoriously gave Czechoslovakia away to Hitler's Germany despite their mutual alliance. On the other hand, the largest Slavic nation, Russia, was considered by the communists as Czechoslovakia's best 'friend' and protector – there again, a vision enhanced by the Red Army liberation from Nazi occupation in 1945.

As a result, Klaus primarily supports a form of isolationist nationalism. Foreign countries and international organizations or structures should not exert any influence on Czech politics, and the Czech state correspondingly should not meddle in foreign affairs. On the occasion of Kosovo's recently proclaimed independence, for instance, he and other representatives of conservative currents in Czech politics expressed their scepticism. They underlined Slavic solidarity and delayed Czech recognition of this independence for as long as possible.[23] There again, the Kosovo question is reminiscent in the Czech context of the ever-present Sudeten German issue: the implicit Czech conservative argument is that citizens who do not behave loyally to a Slavic state should leave – or be forced to leave.

Klaus is of course not as openly supportive of the former 'Big Brother' as the former regime leaders, but he still is sympathetic to his Eastern neighbour and

---

[22] See Řiháčková and von Seydlitz 2007.

[23] The best proof of Slavic solidarity being that Yugoslavia did not take part in the invasion of Czechoslovakia in 1968, but as Petr Uhl mischievously remarked, 'Probably no one told them that if Yugoslavia didn't intervene in Czechoslovakia in 1968 along with the Warsaw Pact troops, it's only because it was not asked to.' See the round table 'Le printemps de Prague', Prague, Komerční Banka, 21 May 2008, organized by Marie-Claude Maurel (Centre français de recherche en sciences sociales).

occasionally takes Russia's side in international affairs, even against the European Union's better judgement – which does not prevent him from sometimes taking America's side against Russia, too. The only exception to the self-proclaimed rule of not intervening in other countries' affairs occurred during such a Klausian episode of vehement pro-Russian attitude, with his support of the Kremlin in the summer of 2008 during the war with Georgia. Unsurprisingly, he was also opposed to the bombing of Serbia, to the war in Iraq, and to the installation of American radars on Czech soil.[24] These radars, coupled with missile shields installed in Poland, were justified by President Bush in order to protect Europe, NATO, and the US against potential missiles coming from the so-called 'rogue states', in particular Iran (though President Obama seems in the meantime to have abandoned the project). Indeed, their installation caused great distress and a strong, threatening reaction on the part of Russia, which is keen on asserting its veto right over what it still considers its sphere of influence, i.e. Central Europe – hence the strategic importance of Central Europe in the Czech European debate. Václav Klaus' support was rewarded: his latest book was translated into Russian thanks to a subsidy from Lukoil, a subsidiary of the Russian gas giant Gazprom.[25]

Václav Klaus' open contempt of the West goes so far that he distinguished himself in the 1990s by what Western observers have generally considered as arrogant behaviour, namely by lecturing the European Union on what the Czech Republic could bring to it rather than the other way round. In his seminal 2005 (i.e. post-accession) speech ironically entitled 'View from a post-communist country in a predominantly post-democratic Europe' given in Rekjavik, Iceland, Václav Klaus – who defines himself not without humour as an 'EU dissident' – warned against 'Europeanism', mixing his opposition with Havel's world in one overall set of values (Belien 2005).

Portraying himself as an indomitable defender of liberty in Margaret Thatcher's mould, he underlined that 'Europeanism' and 'NGOism' were 'substitute ideologies' to late socialism (sic) because they were based on 'similar illiberal or antiliberal views'. Among these damaging ideologies, he also included environmentalism with its 'Earth First, not Freedom First principle', 'radical human-rightism', the ideology of 'civic society' or communitarianism, 'which is nothing less than one version of post-Marxist collectivism which wants privileges for organized groups, and in consequence, a re-feudalization of society' (sic), multiculturalism, and feminism (Belien 2005). According to President Klaus, these dangerous ideologies share with 'old-style socialism' the same 'limiting (or constraining) of human freedom', the same 'ambitious social engineering',

---

[24] Noting, however, that the relationship to the United States is not a question of 'right' or 'left', but of pro-American 'humanitarian' interventionism against isolationist nationalism à la Klaus.

[25] Soukup and Benešová 2008.

the same 'immodest "enforcement of a good" by those who are anointed on others against their will', the same 'crowding out of standard democratic methods by alternative political procedures', and last but not least, the same 'feeling of superiority of intellectuals and of their ambitions' (Belien 2005).

He urged all freedom-loving Europeans to 'understand that this is a contemporary version of worldwide socialism'. He opined that these 'alternative ideologies' were successful especially in Europe (as opposed to the United States) because they found there a 'fertile ground', where 'freedom (and free markets) have been heavily undermined by long-lasting collectivistic dreams and experiences and where intellectuals have succeeded in getting and maintaining a very strong voice and social status' (Belien 2005).

At this point his hostility to Havel, 'Europe', and the European Union mingle into one, clear object of severe criticism: 'It is Europe where we witness the crowding out of democracy by post-democracy, where the EU dominance replaces democratic arrangements in the EU member countries, where [some people] do not see the dangers of empty Europeanism and of a deep, and ever deeper, but only bureaucratic unification of the whole European continent.' The 'European political system' is allegedly endangered by a 'postmodern interpretation of human rights' with its 'dominance of group rights and entitlements over individual rights and responsibilities' and its 'denationalization of citizenship'. Klaus explicitly opposed the 'weakening of democratic institutions, which have irreplaceable roots exclusively on the territory of the states' (Belien 2005). In this respect, his positions recall those of some currents in French political thought which denounce the 'religion of human rights' allegedly embodied by Europe – see the chapter on France in this volume.

Unsurprisingly in the context of the Europe-wide debate in 2005 on the European 'constitution', Václav Klaus concludes: 'The European constitution was an attempt to set up and consolidate such a system in a legal form. It was an attempt to constitute it. It is, hence, more than important that the French and Dutch referenda put an end to it, that they interrupted the seemingly irreversible process towards an "ever-closer Europe".' Indeed, President Klaus himself appealed to the population to vote 'no' in a potential referendum in the Czech Republic, and the state of opinion polls at the time indicates that the Czech public was ambivalent about its potential response: as always,[26] opponents of

[26] Opponents of the European Union and generally people who are dissatisfied about the economic and political situation in the Czech Republic massively abstain from voting. That is why the voter turnout is regularly very low in the Czech Republic, as in the other post-socialist countries. Electoral abstention reached in October 2006 a historical high in the Czech senatorial elections, with an electoral participation of only 20.73 per cent in the second round (see the official results at <http://www.volby.cz>.) This lack of involvement and interest in the public sphere also explains why the actual results concerning the EU (referendum in 2003 where 75 per cent of the public voted yes, potential referendum on the EU Constitution in 2005) show much more positive results than the current state of public opinion.

the EU were planning en masse not to vote, while the rest of the public was split. Only 45 per cent of the population planned to take part if a referendum had been organized on the issue of the EU Constitution, while 29 per cent said they would not vote and 16 per cent didn't know yet. Among those who would have voted, as of June 2005, 41 per cent would have said yes, 34 per cent would have said no, and 25 per cent were undecided.[27] But at the same time, President Klaus was the most trusted politician of the Czech Republic, with a 67 per cent score.[28]

The Czech Republic was the last country in the EU to start ratifying the Lisbon Treaty. President Klaus continued to claim that he would not sign it for months – even though his country was presiding over the EU at the relevant time (first half of the year 2009).[29]

What should the European Union be, then, for President Klaus? It should be an entity based on 'freedom, personal responsibility, individualism, natural caring for others and genuine moral conduct of life'. It is a 'system of relations and relationships of individual countries, which must not be based on false internationalism, on supranational organizations and on misunderstanding of globalization and of externalities, but which will be based on good neighbourliness of free, sovereign countries and on international pacts and agreements' (Belien 2005).

Having emerged from the post-1989 professional political milieu more than from intellectual dissent, and in view of his scathing criticism, President Klaus does not enjoy much support among established intellectuals. A handful of conservative individuals, who have sometimes also been politically engaged, do share some of his views, but primarily as an attempt to defend national pride. For instance, the aggressive anti-European discourse of yet another Václav, Václav Benda – formerly contributor to the review *Střední Evropa* (Central Europe) and author of the dissident concept of *Parallel Polis*[30] – was until his death in 1999 rooted in his resentment that the West had not fought for enlargement before 1989.[31] Václav Bělohradský, a philosopher who emigrated to Italy under communism, also criticizes the EU, and especially its regionalization programme, as a danger for democracy. Democracy can only be national. Bělohradský could believe in a European nationalism only if it were based on

---

[27] Horáková 2005a (CVVM). CVVM is one of the best Czech polling institutes, attached to the Social Institute of the Academy of Sciences (see <http://www.cvvm.cas.cz>).

[28] Horáková 2005b.

[29] See Kopecký 2009; see also Hanák 2008 and Uhl 2008.

[30] 'In a repressed state, Benda argues that it is impossible to overturn corrupt social, economic and political institutions. Such efforts are futile. Instead, he suggests the creation of new "parallel institutions" that are more responsible to human needs. In time, he further argues, these more credible institutions may supplant the old corrupt ones': see the Wikipedia page (in English) for the entry 'Parallel Polis'.

[31] See his speech at the ODS Congress, 13–14 December 1997.

ecology, while the idea of a federal Europe seems the most dangerous to him (Bělohradský 2005).

A few left-wing intellectuals, however, also support national centralism in a way comparable to that of Václav Klaus. Karel Kosík, the most important Czech Marxist philosopher, who also was a dissident under the communist regime, criticized EU construction for social reasons before his death in 2003. He believed that a social state was easier to construct on the national level (Kosík 2003). Also bordering on national centralism, although not one of Klaus' group of supporters, the formerly communist intellectual writer and later dissident Ludvík Vaculík regularly expresses his fear of the EU in the Czech media while underlining an alleged 'German domination' on the continent as a danger (Dupré-Latour 2006; Vaculík 2005). It must be underlined again that the main ingredient cementing this (mostly unacknowledged and otherwise improbable) alliance of certain right- and left-wing intellectuals with Klaus' 'camp' is this centralistic relationship to the state and to the nation.

We have now presented the main arguments and frames of reflection on Europe among prominent Czech intellectuals, and underlined the historical reasons behind the extreme politicization of the European question. Since Europe is debated almost exclusively in the political sphere and by politicians – albeit admittedly of intellectual background – it is particularly relevant to study the application of these conceptions of Europe and the policies advocated by these very same political actors. The specificity of post-socialist countries after 1989 is, after all, that intellectuals came to power.

The relativity of discourses on Central Europe and Europe in practice

The accession to presidency in 1989–90 of such emblematic intellectuals as Lech Wałęsa in Poland, Václav Havel in Czechoslovakia, and Árpád Göncz in Hungary promised a revolution in politics. The former dissidents, as we saw previously, had very much supported the Central European idea for as long as they were opposed to the communist regimes.

The post-1989 period, however, was to bring a rather stark and unexpected – although perhaps not so surprising – return to realpolitik. At first, the cooperation between the three countries seemed to function effectively: the Warsaw Pact and the Comecon linking Central Europe to the Soviet Union were, for instance, swiftly and successfully dismantled. But discourses on Central European solidarity were rapidly overshadowed by the competition over EU accession, and the willingness to cooperate faded; Czechoslovakia fell apart, Wałęsa failed to be re-elected in 1995, and both Havel and Göncz remained as little involved in daily politics as they could. These former dissidents were in favour of Central Europe; all in all, however, they have done little more than create the Visegrád group on paper.[32]

On the other hand, so-called 'pragmatic' politicians in the Czech Republic, Slovakia, Poland, and Hungary[33] – also less charitably dubbed 'populists', if not 'opportunists'[34] over the years – spoke of national interest much more than of Central European cooperation. They made no secret in their domestic political discourses of a feeling of superiority over each of the other three countries (Novotný 1996; Szakács 2003). Prime Minister Václav Klaus (1992–7)[35] saw in regional cooperation a constraint on the Euro-Atlantic integration of the Czech Republic.[36] Prime Minister Vladimír Mečiar (1992–8) led Slovakia towards growing isolation and a semi-authoritarian regime (Fish 1999). Hungarian Prime Minister Viktor Orbán (1998–2002) threatened to sabotage Slovakia's accession to NATO and suggested in front of the European Parliament that the Czech Republic and Slovakia could not enter the EU without abrogating the Beneš decrees. The Visegrád summit due to take place in spring 2002 to define a common policy on EU negotiations was postponed, then cancelled altogether. Yet, as officially hostile to each other as they might have been, these prime ministers did not take significant concrete steps to block each other from achieving EU accession. They claimed to oppose Central Europe, but they have at least maintained the Visegrád group on paper.

The same general pattern as with 'Central Europe' can of course be observed in Prague about Europe in general. The EU is often criticized in the public sphere, and official speeches are sometimes severe; yet no one, and especially no leading politician, has attempted to slow down the pace of integration of the Czech Republic, nor even questioned the legitimacy of the Czech Republic's membership of the European Union. Despite Václav Klaus' numerous scornful comments, the Czech Republic has not been known to undermine the Union's daily functioning in any spectacular way – as, for instance, Poland has (to some extent). In addition – even though he was vehemently opposed to it and was the last in Europe to do so – Klaus did, after all, appose his signature to the Lisbon Treaty.

Why this dichotomy between the theory and the practice, between the speeches and the realpolitik of Europe? The Czech political scene resembles the French one (and probably others in Europe) in so far as both the main right- and

---

[32] Which happened on 15 February 1991 in the town of Visegrád (Hungary). The signed document was entitled 'Declaration on the cooperation of The Czech and Slovak Federal Republics, Poland and Hungary on the road to European integration'.

[33] They were joined in Poland a few years later by the Kaczyński brothers, Lech and Jarosław, in the posts of president (2005–10) and prime minister (2005–6) respectively.

[34] See for instance Haraszti 2002. The Slovak regime under Mečiar was even coined 'anti-democratic': see Mesežnikov 2004.

[35] Later president (2003–present).

[36] To the point that he had all references to Visegrád erased from the official documents. See Vincze 2002.

271

left-wing parties are strong partisans of state control, whereas the centre is social liberal in diverse forms, and more pro-European. In Czechia, although political power is usually attached to these right- and left-wing main parties, the centrist intellectual and journalistic spheres are acknowledged and respected, and therefore do exert a significant influence on political platforms. That is why, even when parties or politicians who profess to be 'anti-European' with the aim of seducing a larger part of the electorate do hold the majority in Parliament (for instance during the 'Grand Coalition' between the ODS and the left wing of the ČSSD which has characterized a large part of the 2000s), official Czech policy remains pro-European in practice.

Conclusion: The limits of the Czech debate on Europe

The debate on Europe in the Czech Republic is characterized by two elements. First of all, it is political as much as philosophical. The tension between these two spheres gives all its meaning to the debate between the two Václavs. Europe makes its presence felt almost exclusively in the shape of the European Union, and the intellectual debate on Europe is structured almost exclusively according to its interaction with political life. Second, the debate on Europe is largely theoretical, and does not affect concrete official policy even when one or the other of the opposing camps accedes to power.

The major fracture line in the intellectual field concerning Europe, as symbolized by the debate between the 'two Václavs', relates to the essential dichotomy between structure and discourse, statism and self-management, pragmatism and idealism, or republicans and democrats. For the first, represented by Václav Klaus, it is useless to try to change the world through social action. What counts above all is a centralized nation-state. Nothing should stand in the way between citizen and state, and nothing should stand above the state. In this vision, civil society and Europe participate in the same harmful ideology.

For the second, Václav Havel, the world is not just divided between the domineering and the dominated, the rich and the poor, the powerful and the powerless.[37] On the contrary, there is meaning in people's action. The existence of civil society is a goal in itself. People can be idealistic and engaged, and this engagement is meaningful in its very existence, for instance in the dissident movement. Words have an ethical dimension beyond power questions, and Europe is a philosophical project, not just a free-trade area. Life in the national community includes different complex levels where Europe and civil society must be taken into account, respected, and appreciated.

---

[37] To refer to one of his most famous essays, 'The power of the powerless', where he invites the 'powerless' population to take their own fate into their hands and challenge the communist regime by simply speaking the truth.

All in all, however, the opposition between Havel and Klaus is not merely moral and political, but results from the process of democratic reconstruction after 1989. Václav Klaus cannot derive any measure of intellectual legitimation from a dissident past because he was not officially a dissident. He nevertheless proved – like other leaders in other countries, East and West – that populism and nationalism are resources which are even easier to mobilize than intellectual concepts. The case of Václav Havel on the other hand – though this is again true for all Central European countries – points to the particular path followed by intellectuals and artists from their original post-1989 'position', as we defined it, to democracy. The legitimacy deriving from their former dissident status has been melting away, while professional politicians have been taking over. Even if the latter include populistic elements, the erosion of intellectuals' influence – since it is tantamount to a progressive consolidation of democracy – cannot be seen as negative.

What is most remarkable of all, however, is the European apathy of the Czech public, whose main interest lies much more in its standard of living and in the state of economic transition than in intellectual debates on Europe. In this respect, it can be concluded that the heritage of forty-year-long communist propaganda is still largely felt. Europe as a concept, which had been so present in the media and intellectual life before the war, was effectively chased out of Czech intellectual and public discourse after 1948 and replaced by a Marxist-Leninist analysis revolving around imperialism (Reijnen 2008: 111);[38] it has never really made its comeback since. Instead, the bipolar Cold War perspective endures today under a new form, the fight against globalization or Europeanization, with an all-too-similar mechanism of exclusion.

We mentioned the Visegrád group as the symbol of the defeat of intellectual conceptions of Central Europe by realpolitik, but also of the relativity of conservative criticism of the Central Europe notion. What is most revealing, however, is the perception by the Czech public of what 'Visegrád' meant and what the four members of the Visegrád group could bring to the European Union: where Slovaks stressed their hard work and diligence, Poles accentuated their traditions, moral value, religion, and quality agriculture, and Hungarians took pride in their culture and arts, Czechs stressed only their tourist attractions and their cheap labour force, and considered the opening of the market to products from other EU countries to be the element of greatest importance (Seidlová 2004).

In practice, the Czech population's approbation of Europe on a general and abstract level mingles with a stark criticism of particular aspects of European

---

[38] Cf. the Jdanov doctrine dividing the world into the camps of the 'anti-imperialist, democratic' Soviet Union, and 'imperialist, anti-democratic' United States, which he introduced at the founding conference of the Cominform in Szklarska Poreba (Poland) in September 1947. See Procacci 1994.

policy.[39] The results are contradictory in many ways: the public is not sure where the main political parties stand on the European issue, and the main political parties are equally unsure where the public stands on the European issue.[40] As for intellectuals, their conceptions have been moulded respectively by their engagement in communism, by their dissidence under communism, by the exile experience that many of them went through, by national construction, and by universalism.[41] In those contradictions, they are very European. However, their strong European commitment and identity is no doubt best documented by their eagerness to maintain a positive image among other European nations (Blaive 2008).

---

[39] See for instance the oral history project undertaken by Muriel Blaive and Berthold Molden for the Ludwig Boltzmann Institute for European History and Public Sphere at the Czech–Austrian border (České Velenice/Gmünd): the interviews showed that the European Union was the regular recipient of verbal abuse and of much bitterness, pointing to the deficiencies of its agricultural policy, the bureaucracy allegedly imposed by EU norms and numerous other small aspects of daily life allegedly undermining Czech (or Austrian, for that matter) national sovereignty: for instance, requiring restaurants to have hot water in the toilets, or the packing of doughnuts in cellophane paper. See <http://ehp.lbg.ac.at>.

[40] In opinion polls, notably one undertaken in 2004 which attempted to measure political support in relation to the European question, respondents designated the Social-Democrats and Christian-Democrats as most supportive of the EU, but without clearly themselves supporting an advancement of EU integration. The conservative and centre-right parties were considered to be semi-supportive of the EU. Only the communist party was clearly understood as being against further EU integration. It is remarkable that in the same poll, almost a third of respondents declared themselves to have no sympathy for any political party. The score on 'probable vote' at next election gave confused results, almost impossible to interpret. See Horáková 2004.

[41] This question recalls Katy Hayward's contribution in this volume on Ireland, with a similar lack of vision concerning the place of the nation in Europe.

Part V

Outliers

14

Progressive Nationalism?
Norwegian Intellectuals and Europe*

John Erik Fossum and Cathrine Holst

Introduction

European integration is widely depicted as an intrinsic part of, and perhaps even a vanguard for, a broader pattern of transformation of the nation-state. Great uncertainty surrounds this process. The European Union is an essentially contested project without an agreed-upon final goal or end state. Many analysts and decision-makers alike also highlight its experimental character as a testing ground for ideas, principles, procedures, and institutional arrangements.[1]

From this perspective, 'Europe' represents a potentially new arena for the intellectual: an *opportunity* for truly pan-European public discussions, with intellectuals occupying a prominent position. Arguably, a European experiment even *requires* intellectuals; figures who are able to liberate themselves from institutional and cultural bonds, to speak freely and openly to the challenge of building and re-building Europe in a world where familiar nation-state-based categories and arrangements are increasingly challenged. This includes responding to the many critics – many within their own ranks – who argue that the European integration process is simply the offshoot of a global process of marketization, commodification, and political estrangement. Thus, an important question on which this book sheds light is whether intellectuals across Europe are mainly concerned with 'writing the Union into existence', or with debunking the European project.

However, as the editors make clear in the introductory chapter, the question of Europe is not simply a matter of being for or against the EU. There is a range

---

* We have received valuable comments on earlier drafts of this chapter from Marianne Riddervold, Erik Ryen, the editors, and participants at the workshop in Oxford, 2009.

[1] This is reflected in notions such as 'integration through deliberation' (see Eriksen and Fossum 2000) and 'reflexive integration' (E. Eriksen 2005).

of stories told that speak to widely different conceptions of the EU and of Europe. What are these stories? Or more to the point, as this chapter deals with Norway: what stories are told by Norwegian intellectuals? What conceptions of the EU and Europe mark the Norwegian intellectual landscape?

To some our endeavour is rather absurd. A claim often made by Norwegian – well, intellectuals – is that there are not, and cannot be, any 'real' intellectuals in Norway, due to peculiar 'Norwegian' characteristics. The country is small; we all have to wear several hats (very few specialize in being 'intellectuals', so to speak); there are close relationships between academics, politicians, and government officials; Norway is imbued with a political consensus culture; there is an anti-intellectual tenet in Norwegian egalitarian culture, and so forth.

Our assumption is that it is meaningful to speak of intellectuals of different categories also in Norway. In the following, we will examine how a select number of Norwegian *academic intellectuals* have conceived of Europe, the European integration process, and Norway's relationship to the rest of Europe. More precisely, we discuss their approach in relation to three conceptions of the EU: the EU as a problem-solving entity, as a value community, and as a rights-based union (Eriksen and Fossum 2004).[2] According to the first conception, the EU is an international organization set up by and for the member states. Its main purpose is to solve their problems and to propound their interests. Neither a set of shared European values nor a common sense of identity is required, and the member states set and enforce clear limits on the scope of EU-level political integration. Political identity, but also democracy, remain the preserve of the nation-state.

The second conception sees the EU as a distinct value community. In this view, the EU is based on and propounds a set of values that are designative of European history and tradition. One European value-source is a set of revitalized and modernized Christian values. However, this value system also encompasses the notion of a distinct European tradition of *Bildung* and self-realization, and a particular European 'social' tradition that stresses equality, solidarity, and collectiveness, in opposition to unbridled American individualism. European values, of one kind or another, motivate the drive to entrench a deeper sense of unity, community, and thick European identity wherein people of different nationalities become European compatriots willing to take on new collective obligations and provide for each other's well-being. The European value community is generally understood to be embedded in a soon-to-emerge European federal state.

The third and final conception sees the EU as a regional actor within a larger global order steeped in cosmopolitan principles. The EU is a rights-based entity; EU citizens possess fundamental civil and political rights and embrace a thin,

---

[2] These three conceptions underpinned the Fifth Framework integrated project Citizenship and Democratic Legitimacy (CIDEL). They are derived from Habermas' (1993) three legitimation discourses.

post-national, European identity; the EU is regarded neither as a mere instrument for the member states (i.e. the first conception) nor as a European federal state in the making (i.e. the second conception). The third conception instead posits that the EU is a central component – and driver – in the move from a world organized around sovereign nation-states to a multi-level cosmopolitan global order.

Why these three conceptions? For one, they focus on legitimacy and link identity, community, and polity in such a manner as to capture some of the basic features of discussions over Europe that occur across Europe. Moreover, they allow us to pay particular attention to nation-state thinking or nationalism. A key reason for why Norway has not become a member of the EU lies in a strong popular attachment to nationalism: people's commitment to democracy and community has tended to be closely linked to their belief in and loyalty to the nation-state.[3] The question is to what extent popular nationalism is challenged or affirmed by Norwegian intellectuals.

The first, problem-solving conception of the EU is the most obvious indicator of nationalism, because it posits that democracy and political identity are inherent in the member nation-states. The problem-solving conception does not, however, exhaust the national dimension. The second notion, that of the EU as a value community, is also ultimately embedded in nation-state thinking, in the sense that EU integration is conceived of in terms of a nation-building process at the European level. Arguably, the value-community conception simply replaces member-state nationalism with European-level nationalism. Hence, whether Norwegian intellectuals think fundamentally differently with regard to questions of identity, community, and political legitimacy will become apparent in so far as they understand the EU as a post-national union. It may well be that a greater proportion of Norwegian academic intellectuals support the making of a European value community and federal state than do ordinary Norwegian citizens; if so, our analysis will shed light on this. However, our point here is this: to challenge the prevalent nation-state thinking requires something more, namely a qualitative leap to the third EU conception outlined above. To what extent is such a shift taking place? To what extent do Norwegian intellectuals enter a qualitatively different conceptual and normative terrain when discussing Europe?

Two referenda have been held on whether Norway should formally join the EU (in 1972 and 1994). On both occasions a small majority said 'no'. Our analysis will focus on interventions by the academic intellectuals during the

---

[3] Bjørklund (2005: 189), in his analysis of the popular EU referenda, shows that national independence and national democratic self-rule was the opponents' main argument. Kvalvåg (1999: 176) argues that opponents and proponents shared an unexpressed ethical consensus on the salience of Norwegian national identity and values. Archer (2005: 2) notes that especially the 1972 vote was 'a fight between "them" and "us" over the soul of Norway. It was a continuing struggle between those representing government and those who claimed to voice the nation's feeling, with the battleground being in the realms of civil society.'

1994 referendum debate and afterwards.[4] Such an engagement will be marked by historical factors: intellectuals' role and status in society; their affiliation to and identification with the national project; and their engagement with the lines of conflict in Norwegian society, as for instance entrenched in political cleavage patterns. We start by identifying central elements of sovereignty, community, and identity over the last centuries.

La longue durée

Historical unions

In his analysis of state formation and nation-building across Europe, Stein Rokkan (1975: 573) shows that the three dominant stages of Norwegian state formation and nation-building unfolded under Danish and Swedish auspices. Norway was part of a union with Denmark (1389–1814), and thereafter entered a monarchical union with Sweden (1815–1905). In both cases, Norway was the junior partner. These two unions had clear bearings on the role of intellectuals in Norwegian society. Notably in the union with Denmark, Norwegian intellectuals had to go abroad, mainly to Copenhagen, for their education and training. One issue this raised was that of 'whose intellectuals' they were. Another was that an important impetus in Norway's cultural and democratic development came from Norwegian intellectuals bringing European ideas home with them, notably from Copenhagen. An important forum was the literary *Norske Selskab* (established in 1772 and counting over 250 members). It has generally been understood as having stimulated Norwegian patriotic sentiment from the late 1700s, but recent research has shown that the members were more internationally oriented (Bliksrud 1999). This suggests that intellectuals could have quite complex bonds of allegiance: were they Danes or Norwegians, or both?

The great power politics during and after the Napoleonic wars led to the 1814 Treaty of Kiel, which stipulated that the King of Denmark cede Norway to the King of Sweden. Norwegians, inspired by the examples of the American and French revolutions, imagined that they could seize the occasion to forge independence through writing a Norwegian constitution. A union with Sweden came about under the terms that Norway would share a monarchy with Sweden, and that the union's foreign policy was to be run from Stockholm.

---

[4] This chapter draws on a select group of Norwegian academic intellectuals. We have chosen those we consider most central and visible and have consulted their contributions as they appear in written media (quality newspapers), books, and journals. We undertook systematic library and internet searches. The sources listed here are a select number of the ones we consulted. We have also consulted more specialized contributions from our select group when such contributions could shed light on perspectives and arguments. For this survey we have received excellent research assistance from Mads Skogen.

Nonetheless, Norway got its democratic constitution, and was recognized as a country with full internal sovereignty.

Norway's monarchical union with Sweden is thus best understood as a century-long process of Norwegian national identity formation and institution-building. The union with Sweden was never able to put its stamp on Norway's internal affairs to the same extent as the union with Denmark. The separation from Sweden in 1905 therefore simply marked the end of a long process of entrenching Norwegian constitutional democracy in symbolic and substantive terms within a national frame.

Norway's long history as the junior partner in the two unions has figured centrally in current academic debates, among historians in particular, on whether unions have been 'good' or 'bad' for Norway. Popular opinion is perhaps more set: unions are 'bad'; national independence is 'good' – or at least better than having one's sovereignty constrained by foreign governments. This relates to another well-established view that is predominant both in the public arena and among academics and intellectuals, namely that Norwegian nationalism eventually advanced the democratization process. Norway's separation from Sweden is widely cast as the culmination of a century-long peaceful struggle for national independence; for many, it carries with it the symbolic portent of nationalism serving the *progressive* cause by entrenching constitutional democracy in a national Norwegian community.

The Norwegian political system and cleavage structure

Furthermore, Norway's historical incorporation in unions with its closest neighbours affected the political system, including the cleavage structure and the party system (Rokkan 1970). The National Revolution, much of which unfolded before formal independence in 1905, represented an important territorial–cultural conflict that pitted the first two political parties, Liberals and Conservatives, against each other, with the Liberals representing the independence party and the Conservatives the more union-friendly. The Liberal Party itself represented an attempt to resolve several sets of cleavages brought on by the National Revolution. One such was territorial, and pitted urban progressives against farmers; this was amplified by a socio-cultural division which set progressives in urban areas against peripheral adherents of 'counter-cultures' (based on a different, less 'Danish' version of the Norwegian language – 'Nynorsk' – and on puritan versions of Protestantism, such as 'haugianismen'). Later came the Industrial Revolution, which brought about the political mobilization of the working class through the Labour movement and the Labour (and Communist)[5] party. This mobilization was then channelled into the already existing complex tapestry of

---

[5] Norges Kommunistiske Parti (NKP) was established in 1923.

cleavage lines and party configurations. The latter served to modify the class-based political thrust and the left–right alignment of the political landscape generally associated with the Industrial Revolution.

Moreover, the ensuing complex multi-dimensional pattern of cultural, territorial, and socio-economic conflict was such as to have been *managed* rather than truly resolved over time. Of central importance in this connection is of course the development of a 'social-democratic' welfare state (Esping-Andersen 1990), based on a set of compromises, a capital–labour compromise, a centre–periphery compromise, and so on, and contributing to making Norway into a typical consensus-democracy (Lijphart 1999). This structure again has bearings on the manner in which controversial issues are handled. Consensus-oriented systems, notably those with deep-seated conflicts, have a strong propensity to bracket off conflicts, either through addressing them in closed fora or by seeking out means of issue avoidance. As we will illustrate shortly, Norway's relationship to the EU is a highly illustrative example.

Norway and the issue of EU membership

Norwegian EU membership has been a highly contentious issue that has divided both the population and the Norwegian political establishment. Three governments have fallen on the EU membership issue, in 1971, 1972, and 1990 (Bjørklund 2005: 73). The two referenda rejections produced very narrow 'no' majorities.[6] Divisions over EU membership are evident in all three major channels into the political system: the political party channel, the organizational channel, and the media channel.

According to Henry Valen (1999: 106), one of the reasons for the intensity of conflict is that the EU membership issue has tended to activate the cleavage lines identified by Rokkan. In this perspective, it is interesting to observe that the last referendum was, notes Tor Bjørklund (2005: 183), a 'carbon copy' of its predecessor in terms both of the general outcome and of the results in the various constituencies. Both the 1972 and the 1994 results showed a strong split between centre and periphery: while economic and political elites were in favour of EU membership, peripheral areas and counter-cultures furnished no-voters during both referendum campaigns (Bjørklund 2005).

Nevertheless, the EU membership issue was not simply a case of reactivation of old cleavages. A central issue was also the role and status of the welfare state in an EU context. This issue weighed more heavily in the eventual rejection of membership, and is linked to the clear gender dimension to the membership debate and decision (Bjørklund 2005): men were clearly more favourable to EU

---

[6] In 1972 53.5 per cent voted against membership and 46.5 per cent voted for, and in 1994 52.2 per cent voted against, whereas 47.8 per cent voted in favour.

membership than were women, who often conceived of the EU as a threat to the Scandinavian 'woman-friendly' welfare model (Hernes 1987). Another significant variable was position on the left/right-continuum. The social democrats were deeply divided (with roughly 60 per cent in favour and 40 per cent against) on the EU membership issue in 1994. However, the largest national workers' union said 'no', together with leftist civil society organizations, movements, and pressure groups and a huge majority of socialist and communist party voters.[7] Conservative party voters were overwhelmingly 'pro', as were leading business organizations and lobby groups.

Norway's present relation to the EU: close incorporation without formal membership

Nonetheless, Norway – albeit having turned down a negotiated membership agreement twice (1972 and 1994) – has since 1992, when it entered into the European Economic Area (EEA) Agreement with the EU (and thus starting before the second membership negotiation round), become tightly integrated in the EU.[8] Given that Norway is also an associated member of the Schengen Agreement, is involved in battlegroups, and other arrangements, it is in some respects more integrated in the EU than, for instance, the UK. Clive Archer (2005: 188) has noted that '[s]ince 1994, Norway's relationship with the process of European integration, as led by the EU, has been as close as possible without full membership'. The present ambiguous situation of non-membership matched with tight incorporation is somewhat ironic, given that the main reason for rejecting EU membership was to protect Norwegian sovereignty and democracy (Bjørklund 2005: 189; Oskarson and Ringdal 1998: 153–66).

The Norwegian political system has found the controversial EU membership issue too hot to handle. Janne Haaland Matlary (2007) has noted that '(r)egardless of which coalition government we have, the EU is not on the agenda'. The political system has instituted a set of self-imposed constraints – or 'gag-rules' – against discussing EU membership with implications for the discussion of EU-related questions generally (Fossum 2010). At the same time, a wide range of measures have been taken to ensure a dynamic 'backstage' process

---

[7] Sosialistisk Venstreparti (SV) was established in 1975. The revolutionary Marxist party, Rødt has replaced NKP as the largest communist party.

[8] A brief overview includes the following, which encompasses all three EU pillars: through the EEA Agreement well over 6, 000 legal provisions have been incorporated into Norwegian law since 1994. Further, Norway participates in a broad range of EU programmes (such as research and development, culture, etc.) and a host of EU bureaus (see Sejersted 2008). Norway is a member of the Schengen Agreement; is attached to the Dublin network; has a cooperation agreement with Europol and Eurojust; and has negotiated a parallel agreement to the European Arrest Warrant (see Finstad 2008 for overview). Within security and defence Norway takes part in the EU's civilian and military crisis management, including the EU battlegroups (for an overview see Sjursen 2008).

of Norwegian inclusion in most of the issue-areas that the EU deals with. Obviously, this makes the role of the intellectual harder, but also more crucial: potentially, *intellectuals* can be the ones who 'un-gag' discussions and bring them 'front stage'.

What are Norwegian academic intellectuals' contributions in this perspective? When do they intervene? And how do they do it? What are the characteristics of Norwegian intellectuals' debates on the question of Europe? This is the topic of the following pages.

Europe and Norwegian intellectuals: Central assumptions and positions

Methodological nationalism

A first striking feature of many Norwegian intellectuals' approach to the EU is what we might refer to as 'methodological nationalism', to use Ulrich Beck's (2003) by now influential term. An underlying normative assumption of the right of every nation to self-determination contributes to shaping and 'nationalizing' the intellectual discourse on Europe and the EU, even when what is said is seemingly purely descriptive. History, culture, and society are typically described and analysed within a national horizon. The focus is on Norway, as a nation and a nation-state, and Norway as a nation/nation-state alongside and/or compared to other nations/nation-states. Europe and 'European' units, such as the European Union, are downplayed. Europe is still framed as a collection of nation-states. Patterns of cooperation and conflict that are highlighted are those between nation-states. What counts are consequences, good and bad, for nation-states, and what is understood as democracy and justice is what transpires within the limits of the nation-states.

There are also explicit justifications for the focus on nation-states. As we will return to, nationalism is not simply 'methodological'. However, these explications are embedded in a general stance of taking the prevalence of the national frame for granted, an assumption that moreover cuts across positions of 'yes' or 'no' to EU membership to a certain extent – and across different academic disciplines.

Norwegian historians could serve as an example (Stråth et al. 2008). Historically, Norwegian historians have been highly nationally focused in their research orientation. However, even today the national dimension continues to figure strongly. To be sure, historians have played a particularly significant role in the shaping of the Norwegian national imaginary. However, the national orientation seems to be a characteristic feature of several disciplines[9] – and,

---

[9] For a recent analysis of the methodological nationalism of Norwegian law, see C. Eriksen 2009).

unsurprisingly, this is also brought to the fore when academics leave academia for a while, and enter the public sphere as intellectuals.

We see it, for instance, in the debate on how influential 'Norway' would be as an EU member. Most argue that Norway's influence would be minimal. As noted by the historian Kåre Lunden (1994: 48), even if more decisions were moved from the Council to the European Parliament, a democratic problem would remain: Norway would still only have a representation in the Parliament corresponding to the – in a European context, small – size of the Norwegian people. In the end, 'we' would not get a chance to make much difference.

There are, on the other hand, more optimistic voices arguing that Norway would have influence in the EU through the European Parliament and the Council by means of lobbying and so on, and that other 'Norwegian-friendly' voices must be added if we are to get a proper picture of Norway's potential influence in the EU. Typically, these voices are those of the other Nordic countries. Accordingly, people thinking along these lines often consider the fact that Finland, Sweden, and Denmark are now members, whilst Norway is not, a 'lost opportunity'. Political scientist and anthropologist Iver B. Neumann complained in 1993 that inter-Nordic cooperation in the future would be reduced to cooperation on trivial and low-salience issues if Norway did not join forces with the other Nordic countries *in* the Union to promote the common interests of the Nordic countries, for example with regard to defence and security issues. (Norway does participate in such cooperation now.)

In other words, a widely held assumption – across disagreements on the membership issue[10] – is that what ultimately counts is 'Norway's' vote – and not for example the vote of the working class, of liberals, of social democrats, of women, of primary industries, of individual citizens, or of other politically relevant units that one might think of. The decisive factor is taken for granted as the influence and scope of action of the Norwegian nation-state.

This is not to deny the numerous analyses and criticisms of methodological nationalism in several relevant academic disciplines (sociology, social anthropology, political science, etc.);[11] our remarks fall into this pattern. However, what is also notable is that in the Norwegian context, these critical discussions have only to a very limited extent been translated into alternative approaches to Europe and the EU. This is in part because the criticism of methodological nationalism is in the end something to which one pays lip-service: an abstract criticism of national parameters that can, seemingly, very well be combined with continuing more concrete discussions safely within the framework of the national. There are, moreover, other concepts and units to invest in that are on the one hand beyond the national template, and on the other not as

---

[10] Lunden has for many years been a profiled defender of a 'no' position in the membership debate, whereas Neumann is pro EU-membership.
[11] Neumann explores a different 'conceptual' terrain in other writings.

conflict-laden as that of Europe and the EU. It is 'easier' and less controversial to talk about 'the Nordic model' and 'the Scandinavian system', about the UN and 'a new world order', or about transnational networks, 'the diaspora', 'the multitude', and 'new social movements'. Typically, the national paradigm is challenged without addressing the question of European integration.

Normative nationalism: National democracy

However, as already suggested, nationalism is not only taken for granted and 'methodological'; it is also, very often, normative and explicit. The European nation-state as we know it is presented and defended, by many, as the most viable carrier of political democracy. This is on the one hand steeped in an empirical assessment of the likely trajectory of EU developments, and on the other in a normative assessment of EU democracy. The contributions by political scientist Øyvind Østerud exemplify this trend.[12] Østerud (1990: 60–1) depicts the EU as a non-state entity, as something 'more' than a confederation but 'less' than a federation. Exactly because the EU is not only an international, problem-solving unit (i.e. the first conception above), but an organization with independent polity traits and democratic ambitions, the question of democracy becomes central. Federalization cannot, however, as Østerud sees it, result in a convincing solution to what he refers to as 'the democratic dilemma' of European integration. Whereas integration enhances steering capacity or the ability to influence the external conditions on which everybody is dependent, the transfer of power to supranational entities weakens local proximity to and control over decision-making centres. The upshot is that 'the political entity's *size* is a democratic dilemma' (Østerud 1993: 257 – authors' translation), where it is impossible to have both decision-making influence and sovereignty.

Furthermore, the EU in its current neoliberal trappings places severe constraints on the scope for action for the EU itself and for national governments. In other words, the EU is a risky experiment; there are no clear guarantees for EU democracy; and at the same time, national democracy is put under great pressure. Moreover, EU enthusiasts take as their point of departure a 'hyper'-thesis of globalization as something dramatic and irreversible. The nation-state is undermined and other actors take over. Østerud refers in this connection to Jürgen Habermas. However, the 'hyper'-thesis is far from empirically confirmed (Østerud 1999: 293–5) – and nationalism is far from outdated: 'it is quite possible, perhaps highly likely, that European integration in a federal direction will encounter crises that produce nationalist counter-reactions' (Østerud 1990: 69 – authors' translation).

---

[12] Østerud was chair of the government appointed and funded Norwegian Study on Power and Democracy (1998–2003). The mandate was to consider the terms of Norwegian parliamentary democracy and possible alterations to these terms.

Thus far we have seen Østerud's analysis. However, the examples are many and varied. Norwegian intellectuals state their concerns about the future of national democracy clearly, frequently, and in different (disciplinary and other) vocabularies. A majority understands the EU as a part of the problem. Several economists have for example expressed deep concerns about the loss of national sovereignty, in particular with regard to decision-making on economic policy. This is considered as intimately linked to how the EU – but also the EEA – restricts and weakens political democracy. In the 1994 pre-referendum debate, economists such as Steinar Strøm (1994) and Tore Thonstad (1993) criticized the Maastricht Treaty, the congruence criteria, the European Monetary Union, and so on, for limiting national governments' scope of action in fiscal and monetary policy-making.

There are also examples from law. One of the leading Norwegian public law professors in the last decades, the late Torstein Eckhoff, argued persistently along the lines of Østerud, Strøm, and Thonstad. Eckhoff was very active and influential in the years preceding the 1994 referendum, and challenged pro-membership ministers who claimed that EU membership (and the EEA) would have no negative effects on national democracy and sovereignty. Several lawyers have followed up on his approach since then.

Recent analyses have highlighted the problems associated with the EEA Agreement. EEA law expert Ole Gjems-Onstad (2000: 7) notes that 'in slogan form one might denote the EEA a form of voluntary colonization or vassalage' (authors' translation). Fredrik Sejersted (2008), director of the European Law research centre at the University of Oslo, concurs with this assessment, but also criticizes governments for passivity. Governments can do more to defend and cultivate national democracy, even within the bounds set by the EEA. The EU *is* a democratic problem in terms of national democracy, but the problem must not be overstated.

What's in it for us?

Yet another striking characteristic of Norwegian intellectuals' approach to the EU is instrumentalism: the EU is conceived of as an instrument to serve the member states. The question is then 'what can Europe/the EU do for us?', meaning 'us' in Norway. Policy outcomes in various issue-areas become decisive. The economists may once more serve as an example. Typically, they emphasize macroeconomic implications, the consequences of EU membership, of the EEA, of the EU enlargements, of the monetary union, and so on, on growth, employment, innovation, distribution, the future of the welfare state, and the future of primary industries.

Given the focus on outcomes and consequences, the ultimate question then becomes that of whether these are 'good' or 'bad'. The EU: what's in it for us? There are, basically, three answers to this question. First, it is sometimes claimed that the EU does not make much of a difference. This has been the basic message from University of Oslo economist Karl Ove Moene. EU membership or not, EEA or not, the Scandinavian welfare and labour relation model remains (Barth, Moene, and Wallerstein 2003). The experienced welfare-state researcher and political scientist Stein Kuhnle's (1990) basic message before the 1994 referendum was very similar: the Scandinavian welfare model could be maintained if Norway joined the EU, or – more to the point – whatever threatens this model threatens it whether Norway joins or not. Second, some – mostly right-wing – economists argue that outcomes are good. However, the third and perhaps most common answer is that outcomes are bad. In the debate before the 1994 referendum, economists such as Thonstad and Strøm warned against the 'anti-social' implications of Norway joining the EU. They feared unemployment, social dumping, and productivity losses as effects of integrating Norwegian economic policies with the Union's.

Neoliberal Europe

We have, then, already indicated our next point: the EU is very often linked to notions such as 'neoliberalism' and 'free market capitalism'. Many link Europeanization to 'neoliberalization', and the EU is considered as a vehicle for a neoliberal ideology.

Most Norwegian academic intellectuals regard what they see as the EU's neoliberal framework as deeply problematic; there is, to be sure, a certain social-democratic hegemony in the contributions we have analysed. The sociologist Ottar Brox is a prominent example. Brox has long played a crucial intellectual role on the Norwegian left. Starting with his *Hva skjer i Nord-Norge?* (What is happening in the North of Norway?) in 1966, he has been a significant figure in the public debate on a range of political issues. His political position has been described – including by himself – as populist: the title of his book from 1972 is *Politikk: Bidrag til populistisk argumentasjon* (Politics: Contribution to populist argumentation). His vision is a society of lively, self-governing local communities within the framework of an independent, democratic nation-state. Brox's vision has, of course, been 'modernized' and adapted to new issues over the decades. His latest book is about the climate crisis – or rather, characteristically, about how we can meet this crisis in our daily life, both on the local and national level (Brox 2009). However, an important condition – for this, as for left-wing political success generally – is to avoid EU membership.

The EU and what is wrong with it has been a recurrent preoccupation for Brox. One of his strategies has been to identify and criticize policy outputs: negative effects on Norway from the EEA and the EU's influence pertaining to primary industries, the welfare state, unemployment, the environment, and so on. However, the 'badness' has a particular ideological source: Brox regards the

Union as a vehicle for neoliberalism. The argument is often put in the following manner: neoliberalism prescribes free markets; this and that follows when markets are not regulated; this and that is 'bad'; therefore, the EU is 'bad' since its ideological foundation is neoliberal. This overall argument is then supplemented with detailed knowledge about particular unfortunate policy outputs, typically cases where the EU arguably demonstrates its neoliberal side.

There are also less critical voices, however: commentators and right-wing economists who point out how neoliberalism may deliver positive outcomes and represent a kind of 'market democracy'. Neoliberalization is equated with democratization because it enhances consumer choice and economic freedom – or so it is argued. Thus, if more 'Europe' means more free-market capitalism, this is good for business and profits – and for all the things business and profits are to finance (for example fundamental welfare) – but also for democracy. The important thing here is not what the EU may mean for political democracy, but the EU as an expanding market that increases economic choices and possibilities, and so enhances the fulfilment of individual preference.

To reiterate: the EU's neoliberal tenet is most often presented as an 'evil'. This puts pro-membership critics of neoliberalism in a difficult position: why be 'pro' something (EU) that you are in reality against (neoliberalism) which is, in the end, what the EU has to offer?

The promise – or threat – of Europe

So far we have stressed how the Norwegian intellectual debate has a strong anchoring in traditional nation-state thinking. Most consider the EU as an international organization 'giving' to or 'taking' from 'us in Norway', or as something 'more' causing serious and seemingly unsolvable democratic problems.

However, the picture is more mixed. There are also notions of the EU as a more self-sufficient political unit in the sense of a rudimentary federal state (i.e. the second conception above). The most explicit articulations of the EU as an independent polity – in the sense of a fledgling state – are to be found among the strongest opponents to Norwegian EU membership. Johan Galtung's well-known book from 1973 has the telling title *The European Community: A Superpower in the Making*. Here, Galtung argues that the EU is well on the way to becoming a superpower, and that through this it will reintroduce European colonialism on the world stage. This is symptomatic: the EU's emerging state-based character is a theme that is frequently reiterated among membership opponents (Moen et al. 2004: 202ff.). Moreover, the European Union is often associated with Norway's historical unions with Denmark and Sweden (Køber 2001; Neumann 2002; Rian, Rudd, and Tangen 2005). European construction is thus presented as a direct threat to sovereign statehood. The implication is that as an emerging superstate or a federal state it will subject Europe's independent states to the same homogenizing thrusts as those found in the US, with the effect that Norway will be transformed from an independent state into a subservient entity akin to a German Land or a US state.

Europe as value community

There are also – in accordance with the second conception – thoughts about Europe as a particular value community. Speaking explicitly to the EU, Janne Haaland Matlary (2003b) – a political scientist, well-known public figure, and pro-EU-membership Conservative – notes that the EU was forged by Christian Democrats and that its foundation is Christian democratic values. 'Europe is the cradle of Christian democracy, and Europe, for better or worse, is in many different ways built on a Christian value foundation' (authors' translation). Matlary (2003a: 9) describes a Christian value foundation that is universal in its orientation; it is not particularly closely linked to the nation-state and does not imbue the nation-state with any special value. The EU is a peace project: it promotes peace and solidarity through integration – including notably through the latest rounds of enlargement. Matlary criticizes Norwegians and Norwegian policy for failing to appreciate this. She also notes how Norwegian activism in relation to the UN stands in marked contrast to Norwegian passivity in relation to the EU. She finds this 'jumping over Europe' unfortunate, and links it to how Norwegian authorities conceive of an appropriate Norwegian foreign policy: rule-oriented multilateralism associated with UN action has taken pride of place over the pursuit of power and realpolitik that a direct presence in the EU would offer. An important concern for Matlary is thus to point out that Norwegian authorities do not serve Norwegian *interests* well enough. Thus, there is some ambivalence in Matlary's approach, when considered in relation to the three conceptions of the EU presented above. Europe must be recognized as a value community and a political actor, but national interests are far from obsolete.

The idea of Europe as a value community is also articulated on the opposite side of the political spectrum. Among Norwegian left-wing intellectuals there is indeed an idea of Europe as 'culture', or more specifically of Europe as *high* culture, as *Bildung*, as excellence in art and philosophy, and so on. This idea is intimately linked to the notion that the 'real' Europe is something different from and also more than the (neoliberal) EU. It also has clear links with anti-Americanism (the US represents commercialization, mass culture, etc.). However, it does not necessarily manifest itself in a clearly articulated *political* vision of Europe. These elements actually go hand in hand: an idealization of intellectual/high-culture Europe on the one hand, and of the nation-state – and *not Europe* – as a political unit, on the other. A prominent example is the historian and politico-legal theorist Rune Slagstad, a former member of the leadership of the Socialist Party. Slagstad has had a defining intellectual role on the Norwegian left.

Tellingly, the title of one of his most read articles is 'Sosialisme på norsk' (Socialism in Norwegian) from 1980. The deepening of political democracy is intimately linked to the deepening of national democratic institutions and publics, and to the more or less fortunate choices of the shifting 'national strategists', to quote the title of Slagstad's 500-page magnum opus on modern Norwegian history (*De nasjonale strateger*) from 1998. The idea of 'Europe' as a set of rich cultural/intellectual traditions is contrasted with American shallowness. Thus, 'Europe' denotes high culture, *Bildung*, and a long history of excellence in art, philosophy, and intellectual life. 'Europe' is, however, not really conceived of as a potent political space. There is some mention of the prospects of 'Eurocommunism' in Slagstad's writings before 1989. Even then, however, it is the promise of Europe's nation-states that is at the centre, and not the EU.[13]

Cosmopolitanism and the EU

Finally, there *are* also academic intellectuals with positive political visions for Europe that reach beyond the idea of the EU as an international organization or as a value community and/or a state-type entity. That is, there are adherents of some version of a post-national Europe (conception three) in Norwegian intellectual discourse. There are two strands to this argument, both with a clear cosmopolitan slant. On the one hand there are those who argue that the EU is distinct in that it holds clear traits of 'integration through deliberation' (Eriksen and Fossum 2000); as such, it is a distinctly *modern* creation wherein power must be justified with reference to modern liberal conceptions of justice. In the Norwegian public space it is in particular political scientist Erik Oddvar Eriksen, drawing mainly on Habermas' approach, who has sought to outline the contours of such an entity. A similar view is defended by Helge Høibraaten, a philosopher and intellectual who has for the last several decades played a central role in bringing German philosophy and current intellectual-political debates in Germany to Norway (for his recent deliberations on the EU, see Høibraaten and Hille forthcoming). There is also an emerging 'cosmopolitical' approach to the EU among lawyers (C. Eriksen 2009; Kinander 2005).

The other strand takes a more post-modern tack, and is notably reflected in the writings of Iver B. Neumann and the social anthropologist Thomas Hylland Eriksen. Iver B. Neumann has written extensively on questions of European identity. He notes on the one hand how the EU functions as 'the other' in the construction of Norwegian identity. On the other hand he is concerned with the prospects for a more inclusive EU than those we see today. Thomas Hylland Eriksen pins his hopes on a regional-cosmopolitan Europe. In a recent book the

---

[13] In a recent article Slagstad (2009) includes some self-critical remarks with respect to the national embedding of his earlier thinking on democracy.

EU is held up as a potentially new type of polity, a polity that departs from the state because it does not distinguish categorically between those inside and those outside, and as such is based on fluid borders (Eriksen and Tretvoll 2006). The hallmark of this 'cosmopolitics' model is respect for difference and diversity. With regard to the more specific institutional character of the EU, the model is somewhat vague. The important concern is to stake out a normative and conceptual direction; to pave the way for talking about the EU in a vocabulary that is different from the familiar nation-state-based one.

Finally, there are also Eurosceptic left-wing intellectuals who espouse a global cosmopolitan position, but who basically 'jump over the EU'. Instead, they highlight the need for Norway to stay out of the rich man's club, the European Union, in order to aid the developing countries. This argument has presumably lost some of its sting after the two latest bouts of EU enlargement.

Conclusion

The Norwegian intellectual debate on the EU, we have found, is largely a self-referential debate embedded in nation-state thinking and opposition to EU membership. The latter is interesting given that Norwegian elites have been more positive about Norwegian EU membership than the population in general. Our findings suggest that academic intellectuals tend to mirror popular attitudes on this point.

Many of the academic intellectuals we have examined highlight the historically progressive role of nationalism in entrenching Norwegian democracy; they therefore consider the democratic nation-state as the appropriate normative foundation. What is also important to note is that this view cuts to a large extent across the yes/no divide on the membership question.

When faced with the challenge of European integration, the natural response has been to underline the need to protect nationally based democracy; thus, the favoured conception of the EU is the first, which depicts it as a democratically derivative entity (from the member states) and as a mere instrument for problem-solving. This position accords only a limited licence to political integration; it offers more scope for economic integration, but this also has to be justified with reference to the beneficial *results* – *to us*, the democratically justified national community with exclusive authority to assess whether the benefits of cooperation exceed the costs. Even the pattern of economic integration, however, has been found to be problematic, notably by those who see the EU as an emerging neoliberal juggernaut.

We have found that there are alternative voices, but that they have not effectively challenged the dominant national position. Even those who are highly critical of the national framing expend more of their energies on criticizing this than on attempting to hammer out a viable alternative vision. The debate is not therefore over three self-standing and equally well-expanded conceptions of the EU; rather, it is a highly lopsided debate in which efforts to sketch alternatives continue to be considered and evaluated from the national perspective. The result is that far more emphasis is placed on the alleged negative effects of the European project and European governance on politics, autonomy, agency, sovereignty, republican ideals, and so on. The same can be said of how Norwegian academic intellectuals – or at least several among them – consider the relationship between Europe-as-values and Europe-as-prosperity. There is a well-entrenched notion that Europe is a 'rich man's club', a conviction that has remained largely unscathed through the last two rounds of EU enlargement. These enlargements have nevertheless precipitated a subtle shift from the notion of the EU as a 'rich man's club' towards the notion of the EU as a businessman's club, as a fountain for an all-permeating neoliberal economics. Many of Norway's political progressives also underline that Norway should fulfil its historical mission as one of the West's few 'true' friends of the Third World. This is part of a programme to promote international democracy, but here, generally speaking, the EU does not figure; the tendency is to 'jump over' Europe.

We noted in the introduction that today's Europe represents a unique opportunity for a truly pan-European public discussion, with intellectuals necessarily occupying a prominent position. Generally speaking, only a few intellectuals in Norway have found the EU interesting in this regard. Our overarching conclusion is that the Norwegian academic intellectual milieu has done little in terms of challenging the 'gag-rules' and taking on board and exploring this unique opportunity.

15

Convergence and Resistance

The European Dilemma of Turkish Intellectuals

Nora Fisher Onar and Ahmet Evin

A widespread perception, both within and outside Turkey, is that there is something unique about its relationship with and place in 'Europe'. What other country, after all, is at one and the same time the quintessential 'Other' of the European collective imagination, a core member of the European strategic alliance, and a controversial candidate for inclusion in the European Union? Tellingly, arguments both for and against Turkish membership of the EU cite its geography, size, demographics, and economy, as well as history, culture, and religion, as compelling reasons for its place – or lack thereof – in Europe. Yet if there is one thing common to visions of Europe in countries on the continent's limes, it is a sense of exceptionalism about the dilemmas faced in engaging with Europe. As the chapters in this volume reveal, pundits in many successor states of the Austro-Hungarian and Ottoman Empires have produced narratives in which 'Europe' is construed as both beacon and threat. Góra and Mach (Chapter 11), for example, juxtapose Polish calls for a 'return to Europe' as panacea for economic and political woes, and nativist fears for the integrity of Polish culture. Barbu too (Chapter 12), points to the Romanian intellectual tradition of critiquing 'Europe' as a site of modern, rational, bureaucratic, capitalist disenchantment which is contrasted with an 'East' said to serve as a bastion of 'authentic' European religiosity and culture. For Pagoulatos and Yataganas (Chapter 9), a similar dichotomy is evident in discourses on the fringes of contemporary Greek intellectual and political life. To what extent, then, is the ambivalence that animates Turkish intellectuals' European dilemma unique, and what does the answer tell us about the nature and prospects of the relationship?

We address this question by suggesting that certain features of Turkish discourses on Europe are fairly constant both over time and across the political spectrum at any given time. Other elements, however, appear contingent upon the proclivities of particular intellectuals and the intellectual traditions to which they adhere, as well as evolving domestic and international context. The interplay between the more constant and more contingent features means that intellectuals' views on 'Europe' span a spectrum. They range from those who advocate *selective* engagement, to those who take a *syncretic* approach, to those who call for *unequivocal* convergence with that which they understand 'Europe' to represent. Employing this spectrum as a heuristic device, this chapter traces continuity and change in several schools of thought on 'Europe' from the inception of Ottoman Westernization to the present. It does so by schematically showcasing the views of specific intellectuals as representative of different traditions of thought. It then turns to key moments in the 1999–2009 period during which public debates on 'Europe' were particularly intense in light of Turkey's acquisition of candidate status to the EU in 1999.

Before proceeding, it is worth clarifying that we use the term 'intellectual' loosely to refer to individuals such as journalists, political activists, novelists, poets, and spiritual leaders who shape public debates. Since the nineteenth century, such figures have confronted Turkey's European dilemma, or 'Western question' (Berkes 1975) – through editorials and serialized publications in newspapers, journals, books, and, more recently, televised debates. The considerable deference accorded such personalities is evident in the large contingents of columnists employed by even minor newspapers. In the Turkish context, especially seen from a historical point of view, bureaucrats and politicians have also fulfilled the function of public intellectuals in the sense of defining the parameters of debate on Turkey's place in 'Europe'. The emphasis in this chapter is therefore on perceptions of 'Europe' as they relate to intellectuals' *political* views.

Bearing this in mind, it is also important to note that political labels like 'liberal' and 'left', and 'Kemalist' and 'Islamist' are quite ambivalent in the Turkish context. Figures who are often described – and describe themselves – as affiliated with these camps espouse ideas which might display a modicum of, say, liberal thought in terms of a commitment to certain tenets of liberal democracy, but which are also infused with layers of meaning idiosyncratic to their experience and the Turkish context more broadly (such as prior affiliation with the radical left). Likewise, except for members of the bona fide but short-lived communist movement of the 1910s and early 1920s which was crushed following independence, Turkish 'leftists' share a commitment to redistributive policies. But their views tend to be informed above all by anti-imperialism and may be fused with a range of preferences from *étatisme* to Alevi collective identity and even Kurdish nationalism. 'Kemalism' meanwhile is a label early republican followers of Mustafa Kemal Atatürk may not have used, but it is regularly ascribed to such figures as well as those today who are passionately committed to the tenets of Atatürkist thought. Finally, 'Islamist', and even the notion of 'moderate Islamist', carries connotations of radicalism in English which obscure the particularities of religious-informed political thought in

Turkey, especially today. We nevertheless employ these labels as a chapter of this length cannot aspire to propose a new and unfamiliar pantheon of signifiers. We ask only that the reader recognize that such terms may not correspond precisely to the meanings they bear in continental Europe or Britain.

Constant and contingent features of narratives of 'Europe'

We argue that there are a number of constant as well as contingent features to Turkish intellectuals' discourses on 'Europe'. Constant features of any narrative, as Freeden might argue, are not stable but rather 'ineliminable' themes the precise meaning of which at any point in time depends upon their association with other, contingent elements.[1] The source of constants in Turkish narratives of Europe may be the structural condition of relative weakness that has prevailed since at least the nineteenth century. At that time, the Ottomans were compelled to renounce their own universalistic pretentions to launch a project of defensive modernization based on the selective adoption of technologies and ideas emanating from Western Europe. From the mid-1800s onwards, a consensus emerged amongst the Ottoman reformist intelligentsia and leadership that the material aspects of 'European' civilization, including the modern state and instruments of government, reflected and contributed to progress. Commitment to a 'European' programme for change was heightened, ironically enough, by the experience of defeat and near-dismemberment at Allied hands after the First World War. At that juncture, the traumatized founding fathers upped the ante, rebuilding Turkey as a sovereign nation-state in accordance with models prevalent in contemporary Europe. The intense, if paradoxically defensive, project of Westernization was amplified by the secularist cultural revolution, undertaken much to the chagrin of Islamist quarters. Yet many amongst religious cadres, like their counterparts in the secularist camp, continue to this day to endorse the task of achieving 'contemporary', i.e. European, civilization, at least in material terms.

Coming of age in a world circumscribed by European hegemony and its legacy means that for the Turkish intellectual there is something ubiquitous about the signifier 'Europe' regardless of the substance attributed to the concept. For, at each step along the way, it was public intellectuals who interpreted and transmitted the 'European' experience as they understood it to the political classes and public. Even advocates of alternative paths to modernity were compelled to do so through juxtaposition with what they took to be the 'European' way. This is reflected in the very word that renders the concept of 'intellectual' in Turkish: *aydın*. Literally meaning 'one who is enlightened', it

---

[1] Michael Freeden (1996) uses the terms 'core' and 'ineliminable' in his seminal work on the concept of ideology.

could be read as privileging the rationalist and positive knowledge of the Enlightenment thinker. Indeed, a recurrent and self-disparaging feature of many intellectuals' discourse is lamentation that the country has not produced intellectuals of the calibre of a Descartes or Newton. Even those who reject this view, such as Islamists or ultranationalists, assert that debates in Turkey are feeble precisely because Westernist intellectuals display this self-Orientalizing tendency.

The historically subordinate subject position gives rise to at least three constant or ineliminable features of discourses on 'Europe'. One such feature is the enduring resonance of certain traumatic episodes in the Turkish collective imagination. These include the so-called 'Capitulations'[2] and 'Sèvres'[3] syndromes, which emanate from the experience of semi-colonization by the Great Powers during the late Ottoman period. The visceral power of such memories – and their mobilizing potential – are reinforced by cognizance of the negative perception of Muslim peoples in certain European quarters, both historically and in the post-9/11 context.[4] These neuralgic buttons are pressed – sometimes reflexively, sometimes instrumentally – by public intellectuals across the political spectrum, especially at times when relations with European actors are volatile.

A second effect of power asymmetry is a tendency to view 'Europe' not as a complex heterogeneous enterprise, but as a given, a foil to intellectuals' own struggle to understand the challenges associated with processes of modernization in Turkey. Part and parcel of this is a tendency to treat 'Europe' as a monolithic actor. Thus, with the exception of a small community of academic and policy experts on European affairs, intellectuals habitually refer to entities such as the EU, its constituent organs, member states, the Council of Europe (CoE), its European Court of Human Rights (ECtHR), and similar bodies as one amorphous 'European' entity. At other times, the notion of 'Europe' is elided with 'the West', as was the case throughout the Cold War.[5] This is almost a reflex: when pressed, most intellectuals are aware of European diversity yet the habit of referring to 'Europe' in monolithic terms is pervasive nonetheless. It means, furthermore, that interest in developments in 'Europe' per se comes second to concern for how such developments impact upon relations with

---

[2] Capitulations were economic concessions granted to citizens of European states and their non-Muslim Ottoman protégés.

[3] The Treaty of Sèvres (1920), if implemented, would have carved the Empire up into British, French, Italian, and Greek holdings, as well as establishing an independent Armenia and Kurdistan.

[4] A powerful expression of such sentiments may be found in *The Moral Bankruptcy of Western Policy towards the East*, a treatise published by Ahmet Riza, founder of the Young Turks, shortly before his death. Anticipating many of the arguments of Edward Said, Riza (1979) calls European actors to task for employing double standards towards Muslim peoples.

[5] Discussion of perceptions of 'Europe' during the Cold War in this chapter will accordingly use the terms 'Europe' and 'the West' fairly interchangeably.

Turkey. An important if somewhat tautological corollary of this is that Turkish estimations of 'Europe' tend to fluctuate in tandem with Turkish assessments of the justice or injustice of 'European' treatment of Turks (Fisher Onar 2009a). This can fuel a selective reading of European debates on Turkey, which either exaggerates the centrality of Turkey to a particular question, or hones in on negative representations of the country by European actors whilst ignoring neutral or positive views.

The vision of 'Europe' as a static set of givens has a further important consequence: a tendency to treat 'Europe' as a menu. This gives rise to a habit of selectivity, a belief that some items on the menu may be ingested whilst others are best avoided. The tendency is evident in the considerable consensus since at least the late Ottoman era on the desirability of adopting the material aspects of 'European' civilization from which European actors' strength was thought to emanate (e.g. military technologies, scientific innovations, the industrial mode of production, a bureaucratized, centralized state).[6] It is likewise apparent in the lack of commensurate consensus on adoption of 'European' norms and values.[7] Thus, since the late Ottoman period, we encounter figures who limit their engagement to *selective* importation of hardware and know-how, like the early modernizing sultans. Others went further, seeking synthesis by embedding 'European' conceptions of liberal, democratic governance into an Ottoman-Islamic idiom. The Islamist-rooted Justice and Development Party (*Adalet ve Kalkınma Partisi* – AKP) has recently displayed a similar *syncretic* impulse by defending the Muslim veil as both right and religious obligation (Fisher Onar 2009b). Still others have advocated *unequivocal* adoption of (their reading of) 'European' norms and values. The case par excellence is surely republican rejection of the dynastic and religious sources of Ottoman authority and importation of civil, penal, and family law from extant European codes.

Yet norms and values are internalized in specific contexts, and in time these change – for 'Europe', of course, is not uniform or static. Altered circumstances can lead to a renewed drive for convergence, or to expressions of resistance. For example, Kemalist Westernism – like that of the Young Turks – entailed a powerful will to adopt both the material and normative/institutional features of 'European' civilization in the 1920s and 1930s, from the nation-state form of socio-political organization to secularism (or, more precisely, *laïcité*). Today, however, attraction to the EU is diminished by the requirement of relinquishing sovereignty in certain key areas. It is also muted by concern that EU-accession-oriented democratization could endanger secularism by empowering populist pro-religious political forces and eliminating the reserve domain allotted to the military as guardian of secularism. Thus, there is considerable contingency in

---

[6] Karpat 2000 dates mainstream Islamist intellectuals' abandonment of traditional advocacy of aestheticism, in favour of 'European' scientific civilization, to the mid-nineteenth century.

[7] For how this plays out with reference to pluralism and secularism, see Fisher Onar 2009b.

discourses on 'Europe'. Contingency is a function of the preferences of an individual and the intellectual tradition to which s/he subscribes, as well as of evolving domestic and international circumstances.

In short, there are a number of structurally induced ineliminable features common to Turkish intellectuals' perceptions of Europe both across the political spectrum and over time. These include a tendency to perceive 'Europe' as a ubiquitous and monolithic actor, a set of traumatic memories, and a habit of regarding the 'European' experience as furnishing a 'menu' of choices. Since the late Ottoman era, most intellectuals have agreed on the need to adopt the material features of that experience, but disagreed on whether to embrace 'European' codes of conduct in normative terms. As such, we may situate intellectuals' views along a spectrum that reaches from desire for convergence (with 'European' norms however understood) to desire for resistance. The will to converge, moreover, ranges from *selective* to *syncretic* to *unequivocal*, depending on the preferences of the individual intellectual and the intellectual tradition in question, and the domestic and international context. By using the spectrum as a heuristic device, and by honing in on intellectuals whose views are seminal to particular schools of thought on 'Europe', we may tackle the substance of perceptions from the late Ottoman period to the present. For only by understanding the interplay of constant and contingent features of intellectuals' discourse over time can we understand the many apparent contradictions associated with different factions' apprehensions of 'Europe' today.

The nineteenth- and twentieth-century crucible of views on 'Europe'

There is an ongoing, highly politicized debate in Turkish historiography over whether there was greater continuity or rupture in the transition from Ottoman Empire to the Turkish Republic (see Fisher Onar forthcoming). What is certain is that many contemporary schools of thought have roots in the crucible of the late Ottoman/early Republican era. At this juncture, pundits across the political spectrum were gripped by the painful yet urgent question of how to adapt to pressures emanating from ascendant Western Europe. In the face of successive military defeats at the hands of European armies, early reformers engaged with 'Europe' by importing military expertise.[8] But the invocation of French revolutionary ideals by the ideologists of the Greek War of Independence

---

[8] As early as the 1730s, the Comte de Bonneval (1674–1747), who became an Ottoman officer and took the name Humbaraci Ahmet Paşa, introduced and commanded light cavalry; Baron de Tott (1733–1793) was instrumental in the establishment of modern naval and military schools. Selim III (1789–1807) declared a 'New Order' (*Nizam-i Cedid*) and sought information about developments in Europe. His bid to replace the Janissaries with a Western-style army cost him his life. The task was completed by Mahmut II (1808–1839).

(1821–9) – and the appeal of such ideals for other communities within the heterogeneous empire – suggested a need for deeper engagement with 'European' ideas and institutions (Erdem 2005). Yet there was also awareness that Westernization would engender resistance amongst conservative elements within the elite and populace.

The Tanzimat reforms (1839–71) accordingly launched concerted Westernization, framed in a syncretic fashion. The Decree of Gülhane of 1839, for example, like the Imperial Reform Edict of 1856, guaranteed subjects' life and property in terms congruent with the Declaration of the Rights of Man and Citizen, but also with the Hanafi school of Islamic jurisprudence to which the Ottoman dynasty subscribed.[9] Similarly, Ahmed Cevdet Pasha, a renowned *alim* (religious scholar) and civil servant under multiple sultans, codified the *Shari'a* in accordance with Western forms. The Tanzimat led to the gradual restructuring of Ottoman state and society along European lines. In the process, however, many amongst the Tanzimat intelligentsia acquired ostentatiously Westernized habits which rankled with their juniors and conservative elements in society at large.

One group – the Young Ottomans – believed they possessed a deeper sense of what 'Europe' represented, and sought to synthesize European science and liberal political institutions with their vision of the Ottoman-Muslim soul. To this end, a leading intellectual, Namik Kemal, pleaded for his countrymen to accept the example of 'European' civilization with regard to medicine, engineering, the arts, commerce, and advances in law, pointing to Ottoman-Islamic sources for notions like the 'social contract' and 'freedom'.[10] Yet he insisted on retaining an autonomous, authentic Ottoman-Muslim sphere:

We will accept every kind of progress achieved by Europeans.... [but] we must never become Europeans, for God's sake. The insistence by the Muslim on not becoming Europeanized is a hundred times more apparent than it has ever been. (Hanioğlu 1995: 14)

This tendency to distinguish between desirable (science, liberal institutions) and undesirable aspects of the 'European' experience (ethics and religiosity, or perceived lack thereof) would prove a constant feature of pious intellectuals' discourse over the next century. Interestingly, it also echoes the dichotomous representation of soulless Western Europe versus the spiritual 'East' in Orthodox Christian discourses (see, for example, the chapters on Romania and Greece in this volume).

The Young Ottoman programme failed to stem secessionism amongst non-Muslims of the Empire. In a bid to bolster solidarity amongst remaining Muslim elements, the autocratic Abdülhamit II employed pan-Islamist rhetoric. Ever aware, however, of the need to keep pace with developments in Europe, he also

---

[9] For more on the syncretic nature of Ottoman reformers see Fisher Onar 2009c.

[10] The name of his journal, *İbret*, was telling: it meant 'to learn a lesson from misfortune'.

expanded Western-style education and military reform with the help of Prussian experts. A new generation of 'Young Turks' was thus exposed to European ideas. This led some to abandon the syncretism of earlier reformists and embrace the positivism of social engineers such as Saint Simon and Comte. In so doing, they established the foundations of Turkish secularism in its liberal and nationalist variants, and many travelled to European capitals as students (or political exiles). Positivism was attractive because by treating science as a religion, it facilitated what these intellectuals deemed necessary for survival in the Europe-dominated modern world: a leap from a sacred to a rational ontology. Not all were able to weather that leap, as demonstrated by the example of one suicidal writer who diligently recorded his impressions until losing consciousness in order to prove there was no life after death. Others, like Prince Sabahattin – the father of Turkish liberalism – found meaning in works like Demolins' 'A Quoi Tient La Supériorité des Anglo-Saxons' (Kadioğlu 2007). Blaming Ottoman decline on the intrusiveness of the state and communitarianism of the people, he called for reforms to inculcate citizens with a more individualistic and entrepreneurial spirit along British lines (Mardin 1989). Still other positivists turned to constructs of ethnicity increasingly prevalent in contemporary Europe. These budding nationalists recovered from European usage the notion of the 'Turk', a marginal construct for the Ottomans.[11] They used it to mobilize Ottoman Muslims, many of whom had been displaced to Anatolia by fighting in the Balkans and Caucasus. For some such émigrés, especially those such as Yusuf Akçura who had encountered Russian pan-Slavism, the lure of ethnicity translated into pan-Turkist schemes. These proved impracticable, not least because the almost continuous war effort from the Balkan Wars through to the War of Independence (1912–23) required all available resources.[12]

Others, like Ziya Gökalp, rejected irredentism, delimiting the Turkish homeland to Anatolia. Within these territorial confines, and influenced by Durkheimian solidarism, Gökalp envisaged 'Turkishness' as ethnicized Muslimness. The frame was thus inclusive of all Muslim communities living in Anatolia, which included Kurds, Turkmen, Circassians, Abkhazians, Laz, Bosniaks, Albanians, and many others. In elaborating his formula, Gökalp drew on the German distinction between civilization and culture according to which the former is universal and scientific, a 'consciously created artefact of human reason' which does not relate to the values of any given society (Evin 1984; Kalaycioğlu 2005). Culture, on the other hand, refers to particulars – the language and value system of a society; it is therefore indigenous and non-transferable. Gökalp argued that

[11] If Europeans used the term 'Turk' broadly to describe any Muslim associated with the Ottoman Empire, the Ottomans played down the ethnic element in favour of dynastic and religious sources of authority.

[12] That said, Enver Pasha of the Young Turk triumvirate perished fighting for the pan-Turkist cause in what is today Uzbekistan. The early republicans roundly condemned his exploits as wasteful, utopian adventurism.

Turks (i.e. Anatolia-based Muslims) must abandon an Islamic civilization that had fallen behind in technical terms. But in joining 'Europe', today at the vanguard of scientific civilization, 'Turks' would not have to abandon their Muslim culture, which would continue to be a font of ethics and aesthetics. This synthesis could be achieved by ensuring that religion became a matter of private conscience, and culture an expression of the societal ethos. By thus collapsing religion into culture, Gökalp was able to embrace European positivism unequivocally.

The founders of the Turkish Republic took Gökalp's vision to heart. Scarred by defeat in the First World War and the high price of victory in the War of Independence, they rejected Ottoman heterogeneity and religiosity, which they blamed for the Empire's collapse. Instead, they established Turkey as a unitary and secular nation-state along contemporary European lines. Their highly solidaristic vision of national belonging was reinforced by the salience of Durkheim in Kemalist thinking, transferred via Gökalp. Their Jacobin secularism, moreover, reflected contemporary European Orientalists' view of Islam as inimical to progress (Toynbee and Kirkwood 1926). This unequivocal embrace of what 'Europe' was thought to represent (for the paradoxical purpose of keeping 'Europe' at bay) was internalized by many, especially amongst urban elites.

Challengers, 1923–1999

Yet the Westernist project also engendered resistance. This was expressed within and outside the Kemalist mainstream, during the single- and multi-party periods, by intellectuals on both the left and right. Leftist thought in Turkey presents a fragmented tableau because it has appealed to diverse figures for manifold, often contradictory reasons. There are, nevertheless, a number of constants to leftist discourses such as a commitment to secularism and progressive social policies, often defended through recourse to European referents. At the same time, views of 'Europe' for leftists of most stripes are informed by the memory of subordination to European powers, and they use anti-imperialist language, often with strong nationalist inflections.

In the late Ottoman period, socialist and communist ideas circulated most vigorously in non-Muslim circles, where they often fused with (or were trumped by) nationalist sentiments (Ciddi 2009). A fledgling communist movement was also tolerated by the nationalist leadership during the years of resistance against occupying Allied forces, not least in return for Bolshevik gold. But a common refrain amongst contemporary Turkish observers, including Atatürk, was that socialism would find scant followers in pre-industrial Muslim Turkish society. There was, nonetheless, some sympathy for its anti-imperialist platform. This spurred intellectuals associated with the *Kadro* journal, such as

Şevket Sürreya Aydemir and Yakup Kadri Karaosmanoğlu, to develop a Kemalist–Marxist synthesis according to which Turkey would lead a revolt of semi- or post-colonial societies against the industrial West (Ahmad 2004). For other intellectuals, such as poet Nazim Hikmet, communism provided an idiom for coming to terms with the jarring transformations of the early Republican era.

Though the communist party was never permitted to flourish, the Kemalist Republican People's Party (*Cumhuriyet Halk Partisi* – CHP) turned to social democracy under the leadership of charismatic poet Bülent Ecevit in the 1960s.[13] Ecevit's synthesis bore affinities to both European social democracy and third-worldist socialisms. It was predicated on social justice, economic development, democratic *étatisme*, secularism, and nationalism (Altunişik and Tür 2005). In the same period, radical leftist groups were galvanized by the first freely circulating translations of Marx, Lenin, and Mao. Radicalism was further fuelled by the diminished salience of the Western peg of Turkish identity after a series of humiliating episodes involving Western allies.[14] This contributed to what was later viewed as a historic lost opportunity when Ecevit snubbed the EEC – with which Turkey had had an Association Agreement since 1963 – when the body invited Ankara to apply for membership at the same time as Athens.

Leftists of all stripes were repressed during the 1971 and 1980 military interventions. Some Kemalist leftists of Ecevit's generation nevertheless continue to propound an ambivalent vision of 'Europe' as both progressive beacon and neo-imperialist threat in fora like the newspaper *Cumhuriyet* (Republic). Meanwhile, over the course of the 1980s and 1990s, many former radicals began to employ the vocabulary of economic and political liberalism – though their critics doubt whether they have internalized liberalism in any meaningful way. Today, some such 'liberals' or 'liberal-leftists' as they are sometimes and rather oxymoronically described, use dailies like *Radikal* (Radical), *Zaman* (Time), and *Taraf* (Side) to champion convergence with EU standards of human rights, rule of law, and democracy.

Kemalist Westernism also provoked the emergence of several schools of thought on the right, from ultranationalist and religious currents to the centre-right. A constant across the three camps is a will towards selective or syncretic engagement with European know-how in order to empower Turks in their dealings with the West. They differ, however, on the degree to which they believe that the rehabilitation of Muslim religiosity – which most, though not all, right-leaning intellectuals endorse – is compatible with Turkey's European vocation.

---

[13] Former party leader İsmet İnönü launched the process, but it was only under Ecevit that the turn to social democracy was completed.

[14] Specific incidents were the Kennedy administration's disregard for Turkish preferences during the Jupiter missile crisis, and the 'Johnson letter' of 1964 in which the US president employed condescending language to reprimand Turkey over its position on Cyprus.

The intellectual godfather of Turkish ultranationalism, novelist Nihal Atsiz, was thoroughly rejectionist in his attitude towards Europe, to which he thought Kemalism was pathetically beholden. Atsiz claimed to dismiss all foreign 'ideologies' including liberalism, communism, Islam, and fascism (to which his ideas nevertheless bore a family resemblance). Alien value systems had polluted the great Turkic nation, which would be rejuvenated when social and political life was thoroughly Turkified by heroic bloodshed and strife (Üzer 2002).[15] His militarism would prove a constant of ultranationalist discourses. But Atsiz's total rejection of religion and European referents for modernization did not appeal to either the masses or the political elite. Ultranationalism received a boost with the establishment, in the 1960s, of the 'Hearth of the Enlightened' (*Aydinlar Ocaği*). Hearth intellectuals attacked humanists, cosmopolitans, atheists, Christians, and leftists as enemies of the nation (Poulton 1997). They nevertheless argued for selective engagement of 'Europe' in material terms whilst insisting on the retention of a 'pure' Turkish-Muslim identity. This (re-)coupling of Turkishness and Islam in right-wing nationalist thought was echoed, after the mid-1960s, by Alparslan Türkeş, founder of the Nationalist Action Party (*Milliyetçi Hareket Partisi* – MHP). In his 'Nine Lights and Turkey' (*Dokuz Işik ve Türkiye*), Türkeş also continued to argue that economic development along European lines was necessary to cast off the Western yoke (Türkeş 1994).

The nationalist right's Turkish-Islamic synthesis (TIS) was appropriated by the generals behind the 1980 coup, who believed it could serve as a bulwark against communism. Indeed, two Hearth intellectuals were on the committee responsible for drafting the new constitution (Yavuz 2003). It was at this juncture, then, that a strain of nationalist Kemalism devoid of leftist inflections became intertwined with right-wing nationalist thought, although the generals rejected the anti-Western subtext of the TIS. The restrictive, TIS-informed constitutional order nevertheless went against the grain of developments in contemporary Europe, where bodies like the CoE and EP were increasingly trumpeting a vision – attainable or otherwise – of 'Europe' as liberal and cosmopolitan. The result is that those nationalist Kemalists who invested in the post-1980 regime, alongside ultranationalists, are today amongst the most Eurosceptic figures in Turkey.

Meanwhile, a second major strain of right-wing response to Kemalist Westernism came from religious cohorts who resented, above all, the secularist cultural revolution. Poets such as Mehmet Akif Ersoy and Necip Fazil Kisakürek – iconic figures for Islamists to this day – echoed their ultranationalist counterparts in declaring the 'miraculous refinement of the West' to be 'etched on a background of plastic' disguising 'ruin and darkness; a civilization condemned to hit its head

---

[15] Atsiz's views, though more extreme, struck a chord with a highly ethnicist conception of Turkishness prevalent amongst some Kemalists in the 1930s. Influenced by racist currents in contemporary European thought, these cohorts developed the Turkish History and Sun Language Theses according to which all nations of the world descended from Turkish stock.

against one wall after another' (Kisakürek, cited in Mardin 1994: 198–9). But whilst many on the religious right employed the *leitmotif* of European decadence versus Turkish-Muslim virtue, they too advocated selective or even syncretic adoption of the material aspects of 'European' civilization. For instance, figures like Said Nursi, founder of the influential Nurcu movement – a branch of which is led today by Fethullah Gülen – advocated an 'inner *hijra*' or pilgrimage to escape what he considered to be the corrosive effects of Kemalist secularism; yet, he simultaneously argued that the Koran should be read through the lens of scientific discoveries (Yavuz 2003).

Religious resistance to Kemalist Westernism found political expression with the establishment, in the 1960s, of the National View (*Milli Görüş* – MG) movement by Necmettin Erbakan. Erbakan belonged to a sect led by the formidable Sheik Zaid Kotku, spiritual godfather to many a pious politician. Kotku was not opposed to engaging with the material dimension of European modernity. Like his ultranationalist counterparts, he believed that instrumental adoption of European expertise would enable Muslim Turks to overcome subordination in political and existential terms. To illustrate this, Kotku modified the old Sufi expression 'a morsel, a cloak', which meant that all a person needs to survive is food and clothing. In its stead, he declared the basics to be: 'a morsel, a cloak, a Mazda' (*Bir lokma, bir hirka, bir Mazda*, cited by Yavuz 2003: 142). As pious cohorts prospered with economic and political liberalization in the 1980s and 1990s, this religious-capitalist synthesis acquired ever wider purchase. One of Kotku's successors even described market forces and the invisible hand as tantamount to the workings of God (Yavuz 2003). Such views found political voice with the foundation of the 'moderate Islamist' AKP which, despite its roots in political Islam, claims to have abandoned anti-systemic, anti-Western religious nationalism to become a socially conservative but economically and politically liberal movement that favours Turkey's accession to the EU.

In so doing, the party has become heir apparent to a centre-right tradition which has long sought to forge a 'mid-way between the scientistic-positivis[m] ... of republican factions and Islamic orthodoxy' (İrem 2004: 90). The project dates back at least to the foundation of the Republic, when close affiliates of the regime, such as Ahmet Ağaoğlu, found themselves drawn to the 'other West' of romanticism, spiritualism, and Bergsonism. Indeed, a member of this group is credited with telling an audience at the Ninth Philosophy Conference in Paris of 1936 that, 'today, Turkey is constructing herself in the way Mr Bergson has defined' (İrem 2004: 104). Ağaoğlu's eclectic synthesis of liberal and conservative, nationalist and westernist ideas acquired a mass following under the banner of the centre-right with the transition to multi-party politics. Ideologues affiliated with a series of centre-right parties[16] accordingly pursued economic

---

[16] The Democrat Party (*Demokrat Parti* – DP, 1946–60), the Justice Party (*Adalet Partisi* – AP, 1961–92), and the Motherland Party (*Anavatan Partisi* – ANAP, 1983–2009) were arguably the

and political liberalization indexed to a Western referent, whilst relaxing restrictions on Islamic practice in public spaces.

A trailblazer in this respect was Turgut Özal, who dominated post-1980 civilian politics until his death in 1993. Though not an intellectual himself, Özal gathered around his person minds like former leftist radical Cengiz Çandar. A journalist, Çandar helped develop 'neo-Ottomanism', a doctrine which cited Ottoman heterogeneity as a source of tolerance in contemporary social and political life, and pointed to historical, cultural, and linguistic ties with former Ottoman territories in the Balkans, Caucasus, and Middle East as bases for building constructive relations with these regions.[17] This attempt to pluralize Turks' international horizons was part and parcel of intellectuals' and politicians' struggle to redefine Turkish identity after the Cold War. In this respect, the collapse of the Iron Curtain in 1989, and the bid, following the Maastricht Treaty of 1992, to construct a 'thicker' European collective identity were important turning points. For whilst the events did not have as immediate an impact on Turkey as they did on former communist countries and EU members respectively, they marked a shift in attitudes towards Turkey on the part of partners in Europe and the West. One sign of this was the critique of Turkey's European credentials developed by mainstream figures in the EU, many of whom were associated with the Christian Democrat tradition. Neo-Ottomanism, in effect, sought to compensate for this by situating Turkish identity at the interstices of several regions, whilst simultaneously seeking to secure the country's place in 'Europe'. Thus, in *Turkey in Europe* (1991), Özal – or rather his presumed ghost writer, former diplomat and public intellectual Gündüz Aktan – characterized 'Europe' as a 'way of life based on freedom, democratic liberties, and respect for human rights'; Turkey had a rightful place in such a Europe, given the commitment of generations of Ottoman and Turkish reformers towards the 'universal values of Western civilization'. But watchdog groups like the EP who were highly critical of Turkey's human rights record throughout the 1980s and 1990s begged to differ. In response, many Turkish pundits, including Aktan, began to argue that the human rights critique masked a deeper animosity steeped in culturalist exclusionism.

Convergence and resistance: 1999–2009

Acquisition of full candidate status to the EU in December 1999 marked a major turning point, in that 'Europe' became a referent onto which the aspirations of the rival factions were projected. Thus, from 1999 until roughly 2004, a

dominant force in civilian politics – albeit often in coalition with other, more radical parties of the right – for much of the second half of the twentieth century.

[17] For a comparison of variants of neo-Ottomanism in Turkey today see Fisher Onar 2009d.

cross-cutting consensus emerged on the imperative of Europeanization leading to a 'veritable legal revolution' and spurring commentators to cite a 'European' prerogative or precedent for almost any course of action.[18] The honeymoon lasted as long as the nitty-gritty details of the accession process, their transformative impact on domestic social and political life, and the winners and losers in these processes remained unknown.

Many Kemalists, for instance, felt closer than ever to achieving the holy grail of integration with 'Europe', and were reconciled with the democratic opening this required. A case in point was willingness to delay the mandatory parliamentary vote on the Kurdish terrorist leader Abdullah Öcalan's death sentence and wait until the ECtHR decision on the appeal,[19] a political move which paved the way for abolition of capital punishment. Some, like Ecevit, argued for abolition in instrumentalist terms as a necessary step on the path to EU accession. But others, like Seyfi Oktay and Ercan Karakaş – public intellectuals who had previously served as ministers of justice and culture respectively – believed that eliminating capital punishment was a categorical imperative to which Kemalism was reconciled as part and parcel of its commitment to European-cum-universal values.[20]

Not dissimilarly, when the self-proclaimed 'Muslim Democrat' AKP came to power on a pro-EU, pro-democratization platform in 2002, intellectuals affiliated with the religious right pronounced the compatibility of moderate Islamist and EU demands for civilianization, democratization, and cultural pluralism (Ilicak 2000). Enthusiasm for convergence with 'European' political values was also notable in the retreat of intellectuals like Ali Bulaç and Ahmet Davutoğlu from the profound critique of European modernism and universalism that each had developed in what many considered their *magna opera*. Bulaç's 'Medina Contract', for example, invoked the early Islamic community and Ottoman *millet* system to condemn modernist nationalism. He called instead for the instantiation of a neo-Ottoman polity based on legal pluralism for autonomous, religiously-defined communities.[21] Similarly, Davutoğlu, in his *Civilizational Transformation and the Muslim World* (2004), deconstructed Fukuyama and Huntington to critique Western universalism as a totalizing project. A reinvigorated *umma*, he argued, offered an attractive alternative for broader humanity. Yet, in this period, both intellectuals became champions of EU accession – Bulaç via his columns at high-circulation *Zaman*, Davutoğlu as advisor to the prime minister.

---

[18] For a comprehensive account of the reforms and their implications for civil liberties, see Özbudun 2007.

[19] According to Turkish law prior to the abolition of the death penalty *in toto*, sentences had to be approved by parliament.

[20] Interviews by one of the authors with Seyfi Oktay in February 2007, and Ercan Karakaş in May 2007.

[21] Ali Bulaç, *Medine Vesikasi*, available at: <http://www.yeniumit.com.tr/yazdir.php?konu_id= 385>.

Secular liberals were also thrilled by the European anchor for dismantling the authoritarian legacy of 1980. Many also piggy-backed on the moderate Islamist reformist drive to give their own agenda wider societal purchase. Thus, public intellectuals like Şahin Alpay and Ali Bayramoğlu disseminated their pro-EU message to audiences at *Zaman* and *Yeni Şafak* (New Horizon), whilst also devoting energies to reassuring secularist audiences that the moderate Islamist conversion to political liberalism was sincere. As Turkish-Armenian commentator Etyen Mahçupyan put it: 'As long as religion is left out of the picture, the EU is a very important universal reference point and very functional. It can affect everyone independently of their identity – Kurdish, Islamist, secularist, Turk – everyone talks about human rights, democratization, and freedoms; and they want the same standards here that people have in other parts of the world.'[22]

Interestingly, during this period even ultranationalist politicians appeared conciliatory at a time of broad societal consensus on the desirability of convergence with the EU. They accordingly endorsed accession-oriented reforms such as abolition of capital punishment and measures enhancing minority language rights. But such moves engendered deep dismay amongst many an ultranationalist commentator who warned, like a columnist at *Orta Doğu* (Middle East), that those who had sold Turkey out to nefarious 'European' interests would 'drown in the blood' of martyrs (Topdur 2000). The dissonance between ultranationalist political practice and commentary evaporated, however, when the MHP failed to pass the electoral threshold in 2002. Nationalist backlash became even more pronounced as the ripple effects of 9/11 and the Iraq war began to be felt across the world. It fed too on the ever more explicit denial of Turkey's European character by leading figures within the EU.

Joined by a growing chorus of Eurosceptic voices from both republican and Islamist circles, ultranationalists developed a discursive repertoire aimed at discrediting 'liberal' and pro-AKP intellectuals' arguments for the compatibility of Turkish identity, secular or otherwise, and 'European' values. One way they did so was by using Article 301 of the Turkish penal code, which bans insults to 'Turkishness'. They invoked the item to charge journalists and novelists who had challenged the official line on a wide range of topics. The purpose, argued Baskin Oran, a leading liberal scholar and public personality, was to discredit Turkey's reformist credentials in the eyes of European and international commentators as much as it was to intimidate revisionists in Turkey.[23] The strategy registered success on both counts. On the international front, for example, the likes of Salman Rushdie lambasted 'Turkey' in general terms (rather than the ultranationalist campaign per se) for prosecuting renowned author Orhan Pamuk. Meanwhile, the argument developed by ultranationalists for domestic consumption played upon the traumas of yesteryear to suggest that European

---

[22] Interview by one of the authors with Etyen Mahçupyan, December 2006.
[23] Interview by one of the authors with Baskin Oran, March 2007.

actors, with the collusion of liberals, Kurds, and other 'traitors', were seeking through the accession process to complete the unfinished task of dismembering Turkey. In a classic invocation of ultranationalist tropes, the author and host of the popular *Cevizli Kabuğu* (Nutshell) debate programme, Hulki Cevizoğlu (2007) declared that 'internal and external agents' were increasingly 'playing games over the country' at a time when Turkey 'is being increasingly colonized'.

In the same period, the moderate Islamist love affair with 'Europe' turned into heartache when it became clear that the normative framework upheld by the EU and the CoE did not provide Islamists with leverage in their challenge to Kemalist secularism (if not necessarily to secularism per se). A major catalyst in this respect was the move of the ECtHR to uphold a secularist ban on veiling in public institutions including universities in the case of *Leyla Şahin* v. *Turkey* (June 2004; November 2005). Pro-religious commentators widely interpreted the verdicts as a racist and Islamophobic misreading of legitimate demands on the part of Muslim citizens. The verdicts represented a major blow to those, like Fehmi Koru, editor of *Yeni Şafak*, who had argued in syncretic terms that 'European' justice would vindicate the demands of pious citizens. There was also disappointment at the clear constituency in some quarters within the EU for a reference to Christianity in the draft constitution. For Koru, this not only denied the Aristotelian underpinnings of Islamic jurisprudence and the debt to Islam for preserving, developing, and transmitting Classical Greece back to 'Europe', but also disenfranchised millions of Muslim Europeans.[24] Disappointment also meant that intellectuals like Bulaç slipped back into their earlier estimation of 'Europe' as a 'totalitarian' project ontologically incapable of acknowledging the truths of 'Others'.[25]

Pro-EU figures, concentrated amongst liberals/liberal-leftists, watched in dismay as the societal consensus and political will driving convergence with 'European' norms appeared to fade. The flagging commitment to reform in turn took the bite out of the critique advanced by intellectuals from all quarters that European rejectionism of Turkey was animated by 'double standards' towards Turkish Muslims. One strand of response to these developments was the cosmopolitan arguments developed by figures like Fuat Keyman, an academic, columnist, and public personality. According to this line of reasoning, the ability of 'Europe' to evolve into a post-national polity predicated on inclusive, civic values – the 'Europe' desired by many amongst the crème de la crème of the European intellectual elite – was dependent upon Europeans' ability to accept Turkey as an equal partner if and when Turkey meaningfully internalized the political criteria for accession (Aydin and Keyman 2004; Baban and Keyman 2008). However, given the persistence of exclusionary discourses on the part of key figures like Nicolas Sarkozy and Angela Merkel, other

---

[24] Interview by one of the authors with Fehmi Koru, December 2006.
[25] Interview by one of the authors with Ali Bulaç, May 2007.

champions of 'European' values within Turkey increasingly came to fear that 'European' stances on Turkish membership might actually be diminishing the lure of 'European' values.[26] Meanwhile, as the European 'anchor', 'carrot', or 'dream' appeared to slip into the background, a battle between pro-religious forces and the old republican establishment rose to the fore, further polarizing the country.

Conclusion

In sum, the modern Turkish project, like that of neighbouring Greece and other successor states of the Austro-Hungarian and Ottoman Empires, was conceived in the shadow of European modernity. This has given rise to ambivalent engagement of European values and practices on the part of national intellectuals.[27] Is then the dilemma of Turkish intellectuals vis-à-vis 'Europe' really so different from that of counterparts in other 'peripheral' states? This chapter has shown that whilst other national intellectuals construe 'Europe' in essentializing yet dichotomous terms as both lighthouse and shoal, there are several unique dimensions to the Turkish case. Amongst these is the fact that Turkey achieved its 'independence' through warfare with European Great Powers and their protégées amongst Ottoman minorities. Anti-imperialist nationalism and suspicion of the identity pluralism that is said to underpin the EU project can therefore fuel a heightened sense of exceptionalism vis-à-vis 'Europe'. A second important factor is the fact that unlike Polish or Greek Europeanists who can cite embeddedness in 'European' cultural space by virtue of their Christianity on one hand, and experience of the Enlightenment on the other, Turkish Europeanists encounter persistent resistance from diverse quarters within the EU as to their European credentials.

Nevertheless, the signifier 'Europe' is a locus of attraction and resistance, with intellectuals across the political spectrum drawn to the material aspects of the 'European' experience, but displaying ambivalence towards 'European' norms and values. This has given rise to platforms advocating selective, syncretic, or unequivocal embrace of what 'Europe' is understood to represent. In the debate today, hardliners – who can come from republican and Islamist as well as right-wing nationalist ranks – are often outright rejectionist in their attitudes towards 'Europe', whilst 'moderate Islamists' have tended to display a syncretic approach, fusing EU-oriented liberal language with religious idiom. The only unequivocal advocates of a 'European' path in normative terms are liberals/liberal-leftists who – in the face of hostile attitudes towards Turkish membership within the

---

[26] Interviews with Şahin Alpay, December 2006; Zekeriya Akçam, February 2007; Erol Tuncer, April 2007.

[27] For a comparison of the Turkish and Greek experiences see Fisher Onar 2009a.

EU itself – increasingly emphasize the need to conform to European standards of democracy, rather than accession per se.

That said, important transformations in perceptions of 'Europe' have occurred in the past decade. Lively debates over the nature and implications of EU-oriented reform have led to the shattering of numerous taboos. There has also been a learning curve with regard to Turks' understanding of actors and dynamics in Europe. The institutional integration that accompanied candidate status – such as Turkish adhesion to the Erasmus academic exchange programme – has furthered this process of strategic, cognitive, and sociological learning, especially amongst academics, activists, and policy-makers. In the view of some commentators, there has been a similar learning curve amongst Turkey's interlocutors within the EU, notably amongst Social Democrats and Greens who, it is believed, have acquired a more nuanced understanding of Turkish society and politics. Thus whilst disappointment at EU actors from 2004 to roughly 2007 may have diminished what, for many, had been the grail-like allure of 'Europe', increased exposure to the diversity of voices within the EU may ultimately furnish the basis for a healthier relationship. For now, engagement appears to be based above all on pragmatism. Thus, figures like Davutoğlu – foreign minister since May 2009 and an advocate of neo-Ottomanism – have been seeking to augment Turkey's 'soft power' in its region(s) by reaching out to neighbours, as well as by establishing the country as an energy hub. This entails a certain irony: at a time when the EU peg for Turkey's transformation may be diminishing, yet in light of two centuries of ambivalent engagement with 'European' norms, Turkey may nevertheless be on the road to becoming something of a 'soft power' in line with the normative foundations of the contemporary 'European' project.

Part VI

One Story or Many?

16

Europe's Political Identity
Public Sphere and Public Opinion

Juan Díez Medrano

Fifteen years ago, my interest in the topic of European integration was ignited upon reading a nice little book edited by Wolfgang Mommsen and prefaced by Walter Lacqueur (1994). The book's title was *The Long Way to Europe* and it included beautifully written essays by well-known scholars such as François Bédarida, Valerio Castronovo, William Wallace, and Ivan Berend, on how the elites in their respective countries had approached European integration. Thus the chapters had titles like 'France and Europe – From Yesterday to Today', 'Hungary's Place in Europe: Political Thought and Historiography in the Twentieth Century', or 'The British Approach to Europe'. The book was in many ways the scholarly counterpoint to Hans Magnus Enzersberger's literary and generally witty collection of essays entitled *Europe, Europe* (1989) and shared with it a renewed fascination with Europe in the context of the fall of the Berlin Wall and the drafting of the Treaty of European Union. The contributions to this volume connect with this tradition of examining the various stories that public intellectuals in different parts of Europe have knitted together as they reflect on Europe. The stories are gripping, and like those told by Mommsen, his collaborators, and Enzersberger, they naturally resonate with the national cultures in which they are embedded.

The accent of my previous work on European integration has been on the explanation of citizens' attitudes towards European integration. I therefore focus on citizen representations and, more generally, on views on Europe expressed by actors in the public sphere. While occasionally these actors are intellectuals, they are more often than not politicians or representatives from interest groups. Their views on Europe are sometimes inspired by those of public and scholarly intellectuals but only partially overlap with them. Either because European stories lose their national-specific narrative structure as they travel from intellectuals to public actors and citizens or because public actors and citizens autonomously develop their representations of Europe, the fact is that national public spheres portray the European Union and the European integration process and imagine the future of the European Union in very similar ways. Therefore, I will argue that viewed from the public sphere's and the citizens' perspective, the most relevant story to be told about the European Union is one of similarity.

I also argue that the content of debates on European integration in the public sphere and citizens' views on European integration suggest that the European Union is unlikely to move beyond consolidation of the current architecture. It may become more efficient and even larger, but not much more integrated. This is because the political elites' projects for a European political identity do not imply sharing a great deal more sovereignty than at present in the second and third pillars. The populations of the European Union largely share the elites' political identity project and, lacking a deep sense of identification with Europe that would lead them to develop more than a pragmatic interest in the European Union, they are unlikely to become a driving force of integration.

Although there is a broad consensus on the type of Europe that both elites and populations want, European political elites still quarrel about details or about semantic issues with an eye to their domestic audiences. Drawing on themes that resonate with national cultures, and that through sheer repetition have become part of these same national cultures, elite discourses thus shape public frames of reference about European integration. These different frames in turn can, and in some cases do, have a concrete impact upon public attitudes to European integration.

The following sections develop the points made above. I draw mainly on my own research on how people frame European integration and on the European public sphere, but also on data provided by surveys and secondary sources. I begin with a focus on political elite discourses on the European Union and the European integration process, as portrayed in the media. Partial as it may be, this analysis gives us access to political elites' representations of the European Union and to their political identity projects. I then move to examine ordinary citizens' representations of the European Union, political identity projects, and degrees of identification with Europe.

Europe viewed from the public sphere

Frames about Europe among political elites

Between 2001 and 2003 some colleagues and I coded thousands of newspaper articles in seven European countries in order to examine public discourse on the European Union between 1990 and 2002. These countries were France, Germany, Italy, the Netherlands, Spain, Switzerland, and the United Kingdom.

The Europub.com project, as this research endeavour was called, allowed me to expand on insights I had drawn from a previous study of media frames in Germany, Spain, and the United Kingdom. The Europub.com data demonstrate that political elites in this broad range of countries tend to represent the European Union broadly speaking in the same way: namely, as a market founded on democratic values (see Table 16.1). In the period we analysed, the Euro, European Central Bank policies, and EU enlargement were the issues that prompted the use of economic frames. They were presented in slightly different ways in different countries, however. In Germany, and to a lesser extent in the Netherlands and Switzerland, for instance, the Euro and European Central Bank policies were framed predominantly in terms of their contribution to stabilizing prices. In France, Italy, and to a lesser extent in Spain, the focus was on trade-offs between budgetary discipline, a strong Euro, and price stability on the one hand, and economic growth and unemployment on the other. In Britain, together with a great deal more discussion of the economic trade-offs involved in pursuing a monetary policy basically inspired by that of the Bundesbank, aversion to membership led public actors to debate the EMU with reference to a broader range of economic topics such as investment, export opportunities, and convergence (or lack of it?) between the British and the EU's economic cycles. Other subtle contrasts also distinguished countries in their discussions of European Union enlargement. Although enlargement was predominantly framed as an opportunity for economic growth for both old and new members, concern over a decline in social standards ('Lohn-Dumping') induced by outsourcing and labour immigration was greater in Germany and the Netherlands than in the rest of the countries. British public actors were those who framed enlargement in the most positive terms, as when British Prime Minister Tony Blair said that 'enlargement is about the stability provided by national working together rather than fighting together and the prosperity that comes from the single biggest market in the world' (*The Times*, 8 December 2000).

As mentioned above, only slightly less prevalent than the representation of the European Union as an economic space is the representation of the European Union as a project grounded in and upholding democratic values. In the period that we analysed, this framing of the European Union emerged in discussions over EU enlargement to Central and Eastern Europe and to Turkey, and very frequently too during the debate over sanctions to Austria prompted by the participation of Jörg Haider's party in the coalition government. Democracy as a frame was also used in public discourse, however, to criticize the alleged democratic deficit of the European Union institutions and procedures. This was the case especially in the United Kingdom.

While conceptualizations of the European Union as a market embedded in democratic institutions prevail over any other conception, images of Europe are much more diverse, and national contrasts often stem from the relative prevalence of these less frequent frames. Among these other frames, the EU's impact

Table 16.1 Most-mentioned political and media actors' frames, by country (% of claims with a particular frame)

	Germany	Spain	France	Italy	Netherlands	United Kingdom	Switzerland	Total
Economy, trade, and prices	22.3	4.8	16.6	20.9	29.8	30.4	14.0	19.8
Democracy and rights	9.6	20.1	13.3	16.1	10.1	8.4	12.5	12.9
Sovereignty	6.3	12.7	13.3	10.0	3.2	21.3	9.5	10.9
Security and peace	12.6	6.3	6.0	10.4	7.7	6.6	11.6	8.8
Historical	9.0	10.1	13.0	3.5	11.6	6.8	5.7	8.2
Strong bloc	7.6	6.3	9.2	6.8	6.4	12.4	2.7	7.3
Equality	9.6	15.9	9.5	6.3	6.2	4.8	5.1	8.2
Efficiency	5.6	5.8	6.8	7.3	10.3	4.8	3.0	6.2
Citizen	8.7	9.0	9.6	4.1	6.4	4.8	5.4	6.9
Community of values	4.1	9.0	7.8	12.9	4.5	1.0	3.3	6.1
Exclusion	1.4	3.7	3.8	9.0	4.9	1.5	3.9	4.0
National interest	1.9	0.5	4.1	0.8	1.1	8.6	6.8	3.4
Globalization complex	1.1	2.6	4.7	1.5	3.8	3.0	1.5	2.6
National identity	1.7	2.1	4.2	1.5	3.8	3.3	0.9	2.5
N	934	189	664	603	533	395	336	3,654

Source: Europub.com. See Ruud Koopmans, *The Transformation of Political Mobilization and Communication in European Public Spheres*. Fifth Framework Programme of the European Commission. Contract Number HPSE-CT2000–00046.

Note: Each frame represents descriptions of what the European Union is/is not, leads/does not lead to, and should/should not lead to:

Economy, trade, and prices: Descriptions that portray the European Union as a market or that highlight the European Union's economic effects.
Democracy and rights: Descriptions that portray the European Union as founded on democratic values and rights or as promoting them.
Sovereignty: Descriptions that refer to the European Union's impact on national sovereignty.
Security and peace: Descriptions that refer to the European Union's contribution to security and peace, as well as to understanding between the peoples of Europe.
Historical: Descriptions that link the European Union and European integration to particular historical events.
Strong bloc: Descriptions that portray the European Union as a strong bloc, able to compete economically and politically with other great powers in the world.
Equality: Descriptions that link the European Union to social and regional cohesion in Europe.
Efficiency: Descriptions related to the European Union institutions' efficiency in carrying out their assigned tasks.
Citizen: Descriptions related to the European Union's transparency and openness to citizen participation.
Community of values: Descriptions that relate to the European Union's values and to the degree of shared values across countries.
Exclusion: Descriptions that relate to the contribution of the European Union to addressing problems of social and/or ethnic exclusion.
National interest: Descriptions that connect the European Union to the national interest and/or discuss its impact on it.
Globalization Complex: Descriptions that connect the European Union and European integration to the conditions created by globalization.
National Identity: Descriptions that link the European Union to national identity.

on sovereignty and its actual and potential contribution to peace and security stand out. Meanwhile, the civic, republican conception of the European Union outlined above is not matched by an equally powerful 'ethno-cultural' representation. Cultural understandings, shared values, and collective identities are seldom drawn on by public actors in their constructions of the EU, and when they are, they cover a wide range of themes. Among these, the conceptualization of the EU as a community of values ('community of values', 'Western values', 'Christianity/(Judeo)-Christian values/culture') and the EU's impact on national identity ('national identity') are the two most frequently mentioned ones. Other, less frequently mentioned, ethno-cultural frames are religious beliefs such as Christianity or Islam, ideologies such as neoliberalism or cosmopolitanism, and general principles like diversity, unity, or civilization.

A lack of an anchoring point is also observed with respect to the historical events or periods that appear in public discourse on the European Union. Although public actors often frame the European integration project through references to historical events or periods, these historical events or periods cover a very wide range of themes, from references to antiquity to the September 11 attacks. The most mentioned events, historical periods, or historical characters or groups are antiquity, the Second World War, the Nazis/fascism, communism, the Cold War, divided Germany, Franco-German cooperation, and war in general. The classic Greco-Roman heritage, war, Franco-German cooperation/rivalry, communism, and fascism thus seem to be the main anchoring points of the historical memory of the countries in the Europub.com study.

The most striking finding in our investigation was the surprising cross-national similarity in the way political actors frame or represent the European Union and the European integration process in public debates. That is, political actors describe the characteristics, rationale, foundations, and objectives of the European Union and the European integration process in pretty much the same ways across countries. There is broad cross-national similarity in the range of topics that are referred to in the public sphere and in their relative salience. This point must be stressed before moving on to examine the most salient contrasts. The image of the European Union as a market and as a democratic club is pervasive across European public spheres. Nonetheless, contrasts there are and it is on these that I focus now. Generally speaking, the main cleavage across countries is that between those countries that construct the European Union in politico- or ethno-cultural terms with a comparative disregard for national interest, and those that represent the Union in terms of national interest while neglecting political and ethnic cultural homogeneity.

By far the main cleavage in our sample of countries is that between the United Kingdom and the rest of the countries. While the range of themes covered in British public discourse mimics that found in other countries, political discourse in the United Kingdom stands out for its representation of the European Union in terms of national interest, for a lack of perception of a common European culture, for an overt and literal emphasis on sovereignty, and for a disproportionate presence of negative economic images (Figures 16.1–3). In particular, a qualitative analysis of the frame data reveals that the sovereignty frame was used in connection with general discussions about the reform of the European Union's architecture – as in 1990 and in 2000–2 (i.e. Maastricht and

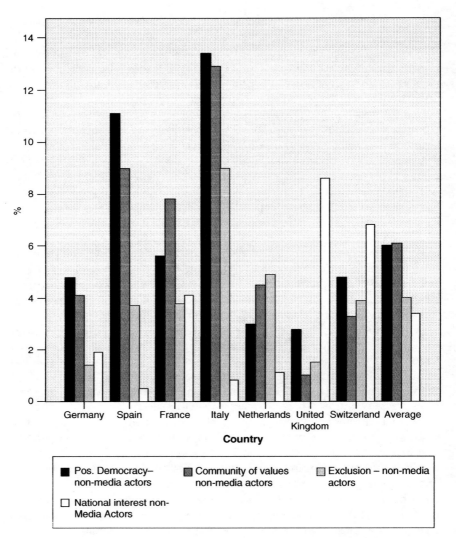

Figure 16.1 Percentages of claims with 'positive democracy', 'community of values', 'exclusion', and 'national interest' frames, by country

Source: Europub.com. See Ruud Koopmans, *The Transformation of Political Mobilization and Communication in European Public Spheres*. Fifth Framework Programme of the European Commission. Contract Number HPSE-CT2000–00046.

Note: *Non-media actors*: Actors whose claims in the public sphere are reported in the media, but who do not represent the media's own views.

Pos. democracy: Frames that speak to the European Union's foundation on democratic values.

Community of values: Descriptions that relate to the European Union's values and to the degree of shared values across countries.

Exclusion: Descriptions that relate to the contribution of the European Union to address problems of social and/or ethnic exclusion.

National interest: Descriptions that connect the European Union to the national interest and/or discuss its impact on it.

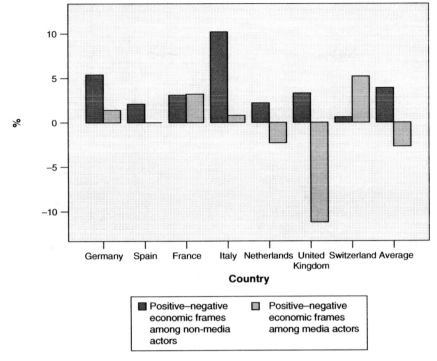

Figure 16.2 Net valence of economic representations of the European Union, by country (non-media and media actors) (% claims with positive economic frames minus % of claims with negative economic frames)

Source: Europub.com. See Ruud Koopmans, *The Transformation of Political Mobilization and Communication in European Public Spheres*. Fifth Framework Programme of the European Commission. Contract Number HPSE-CT2000–00046.

Note: *Non-media actors*: Actors whose claims in the public sphere are reported in the media, but who do not represent the media's own views.
Media actors: Actors whose claims in the public sphere represent the media's own views.
Positive-negative economic frames: Frames that portray the European Union's impact on the economy in positive or negative terms.

Constitutional Treaties respectively) – as well as European Monetary Union, foreign and defence policy, and adherence to the Social Charter. Alan Sked's remarks in his *Times* article of 28 August 1990 exemplify general critiques in the early 1990s of the Treaty of European Union. Sked was at the time a member of the Faculty at LSE and a vocal critic of the European Community. On the occasion of the Helsinki Conservative Leaders' summit, Sked invited Margaret Thatcher, then the UK Prime Minister, to resist short-term moves to create a European government, central bank, or a common foreign and defence policy, and to protect British national sovereignty 'at all costs':

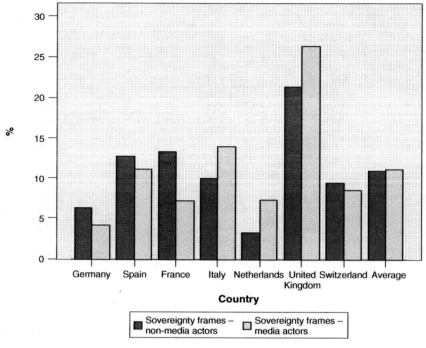

Figure 16.3 Percentage of claims with a sovereignty frame, by country (non-media and media actors)

Source: Europub.com. See Ruud Koopmans, *The Transformation of Political Mobilization and Communication in European Public Spheres*. Fifth Framework Programme of the European Commission. Contract Number HPSE-CT2000–00046.

Note: Non-media actors: Actors whose claims in the public sphere are reported in the media, but who do not represent the media's own views.
Media actors: Actors whose claims in the public sphere represent the media's own views.
Sovereignty: Descriptions that refer to the European Union's impact on national sovereignty.

Europe's response to war, terrorism, aggression, and blackmail is likely to be so inadequate that British national sovereignty must be protected at all costs...The Prime Minister's task in Europe is crystal clear...to support the creation of the single market, while resolutely resisting federalism. Yet what chance does she have of defeating the federalists? (*The Times*, 28 August 1990)

The 'sovereignty' frame is used in multiple contexts and by multiple actors. It is not always actors who oppose steps to European integration who contribute to its diffusion. Very often it is public actors, generally foreign, who involuntarily strengthen the presence of this frame in the British public sphere by using it to counter claims that the EU contributes to erosion of the UK's sovereignty. As Marc Steinberg shows in his dialogical discourse analysis of nineteenth-century class conflict in England, the weak (in the UK, those in favour of

European integration) usually find themselves using their opponents' frames, even though they try to turn them against these opponents (Steinberg 1999). This puts them at a rhetorical disadvantage, and at any rate ends up reinforcing the dominant frames. Thus, we read Douglas Hurd, Foreign Affairs Secretary and a moderate in the Thatcher and Major governments, saying during the debate on the Treaty of European Union: 'We are going to keep our separate governments, our legal systems, our constitutions, our traditions. At the same time we will hold more and more practical policies in common. This is not eroding sovereignty, it is using it' (11 June 1990). Similarly, we also read Jacques Santer, President of the European Commission between 1995 and 1999, saying in an interview to the BBC reported in *The Guardian*, that despite the extension of qualified majority voting and EMU Britain would preserve its identity. If his own country had not lost its identity, there was no reason why Britain should lose its own: London would retain its artistic traditions, cabbies' banter, smell of freshly mown lawn, and so on ... (*The Guardian*, 5 May 1995).

Political identity projects

The previous section has examined European identity as representation. I now move to examine the European Union as a political identity project. The question that this discussion will address is what kind of Europe political actors want as inferred from what they say in the public sphere. The answer that emerges from a systematic analysis of claims is as clear as the answer to the question of representations of the European Union. Political actors in different European countries want a European Union that is both an economic and political actor, and while they do not object to the sharing of an increasing number of competences between European Union and state institutions, they generally shy away from advocating further transfers of sovereignty to the European Union. The Euro will probably have been the last meaningful transfer of sovereignty to the European Union in a long time.

Despite the general consensus on the broad contours of the European Union's institutional design, three major issues of contention help explain the paralysis in today's European Union and animate an otherwise lacklustre political debate (see Table 16.2). The first concerns the limits of supranationalization. This issue of contention pits intergovernmentalists against supporters of a mixed supranational-intergovernmental model. The former question the degree of sovereignty already transferred to the EU, and often oppose steps towards a political Europe. The latter accept the status quo and support a political Europe, but without really specifying what they mean by that. This cleavage largely corresponds to Lacroix's and Nicolaïdis' distinction in the book's introduction between 'nationalist' and 'transnational' perspectives on Europe, but with much less detail.

Table 16.2 Publicized political identity projects in the EU (Examples)

	Dual supranational-intergovernmental		Intergovernmental
	Federal parliamentarian	*Presidentialist*	
Non-social*	German political elites	French political elites	British political elites
	Dutch political elites		Polish political elites
Social	Spanish public actors, both political and civil		
	Trade unions in all countries		

* Means that they do not openly call for a social Europe in public discourse and stress economic growth instead.

Source: Based on data from Europub.com. See Ruud Koopmans, *The Transformation of Political Mobilization and Communication in European Public Spheres*. Fifth Framework Programme of the European Commission. Contract Number HPSE-CT2000–00046.

The Europub.com dataset does not show clear trends of support for transfers of sovereignty to the European Union in the period considered here. This may be partly due to the paucity of data points considered and to the small number of claims that deal with institutional design in the European Union. My qualitative examination of a large number of newspaper editorials between 1990 and 1997 (Díez Medrano 2003) suggested, however, that the debate on European Monetary Union was the first symptom of an emerging elite split between those still wanting a greater transfer of sovereignty to the European Union and those content with leaving things as they currently stood. I thus demonstrated that in Britain, Germany, and Spain, conservative newspapers were significantly more reluctant to abandon the national currency than were more progressive ones. Lack of or limited progress since then on a number of issues where sovereignty cannot be shared by different levels of governance – whether economic policy, taxes, or armies – suggest that the EMU episode was not a one-off. National elites still support that some new competences be shared between national governments and the EU (for example, energy policy or environment), but they do not want to forgo their veto power on issues like macroeconomic policy, foreign relations, and defence.

The second issue of contention in today's European Union concerns its parliamentarian or presidentialist design. This issue has long pitted German against French political elites. In the years covered by this sample, German proposals for a federal Europe (e.g. Fischer's speech at the European Parliament) were strongly rejected by segments of the French political elite on the grounds that Germany was trying to force its own political system onto Europe. As Lacroix points out in Chapter 5, the federalist supranationalist perspective is absent from French discourse. One may argue, however, that opposition to a federal Europe among French political actors mainly expresses a rejection of the specifically parliamentarian supranational structure proposed by Germans.[1] This federal structure pivots around a strong parliament (with or without a second chamber composed of one delegate per member state) and a strong Commission, acting as the parliament's executive branch. Instead, the institutional model of French political actors pivots around the Council of Ministers, where the bulk of decisions would be reached through qualified majority voting (the concentration of power in the Council of Ministers, but not the extension of QMV, was the traditional Gaullist consensus, only recently broken by anti-Europeans and French federalists – see Goulard 2002).

The empirical analysis of the public sphere indeed shows that French actors invoke the extension of qualified majority vote at the Council of Ministers more often than do German actors, whereas German actors call more often than do French actors for the extension of the legislative powers of the European Parliament. Therefore, while it is objectively true that the term 'federal' is not part of French discourse on Europe, one should be careful when concluding that the French are less favourable to a supranational Europe than are Germans. What French and German elites seem to be defending are in fact different models of supranationalism, anchored in their respective political traditions – presidentialist and parliamentarian respectively.

Without taking into account the competences that French and Germans want to transfer to the European level, or how these competences would be allocated across different levels of government, it is problematic to attribute a greater nationalist bias to French political actors than to Germans. For one, German political actors have often stressed strict application of the subsidiarity principle. Also, the German federal system is one where competences are not allocated as strictly between the federal and the state levels as they are in the US. Instead, competences tend to be shared, with the federal government providing the main legislative or policy framework and states implementing it with a great deal of autonomy. Finally, in a critical domain such as foreign affairs and defence policy, the European Union's second pillar, German public actors have rarely expressed a willingness to move decisively towards qualified majority decision-making or to the creation of a European army. In sum, one cannot exclude the possibility that a presidentialist approach to Europe-making, in which a Council of Ministers would adopt decisions through qualified majority voting, might develop into a model at least as supranational in its effects as the architecture that German political actors propose. Again, the Europub.com data show no distinctive trend in support of either the presidentialist or parliamentarian model of integration between 1990 and 2002. The European

---

[1] The argument that German political elites view Europe as an extension of their own institutional arrangements is also discussed in Jachtenfuchs 2002: 286; see also Katzenstein 1997 for a discussion of the institutional similarities between Europe's and Germany's systems of governance and Nicolaïdis and Weatherill 2003.

Constitution, however, expressed a slight shift towards the latter, but stopped short of the federal model advocated by political leaders such as Joshka Fischer. One can easily envisage that this issue of contention will continue to pit France and Germany against each other in years to come.

Finally, the third issue of contention in today's European Union concerns the neoliberal or social spirit that guides both institution-building and policy in the European Union. The Europub.com data show very clearly that trade unions are much more vocal than political elites in supporting the maintenance of a strong social dimension in Europe. I would argue that this split between political elites more concerned with gross economic performance and trade unions still attached to the European social model reflects a broader split between political elites and citizens, which underlies the latter's lack of enthusiasm for the Euro, enlargement, and the European Constitution. The greater interest of political elites in economic growth than in the maintenance and strengthening of Europe's 'social model' favours the channelling of frustration by Europe's have-nots towards both national and European institutions. This frustration takes the form of abstention in electoral contests or of opposition to European developments such as the Euro, the enlargement process, and the European Constitution. The Europub.com data do not provide enough information to test the hypotheses outlined here in a more systematic fashion.

Europe from below

The analysis of political discourse in the public sphere above shows a rough overlap between the representations of and political identity projects for the European Union in different European countries. The contours of these representations and political identity projects roughly coincide with the current institutional and procedural characteristics of the European Union. Elites are prepared to tinker with the current 'acquis' and make the European Union more efficient, but not to advance significantly beyond the current state of affairs. Whether this is a good or a bad thing is not a question that concerns me in this chapter. One may wonder, however, whether Europe's populations differ from their political leaders in both representations and projects. We might also ask whether fifty years of European construction have managed to instil in European populations any sense of membership in a community called Europe strong enough to make the European Union an irreversible project and even move it forward.

Identification with Europe

By way of background, we can point out that mass movements moved by national sentiment have rarely created states. More often than not, it is states that have created nations (see Weber 1983). Based on the historical record, one should therefore not count on the peoples of Europe to push European integration forward. Europeans, as was the case with many peoples before them whose states moulded them into nations, lack a strong sense of identification with Europe. The task of making Europe is made more difficult because of the fact that the European Union is built above pre-existing nations, created and moulded by states throughout the nineteenth and twentieth centuries (see Breuilly 1981; Gellner 1983; Hobsbawm 1989). This means that even an ideal scenario where the welfare competences that most directly affect people's sense of material security would be transferred to and guaranteed by the European Union would fail to create a sense of identification with Europe comparable to national loyalties. The examples of Catalonia in Spain and Scotland in Britain demonstrate how little states can do when their welfare and democratic structures are built on those of pre-existing nations.

The peoples of Europe remain primarily attached to their states, or nations below their states, and this has not changed despite the deep transformations that the European Union has experienced since approval of the Treaty of European Union back in the early 1990s. Only about one in ten inhabitants in the European Union identified and still identify themselves primarily as Europeans (Table 16.3). In fact, about half of the population of Europe identifies only with their national community. This is hardly surprising. National communities have congealed into half-republican, half-cultural nations, with language at their centre. Indeed, the International Social Survey Programme (ISSP) module on national identity showed that between eight and nine out of ten individuals in European countries consider both language and respect for a country's political institutions as preconditions to being considered a member of the nation. The fact that linguistic distinctiveness has been constructed as the central marker of nationhood in most European countries is a minor tragedy for those hoping for the emergence of a European identity. Indeed, despite overwhelming cultural similarities (see Inglehart 1997), Europeans remain separated by language. The diffusion of English as a lingua franca would

Table 16.3 Trends in relative identification (1992–2004)

	1992	1996	2000	2004	2005
Nationality only	40.0	53.3	39.5	41.4	41.0
Nationality and European	47.3	35.4	47.5	46.9	48.0
European and nationality	6.1	5.5	6.3	6.9	7.0
Only European	3.2	3.5	3.4	3.1	2.0
Don't know	3.4	2.3	3.2	1.8	2.0

Source: Eurobarometer (European Commission).

certainly help overcome this problem, and it is certainly the case that more and more Europeans command a second and even third European language. We are still far, however, from a multilingual Europe.

What we thus have is a population that has at best developed a vague and superficial sense of identification with Europe. The stability of levels of identification with Europe despite huge strides towards integration in the last two decades should make us suspicious about the depth of any affective sense of belonging to Europe. Qualitative analysis of what it really means for people to identify with Europe helps to substantiate this point. Between 1996 and 1997 I interviewed Germans, Britons, and Spaniards about their attitudes towards European integration and about their sense of identification as members of their state, their region, and Europe. What transpired was that when people say that they identify as Europeans, what they mean is very different from what they mean when they say that they identify as members of their region or state. Emotion is largely absent in the former case. For most people, to identify as European is synonymous with acknowledging that one was born or lives in a geographical, perhaps even political, space called Europe. Other people equate identifying as European with being in favour of European integration, such as the following British citizen who says: 'If you're for a central bank, if you're for a common, a European foreign currency, and you are for international freedom, then you've got to be European, at the end of the day.' It is not that identity causes support, as many researchers would wish to believe; it is simply that individuals interpret the question of identification as a question about their support for the European unification process.

Yet another group of people use the opportunity afforded by the interviewer who asks them whether they identify as European to condense in their assertion of a European identification the sense of distinction to which they feel entitled because of having travelled abroad or learned foreign languages. Finally, in multinational states like Spain or Britain, disaffected members of the Spanish state say European when they want to say *Not National*. To be sure, one encounters the occasional individual who genuinely expresses a sense of identification with Europe based on love for its culture or appreciation of the European Union's economic and political achievements. But individuals like these are so hard to find that one could as well accept that Europe does not even exist as an emergent community. I would even go further and venture, with Favell (2008), that the European economic and political space promotes instead the emergence of denationalized/post-national individuals and offers them the possibility of staying away from the oppressive nationalism of their countries of origin.

One may speculate about the implications of building Europe on such a flimsy communal basis as described above. What meets the eye, however, is how far European integration has gone without a population imbued with a sense of Europeanness. Either the artichoke's heart is much smaller than

Hoffman (1966) thought or one has to agree that European citizens are more receptive to the idea of a post-national state than most scholars of nationalism would ever have expected. Of course, there is a third possibility, not to be ruled out: that citizens are largely unaware of the European Union's actual impact on their lives and the degree to which sovereignty has been transferred from states to European Union institutions. The main problem is that the lack of a strong political or cultural identity foundation makes the project of European integration more vulnerable to reversal than it would be if a stronger community of people identified as Europeans sustained it. For those who think that the European Union is a guarantee of peace in Europe, this should come as a rather bleak prospect. On a more optimistic vein, one could place one's bets on the possibility that the gradual expansion and encompassing character of transnational networks may provide the necessary glue for the irreversibility of the European project.

Framing Europe

Individuals are both agents and products of socialization processes, which more than ever take place through mass media. The more removed an issue is from the individual, the more he or she is subject to these secondary socialization processes. European integration and the European Union fall into the category of objects that are far removed from daily personal experiences. The European Union certainly affects its citizens' lives. But it operates through national administrations, thus sustaining the illusion among citizens that it is governments and not the EU who are responsible for the laws and policies that impact on their lives. National governments themselves do little to enlighten citizens about the fact that all they very often do is transpose or execute European Union policies.

Europeans are increasingly aware, however, of experiences and changes in their lives that they owe to the European Union. Surveys reveal, in particular, that people now recognize European Union achievements such as the Euro, the Erasmus Program, and European Union funding for infrastructural projects. This is still little, however, and popular representations of the European Union still mirror those portrayed in media discourse. Because of this, a shared representation of the European Union as a primarily economic and democratic space has spread across Europe (see Table 16.4). This shared representation includes other elements emphasized in media accounts of the European Union, such as the erosion of national sovereignty and the chaotic character of the European Commission's bureaucracy. European populations emerge as agents of their own representations of Europe only when they imagine it as a geographic space that allows for the free movement of persons. This is indeed, one of the most prevalent representations of Europe among the population, as demonstrated both by European-wide surveys (see Eurobarometer 67.1 from

Table 16.4 Representations of the European Union and European integration in Germany, Spain, and Britain, by city (number of respondents who mention a particular topic)

	Germany	Spain	United Kingdom	Total
Economic themes (trade, market)	45	39	45	129
States are too small to compete	26	30	23	79
Removal of barriers to movement	23	19	25	67
EU governance	22	18	30	70
Consequences of free movement on competition	**20**	1		21
Democratic deficit	17	4	6	27
WWII as motive for support	**19**			19
Peace	20	5	17	42
Understanding between peoples	21	15	17	53
Modernization of the country	1	**17**	6	24
CAP	5	27	15	47
Structural/regional funds	2	22	15	39
Against the country's isolation	1	**12**	2	15
Lack of voice on European affairs	2	12	6	20
Sovereignty and identity	3	4	**18**	25
Social benefits	3	8	13	24
Total	56	51	53	160

Source: Personal interviews with ordinary citizens and local elites (1996–7).

2007) and my own ethnographic work in Germany, Spain, and the United Kingdom. The peoples of Europe also slightly depart from elites in placing greater emphasis on the European Union's historical contribution to peace and understanding (for similar findings in Poland, see Bücker forthcoming).

One can thus assert the existence of a shared image of Europe across the European Union's member states. In other words, the beast looks approximately the same whether one looks at it from Estonia or from Portugal. Nevertheless, one still discovers cross-national contrasts. These contrasts are interesting from the viewpoint of a sociology of European culture, even though they do little more than shape the discursive styles around the topic of the European Union. German citizens' emphasis on the Second World War or Spanish citizens' emphasis on the European Union's expected impact on Spain's modernization, or in making Spain a significant actor on the world stage, are examples of relatively inconsequential frames. They are used widely, but they are used both by those who criticize and by those who support European integration and the European Union. The former sometimes refer to them only to then invoke even more powerful arguments in order to oppose European integration or to express lassitude or contempt for those who use them in support of European integration. Meanwhile, the latter refer to them as the main reason why they stand behind the European project.

Sometimes, however, framing contrasts are consequential, for they decisively shape attitudes to European integration. The main example of such frames is the British representation of the European Union as an institutional framework that threatens Britain's national identity. Statistical analysis demonstrates that not only does this representation generally differentiate supporters from opponents of European integration but that it decisively contributes to the explanation of the relatively low levels of support for the European Union in Great Britain. In fact, if it does not completely account for the contrasts in support for the European Union between Great Britain and other countries, it is because an expression of fear for the loss of national identity is often just a pious way of expressing one's rejection of membership in the European Union.

Consequential or not for the process of European integration, the distinctive features of national representations of the European Union, whether at the elite or citizen levels, resonate with salient aspects of these countries' political cultures, including the public intellectuals' discussions on Europe. The use of the Second World War frame by West Germans resonates with the continuing but now declining importance of the Second World War in West German political discourse and historical memory. The emphasis on modernization and on breaking with the country's international isolation in Spanish representations of the European Union echoes long-standing intellectual and political debates dating back to the last third of the nineteenth century. Although this debate is over, as Closa and Barroso point out in Chapter 10, largely because the debate was won by the pro-Europeans, the modernization and isolation frames loom large in both public and citizen discourse on Europe. Finally, the emphasis on national identity, on Britain's cultural distinctiveness, has been a constant in British twentieth-century political and cultural debates. The *Xenophobe's Guide to Europe*, a series edited in London and found in many airports, provides an extreme illustration of this widespread British view of Europe as both alien and hopelessly diverse.

The citizens' Europe

Just as popular representations of Europe largely mirror those of political elites, citizens' political identity projects for Europe, sketchy as they are, strongly resemble those discussed in the public sphere. Needless to say, the majority of the population has never reflected on the European Union as a project. They take it as it comes. Occasionally, they even reject proposals submitted to their approval. But these 'No' votes express less a rejection of the specific integration projects on which they are voting than deep unease among large segments of the population about larger processes such as global competition and migration. Lack of clear commitment by political elites to a social Europe may contribute to the citizens' channelling of frustration against the European Union whenever they are asked to vote on a reform treaty.

331

Surveys have shown quite consistently that populations are ahead of their political elites in calling for a strong European foreign policy and even a European army. On close inspection, however, there is little difference between the rhetorical calls for a political Europe that one constantly hears from political elites and people's support for common foreign affairs and defence policies. Once one scratches below the surface, as I did in my qualitative study of German, British, and Spanish conceptualizations of the European Union, it becomes clear that almost no one contemplates more than intergovernmental cooperation and consensus-seeking methods. What people really express through their calls for a common foreign affairs and defence policy is their desire for a Europe that speaks with one voice; that is, that they ALL agree on the issues discussed. More generally, the citizens of Europe rarely go beyond imagining a European Union with more competences but little surrender of sovereignty. In fact, many citizens that I interviewed were surprised and even discomfited upon learning how much sovereignty has already been transferred to the European Union. The reality is that most citizens are unaware of the extent to which decisions in the European Union can be taken without the country representatives' consent. One reason why Britons lean on the side of those opposed to more transfers of competences is precisely that they have been repeatedly told that transfers of competences very often mean a surrender of sovereignty.

Conclusion

This chapter has examined the prevalence of 'European stories' from various angles, all related to different meanings and uses of the term 'identity'. I have examined how political elites and ordinary citizens conceptualize or represent Europe. This is a story about 'identity' as self-representation, the third sense of Brubaker's and Cooper's discussion of the term identity (Brubaker and Cooper 2002). I have examined the degree to which ordinary citizens identify as 'Europeans', thus connecting my discussion of 'identity' to Brubaker's and Cooper's second understanding of the term, as 'identification'. Finally, I have examined political elites' and ordinary citizens' political identity projects. While this use of the term 'identity' again corresponds to Brubaker's and Cooper's equation between identity and self-understanding, it is better captured by Checkel's and Katzenstein's conceptualization of identity as process (Checkel and Katzenstein 2008).

However one uses the term identity in connection with European integration and the European Union, what one sees is that public actors and citizens pretty much share the same 'European story', with similar cross-national representations of the European Union and a common political identity project. This similarity in the European story shared by public actors and the populations at large contrasts with the diversity of European stories that we find among the intellectuals covered in this book. It would be worth the effort to enquire about the mechanisms that explain why the stories told by intellectuals do not feature more prominently in the public sphere. Does it have to do with their lack of institutionalization in educational curricula? Does it have to do with inequalities in access to education? Or does it reflect the national intellectuals' failure to persuade their populations?

Some researchers would not be very happy with the 'European story' that prevails among publics and citizens that I have told above, because they would like the European Union to be more than an efficient bureaucratic machine, a guarantee of peace, and a space where individuals can move freely. This is a reason why they revel in the little battles at the helm of the European Union and in the contrasting levels of support one observes in different countries, as if this exercise would help exorcize the sober realization that after fifty years the European project may have reached its natural limits. But reality is stubborn, and this is a reason why the nicely packaged reform treaties of the last few years have been defeated not in Eurosceptic Britain, Austria, or Poland, but rather in Europhile France, the Netherlands, and Ireland. More ambitious 'Europhiles' may have to come to grips with this reality after all and look elsewhere for solutions to Europe's ills and secular decline.

Conclusion

Echoes and Polyphony

In Praise of Europe's Narrative Diversity*

Janie Pélabay, Kalypso Nicolaïdis, and Justine Lacroix

> *'Ni tout à fait la même,*
> *ni tout à fait une autre'*
>
> (Marcel Proust, *Albertine disparue*)

Behold our Europes! Europe invented, possessed, reified in the core – Germany, France, Italy; Europe othered, appropriated, enlisted in its borderlands – Great Britain, Greece, Ireland, or Spain; Europe returned, revealed, defied in the East – Poland, the Czech Republic, or Romania; Europe imagined, revered, resented in the limes – Norway or Turkey. If this book tells one story, it is that Europe is debated, deconstructed, debunked, and demystified in thousands of different ways across Europe. And as they do so, European intellectuals from different traditions seem to disagree about an evanescent Europe, *pas tout à fait la même, pas tout à fait une autre*, across ideologies, national traditions, and disciplinary biases.

In this conclusion to *European Stories*, we seek to draw together common threads from the chapters presented in this volume, each analysing specific national debates. What do we find?

First, we conclude that the quest for a unique and unanimous 'European narrative' as an answer to the EU's legitimacy challenge is a non-starter. The pluralism that characterizes Europe's cultures and politics, Europe's socio-economic systems, and Europe's national bargains extends perhaps even more deeply to its intellectual traditions, thus giving rise to a 'deep diversity' of narratives about Europe and the EU.[1] More importantly for our purposes, as

---

* We would like to express our gratefulness to Gabi Maas for her insightful comments on this chapter.

[1] For prior work on narrative diversity in Europe, see Nicolaïdis and Pélabay 2007 and 2008.

our national accounts make clear, this narrative diversity that animates intellectual debates, and beyond them the EU's political life, should not be reduced to the mere juxtaposition of supposedly clear and homogeneous national narratives about Europe. This book makes a case for insisting that we must resist the tendency to ascribe specific European narratives to different national 'collective selves'. In this volume, we find different focuses and cleavages, grounds for different fears and hopes, *within* each national debate about Europe; and despite the difficulty of translation between different intellectual 'languages' – as well as between our national languages literally speaking[2] – we also find multiple echoes between these conversations that are woven into a polyphony of sorts, the European way.

In short, consistent with Liebert's insightful notion of contentious European democracy,[3] the chapters in this book tell us not only about the inner tensions within each national context, but also about a number of transverse cleavages and – still fragile – transnational narratives emerging from lines of contestation that cut across the boundaries between member states. Could it be their combination into a grand and extravagant polyphony that is the ultimate European story?

Intellectuals, of course, do not speak like politicians: their views on the EU tend to be shaped by a core of abstract and normative statements. This principles-oriented approach is applied to what John Erik Fossum and Cathrine Holst qualify as the European experiment, that is, the EU apprehended as 'a testing ground for ideas, principles, procedures, and institutional arrangements'.[4] This is not to say that intellectuals' views are not context-dependent or historically framed: on the contrary, intellectual debates about the EU are significantly coloured by the discursive contents of each political culture, including *longue durée* frames of reference, from the birth of some European nations in the nineteenth century to the earlier foundational myths of ancient Greeks, Celtic times, or Ottoman grandeur.[5] So much so that the reference to each specific national project may appear unrelenting and somewhat obsessive in the debate over a Europe that is supposed to transcend them. Yet the debates that we witness across Europe do not generally oppose one national project to another but highlight diverging visions *inside* each country on how the European project affects the nation and vice versa.

Which brings us to the normative front where we emerge from this intellectual journey. We find solid reasons to counter the idea that often refers to thick

---

[2] It is interesting to note in particular that the impression that English has become the lingua franca of intellectuals around Europe is clearly biased, as it simply reflects the segment of European debate that can be accessed across borders. Most of our chapters cite extensively from works in the national language.

[3] See Ulrike Liebert, in this volume.

[4] See John Erik Fossum and Cathrine Holst, in this volume.

[5] See Mario Telò, in this volume.

consensus on representation of the polity as a necessity if the country is to hold together – or rather, the idea that this axiom necessarily applies to the EU construct. Instead, the concept of deep diversity[6] allows for a plurality of equally acceptable ways of belonging and feeling allegiance to the political community, at least when the political entity at issue is the EU. Indeed, this 'union of states and of peoples', this 'demoi-cracy in the making' (Nicolaïdis 2004a), rests on practices of interpretation and negotiation that reflect strong – yet reasonable – disagreements between its many component parts on the norms and goals that underpin the process of European integration. In the end, we believe that democratic life in the EU can only be enhanced by such a great variety of diverging and competing stories about Europe as a whole, and about its current institutional translation through the EU.

Our praise of narrative diversity, however, does not imply a denial of any common core. To be sure, European citizens, peoples, and member states do seem to share a certain inclination for reiterating their commitment to universal political principles and purposes – freedom, peace, the rule of law, prosperity, solidarity, fundamental rights, and social justice, for example (Garton Ash 2007c). These common principles are arguably the object of a 'soft consensus' within the EU. A similar kind of consensus is depicted by Juan Díez Medrano, who argues in the preceding chapter that political elites and ordinary citizens tend to converge in their stories about the EU, since they apprehend Europe in the same way, namely, as a market founded on democratic values.[7]

In our view, however, such a common core does not take us very far. The vague image of the EU as both 'a market and a democratic club' is too general to prevent the disagreements and cleavages identified in this volume. For the kind of pluralism that most of the authors emphasize when investigating their national landscape has to do with how various intellectuals translate a set of fundamental but abstract norms into the concrete workings of the EU polity. When it comes to offering an interpretation of the so-called 'shared values' or giving an account of what 'market democracy' means in practice, narrative diversity prevails.

Far from convergent and consensual, the various 'European stories' which emerge from the intellectual debates considered in this volume thus provide deeply contrasting visions of what the Union *is*, or *should* be. There is of course the divide between the EU's discontents and the EU's cheerleaders. We might also simply contrast descriptive accounts of European integration which seem hardly compatible. Other visions again put forward normative propositions for the future EU that are grounded on conflicting expectations. And even where there is overwhelming support for the EU – as in Spain where Europe is

---

[6] The concept of 'deep diversity' is articulated by Taylor 1993. For a study of this concept applied to the EU, see Pélabay 2009.

[7] See Juan Díez Medrano, in this volume.

conceived as a 'national project',[8] or in Germany where European integration has long appeared as 'an unquestioned, or even unquestionable, good'[9] – the intellectual debates about the EU act as a catalyst of disagreements, revealing profound axiological cleavages – notably with regard to political ideals inherited from modernity as will be discussed below, as well as the nature and scope of liberal democracy.

Unsurprisingly, intellectuals have found a wide selection of labels to designate the object of their scorn or desire that is 'Europe'. Those who disapprove of EU membership tend to portray the Union as an artificial construct, since for them there is no European heritage, identity, or people, but only national ones; some go further and see the EU as an identity threat – to give a radical example, the *civitas diaboli* picture remobilized by some Polish Catholic conservatives;[10] or as an 'ethical hazard' which in Noica's view has replaced the ideology of state socialism; or, most succinctly, as a 'giant supermarket' exclusively focused on material goals.[11] On the other side of the spectrum, Europhiles find a variety of labels to express their approval, from an established Western civilization to a moral 'community of values' consistent with the image of a humanist Europe,[12] a legal community based on human rights, an 'anchor for democratic consolidation',[13] a provider of social goods, or a normative power capable of transforming the world in its own image. One of the contributions of this book is to take us on a journey beneath the labels attached to the traditional Europhobe–Europhile debate.

The range of contentious issues in the deliberative space carved by our European intellectuals is huge. In this concluding chapter, we identify four types of debate which we believe constitute the main common threads that run through our chapters.[14] In each case we specify the nature of the debate, the object of the debate, and what can be seen as the normative horizon of the debate, seen as a promise by some and contested by others. The first debate we call *relational* in that it focuses on the theme of identity, broadly understood, and on the implicit or explicit disagreements on whether, and how, mutual recognition is to be achieved both inside and outside the EU. The second debate, which is *civilizational* in nature, deals with the issue of progress as the contested promise of European modernity. The third debate is *political*, dealing

---

[8] See Carlos Closa and Antonio Barroso, in this volume.

[9] See Jan-Werner Müller, in this volume.

[10] See Magdalena Góra and Zdzisław Mach, in this volume.

[11] For the last two 'labels', see Daniel Barbu, in this volume.

[12] See, for instance, the chapter on Norway by John Erik Fossum and Cathrine Holst; but a similar vision appears in the chapters devoted to Greece and Italy.

[13] See the chapter on Spain, by Carlos Closa and Antonio Barroso, in this volume.

[14] We can think of these as transnational contentions in the sense of 'contentious politics', and focusing on ordinary people (as opposed to elite interaction). A quantitative research work devoted to mapping transnational contention has been undertaken by Imig and Tarrow 2001 in the field of political sociology.

as it does with the core idea of integration – in other words, the challenge of 'unity in diversity' and the contested promise of liberal democracy. And with the fourth, *definitional*, debate we enter the controversy on the very nature of the European polity and the question of its *finalité*. Finally, with a view to clarifying what is theoretically and practically at stake in Europe's narrative diversity, we contrast two competing modes for debating Europe, namely self-clarification and public justification.

A relational debate: Identity and the contested promise of mutual recognition

Unsurprisingly, most of the chapters in this volume reveal the crucial import-ance of the reference to their own national project as the preferred prism through which many intellectuals tackle the EU. To be sure, this obsession does not contradict our central argument that there is no such thing as a *French* or *Polish* vision of Europe, since part of the national debate is precisely *over* this national referent, whether it is pertinent or not, and if it is pertinent what it implies: the national prism to discuss Europe can accommodate radically differ-ent ideas about Europe, about the national project, and about the relationship between the two.

More generally, whether national identity is seen as bolstered or denied intellectuals worry about how Europe affects it and how it affects Europe in return. But while we find such identity warriors across member states we also find their counterparts, intellectuals who worry that identity-talk is generally dangerous, or at least misguided. Indeed, the debate – within and across bor-ders – often pits those who seek to ground identity through othering against those who are more interested in mutual recognition between peoples, turning away from essentialist identity preoccupations. These identity debates, we find, are always relational in one way or another, whether the relation is to one's neighbours, one's past or some other 'other'. Before we review these different angles, we start by embedding the national prism in a broader context.

From national to European: the mosaic of intellectual prisms

Again and again, Europe and its EU incarnation serve as a foil to the fate of each country in their respective domestic debating spaces (Díez Medrano 2003; Leerssen 2007). Certainly, the EU is discussed first and foremost not as an object in itself, but rather in terms of how it either reinforces or endangers the nation – or more precisely a specific national project and particular vision. In other words, the debate is less about the EU itself than about what the EU means for *France*, for *Italy*, for *Poland* – or for *Britishness, Greekness, Germanness*. The positive assessment expressed in the slogan 'Europe is good for Ireland' illustrates the tendency to view the EU through the exclusive prism of national identity and interest. The same goes for those intellectuals in Poland or Germany who apprehend Europe as protecting the nation from its internal evils, or for the Europeanist views articulated in Spain and Greece that represent the EU as the best solution to the country's problems. On the other side, we find the same reference framing intellectual visions of the likely negative effects of European integration on the nation. The various facets of these debates all revolve around a series of 'relational' questions: to what extent is the EU itself like 'our country' or antithetic to 'our values', 'our story', 'our national project'? Can this new kid on the block, the EU, even perhaps allow us to reinvent the national? Or is the EU the conduit for the domination of 'our country' by bigger ones? In short, national debates about Europe do not generally start with the *abstract* notion of the nation-state and its relations to Europe, but rather with the *specific* nation-building project at hand, and – what is more – with contrasting interpretations of it.

Inescapable though it may seem, the nation is not the only prism through which intellectual debates on the EU are framed and articulated. In the chapters collected in this volume, we also find other 'intellectual gates' to discussing European integration which serve as 'connecting points' between the domestic sphere and the European level.[15] These can be 'regional' narratives, like the 'Nordic model'[16] and the paradigmatic 'Central Europe' considered by Jan Křen as 'a conceptual stage on the way to Europe as a whole',[17] or 'cultural' narratives, like Hellenism or Celtic heritage. Finally, there are narratives whose subject is 'Europe' as such – whether this term refers to a European 'spirit' or self or whether it designates a political project, a set of institutions and policies, or even a bureaucratic body also named 'Brussels'.

Peripheral angst: Self-assertion through recentring

From these intellectual prisms, the dichotomy 'centre versus periphery' emerges in full relief. To start with, references to nationhood are predominantly associated with Eurosceptical attitudes. In reaction to what the likes of Václav Klaus see as the denationalization of citizenship associated with the EU – and against their compatriots who support it – a brand of intellectuals found especially in Poland, the Czech Republic, and Ireland converge in championing their vision of nationhood in a *defensive mode*. The Polish debate on this issue is animated by the resurgent polarization between, on one hand, a homogenized

---

[15] We borrow the phrases 'intellectual gate' and 'connecting point' from Muriel Blaive and Nicolas Maslowski and from Katy Hayward respectively.

[16] See John Erik Fossum and Cathrine Holst, in this volume.

[17] See, for instance, the chapter on the Czech Republic, by Muriel Blaive and Nicolas Maslowski, in this volume.

and essentialist vision of nationhood inspired by Roman Dmowski's integral nationalism and, on the other, a multi-ethnic vision inspired by Józef Piłsudski. As Mach and Góra show in their chapter, a post-romantic speech now places 'national uprising, messianism, martyrdom, the Christian crusade' at the core of Polishness.[18] Similar views on identity and nationality are widespread in the Czech Republic via Václav Klaus' discourse which reactivates the pan-Slavist and anti-Western ideology inherited from the communist regime. Another variant of the *defensive mode* can be found in countries such as Greece, where Diamandouros' culture of the underdog (Diamandouros 1997) leads to an ethnocentric exaggeration of both past glory and present misery, as discussed by Pagoulatos and Yataganas in this volume. In these debates, Europe is targeted by one camp as a cause of national demise and enlisted by the other as its remedy.

Indeed, if peripheral countries are often home to intellectuals who perceive the EU as a threat to the nation, they are also home to what we could call intellectual strategies of recentring: 'our nation may be small but it is at the core'. This is the case of Irish or Greek claims to have played a vital role in moulding European culture: the struggle for leadership within the competitive market of cultural foundations and the assertion of a civilizational centrality reflects, on the narrative front, the institutional squabbles regarding state equality. In these two countries, the rhetoric of exceptionalism echoes the complex dialectic between senses of superiority and inferiority, as with the claim for Romania's contribution to European integration as an effort to keep alive the 'pre-political spirit of Europe'.[19] A similar version of the centre/periphery antagonism underlies Norwegian debates about EU membership, which reactivate structural socio-cultural and territorial cleavages that strongly marked *longue durée* national memory in that country. As for regional prisms, the use of the concepts of Slavism, Central Europe, or even Central-Europeanness in Poland and the Czech Republic serves as a remedy to the existential (much more than geopolitical) peripheral role ascribed to Eastern member states.

Arguably, many of the criticisms advanced by intellectuals 'from the periphery' are not targeted at Europe and the EU in general; rather, they express a reluctance to adhere to a hegemonic, ready-made narrative of European integration. To put it differently, what is refused is a form of 'Europeanization through imitation'. Europeanization – they argue – is a multi-faceted process with many possible paths. Consequently, they urge the self-confident laudators of 'Europe' in their own country to admit that their dominant view is controversial. Grounded on the memory of past domination or colonialism, or based on what the Turkish intellectual Ali Bulaç considered to be an ontological

---

[18] See Magdalena Góra and Zdzisław Mach, in this volume.
[19] See Daniel Barbu, in this volume.

incapacity in mainstream European circles of 'acknowledging the truths of "Others"',[20] such a claim finds growing support. This is particularly the case amongst intellectuals from the 'new' member states. An illustration of this is the Central European appeal for an expansion of European understanding launched by Marek A. Cichocki. In his view, the time is ripe to acknowledge that there was not just one 'European Enlightenment' from which we can derive practical conclusions for the European Union, and that the 'predominantly Franco-German narrative is no longer appropriate'. Hence he makes a case for the enrichment of the European narrative with a variety of different forms of the Enlightenment occurring side by side (Cichocki 2007).

It is now, of course, generally accepted that what Cichocki calls the Franco-German narrative is of little relevance to the contemporary EU. Indeed, there are plenty of intellectuals on both sides who also fear that their national identity might be soluble in Europe. And often, support for the EU in France and Germany is also framed – just as in Ireland or Greece – by the conviction that the Union is simply a France or Germany writ large. Implicitly or explicitly, the argument goes, Europe is good because and when it is made in our image, or better still because it is of our making.

Neighbours and frères-ennemis: from 'them' to 'us'?

Peripheral angst is but one variant of a more general line of debate revolving around the relation to the Other, within or outside the EU. Here, the dividing line across countries pits those who are prone to adopt a rhetoric of 'us' versus 'them' against those who resist this logic. The 'us' language prevails in narratives which insist that EU member states are part of a larger 'European we'. Conversely, when the relations between member states are viewed on the model of international relations or foreign affairs, the use of 'us' is reserved for the national community, while 'them' refers to the rest of the EU. As analysed in the chapter on Poland, the transition from 'them' to 'us' is typically made possible through a change in the perception of previous neighbours – Germany in the case at hand – from a threat to a possible cooperation partner, or even an ally, often with the help of the EU. But whether the *frère-ennemi* turned partner transforms all other Europeans into members of a 'we' is open to debate.

When applied to 'external' Others, we of course find debates about Europe and Islam, be it within or outside its borders. But at least in the chapters that make up this book, this relational debate is mainly about the appropriate partnership between Europe and the United States. Some intellectuals argue in favour of a strong EU–US partnership – from Václav Havel or Timothy Garton Ash to the Italian pro-Atlanticist shift identified by Mario Telò as a by-product

---

[20] See Nora Fisher Onar and Ahmet Evin, in this volume.

of the 'Berlusconian revolution'. In contrast, a 'Mediterranean Europe' has emerged as a possible anti-imperialist EU, converging with the concerns expressed from within the British left by Perry Anderson – who deplores the lack of independence from the US – and by Tom Nairn, who feared that the suggestion of increasing European–American partnership would turn into a process of 'self-colonization'. The US, then, is the common topic of discussion around which European debate has constantly gravitated, even if Europeans passionately disagree on whether it is about a 'we' or a 'them'.

A community of memory? Whose memories?

Ultimately, debates over identity tend to turn around memory and intellectuals' relationships with the intertwined national and European pasts. Perhaps the past, loved or loathed, is the real other of Europe. Here, the fundamental cleavage is mainly between an apologetic approach to national history and a self-critical thinking applied to collective memory. In Poland, for instance, many have advocated the 'defalsification' of a collective memory marked by decades of communism, and subsequently a critical rethinking of the national past in order to build a double identity, both national and European – or even a 'European-oriented' new identity. But at the same time, our Polish chapter documents the weak propensity in Poland for recognizing the harm and historical injustice done to others, thus noting that Polish opinion seems to be devoid of any 'post-colonial complex'. And indeed, self-criticism finds little room in an intellectual environment dominated by discourses warning against 'nothingness' and the 'lack of memory foundations'.[21]

Such a tension between self-reflection and apologia can be found in other national debates too. In Ireland, the experience of colonialism teaches that the European past is composed of national traditions which are capable of 'barbarism' as well as 'beauty'. This is a crucial lesson if we are to learn from the negative aspects of national history and give impetus to mutual recognition. But, as argued by Hayward, this self-critical attitude is far from predominant. Instead, a rather apologetic relation to the national 'heritage' tends to focus the debate towards 'how best to reclaim Ireland's past', even at the risk of verging on an intoxication with such a mythical history.[22] This 'hyperbolic' sense of the past is arguably shared by a large number of Greek intellectuals, except that in their case – they claim – the national inheritance has benefited the whole of Europe, and indeed, the world.[23] By contrast, the anti-nationalist and pacifist narratives analysed by Mario Telò tend to encourage critical self-appropriation of the past in Italy. This is all the more so in the case of Germany, where the

---

[21] See Magdalena Góra and Zdzisław Mach, in this volume.
[22] See Katy Hayward, in this volume.
[23] See Georges Pagoulatos and Xenophon Yataganas, in this volume.

contribution to the construction of a united and peaceful Europe proceeds from a desire for 'moral rehabilitation' grounded on historical sin.

Finally, the dichotomy 'continuity versus discontinuity' appears in several European stories analysed in this book, with both perceptions usually coexisting for the same country depending on *which* history is referred to.[24] Hence the gap between, on one hand, EU membership as an extension of the nation's history – or more precisely of what is perceived and glorified as its most positive achievement – and, on the other, EU membership as a break with what is perceived as its most contemptible past (communism, fascism, collaboration, colonialism). For Italians, the EU vindicates their turning their back on Mussolini, while for the French it reverberates with memories of revolution and resistance. For Greece or Ireland, EU membership has been viewed by the mainstream as a means to free the nation from the colonial yoke, but at the same time as a reconnection with a more remote past. The 'myth of continuity' that George Pagoulatos and Xenophon Yataganas discern in Greek intellectuals' visions of Europe may well reveal some anxieties about the future in general, and about the possible role of Greece within the EU in particular. We also see how historical rivalries throughout Europe are offered up to the altar of a project meant to remember and transcend them (France and Germany, France and Britain, Greece and Turkey, Poland and Germany, etc.). Alternatively, the EU may entrench elements of some traditional dominances (France, Italy), or it may help to enhance a country's power on the continent (small states in general, post-communist states). To sum up, all EU members use the EU in one way or another as a means of renegotiating their own history and the relationship between their respective histories. Just like national identities in general, patterns of continuity and discontinuity are thus constructed to *Europeanize* national history to one's national advantage.

Turning to the European prism, these national differences can of course be apprehended under an overarching tension when it comes to the past of Europe as a whole. Many intellectuals across member states tend to chime with the idea of the EU as a 'community of memory', a means of atonement for Europe's cardinal sin, the transformation of two continent-wide civil wars into world wars. Others, however, prefer to put a more positive emphasis on Europe's Enlightenment heritage – a continuity argument – or conversely on its break with the various pasts of some of its member states – a discontinuity argument. Under the latter, 'virgin birth' understanding, the EU was designed on a blank slate and does not need to atone for the colonial legacies of the former metropolises in its midst. It is noteworthy, however, that the colonial pasts of some of the member states and the EU's pattern of relations with previously colonized non-European peoples is scarcely discussed by the intellectuals considered in

---

[24] We are grateful to Gabi Maas for helping us to clarify this point.

this volume. In this, they may simply reflect a general pattern of denial in European societies. The memory of European intellectuals, as well as European publics, is indeed selective.

To sum up, we have indicated here just some of the variants of the identity debates that readers will find scattered across the chapters of the book. It is remarkable, however, to note that underlying much of the argument around identity lies an almost universally shared sense of the exceptionalism of one's national project, the conviction that one's national history is not only unique but uniquely related – positively or negatively – to European history. Given the relatively (though increasingly less) closed nature of these national debates, it is even doubtful that we can observe an actual 'clash of exceptionalisms'. Instead, we find a happy coexistence between similar yet contradictory claims to exceptional status, that are each oblivious to such ironies. It remains to be seen whether the alternative gates or prisms used by intellectuals to 'enter' debates around Europe will eventually diversify, leaving their *patrie* to compete with other frames for their musings about Europe.

A civilizational debate: Progress and the contested promise of European modernity

We can now turn from the range of particulars, each concerned with the fate of their own national project, to more generic transnational cleavages. As far back as we can go – i.e. six or seven centuries ago (see the discussion on emergence of intellectuals in the introduction to this volume as well as Francis Cheneval's chapter) – 'intellectuals' in Europe have clashed around the issue of unification of the continent, and about whether such unification could in turn be seen as one version of the bigger question of what constitutes progress, however this may be defined in a given era and by a given author or group of authors. Is progress best served by forming smaller or larger political entities? Does it point in the direction of state sovereignty or continental unity? In our introduction, we referred to this *longue durée* discussion over the nature of progress as the first-order debate that underpins the continuous pendulum between the national and supranational poles. At the end of our intellectual journey, we find that the EU is discussed as the embodiment of 'European modernity' and its promise of progress. The question as to whether this promise has been kept or broken is at the core of our intellectual debates, thus reminding us that progress is neither unequivocal nor irrevocable.

Modernity and its European nemesis

For many intellectuals, European integration has come to epitomize progress, whilst for others it is the most evident symptom of the 'diseases' caused by modernity in the public domain. Almost all of our countries have seen modernity and its European nemesis alternatively celebrated and put on trial, although on different grounds and with different reference points.

Those who regard the process of modernization by and large through the lens of progress tend to define it broadly, notably through its extension to the requisites of social justice or to certain forms of egalitarianism or multiculturalism.[25] The fact remains, however, that they tend to consider the ideals attached to the Enlightenment, political modernity, rationalism, secularism, and universalism to be self-evident normative benchmarks for the European project. In this 'Europeanist-modernist' perspective – widely represented in Spain and Italy – European integration is viewed as an obvious path towards democratization, social progress, and the implementation of modern values. But precisely because this diagnosis is presented as so unproblematic, it prompts concern among those who fear that a process of Europeanization unilaterally conducted in the name of 'modernity' will act as a straitjacket for many countries. Scholars in this vein resent the one-size-fits-all, EU-led hegemonic interpretation of 'European modernity'.

These anxieties may take various forms. One of them opens a debate about the *sources* of the 'modern European self'. In this debate, alternative sources – most noticeably Romanticism and Christianity – are invoked with a view to counterbalancing what is perceived as a dominant yet truncated picture of 'Enlightened Europe'. The predominance of a European narrative embedded in the legacy of Western Enlightenment is especially contested by intellectuals from the post-communist member states. Thus for instance, in the face of a universalistic rhetoric, 'post-romantic speeches' and calls for the community's distinctiveness have found a significant audience in Poland and the Czech Republic. To be sure, the dichotomy between universalism and particularism might appear too simplistic; but it clearly surfaces in intellectual debates on the EU.

The latter brings out another important aspect of modernity: secularism. On that subject, Polish pleas for the recognition of the Christian/Catholic sources of the 'European ethos' are paradigmatic. Behind this claim lie slightly different purposes: based on the concept of the *'ante-murale'* and supported by the discourse of 'martyrdom' and 'Christian crusade' as discussed above, some intellectuals exhort the Polish citizenry to engage in a double quest for moral integrity and cultural purity that tends to fuel a defensive and mistrustful attitude towards European integration; others encourage a more offensive attitude aiming to fulfil Poland's mission of 'bringing Christianity back to Europe'.

---

[25] This stance can be exemplified, among others, by Habermas' moral and political philosophy and its attempt to reformulate the Enlightenment ideal of progress through a 'post-metaphysical' vocabulary based on the notions of learning process, deliberative opinion formation, or cosmopolitan law.

This narrative of the saviour bears striking similarities with de Valera's speech on Ireland's religious and spiritual task in Europe. This discourse, with Herderian undertones, presents the Irish people as having made a unique contribution to 'European culture' and therefore deserving of special recognition. The 'Irish genius' – the argument goes – lies in its capacity to protect Europe from the dangers, and the decadence, that stem from a public culture disconnected from any transcendent framework and perverted by consumerism and the pursuit of material goods.[26] One might also refer to Greek 'communitarian' thinkers such as Yannaras, especially the members of the so-called 'neo-Orthodox movement', who promote a sense of 'particularist loyalty' to a 'warm' community shaped by the Greek-Christian tradition and worldview.[27]

It is worth pointing out that the controversy over the religious ethos and telos of the EU has gained a wider audience not only at the societal level but also within European academia where secularism, multiculturalism, and the accommodation of religious differences have become widely debated.[28] The debate mobilized and polarized large portions of public opinion around Europe, especially in Spain, Italy, Portugal, and France, where issues related to secularism are highly sensitive. Here, the divide is between secularism as a prerequisite for any political regime respectful of a plurality of comprehensive worldviews and secularism as a cause for the failure of Europe on the front of culture and civilization.

Universalism and secularism are thus two bones of contention that merge into a broader tendency which consists in appraising the EU in terms of the benefits and damages attributed to 'European modernity'. To be sure, except for those who lament the loss of 'organic solidarities' and 'holistic worldviews',[29] there are few intellectuals who explicitly contest the value attached to political modernity in general, and to the principles of liberal democracy in particular. Nevertheless, as we shall see, this does not preclude deep disagreements about the appropriate interpretation of these principles and their implementation within the EU. Moreover, emphasis put on progress in terms of freedom, education, or prosperity can coexist with a critical stance towards the consequences of modernization for public culture and democratic life in contemporary European societies.

---

[26] See Katy Hayward, in this volume.

[27] See George Pagoulatos and Xenophon Yataganas, in this volume.

[28] The debates were triggered by the question as to whether a reference to Europe's Christian roots should be included in the European Charter of Fundamental Rights and later in the Preamble of the Constitutional Treaty. See, for instance Weiler 2003b: in this essay, the prominent lawyer and transnational intellectual, well known in academia for his notion of 'constitutional tolerance', made a case against the 'denial' of the Christian roots of Europe. For critical reviews, see Howse 2004; Menéndez 2005; Pélabay 2008.

[29] See the analysis of the Romanian debate by Daniel Barbu, in this volume.

Europe and the pathologies of modernity

The latter line of debate is reminiscent of the philosophical discourse about the 'malaise of modernity',[30] a prevailing theme throughout this book – from the pleas for a 'return to metaphysics' and holistic (religious) orders to Václav Klaus' case against 'radical human-rightism', or the arguments about the shortcomings of modern individualism and procedural citizenship. The uncontrolled development of atomism and narcissism, the dominance of instrumental reason, the bureaucratization of state action, and the decline in civic participation appear frequently on the list of the 'pathologies' characteristic of this truncated vision of modernity. According to this diagnosis, some of the most complex problems currently faced by the European polity, including its 'democratic deficit', must be understood as a manifestation or radicalization of such 'pathologies'.

Finally, let us pick up the most radical vein within the rhetoric on the 'loss of meaning' associated with modernity and the European project, namely the discourse of those intellectuals who see the very process of European integration as synonymous with a decline in morality, culture, and religion. These radical critics – such as those we encounter, for instance, in Polish and Greek intellectual circles – warn against the extreme ethical and spiritual poverty of the EU caused by the erosion of any 'superior', transcendent horizon and of any traditional authority. These visions of Europe express a profound mistrust – if not an outright rejection – of modern ideals and processes, including the rationalization and autonomization of the political order. One of the most characteristic illustrations of this stance is provided here by the 'historicist counter-narrative of Europe' spread by the Orthodox Church in Romanian society and 'the revival of metaphysics' propped up by followers of Noica.[31]

This is not to say that intellectual debates about the EU have returned to rekindling the quarrel between *the Ancients and the Moderns*. At the very least, however, we have to admit that the 'European stories' told by certain branches of thought contribute to shaping a much contrasted picture of 'European modernity', which in turn supports a series of extremely ambivalent positions on EU membership. More often than not, the ambivalence lies in an attitude which consists in celebrating the great strides made in science and technology, the political advances in freedom of movement, and especially the increase in economic prosperity, while rejecting the spiritual, moral, and cultural impoverishment deemed to symbolize the 'negative' aspect of Europeanization. The separation of these two contrasting faces of modernity is exemplified in the Turkish debate by the 'tendency to treat "Europe" as a menu', that is, to adopt

---

[30] On this philosophical debate, see Habermas 1987; Taylor 1991.
[31] See Daniel Barbu, in this volume.

'the material aspects of "European" civilization' and to avoid embracing the underlying values and worldviews.[32]

Interestingly, this traditionalist and conservative intellectual sensitivity bemoaning the dominance of the market, the material, and the foreign in today's Europe converges with a left-wing anti-market and anti-globalization stance found across all member states. Both perceive the EU as a Trojan horse for cultural globalization, 'homogenization', and consumerism, which are the hallmarks of modernity's pathologies.

Ultimately, this 'civilizational' debate over European modernity not only pits different opinions about whether Europe contributes to progress against each other; it also spawns polarized views about what kind of progress actually matters – material, political, or spiritual. One sort of European modernity does not fit the bill for all.

A political debate: Integration and the contested promise of liberal democracy

If we take the idea of progress down one level of specificity and move from civilizational to more political controversies, we find that intellectuals across Europe disagree passionately on the most appropriate foundations for and forms of integration in a political community. In these debates, the various meanings of integration within states echo those attached to the EU as a whole, since on either level the question is how to reconcile unity and diversity, cohesion and tolerance, not only in the cultural realm where all tend to agree, but more controversially on the political and socio-economic planes. In short, how can different models of integration accommodate the requirements of pluralism in a given polity, on whatever scale?

In this sense, even if we follow Rawls' minimalist requirement for a consensus on the norms of justice within a 'well-ordered society' – a 'social union of social unions' – the EU would need to develop an overlapping consensus of overlapping consensuses, a contract between different social contracts as it were.[33] So to the extent that the EU makes them coexist it is legitimate for intellectuals to argue over what each of the component consensuses should be made of. And it is this normative agenda that is at stake as we watch debates unfold both over liberalism in general and over liberal democracy in particular.

---

[32] See Nora Fisher Onar and Ahmet Evin, in this volume.
[33] See Nicolaïdis and Pélabay 2007 and 2008.

Liberalism and its discontents

Throughout Europe, some criticize the EU for being too liberal, and others for not being liberal enough. As shown by Georgios Varouxakis, the suspected illiberalism of Continental Europe has long served as a cause of Euroscepticism in Britain, and still today British intellectuals' distrust of the EU is partly due to its lack of liberal credentials. On the other hand, there are critics of the EU who lament its liberal orientation, whether that means the drift towards a procedural pattern of democracy (as argued by the republican proponents of a robust democracy in France or Poland) or the hegemony of a neoliberal pattern of free market economy (as lamented by left-leaning intellectuals in many countries analysed in this volume). Along this ideological fault line, the debated attributes of liberalism include pluralism, legalism, state neutrality, and state–society relationships.

In line with British liberal intellectuals who have expressed concern about a perceived obsession with the uniformity of Continental Europe, one finds converging views of pluralism as a mainstay of European democracy in the Polish, French, German, and Italian contexts. These are currents of thought which celebrate the expression of social pluralism, the free flow of ideas and the plurality of worldviews as so many antidotes to totalitarianism and a political order based on what Ingolf Pernice called 'legal monism'.[34] In contrast, consistent with the Schmittian assumption that interest-group pluralism represents a threat to sovereign statehood, some intellectuals fear that the promotion of pluralism would undermine democracy, allowing for the capture of the state by special interests. Reiterating the conceptual opposition between holism and atomism that is a crucial aspect of the controversy on the 'malaise of modernity', intellectuals disagree about whether European integration has homogenizing or fragmenting effects: is the EU the incarnation of the dream of homogeneity or of the 'art of separation'?[35] Should the EU be contested for being a 'superpower' with homogenizing and imperialistic tendencies, or rather, in Noica's view, for realizing a 'civilization characterized by total disconnections and multiple partitions'?[36]

More generally, the kind of pluralism so feared by neo-Schmittians is often defended through rights-based discourses. Clashes over pluralism therefore lead to disagreements over the place that the rule of law should have in society. To be sure, the same fears as those found over pluralism also underlie the various critical stances about the prevalence of legal norms over civic virtues or, to put it differently, about the primacy of rights over duties. Echoing the idea expressed

---

[34] See Jan-Werner Müller, in this volume.

[35] This phrase is used by Walzer 1984 to criticise the liberal atomistic view of social and political order.

[36] See Daniel Barbu, in this volume.

by many Romanian intellectuals that the priority of rights is a self-defeating theory,[37] French intellectuals such as Gauchet view the EU as being in the grip of a 'religion of law' which exacerbates the damages caused by individualism and quite simply undermines the popular basis of democracy. Conversely, the picture of the EU drawn by French 'liberal-revolutionary' intellectuals emphasizes the anti-oppressive dimension of the claim for rights as well as their socially 'binding effects'. According to them, it is rather the inadequacy of the EU in implementing 'human rights politics' that reveals its democratic failure.[38]

Intellectuals also disagree over another tenet of political liberalism, namely state neutrality. Consistent with the civilizational claims analysed above, some Polish and Romanian intellectuals attack liberal impartiality and criticize that ideal for preventing the assertion of collective identity and memory in an affirmative way. Fustigating 'European amnesia', Romanian 'metaphysicians'[39] associate state neutrality with diseases such as relativism, secularism, and estrangement from tradition, while their Polish counterparts advocate 'a Roman-inspired system of law' and call for the consolidation of morality by faith and the return of the nation as a medium between the citizenry and what they call 'the absolute'. And while the nation is best placed to uphold the moral values in question, these critics also turn to the European project to urge their fellow Europeans to accept their own cultural, axiological, and religious partiality.

But then what should come first, state or civil society? And how should the EU affect state–society relations? A brand of intellectuals around Europe passionately resists the liberal 'primacy of politics', since the conduct of modernization/Europeanization from a purely political perspective is suspected of preventing marginalized cultures from wielding their spiritual influence over the continent.[40] This debate over 'the autonomy of the political' results, in a more precise form, in normative standpoints that set 'centralism' *against* 'independence of civil society' and 'statism' *against* 'constitutionalism', and converge in their extreme suspicion of the public domain per se. In this respect, Václav Klaus' assertion that the lack of state control over 'civil society' represents a danger to democracy is emblematic.[41]

On the other side, in Petr Pithart's view, a highly developed civil society is the best means of curbing the tendency to succumb to totalizing ideologies such as fascism or communism. Indeed, as Jan-Werner Müller points out, any attempt to restore the idea of a unitary state with a hierarchical administration is regarded by a number of German intellectuals as the potential reactivation of

[37] See Daniel Barbu, in this volume.
[38] See Justine Lacroix, in this volume.
[39] The calls for a 'return to metaphysics' (see Barbu's chapter in this volume) can be understood as opposed to Rawls' famous defence of his theory of justice as being 'political and not metaphysical'.
[40] See Daniel Barbu, in this volume.
[41] See Muriel Blaive and Nicolas Maslowski, in this volume.

political and intellectual traditions deeply compromised by Nazism. Furthermore, as explained by Muriel Blaive and Nicolas Maslowski, Václav Havel and his fellow opponents of communism celebrated Europe precisely for recognizing and protecting intermediary bodies between state and citizenry. Of course, this debate can be found across Europe, but it is perhaps especially acute in the new member states.

Finally, these debates often find another variant around the advocacy of American versus European versions of liberalism, a debate most famously addressed in 2003 by Habermas and Derrida, expanding on Habermas' vision of a distinctive 'European mentality'. As for this dichotomy, we can contrast a procedural and rights-based vision of justice characteristic of 'American' liberalism with a model supposedly more in line with a republican approach to political integration. In this volume, however, the most frequently discussed occurrence of such a dichotomy pertains to egalitarianism and social democracy. Across European debates in Poland, Italy, Britain, Germany, Greece, and Norway, a leftist-feminist-green and anti-globalization intellectual coalition emerges against an 'American' version of liberalism, associated with capitalism and the free market economy. A number of intellectuals in these countries condemn the EU for having being converted to economic neoliberalism, and call for re-orienting Europeanization towards a model more concerned with social justice, gender equality, and ecology. Alternatively, assuming that there is no going back, many among the British New Left proponents, including Anderson, have lost hope that the EEC/EU could be 'a vehicle for socialist reform'.[42] In Greece and Norway, meanwhile, the link between Europeanization and liberalization fuels intellectual resistance to European integration and the defence of national sovereignty. And yet, as explained by John Erik Fossum and Cathrine Holst, this attitude can also support a conception of the EU as 'a value community', in that it can give grounds for the promotion of the European social model which stands 'in opposition to unbridled American individualism'.

The preconditions of democracy and the national premise

Unsurprisingly, our chapters show that many intellectual debates on Europe revolve around the preconditions of democracy – understood in a broad sense as including both self-government and some kind of social equality. In particular, these discussions focus on the relevance of nationhood, both in its cultural facet (based on a common sense of ethnicity and cultural distinctiveness) and, more often, in its political dimension (pertaining to arguments such as statehood and popular sovereignty). Here, intellectual stances consist in reasserting

---

[42] See Georgios Varouxakis, in this volume.

or questioning the basic idea that there can be no democracy beyond the nation-state.

In the different chapters of this book, this premise comes in a variety of forms. In Norway, it impregnates what John Erik Fossum and Cathrine Holst depict as a 'taken-for-granted nationalism' espoused by the vast majority of academic intellectuals. In this ideological context, any infringement of state sovereignty is deemed to be so untenable that many prefer to adopt, so to speak, a politics of avoidance on such matters. By contrast, in Germany, France, and Britain, the controversy over the 'no democracy beyond the nation' axiom serves as the main motivational vector for embarking on the European debate. In Germany, the few suspicious attitudes towards European integration are framed by references to statehood as a precondition of democracy and constitutionalism.[43] Firmly established in the French political imaginary, this premise underlies criticisms of the EU advanced by the French 'national-republicans' who reiterate the classical idea that democratic legitimacy requires citizens to exert political authority.[44]

To this civic plea for an effective popular sovereignty some intellectuals add that the national embodiment of democracy is a prerequisite for implementing social justice policies, thus echoing the key thesis of Miller's 'liberal nationalism' as well as the British left-leaning criticism of the EU developed in the name of egalitarianism and progressive politics. On the opposite side of the British political spectrum, the very same premise leads right-wing Eurosceptics to consider the concept and practice of sovereignty pooling to be an 'absurdity'. Thus, according to Noel Malcolm, any sort of democratic politics is dependent not only on a real political authority over the legal order, but also on an 'established political community', where 'established' means that people should share 'the same customs, political traditions, and, above all, the same language'.[45]

At that point, political criticisms of sovereignty pooling meet culturalist claims for national integrity – such as that voiced in Britain by Roger Scruton, who asserts that England should be protected against its undoing by European 'transnational legislation'.[46] Moreover, these criticisms also bring tensions between the universal and the particular back to the fore, as shown by the French and German debates about constitutional patriotism. On this matter, thinkers close to the 'national-republican' paradigm in France and proponents of 'liberal nationalism' in Britain once again converge in reproaching an abstract universalism and a disengaged cosmopolitanism for underestimating the importance of a sense of belonging required by democratic politics. Associated by Pierre

---

[43] See Jan-Werner Müller, in this volume.
[44] See Justine Lacroix, in this volume.
[45] See Georgios Varouxakis, in this volume.
[46] Ibid.

Manent with a 'passion for similarities', the 'reign of legal universalism' and the unencumbered view of the self on which it rests are suspected of eventually leading towards an undifferentiated society, thus defeating democracy.[47]

The question of whether – and to what extent – the rational, formal, and abstract principles of democratic citizenship can be disentangled from the nation in turn highlights the conceptual link between assertion of state sovereignty and the notion of 'territory' or political 'body'. On the opposite side of the French debate, one finds Rancière's idea that democracy is 'anybody's government', complemented as it is by the French 'liberal revolutionaries' who conceive Europe as a potential testing ground for a new kind of citizenship dissociated from nationhood and as the ideal locus for radical democratic ambitions. For instance, Etienne Balibar and his followers attempt to reappraise the myth of the sovereign nation-state by giving priority to an anti-discriminatory language which denotes a more specific concern for non-EU nationals.[48] In a slightly different vein, the 'anti-nationalist' stance that Mario Telò identifies at the centre of Italian political culture[49] contributes to stressing the practical link between the limitations of national sovereignty and the achievement of peace and justice. This stance also resonates with the German intellectual enterprise of 'Gruppe 47', nowadays supported by post-nationalist and left-liberal thinkers, united in their rejection of the nation-state as 'a prime moral imperative'.[50]

In sum, diverging conceptions of democratic principles lead to diverging conceptions of the European project. The language in which this disagreement is expressed may itself be deeply embedded in distinct national cultures. But, against the cliché according to which there would be 'a' French, 'a' Polish, or 'a' German vision of Europe, disagreements within each of these contexts over what should be a political community lead to distinct conceptions of what the European polity is, and should be.

A definitional debate: *Finalité* and the contested nature of the European polity

The debates over the keys to political integration and the desirability of liberal democracy in individual member states are intrinsically interwoven, as we have just seen, with debates over the nature of the EU as a political community in itself. At this level, we could simply say that intellectuals disagree over the definition to be attached to the strange animal, unidentified object, *sui generis* project, unprecedented experiment – or whatever other metaphors we might

---

[47] See Justine Lacroix, in this volume.   [48] Ibid.
[49] See Mario Telò, in this volume.
[50] See Jan-Werner Müller, in this volume.

use to describe this state of definitional limbo. Ultimately, intellectuals disagree not only over the appropriate definition of the EU as it *currently* stands, but over what should be its *finalité* and even whether it should have a *finalité* at all – or is it the journey that matters?

Conceptual triangulation: Nationalism, supranationalism, and the transnational third way

There are, of course, several dividing lines. Among the thinkers who expect the EU to become a true 'political body', the dividing line is between the advocates of a Europe of nations and the proponents of a federal Europe. The former option can be connected with the Mazzini-inspired idea of a 'Europe of nations' as 'a third alternative to the utopia of importing the American federal model and the reality of the existing European Concert'.[51] The federalist option is much more multiform. As for Britain, seminal variations are given by Larry Siedentop's Euro-federalism and Glyn Morgan's plea for a European sovereign state. The latter contrasts with the federalist idea defended by Spinelli, Colorni, and Rossi, according to a Hamiltonian model. Within the German federalist camp, there is a conceptual division between 'a federation of states' and 'a federal state' which has made the picture even more complex.[52] Despite their differences, all these representations of the EU as a supranational body with federalist features share the 'embodiment' premise described above, be it in its thin or thick version. By contrast, those in Romania, the Czech Republic, Britain, or Norway who represent the EU as an intergovernmental organization insist that the association between European sovereign states should be as flexible as possible, according to a 'problem-solving' logic.[53]

In the introduction to this book, we suggested a way of simplifying our grasp of all these variants found across countries around the question of what the EU is or should be. We argued in two steps: first, that we could most simply arrange traditions of thought around the two poles which have served to discuss progress and its relation to Europe, that is whether they are closer to a nation-centred or supranational understanding of the EU. However, as also suggested in the introduction, not all debates about Europe can be framed around the question of substantive progress, at least to the extent that it is framed as a choice between the national and the supranational. Rather, in a second step, we see a set of intellectuals enter the fray who prefer to ask how integration can accommodate diversity per se. In the introduction, we labelled this generic third-way leaning 'transnationalism', although the differences of national contexts make it impossible to aggregate all the viewpoints associated with it.

---

[51] See Mario Telò, in this volume.
[52] See Jan-Werner Müller, in this volume.
[53] See John Erik Fossum and Cathrine Holst, in this volume.

Nevertheless, what we do find is a set of debates which may pit the *same* intellectuals against sovereigntists on one hand, *and* supranationalists on the other.

As we saw, the national(ist) premise works towards denying both the possibility and appropriateness of separating democratic politics from national identity. And yet, the diagnostic of the non-existence of a European unified people and active popular will could, by the same token, create the normative grounds for a federal state as a new political body based on a strong sense of European belonging. Under the label of 'post-nationalism', therefore, two different patterns of European democracy can be articulated: supranationalism and transnationalism, the former reproducing the national trope at the supranational level (one polity/one people), whilst the latter seeks to transcend it. Thus intellectuals writing in the transnational vein can be seen as oriented towards the conceptualization of a pluralistic political order of a new kind; and we see them asking, across the member states discussed in this volume, whether Habermas' plea for a 'core Europe' should not be seen as hedging in the direction of a Euro-nationalist or Euro-patriotic temptation – a controversy which brings together in this book Jan-Werner Müller, Ulrike Liebert, and (via the chapter on Britain) Timothy Garton Ash and Ralf Dahrendorf. Together with the supranational thinkers, the representatives of the still emerging transnational constellation attach – to use Jan-Werner Müller's phrase – 'no ethical significance' to nationality. At the same time, they warn against the exclusionary and homogenizing tendencies stemming from the supranationalist hope of anchoring European democracy in a unified people. This transnational stance is articulated through a 'post- or anti-statist language'[54] developed in its most sophisticated version in Germany.

A new generation of European intellectuals is thus trying to conceptualize the EU as a polity of a new kind by rejecting both nationalism and supranationalism, and defining functional equivalents of democracy able to resist the transposition of statism to the European polity. They include *inter alia* Pernice's and Teubner's theories of 'multilevel constitutionalism', Robert Cooper's visions of the EU as a 'voluntary empire', the 'Europolity' defended by Bellamy and Castiglione under the ambivalent notion of 'cosmopolitan communitarianism', Kalypso Nicolaïdis' notion of 'European demoi-cracy', and the concept of 'a democratic association (or community) of semi-sovereign nations' developed by Anthony Giddens according to an approach qualified as 'cosmopolitan nationalism'.[55]

Is 'definitional instability' an asset of the European project or a sign of its weakness? This question partly revives the disagreements over whether EU institutional arrangements on the balance of powers, the respective competences of

---

[54] See Jan-Werner Müller, in this volume.
[55] See Georgios Varouxakis, in this volume.

the EU and the member states, and so on should be constitutionally settled once and for all; whether its borders should be drawn permanently; and whether the *finalité* of the EU should be laid down by constitutional law. Those who argue for 'undefinition' view the EU as a political project in the making that has to remain so for the indefinite future. Illustrating this stance, Petr Pithart depicted European integration as 'a "story without ending"... where the process of construction constitutes a goal in itself'.[56] The opposite camp, however, sees its ranks bolstered in times of uncertainty – after half a century, they argue, the EU has reached an equilibrium and constitutional maturity. It is time for Europeans to call Europe by a name, whether federation, association of states, or any other appropriate label; and, if its *finalité* still seems unknown, Europeans must now invent it.

What is the glue that binds us together?

Such reinvention involves deeply contrasting views about what binds European citizens, peoples, and states together. Is the vector of belonging to the EU a common identity, a shared ethos, a core of basic rights, a set of procedures and rules of government, a series of common interests? And depending on the answer, what is Europeanization supposed to achieve?

Here again, a great variety of answers emerge from the intellectual debates analysed in this book. According to a consequentialist approach to European integration, some consider that the EU's task is to supply social goods and increase economic prosperity, thus reducing the European project to its economic dimension – and provoking the rebuttal of the anti-modernity camp encountered earlier. Instead, emphasizing its political dimension, others view the EU as a 'democratic anchor' whose task is to secure and enhance democracy in its member states.[57] Others expect the EU to promote the mutual recognition of each other's cultural, economic, and political identity among the nations that compose it. This European 'politics of recognition' transcends the liberal model of tolerance and allows each nation to exercise a direct and active influence on others, so as to promote the nation's particular vision and to spread its specific values.[58] In this perspective, EU policies can be considered as legitimate to the extent that they adapt to national identities, and not the opposite. More often than not, those who follow this line of reasoning consider that the attempt to consolidate a European identity is both utopian and dangerous. However, one also finds vibrant discourses about the need to construct a new, 'European-oriented' collective identity, for instance in Poland, Greece, or

---

[56] See Muriel Blaive and Nicolas Maslowski, in this volume.

[57] As shown by Carlos Closa and Antonio Barroso, in this volume, this vision of the EU is predominant among Spanish intellectuals.

[58] See, for instance, the chapter on Poland, where Magdalena Góra and Zdzisław Mach, in this volume, show that some intellectuals insist on the need to 'make Europeans more Polish'.

Turkey. These discourses echo some Italian intellectuals' calls for the creation of a 'new European consciousness' which might frame international relations.

Given the crucial role played by the notion of territory, it is no surprise that the 'embodiment' question eventually leads to the issue of borders: Are they to be consolidated or expanded? This issue is discussed in Spain as the 'European dilemma', that is, the need to specify the EU's 'final territorial horizon',[59] especially with regards to Turkey's accession. As illustrated by the French debate, the emphasis put on the notion of territory entails an opposition to the vision of the EU as 'a heterogeneous, multi-polar Europe with ever-evolving frontiers'.[60] According to Pierre Manent, 'intangible borders' are needed in order to protect the most vulnerable people, in particular against the pervasive forces of globalization. By contrast, Balibar and his followers warn against the current obsession with borders control, which reveals the exclusionary tendency of the EU as well as signs of a new European racism against third-country nationals, asylum seekers, and migrant workers. In Greece and Poland, meanwhile, we see the 'fear of Balkanization' giving rise to two opposite attitudes: in Greece, it stirs up isolationist reflexes based on the 'foreign surrounding' syndrome, whereas in Poland the same fear prompts the recommendation of reducing the value attached to borders.

The chapters provided in this volume discuss numerous other instances of such definitional wars. Ultimately, we are interested in asking how such contrasting claims, concerns, and anxieties contribute to furthering the debate about the EU. We also investigate how they can be turned into 'reasonable disagreements', thus encouraging thinkers who speak the language of self-criticism and mutual recognition to use it in order to define European integration in a more inclusive and decentred way.

In praise of narrative diversity

Michael Freeden asked at the beginning of this volume whether the 'European stories' that are told across Europe are dedicated to *interpreting* or *changing* the EU; and he is right to highlight the tension between the identity and hermeneutic dimensions of story-telling on the one hand, and the normative task of political theory on the other. This tension appears clearly in civilizational debates about European modernity, where different identity-based discourses seek to preserve or restore what the intellectuals involved see as the 'authentic' sources of the 'European self'. These are 'stories' in the sense conjured up by Michael Freeden and, true, their problematic dimension lies in a normative

---

[59] See Carlos Closa and Antonio Barroso, in this volume.
[60] See Justine Lacroix, in this volume.

deficit in rational critique. In this concluding part, we examine the differences between these two divergent modes of debating Europe and what they imply.

Self-clarification versus public justification

Self-clarification corresponds to what Antonio Barroso and Carlos Closa refer to in their chapter on Spain as 'an "introspective" view' dedicated to disclosing, clarifying, and emphasizing a country's or a culture's distinctive values as they relate to Europe. In this view, any culture – be it 'ethnic' or 'civic' – is to be conceived of as a shared fund of semantic contents, as a sediment of historical, religious, or ethical experiences that take the form of a 'legacy', or – in Daniel Barbu's words[61] – 'a cultural repository of meanings'. Such viewpoints are oriented towards promoting the distinctiveness or uniqueness of the community's *ethos*. The search for authenticity leads to a 'politics of survival', the purpose of which is to protect what makes the community so specific vis-à-vis some 'significant others' – the rival neighbour discussed above or, for Europe as a whole, the US, Turkey, or 'Islam' – and to preserve its cultural and/or moral integrity in the face of external (and, occasionally, internal) influences which might threaten it. Obviously, this approach goes hand in hand with a civilizational view and a moralistic definition of the EU as an entity loaded with a set of substantial ethical values, in particular a Christian definition of the good life. In all, the self-clarification approach is both foundational in nature, since it focuses on the founding features of a given culture, and defensive in practice since their protection is a predominant preoccupation, far beyond the search for fundamental or social justice.

It should be noted that the self-clarification approach may be applied to the nation, to a regional identity, to Europe as a civilization, or even to the EU *qua* polity. On all these scales, political integration is grasped through the prism of self-definition, that is the elucidation of what is genuinely *constitutive* of collective identity. According to this communitarian perspective, the 'European community' should be entrenched in a common tradition of values, virtues, and spiritual traits to be cherished for giving a 'substance' to the European project. In other words, this approach to European integration, often designed against liberal individualism, paves the way to a community-building process devoted to the stabilization of a 'thick' collective identity.[62]

On the other hand, one finds intellectual debates about the EU which are oriented towards legitimation issues. This line of reasoning (see for instance E. O. Eriksen 2009) can be seen as 'justificatory': not in the sense that its representatives are unquestioning supporters of the present-day EU, but

---

[61] See Daniel Barbu, in this volume.
[62] See, for instance, Etzioni's (2007) communitarian conceptualization of European integration.

because they are primarily concerned with the problem of finding a basis for 'public justification'[63] based on rules, principles, and norms that might be viewed as criteria for critical assessment of state action and the legitimacy of the polity. Differently put, this approach leaves room for competing normative viewpoints on the choices and trade-offs associated with integration to be set against each other in the public domain. Debates in this vein are thus 'normative' in nature, including political, legal, economic, institutional, and constitutional issues, since they express disagreements about the path that should be followed in order to reach a just, fair, or 'sustainable' integration within the EU.

In this realm, disagreements are about what balance is best to be struck between different political purposes (e.g. social peace versus international peace, redistribution versus growth, power versus equality considerations, political unity versus respect for national, cultural, and linguistic diversity). They are also about which institutions, rules, and procedures are to support such a process, and about how various actors ought to participate in it. Perhaps the most fundamental divide here is between those whose legitimation strategies are based on applying to the greatest extent possible the pattern of nation-building, and those who stress the openness of the political project (Beck and Grande 2007; Grande 2009: 54).

These two lines of argument follow divergent logics. It is one thing to attempt to clarify the buried sources of the 'European self',[64] deemed – rightly or wrongly – to be the grounds of our common 'Europeanness'; but it is quite another to look for a basis of public justification to debate European integration as a political process and project. The differences between these two tasks lie in their respective normative and critical potential. The self-clarification approach, moreover, suffers from at least three normative and pragmatic deficits. First, when exploited for 'identification' ends, the mode of narration is limited to articulating, expressing, and even reproducing a background of shared meanings. Second, the 'common values' frequently invoked may not be so common as might be expected. As illustrated by the failed attempt to refer to Christian heritage during the debate on the late Constitutional Treaty, there is little if any agreement on the various components of a European civilization. Consequently, any call to common values may spark off conflicts between European societies (Grande 2009: 52). Third, reifying the 'European mentality' might ossify oppositions that hinge on the modernity issue (Lacroix 2009: 141). This is what Habermas seems to have in mind when he deplores the 'hysterical call for the

---

[63] A number of political theorists, including John Rawls, Jürgen Habermas, and Bruce Ackerman in one way or another ground their theory within the framework of 'public justification'. For a study of the concept and a critical analysis of its use in the field of contemporary political theory, see: D'Agostino 1996.

[64] Through this phrase, we of course allude to Charles Taylor's seminal book, *Sources of the Self: The Making of the Modern Identity* (1989) which falls within the 'self-clarification' approach.

defence of our values' which is apparently nothing 'but a semantic armament against an unspecified domestic enemy'.[65]

It is precisely this crucial tension between the descriptive and (implicit) prescriptive dimensions of self-clarification which takes us back to the question of the theoretical and practical status of the EU's 'narrative diversity'.

What is at stake? Unity through diversity

The competing visions of Europe represent an inescapable element of the EU's political life. At the same time, is 'narrative diversity' more than a mere *fact*? More precisely, could it be considered as a *practice*? Here, a practical approach to 'narrative diversity' raises the question as to whether the 'European stories' over which public intellectuals – and, partly influenced by them, wider sections of public opinion – agree or disagree could provide the basis for a transnational deliberation about European integration. In other words, beyond *intergovernmental* bargains, is the EU still amenable to *inter-societal* debates devoted to public discussion of the similarities and differences between competing visions of the EU among its citizenry?[66]

In so far as the permissive character of the EU project is increasingly elusive, encouraging the 'reasonable confrontation' of European narratives has become a more urgent task. However, this requires framing the antagonism between narratives as clearly as possible. We must therefore start by shedding the illusion of narrative unanimity. It is indeed pointless to seek one single and official 'European grand narrative', now more than ever, as politicians try to accommodate the many contradictory grounds of existence for the EU. In this respect, we consider that the very idea of 'narrative diversity' has a positive role to play in fostering the EU's democratic life. Therefore, by way of conclusion, let us suggest what a public process of 'confrontation-cum-legitimation' might look like.

Such a process should represent an alternative to the collective self-clarification approach. Indeed, we should abandon the criterion of 'narrative truth'[67] as we internalize the idea that 'reasonable pluralism', including a range of divergent views about what brings us together, should be a fact of life in a transnational demoi-cracy like the EU. Here, the idea is to break away from the correlation between identity and legitimacy, that is, to 'refuse to tie Europe's legitimacy to an identification logic' (Lacroix 2009). This orientation is intended to take into account that 'the glue that binds the EU together is not a shared identity; it is, rather, a shared project and shared objectives' (Nicolaïdis

---

[65] The article originally appeared in German in the *Kölner Stadtanzeiger* on 8 November 2006, and in French in *Le Monde* on 28 December 2006.

[66] For a preliminary discussion see Nicolaïdis and Pélabay 2008.

[67] As Rawls explains, 'holding a political conception as true', and 'for that reason alone' as the one suitable for public agreement 'is exclusive, even sectarian, and so likely to foster political division': see Rawls 1993: 129.

2004a: 103). As a result, we consider that a 'processual scenario'[68] focused on public justification should be prioritized over a substantialist one, so as to exploit Europe's 'narrative diversity' in a dynamic and inclusive manner.

Importantly, the latter conditions – i.e. dynamism and inclusiveness – rule out two common understandings of the 'narrative' mode. First, they preclude the political or managerial use of 'story-telling' as a technique to control and manipulate peoples' behaviours.[69] Instead, a public process of 'confrontation-cum-legitimation' is intended to transform the political debate on the EU by creating a common deliberative space precisely through disagreements. Second, our emphasis on the processual dimension thus conflicts with the communitarian concept of the narrative self.[70] To begin with, a processual model is predicated on a fluid and plural notion of identities. As stated by Ricœur (1995: 6), 'narrative identity takes part in the story's movement, in the dialectic between order and disorder', and remains open to criticism and revision. Thus conceived, the narrative mode gives rise to self-reflexive practices, and points to a politics of mutual recognition. This is what Jean-Marc Ferry conceptualizes through what he qualifies as 'an ethics of reconstruction': 'the strictly procedural ideal of reconstructive justice consists in an open, cooperative confrontation that is self-critical on both sides, listening to all of the stories that narrate conflicting experiences and understanding the possible interpretations that we might give to them in a comprehensive way' (Ferry 2000: 147; authors' translation).

How, then, might such a confrontational process unfold? A first step consists in assuming that the various European narratives may act as so many 'comprehensive interpretations' to be publicly discussed and questioned across borders, which in turn calls for a much more ambitious and systematic work of *translation* across borders than we see today. To go beyond a purely hermeneutic and contextualist – most likely conservative – enterprise of self-clarification, the 'authenticity claims'[71] advanced through competing narratives ought to be translated into *normative statements* about different options for integration. Such translation is made possible through the 'public use of reason', that is, a

---

[68] This is a scenario of the kind which Jean-Marc Ferry (2005) proposes under the name of 'consensus through confrontation'.

[69] For a fascinating and very well-researched critical study on 'storytelling', see Salmon 2009.

[70] A version of this concept is provided by the notion of 'cognitive self' as expounded by Sandel 1982 against the liberal, 'voluntarist' approach to identity. The constitutive role of the narrative exploration of one's prior attachments to community is also at the core of MacIntyre's concept of narrative: 'What I am . . . is in key part what I inherit, a specific part that is present to some degree in my present. I find myself part of a history and that is generally to say, whether I like it or not, whether I recognise it or not, one of the bearers of a tradition' (MacIntyre 1984: 221). For a critique of the communitarian concept of the narrative self, see Hunyadi 1992.

[71] Here we refer to Habermas 1984: 8–23, where he distinguishes between different forms of 'validity claims', namely: truth, rightness, and authenticity claims. The latter claims pertain to the particularistic values and cultural integrity of a given community or historical tradition, while 'rightness' claims pertain to a legal-political sphere of public deliberation.

public deliberation where 'reasonableness' means respecting principles such as reflexivity, equal consideration, and mutual recognition. As Michael Freeden rightly pointed out, the aim is not to agree on what it means to *be* European; instead, we can agree on explaining to each other how we each conceive of the European project.

To be sure, the process of translation we must confront represents a triple challenge. First, and most obviously, if one is to affect a transnational sphere, there is the challenge of translation between national languages, traditions, and political cultures so as to build a discursive framework within which to debate the sense and nature of European integration. Second, we need better translation between various disciplinary and professional spheres that correspond to different intellectual vocabularies and epistemological maps. Thus, for instance, the ethical-existential realm is concerned with the 'good' life and the 'good' citizen; in the normative realm, we speak the language of constitutionalism, the rule of law, and, more broadly, share concerns about the fate of modernity; in the world of experts and bureaucracy, we dissect and shape regulations, decision-making procedures, and modes of governance; and in the political perspective, we engage in a pragmatic search for a new type of democratic polity. In short, we need clues and words to speak across, rather than over, these various languages and spheres. The third and final challenge, which to some extent subsumes the other two, is that of translation between the worlds of scholarship and of politics. Here, we need to find conduits and bridges for stark images and subtle arguments. The *political* message that can inspire the journey ahead for a European Union that is perhaps at last ready to look beyond its confines may well be a compound of our European stories, a sparkling of their various insights and inspirational powers. Among these stories, European citizens can find the material for their own individual interpretations of the common project. Perhaps scholars themselves can learn to translate and channel their own disagreements into the message of mutual recognition, deep diversity, and demoi-cracy at the heart of the EU.

Some may argue that the 'narrative restraints' that we advocate in the name of reasonable pluralism tend simply to cover up the most profound causes of contention, and to limit drastically the range of contestation over the EU; others may fear that the focus on 'reasonable disagreements' precludes the achievement of consensus, and eschews the goal of ever closer union. We believe that what is at stake is of a different nature: when incorporated into this confrontational practice, the various 'European stories' that we have explored lose their self-evident dimension as well as their purely contextual validity. They become part of a larger multi-faceted whole, part of a logic that we can only wish for, a logic of reflexive appropriation, decentring, and mutual learning. If we can amplify the echoes between them and hear them together in a new kind of political polyphony intended to take the competing visions of Europe seriously, we may start to turn 'unity in diversity' into more than just a pleasing motto.

References

AAVV (1963), *Libertad y organización*, Madrid: Ed. Insula.

Agnelli, Giovanni and Attilio Cabiati (1918), *Federazione europea o lega delle nazioni?*, Milan: Fratelli Bocca.

Ahern, Bertie (2000), 'Statement by the Taoiseach on the European Council in Nice, 7–11 December 2000', Dáil Éireann, *Dáil Debates*, vol. 528, cols. 444–52, 13 December.

Ahmad, Feroz (2004), *The Making of Modern Turkey*, London: Routledge.

Aldecoa, Francisco and José María Gil Robles (2005), 'Salto cualitativo en la construcción de la UE', *El País*, 31 January.

Allison, Graham T. and Kalypso Nicolaïdis, eds. (1997), *The Greek Paradox: Promise vs. Performance*, Cambridge, MA: MIT Press.

Alter, Karen (2003), *Establishing the Supremacy of European Law*, New York: Oxford University Press.

Altunişik, Meliha and Özlem Tür (2005), *Turkey: Challenges of Continuity and Change*, New York: Routledge.

Álvarez Miranda, Berta (1996), *El sur de Europa y la adhesión a la Comunidad: Los debates políticos*, Madrid: Centro de Investigaciones Sociológicas.

Amato, Giuliano (2006), 'The future of Europe', in Detler Albers, Stephen Haseler, and Henning Meyer, eds., *Social Europe: A Continent's Answer to Market Fundamentalism*, London: London Metropolitan University.

——(2007), *Génèse et destinée de la constitution européenne*, Brussels: Bruylant.

Anastasakis, Othon, Kalypso Nicolaïdis, and Kerem Öktem, eds. (2009), *In the Long Shadow of Europe: Greeks and Turks in the Era of Postnationalism*, Leiden/Boston, MA: M. Nijhoff.

Anderson, Perry (1980), *Arguments within English Marxism*, London: Verso.

——(1992a[1964]), 'Origins of the present crisis', in *English Questions*, London: Verso.

——(1992b[1991]), 'The Light of Europe', in *English Questions*, London: Verso.

——(2005), 'Dreams of Central Europe: Timothy Garton Ash', in *Spectrum: From Left to Right in the World of Ideas*, London: Verso.

——(2007), 'European hypocrisies', *London Review of Books* 29 (18), 20 September, 13–21.

——(2009), *The New Old World*, London: Verso.

Anderson, Peter (2004), 'A flag of convenience? Discourse and motivations of the London-based Eurosceptic press', *European Studies* 20 (1), 151–70.

Andreescu, Gabriel and Adrian Severin (2001), 'Un concept românesc al Europei federale' [A Romanian concept of federal Europe], in R. Weber, ed., *Un concept românesc privind viitorul Uniunii Europene* [A Romanian concept on the future of the European Union], Iaşi: Polirom.

363

References

Annan, Noel (1990), *Our Age: Portrait of a Generation*, London: Weidenfeld and Nicolson.

Archer, Clive (2005), *Norway Outside the European Union: Norway and European Integration from 1994 to 2004*, London: Routledge.

Areilza Carvajal, José María (2001), 'La reforma de Niza ¿Hacia qué unión Europea?', *Política Exterior* 79, 104–19.

——(2002), 'España en el debate federal europeo', *Revista de Occidente* 249, 5–11.

——(2003), 'La Convención Europea: un balance', *Política Exterior*, June, 94.

——(2005), 'La Constitución Europea: el regreso a la Comunidad Europea', in C. Closa and N. Fernández, eds., *La Constitución de la Unión Europea*, Madrid: Centro de Estudios Políticos y Constitucionales.

Arnold, Matthew (1965), *The Complete Prose Works of Matthew Arnold*, ed. R. H. Super, vol. 5: *Culture and Anarchy*, Ann Arbor: University of Michigan Press.

Aron, Raymond (1966), *Peace and War: A Theory of International Relations*, London: Weidenfeld and Nicholson.

——(1974), 'Is multinational citizenship possible?', *Social Research* 41 (4), 638–58.

Aydin, Senem and Fuat Keyman (2004), 'European integration and the transformation of Turkish democracy', EU-Turkey Working Papers No. 2, Brussels: Centre for European Studies.

Baban, Feyzi and Fuat Keyman (2008), 'Turkey and post-national Europe', *European Journal of Social Theory* 11 (1), 107–24.

Bachoud, Andrée, Josefina Cuesta, and Michel Trebitsch, eds. (2000), *Les intellectuels et l'Europe de 1945 à nos jours*, Paris: Publications Universitaires Paris Diderot.

Baconsky, Theodor (2002), 'Decadenţa etatismului şi renaşterea ortodoxă' [The decadence of etatism and the revival of orthodoxy], in I. I. Ică Jr. and G. Martino, eds., *Doctrina socială a Bisericii: Fundamente, documente, analize, perspective* [The social teaching of the Church: Fundamentals, documents, analysis, perspectives], Sibiu: Deisis.

Balibar, Etienne (1992), *Les frontières de la démocratie*, Paris: La Découverte.

——(2001), *Nous citoyens d'Europe? Les frontières, l'Etat, le peuple*, Paris: La Découverte.

——(2002), *Droit de cité*, Paris: Presses Universitaires de France.

——(2003), *L'Europe, l'Amerique, la guerre: Réflexions sur la médiation européenne*, Paris: La Découverte.

——(2005a), *Europe, Constitution, Frontières*, Bordeaux: Editions du Passant.

——(2005b), 'Oui mais . . . non car', *Libération*, 25 May, 28.

Barbé, Esther (1999), *La política europea de España*, Barcelona: Ariel.

Barbu, Daniel (2002), 'The burden of politics: Public space, political participation, and state socialism', *Studia Politica: Romanian Political Science Review* 2 (2), 329–46.

——(2007), 'The state vs. its citizens. A note on Romania, Europe and corruption', *Studia Politica: Romanian Political Science Review* 7 (1), 9–12.

——and Cristian Preda (2006), 'Building the state from the roof down: Varieties of Romanian liberal nationalism', in I. Z. Dénes, ed., *Liberty and the Search for Identity: Liberal Nationalisms and the Legacy of Empires*, Budapest and New York: Central European University Press.

Barratt Brown, Michael (1961), 'Neutralism and the Common Market', *New Left Review* I/12 (November–December).

Barth, Erling, Moene Kalle, and Michael Wallerstein (2003), *Likhet under press: Utfordringer for den skandinaviske fordelingsmodellen*, Oslo: Gyldendal.

Bartoszewski, Władysław (2001), 'Vision and potential: For a new direction in European integration. Speech at the Centre for European Policy Studies, Brussels, 25 July 2000', in *Above Divisions: Selected Speeches and Interviews, July–December 2000*, Warsaw: Ministerstwo Spraw Zagranicznych.

Bauman, Zygmunt (2007), *La décadence des intellectuels? Des législateurs aux interprètes*, Paris: Chambon.

Beaud, Olivier (2007), *Théorie de la Fédération*, Paris: Presses Universitaires de France.

Beaumont, Gustave de (2007 [1839]) *Ireland: Social, Political, and Religious*, introduced by T. Garvin and A. Hess, Cambridge, MA: Harvard University Press.

Beciu, Camelia (2006), 'L'espace publique des débats sur l'Europe. Traitements médiatiques et modes de généralisation', in S. Marton, ed., *Europe in Its Making: A Unifying Perception on Europe*, Iaşi: Institutul European.

Beck, Ulrich (2003), 'Toward a new critical theory with a cosmopolitan intent', *Constellations* 10 (4), 453–68.

——and Edgar Grande (2004), *Das kosmopolitische Europa: Gesellschaft und Politik in der zweiten Moderne*, Frankfurt am Main: Suhrkamp.

——(2007), *Cosmopolitan Europe*, Cambridge: Polity Press.

Belien, Paul (2005), 'Czech president warns against "Europeanism"', *The Brussels Journal: The Voice of Conservatism in Europe*, 28 August, <http://www.brusselsjournal.com> (accessed 5 November 2009).

Bell, Duncan (2007), *The Idea of Greater Britain: Empire and the Future of World Order, 1860–1900*, Princeton, NJ: Princeton University Press.

Bellamy, Richard (2001), 'Intellectuals and politics in Italy from Vico to Eco', *Journal of Modern Italian Studies* 6, 151–264.

——(2004), 'Which constitution for what kind of Europe? Three models of European constitutionalism', Paper for the CIDEL Workshop 'Constitution-Making and Democratic Legitimacy in the EU', London, 12–13 November.

——(2006a), 'The European Constitution is dead, long live European constitutionalism', *Constellations* 13 (2), 181–9.

——(2006b), 'Between past and future: The democratic limits of EU citizenship', in R. Bellamy, D. Castiglione, and J. Shaw, eds., *Making European Citizens: Strategies of Civic Inclusion in Pan-European Civil Society*, Basingstoke: Palgrave.

——(2007), *Political Constitutionalism: A Republican Defense of the Constitutionality of Democracy*, Cambridge: Cambridge University Press.

——and Dario Castiglione (1998), 'Between cosmopolis and community: Three models of rights and democracy within the European Union' in D. Archibugi, D. Held and M. Koehler, eds., *Re-Imagining Political Community*, Cambridge: Polity Press.

————(2003), 'Legitimising the European Union and its regime: The normative turn in EU studies', *European Journal of Political Theory* 2 (1), 7–34.

————(2004), 'Lacroix's European constitutional patriotism: A response', *Political Studies* 52, 187–93.

Bělohradský, Václav (2005), 'Proč jsem znovu disidentem' [Why I became a dissident again], <http://www.multiweb.cz/hawkmoon/eurohybrid.htm> (accessed 21 December 2009).

References

Benda, Julien (1955), *The Betrayal of the Intellectuals*, Boston, MA: Beacon Press.
——(1992), *Discours à la nation européenne*, Paris: Folio.
Beneyto, José María (1999), *Tragedia y razón: Europa en el pensamiento español del siglo XX*, Madrid: Taurus.
——(2002), 'Tesis para la discusión sobre el reparto de competencias en la Unión Europea', *Seminario Hispano Alemán*, 21–22 February.
Benhabib, Seyla (2009), 'Claiming rights across borders: International human rights and democratic sovereignty' *American Political Science Review* 103 (4), 691–704.
Berkes, Niyazi (1975), *Türk Düşüncede Batı Sorunu*, Istanbul: Bilgi.
Berlin, Isaiah (1969), *Four Essays on Liberty*, Oxford: Oxford University Press.
——(2002), *Liberty*, Oxford: Oxford University Press.
——(2009 [1953]), *The Hedgehog and the Fox: An Essay on Tolstoy's View of History*, London: Phoenix.
Berman, Sheri (1998), *The Social Democratic Moment*, Cambridge, MA: Harvard University Press.
Bernath, Mathias (1972), *Habsburg und die Anfänge der Rumänischen Nationsbildung*, Leiden: E. J. Brill.
Bielecki, Jędrzej (2007), 'Myślą o Polsce a nie o Europie'. *Dziennik: Polska-Europa-Świat*, 6 July.
Bikont, Anna (2007), 'Wolne, równe, dyskryminowane? dyskusja wokół "Czarnej księgi kobiet"', *Gazeta Wyborcza*, 7–9 April.
Bjørklund, Tor (2005), *Hundre år med folkeavstemninger*, Oslo: Universitetsforlaget.
Blackledge, Paul (2004), *Perry Anderson, Marxism and the New Left*, London: Merlin Press.
Blaive, Muriel (2002), 'Tchèques, Allemands, Autrichiens: La gestion d'un passé douloureux. Commentaire sur l'article de Jacques Rupnik "Das andere Mitteleuropa: Die neuen Populismen und die Politik mit der Vergangenheit"', Tr@nsit online, 23, <http://www.iwm.at/transit>.
——(2006), 'Up from communism: The legacies of the Cold War and its collapse', in Thomas Row, ed., *Does Central Europe Still Exist?*, Favorita Papers 3/2006, Vienna: Diplomatic Academy.
——(2007), 'De la démocratie tchèque et des décrets "Beneš"', in G. Mink and L. Neumayer, eds., *L'Europe et ses passés douloureux*, Paris: La Découverte.
——(2008), 'Češi a Evropa' [Czechs and Europe], in M. MacDonagh-Pajerová and J. Hrom, eds., *Evrpané píší o Evropě* [Europeans write on Europe], Prague: Ano pro Evropu.
——and Georges Mink, eds. (2003), *Benešovy dekrety: Budoucnost Evropy a vyrovnávání se sminulostí* [The Beneš decrees: Europe's future and its dealing with the past], Prague: Dokořán.
Bliksrud, Liv (1999), *Den smilende makten: Norske Selskab i København og Johan Herman Wessel*, Oslo: Aschehoug.
Bobbio, Norberto (1975), 'Il federalismo nel dibattito politico e culturale della Resistenza', in S. Pistone, ed., *L'idea dell'unificazione europea tra la prima e la seconda guerra mondiale*, Turin: Fondazione Einaudi.
——(1990), *Saggi su Gramsci*, Milan: Feltrinelli.
Böckenförde, Ernst-Wolfgang (1999), 'Begriff und Probleme des Verfassungsstaats', in *Staat, Nation, Europa*, Frankfurt am Main: Suhrkamp.
Bodei, Remo (1998), *Il noi diviso*, Turin: Einaudi.

Bogdandy, Armin von (2005), 'The European Constitution and European identity: Text and subtext of the Treaty establishing a constitution in Europe', *International Journal of Constitutional Law* (I.CON) 3 (2/3), 295–315.

Bogdanor, Vernon (2005), 'Footfalls echoing in the memory. Britain and Europe: The historical perspective', *International Affairs* 81 (4), 689–701.

Bohman, James (2007), *Democracy across Borders: From Dêmos to Dêmoi*, Cambridge, MA: MIT Press.

Bohrer, Karl Heinz (2000), 'Die europäische Differenz', *Merkur* 54, 991–1003.

Boltanski, Luc and Laurent Thévenot (1991), *De la justification*, Paris: Gallimard.

Borodziej, Włodzimierz (1990), *Od Poczdamu do Szklarskiej Poręby: Polska w stosunkach międzynarodowych 1945–1947*, Londyn: ANEKS.

Bosco, Andrea, ed. (1991), *The Federal Idea*, vol. 1: *The History of Federalism from the Enlightenment to 1945*, London: Lothian Foundations Press.

Botopoulos, Costas (2007), Η Ευρώπη με ανοιχτά μάτια [Europe with open eyes], Athens: PSE.

Bozóki, András, ed. (1999), *Intellectuals and Politics in Central Europe*, Budapest: Central European University Press.

Brague, Rémi (1992), *Europe: la voie romaine*, Paris: Folio Essais.

Breathnach, Edel (2007), 'Celebrating Louvain 400', <http://www.ucd.ie/expertiseatucd/researchshowcase/louvain400/index.html> (accessed July 2009).

Breuilly, John (1981), *Nationalism and the State*, Chicago: University of Chicago Press.

Brox, Ottar (1966), *Hva skjer i Nord Norge? En studie i norsk utkantpolitikk*, Oslo: Pax.

——(1972), *Politikk: Bidrag til populistisk argumentasjon*, Oslo: Pax.

——(2009), *Klimakrisen – hva kan vi gjøre?*, Oslo: Aschehoug.

Brubaker, Rogers and Frederick Cooper (2000), 'Beyond identity', *Theory and Society* 29 (1), 1–47.

Brunkhorst, Hauke (2007), 'Die Verfassung als Verkörperung kommunikativer Macht. Zu Hannah Arendts komplexer Theorie der Macht', *Internationale Zeitschrift für Philosophie* 1, 28–51.

Bücker, Nicola (forthcoming), 'Attitudes toward the EU in East Germany and Poland', PhD dissertation, in progress.

Bugge, Peter (2000), 'Czech perceptions of the perspective of EU membership: Havel vs. Klaus', Working Paper, Robert Schuman Centre for Advanced Studies, San Domenico: European University Institute, <http://hdl.handle.net/1814/1650>.

Bryk, Andrzej, Tomasz Lis, Jan M. Rokita, and Andrzej Zoll (2007), 'Być i mieć w Europie' (Debate with Tygodnik Powszechny), *Tygodnik Powszechny*, 1 April.

Cacciari, Massimo (1994), *Geofilosofia dell'Europa*, Milan: Adelphi.

Case, Holly (2008), 'Being European: East and West' in J. Checkel and P. Katzenstein, eds., *European Identity*, Cambridge: Cambridge University Press.

Castoriadis, C. (2006–8), *Ce qui fait la Grèce*, 2 vols., Paris: Seuil.

Cattaneo, Carlo (1991), *Stati Uniti D'Italia*, Milan: Mondadori.

Cautrès, Bruno (2005), 'Une fracture générationelle?', in A. Mergier et al., *Le jour où la France a dit non*, Paris: Plon.

Cevizoğlu, Hulki (2007), 'Daha Da Kaşıyacaklar', *Yeniçağ*, 23 January, <http://www.cevizkabugu.com.tr/yazilar.asp?procid=144&page=9> (accessed 26 June 2010).

Chabod, Federico (1961), *Storia dell'idea d'Europa*, Bari: Laterza.

References

Chabot, Jean-Luc (2005), *Aux origines intellectuelles de l'Union européenne: L'idée d'Europe unie de 1919 à 1939*, Grenoble: Presses Universitaires de Grenoble.

Charles, Christophe (1990), *Les intellectuels en Europe au XIXe siècle? Essai d'histoire comparée*, Paris: Seuil.

Checkel, Jeffrey and Peter J. Katzenstein (2008), *European Identity*, Cambridge: Cambridge University Press.

Chemillier-Gendreau, Monique (2005), 'Quelle citoyenneté adaptée à la pluralité du monde', *Tumultes* 24, 165–78.

Cheneval, Francis (1995), *Die Rezeption der Monarchia Dantes bis zur Editio Princeps im Jahre 1559: Metamorphosen eines philosophisches Werkes*, Munich: Fink Verlag.

——(2002), *Philosophie in weltbürgerlicher Bedeutung*, Basel: Schwabe.

——(2005), *La Cité des peuples. Mémoires de cosmopolitismes*, Paris: Cerf.

Chryssochoou, Dimitris N. (2009), *Theorizing European Integration*, 2nd edn, London and New York: Routledge.

Chun, Lin (1993), *The British New Left*, Edinburgh: Edinburgh University Press.

Cichocki, Marek (2004), *Porwanie Europy*, Cracow/Warsaw: Ośrodek Myśli Politycznej.

——(2007), 'New countries, old myths: A Central European appeal for an expansion of European understanding', *IP-Global* 8 (Winter), 68–71.

Ciddi, Sinan (2009), *Kemalism in Turkish Politics: The Republican People's Party, Secularism and Nationalism*, London: Routledge.

Ciliberto, Michele, ed. (2008), *Biblioteca laica: Il pensiero libero dell'Italia moderna*, Rome: Laterza.

Cioran, Emil (1995), *Scrisori către cei de-acasă* [Letters to those at home], ed. G. Liiceanu and T. Enescu, Bucharest: Humanitas.

Ciorănescu, George (2005), *L'Europe unie: De l'idée à la fondation*, ed. S. Delureanu, Bucharest: Paideia.

Closa, Carlos (2004a), 'Deliberative constitutional politics and the EU value-based constitution', in C. Closa and J. E. Fossum, *Deliberative Constitutional Politics in the EU*, ARENA Report, 5/04, <http://www.arena.uio.no/cidel/Reports/Albarracin_Report.htm>.

——(2004b), 'El fracaso del Consejo Europeo de Bruselas y el futuro de la Constitución', *Análisis del Real Instituto Elcano* 14.

——(2004c), 'Ratification of the constitution of the EU: A minefield', *Análisis del Real Instituto Elcano* 120.

——(2005), 'The Spanish intellectual debate on the future of the EU: Who was mobilized and with what effects?', in S. Lucarelli and C. Radaelli, eds., *Mobilizing Politics and Society? The EU Conventions Impact on Southern Europe*, London: Routledge.

——and Paul Heywood (2004), *Spain and the European Union*, Basingtoke: Palgrave.

Collignon, Stefan (2009), *European Republic: Reflections on the Political Economy of a Future Constitution*, London: Federal Trust for Education and Research.

——(2006), *Absent Minds: Intellectuals in Britain*, Oxford: Oxford University Press.

——and Christian Paul (2008), *Pour la république européenne*, Paris: Odile Jacob.

Cooper, Robert (2000), *The Post-Modern State and the World Order*, 2nd edn, London: Demos.

——(2003), *The Breaking of Nations: Order and Chaos in the Twenty-First Century*, London: Atlantic Books.

368

Costa, Joaquín (1981), *Reconstitución y Europeización de España y otros escritos*, Madrid: Instituto de Estudios de la Administración Local.

Cotarelo, Ramón (1992), 'Altos y bajos de la unidad política europea', *Cuenta y razón de pensamiento actual* 71–72, 2–7.

Couloumbis, Theodore (2007), 'Η αποβαλκανιοποίηση των Βαλκανίων' [The debalkanization of the Balkans], *Kathimerini*, 11 February.

Crapez, Marc (2005), 'Les élites et le droit européen', *Commentaire* 112, 827–31.

Croce, Benedetto (1932), *Storia d'Europa del XIX secolo*, Bari: Laterza.

Cronin, Ciaran (2003), 'Democracy and collective identity: In defence of constitutional patriotism', *European Journal of Philosophy* 11 (1), 1–28.

Crouch, Colin (2004), *Post-Democracy*, Cambridge: Polity Press.

——and Wolfgang Streeck, eds. (2006), *The Diversity of Democracy: Corporatism, Social Order and Political Conflict*, Cheltenham: Elgar.

Curcio, Carlo (1958), *Europa. Storia di un idea*, Florence: Vallechi.

Cywiński, Bogdan (1985), *Rodowody niepokornych*. Paris: Editions Spotkania.

D'Agostino, Fred (1996), *Free Public Reason: Making It Up As We Go*, Oxford: Oxford University Press.

Daddow, Oliver J. (2006), 'Euroscepticism and the culture of the discipline of history', *Review of International Studies* 32, 309–28.

Dahrendorf, Ralf (1959), *Class and Class Conflict in Industrial Society*, Palo Alto, CA: Stanford University Press.

——(1973), *Plädoyer für die Europäische Union*, Munich: Piper and Co.

——(1994), 'Die Zukunft des Nationalstaates', *Merkur* 48, 751–61.

——(2001), 'Can European democracy survive globalization?', *National Interest* 65 (Fall), <http://www.nationalinterest.org/General.aspx?id=92&id2=12516>.

——(2004), *Der Wiederbeginn der Geschichte: Vom Fall der Mauer zum Krieg im Irak*, Munich: C. H. Beck.

——and Timothy Garton Ash (2003), 'Die Erneuerung Europas', *Süddeutsche Zeitung*, 4–5 July.

Davie, Grace (2007), 'Vicarious religion: A methodological challenge', in N. T. Ammerman, ed., *Everyday Religion: Observing Modern Religious Lives*, Oxford and New York: Oxford University Press.

Davies, John Kenyon (1993), *Democracy and Classical Greece*, 2nd edn, Cambridge, MA: Harvard University Press.

Davies, Norman (1996), *Europe. A History*, Oxford: Oxford University Press.

Davis, Howard (1997), 'Revisiting the concept of the public intellectual', in J. Jennings and A. Kemp-Welch, eds., *Intellectuals in Politics from the Dreyfus Affair to Salman Rushdie*, London: Routledge.

Davutoğlu, Ahmet, (2004), *Civilizational Transformation and the Muslim World*, Istanbul: Bilim ve Sanat Vakfi.

Daye, Barbara (1999), *The Velvet Philosophers*, London: Claridge Press.

De Giovanni, Biagio (1992), *L'ambigua potenza dell'Europa*, Naples: Guida.

——(2002), *L'ambigua potenza dell'Europa*, Naples: Guida.

——(2004), *La filosofia e l'Europa moderna*, Bologna: Il Mulino.

Debray, Régis (1981), *Teachers, Writers and Celebrities: The Intellectuals of Modern France*, trans. D. Macey, London: Verso.

References

Debray, Régis (1999), *Le Code et le glaive. Après l'Europe, la nation?*, Paris: Albin Michel.

Delureanu, Ştefan (2006), *Le Nouvelles Equipes Internationales: Per una rifondazione dell'Europa (1947–1965)*, Soveria Mannelli: Rubbettino.

——(2007), *Uniunea Europeană a Federaliştilor şi promotorii români ai Europei Unite: Mărturie şi memorie (1947–1957)* [The European Union of federalists and the Romanian promoters of united Europe: Testimony and memory (1947–1957)], Bucharest: Paideia.

Derrida, Jacques (1992), *The Other Heading*, Bloomington: Indiana University Press.

——and Jürgen Habermas (2003), 'February 15, or what binds Europeans together: A plea for a common foreign policy, beginning in the core of Europe', *Constellations* 10(3): 291–7.

Diamandouros, Nikiforos (1994), 'Cultural dualism and political change in postauthoritarian Greece', *Instituto Juan March de Estudios e Investigaciones*, Working Paper 50, February (also in Greek: '*Πολιτισμικός Δυισμός και Πολιτική Αλλαγή στην Ελλάδα της Μεταπολίτευσης*', Athens: Alexandria Publications, 2000).

——(1997), 'Greek politics and society in the 1990s,' in G. T. Allison and K. Nicolaïdis, eds., *The Greek Paradox: Promise vs. Performance*, Cambridge, MA: MIT Press.

Díaz, Elías (1974), *Pensamiento español 1933–1973*, Madrid: Cuadernos para el Diálogo.

Díez Medrano, Juan (2003), *Framing Europe: Attitudes to European Integration in Germany, Spain, and the United Kingdom*, Princeton, NJ: Princeton University Press.

Dimier, Véronique (2004), 'Unity and diversity: Contending conceptions of the French nation and republic', *West European Politics* 27 (5), 837–95.

Dmowski, Roman (1903[1996]), *Myśli nowoczesnego Polaka*, Wrocław: Wyd. Nortom.

Dobroczyński, Michał (2003), *Poland in the European Union*. Toruń: Wydawnictwo Adam Marszałek.

Dooley, Mark (2009), *Roger Scruton: The Philosopher on Dover Beach*, London: Continuum.

Drake, David (2002), *Intellectuals and Politics in Post-War France*, Basingstoke: Palgrave.

Dryzek, John S. (2006), *Deliberative Global Politics: Discourse and Democracy in a Divided World*, Cambridge: Polity Press.

Duchenne, Geneviève (2008), *Esquisses d'une Europe nouvelle. L'européisme dans la Belgique de l'entre-deux guerres (1919–1939)*. Brussels: PIE-Lang.

Ducreux, Marie-Elizabeth (1990), 'Entre catholicisme et protestantisme: l'identité tchèque', *Le Débat* 59, 106–25.

Duggan, Christopher J. (2008), *La forza del destino*, Rome/Bari: Laterza.

Dupré-Latour, Nathanaël (2006), 'Le retour à l'Europe: La pensée dissidente tchèque (tchécoslovaque) et le projet européen', PhD dissertation, IEP Paris.

Duroselle, Jean-Baptiste (1965), *L'idée d'Europe dans l'histoire*, Paris: Denoël.

Duţu, Alexandru (1999), *Ideea de Europa şi evoluţia conştiinţei europene* [The idea of Europe and the evolution of the European consciousness], Bucharest: All Educational.

Dwan, David (2009), *The Great Community: Culture and Nationalism in Ireland*, Dublin: Field Day.

Dyson, Kenneth (1979), *The State Tradition in Western Europe: A Study of an Idea and Institution*, Oxford: Martin Robertson.

Eco, Umberto (1994), *La recherche de la langue parfaite*, Paris: Seuil.

Einaudi, Luigi (1950), *La guerra e l'unità europea*, Milan: Comunità.

Eisler, Jerzy (1991), *Marzec 1968. Geneza, przebieg, konsekwencje*, Warsaw: Państwowe Wydawnictwo Naukowe.

Eliade, Mircea (1937), 'Where does the mission of Romania begin?', *Vremea* 10 (477), 28 February, 3. (Reprinted in M. Eliade, *Texte 'legionare' și despre 'românism'* [Texts from the Legion period and on 'Romanianism'], ed. M. Handoca, Cluj/Napoca: Dacia, 2001.)

Ellison, James (2000), *Threatening Europe: Britain and the Creation of the European Community, 1955–58*, Basingstoke: Macmillan.

English, Richard and Joseph Morrison Skelly, eds. (1998), *Ideas Matter: Essays in Honour of Conor Cruise O'Brien*, Dublin: Poolbeg Press.

Enzersberger, Hans Magnus (1989), *Europe, Europe*, New York: Random House.

Erdem, Hakan (2005), '"Do not think of the Greeks as agricultural labourers": Ottoman responses to the Greek War of Independence', in F. Birtek and T. Dragonas, eds., *Citizenship and the Nation-State in Greece and Turkey*, New York: Routledge.

Eriksen, Christoffer Conrad (2009), 'Europeisk rett og norsk politikk – et konstitusjonelt perspektiv', *Nytt Norsk Tidsskrift* 2, 194–200.

Eriksen, Erik Oddvar, ed. (2005), *Making the European Polity: Reflexive Integration in Europe*, London: Routledge.

——(2009), *The Unfinished Democratization of Europe*, Oxford: Oxford University Press.

——and John Erik Fossum (2000), *Democracy in the European Union: Integration through Deliberation?*, London: Routledge.

————(2004), 'Europe in search of legitimacy: Strategies of legitimation assessed', *International Political Science Review* 25 (4), 435–59.

————(2007), 'Europe in transformation. How to reconstitute democracy?', *RECON Online Working Papers* 1, <http://www.reconproject.eu/projectweb/portalproject/RECON-WorkingPapers.html> (accessed 23 June 2010).

————(2009), 'Europe's challenge: Reconstituting Europe or reconfiguring democracy?', in *RECON Theory in Practice* (ARENA Report No. 2/09, RECON Report No. 8).

Eriksen, Thomas Hylland and Halvor Finess Tretvoll (2006), *Kosmopolitikk: En optimistisk politikk for det 21. århundre*, Oslo: Cappelen Damm.

Esping-Andersen, Gøsta (1990), *The Three Worlds of Welfare Capitalism*, Cambridge: Polity Press.

Estella, A. (2004), '¿Son tan importantes los votos en el Consejo Europeo?', *El País*, 5 April.

Etzioni, Amitai (2007), 'The community deficit', *Journal of Common Market Studies* 45 (1), 23–42.

Evin, Ahmet (1984), 'Communitarian structures and social change', in *Modern Turkey: Continuity and Change*, Hamburg and Opladen: Leske Verlag und Budrich.

Eyerman, Ron (1994), *Between Culture and Politics? Intellectuals in Modern Society*, Cambridge: Polity Press.

Fabbrini, Sergio and Simona Piattoni, eds. (2008), *Italy in the European Union: Redefining National Interest in a Compound Polity*, Plymouth: Rowman & Littlefield.

Fanning, Bryan (2008), *The Quest for Modern Ireland: The Battle of Ideas 1912–1986*, Dublin: Irish Academic Press.

Faraldo, José M., Paulina Gulińska-Jurgiel, and Christian Domnitz, eds. (2008), *Europa im Ostblock: Vorstellungen und Diskurse (1945–1991)*, Cologne: Böhlau.

Favell, Adrian (2008), *Eurostars and Eurocities*, London: Blackwell.

Fawn, Rick (2003), 'Ideology and national identity in post-communist foreign policies', *Journal of Communist Studies and Transition Politics*, 19 (3), 1–41.

References

Ferguson, Niall (2004), 'The end of Europe?', American Enterprise Institute Bradley Lecture, Washington, DC, 1 March.

Ferry, Jean-Marc (1998), 'La Communauté européenne entre Etat fédéral et fédération d'Etats', *Swiss Political Science Review* 4 (4), 11–31.

——(2000), *La question de l'Etat européen*, Paris: Gallimard.

——(2005), *Europe? la voie kantienne*, Paris: Cerf.

Feuer, Lewis S. (1975), *Ideology and the Ideologists*, New York: Harper & Row.

Feuerstein, Burkhard (2007), 'Mariazell: Pope Benedict XVI visits Marian Shrine in the heart of Europe', <http://www.catholicnewsagency.com/austria07/mariazell.htm> (accessed July 2009).

Finkielkraut, Alain (2007), *Qu'est-ce que la France?*, Paris: Stock.

Finstad, Fredrik Bøckman (2008), 'Norges tilknytning til EUs justis- og innenrikspolitikk', *Nytt Norsk Tidsskrift* 4, 336–47.

Fischer, Joschka (2000), 'Vom Staatenbund zur Föderation – Gedanken über die Finalität der europäischen Integration', and ' "9. November als Feiertag": Aussenminister Joschka Fischer über den Kampf gegen den Rechtsextremismus und eine angemessene Rückbesinnung auf den Nationalstaat', *Der Spiegel*, 21 August.

Fischer-Lescano, Andreas and Gunther Teubner (2006), *Regime-Kollisionen: Zur Fragmentierung des globalen Rechts*, Frankfurt am Main: Suhrkamp.

Fish, Steven (1999), 'The end of Meciarism', *East European Constitutional Review* 8 (1–2), 47–55.

Fisher Onar, Nora (2009a), 'The lure of Europe: Reconciling the European other and the national self in Turkey and Greece,' in O. Anastasakis, K. Nicolaïdis, and K. Öktem, eds., *Under the Long Shadow of Europe: Greeks and Turks in the Era of Post-Nationalism*, Leiden: Brill.

——(2009b), 'Beyond binaries: "Europe", pluralism, and a revisionist-status quo key to Turkish politics', 2nd place, Sakip Sabanci International Research Award, May, <http://www.sabanciuniv.edu/tr/arastirma/sakip_sabanci_uluslararasi_arastirma_odulu/images/Nora_Fisher_Onar_Sabanci_Essay_Contest_2009_Final.pdf>.

——(2009c), 'Transcending the "West"/"Islam" binary?: Turkey and the post-Ottoman Mediterranean', in K. Nicolaïdis and D. Bechev, eds., *Mediterranean Frontiers: Borders, Conflict and Memory in a Transnational World*, London: I. B. Tauris.

——(2009d), 'Echoes of a universalism lost: Rival representations of the Ottomans in today's Turkey,' *Middle Eastern Studies* 45 (2), 229–41.

——(forthcoming), 'Continuity or rupture? The historiography of the Ottoman past and its political applications', in K. Nicolaïdis and B. Sebe, eds., *Echoes of Colonialism*, Cambridge: Cambridge University Press.

Fleck, Christian, Andreas Hess, and E. Stina Lyon, eds. (2009), 'Introduction' in Fleck, Hess and Lyon, *Intellectuals and their Publics: Perspectives from the Social Sciences*, Farnham, Surrey: Ashgate.

Foerster, Rolf Hellmut (1967), Europa, Geschichte einer politischen Idee. Mit einer Bibliographie von 182 Einigungsplänen aus den Jahren 1306 bis 1945, Munich: Nymphenburger Verlagsbuchhandlung.

Föllesdal, Andreas, and Simon Hix (2006), 'Why there is a democratic deficit in the EU: A response to Majone and Moravcsik', *Journal of Common Market Studies* 44 (18).

Fonseca, Francisco J. and Juan A. Martín (1992), 'La Unión Europea: génesis de Maastricht', *Revista de Instituciones Europeas* 19 (2), 517–64.

Fossum, John Erik (2010), 'Norway's European "gag rules"', *European Review* 18 (1), 73–92.

——and Philip Schlesinger (2007), *The European Union and the Public Sphere: A Communicative Space in the Making?* Routledge Studies on Democratizing Europe. London: Routledge.

Fox, Inman (1997), *La invención de España*, Madrid: Cátedra.

Frank, Robert (2000), 'Raymond Aron, Edgar Morin et les autres: le combat intellectuel pour l'Europe est-il possible après 1950?' A. Bachoud, J. Cuesta, and M. Trebitsch, eds., *Les intellectuels et l'Europe de 1945 à nos jours*, Paris: Publications Universitaires Paris Diderot.

——(2002), 'The meaning of Europe in French national discourse: A French Europe or a Europeanized France ?', in M. Malmborg and B. Strath, eds., *The Meaning of Europe*, Berg: Oxford.

Freeden, Michael (1996), *Ideologies and Political Theory: A Conceptual Approach*, Oxford: Clarendon Press.

——(2005), 'What should the 'political' in political theory explore?', *Journal of Political Philosophy* 13, 113–34.

Fusi, Juan Pablo (2000), *España, la evolución de la identidad española*, Madrid: Temas de Hoy.

Galtung, Johan (1973), *The European Community: A Superpower in the Making*, London: Allen & Unwin.

Garton Ash, Timothy (1983), *In Europe's Name: Germany and the Divided Continent*, London: Jonathan Cape.

——(2004), *Free World: Why a Crisis of the West Reveals the Opportunity of our Time*, London: Random House.

——(2005), 'Dreams of Central Europe', in P. Anderson, ed., *Spectrum: From Right to Left in the World of Ideas*, London: Verso.

——(2007a), 'Today's European Union is 27 states in search of a story', *The Guardian*, 4 January.

——(2007b), 'What's our story?', *The Guardian*, 16 March.

——(2007c), 'Europe's true stories', *Prospect* 131, 36–9.

Garton Ash, Timothy (2009), *Facts Are Subversive: Political Writing from a Decade Without a Name*, London: Atlantic Books.

Garvin, Tom (2005), *Preventing the Future: Why was Ireland so Poor for so Long?* Dublin: Gill and Macmillan.

GATT (1947), General Agreement on Tariffs and Trade, <http://www.wto.org/english/docs_e/legal_e/06-gatt_e.htm> (accessed 7 June 2010).

Gauchet, Marcel (2002), *La démocratie contre elle-même*, Paris: Gallimard.

——(2005a), *La condition politique*, Paris: Gallimard.

——(2005b), 'Comment l'Europe divise la France', conversation with René Rémond, *Le débat* 136, 4–19.

Geenens, Raf (2008), 'Democracy, human rights and history: Reading Lefort', *European Journal of Political Theory* 7 (3), 269–86.

Gellner, Ernest (1983), *Nations and Nationalism*, Ithaca, NY: Cornell University Press.

Geremek, Bronisław (2004), *Szansa i Zagrożenie: Polityka i dyplomacja w rodzinnej Europie. Rozmawia Dorota Maciejewska*, Warsaw: Wydawnictwo Studio EMKA.

References

Giakovaki, N. (2006), Ευρώπη μέσω Ελλάδας [Europe via Greece], Athens: Estia.

Giddens, Anthony (2007), *Europe in the Global Age*, Cambridge: Polity Press.

——and Ulrich Beck (2005), 'Nationalism has now become the enemy of Europe's nations', *The Guardian*, 4 October, <http://www.guardian.co.uk/politics/2005/oct/04/eu.world> (accessed 26 May 2008).

——Patrick Diamond, and Roger Liddle, eds. (2006), *Global Europe, Social Europe*, Cambridge: Polity Press.

Giedroyc, Jerzy and Juliusz Mieroszewski (1999), *Listy 1949–1956*, Warsaw: Czytelnik.

Gil Ibañez, Alberto (1994), 'Spain and the ratification of the Maastricht Treaty', in F. Laursen and S. Vanhoonacker, eds., *The Ratification of the Maastricht Treaty: Issues, Debates and Future Implications*, Maastricht: European Institute of Public Administration.

Gil Robles, José María (2005), 'Votar la Constitución Europea: un acto de patriotismo', *ABC*, 25 January.

Gillespie, Paul (2009), 'Parallels of accession states and Ireland', *Irish Times*, 2 May.

Gillet, Olivier (1997), *Religion et nationalisme: L'idéologie de l'Eglise Orthodoxe Roumaine sous le communisme*, Brussels: Editions de l'Université de Bruxelles.

Ginzborg, Paul (1989), *Storia d'Italia dal dopoguerra ad oggi*, Turin: Einaudi.

Gjems-Onstad, Ole (2000), *EØS-avtalen og EØS-loven med kommentarer*, Oslo: Gyldendal.

Gladwyn, Lord (1972), *The Memoirs of Lord Gladwyn*, London: Weidenfeld and Nicolson.

Goldfarb, Jeffrey (1998), *Civility and Subversion: The Intellectual in Democratic Society*, New York: Cambridge University Press.

Goldring, Maurice (1987), *Faith of our Fathers: A Study of Irish Nationalism*, Dublin: Repsol.

——(1993), *Pleasant the Scholar's Life: Irish Intellectuals and the Construction of the Nation-State*, London: Serif.

Göllner, Carol (1973), *Regimentele grănicereşti din Transilvania 1764–1851* [The border regiments of Transylvania 1764–1851], Bucharest: Editura Militara.

Goodhart, David (2004), 'Too diverse?', *Prospect* 95 (February).

——(2006), *Progressive Nationalism: Citizenship and the Left*, London: Demos.

——(2008), 'The baby-boomers finally see sense on immigration', *The Observer*, 24 February.

Goulard, Sylvie (2002), 'Frankreich und Europa: die Kluft zwischen Politik und Gesellschaft', in M. Meimeth and J. Schild, eds., *Die Zukunft von Nationalstaaten in der europäischen Integration: Deutsche und französische Perspektiven*, Opladen: Leske and Budrich.

Gowan, Peter and Perry Anderson, eds. (1997), *The Question of Europe*, London: Verso.

Goytisolo, Juan (1962), 'L'Espagne et l'Europe', *Les Temps Modernes* 194, 128–46.

Gramsci, Antonio (1971), *Selections from Prison Notebooks*, ed. Q. Hoare and G. Nowell Smith, London: Lawrence and Wishart.

——(1975), *Quaderno sul Machiavelli*, Torino: Einaudi.

——(1978), *Selections from Political Writings (1921–1926)*, trans. and ed. Q. Hoare, London: Lawrence and Wishart.

Grande, Edgar (2009), 'Europe identity: A dangerous obsession', in O. Cramme, ed., *Rescuing the European Project: EU Legitimacy, Governance and Security*, London: Policy Network.

Greenwood, Sean (2008), *Titan at the Foreign Office: Gladwyn Jebb and the Shaping of the Modern World*, Leiden and Boston, MA: Martinus Nijhoff.

Grimm, Dieter (1995), 'Does Europe need a constitution?', *European Law Journal* 1, 282–302.

——(2005a), 'Integration by constitution', *I-CON* 3 (2/3), 193–208.

——(2005b), 'The constitution in the process of denationalization', *Constellations* 12, 447–63.

Gross, Jan T. (2000), *Sąsiedzi: Historia zagłady żydowskiego miasteczka*, Sejny: Pogranicze.

Guénon, René (2008), *Criza lumii moderne*, trans. and intr. A. Manolescu, Bucharest: Humanitas.

Guizot, François (1985), *Histoire de la civilisation en Europe*, ed. P. Rosanvallon, Paris: Hachette.

Günther, Frieder (2004), *Denken vom Staat her: Die bundesdeutsche Staatsrechtslehre zwischen Dezision und Integration 1949–1970*, Munich: Oldenbourg.

Haas, Ernst B. (1976), 'Turbulent fields and the theory of regional integration', *International Organization* 30 (2), 173–212.

Habermas, Jürgen (1984), *Theory of Communicative Action*, vol. 1, Boston, MA: Beacon Press.

——(1987), *Theory of Communicative Action*, vol. 2, Boston, MA: Beacon Press.

——(1993), *Justification and Application: Remarks on Discourse Ethics*, Cambridge, MA: MIT Press.

——(1996), *La paix perpétuelle: le bicentenaire d'une idée kantienne*, Paris: Cerf.

——(1998), *Die postnationale Konstellation: politische Essays*, Frankfurt am Main: Suhrkamp.

——(2001a), 'Warum braucht Europa eine Verfassung? Nur als politisches Gemeinwesen kann der Kontinent seine in Gefahr geratene Kultur und Lebensform verteidigen', *Die Zeit* 27.

——(2001b), 'Why Europe needs a constitution', *New Left Review* 11 (September/October), 11–32.

——(2001c), 'Pas d'Europe sans une Constitution commune!', *Le Point* 1491, 102–4.

——(2004), 'Ein Ruck muss durch Europa gehen', *Weltwoche* 21 (19 May), <http://www.weltwoche.ch/ausgaben/2004–21/artikel-2004–21-ein-ruck-muss-durch-europa-gehen.html> (accessed 10 January 2008).

Habermas, Jürgen (2006a), 'Religion in the public sphere', *European Journal of Philosophy* 14 (1), 1–25.

——(2006b), *The Divided West*, Cambridge: Polity Press.

——(2008), 'Nach dem Bankrott: Der Privatisierungswahn ist an sein Ende gekommen. Nicht der Markt, sondern die Politik ist für das Gemeinwohl zuständig – Ein Gespräch mit dem Philosophen Jürgen Habermas', *Die Zeit* 46.

——(2009) 'Habermas über Dahrendorf. Die Liebe zur Freiheit', *Frankfurter Allgemeine Zeitung*, 2 May 2009.

——and Jacques Derrida (2003), 'Nach dem Krieg: Die Wiedergeburt Europas Frankfurter Allgemeinen Zeitung', 31 May. Reprinted in English in D. Lévy, M. Pensky, and J. Torpey (2005), *Old Europe, New Europe, Core Europe: Transatlantic Relations after the Iraq War*, London and New York: Verso.

——(2005), 'Feb. 15 or, what binds Europeans together: Plea for a common foreign policy, beginning in core Europe', in D. Lévy, M. Pensky, and J. Torpey, eds., *Old Europe,*

References

New Europe, Core Europe: Transatlantic Relations after the Iraq War, London and New York: Verso.

Halberstam, Daniel and Christoph Möllers (2009), 'The German Constitutional Court says "Ja zu Deutschland"', *German Law Journal* 10(8), 1241–57.

Halecki, Oskar and Andrew L. Simon (2000), *Borderlands of Western Civilization: A History of East Central Europe*, Simon Publications (original publication New York: Ronald Press, 1952).

Hall, Stuart and Perry Anderson (1961), 'The politics of the Common Market', *New Left Review* I/10 (July–August), 1–14.

Hanák, Jiří (2008), 'Václav Klaus reiterates his "no" to Lisbon', *Eurotopics*, 26 November, <http://www.eurotopics.net> (accessed 13 July 2010).

Hanioğlu, Şükrü (1995), *The Young Turks in Opposition*, Oxford: Oxford University Press.

Haraszti, Miklós (2002), 'The real Viktor Orbán', *Open Democracy* (1 May), <http://www.opendemocracy.net> (accessed 14 July 2010).

Harrison, Brian (2009), *Seeking a Role: The United Kingdom 1951–1970*, Oxford: Oxford University Press.

Havel, Václav (1989), *Essais politiques*, Paris: Calmann-Lévy.

Hayward, Katy (2009), *Irish Nationalism and European Integration: The Official Redefinition of the Island of Ireland*, Manchester: Manchester University Press.

Hazard, Paul (1953), *The European Mind 1680–1715*, London: Hollis and Carter.

Heine, Sophie (2009), *Une gauche contre l'Europe? Les critiques radicales et altermondialistes contre l'Union européenne en France*, Brussels: Editions de l'ULB.

Hennessy, Peter (2006), *Having It So Good: Britain in the Fifties*, London: Allen Lane.

Hennis, Wilhelm (1959), 'Zum Problem der deutschen Staatsanschauung', *Vierteljahrshefte für Zeitgeschichte* 7, 1–23.

Hernes, Helga (1987), *Welfare State and Woman Power: Essays in State Feminism*, Oslo: Universitetsforlaget.

Herrero de Miñón, Miguel (1992), 'Europa: integración sin esquizofrenia', *El País*, 10 June.

Hilton, Dominic (2005), 'Beyond the barbarians at the gate: Timothy Garton Ash interviewed', *Open Democracy* (24 February), <http://www.opendemocracy.net/democracy-americanpower/article_2352.jsp> (accessed 25 May 2008).

Hix, Simon (1999), 'Dimensions and alignments in European Union politics: Cognitive constraints and partisan responses', *European Journal of Political Research* 35, 69–106.

——(2008), *What's Wrong with the EU and How to Fix it*, London: John Wiley and Sons.

——and Andreas Føllesdal (2005), 'Why there is a democratic deficit in the EU: A response to Moravcsik and Majone', *Journal of Common Market Studies* 44 (3), 533–62.

Hobsbawm, Eric (1989), *Nations and Nationalism since 1789*, Cambridge, MA: Harvard University Press.

Hoffman, Stanley (1966), 'Obstinate or obsolete? The fate of the nation-state and the case of Western Europe', *Daedalus* 95 (3), 862–916.

Høibraaten, Helge and Jochen Hille, eds. (forthcoming), *Northern Europe and the Future of the EU*, Berlin: Wissenschafts-Verlag.

Holmes, Martin, ed. (1996), *The Eurosceptical Reader*, Basingstoke and London: Macmillan.

Hooghe, Liesbet and Gary Marks (2009), 'A postfunctionalist theory of European integration: From permissive consensus to constraining dissensus', *British Journal of Political Studies* 39, 1–23.

Hoppe, Jiří (2004), *Pražské jaro v médiích: Výběr z dobové publicistiky* [The Prague Spring in the media: Selection of writings], Prague: ÚSD.

Horáková, Naděžda (2004), 'Political parties and European integration in Czech public opinion', *CVVM*, 3 September, <http://www.cvvm.cas.cz>.

——(2005a), 'Agreement on EU Constitution in eyes of the Czech public', *CVVM*, 23 August, <http://www.cvvm.cas.cz>.

——(2005b), 'Confidence in constitutional institutions and satisfaction with political situation', *CVVM*, 6 May, <http://www.cvvm.cas.cz>.

Horciani, Ferhat, Danilo Zolo, and Orsetta Giolo (2005), *Mediterraneo: un dialogo tra le due sponde*, Rome: Jouvence.

Horel, Catherine (2009), *Cette Europe qu'on dit centrale: Des Habsburg à l'intégration européenne 1815–2004*, Paris: Beauchesne.

Howse, Robert (2004), 'Piety and preamble', review of J. H. H. Weiler, *A Christian Europe*, *Legal Affairs* 3 (3), 60–2.

Hunyadi, Mark (1992), 'Je suis ce que je me raconte. L'impuissance du modèle narratif', in J. Lenoble and N. Dewandre, eds., *L'Europe au soir du siècle*, Paris: Éditions Esprit.

Hurrell, Andrew (1990), 'Kant and the Kantian paradigm in international relations', *Review of International Studies* 16, 183–205.

Hurwic-Nowakowska, Irena (1996), *Żydzi polscy 1947–1950. Analiza więzi społecznej ludności żydowskiej*, Warsaw: IFIS PAN.

Hutchinson, John (1987), 'Cultural nationalism, elite mobility and nation-building: Communitarian politics in modern Ireland', *British Journal of Sociology* 38 (4), 482–501.

Ică Jr., Ioan I. (2002), 'Dilema socială a Bisericii Ortodoxe Române: Radiografia unei probleme' [The social dilemma of the Romanian Orthodox Church: The radiography of a problem], in I. I. Ică Jr. and G. Martino, eds., *Doctrina socială a Bisericii: Fundamente, documente, analize, perspective* [The social teaching of the Church: Fundamentals, documents, analysis, perspectives], Sibiu: Deisis.

Ilicak, Nazli (2000), 'Türkiye ve Avrupa Birliği', *Yeni Şafak*, 9 November, <http://yenisafak.com.tr/arsiv/2000/kasim/09/nilicak.html> (accessed 26 June 2010).

Imig, Doug and Sidney Tarrow (2001), *Contentious Europeans: Protest and Politics in an Emerging Polity*, Oxford: Rowman & Littlefield.

Inglehart, Ronald (1997), *Modernization and Postmodernization: Cultural, Economic, and Political Change in 43 Societies*, Princeton, NJ: Princeton University Press.

Inglis, Tom (2009), 'Getting and spending', review of F. Bradley and J. J. Kennelly, *Capitalising on Culture, Competing on Difference: Innovation, Learning and Sense of Place in Globalising Ireland* (Dublin: Blackhall, 2008), *Dublin Review of Books* 9, Spring 2009, <http://www.drb.ie/more_details/09-03-20/Getting_and_Spending.aspx>.

Institut des hautes études de la Défense nationale (2003), *Perspectives et capacités pour la Défense européenne*, Paris: Institut des hautes études.

Ioakimidis, Panagiotis C. (1998), *Η Ευρωπαϊκή, Ένωση και το Ελληνικό Κράτος, Συνέπειες της συμμετοχής στην ενοποιητική διαδικασία* [The European Union and the Greek state: Consequences of participation in the integration process], Athens: Themelio.

——ed., (2002), *Το μέλλον της Ευρώπης και η Ελλάδα* [The future of Europe and Greece], Athens: EKEM/ Sakkoulas.

——(2007a), *Η θέση της Ελλάδας στο Διεθνές, Ευρωπαϊκό και Περιφερειακό Σύστημα* [Greece's place in the international, European and regional system], Athens: Themelio.

References

Ioakimidis, Panagiotis C. (2007b), *Will the European Union Survive?*, Athens: Papazissis.

Ipsen, Hans Peter (1972), *Europäisches Gemeinschaftsrecht*, Tübingen: Mohr.

——(1973), 'Über Supranationalität', in H. Ehmke, ed., *Festschrift für Ulrich Scheuner zum 70. Geburtstag*, Berlin: Ducker & Humblot.

——(1994), 'Zehn Glossen zum Maastricht-Urteil', *Europarecht*, 29 (1), 1–21.

İrem, Nazim (2004), 'Undercurrents of European modernity and the foundations of modern Turkish conservativism: Bergsonism in retrospect', *Middle Eastern Studies* 40 (4), 79–112.

Jachtenfuchs, Markus (2002), *Die Konstruktion Europas: Verfassungsideen und Institutionelle Entwicklung*, Baden Baden: Nomos.

Janion, Maria (2007), *Niesamowita słowiańszczyzna. Fantazmaty literatury*, Cracow: Wydawnictwo Literackie.

Jedlicki, Jerzy (2007), 'Polskie położenie i europejska szansa', in *Gazeta Wyborcza*, 31 March–1 April.

Jennings, Jeremy (1993), *Intellectuals in Twentieth-Century France: Mandarins and Samurais*, London: MacMillan.

——(2000), 'Intellectuals and political culture', *The European Legacy* 5/6, 781–94.

——and Anthony Kemp-Welch, eds. (1997), *Intellectuals in Politics from the Dreyfus Affair to Salman Rushdie*, London: Routledge.

Jerez Mir, Miguel (1999), *Ciencia política, un balance de fin de siglo*, Madrid: Centro de Estudios Políticos y Constitucionales.

Joerges, Christian (2003), 'Europe a *Großraum*? Shifting legal conceptualizations of the integration project', in C. Joerges and N. Singh Ghaleigh, eds., *Darker Legacies of Law in Europe*, Oxford: Hart.

Judt, Tony (1992), *Past Imperfect: French Intellectuals 1944–1956*, Berkeley: University of California Press.

——(1996), *A Grand Illusion? An Essay on Europe*, London: Penguin.

——(2005), *Postwar: A History of Europe since 1945*, London: William Heinemann.

——(2008), 'The Good Society: Europe vs. America', in *Reappraisals: Reflections on the Forgotten Twentieth Century*, London: William Heinemann.

Kadioğlu, Ayşe (2007), 'An oxymoron: The origins of civic-republican liberalism in Turkey', *Critique: Critical Middle Eastern Studies* 16 (2), 171–90.

Kaelble, Hartmut (2009), 'Identification with Europe and politicization', in J. Checkel and P. Katzenstein, eds., *European Identity*, Cambridge: Cambridge University Press.

Kalaycioğlu, Ersin (2005), *Turkish Dynamics: Bridge across Troubled Lands*, New York: Palgrave Macmillan.

Kaldor, Nicholas (1971), 'The truth about the dynamic effects', *New Statesman*, 12 March.

Karavidas, C. (1931), *Αγροτικά· Συγκριτική έρευνα της κοινωνικής μορφολογίας της Ελλάδας και των γειτονικών σλαβικών χωρών* [Agrotica: Comparative research on the social morphology of Greece and neighbouring Slavic countries], Athens.

Karpat, Kemal, ed. (2000), *Ottoman Past and Today's Turkey*, Leiden: Brill.

Katzenstein, Peter K., ed. (1997), *Tamed Power: Germany in Europe*, Ithaca, NY: Cornell University Press.

Kawalec, Krzysztof (2000), *Spadkobiercy niepokornych: Dzieje polskiej myśli politycznej 1918–1939*, Wrocław: Zakład Narodowy im. Ossolińskich.

——(2006), 'Narodowa Demokracja wobec procesów modernizacyjnych. Dylematy, recepty, racje', in *Drogi do nowoczesności: Idea modernizacji w polskiej myśli politycznej*, Cracow: Ośrodek Myśli Politycznej.

——and Teresa Kulak (1992), 'Endecja wobec kwestii żydowskiej (lata 1893–1939)', in E. Grześkowiak-Łuczyk, ed., *Polska – Polacy – Mniejszości narodowe*, Wrocław: Zakład Narodowy im. Ossolińskich.

Kazakos, Panos (1991), *Η Ελλάδα μεταξύ Προσαρμογής και Περιθωριοποίησης· Δοκίμια Ευρωπαϊκής Οικονομικής Πολιτικής* [Greece between adjustment and marginalization: Essays on European economic policy], Athens: Diatton.

Kearney, Richard (1984), *The Irish Mind: Exploring Intellectual Traditions*, Dublin: Wolfhound Press.

——(1992), *Visions of Europe: Conversations on the Legacy and Future of Europe*, Dublin: Wolfhound Press.

——(1995), *States of Mind: Dialogues with Contemporary Thinkers on the European Mind*, Manchester: Manchester University Press.

——(1997), *Postnationalist Ireland: Politics, Culture, Philosophy*, London: Routledge.

Kende, Pierre (2001), *Raymond Aron et la liberté politique: Actes du colloque international des 6 et 7 octobre 2000*, Paris: de Fallois.

Kennedy, Fiachra and Sinnott, Richard (2007), 'Irish public opinion toward European integration', *Irish Political Studies* 22 (1), 61–80.

Kenny, Michael (1995), *The First New Left: British Intellectuals After Stalin*, London: Lawrence & Wishart.

Kersten, Krystyna (1993), *Między wyzwoleniem a zniewoleniem: Polska 1944–1956*, London: Aneks.

Kertesz, Imre (2003), *Die exilierte Sprache: Essays und Reden*, Frankfurt am Main: Suhrkamp.

Kielmansegg, Peter Graf von (2003[1996]), 'Integration und Demokratie', in M. Jachtenfuchs and B. Kohler-Koch, eds., *Europäische Integration*, Opladen: Leske and Budrich.

Kinander, Morten, ed. (2005), *Makt og rett: Om Maktutredningens konklusjoner om rettsliggjøring av politikken og demokratiets forvitring*, Oslo: Universitetsforlaget.

Kirchhof, Paul (1993), 'Europäische Einigung und der Verfassungsstaat der Bundesrepublik Deutschland', in J. Iseensee, ed., *Europa als politische Idee und als rechtliche Form*, 2nd edn, Berlin: Duncker & Humblot.

Kitromilides, Paschalis (1995), 'Europe and the dilemmas of Greek conscience', in P. Carabott (ed), *Greece and Europe in the Modern Period: Aspects of a Troubled Relationship*. London: King's College, Centre for Hellenic Studies.

——(2000), *Διαφωτισμός: οι πολιτικές και κοινωνικές ιδέες* [Enlightenment: The political and social ideas], 3rd edn, Athens: National Bank of Greece Cultural Foundation (MIET).

Klaus, Václav (2005), 'The intellectuals and socialism as seen from a post-communist country situated in predominantly post-democratic Europe', 22 August, <http://www.klaus.cz/clanky/2171>.

Kłoczowski, Jerzy (2002), *Polska-Europa: Od Gniezna 1000 roku do Polski w Unii Europejskiej*, Gdańsk: Novus Orbis.

Køber, Lars Kjetil (2001), 'Verre enn unionen med Sverige' – om bruken av unionsbegrepet og historiske sammenligninger med unionen med Sverige i EEC/EF/EU-debattene 1961–1994. Hovedoppgave i historie, Universitetet i Oslo.

References

Kojève, Alexandre (2004 [1945]), 'Outline of a doctrine of French policy', *Policy Review* 3/4, 3–40.

Koliopoulos, John S. and Thanos M. Veremis (2010), *Modern Greece: A History since 1821*, Oxford: Wiley-Blackwell.

Kontogeorgis, Giorgos (2005), 'Hellenism as nation cosmosystem', address at the Foundation of the Hellenic World, 19 October.

Kopeček, Michal (2005), 'The ups and downs of Central Europe. Chapters from Czech symbolic geography', in Z. Hlavíčková and N. Maslowski, eds., *The Weight of History in Central European Societies of the 20th Century*, Prague: CES (Collection of Central European Studies in Social Sciences).

Kopecký, Josef (2009), 'The Lisbon treaty still has a long way to go in Prague', *Eurotopics* (translated from the daily *Mladá fronta Dnes*), 19 February, <http://www.eurotopics.net> (accessed 13 July 2010).

Koryś, Piotr (2006), 'Jaka nowoczesność?', in *Drogi do nowoczesności. Idea modernizacji w polskiej myśli politycznej*, Cracow: Ośrodek Myśli Politycznej.

Kosík, Karel (2003), 'Un troisième Munich', in *La crise des temps modernes: Dialectique de la morale*, Paris: Editions de la Passion.

Koskenniemi, Martti (2007), 'The fate of public international law: Between technique and politics', *Modern Law Review* 70, 1–30.

Kouřil, Vít (2008), 'Ženy u nás mají slušnou pozici – Rozhovor s Jiřinou Šiklovou' [Women have a decent position in our country – Interview with Jiřina Šiklová], *Sedmá generace* 1, <http://www.sedmagenerace.cz/index.php?art=clanek&id=304> (accessed 13 June 2010).

Krasnodębski, Zdzisław (2005), *Demokracja peryferii*, Gdańsk: Wydawnictwo słowo/obraz terytoria.

——(2008), 'Poland's civil religion and its "liberal" deconstruction', in W. Rothholz and S. Berglund, eds., *Vom Symbol zur Realität: Studien zur politischen Kultur des Ostseeraums und des östlichen Europas*, Berlin: Berliner Wissenschafts-Verlag.

Krastev, Ivan (2004), 'We are all Brits today: Timothy Garton Ash's "Free World"', *Open Democracy* (6 September), <http://www.opendemocracy.net/democracy-europe_constitution/article_2078.jsp> (accessed 25 May 2008).

Křen, Jan (2005), *Dvě století střední Evropy* [Two centuries of Central Europe], Prague: Argo.

Krytyki Politycznej Przewodnik Lewicy: Idee, daty i fakty, pytania i odpowiedzi (2007), Warsaw: Wydawnictwo Krytyki Politycznej.

Kuhling, Carmen and Kieran Keohane (2007), *Cosmopolitan Ireland? Globalisation and Quality of Life*, London: Pluto Press.

Kuhnle, Stein (1990), 'Velferdsstaten og europeisk utvikling', *Nytt Norsk Tidsskrift* 3, 244–56.

Kundera, Milan (1983), 'La tragédie de l'Europe centrale ou un Occident kidnappé', *Le Débat* 27 (November), 3–22. English translation in *New York Review of Books*, 26 April 1984, 33–8.

Kuźniar, Roman (2008), *Droga do wolności: Polityka zagraniczna III Rzeczpospolitej*, Warsaw: Scholar.

Kvalvåg, Svein (1999), *Argumentasjonsbruk i den norske EU-debatten: En sammenligning av EU-debatten i 1972 med EU-debatten i 1994* [Arguments used in the Norwegian EU debate: A comparison of the EU debate in 1972 with the debate in 1994], Bergen: LOS-Senteret Rapport R9911.

Kwiek, Marek and Wolf Lepenies (2003), 'Homo Europaeus intellectualis revisited', in E. Czerwinska-Schupp (ed.), *Philosophie an der Schwelle des 21. Jahrhunderts*, Frankfurt am Main and New York: Peter Lang.

La Palombara, Joseph (1987), *Democracy Italian Style*, New Haven, CT: Yale University Press.

Laborde, Cécile (2001), 'The culture(s) of the republic. Nationalism and multiculturalism in contemporary French republican thought', *Political Theory* 29 (5), 716–35.

Lacroix, Justine (2002), 'For a European constitutional patriotism', *Political Studies* 50, 944–58.

——(2004a), 'A reply to Bellamy and Castiglione', *Political Studies* 52, 194–6.

——(2004b), *L'Europe en procès: Quel patriotisme au-delà des nationalismes?*, Paris: Cerf.

——(2008), *La pensée française à l'épreuve de l'Europe*, Paris: Grasset.

——(2009), 'Does Europe need common values? Habermas vs. Habermas', *European Journal of Political Theory* 8 (2), 141–56.

——and Paul Magnette (2009), 'French Republicanism and the European Union', in S. Besson and J. L. Marti, *Legal Republicanism: National and International Perspectives*, Oxford: Oxford University Press.

Laffan, Brigid and Jane O'Mahony (2008), *Ireland and the European Union*, Basingstoke: Palgrave Macmillan.

Laignel-Lavastine, Alexandra (2000), 'La double dissidence de Jan Patočka? entre pratique politique et européanité critique', in A. Bachoud, J. Cuesta, and M. Trebitsch, eds., *Les intellectuels et l'Europe de 1945 à nos jours*, Paris: Publications Universitaires Paris Diderot.

——(2005), *Esprits d'Europe – Autour de Czeslaw Milosz, Jan Patocka et Istvan Bibo*, Paris: Calmann-Lévy.

Lane, Thomas (2008), 'East European exiles and their interpretations of the meaning of Europe', in J. Faraldo, P. Gulińska-Jurgiel, and C. Domnitz, eds., *Europa im Ostblock*, Cologne: Böhlau.

Laporta, Francisco (2005), 'El referéndum y la falsa seducción', *El País*, 14 June.

Lavdas, Kostas A. (2001), 'Republican Europe and multicultural citizenship', *Politics* 21 (1), 2–11.

——(2009), 'A European republic in a polycultural setting: Authority and diversity in Europe's emerging polity', in S. Stavridis, ed., *Understanding and Evaluating the European Union: Theoretical and Empirical Approaches*, Nicosia: Nicosia University Press.

Lazorthes, Frédéric (2005), 'L'attente confuse d'un pays en mal d'avenir', *Le débat* 136, 58–68.

Le Duc, Gwenaël (1994), 'The contribution to the making of European culture of Irish monks and scholars in the medieval times', in J. P. Mackey, ed., *The Cultures of Europe: The Irish Contribution*, Belfast: Institute of Irish Studies, Queen's University Belfast.

Le Goff, Jacques (1985), *Les intellectuels au moyen âge*, Paris: Seuil.

——(2005), 'Le malaise français au miroir de l'Europe', *Le débat* 136, 44–57.

Lee, Joseph (1989), *Ireland 1912–1985: Politics and Society*, Cambridge: Cambridge University Press.

Leerssen, Joep (2007), *National Thought in Europe: A Cultural History*, Amsterdam: University of Amsterdam Press.

Lefort, Claude (1980), *L'invention démocratique*, Paris: Fayard.

References

Leggewie, Claus, ed. (2004), *Die Türkei und Europa: Die Positionen*, Frankfurt am Main: Suhrkamp.

Lemayrie, Michel (2008), 'Intellectuels', in Y. Bertoncini et al., *Dictionnaire critique de l'Union européenne*, Paris: Armand Colin, 237–43.

——and Jean-François Sirinelli (2003), *L'histoire des intellectuels aujourd'hui*, Paris: PUF.

Lepenies, Wolf (1992), *La fin de l'utopie et le retour de la mélancolie. Regards sur les intellectuels d'un vieux continent*, Paris: Collège de France. (Translated as *Melancholy and Society*, trans. J. Gaines and D. Jones, Cambridge, MA: Harvard University Press.)

——(2007), *Qu'est-ce qu'un intellectuel européen? Les intellectuels et la politique de l'esprit dans l'histoire européenne*, Paris: Seuil.

Lepsius, Oliver (2004), 'Braucht das Verfassungsrecht eine Theorie des Staates?', *Europäische Grundrechte-Zeitschrift* 31, 370–81.

Lévy, Daniel, Max Pensky, and John Torpey, eds. (2005), *Old Europe, New Europe, Core Europe*, New York: Verso.

Libéra, Alain de (1991), *Penser au moyen âge*, Paris: Seuil.

Licata, Laurent and Olivier Klein (2002), 'Does European citizenship breed xenophobia? European identification as a predictor of intolerance towards immigrants', *Journal of Community and Applied Social Psychology* 12 (5), 323–37.

Liebert, Ulrike (2007), with T. Evas, S. Maatsch, K. Packham, P. Rakusanova, A. Wyrozumska, 'Europe in contention: Debating the Constitutional Treaty', in *Perspectives on European Politics and Society*, 8 (3), special issue, 235–413.

——(2010), 'More democracy in the European Union? Mixed messages from the German Lisbon ruling', in A. Fischer-Lescano, C. Joerges, A. Wonka, eds., *The German Constitutional Court's Lisbon Ruling: Legal and Political Science Perspectives*, ZERP Diskussionspapier (University of Bremen, Zentrum für Europäische Rechtspolitik, 1/2010).

Liiceanu, Gabriel (1983), *Jurnalul de la Păltiniş: Un model paideic în cultura umanistă* [The Păltiniş diary: A paideic model in the humanist culture], Bucharest: Cartea Românească.

——(1987), *Epistolar*, Bucharest: Cartea Românească.

——(1991), 'În loc de prefață – Ce înseamnă a fi european în Estul postbelic?' [In place of a foreword – What does it mean to be a European in the post-war East?], foreword to *Jurnalul de la Păltiniş*, 2nd edn, Bucharest: Humanitas.

Lijphart, Arend (1999), *Patterns of Democracy: Government Forms and Performance in Thirty-Six Countries*, New Haven, CT: Yale University Press.

Lilla, Mark (1994), *New French Thought*, Princeton, NJ: Princeton University Press.

——(2001), *The Reckless Mind: Intellectuals in Politics*, New York: New York Review of Books.

Livezeanu, Irina (1995), *Cultural Politics in Greater Romania: Regionalism, Nation Building and Ethnic Struggle, 1918–1930*, Ithaca, NY and London: Cornell University Press.

Longhurst, Kerry and Marcin Zaborowski (2007), *The New Atlanticist: Poland's Foreign and Security Policy Priorities*, London: Chatham House.

López Castillo, Autonio (2005), '¿Si ya hay Tratados Constitucionales, para qué una Constitución Europea?', *Noticias de la Unión Europea* 21 (250), 7–18.

López Garrido, Diego (1992), 'Un sí que vale', *El País*, 24 September.

Lübbe, Hermann (1994), *Abschied vom Superstaat: Vereinigte Staaten von Europa wird es nicht geben*, Berlin: Siedler.

Lunden, Kåre (1994), 'Politisk handling, nasjonalisme og EU-motstand', *Mål og makt* 24 (4), 45–53.

Lygeros, Stavros (2008), Στο όνομα της Μακεδονίας· Ο διπλωματικός πόλεμος [In the name of Macedonia: The diplomatic war], Athens: Livanis.

MacDonagh, Oliver (1983), *States of Mind: A Study of Anglo-Irish Conflict, 1780–1980*, London: Allen and Unwin.

——(1984), *After Virtue: A Study in Moral Theory*, Notre Dame, IN: University of Notre Dame Press.

Mackey, James P., ed. (1994), *The Cultures of Europe: The Irish Contribution*, Belfast: Institute of Irish Studies, Queen's University Belfast.

MacLean, Ian, Alan Montefiore, and Peter Winch, eds. (1990), *The Political Responsibility of Intellectuals*, Cambridge: Cambridge University Press.

Mach, Zdzisław (1993), *Symbols, Conflict and Identity: Essays in Political Anthropology*, Albany, NY: SUNY Press.

McNally, Mark (2008), 'Conor Cruise O'Brien's conservative anti-nationalism: Retrieving the postwar European connection', *European Journal of Political Theory* 7 (3), 308–30.

Magnette, Paul (2007), 'Comment peut-on être européen?', *Raison publique* 7, 99–113.

——and Yannis Papadopoulos (2008), 'On the politicization of the European consociation: A middle way between Hix and Bartolini', *European Governance Papers (EUROGOV)* No. C-08–01, <http://www.connex-network.org/eurogov/>.

Magris, Claudio (1986), *Danubio*, Milan: Garzanti.

Majone, Giandomenico (2010), 'Transaction-cost efficiency and the democratic deficit', *Journal of European Public Policy*, 17 (2), 150–75.

Malcolm, Noel (1991), *Sense on Sovereignty*, London: Centre for Policy Studies.

——(1995), 'The case against "Europe"', *Foreign Affairs* (March/April).

——(2003), 'A federal constitution with the heart of a manifesto', *Daily Telegraph*, 28 July, 18.

Malefakis, Edward (1995), 'The political and socioeconomic contours of southern European history', in R. Gunther, P. N. Diamandouros and H.-J. Puhle, eds., *The Politics of Democratic Consolidation: Southern Europe in Comparative Perspective*, Baltimore, MD: Johns Hopkins University Press.

Manent, Pierre (2006a), *La raison des nations: Réflexions sur la démocratie en Europe*, Paris: Gallimard.

——(2006b), 'Manent, libéral-patriote', interview with Elisabeth Lévy, *Le Point* 1746, 91–3.

——(2007), *Democracy without Nations? The Fate of Self-Governance in Europe*, Wilmington, DE: ISI.

Mangas Martín, Araceli (2005), 'Sobre la primacía del Tratado Constitucional. ¿Tensiones Constitucionales a las vista?', in C. Closa and N. Fernández, eds., *La Constitución de la Unión Europea*, Madrid: Centro de Estudios Políticos y Constitucionales.

Manitakis, Antonis (2004), Το Σύνταγμα της Ευρώπης εναντίον της εθνικής και λαϊκής κυριαρχίας [The constitution of Europe against national and popular sovereignty], Athens: Papazissis.

——(2007), 'Το τέλος της Ευρωπαϊκής Συνταγματοποίησης ή η αρχή μιας άλλης' [The end of European constitutionalization or the beginning of another?], special issue of Το Σύνταγμα, ed. Sakkoulas, 3–23.

Manners, Ian (2002), 'Normative power Europe: A contradiction in terms?', *Journal of Common Market Studies* 40 (2), 235–58.

References

Mannheim, Karl (1936), *Ideology and Utopia*, New York: Harcourt, Brace & Co.

Mardin, Şerif (1989), *Jön Türklerin Siyasi Fikirleri 1895–1908*, Istanbul: İletişim.

——(1994), 'Culture change and the intellectual: A study of the effects of secularization in modern Turkey, Necip Fazil Kisakürek and the Nakşibendi', in *Cultural Transitions in the Middle East*, Leiden: Brill.

Marías, Julián (1992), 'Europa, la segunda salida', *Cuenta y razón de pensamiento actual*, 71–2, 7–10.

——(2000), *Ser español: Ideas y creencias en el mundo hispánico*, Barcelona: Planeta.

Marino, Adrian (2005), *Pentru Europa: Integrarea României; Aspecte ideologice şi culturale* [For Europe? The integration of Romania; ideological and cultural aspects], 2nd edn, Iaşi: Polirom.

Marquand, David (1979), *Parliament for Europe*, London: Jonathan Cape.

——(2008), *Britain Since 1918: The Strange Career of British Democracy*, London: Weidenfeld & Nicolson.

Martino, Antonio (1994), *La rivolta liberale*, Milan: Sperling & Kupfer.

Maslowski, Nicolas (2007), 'W cieniu Wacławów' [In the shadow of the Václavs], *Tygodnik powszechny* 13 (4), 15.

——(2008), 'Republika nebo demokracie. Rozhovor s Michelem Wiewiorkou' [The republic or democracy; discussion with Michel Wieviorka], *Babylon*, January, pp. 1, 5.

Mastellone, Salvo (2000), *La democrazia etica di Mazzini*, Rome: Izzi.

Matlary, Janne Haaland (2003a), 'EU gir solidaritet', *Aftenposten*, 7 January, 9.

——(2003b), 'Kristendemokratene og EU', *Aftenposten*, 8 July, 6.

——(2007), 'Ny EU-debatt kan bli tvunget frem', *Aftenposten*, 30 August.

Mayer, Françoise (2003), *Les Tchèques et leur communisme*, Paris: EHESS.

Mayne, Richard and John Pinder (1990), *Federal Union: The Pioneers; A History of Federal Union*, Basingstoke: Palgrave Macmillan.

Mazower, Mark (2008), *Hitler's Empire: How the Nazis Ruled Europe*, New York: Penguin.

——(2009), *No Enchanted Palace: The End of Empire and the Ideological Origins of the United Nations*, Princeton, NJ: Princeton University Press.

Mazzini, Giuseppe (2001), *Thoughts upon Democracy in Europe*, ed. S. Mastellone, Florence: CED.

Meagher, Denise M. (2001), 'Academic rites: An anthropology of contested reproductions of modern Irishness', Unpublished PhD thesis, National University of Ireland Maynooth.

Meller, Stefan (2007a), 'Razem' powinno być najważniejszym słowem we wzajemnych stosunkach polsko-niemieckich', *Dziennik: Polska-Europa-Świat*, 21 August.

——(2007b), 'Polska dołączy do najważniejszych państw Unii', *Dziennik: Polska-Europa-Ś wiat*, 24 July.

Menéndez, Agustin José (2004), 'Comment on "A Convention without Law"? Legitimating "legal" constitution-building in Europe', in C. Closa and J. E. Fossum, *Deliberative Constitutional Politics in the EU*, ARENA Report, 5/04, <http://www.arena.uio.no/cidel/Reports/Albarracin_Report.htm>.

——(2005), 'A pious Europe? Why Europe should not define itself as Christian', *European Law Review* 30 (1), 133–48.

Mény, Yves (2002), 'Constituer l'Europe', *Le Monde*, 27 February, 1.

——(2009), 'The "Democratic Principle" and the European Union: The Challenge of a Post-National Democracy', in C. Moury and L. de Sousa, eds., *Institutional Challenges in Post-Constitutional Europe: Governing Change*, London: Routledge.

Mergier, Alain (2005), 'Pourquoi le non était possible', in A. Mergier et al., *Le jour où la France a dit non: Comprendre le référendum du 29 mai 2005*, Paris: Plon.

Mesežnikov, Grigorij (2004), 'Slovakia: From ugly duckling to swan', *The New Presence* (March), <http://www.ceeol.com>.

Michalski, Krzysztof, ed. (2006), *What Holds Europe Together?*, Budapest and New York: Central European University Press.

Michlic, Joanna (2004), '"The Open Church" and "the Closed Church" and the discourse on Jews in Poland between 1989 and 2000', *Communist and Post-Communist Studies*, 37 (4), 461–9.

Michnik, Adam (1985), *Letters from Prison and Other Essays*, Berkeley: University of California Press.

——(1990), 'Notes from the revolution', *New York Times Magazine*, 11 March.

——(1995), *Diabeł naszego czasu: Publicystyka z lat 1985–1994*, Warsaw: NOWA.

——(2005), *Wściekłość i wstyd*, Warsaw: Zeszyty Literackie.

——Józef Tischner, and Jacek Żakowski (1995), *Między panem a plebanem*, Cracow: Znak.

Miller, David (1995), *On Nationality*, Oxford: Clarendon Press.

——(2000), 'Communitarianism: Left, right and centre', in *Citizenship and National Identity*, Cambridge: Polity Press.

——(2007), *National Responsibility and Global Justice*, Oxford: Oxford University Press.

Milner, Jean-Claude (2003), *Les penchants criminels de l'Europe démocratique*, Paris: Verdier.

Miłosz, Czesław (1964), *Une autre Europe*, Paris: Gallimard.

——(1994), *Rodzinna Europa*, Cracow: Wydawnictwo Literackie.

Milward, Alan (1992), *The European Rescue of the Nation State*, London: Routledge.

Moen, Jo Stein, Wegard Harsvik, Anne Margit Bjørnflaten, and Tore O. Sandvik (2004), *Et nytt nei*, Oslo: Spartacus.

Möllers, Christoph (2000), *Staat als Argument*, Munich: C. H. Beck.

——(2007), '"We are (afraid of) the people": Constituent power in German constitutionalism', in M. Loughlin and N. Walker, eds., *The Paradox of Constitutionalism: Constituent Power and Constitutional Form*, Oxford: Oxford University Press.

——(2008), *Der vermisste Leviathan: Staatstheorie in der Bundesrepublik*, Frankfurt am Main: Suhrkamp.

——(2009), 'Was ein Parlament ist, entscheiden die Richter', *Frankfurter Allgemeine Zeitung*, 16 July.

Mommsen, Wolfgang, ed. (1994), *The Long Way to Europe*, Chicago, IL: Edition Q.

Monnet, Jean (1997), *Mémoires*, Paris: Fayard.

Montefiore, Alan (1990), 'The political responsibility of intellectuals', in I. Maclean, A. Montefiore, and P. Winch, eds., *The Political Responsibility of Intellectuals*, Cambridge: Cambridge University Press.

Montes, Pedro (1993), *La integración en Europa*, Madrid: Trotta.

Morata, Francesc (1998), 'Spain: Modernization through integration', in K. Hanf and B. Soetendorp, eds., *Adapting to European Integration: Small States and the European Union*, London: Longman.

References

Moravcsik, Andrew (2001), 'Despotism in Brussels? Misreading the European Union', *Foreign Affairs* (May/June).

—— (2002), 'In defence of the democratic deficit: Reassessing legitimacy in the European Union', *Journal of Common Market Studies* 40 (4), 603–24.

—— (2006), 'What can we learn from the collapse of the European constitutional project?', *Politische Vierteljahresschrift* 47 (2), 219–41.

Moreno Juste, Antonio (2000), 'Las relaciones España/Europa en el siglo XX: Notas para una interpretación', *Cuadernos de Historia Contemporánea* 22, 95–133.

Morgan, Glyn (2005), *The Idea of a European Superstate: Public Justification and European Integration*, Princeton, NJ and Oxford: Princeton University Press.

Morin, Edgar (1987), *Penser l'Europe*, Paris: Gallimard.

Morley, John (1874), *On Compromise*, London: Macmillan.

Moses, A. Dirk (2007), *German Intellectuals and the Nazi Past*, Cambridge: Cambridge University Press.

Mosse, George (1974), *The Nationalization of Masses*, New York: Howard Fertig.

Mount, Ferdinand (2001), 'Britain and the intellectuals', *The National Interest*, 22 June.

Moury, Catherine and Luís de Sousa, eds. (2009), *Institutional Challenges in Post-Constitutional Europe: Governing Change*, London: Routledge.

Mouzelis, Nicos (2002), *Από την αλλαγή στον εκσυγχρονισμό* [From change to modernisation], Athens: Themelio.

—— and George Pagoulatos (2005), 'Civil society and citizenship in postwar Greece' in F. Birtek et al. eds., *Citizenship and Nation State in Greece and Turkey*, London: Frank Cass.

Moynihan, Maurice, ed. (1980), *Speeches and Statements by de Valera, 1917–1973*, Dublin: Gill and Macmillan.

Müller, Jan-Werner (2000), *Another Country: German Intellectuals, Unification and National Identity*, New Haven, CT: Yale University Press.

—— (2003), *A Dangerous Mind: Carl Schmitt in Post-War European Thought*, New Haven, CT: Yale University Press.

—— (2006), 'Julien Benda's Anti-Passionate Europe', *European Journal of Political Theory* 5 (2), 125–37.

—— (2007), *Constitutional Patriotism*, Princeton, NJ: Princeton University Press.

—— (forthcoming), 'Three constitutionalist responses to globalization', in S. Macedo and J. Tullis, eds., *The Limits of Constitutional Democracy*, Princeton, NJ: Princeton University Press.

Mummendey, Amélie and Sven Waldzus (2004), 'National difference and European plurality: Discrimination or tolerance between European countries', in R. K. Herrmann, T. Risse, and M. B. Brewer, eds., *Transnational Identities: Becoming European in the EU*, Lanham, MD: Rowman & Littlefield.

Münch, Richard (2008), *Die Konstruktion der europäischen Gesellschaft*, Frankfurt am Main: Campus.

Murray, John (1952), 'This growing sense of Europe', *Studies*, 41 (163–4), 268–80.

Muszyński, Henryk (2007), 'Kościół obawia się Karty', *Dziennik: Polska-Europa-Świat*, 12 November.

Nairn, Tom (1971), 'British nationalism and the EEC', *New Left Review* I/69 (September–October), 3–28.

——(1972), 'The left against Europe?', special issue, *New Left Review* 1/75 (September–October).

——(1973), *The Left against Europe?* London: Penguin.

——(2004), 'The free world's end?', *Open Democracy*, <http://www.opendemocracy.net/democracy-americanpower/article_2249.jsp> (accessed 26 May 2008).

Nanz, Patrizia (2006), *Europolis: Constitutional Patriotism Beyond the Nation State*, Manchester: Manchester University Press.

Napolitano, Giorgio (1992), *America ed Europa dopo il 1989*, Rome-Bari: Laterza.

——(2002), *Europa politica*, Rome: Donzelli.

——and Eric Hobsbawm (1976), *La politique du PCI, entretien avec Eric Hobsbawm*, Paris: Editions Sociales, Notre Temps/Monde.

Năstase, Adrian (2004), *De Karl Marx à Coca-Cola* [From Karl Marx to Coca-Cola], Bucharest: Nemira.

National Intelligence Council (2008), 'Global Trends 2025: A Transformed World', <http://www.dni.gov/nic/PDF_2025/2025_Global_Trends_Final_Report.pdf> (accessed 27 November 2008).

Neamțu, Mihail (2008), *Bufnița printre dărâmături: Insomnii teologice în România post-ocmunistă* [The owl among the rubble: Theological insomnia in post-communist Romania], Iași: Polirom.

Negri, Antonio and Michael Hart (2000), *Empire*, Cambridge, MA: The President and Fellows of Harvard College.

Nejedlý, Zdeněk (1950 [1946]), *Komunisté: Dědici velkých tradic českého národa* [The communists: The great inheritors of the Czech nation's tradition], Prague: Československý spisovatel.

Neumann, Iver B. (1993), 'Nordens skjebne frem mot år 2000' (Op. Ed.), *Aftenposten* 6 July, 7.

——(2002), 'This little piggy stayed at home – Why Norway is not a member of the EU', in L. Hansen and O. Wæver, eds., *European Integration and National Identity*, London: Routledge.

Nicolaïdis, Kalypso (2001), 'Conclusion: The federal vision beyond the federal state', in K. Nicolaïdis and R. Howse, *The Federal Vision: Legitimacy and Levels of Governance in the United States and the European Union*, Oxford: Oxford University Press.

——(2003a), 'Our European demoï-cracy: Is this constitution a third way for Europe?', in K. Nicolaïdis and S. Weatherill, eds., *Whose Europe? National Models and the Constitution of the European Union*, Oxford: Oxford University Press.

——(2003b), 'The new constitution as European demoi-cracy?', London: Federal Trust for Education & Research, online paper 38, <http://www.fedtrust.co.uk/uploads/constitution/38_03.pdf> (accessed 27 June 2010).

Nicolaïdis, Kalypso (2004a), 'We, the peoples of Europe . . . ', *Foreign Affairs* 83 (6), 97–110.

——(2004b), 'The new constitution as European demoicracy?', *Critical Review of International Social and Political Philosophy* 7(1), 76–93.

——(2005), 'UE: Un moment tocquevillien', *Politique étrangère* 3, 459–509.

——(2007), 'Trusting the Poles? Constructing Europe through mutual recognition', *Journal of European Public Policy* 14 (5), 682–98.

——and Robert Howse, eds. (2001), *The Federal Vision. Legitimacy and Levels of Governance in United States and the European Union*, Oxford: Oxford University Press.

References

Nicolaïdis, Kalypso and Janie Pélabay (2007), 'Comment raconter l'Europe tout en prenant la diversité narrative au sérieux?', *Raison Publique* 7, 63–83.

——(2008), 'One union, one story? In praise of Europe's narrative diversity', in D. Phinnemore and A. Warleigh-Lack, eds., *Reflections on European Integration*, Basingstoke: Palgrave.

——and Stephen Weatherill, eds. (2003), *Whose Europe? National Models and the Constitution of the European Union*, Oxford: Oxford University Press.

Nida-Rümelin, Julian and Werner Weidenfeld, eds. (2007), *Europäische Identität: Voraussetzungen und Strategien*, Baden-Baden: Nomos.

Niess, Frank (2001), *Die europäische Idee – aus dem Geist des Widerstands*, Frankfurt am Main: Suhrkamp.

Nilsson, Dick (2000), 'Yet another Europe?', *Central Europe Review* 2 (36), October, <http://www.ce-review.org/00/36/books36_nilsson.html>.

Noica, Constantin (1988), *De dignitate Europae*, Bucharest: Kriterion Verlag.

——(1993), *Modelul cultural European* [The European cultural model], Bucharest: Humanitas.

Novotný, Dušan (1996), *Une dangereuse méprise*, Paris: Charlot.

Ó Raifeartaigh, Tarlach F. (1972), *Ireland and the EEC: The Cultural Aspects*, Dublin: Irish Council of the European Movement.

O'Brien, Conor Cruise (1988), *God Land: Reflections on Religion and Nationalism*, Cambridge, MA: Harvard University Press.

O'Dowd, Liam (1985), 'Intellectuals in twentieth century Ireland and the case of George Russell (Æ)', *The Crane Bag* 9, 6–25.

——(1996), *On Intellectuals and Intellectual Life in Ireland: International, Comparative and Historical Contexts*, Belfast: Institute of Irish Studies, Queen's University Belfast.

O'Grady, Desmond (2001), *The Wandering Celt*, Dublin: Dedalus Press.

O'Mahony, Jane (2010), 'Ireland's EU referendum experience', in K. Hayward and M. C. Murphy, eds., *The Europeanization of Party Politics in Ireland, North and South*, London: Routledge.

O'Mahony, Patrick and Delanty, Gerard (1998), *Rethinking Irish History: Nationalism, Identity and Ideology*, Basingstoke: Macmillan Press.

O'Neill, Michael (1996), *The Politics of European Integration: A Reader*, New York: Routledge.

Offe, Claus, ed. (2003), *Demokratisierung der Demokratie: Diagnosen und Reformvorschläge*, Frankfurt am Main: Campus.

——and Ulrich K. Preuss (2006), 'The problem of legitimacy in the European polity: Is democratization the answer?', in C. Crouch and W. Streeck, eds., *The Diversity of Democracy: Corporatism, Social Order and Political Conflict*, Cheltenham: Elgar.

Ortega, Andrés (1994), *La razón de Europa*, Madrid: Editorial Aguilar.

——(2007), 'Demoicracia', *El País*, 25 January.

Ortega y Gasset, José (1910), 'España como posibilidad', in *Obras Completas, Tomo I*. Madrid: Taurus.

Ory, Pascal and Jean-François Sirinelli (1992), *Les intellectuels en France de l'affaire Dreyfus à nos jours*, Paris: Armand Colin.

Oskarson, Maria and Kristen Ringdal (1998), 'The Arguments', in A. T. Jenssen, P. Personen, and M. Giljam, eds., *To Join or Not to Join*, Oslo: Scandinavian University Press.

Østerud, Øyrind (1990), 'EF 1992 – mot en europeisk superstat', *Nytt Norsk Tidsskrift* 1, 59–69.

——(1993), 'Grenser for europeisk integrasjon', *Nytt Norsk Tidsskrift* 3–4, 256–70.

——(1999), 'Den postnasjonale utfordringen', *Nytt Norsk Tidsskrift* 4, 285–96.

Özal, Turgut (1991), *Turkey in Europe and Europe in Turkey*, Nicosia, N. Cyprus: K. Rustem and Brother.

Özbudun, Ergun (2007), 'Democratization reforms in Turkey, 1993–2004', *Turkish Studies* 8 (2), 179–96.

Packham, Kathrin (2007), 'From the contentious constitution to the awkward other... social model: The constitutional debate in the British print media', in U. Liebert et al., eds., 'Europe in contention: Debating the Constitutional Treaty', special issue of *Perspectives on European Politics and Society* 8 (3), September.

Padoa Schioppa, Tommaso (2004), *The EU as a Gentle Power*, London: Federal Trust.

Pagden, Anthony (2000), 'Stoicism, cosmopolitanism, and the legacy of European imperialism', *Constellations* 7(1), 3–22.

——(2002), *The Idea of Europe*, Cambridge: Cambridge University Press.

Pagoulatos, George (2002), 'Greece, the European Union, and the 2003 Presidency' (foreword by President Jacques Delors), Notre Europe Institute, *Research and European Issues* 21 (December), <http://www.notre-europe.eu/> (available in English and French).

——(2004), 'Believing in national exceptionalism: Ideas and economic divergence in southern Europe', *West European Politics* 27 (1), January, 43–68.

——(2007), 'Ασφάλεια και Ανάπτυξη: Στρατηγική για τη συμμετοχή στα οφέλη μιας ισχυρής Ευρώπης' [Security and growth: A strategy for participation in the benefits of a strong Europe], *Vima Ideon* 1 (special edition of *To Vima*), May.

Pamfil, Laura (2007), *Noica necunoscut: De la uitarea fiinţei la reamintirea ei* [Noica unknown: From the oblivion to the remembrance of being], Cluj: Biblioteca Apostrof and Casa Cărţii de Ştiinţă.

Pantazopoulos, Nicolaos (1967), Κοινοτικός βίος στη Θεσσαλία [Communitarian life in Thessaly], Thessaloniki.

——(1993), Ελληνικός κοινοτισμός και σύγχρονη ελληνική παράδοση [Greek communitarianism and modern Greek tradition], Athens: Parousia.

Papadimitriou, George (1995), 'Ευρωπαϊκή ενοποίηση και εθνικό Σύνταγμα' [European integration and national constitution], in N. Maravegias and M. Tsinisizelis, eds., Η ολοκλήρωση της Ευρωπαϊκής 'νωσης [The integration of the European Union], Athens: Themelio.

——(1996) 'Η σημασία της συνταγματικής θεμελίωσης' [The relevance of constitutional basis], in Η Ελλάδα στην Ευρωπαϊκή Ένωση· Τα πρώτα 15 χρόνια· Απολογισμός και προοπτικές [Greece in the European Union: The first 15 years; Evaluation and perspectives], Athens: Papazissis.

Paparrigopoulos, Constantine (1858), Ιστορία του Ελληνικού 'θνους [History of the Greek Nation], Athens: Eleftheroudakis.

Parry, Jonathan (2006), *The Politics of Patriotism: English Liberalism, National Identity and Europe, 1830–1886*, Cambridge: Cambridge University Press.

Pašeta, Senia (1999), *Before the Revolution: Nationalism, Social Change and Ireland's Catholic Elite, 1879–1922*, Cork: Cork University Press.

References

Pasquier, Roman and Margarita León (2001), 'Spanish political science and European integration', *Journal of European Public Policy* 8 (6), 1052–9.

Patapievici, Horia-Roman (1996), *Politice*, Bucharest: Humanitas.

——(2008), *Omul recent: O critică a modernității din perspectiva întrebării 'Ce se pierde atunci când ceva se câştigă?'* [The recent man: A critique of modernity from the perspective of the question 'What is lost when something is won?'], 5th edn, Bucharest: Humanitas.

——(2009), 'Valorile Europei' [The values of Europe], in M. Neamţu and B. Tătaru-Cazaban, eds., *O filosofie a intervalului: In honorem Andrei Pleşu* [A philosophy of the interval: In honorem Andrei Pleşu], Bucharest: Humanitas.

Patočka, Jan (1992), *Evropa a doba poevropská* [Europe and the post-European era], Prague: Lidové noviny.

Pélabay, Janie (2008), 'Lorsque la clarification des sources se fait politiquement constitutive. À propos de J. H. H. Weiler, *L'Europe chrétienne? Une excursion*', *Raison publique* 8, 165–76.

——(2009), 'La "diversité profonde" selon Charles Taylor: Quelle pertinence pour l'Union européenne?', in G. Cressman, ed., *Multiculturalisme, modernité et citoyenneté/Multiculturalism, Modernity and Citizenship*, RANAM (Recherches Anglaises et Nord-Américaines), Strasbourg: Publications de L'université de Strasbourg.

Pesmazoglu, Ioannis (1962), *Η σύνδεση της Ελλάδος με την Ευρωπαϊκή Οικονομική Κοινότητα* [Greece's association with the European Economic Community], Athens: Bank of Greece.

——(1964), *La Grèce et l'édification de l'Europe, Chronique de Politique Etrangère*, XVII/6. Brussels: Institut Royal des Relations Internationales.

Peters, Anne (2000), *Theorie einer Verfassung für Europa*, Berlin: Duncker & Humblot.

Petreu, Marta (2005), *An Infamous Past: E. M. Cioran and the Rise of Fascism in Romania*, Chicago, IL: Ivan R. Dee.

Pettit, Philip (2006a), *Democracy, Electoral and Contestatory*, Baden Baden: Nomos.

——(2006b), 'Democracy, national and international', *The Monist* 89 (2), 301–24.

Piłsudski, Józef (1919[1999]), 'Przemówienie na otwarcie Sejmu Ustawodawczego 10 lutego 1919', in W. Suleja, ed., *Wybór Pism*, Wrocław: Wydawnictwo Zakład Narodowy im. Ossolińskich.

Pinder, John (1969), *Europe After De Gaulle: Towards the United States of Europe*, London: Penguin.

——(1999), *Foundations of Democracy in the European Union: From the Genesis of Parliamentary Democracy to the European Parliament*. Basingstoke: Macmillan.

Pistone, Sergio, ed. (1975), *L'Italia e l'unità europea*, Turin: Loescher.

Pithart, Petr (2006), 'Evropa a Evropané, evropanství. Na okraj eseje Václava Klause' [Europe, Europeans and Europeanism: Response to Václav Klaus' essay], *Mladá Fronta Dnes*, 20 May, <http://www.idnes.cz>.

Placák, Petr (2009), 'Konec Party u Stinadel' [The end of the Bad Boys], *Babylon* 2, 4.

Pleşu, Andrei (1988), *Minima moralia*, Bucharest: Cartea Românească.

Pocock, John Greville Agard (2005), 'Deconstructing Europe', in *The Discovery of Islands: Essays in British History*, Cambridge: Cambridge University Press.

Pomian, Krzysztof (1999), 'Aktualność Mieroszewskiego', in *Jerzy Giedroyc, Juliusz Mieroszewski. Listy 1949–1956*, Warsaw: Czytelnik.

——(2006), 'Nikt nie rodzi się Europejczykiem', in *Koniec: Rozmowy Jacka Żakowskiego*, Warsaw: Sic!

Porębski, Czesław (2000), *O Europie i Europejczykach*, Cracow: Znak.

Porter, Bernard (1983), '"Bureau and barrack": Early Victorian attitudes towards the Continent', *Victorian Studies* 27 (4), 407–33.

Posner, Richard (2003), *Public Intellectuals: A Study of Decline*, Cambridge, MA: Harvard University Press.

Poulton, Hugh (1997), *Top-Hat, the Grey Wolf and the Crescent*, London: Hurst.

Powell, Charles T. (2007), 'La larga marcha hacia Europa: España y la Comunidad Europea (1957–1986)', in F. Morata, and G. Mateo, *España en Europa: Europa en España (1986–2006)*. Barcelona: Fundación CIDOB.

Prečan, Vilém, ed. (1990), *Charta 77, 1977–1989*, Bratislava: Archa.

Preda, Radu (2004), 'Amnezia unui continent. Raportul Biserică-stat între laicism şi relativism' [The amnesia of a continent: The church–state relations between secularism and relativism], in M. Tătaru-Cazaban, ed., *Teologie şi politică: De la Sfinţii Părinţi la Europa unită* [Theology and politics: From the Church Fathers to united Europe], Bucharest: Anastasia.

——(2008), *Semnele vremii: Lecturi social-teologice* [The signs of time: Social and theological readings], Cluj/Napoca: Eikon.

Procacci, Giuliano, ed. (1994), *The Cominform Minutes of the Three Conferences 1947/1948/1949*, Milan: Fondazione Giangiacomo Feltrinelli.

Prodi, Romano (2000), *Europe As I See It*, London: Polity Press.

Psyroukis, Nikou (1986), *Η ένταξη της Ελλάδας στην ΕΟΚ και ο άλλος δρόμος* [Greece's accession to the EEC and the other road], Athens: Epikairotita.

Puşcaş, Vasile (2007), *România spre Uniunea Europeană: Negocierile de aderare, 2000–2004* [Romania towards the European Union: The accession negotiations, 2000–2004], Iaşi: Institutul European.

Rancière, Jacques (2005), *La haine de la démocratie*, Paris: La Fabrique.

Ranney, Austin and Giovanni Sartori (1978), *Eurocommunism: The Italian Case*, Washington, DC: University of Washington Press.

Raulet, Gérard (1997), 'Kant, européen?' in M. Madonna Desbazeille, ed., *L'Europe, naissance d'une utopie. Genèse de l'idée d'Europe du XVIe au XIXe siècle*, Paris: L'Harmattan.

Rawls, John (1993), *Political Liberalism*, New York: Columbia University Press.

——(1999), *A Theory of Justice*, Cambridge, MA: Harvard University Press.

Raynaud, Philippe (2006), *L'extrême-gauche plurielle*, Paris: Autrement.

Reijnen, Carlos (2008), 'For a true Europe and a new patriotism. Europe and the West from a Czech Stalinist perspective', in J. M. Faraldo et al., *Europa im Ostblock*, Cologne: Böhlau.

Remiro Brotons, A. (1994), 'Tornaviaje a Europa: el agotamiento de la integración', *Revista de Occidente* 157, 87–108.

Renouvin, Pierre (1949), *L'Idée de fédération européenne dans la pensée politique du XIXe siècle*, Oxford: Clarendon Press.

Rezler, André (1976), *L'intellectuel contre l'Europe*, Paris: Presses Universitaires de France.

Rian, Øystein, Harriet Rudd, and Håvard Tangen (2005), *100 År – var det alt?*, Oslo: Nei til EU.

Ricœur, Paul (1995), 'Reflections on a new ethos for Europe', *Philosophy and Social Criticism* 21 (5/6), 3–13.

References

Řiháčková, Věra and Christian von Seydlitz (2007), 'Václav Klaus and the Constitutional Treaty: Czech Euroscepsis or Eurorealism?', *Europeum*, 19 June, <http://www.europeum. org> (accessed 13 June 2010).

Riza, Ahmet (1979), *The Moral Bankruptcy of Western Policy towards the East*, Tunis: Éditions Bouslama.

Robinson, Mary (1992), 'A question of law: The European legacy', in R. Kearney, *Visions of Europe: Conversations on the Legacy and Future of Europe*, Dublin: Wolfhound Press.

Rodríguez Iglesias, Gil Carlos (2002), 'Una constitución para Europa', *El País*, 1 March.

Rokkan, Stein (1970), *Citizens, Elections, Parties*, Oslo: Universitetsforlaget.

——(1975), 'Dimensions of state formation and nation building: A possible paradigm for research on variations within Europe', in C. Tilly (ed.), *The Formation of National States in Western Europe*, Princeton, NJ: Princeton University Press.

Romilly, Jacqueline de (1992), *Pourquoi la Grèce?* Paris: Editions de Fallois.

Rosanvallon, Pierre (1992), *Le sacre du citoyen: Histoire du suffrage universel en France*, Paris: Gallimard.

——(2003), 'Les formes de la démocratie et l'avenir de l'Europe', in A.-M. Gloannec, ed., *Entre Kant et Kosovo: Etudes offertes à Pierre Hassner*, Paris: Presses de Sciences-Po.

——(2006), *Democracy Past and Future*, ed. S. Moyn, New York: Columbia University Press.

Rotfeld, Adam Daniel (2008), 'Germany–Poland–Russia (some thoughts about the past, the present, and the future)', in W. M. Góralski, ed., *Poland–Germany 1945–2007: From Confrontation to Cooperation and Partnership in Europe*, Warsaw: PISM.

Rougemont, Denis de (1965a), *The Meaning of Europe*, Liverpool: Sidgwick and Jackson.

——(1965b), *La Suisse ou l'histoire d'un peuple heureux*, Paris: Hachette.

Rubio Llorente, Francisco (1994), 'Europerplejidad', *Revista de Occidente* 157, 73–86.

——(2002), 'Un eurogalimatías europeo', *El País*, 2 February.

——(2003), 'El referéndum superfluo y el necesario', *El País*, 11 July.

——and Joseph H. H. Weiler (2003), 'Constitución europea y tradición cristiana', *Revista de Occidente* 27, 87–100.

Rupnik, Jacques (1988), *The Other Europe*, London: Weidenfeld & Nicolson.

Rusconi, Gian Enrico (1993), *Se cessiamo di essere una nazione*, Turin: Einaudi.

——(2003), *Germania, Italia, Europa: dallo stato di Potenza alla Potenza civile*, Turin: Einaudi.

Safjan, Marek (2007), 'Żądajmy referendum o Eurokonstytucji', *Gazeta Wyborcza*, 9 March.

Saint-Pierre, Charles Irénée Abbé de (1714), *A project for settling an everlasting peace in Europe. First proposed by Henry IV of France, and approved of by Queen Elizabeth*, London: J. Watts and F. Burleigh.

——(1986a), *Mémoire pour rendre la paix perpétuelle à l'Europe*, Paris: Fayard (orig. pub. Cologne: J. le Pacifique, 1712).

——(1986b), *Projet pour rendre la paix perpétuelle en Europe*, Paris: Fayard (orig. pub. Utrecht: Schouten, 1713).

——(1986c), *Projet de traité pour rendre perpétuelle entre les souverains chrétiens, pour maintenir toujours le commerce libre entre les nations; pour affermir beaucoup davantage les Maisons Souveraines sur le Trône. Proposé autrefois par Henry le Grand, Roy de France*, Paris: Fayard (orig. pub. Utrecht: Schouten, 1717).

Salmon, Christian (2009), Storytelling, la machine à fabriquer des histories et à formatter les esprits, Paris: La Découverte.

Salvadori, Massimo L. (1999), *La sinistra nella storia d'Italia*, Bari: Laterza.

Sánchez Prieto, Juan María (2000), *La España plural: El debate de la identidad*, Bilbao: Fundación Elkargunea.

Sandel, Michael (1982), *Liberalism and the Limits of Justice*, Cambridge: Cambridge University Press.

Sandu, Dumitru (1999), *Spaţiul social al tranziţiei* [The social space of transition], Iaşi: Polirom.

Santoro, Carlo M. (1991), *La politica estera di una media potenza: l'Italia dall'Unità ad oggi*, Bologna: Il Mulino.

Sartre, Jean-Paul (1978), Preface to Frantz Fanon, *The Wretched of the Earth*, trans. C. Farrington, London: Penguin.

Saryusz-Wolski, Jacek (2007), 'Polska znajdzie się na obrzeżach Unii, jeśli będzie walczyć z Kartą Praw Podstawowych', *Dziennik: Polska-Europa-Świat*, 21 November.

Sassoon, Donald (1986), *Contemporary Italy*, London: Longman.

Sauger, Nicolas, Sylvain Brouard, and Emiliano Grossman (2007), *Les Français contre l'Europe: Le sens du référendum du 29 mai 2005*, Paris: Presses de Sciences-Po.

Schlink, Bernhard (1989), 'Die Entthrohnung der Staatsrechtswissenschaft durch die Verfassungsgerichtsbarkeit', *Der Staat* 28, 161–72.

Schmitt, Carl (2005 [1978]), 'Die legale Weltrevolution', in *Frieden oder Pazifismus? Arbeiten zum Völkerrecht und zur internationalen Politik 1924–1978*, ed. G. Maschke, Berlin: Duncker & Humblot.

Schmitter, Philippe C. (2000), *How to Democratize the European Union . . . And Why Bother?*, Lanham, MD: Rowman & Littlefield.

Schönberger, Christoph (1997), *Das Parlament im Anstaltsstaat: Zur Theorie parlamentarischer Repräsentation in der Staatsrechtslehre des Kaiserreichs*, Frankfurt am Main: Klostermann.

Schrag, Claudia (2008), 'Imagined community: Constructing EU legitimacy', PhD dissertation, University of Cambridge.

Schulz-Forberg, Hagen (2008), 'The European public sphere and the transnational history', in J. M. Faraldo, P. Gulińska-Jurgiel, and C. Domnitz, eds., *Europa im Ostblock: Vorstellungen und Diskurse (1945–1991)*, Cologne: Böhlau.

Scoppola, Pietro (1977), *La proposta politica di De Gasperi*, Bologna: Il Mulino.

Scruton, Roger (1980), *The Meaning of Conservatism*, Harmondsworth: Penguin.

——(1990), 'In defence of the nation', in *The Philosopher on Dover Beach: Essays*, Manchester: Carcanet.

——(2000), *England: An Elegy*, London: Chatto & Windus.

——(2004), *England and the Need for Nations*, London: Civitas.

——(2005), 'The dangers of internationalism', *Intercollegiate Review* 40 (2) (Fall/Winter), 29–35.

——(2006), *A Political Philosophy*, London: Continuum.

Seidlová, Adéla (2004), 'Contribution of the Visegrad 4 group to Europe', *CVVM* 27 May, <http://www.cvvm.cas.cz>.

Sejersted, Fredrik (2008), 'Om Norges rettslige integrasjon i EU', *Nytt Norsk Tidsskrift* 4, 313–22.

References

Seneca (1958), *Moral Essays*, vol. 2, trans. J. W. Basore, Cambridge, MA: Harvard University Press.

Shils, Edward (1968), 'Intellectuals', in *International Encyclopedia of the Social Sciences*, New York: Macmillan and Free Press.

Shils, Edward (1990), 'Intellectuals and responsibility', in I. Maclean, A. Montefiore, and P. Winch, eds., *The Political Responsibility of Intellectuals*, Cambridge: Cambridge University Press.

Showstack Sassoon, Anne (1987), *Gramsci's Politics*, London: Hutchinson.

Siedentop, Larry (1994), *Tocqueville*, Oxford: Oxford University Press.

——(2001), *Democracy in Europe*, London: Penguin Books.

Simitis, Costas (1992), Προτάσεις για μια άλλη πολιτική [Proposals for another policy], Athens: Gnossi.

——(2002), Για μια ισχυρή Ελλάδα στην Ευρώπη και στον κόσμο [For a strong Greece in Europe and the world], Athens: Kastaniotis.

——(2008), Η κρίση [The crisis], Athens: Polis.

Sjursen, H. (2008), 'Fra bremsekloss til medløper: Norge i EUs utenriks- og sikkerhets-politikk', *Nytt Norsk Tidsskrift* 4: 323–35.

Skilling, Gordon (1981), *Charter 77 and Human Rights in Czechoslovakia*, London: Allen & Unwin.

Slagstad, Rune (1980), 'Sosialisme på norsk', in S. Hansson and R. Slagstad, eds., *Sosialisme på norsk*, Oslo: Pax.

——(1998), *De nasjonale strateger*, Oslo: Pax.

——(2009), 'Styringsvitenskap – ånden som går', *Nytt Norsk Tidsskrift* 3–4, 411–34.

Sokolewicz, Zofia (2003), 'Polish debate on European Christian values. Some thoughts on marginal issues of Poland's negotiations of membership of the European Union', in A. Z. Nowak and D. Milczarek, eds., *On the Road to the European Union: Applicant Countries' Perspective*, Warsaw: Warsaw University Centre for Europe.

Someritis, Richardos (1996), 'Το Μάαστριχτ ευθύνεται για όλα' [Maastricht is responsible for everything], Το Βήμα, *To Vima*, 5 May.

Sotelo, Ignacio (1992) 'Europa en la estacada', *Revista de Occidente* 157, 51–72.

——(2004), '¿Por qué un referéndum?, *El País*, 23 November.

Soukup, Ondřej and Petra Benešová (2008), 'Překlad Klausovy knihy zaplatil Lukoil. Prezident Václav Klaus si našel pozoruhodného sponzora své kontroverzní knihy, která bagatelizuje dopady globálního oteplování a kritizuje snahy ekologů' [Lukoil paid for the translation of Klaus' book. President Václav Klaus found a striking sponsor for his controversial book, which minimizes the consequences of the global warming], *Mladá Fronta Dnes*, 18 August, <http://www.idnes.cz>.

Spinelli, Altiero (1975), *Il progetto europeo*, Bologna: Il Mulino.

——(1986), *Discorsi al parlamento europeo, 1976–1986*, Bologna: Il Mulino.

——(1989), *Una strategia per gli Stati Uniti d'Europa*, Bologna: Il Mulino.

Stan, Lavinia and Lucian Turcescu (2007), *Religion and Politics in Post-Communist Romania*, Oxford and New York: Oxford University Press.

Staniszkis, Jadwiga (2006), *O władzy i bezsilności*, Cracow: Wydawnictwo Literackie.

Stapleton, Julia (2001), *Political Intellectuals and Public Identities in Britain since 1850*, Manchester: Manchester University Press.

Stefanou, Constantine (1996), *Η θεσμική μεταρρύθμιση της Ευρωπαϊκής 'Ενωσης* [The institutional reform of the European Union], Athens: Papazissis.

Steinberg, Marc (1999), 'The talk and back talk of collective action: A dialogic analysis of repertoires of discourse among 19th century English cotton spinners', *American Journal of Sociology* 105 (3): 736–80.

Stråth, Bo, Thomas Lindkvist, Dorthe Gert Simonsen, Nils Erik Villstrand, and Anette Warring (2008), 'Evaluering av norsk historiefaglig forskning – Borten for nasjonen i tid og rom: fortidens makt og fremtidens muligheter i norsk historieforskning', Oslo: Norsk Forskningsråd.

Stroehlein, Andrew (1997), 'Czechs and the Czech-German Declaration', *Britské listy*, September, <http://www.blisty.cz> (accessed 23 September 2009).

——(1999), 'Three Václavs', *Central Europe Review* 1 (10), 30 August.

Strøm, Steinar (1994), 'Den økonomiske og monetære unionen i EU', *Kritisk Juss* 2, 118–23.

Suk, Jiří (2003), *Labyrintem revoluce: Aktéři, zapletky a křižovatky jedné politické krize (od listopadu 1989 do června 1990)* [In the revolution's labyrinth], Prague: Prostor.

Svoronos, Nikolaos (1973), *Histoire de la Grèce moderne*, Paris: Presses Universitaires de France.

Sweeney, Matthew (2007), *Black Moon*, London: Jonathan Cape.

Szakács, Judit (2003), 'Ex-PM launches "buy Hungarian" campaign', *Transitions Online*, 25 February, <http://www.ceeol.com>.

Szczuka, Kazimiera (2007), 'Niech państwo nie kontroluje sumień', *Gazeta Wyborcza*, 27 March.

Taguieff, Pierre-André (2001), *Résister au bougisme: Démocratie forte contre mondialisation techno-marchande*, Paris: Mille et Une Nuits.

Taibo, Carlos (2005), 'No es lo que nos cuentan', *El País*, 16 January.

Taylor, Charles (1989), *Sources of the Self: The Making of the Modern Identity*, Cambridge, MA: Harvard University Press.

——(1991), *The Malaise of Modernity*, Toronto: Anansi.

——(1993), *Reconciling the Solitudes: Essays on Canadian Federalism and Nationalism*, Montreal: McGill-Queen's University Press.

——(2007), *A Secular Age*, Cambridge, MA and London: Belknap Press of Harvard University Press.

Tazbir, Janusz (1999), 'Europejska wspólnota obronna', in A. Dylus, ed., *Europa: Drogi integracji*, Warsaw: Studium Generale Europa, Uniwersytet Kardynała Stefana Wyszyńskiego.

——(2004), *Polska przedmurzem Europy*, Warsaw: Twój Styl.

Telò, Mario (2004), *Europa potenza civile*, Rome: Laterza.

——and Paul Magnette (1996), 'Vers une démocratie supra-nationale et post-fédérale', in Teló and Magnette, eds., *Repenser l'Europe*, Brussels: Éditions de l'Université de Bruxelles.

Terry, Sarah Meiklejohn (2000), 'Poland's foreign policy since 1989: The challenges of independence', *Communist and Post-Communist Studies*, 33 (1), 7–47.

Teubner, Gunther (2007), 'Globale Zivilverfassungen: Alternativen zur staatszentrierten Verfassungstheorie', in M. Neves and R. Voigt, eds., *Die Staaten der Weltgesellschaft: Niklas Luhmanns Staatsverständnis*, Baden-Baden: Nomos.

References

Theotokas, Giorgos (1976), 'Η Ευρωπαϊκή Ένωση και το μέλλον του ελληνικού έθνους' [The European Union and the future of the Greek nation], address at the European Club of Thessaloniki, 24 March 1958, in Πολιτικά Κείμενα [Political texts], Athens: Ikaros.

Thibaud, Paul (1992), *Discussion sur l'Europe*, Paris: Calmann-Lévy.

——(2006), 'De l'échec au projet', *Le Débat* 140, 17–29.

Thomas, Hugh, ed. (1959), *The Establishment*, London: Anthony Blond.

——(1973), *Europe: The Radical Challenge*, London: Weidenfeld & Nicolson.

Thonstad, T. (1993), 'Tollunion', in T. Thonstad and T. Eckhoff, *Tollunion, ØMU og EFs styringsmuligheter*, Nei til EFs Skriftserie om EF 3.

Todd, Emmanuel (1995), *L'illusion économique: Essai sur la stagnation des sociétés développées*, Paris: Gallimard.

Tóibín, Colm (1994), *The Sign of the Cross: Travels in Catholic Europe*, London: Jonathan Cape.

Topdur, Zakir (2000), 'Şehit Kanı Boğar', *Ortadoğu*, 11 January.

Topolánek, Mirek (2008), 'Rather kiss Merkel than hug the Russian bear', *Eurotopics* (translated from *Mladá fronta Dnes*), 20 November, <http://www.eurotopics.net> (accessed 13 July 2010).

Torreblanca, José Ignacio (2003), '¿Quién teme a la Convención?', *Análisis del Real Instituto Elcano* 26.

——(2004), 'El Gobierno socialista, la Constitución y la doble mayoría', *Análisis de Real Instituto Elcano* 103.

Toynbee, Arnold and Kenneth Kirkwood (1926), *The Modern World: A Survey of Historical Forces*, vol. 6: *Turkey*, London: Ernest Benn.

Trebitsch, Michel and Marie-Christine Granjon (1998), *Pour une histoire comparée des intellectuels*, Brussels: Complexe.

Tremonti, Giulio (2008), *La paura e la speranza*, Milan: Mondadori.

Tresch, Anke and Margit Jochum (2005), 'Europäisierung der Öffentlichkeit als Legitimitätsbedingung der EU', in F. Cheneval, A. Utzinger, and S. Dänzer, eds., *Legitimationsgrundlagen der Europäischen Union*, Münster/London: Lit Verlag.

Tsakalotos, Euclid (2005), Η αξία και οι αξίες της Αριστεράς: αντι-εκσυγχρονιστικό δοκίμιο για την οικονομία και την κοινωνία [The values and the value of the Left: An anti-modernising essay about economy and society], Athens: Kritiki.

Tsatsos, Constantine (1977), *La Grèce et l'Europe*, Lausanne: Centre de Recherches Européennes.

——(1982), Δημοκρατία και Ευρώπη [Democracy and Europe], Athens: Astrolavos/ Efthyni.

Tsatsos, Dimitris (2007a), Ευρωπαϊκή Συμπολιτεία [European sympolity], Athens: Livanis.

——(2007b), Η έννοια της Δημοκρατίας στην Ευρωπαϊκή Συμπολιτεία [The concept of democracy in the European sympolity], Athens: Polis. (Also published in English as *The European Sympolity: Towards a New Democratic Discourse*, Brussels: Bruylant, 2009).

Tsoukalis, Loukas (1995), Ευρωπαϊκά Ανορθόδοξα [European unorthodox], Athens: Papazissis.

——(2006), *What Kind of Europe?*, Oxford: Oxford University Press.

——(2009), Κι αν βγαίναμε από το καβούκι μας; [And if we came out of our shell?], Athens: Papazissis.

Tsoukas, Haris, ed. (2007), Για μια προοδευτική πολιτική [For a progressive policy], Athens: Kastaniotis.

Tuccari, Francesco and Fabio Armao, eds. (2002), *Il governo Berlusconi: Le parole, i fatti, i rischi*, Bari: Laterza.

Turcanu, Florin (2005), *Mircea Eliade: Le prisonnier de l'histoire*, Paris: La Découverte.

Türkeş, Alparslan (1994), *Dokuz Işık ve Türkiye*, Istanbul: Hamle.

Uhl, Petr (2008), 'Klaus remains stubborn', *Eurotopics*, 27 November, <http://www.eurotopics.net> (accessed 13 July 2010).

Urban, George (1978), *Eurocommunism: Its Roots and Future in Italy and Elsewhere*, New York: Universe Books.

Üzer, Umut (2002), 'Racism in Turkey: The case of Hüseyin Nihal Atsız', *Journal of Muslim Minority Affairs* 22 (1), 119–30.

Vaculík, Ludvík (2005), 'Evropská deviace' [The European deviation], *Lidové noviny*, 22 February, <http://www.lidovky.cz>.

Valen, Henry (1999), 'EU-saken post festum', in B. Aardal, H. M. Narud, and F. Berglund, eds., *Velgere i 90-årene*, Oslo: NKS Forlaget.

Vallès, Josep M. (1989), 'Political science in contemporary Spain: An overview', Working Paper, Barcelona: Institut de Ciences Politiques i Sociales.

Varouxakis, Georgios (1995), 'The idea of Europe in 19th century Greek political thought', in P. Carabott, ed., *Greece and Europe in the Modern Period: Aspects of a Troubled Relationship*. London: King's College, Centre for Hellenic Studies.

——(1997), 'A certain idea of Greece: Perceptions of the past and European integration', *Synthesis: Review of Modern Greek Studies* 2 (1), 32–42.

——(2000), 'Is the forgetting of history a prerequisite for the emergence of a European "imagined community"?', in B. Axford, D. Berghahn, and N. Hewlett, eds., *Unity and Diversity in the New Europe*, Oxford and Bern: Peter Lang.

——(2002), *Victorian Political Thought on France and the French*, Houndmills, Basingstoke: Palgrave.

Védrine, Hubert and Dominique Moïsi (2001), *France in an Age of Globalization*, Washington, DC: Brookings, Institution.

Veneziani, Marcello (2002), *La cultura della destra*, Rome: Laterza.

Verdery, Katherine (1991), *National Ideology under Socialism: Identity and Cultural Politics in Ceauşescu's Romania*. Berkeley, CA, Los Angeles, and London: University of California Press.

Veremis, Thanos (2006), Ελλάδα, η σύγχρονη περίοδος· Από το 1821 στις μέρες μας [Greece, the modern sequel: From 1821 to our times], Athens: Kastaniotis.

Vergopoulos, Costas (1997), 'Modernisation or social cohesion?', *Eleftherotypia*, 23 March.

——(2008), 'Η Ευρώπη όλων των κινδύνων' [Europe of all dangers], in S. Tobazos, ed., Η Ευρώπη, ποιά Ευρώπη [Europe, which Europe?], Athens: Ed. Polytropo.

Verhofstadt, Guy (2006), *The United States of Europe*, London: Federal Trust.

Verner, Pavel (2008), 'Klaus sabotages his government', *Eurotopics* (translated from *Právo*), 13 November, <http://www.eurotopics.net> (accessed 13 July 2010).

Verney, Susannah (1996), 'The Greek Socialists', in J. Gaffney, ed., *Political Parties and the European Union*, London: Routledge.

Vidal-Beneyto, José (2009), '¡Los de Múnich, a la horca!', *El País*, 6 June.

Vidal-Foch, Xavier (1992), 'Maastricht y la sopa de ajo', *El País*, 23 September.

Vilá Costa, Blanca (1992), 'La construcción europea, sin eufemismos', *El País*, 5 May.

References

Vincze, Hajnalka (2002), 'Un contre tous, tous contre un: Coup de froid dans le groupe de Visegrád', *Journal Francophone de Budapest*, 15 March.

Voulgaris, Yannis (2008), Η Ελλάδα, από τη μεταπολίτευση στην παγκοσμιοποίηση [Greece, from the Metapolitefsi to globalisation], Athens: Polis.

Voyenne, Bernard (1954), *Histoire de l'idée européenne*, Paris: Payot.

Walicki, Andrzej (2000), *Polskie zmagania z wolnością widziane z boku*, Cracow: Universitas.

Walker, Neil (2008), 'Taking constitutionalism beyond the state', *Political Studies* 56, 519–43.

Walzer, Michael (1984), 'Liberalism and the art of separation', *Political Theory* 12 (3), 325–30.

Wandycz, Piotr (1990), 'Poland's place in Europe in the concepts of Piłsudski and Dmowski', *East European Politics and Societies*, 4 (3), 451–68.

Warleigh, Alex (2003), *Democracy and the European Union: Theory, Practice, and Reform*. London: Sage.

Waters, Sarah (2004), 'Mobilizing against globalization: Attac and the French intellectuals', *West European Politics* 27 (5), 854–74.

Weber, Eugen (1983), *Peasants into Frenchman*, Palo Alto, CA: Stanford University Press.

Weiler, Joseph H. H. (2001), 'Federalism without Constitutionalism: Europe's Sonderweg', in K. Nicolaïdis and R. Howse, eds., *The Federal Vision: Legitimacy and Levels of Governance in United States and the European Union*, Oxford: Oxford University Press.

——(2003a), 'In defence of the status quo: Europe's constitutional Sonderweg', in J. H. H. Weiler and M. Wind, *European Constitutionalism beyond the State*, Cambridge: Cambridge University Press.

——(2003b), *Un'Europa Cristiana: Un saggio esplorativo*, Milan: BUR Saggi.

——Franz Mayer, and Ulrich Haltern (1995), 'European democracy and its critique', *West European Politics* 18 (3), 4–39.

Whelan, Diarmuid (2005), '"The Kimmage Junta": The new left wing of the Irish nation in post-war Ireland', paper presented to the 'Intellectuals and the Nation-State' conference, University College Dublin, 30 November–1 December 2005.

Wildstein, Bronisław (2007), 'Strzeżmy się Karty Praw Podstawowych', *Rzeczpospolita*, 24 July.

Winkler, Heinrich August (2007), *Germany: The Long Road West*, 2 vols., trans. A. Sager, New York: Oxford University Press.

Winock, Michel (1982), *Nationalisme, antisémitisme et fascisme en France*, Paris: Seuil.

——(1997), *Le siècle des intellectuels*, Paris: Seuil.

Wolański, Marian (1996), *Europa Środkowo-Wschodnia w myśli politycznej emigracji polskiej 1945–1975*, Wrocław: Wydawnictwo Uniwersytetu Wrocławskiego.

Wolin, Richard (2004), *The Seduction of Unreason: The Intellectual Romance with Fascism; from Nietzche to Post-Modernism*, Princeton, NJ: Princeton University Press.

Yannaras, Christos (1983), Η ταυτότητα της σύγχρονης Ελλάδας [The identity of modern Greece], Athens: Grigori.

——(1990), 'Θρησκεία και Ρωμιοσύνη' [Religion and Greekness], in D. Tsaoussis, ed., Ιδεολογικοί και βιωματικοί άξονες στη σύγχρονη ελληνική κοινωνία [Ideological and biomatic axes of Modern Greek society], Athens: Estia.

——(1992), Ορθοδοξία και Δυτικός κόσμος στη σύγχρονη Ελλάδα [Orthodoxy and Western world in modern Greece], Athens: Domos.

Yataganas, Xenophon (1990), *Η Ευρώπη και η Αριστερά· Μια προβληματική σχέση* [Europe and the left: Notes about a problematic relationship], Athens: Themelio.

——and Dimitris Kaloudiotis (2009), *Ήπια Ηγεμονία· Η Ευρώπη μετά την κρίση* [Soft hegemony: Europe after the crisis], Athens: Kritiki.

Yavuz, Hakan (2003), *Islamic Political Identity in Turkey*, Oxford: Oxford University Press.

Young, Hugo (1998), *This Blessed Plot: Britain and Europe from Churchill to Blair*, London and Basingstoke: Macmillan.

Żakowski, Jacek (2007), *Nauczka*, Warsaw: Wydawnictwo Krytyki Politycznej.

Zaremba, Marcin (2001), *Komunizm, legitymizacja, nacjonalizm. Nacjonalistyczna legitymizacja władzy komunistycznej w Polsce*, Warsaw: Wydawnictwo TRIO.

Zolotas, Xenophon (1976), *Η Ελλάδα στην Ευρωπαϊκή Κοινότητα* [Greece in the European Community], Athens: Bank of Greece.

Zouraris, Kostas (2009), *Να την χέσω τέτοια λευτεριά, όπου θα κάμω εγώ εσένα πασιά* [To hell with such liberty, where I will turn you into a pasha], Athens: Armos.

Index

Index